Cognitive processes
in eye guidance

Cognitive processes in eye guidance

Edited by

Geoffrey Underwood
Professor of Cognitive Psychology
University of Nottingham, UK

OXFORD
UNIVERSITY PRESS

OXFORD
UNIVERSITY PRESS

Great Clarendon Street, Oxford OX2 6DP

Oxford University Press is a department of the University of Oxford.
It furthers the University's objective of excellence in research, scholarship,
and education by publishing worldwide in

Oxford New York

Auckland Cape Town Dar es Salaam Hong Kong Karachi
Kuala Lumpur Madrid Melbourne Mexico City Nairobi
New Delhi Shanghai Taipei Toronto

With offices in

Argentina Austria Brazil Chile Czech Republic France Greece
Guatemala Hungary Italy Japan South Korea Poland Portugal
Singapore Switzerland Thailand Turkey Ukraine Vietnam

Oxford is a registered trade mark of Oxford University Press
in the UK and in certain other countries

Published in the United States
by Oxford University Press Inc., New York

A catalogue record for this title is available from the British Library

Library of Congress Cataloging in Publication Data
(Data available)

ISBN 0 19 85 66808 (Hbk)
0 19 85 66816 (Pbk)

10 9 8 7 6 5 4 3 2 1

Typeset in Minion
by Cepha Imaging Pvt. Ltd., Bangalore, India
Printed in Great Britain
on acid-free paper by
Biddles Ltd, King's Lynn

Preface

The central question addressed by the contributions to this book is that of how we know where we should next direct our gaze. The focus here is on the influences on the *where* decision, while acknowledging that there is often an interaction between the decisions about where we should look and about how long we should look there. Our eyes do not move randomly over the visual field, and whether we are reading, or looking at a picture, or driving, or solving a problem there are systematic variations not only in the duration of each eye fixation, but also in what we look at. These systematic variations are the basic data showing a sensitivity of the eye guidance mechanism to the material being inspected, and are the variations that will be taken into account by our theoretical descriptions. In the domain of reading, progress towards an accepted theoretical description is at an advanced stage, with a number of competing and well-formed models prompting new experiments in search of the critical decisive evidence. In other domains of perception the formation of formal theories and the search for critical evidence is less advanced, and one of the purposes of this book is to foster the development of theories of eye guidance in domains such as picture perception, driving, and problem solving, as well as making clear the differences between the well-formed models that exist as accounts of how we know where to look next when reading text.

The reader's eyes do not move inexorably forwards in an invariant left-to-right sequence, but sometimes return to a word that has already been inspected. What prompts such a regressive movement? Françoise Vitu describes the evidence of when we make a regressive fixation – when regressives occur, and where they are directed – and concludes that visual, lexical, and linguistic processes are implicated. Incoming information has a minor role, with the decision being informed mainly by prior processing events such as the length of the prior saccade, the frequency of the prior word, and whether a word was skipped during the prior saccade. Regressives are systematic, especially when incoming information can be incorporated. Vitu uses the evidence from studies of regressives to illuminate differences between the major theories of eye guidance in reading, concluding that when we send our eyes back to region of text, then it is relatively low-level visual-oculomotor features that control the guidance mechanism. The guidance of regressive fixations is also the concern of the chapter by Albrecht Inhoff, Ulrich Weger, and Ralph Radach, who distinguish between short-range regressives to the previous word on the same line of text, and the relatively infrequent longer-range regressives that require a spatial map of the previous text if they are to be made accurately. The evidence suggests that these long regressives are generally inaccurate, and that corrective saccades are made to locate the targeted word, indicating that a spatial map of previously read text is not available. Inhoff, Weger and Radach conclude that where spatial indexing may aid short regressives, readers use linguistic knowledge that involves a reconstruction of the textual information when programming longer saccades.

Just as we do not move our eyes along a line of text in a relentless left-to-right sequence, we do not look at every word that is available. The choice of which words to fixate and which words to skip is critical to our attempts to distinguish between models of guidance – is it low-level visual information that drives the decision, or high-level linguistic information? Marc Brysbaert, Denis Drieghe and Françoise Vitu review the evidence to identify the variables that influence word skipping. The evidence sometimes supports the view that it is visual-oculomotor factors that dominate, and sometimes linguistic factors that determine that a word should be skipped. The frequency and predictability of a word not yet fixated can influence the decision, and this analysis argues for a model of eye guidance that is sensitive to both the visual and the linguistic features of the text being inspected. The influence of linguistic variables in reading is demonstrated clearly in the chapter by Jukka Hyönä, Raymond Bertram and Alexander Pollatsek, which concerns the inspection of long compound words. The Finnish language is characterized by the existence of multi-compound words such as the delightful *lumipallosotatantere* (meaning 'snowball fight field') and these provide a basis for comparing whole-word and decompositional models of word recognition during reading. Whereas short compounds can be read with a single fixation, these long words require several fixations each, and their constituents determine the location and duration of fixations. As the frequency of a constituent decreases, foveal load increases, and this influences saccadic programming in support of eye-guidance models that admit linguistic influences.

The next two chapters present alternate views of the guidance mechanism. Shun-nan Yang and George McConkie summarize their Competition/Interaction Model of guidance in which high-level linguistic influences are minimal because their processing is insufficiently advanced at the point that eye guidance decisions are made. This model is representative of a family of recent models that discount cognitive influences in eye guidance. An important task for these models is to explain how fixations can be sensitive to linguistic variables such as word frequency and contextual predictability. Yang and McConkie address this issue in their discussion. In contrast, the E-Z Reader model advocated in the chapter by Keith Rayner, Erik Reichle and Alexander Pollatsek takes into account evidence of both visual-oculomotor influences on guidance behaviour as well as linguistic influences, allowing linguistic information to have an influence on the guidance mechanism. This discussion reviews the critical data that a model of eye guidance should explain, and presents the current version of the model that is claimed to account for these data. The debate between alternate models of influences on the *where* decision is far from resolved, and these two theoretical discussions advance the debate by setting out the issues very clearly.

Whereas the early chapters concern the well-researched domain of reading, and are able to discuss the use of evidence which is being used to develop and distinguish between models of guidance, the later chapters present descriptions that are less well-supported by theoretical accounts. Models of guidance do exist in domains such as visual search, but they are not developed to the same advanced state as models of reading. Quite often we read sentences accompanied by graphics – for example, photographs in newspapers, pictures in magazine advertisements, and line drawings in textbooks – but there is relatively little work in the literature addressing the question of how we integrate the information from these multimedia sources. The chapter by Geoffrey Underwood on scene perception reviews evidence from studies of sentence reading in the presence of graphics, concluding that the typical scanpath is to look briefly at the picture, then read the text, and then inspect the picture more carefully. The purpose of this first brief inspection of the picture is a curiosity. It may be to enable the viewer to acquire the gist of the picture (and there is abundant evidence that the gist can be acquired in the time taken by a single fixation), but this information is insufficient to support judgements about the meaning of the accompanying sentence. Peter De Graef's chapter on real-world scene perception also addresses the question of what can be seen in a very brief glimpse of a picture. There are similarities in the study of picture perception with the question of what kinds of information are used by the eye guidance mechanism during reading, with attempts to distinguish between influences of visual information and semantic information in the two domains. With pictures, the question is whether fixation patterns are driven by visual saliency or semantic saliency. De Graef compares the sensitivity of our eye movements with variations in intensity, colour and orientation and with variations in the congruity of an object in a scene.

The discussion of picture perception is continued in the chapter by John Henderson and Monica Castelhano, who focus on the development of stable representations over the course of inspection of the scene. Recent studies of the change blindness phenomenon have encouraged the conclusion that we have no memory, but the conclusion may be specific to the paradigm, and Henderson and Castelhano argue that detailed representations are created and are used over all time intervals from transsaccadic events to long-term memories for scenes. These representations are a consequence of inspection. The generality of the results from change blindness studies is also questioned in Peter Chapman's chapter, which again deals with our memories of what we have inspected. The absence of our memories for visual events has been greatly exaggerated, we should conclude, and our patterns of fixations are highly predictive of what we can remember.

When we inspect a scene, we often do so with a purpose – we are looking for something or we are looking to guide our behaviour according to the visual input. The chapter by John Findlay and Iain Gilchrist accounts for variations in fixation patterns in visual search tasks, taking the position that an understanding of eye guidance must be integral to a successful theory of search. This is an active model of the search process, with scanning serving to build a representation of the display, using the visual salience of the components to guide successive fixations. When we interact with a dynamic world, our patterns of search reflect our needs, with both low-level visual influences and high-level cognitive influences being observable. This conclusion from David Crundall's discussion of driving is based on studies of drivers negotiating complex environments in which the objects that compete for attention have varying degrees of importance for the task in hand. Crundall considers the implications of the evidence for possible training interventions, which might be designed to aid the new driver to successfully negotiate a rich environment of objects of varying salience.

Inspection patterns vary as a function of differences in the experience of the viewer, as described in Crundall's description of visual search while driving, and it is also a theme of the three chapters on game-playing and problem solving. Jean Underwood presents a study of experienced and less-experienced users of the computer game Tetris, finding that success is associated with lateral eye movements (rather than vertical movements), and this is attributed to the more successful player creating a changed representation of the screen as part of the formation of desired goal states. The absence of differences in fixation durations is interesting in the light of earlier descriptions of variations as a function of cognitive load, and the demands of a dynamic environment must be taken into account by our models. Eyal Reingold and Neil Charness describe differences in the eye movements of skilled and less-skilled chess players, demonstrating the perceptual advantages of experts. Variations in the numbers of fixations as well as fixation sequences distinguish between players of different ability, and Reingold and Charness suggest that parafoveal processing and larger visual spans contribute to the automatic and parallel processing abilities of experts. In the third chapter in this group, Günther Knoblich, Michael Öllinger, and Michael Spivey focus on problems that offer themselves to the experience of insight. Matchstick arithmetic problems are characteristic of insight problems, in that the answer often appears abruptly in the mind of the solver. The direction of gaze can predict the likelihood of a solution appearing however, whether this is known to the problem solver or not.

This collection of essays on the relationship between eye movements and cognitive processes has its origins in the book *Eye guidance in reading and scene perception* (Elsevier, 1998), and many of the contributors to that volume have taken the opportunity of updating their analyses here. The second origin was at the LOVE meeting ('Lake Ontario Visionary Experimenters', allegedly) held at Niagara Falls in February 2004. Most of the contributors to this volume were at the meeting to present their data and their arguments in a lively and supportive forum. The success of that meeting contributed in no small part to the quality of the chapters here, and thanks are due to the organizers of the meeting, Ken McRae and Michael Spivey, and to the regular participants of LOVE for allowing us to take over their annual event. As drafts of chapters arrived in Nottingham after the meeting, Jessica de Andrade Lima and Lee Melton organized a website to enable all the contributors to access all the contributions. The draft chapters were then reviewed, and at least two sets of comments provided on each chapter. The reviewers were mainly the authors and co-authors of other chapters, but in addition Fernand Gobet and Adam Galpin provided valuable comments. Thanks are due to all those involved in this reviewing process. Finally, I would like to thank the authors for their enthusiasm and their intellectual rigour in helping put together a thought-provoking collection of discussions.

Geoffrey Underwood
Nottingham

Contents

List of contributors

Raymond Bertram
University of Turku, Finland

Marc Brysbaert
Royal Holloway, University of London, UK

Monica S. Castelhano
Michigan State University, USA

Peter Chapman
University of Nottingham, UK

Neil Charness
Florida State University, USA

David Crundall
University of Nottingham, UK

Denis Drieghe
Ghent University, Belgium

John M. Findlay
University of Durham, UK

Iain D. Gilchrist
University of Bristol, UK

Peter De Graef
University of Leuven, Belgium

John M. Henderson
Michigan State University, USA

Jukka Hyönä
University of Turku, Finland

Albrecht W. Inhoff
State University of New York
at Binghamton, USA

Günther Knoblich
Rutgers University, USA

George W. McConkie
Beckman Institute, University of Illinois
at Urbana-Champaign, USA

Michael Öllinger
Max Planck Institute for Human
Cognitive and Brain Sciences,
Munich, Germany

Alexander Pollatsek
University of Massachusetts,
Amherst, USA

Ralph Radach
Florida State University,
Tallahassee, USA

Keith Rayner
University of Massachusetts,
Amherst, USA

Erik D. Reichle
University of Pittsburgh, USA

Eyal M. Reingold
University of Toronto, Canada

Michael J. Spivey
Cornell University, USA

Geoffrey Underwood
University of Nottingham, UK

Jean Underwood
Nottingham Trent University, UK

Françoise Vitu
CNRS, Université de Provence,
Marseille, France

Ulrich W. Weger
State University of New York
at Binghamton, USA

Shun-nan Yang
Smith-Kettlewell Eye Research Institute,
San Francisco, USA

1

Visual extraction processes and regressive saccades in reading

Françoise Vitu

Abstract

When reading a text, our eyes mainly move forward by going from one word to the next, although they happen in some instances to return to previous regions of the text. This chapter investigates why and when regressive saccades occur, and where they send the eyes. It reveals that regressive saccades are determined by three types of processes including visuomotor, lexical, and higher-level syntactic and semantic processes, although the former two may be predominant. Most regressions are initiated quickly in response to prior oculomotor and processing events (i.e. the length of the prior forward saccade, whether or not a word was skipped during the prior saccade, and the length and frequency of the prior word), and independently of incoming information. The likelihood of later-triggered regressions may, however, also rely on the processing of currently available word information, although such regressions would not all result from process-related inhibition. The length of regressive saccades is not determined randomly; rather, regressions aim at specific word locations, sending the eyes to one of the prior words (most likely the immediately prior word), or the currently fixated word.

Introduction

While we read a text, our eyes progress along the lines by moving mostly from one word to the next, although sometimes skipping a word, or sometimes making an additional fixation on the currently fixated word. On some occasions, the forward eye movement pattern is interrupted by a regressive saccade that brings the eyes to a previous word or to another location in the currently fixated word. On average, regressive saccades occur in about 13 per cent of cases with adult readers, but their proportion increases to about 33 per cent in second-grade children, and 20 per cent in fifth-grade children (Lesèvre 1964; see also Buswell 1920).

Up to now, very little research has been dedicated to examining the determinants of regressive saccades. Are these saccades determined by the necessities of ongoing processing inherent to the reading task, or are they simply local readjustments made in response to oculomotor inaccuracies? If regressive saccades are cognitively controlled, do they depend on high-level syntactic and semantic integration processes or are they determined by lower-level processes associated with visual word identification? In addition, when the eyes move backwards, are they directed to a specific location in a specific word, or are they sent randomly to the left so as to express the need to interrupt the predominant forward eye movement pattern? Are regressions a substitute for a default forward eye movement pattern, do they need some sort of inhibition of a previously planned progressive saccade in order to occur, or are they as likely to occur as forward saccades, at least at some point during an eye fixation?

The literature on eye movements in reading, from the earliest research conducted at the beginning of the twentieth century, up to very recent theoretical and empirical developments, answers these questions. However, answers may be only preliminary, and more research is certainly needed to investigate the case of regressions.

Three possible accounts for the occurrence of regressive saccades in reading

Several hypotheses have been proposed to account for the occurrence of regressive saccades in reading. These can be grouped into three basic and non-exclusive explanations which involve different levels of processing, from text and sentence comprehension to word identification and low-level visuomotor processes.

Comprehension hypothesis

The comprehension hypothesis attributes regressions to the difficulties of ongoing language processing. It assumes that regressions are made in response to high-level processing demands related to sentence and text comprehension, and that they sometimes serve to re-inspect and re-analyze text information to deeper levels (Bouma and de Voogd 1974; Buswell 1920; Carpenter and Just 1977; Hochberg 1976; Just and Carpenter 1980; Shebilske 1975; Shebilske and Fisher 1983). As shown in several studies, the overall regression likelihood indeed varies with the difficulty of the text, the order of the words, the presence or absence of clarifying punctuation, the presence of a change in word meaning from sentence to sentence, the position of key words for text comprehension, and the tense in which the sentence is written (Bayle 1942; Cunitz and Steinman 1969; Klein and Kurlowski 1974; Shebilske and Fisher 1983; Wanat 1976). In addition, regressive saccades often occur in semantically or syntactically ambiguous sentences where a given word may have different meanings or syntactic functions (for a review, see Rayner and Pollatsek 1989). In ambiguous sentences, the eyes often regress from the disambiguating region back to the ambiguous region or to the beginning of the sentence.

Such findings are compatible with the comprehension hypothesis, but they do not unambiguously demonstrate that regressive saccades in natural reading result from high-level comprehension processes, nor do they indicate the proportion of regressions that could be attributed to such processes. First, when global factors related, for instance, to the difficulty of a text are manipulated, it is difficult to control the visual configuration of the text, and the respective roles of linguistic and low-level visuomotor factors can often not be distinguished. Similarly, sentence reading data need to be interpreted cautiously. When the ambiguity of a word in a sentence is manipulated, this generally involves the comparison of two sentences that differ by the presence or absence of a short word (e.g. 'that'). This may produce differences in the forward eye movement pattern during the first reading pass, and in turn favor differential regression rates which are unrelated to ongoing processing difficulties (see Trueswell *et al.* 1993). On the other hand, ambiguous sentences are generally absent from normal texts, as they might encourage or allow incorrect interpretations (Just and Carpenter 1980). Thus, semantic or syntactic ambiguities cannot be the only source for the occurrence of regressive saccades in natural reading.

Word identification hypothesis

Difficulties associated with ongoing word identification processes may form another basis for the execution of regressive saccades in reading. As proposed by several authors, regressions would be made in response to word recognition failures, or failures to complete the processing of a word before the eyes move on to a next word (Bouma 1978; Bouma and de Voogd 1974; Engbert *et al.* 2002; Pollatsek and Rayner 1990; Shebilske 1975). This hypothesis, referred to as the word identification hypothesis, is supported by several types of data suggesting that word identification processes often lag behind the ocular activity. Due to the influence of low-level visuo-motor constraints, words are frequently skipped irrespectively of whether or not they were previously identified, suggesting, therefore, that a word may be skipped even though not yet identified (for a review, see chapter 3; see also Brysbaert and Vitu 1998; O'Regan 1990). In addition, the identification of a previously fixated word is sometimes delayed until the eyes fixate on another word. Spillover effects, or instances where the lexical characteristics of a word affect the gaze duration and the duration of the first fixation on the following word, attest for it (Inhoff and Radach 1998; Kennison and Clifton 1995; Schroyens *et al.* 1999).

Still in line with the word identification hypothesis, incomplete processing of a previously encountered word appears to favor the execution of regressive saccades. As revealed in two recent studies, regressions depend on the frequency of occurrence of the encountered words, and when they occur they tend to return the eyes to where a difficulty was encountered (Vitu, and McConkie 2000; Vitu *et al.* 1998). Inter-word regressions are more likely when a previously fixated or skipped word is uncommon compared with when it is more frequent, with the effect being more systematic in word-skip instances. In contrast, intra-word regressions remain unaffected by the frequency of the prior word, but rather depend, as suggested in several other studies, on the efficiency of processing associated with the fixated word (Balota *et al.* 1985; Rayner *et al.* 1996; Vitu 1991a; Vitu *et al.* 1990). As the difficulty of processing associated with the fixated word increases, within-word refixations become more likely, these taking the eyes either to the beginning or end of the word depending mainly on the eyes' initial fixation position in the word (see O'Regan and Lévy-Schoen 1987; see also Pynte 1996).

Interestingly, the frequency of regressions in natural reading does not only vary with lexical and linguistic variables, but it also depends on perceptual and visuomotor factors. As shown by Vitu *et al.* (1998; see also Vitu and McConkie 2000) the overall regression likelihood varies first with the length of the prior saccade (when progressive), with more regressions following longer prior saccades (see also Andriessen and DeVoogd 1973; Lesèvre 1964). Second, it depends on whether the prior forward saccade skipped a word, the length of the skipped word, and the launch site or distance of the eyes in front of the word before skipping. Regressions, and more particularly inter-word regressions are more likely in word skip compared with non-word-skip cases, and following the skipping of longer and further words.

The likelihood of intra-word regressions is enhanced in non-word-skip instances (see Vitu and McConkie 2000), and as revealed in prior research on the determinants of within-word refixations, it strongly depends on the eyes' initial fixation position in words. The so-called Refixation-OVP (Optimal Viewing Position) effect is such that there is a higher probability of making an additional fixation on a word after the initial one when the eyes initially fixate towards the beginning or end of the word, than when they are near the center of the word (McConkie *et al.* 1989; O'Regan and Lévy-Schoen 1987; Rayner *et al.* 1996; Vitu *et al.* 1990; Vitu *et al.* 2001). If the initial fixation is to the right of the word's center, the eyes regress to the beginning of the word, while they move towards the end of the word after an initial fixation in the first part of the word. In addition, the likelihood of within-word refixations increases with the length of the fixated word, and it is greater in instances where the word was not available in peripheral vision before being fixated (Balota *et al.* 1985; Vitu 1991a; Vitu *et al.* 1990).

Effects of perceptual and visuomotor variables on the regression likelihood can be accounted for in the framework of a word identification hypothesis. First, the fact that regressions drive the eyes back to a previously skipped word with a probability that depends on both word length and launch site would simply result from visual acuity constraints. Due to the drastic decrease of visual acuity with retinal eccentricity, the likelihood a word can be identified is indeed reduced when the word remains in peripheral vision as in word-skip instances, and it is further reduced with longer skipped words or when the eyes are launched from far from the beginning of a word before skipping. In a similar manner, within-word refixations (hence intra-word regressions and progressions) would be most likely to occur when the eyes are initially near one of a word's ends since the number of letters that can be extracted from a word decreases with the distance of the eyes to the center of the word, which in turn reduces the likelihood the word can be identified in a single eye fixation (McConkie *et al.* 1989; Nazir *et al.* 1991). Within-word refixations would also be more likely with longer words and in the absence of parafoveal processing since the likelihood a word can be identified with a single eye fixation is decreased when the word is longer or when it could not be preprocessed in peripheral vision.

However, as we shall see below, alternative interpretations that do not make recourse to ongoing language processes can still be envisaged in order to account for the influence of perceptual and visuomotor variables, suggesting that regressions may not be purely determined by the difficulties of ongoing processing.

Visuomotor hypotheses

An alternative to both comprehension and word identification hypotheses consists of assuming that regressions are primarily determined by low-level visuomotor processes, and therefore independently of the needs of ongoing processing. This hypothesis which has taken several variants can potentially account for the systematic influence of perceptual and visuomotor variables on the regression likelihood. It suggests that ongoing word identification processes would intervene only as a modulator of a default eye movement pattern.

Learned eye movement patterns

The first visuomotor hypothesis attributes regressions to predetermined or learned eye movement scanning patterns. It assumes that regressions are automatically triggered in response to specific forward eye movement patterns or when the positioning of the eyes does not allow information from the text to be optimally extracted. Although indirectly serving the needs of ongoing processing, regressions are not determined online by ongoing language processes, but rather result from readers' experience with perceptual extraction processes. As originally proposed by O'Regan and Lévy-Schoen (1987; O'Regan 1990, 1992; see also Reilly and Radach 2003; Vitu and O'Regan 1995; Vitu *et al.* 1995), intra-word progressive and regressive saccades would be most likely following an initial fixation near the beginning or end of a word because readers have previously experienced that processing of a word is worst when the eyes are near one end of the word. Thus, after the eyes have landed on a word, a refixation would be automatically programmed with a probability depending on the distance of the eyes to the center of the word. In a similar manner, it can be proposed that regressions and most likely inter-word regressions result from readers' experience that processing of a word is impaired when the word is never displayed in foveal vision, and that the degree of impairment gets higher with longer words and further launch sites. As soon as a forward saccade longer than a given length would be executed, or more likely that a word of a given length and launched from a certain distance would be skipped, a regression would be automatically programmed.

The present hypothesis which attributes regressive saccades to predetermined eye movement scanning patterns is a real challenge to the word identification hypothesis since it can account for the influence of perceptual and visuomotor variables without making recourse to ongoing word identification processes.

Regressions as corrective saccades

Another visuomotor hypothesis was envisaged by Taylor in 1971, which is also consistent with several eye movement reading data. Taylor's view was that regressions in reading respond to oculomotor aiming errors in the same manner as corrective saccades do. As exemplified in several oculomotor studies, when participants are asked to saccade to a visual target present in peripheral vision, their initial saccade rarely brings the eyes at the exact saccade target location, and a secondary or corrective saccade immediately follows that places the eyes at the expected location (for a review, see Becker 1989). A simple observation at the pattern of eye movements during natural reading unambiguously shows that at least a certain proportion of regressions can be assimilated to such corrective movements. When the reader is presented with a full page of text, his (or her) eyes basically move from the beginning to the end of a line, the same pattern being repeated over and over again along the next lines. The return sweep that bring the eyes from one line to the next is generally launched from somewhere towards the end of a line, and it lands in between the beginning and the middle of the next line. This eye movement is generally followed by a regressive saccade towards the very beginning of the line, which very likely corrects for the systematic undershoot of the return sweep.

Aside from regressions associated with a return sweep, regressions also occur while the eyes move within a line of text, and the question of the determinants of regressions in reading actually concerns this latter type of saccades. Whether within-line regressions, or at least part of them, are a response to oculomotor aiming errors remains an open question. To answer that question, we would first need to know whether the eyes aim for specific words and specific locations in words while progressing on the lines of text, but this has never been conclusively shown. Still, several findings are consistent with the common belief that on each fixation in reading, the eyes aim for the center of the next word (or the center of a predefined target word), and that the variability of initial landing sites results from the influence of low-level visuomotor constraints that prevent the eyes in some instances from landing at the expected location (Just and Carpenter 1980; O'Regan 1990, 1992; O'Regan and Lévy-Schoen 1987; McConkie et al. 1988; Reichle et al. 2003; but see Vitu 2003). First, the distribution of initial landing sites in words reveals that the eyes preferentially land towards the center of words, or slightly to the left of it (Rayner 1979). Second, a great part of the variability of initial landing sites around the centers of words can be attributed to the saccades' launch site (or distance of the eyes from the beginning of a word) (McConkie et al. 1988; see also, Rayner et al. 1996; Vitu et al. 1995). When the eyes are launched from close to the beginning of a word, they are more likely to overshoot the center of the word, and as the launch site gets further away, undershoots become more likely. Interestingly, the launch site effect can be well described by a model which assumes that while the eyes aim for the center of words, they may be deviated towards the center of the range of possible target eccentricities or possible saccade lengths (McConkie et al. 1988; see also Kapoula 1985; but see Vitu 1991b).

Even though the hypothesis that forward saccades in reading aim for precise target words may require further investigation, regressions certainly share several characteristics with corrective saccades. First, they are more likely to occur following longer prior saccades, while the latter are associated with a larger degree of error (see McConkie et al. 1988). Second, inter-word regressions are more likely when the prior saccade skips over a word, or when a visual object or presupposed saccade target is missed. Actually, the observation reported below that the eyes tend to land at the very-beginning of the words following word skipping (see Figure 1.6) is consistent with the hypothesis that skipping is not deliberate, and that in most word-skip instances, the eyes intended to land on the word. Third, the likelihood of inter-word regressions increases with the length of the skipped words, while as shown by Reilly and O'Regan (1998; see also O'Regan 1990, 1992), the forward eye movement pattern in reading can well be described based on the assumption that on each fixation in reading, the eyes aim for the longest word in the periphery. If longer words are more likely to become a saccade target, it is understandable that when such words are skipped they are more likely to trigger the execution of a regressive saccade. Fourth, in the same manner as corrective saccades bring the eyes back at the exact saccade target location, inter-word regressions return the eyes to the center of the prior word, which supposedly corresponds to the saccade target (see Radach and McConkie 1998; Vitu *et al.* 1998). Fifth, as reported by Vitu *et al.* (1998), regressions are preceded by shorter fixation durations than forward saccades, while the average latency of corrective saccades is much shorter than the latency of primary saccades (see Becker 1989). Sixth, intra-word regressions intervene mostly when the center of a word is overshot, and they are preceded by shorter fixation durations than inter-word forward saccades.

It must be noted, however, that although regressions and corrective saccades present similarities, they may not have the same role. In particular, the fact that regressions are preceded by shorter fixation durations than forward saccades does not necessarily mean that regressions are initiated quickly in order to compensate for an oculomotor aiming error. Rather, this may indicate that a saccade is initiated faster when it relies on the processing of previously extracted information, than when it relies on the processing of newly extracted information. Furthermore, unlike corrective saccades, both intra-word regressions and progressions rarely bring the eyes back to the center of words which supposedly corresponds to the saccade target (see O'Regan and Lévy-Schoen 1987). Finally, as seen above, inter-word regressions are more likely following the skipping of long words that were launched from far before being skipped. In contrast, previous research has shown that smaller stimuli are more sensitive to effects such as the center-of-gravity effect which deviate the eyes from the aimed-for location (see Findlay 1982; Vitu 1991c). In a similar manner, oculomotor aiming errors that result in saccade target overshoot were only reported for small target eccentricities (Becker 1989; Kapoula 1985; see also McConkie *et al.* 1988). On this basis, we would expect inter-word regressions to be more likely with short and close words rather than longer and more distant words.

Conclusion

In conclusion, it appears that regressions in reading can occur in response to three non-exclusive types of processes, going from low-level visuomotor processes, to higher-level word identification, and sentence comprehension processes. According to our data, visuomotor and lexically-based regressions may, however, be predominant. Overall, as much as 77 and 85 per cent of within-line regressions made by adults and fifth-grade children in reading, respectively, direct the eyes to either another part of the currently fixated word, or to the immediately prior word, and, as discussed, these instances most likely result from visuomotor and/or lexical processes (Vitu *et al.* 1998; Vitu and

McConkie 2000). How many of those regressions act as corrective saccades and/or result from the adoption of low-level visuomotor scanning routines, however, remains to be determined. Recent studies on the spatial and temporal characteristics of regressive saccades, together with recent theoretical developments in the field of eye guidance in reading are presented below. These may further help understanding the purpose of regressive saccades in natural reading.

The temporal characteristics of regressive saccades

How recent models of eye movement control account for regressions

During the last 30 years, several theories and models were proposed in order to account for the variability of the eye behavior in reading (Engbert *et al.* 2002; Henderson and Ferreira 1990; Just and Carpenter 1980; Morrison 1984; O'Regan 1990, 1992; Reichle *et al.* 1998, 2003; Reilly and Radach 2003; Yang and McConkie 2001, 2004). These models make detailed assumptions about the determinants of saccade size and fixation duration, but surprisingly, only the most recent ones attempt to account for the occurrence of regressive saccades in reading. As we shall see, all current views attribute regressions mainly to ongoing cognitive processes, but these make different predictions on the time course of regressions, at least when such predictions can be made.

E-Z Reader

In the E-Z Reader model proposed by Reichle and colleagues, the issue related to regressions is very quickly and vaguely addressed. Inter-word regressions are assumed to result mainly from high-level syntactic and semantic processes, and therefore cannot be accounted for, as the model only deals with word identification processes (see Reichle *et al.* 2003). The possibility remains, however, as suggested in earlier versions of the model (E-Z Reader 3–5, Reichle *et al.* 1998), that some inter-word regressions result incidentally from word identification processes, although this was not further investigated.

A specific mechanism is proposed to account for the occurrence of within-word refixations, but how this would motivate the execution of a regressive vs. forward saccade is not clearly mentioned. Interestingly, within-word refixations would start being programmed quickly after the beginning of an eye fixation with a probability depending on the length of the fixated word. However, they would be executed only if an intermediate word identification stage (i.e. the word familiarity check) is not reached before the labile stage of saccade programming is terminated (or the saccade is about ready to go). Thus, within-word refixations, hence intra-word regressions would occur at relatively short and constant delays following the beginning of a fixation, and their likelihood would be determined early on based on ongoing processing of the fixated word.

SWIFT

Engbert *et al.*'s (2002) SWIFT model proposes more detailed assumptions on the determinants of regressions in reading, but it does not make a specific case out of regressive or refixation saccades. Both inter- and intra-word regressions would depend on ongoing word identification processes in the same manner as inter- and intra-word progressive saccades. The line of text could be compared with a saliency map, with the saliency of the words being a function of their level of lexical activity. Saccades would be generated after a random initiation time, and they would be directed to one of the words within an attentional window around the fixated point with the highest saliency at that point in time. Inter- and intra-word regressions would occur respectively when a word in the left part or at the center of the attentional window requires further processing. Additional inter-word regressions would eventually occur when the attentional window is displaced to another part of the text, while one of the words behind remains unrecognized.

Competition/Inhibition model

The Competition-Inhibition model proposed by Yang and McConkie (2001, 2004) also relies on the principle that saccades are generated after random initiation times. In this framework, however, saccades would not be directed to any place to the left or to the right depending on ongoing processing needs at a given point in time. Rather, regressions would be limited to only two time windows, allowing the occurrence of early and late regressions. Early regressions would occur within the first 125–150 ms of a fixation, a time-frame where both left and right visual fields would compete in determining the direction of the next saccade. They would mainly occur in response to prior oculomotor and processing events as the processing of incoming information would take more time to develop and to influence the eye behavior. Saccades initiated later than 125–150 ms would mostly move the eyes forward since a rightward eye movement bias (in reading European languages) would enhance the activation level in the right visual field from that point in time. Regressions could still occur in that time frame, but only through process-related inhibition. Ongoing processing associated with newly available information would first suppress a default forward saccade planned independently of the needs of ongoing processing, which would in turn dissipate the bias to the right and allow the occurrence of regressions. The influence of visual and lexical processes associated with incoming information being estimated to occur no earlier than 175 ms and 225 ms respectively from fixation onset, late regressions would not occur before such delays.

Comparisons among models

In summary, it appears that the three latest models of eye guidance in reading propose fundamentally different mechanisms in order to account for the occurrence of regressive saccades in reading, and that each model makes different predictions on the time course of regressions in relation with ongoing language processes. The Competition-Inhibition model distinguishes between two types of regressions, the ones that relate to information extracted from previous fixations, and the ones that relate to the processing of newly available visual information, with the assumption that the latter would require longer delays and would result from process-related inhibition. In contrast, E-Z Reader opposes inter- and intra-word saccades, predicting that intra-word regressive and progressive saccades would occur soon after the beginning of a fixation, although relying on information extracted from the current fixation. Finally, SWIFT does not make explicit predictions on the time course of regressions, but due to the temporal constraints associated with the processing of the encountered words, early-triggered regressions would most likely rely on the processing of previously extracted visual information. However, unlike Yang and McConkie's Competition-Inhibition model, SWIFT does not predict that regressions, even those related to information extracted from the current fixation result from saccade inhibition processes.

There are at present relatively few elements in the literature to help distinguish between the different views for the occurrence of regressive saccades. The empirical data that form the basis of Yang and McConkie's Competition-Inhibition model clearly indicate that the visual and lexical properties of the information displayed on a fixation start influencing the eye behavior only after 175 ms and 225 ms from fixation onset respectively. These data can hardly be reconciled with the proposal made in E-Z Reader that ongoing lexical processes associated with the fixated word can influence the likelihood of a within-word refixation, and thus the likelihood of an intra-word regression within the first 187 ms of a fixation (i.e. the estimated mean time to complete the labile stage of saccade programming). In addition, the observation that processing of newly available information massively suppresses forward saccades and in turn favors the occurrence of regressions, supports the notion of a forward eye movement bias that is not envisaged at all in either E-Z Reader or SWIFT.

At the same time, several limitations apply to Yang and McConkie's findings. First, there may be artifacts associated with the experimental manipulation itself since this involved rather severe intra-saccadic display changes, such as replacing the full page of text with a blank page or lines of Xs. However, the possibility envisaged by the authors themselves is rather unlikely given that similar results were obtained in situations that implied more subtle intra-saccadic changes (see below), and in more natural reading conditions that did not imply intra-saccadic changes (see chapter 5). More critically, the authors' manipulation did not allow them to investigate the determinants of early-triggered regressions, nor to determine the proportion of early vs. late regressions in natural reading. The previously noted observation that regressions are more commonly preceded by shorter durations, compared with forward saccades, particularly when a prior word was skipped, is compatible with the notion that regressions related to prior oculomotor and processing events may be determined at an early stage. However, this does not give a precise indication of when the effects emerge, if they rely only on previously extracted information, and whether or not they are associated with process-related inhibition. In a related manner, it is not clear from our previous investigations whether effects related to perceptual and visuomotor variables present the same time course as lexical influences.

Two recent studies which are described below provide further indications on the temporal properties of regressions in natural reading, and may help distinguish between the models. In line with Yang and McConkie's (2001, 2004) previous research, the first reported study indicates that the visual information extracted from a given fixation starts influencing the regression likelihood only after a certain delay from fixation onset. The second study reveals early but long-lasting effects of prior oculomotor and processing events.

The onset time of effects related to new visual information

In a recent study, adults read single lines of a text while their eye movements were registered; during some saccades, the line of text was displaced to the left or to the right by a few characters (Vitu *et al.* 2003; see for a similar manipulation, Huestegge *et al.* 2003). Although readers did not consciously perceive the displacement, their eye behavior was affected by it. The overall regression likelihood was increased when the text was shifted to the left (or when the readers' eyes landed further on the line of text than where they would have normally landed without the shift) compared with when the line of text was replaced by itself during the saccade (the no-shift control condition) or when it was shifted to the right. The effect of text shift was not present at all fixation durations, but only for fixation durations equal to or longer than 150–175 ms. Further analyses revealed that the effect did not result from the eyes being misplaced in the words due to text shift (or the eyes being not at the optimal viewing position for visual word extraction processes), nor did it result from ongoing word identification processes. The effect was also not associated with saccade inhibition. Rather, the effect appeared to result from low-level visual extraction processes signaling to the system that the eyes were not at the expected position on the line of text, or that the line of text was not positioned as it should be. The processes involved would rely on some sort of comparison of positional information between before and after the eye movement.

   Thus, in line with Yang and McConkie's previous research, low-level visual processes associated with the information extracted from a given eye fixation would not start influencing the eye behavior, and more particularly the regression likelihood before 150–175 ms from fixation onset. The fact, however, that the reported effects did not result from process-related inhibition suggests that a bias to the right may not be efficient around that time, which somehow contrasts with the proposal made in the Competition-Inhibition model that forward saccades are the default from about 125–150 ms from fixation onset.

The onset time of effects related to prior oculomotor and processing events

To further investigate the temporal characteristics of regressive saccades in natural reading, and to determine when various types of information start affecting the likelihood of a regression, a series of analyses was conducted on fifth-grade children's eye movement reading data (Vitu *et al.* 1998). These aimed at determining the time course of the effects related to five variables, including the length of the prior forward saccade, the event that characterized the prior forward saccade (word skip vs. non-word-skip), the length and frequency of the skipped word in word-skip instances, and the frequency of the prior word in non-word-skip instances. For that purpose, the likelihood of regression was measured as a function of the five variables, but separately for different fixation duration intervals. The selection procedure applied on fifth grade data was exactly the same as in Vitu *et al.*'s (1998) previous study. For the analysis, fixation durations were initially divided into six 50 ms time intervals from 100 to 400 ms, with an additional interval for fixation durations between 0 and 100 ms.

Due to a low n, the effects could only be tested over six or four intervals in some analyses. The length of prior forward saccades was re-coded into 2- or 4-letter bins depending on the number of data in each condition for a given analysis.

Variable 1: Length of the prior forward saccade

Figure 1.1 presents the overall regression likelihood as a function of the length of the prior saccade when progressive, and the fixation duration. This indicates first, as previously reported, that the regression likelihood increases significantly with prior saccade length ($F(8,232) = 57.30$, $p < 0.0005$ for fixation durations longer than 100 ms). The effect emerges quite early, within about 100–150 ms from fixation onset. For fixations shorter than 100 ms, the premises of an effect can be seen, at least for prior saccades between 6 and 10 letters, n being too low for the effect to be tested with longer prior saccades. Over time, the effect weakens to completely vanish around 300 ms from fixation onset, thus decreasing the proportion of regressions to about 20 per cent. The interaction tested over fixation durations between 100 and 400 ms was significant ($F(40,1160) = 56.51$, $p < 0.0005$); the same was true for the effect of fixation duration ($F(5,145) = 39.04$, $p < 0.0005$). The effect of prior saccade length was significant at all tested time intervals except the one before the last one ($F(4,116) = 3.58$, $p < 0.01$, $F(8,232) = 30.71$, $p < 0.0005$, $F(8,232) = 56.51$, $p < 0.0005$, $F(8,232) = 55.86$, $p < 0.0005$, $F(8,232) = 10.48$, $p < 0.0005$, $F(8,232) = 0.81$, $F(8,232) = 3.47$, $p < 0.001$, respectively for the seven time intervals from 0–100 ms to 350–400 ms). The significant effect found for the final time interval did not result from a systematic increase of the regression likelihood with prior saccade length.

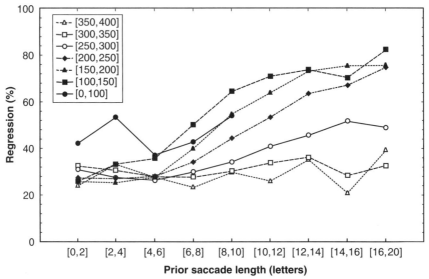

Figure 1.1 Percentage of regressions as a function of the length of the prior forward saccade, separately for seven different fixation duration intervals, from 0 to 400 ms. Prior saccade lengths were grouped in 2-letter bins.

Thus, the time window for the length of a prior forward saccade to influence the regression likelihood is relatively large, starting as early as 100–150 ms from fixation onset (or even before) and lasting up to about 300 ms (for similar findings with adults, see Vitu *et al.* 2003). This finding indicates that the effect related to prior saccade length does not initially rely on new visual information intake as it starts occurring before the information extracted from a given fixation can affect the eye behavior (which is estimated to occur near 175 ms from the beginning of a fixation – see above). It is tempting to interpret the effect in terms of saccade preprogramming (see Becker and Jurgens 1989; Morrison 1984; Yang and McConkie, 2001, 2004), assuming therefore that regressions start being programmed before the prior forward saccade is executed. However, the fact that the effect of prior saccade length can be observed after rather long delays, and after new visual information comes in strongly argues against this hypothesis.[1] Why would the system hold a preprogrammed saccade for as long as 250–300 ms? Actually, a plot of the hazard curves for regressive saccades[2] (not presented here) reveals that it is only from about 100–150 ms from fixation onset that saccadic activity starts rising due to prior saccade length, which more clearly argues against preprogramming. Interestingly, at about 225–250 ms, or around the time where lexical information comes in (see Yang and McConkie, this volume), regressions start being suppressed, progressively reducing the difference initially observed as a function of prior saccade length. Thus, it would take some time before the system could react to prior oculomotor or processing events, and by the time processing of new visual information comes in, the need to return the eyes to previous regions of the text would progressively diminish, and decisions taken early on would be cancelled. An alternative may simply be that early-determined regressions correspond to internally-based corrective saccades (or saccades programmed on the basis of oculomotor feedback). The likelihood of such regressions would drop naturally as time goes by, but independently of the processing of newly available information.

Variable 2: Whether or not a word was skipped during the prior forward saccade

The regression likelihood does not only vary with the length of the prior forward saccade, but it also depends on whether or not a word was skipped during the prior saccade (or prior saccade event): it is higher in word skip than in non-word-skip instances ($F(1,29) = 27.99$, $p < 0.0005$). This effect, shown in Figs 1.2A–F for different fixation duration intervals, also emerges quite early. It is present since at least 100–150 ms from the beginning of a fixation, and remains significant at all tested time intervals ($F(1,29) = 9.33$, $p < 0.005$, $F(1,29) = 6.78$, $p < 0.05$, $F(1,29) = 5.04$, $p < 0.05$, $F(1,29) = 56.09$, $p < 0.0005$, $F(1,29) = 6.28$, $p < 0.05$, $F(1,29) = 5.95$, $p < 0.05$, respectively for the six time intervals, from 100–150 ms to 350–400 ms). Interestingly, the effect varies over time,

---

[1] This suggestion was made by A. Inhoff.

[2] Following Yang and McConkie (this volume), hazard values were calculated by dividing the number of regressive saccades occurring within a given time interval by the number of saccades that still survived at the beginning of the interval.

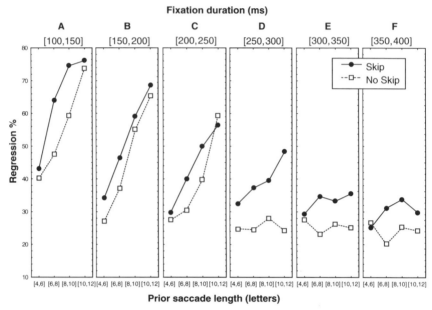

Figure 1.2 Percentage of regressions as a function of the length of the prior forward saccade and whether or not the prior saccade skipped a word, separately for six fixation duration intervals, from 100 to 400 ms (A–F respectively). Prior saccade lengths were grouped in 2-letter bins, with only the data for prior saccades between 4 and 12 letters being represented.

being greater before 150 ms and after 250 ms, particularly when the prior saccade is longer than 8–10 letters. As suggested by a comparison between Figures 1.2A–C and 1.2D–F, the major change that occurs around 250 ms, is a much stronger weakening of the effect of prior saccade length in non-word-skip compared with word-skip cases. The interaction between the prior saccade event and the fixation duration or the prior saccade event and the prior saccade length was significant ($F(5,145) = 2.35$, $p < 0.05$, $F(3,87) = 5.09$, $p < 0.005$, respectively), as well as the three-way interaction ($F(15,435) = 1.69$, $p < 0.05$).

The exact time where a prior saccade event starts influencing the regression likelihood could not be determined here since, due to a low n, the effect could not be tested for fixation durations less than 100 ms. However, it would be rather surprising if influences related to the prior saccade event occurred before those related to the length of the prior saccade. On the other hand, given that word skipping already influences the regression likelihood at about 100–150 ms from fixation onset, the effect cannot rely, at least initially, on incoming information. Rather, regressions would be firstly determined based on prior oculomotor and/or processing events. Later on (or around 250 ms), their likelihood could be influenced in addition, by the processing of newly available information. This would in a first time reduce the likelihood of regressions in instances where no word was skipped during the prior forward saccade, and would then more slowly suppress regressions following word skipping, the former being less damaging to ongoing processing than the latter. An alternative may again be envisaged, which is actually more compatible with Yang and McConkie's view, as it distinguishes between two types of regressions. Early regressions would be initiated in response to prior oculomotor and processing events, some of which corresponding to internally-based corrective saccades (see above). Their likelihood would drop progressively with time. Later regressions would be programmed based on the processing of incoming information. These would be more or less likely depending on prior events since the length of a prior forward saccade and whether or not a word was skipped may indirectly affect the efficiency of processing associated with the fixated word.

Variable 3: Length of a word skipped during the prior forward saccade

In word-skip instances, the regression likelihood depends on several variables including the length of the skipped word. Regressions are more likely with longer than shorter skipped words ($F(3,87) = 10.23$, $p < 0.0005$). As shown in Figures 1.3A–D, this tendency can be observed from at least 150–200 ms ($F(3,87) = 9.42$, $p < 0.0005$). After a delay of 200 ms from the beginning of a fixation, the only trend that remains consistent is a lower regression rate for 1-letter skipped words in comparison with longer words, the

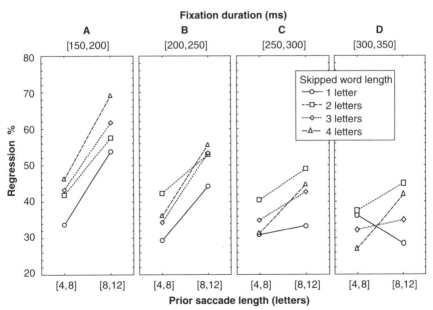

Figure 1.3 Percentage of regressions as a function of the length of the prior forward saccade and the length of the skipped word (1,2,3, and 4 letters), separately for four fixation duration intervals, from 150 to 350 ms (A–D respectively). Prior saccade lengths were grouped in 4-letter bins, with only the data for prior saccades between 4 and 12 letters being represented.

effect being still significant for fixation duration intervals up to 300 ms ($F(3,87) = 9.23$, $p < 0.0005$, $F(3,87) = 6.58$, $p < 0.0005$, $F(3,87) = 1.26$, respectively for the three time intervals, from 200–250 ms to 300–350 ms). The interaction between word length and fixation duration, or word length and prior saccade length was significant ($F(9,261) = 2.45$, $p < 0.05$, $F(3,87) = 3.59$, $p < 0.05$, respectively). Thus, the length of the skipped word affects the proportion of regressions at least at about the same time as incoming visual information becomes available (since it occurs within 150–200 ms from the beginning of the fixation), but it does not seem to be long-lasting. Whether the effect occurs earlier on could not be determined here.

Variable 4: Frequency of a word skipped during the prior forward saccade

In word-skip instances, the regression likelihood also depends on the frequency of the skipped word. The effect illustrated in Figs 1.4A–D for the case of 3-letter skipped words[3] is such that regressions are more likely with low- than high-frequency skipped words ($F(1,29) = 67.47$, $p < 0.0005$). It is present from at least 150–200 ms from fixation onset until about 250–300 ms or even later ($F(1,29) = 18.93$, $p < 0.0005$, $F(1,29) = 37.45$, $p < 0.0005$, $F(1,29) = 67.99$, $p < 0.0005$, $F(1,29) = 3.29$, $p < 0.10$, respectively for the four time intervals, from 150–200 ms to 300–350 ms). The interaction between word frequency and fixation duration was significant ($F(3,87) = 4.21$, $p < 0.01$). The present pattern of data tells us first that the frequency of a skipped word can have early influences on the regression likelihood, since at least 150 ms from the beginning of a fixation, or even before since, due to a low n, the effect could not be tested for shorter fixation durations. This variable intervenes either directly in combination with other variables (prior saccade length, prior saccade event, and skipped word length), or by modulating a decision taken earlier on the basis of low-level visuomotor processes (see above). Given the timing of the effect, it is more likely related to the lexical processing initiated based on previously extracted information. Indeed, as noted by Yang and McConkie (2001), lexical processing associated with incoming information cannot influence the eye behavior before 225 ms from the beginning of a fixation. It may still be the case that the processing of incoming information intervenes at some point in time, reinforcing the difference between high- and low-frequency words. With time, and new visual information, a previously skipped word would be more likely to be identified, and the need to return the eyes to it would become less stringent, at least when the word is easy to process (high-frequency word).

....

[3] For the needs of the present analyses, two word frequency categories were used that were defined based on different criteria than in the original study conducted by Vitu *et al.* (1998). Low- and high-frequency words had respectively a frequency of occurrence of less and more than 7866 occurrences per million according to the American Heritage Corpus (Caroll *et al.* 1971). The present value corresponded to the median of skipped word frequencies, ensuring therefore that a comparable number of data points were available in both word frequency categories, and across prior saccade length and fixation duration intervals.

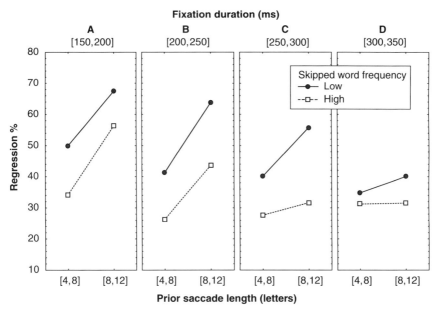

Figure 1.4 Percentage of regressions as a function of the length of the prior forward saccade and the frequency of 3-letter skipped words (high vs. low), separately for four fixation duration intervals, from 150 to 350 ms (A–D respectively). Prior saccade lengths were grouped in 4-letter bins, with only the data for prior saccades between 4 and 12 letters being represented.

Variable 5: Frequency of the prior fixated word in non-word-skip instances

For comparison, additional analyses were performed in instances where no word was skipped during the prior forward saccade (or when the prior word referred to as 'origin' word was fixated). These analyses reveal a pattern of data that is consistent with the observations made in word-skip cases. Figure 1.5 presents the regression likelihood as a function of the frequency of 6-letter origin words[4], and the fixation duration, but only for instances where the prior saccade was between 4 and 8 letters (due to a low n, other saccade length intervals could not be tested). There is again a tendency for more regressions to occur with low- vs. high-frequency origin words ($F(1,29) = 12.72$, $p < 0.005$). The effect is already present at about 150–200 ms from the beginning of the fixation, and it dissipates over time, near about 250 ms. The interaction was not significant ($F(3,87) = 1.60$), but the effect of word frequency was signifi-

[4] As for word-skip cases, two new word frequency categories were used in the present analyses. Low- and high-frequency words had respectively a frequency of less and more than 88 occurrences per million (American Heritage corpus, Carroll *et al.* 1971), which corresponded approximately to the median frequency of 6-letter origin/fixated words.

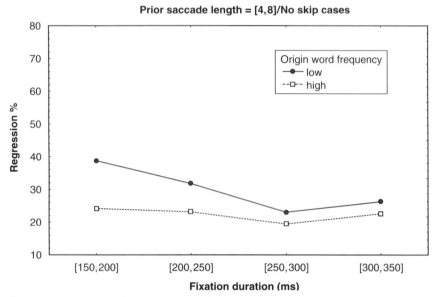

Figure 1.5 Percentage of regressions as a function of the frequency of 6-letter origin words in non-word-skip cases, separately for four fixation duration intervals, from 150 to 350 ms. Prior forward saccade lengths were all between 4 and 8 letters.

cant only for the first two tested time intervals from 150 to 250 ms ($F(1,29) = 10.39$, $p < 0.005$; $F(1,29) = 4.98$, $p < 0.05$, $F(1,29) = 1.16$, $F(1,29) = 0.61$, respectively for the four tested time intervals, from 150–200 ms to 300–350 ms). As for word-skip cases, it is very unlikely that the effect relies on the processing of current information. Rather, this would originate from the processing initiated based on information extracted during the previous fixation. The reason why the effect would stop earlier than in word-skip cases could be attributed to visual acuity constraints, or the fact that more information can be extracted from a word when it is fixated than when it remains in peripheral vision such as in word-skip cases. Thus, when some extra-time is given to the system for identification of the origin word (i.e. the duration of the fixation is longer), the need to return the eyes to it is lower even when the word is uncommon.

How to account for the time course of regressions in relation to information processing

In summary, the regression likelihood in natural reading varies with at least five variables, including the length of the prior forward saccade, the prior saccade event, the length and frequency of the prior skipped word, and the frequency of the prior word in non-word-skip instances. All effects occur relatively early, and they last until quite late during a fixation. The effects related to both prior saccade length and prior saccade event emerge at about 100–150 ms from fixation onset or even before, although it is very unlikely they are already present at the very beginning of an eye fixation.

The effects related to the length and frequency of the prior word start appearing no later than 150 ms after fixation onset. Whether they emerge earlier could not, however, be tested with the present data set. All influences except for those related to word length remain consistent and significant through at least 250–300 ms, with the effects of prior saccade event and skipped word frequency remaining until at least 300–350 ms from fixation onset.

The observed time course of the effects clearly shows that regressions made in response to prior saccade and processing events start being programmed and executed before new visual information comes in. Indeed, we have shown, in line with Yang and McConkie's (2001, 2004) earlier findings, that low-level visual extraction processes affect the eye behavior only from about 150–175 ms from fixation onset (Vitu *et al.* 2003). However, regressive saccades are not completely suppressed by the time processing of incoming information can start affecting the eye behavior. Rather, some regressions made in response to longer prior saccades still occur, and more particularly those made after a low-frequency word was skipped. Two assumptions were envisaged in order to account for the present pattern of data. Following Yang and McConkie (2001, 2004, see also chapter 5), the first assumption distinguishes between two populations of regressions. Early regressions would be initiated in response to prior oculomotor and processing events. While some of them may correspond to internally-based corrective saccades, others would rely on the processing of previously extracted information. In contrast, late regressions would mostly rely on the processing of newly available information, although their likelihood would depend on prior processing events, as the processing of successive words is probably not completely independent from one another. In particular, the processing associated with a fixated word may be somehow impaired or slowed down if the prior word was not identified and/or the prior forward saccade was long. While the likelihood of an early regression would quickly reduce over time, the probability of late regressions would rise slowly, starting when the processing of incoming information begins to influence eye behavior. Although this assumption cannot be rejected based on the present data, it must be noted that in contradiction with Yang and McConkie's proposal, further analyses revealed no trace of process-related inhibition. Thus, the presupposed late regressions here would fundamentally differ from what the authors refer to as late regressions.

The second assumption does not distinguish two populations of regressions, but rather interprets the effects in terms of a continuum. During a fixation regressions would start being planned early on in response to prior oculomotor and/or processing events. Over time, or as the duration of the fixation increases, ongoing processing of previously extracted information together with the processing of incoming information would reduce the need to return the eyes to previous words, thus suppressing regressive saccades. The present assumption does not exclude the possibility that additional regressions may occur later in response to processing difficulties associated solely with new available information, and as a result of process-related inhibition. It is also not opposed to Yang and McConkie's assumption that the eye behavior is biased forward from a certain time during an eye fixation. However, it suggests that the bias may not be efficient while information to the left of fixation still requires further processing. Alternatively, a forward eye movement bias would come into place only when previous information has been fully processed, thus suggesting that it would not influence saccade direction at a constant delay from fixation onset.

The question of how well the present findings can be integrated in the framework of other models of eye guidance in reading remains open. The present data certainly show that a model like E-Z Reader would need to envisage the possibility that regressions occur based on low-level visuomotor and/or lexical processes related to previously extracted information, rather than being simply a result of high-level syntactic processes (Reichle *et al.* 2003).

SWIFT could potentially account for the occurrence of regressions based on prior processing events, but probably not those relying on prior saccade events, at least if both sets of regressions need to be dissociated (Engbert *et al.* 2002). In addition, the hypothesis that saccades are generated based on a random initiation time, with the eyes being directed to the word that presents the highest saliency at a given point in time is consistent with the finding that the saccade directs the eyes either to the left or the right depending on when it is generated. Still to be shown, however, is that the time course of the words' lexical activity level predicted by the model fits the present data, namely that the words presenting the highest saliency shortly after the beginning of a fixation frequently correspond to the words to the left of fixation.

It must be noted that the present data are consistent with the notion that word identification processes follow approximately the same order as words in a sentence. Indeed, when a word is not completely processed while the eyes move on to the next word, the execution of an immediate regression to the word often occurs. However, this does not imply that words are processed sequentially or that two words cannot be processed in parallel. Rather, this shows that while the processing of a word is initiated, the processing of a prior word keeps on progressing, with the latter being most likely to influence the eye behavior early during a fixation. A parallel can be made here with the processing of foveal and parafoveal word information during an eye fixation in reading. The question has been raised whether both sets of information are processed in parallel or sequentially by means of an attentional mechanism, attention allowing supposedly word order to be preserved (Reichle *et al.* 2003; see also chapter 6). The simple fact that visual acuity constraints most likely favor the processing of the fixated word, helps preserve word order, and no recourse to attentional processes is necessary, thus suggesting that adjacent words are also processed in parallel (see Vitu 2003; Vitu *et al.* 2004).

The spatial characteristics of regressive saccades

In reading, the forward eye behavior is subject to significant variability. Sometimes the eyes move to the next word, sometimes they go to one of the words following it (therefore skipping one or several words), and some other times they make an additional fixation on the currently fixated word. When the eyes make a regressive saccade, a variety of eye movement patterns can also be observed, although the eyes land in the majority of cases (77 and 85 per cent in adults and fifth-grade children respectively) either on the currently fixated word or the immediately prior word (Vitu and McConkie 2000; Vitu *et al.* 1998). What determines where the eyes exactly move when making a regressive saccade? Are the eyes sent randomly to the left so as to express the need to interrupt the forward eye movement pattern, or are they sent to precise word locations?

Lengths of regressions: Random or resulting from a saccade target?

At a first sight, research on the determinants of regressions in natural reading may appear as favoring a saccade-target hypothesis or the assumption that regressions aim for precise word locations. It shows, as further detailed above, that the likelihood of inter-word regression mainly varies with prior oculomotor and processing events, while intra-word regressions depend mostly on visuomotor, perceptual and lexical variables related to the processing of the fixated word. Thus, everything happens as if regressions return the eyes to where a processing difficulty and/or an irregularity in the eye movement pattern was encountered. Most findings could, however, also be accounted for by a random hypothesis which according to the eyes move to the left, with saccades being selected randomly from a normal distribution.

As we have seen above, inter-word regressions mainly occur when a word was skipped during a prior forward saccade, while intra-word regressions occur in non-word-skip instances (Vitu and McConkie 2000). Interestingly, the distribution of initial landing sites in words varies as a function of whether or not a prior word was skipped. As shown in Fig. 1.6, when one or several words are skipped, the eyes preferentially land towards the very beginning of words or on the space in front of them, while they land near the center of words or to the right of it in non-word-skip cases.

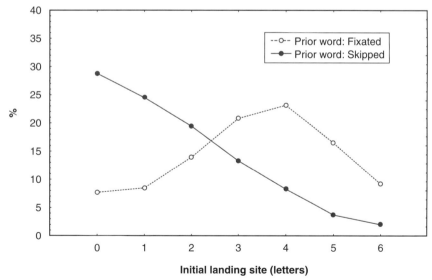

Figure 1.6 Distribution of initial landing sites in 6-letter words following a progressive saccade that skipped or did not skip the prior word(s). Data came from the corpus of fifth grade eye movement reading data (see Vitu *et al.* 1998)

Thus, when regressions are initiated, they are launched from different positions depending on the prior saccade event. In word-skip instances, regressions are mainly launched from the very-beginning of words, while they are launched from the end of words in non-word-skip instances. Under the assumption that saccades are determined randomly from a normal distribution centered around 2–4 characters (i.e. the mode of the distribution of regressive saccades in natural reading – see Vitu *et al.* 1998; Vitu and McConkie 2000), the regressions launched from the very beginning of a word (hence preceded by word skipping) would in most instances return the eyes to the immediately prior word. In contrast, same-size regressions initiated from the end of a word as in non-word-skip cases would mostly correspond to intra-word regressions. In other words, there would be no need for the system to aim for a precise word location when a difficulty is encountered on either prior or current word: executing a saccade of a relatively constant length would do the job equally well. When a difficulty related to a prior word would be encountered, this would generally result from a word being previously skipped, which, in most instances, would then constrain the eyes to return to the prior word. In contrast, if a processing difficulty were to happen at the current word location, this would be most likely associated with a non-word-skip prior event, and an intra-word regression would follow in most instances.

Arguments raised against random control

Several arguments can be raised against a random hypothesis, although further investigation is certainly needed. First, an analysis of the distribution of initial landing sites in words following inter-word regressions reveals a preference for the eyes to land towards the center of words (or a position slightly right of it), with some rather reduced variability around that location (see chapter 2; Radach and McConkie 1998; Vitu *et al.* 1998; see also Coëffé 1985). This result is consistent with the hypothesis that regressions are programmed in order to return the eyes to specific locations in words, although it could also be accounted for by assuming that the eyes are simply sent to the center of gravity of the first blob to the left of fixation (see Findlay 1982; Vitu 1991c).

Another and more convincing argument comes from Radach and McConkie's (1998) analyses of the relationship between launch site and landing site for different types of saccades (see also McConkie *et al.* 1988). A linear relationship can be observed for both inter- and intra-word progressions, as well as intra-word regressions but not inter-word regressions. This finding suggests that inter- and intra-word regressions rely on different processes, and different levels of accuracy. While the former would tend to direct the eyes to the center of a prior word in order to facilitate its identification, the latter would send the eyes to the part of the word that is opposite to where they were initially located in order to obtain complementary visual information. Since intra-word regressions are more likely to be initiated from the end of a word, these would bring the eyes somewhere towards the beginning of the word, but the exact saccade's landing site would not really matter. In a similar manner, when moving forward, the eyes would be sent somewhere further to the right where new visual can be found, without aiming for a precise location (see Vitu 2003).

Radach and McConkie's (1998) study was, however, limited to rather long inter-word regressions that landed on long words (between 5 and 10 letters), and originated from between 0 and 10 characters to the right of the words. In addition, it is very likely that the cases under study mostly corresponded to instances where the prior saccade did not skip a word. First, as suggested by Vitu *et al.*'s (1995) data, the probability of skipping a word between 5 and 10 letters is relatively low, from 0.30 to 0.05. Second, the eyes hardly land further than the first three letters of a word following word skipping (see Fig. 1.6). Does a distinction between inter- and intra-word regressions still apply to shorter regressions, and when word-skip instances are taken into account? Is the distinction limited only to saccades preceded by long fixation durations, or does it apply to all regressions? According to Radach and McConkie (1998), inter-word regressions would be more deliberate and they would be preceded by longer fixation durations. In line with this assumption, Yang and McConkie (2004) reported that the visual and lexical manipulations of the information displayed from the beginning of an eye fixation do not influence the length of regressions, except for regressions initiated after about 250 ms or even 350 ms from fixation onset.

Further arguments against random control: The need to distinguish inter- and intra-word regressive saccades

The analyses reported in the present section confirm the need to distinguish between inter- and intra-word regressions even in the case of short regressions initiated before 250 ms on average, providing further support to the saccade-target hypothesis.

Launch site analysis

To test for the existence of two separate populations of regressions, the distribution of the landing sites of regressive saccades was plotted as a function of the saccades' launch site, with particular attention being paid to instances where regressions were launched from the center of words. As we have seen above, when regressions are launched from the beginning or end of a word, both random and saccade target hypotheses make quite similar predictions on the landing sites of regressive saccades. In short, a single distribution should be observed, which should be centered on the prior word or on the first part of the currently fixated word. This is because fixations towards the ends of words constrain the range of possible regressions' landing sites, while corresponding at the same time to specific prior oculomotor and processing events: initial fixations towards the beginning of a word result mainly from a prior word being skipped, while initial fixations in the end part of a word usually correspond to non-word-skip instances. In contrast, when the eyes are launched from an intermediate location (e.g. the center of a 6-letter word), both inter- and intra-word regressions are equally likely, and word skip and non-word-skip instances are also equally likely (see Fig. 1.6). The question arises whether in those specific cases, the distribution of regressions' landing sites presents one or two separate peaks. According to the saccade-target hypothesis, a bimodal distribution should be observed, with the first part corresponding to inter-word regressions, and the second part to intra-word regressions. In contrast, a random hypothesis which assumes that the length of regressions is randomly determined from a normal distribution centered on about 2–4 characters would predict a distribution with a single mode somewhere near the space in between both words.

To test this specific prediction, analyses were carried out on a corpus of eye movement reading data collected on fifth-grade children. The same data selection criteria were used as in Vitu *et al.*'s (1998) study, except that in addition, only instances where the regressive saccade launch site corresponded to the initial fixation on a word were considered. Furthermore, only regressions crossing four words or less were selected. The length of regressions was on average of about 3.88 characters, and the mean duration of the fixations that preceded regressions was 240 ms. The distribution of landing sites resulting from the execution of regressive saccades was plotted separately for different launch sites (or different fixation locations within a given word), but irrespective of which word was being fixated after the regression (including, therefore, both inter- and intra-word regressions). Initial landing sites were coded relative to the beginning of the current or launch word, with positive and negative values corresponding respectively to intra- and inter-word regressions.

Figure 1.7 presents the results of a first global analysis where the lengths of both current and prior words were not controlled. In accordance with the above predictions, a single distribution is obtained when the eyes are launched from one of the ends of a word.

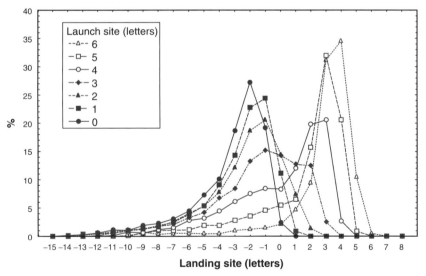

Figure 1.7 Distribution of regressive saccades' landing sites as a function of the launch site (or the position of the initial fixation on the current or launch word). Launch sites and landing sites are expressed in letters, with Letter 0 corresponding to the space in between both words. Positive values correspond to landing sites in the current word, while negative values correspond to landing sites in the prior word or one of the words in front of it. There was no control for length of either current or prior word(s).

Regressions launched from the very-beginning of a word (letters 1 and 2) or from the space in between both words (letter 0), mostly return the eyes to the prior word, while they land on the current word when launched from further away, or from a position that most likely corresponds to the end or the second part of the word. In contrast, when the eyes are launched from intermediate locations (letters 3 and 4), a tendency for a bimodal distribution can be observed. The part of the distribution that is the most represented corresponds to inter-word regressions for launch sites at letter 3, and intra-word regressions at letter 4. These data most likely favor the hypothesis that regressions aim for a precise word location, although further controls are necessary.

Launch site analysis with word length controlled

Since n becomes smaller as more controls are made, it is hard to control for the length of both prior and current words at the same time. A first step consisted, therefore, of controlling for the length of the prior word. In this analysis, two categories of prior word lengths were used that mixed 3- and 4-letter words, and 5-, and 6-letter words, respectively. As can be seen in Figs 1.8A–B, a single distribution of landing sites results from regressive saccades being launched either from the very beginning of a word or from a further position that most likely corresponds to the end of the word. In the former case, the mode of distribution is near the center of the prior word, whatever the length of the word, therefore confirming previous findings (Radach and McConkie 1998; see also, Inhoff *et al*. this volume). In the latter case, the mode of the distribution is centered on letter 3 of the current word, although it cannot be determined whether this corresponds to the first part or the center of the current word since there was no control for the length of the current word. Launch sites in between (letters 3 and 4) tend to produce a bimodal distribution, with the most represented part of the distribution corresponding either to the prior or the current word respectively. This pattern of data is consistent only with a saccade-target hypothesis. It is interesting to note, however, that when regressive saccades are launched from letter 3 in the current word, they are more likely to end up on the prior word when the word is short (3- to 4-letter words) than when it is longer (5- to 6-letter words). This surprising reverse word length effect is likely to be related to the prior saccade event. The need to return the eyes to longer words would be lower since those are less likely to be skipped in a first place.

Figures 1.9A–B present the same analyses, with control for the length of the current word, but the length of the prior word remaining undefined. Two categories of word lengths were used, 5- and 6-letter words, and 7- and 8-letter words respectively. It shows again a single distribution when the eyes are launched from the beginning or end of a word. In contrast, a bimodal distribution can be observed when the eyes are launched from near to the center of a word, with landing sites being either contained in the prior word or the current word. The position where the eyes land following an intra-word regression presents some variation as a function of both word length and launch site. It corresponds neither to the center or the first part of the word. Rather, the eyes appear to be moved a few characters left of their initial location, the distance crossed with the regression increasing as the initial fixation is closer to the end of the word (see for similar findings, Radach and McConkie 1998).

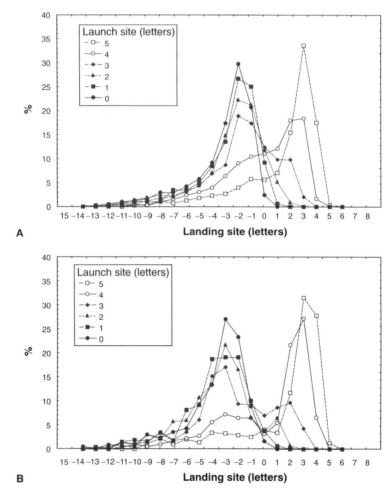

Figure 1.8 Distribution of regressive saccades' landing sites as a function of the launch site (or the position of the initial fixation on the current or launch word). Launch sites and landing sites are expressed in letters, with Letter 0 corresponding to the space in between both words. Positive values correspond to landing sites in the current word, while negative values correspond to landing sites in the prior word or one of the words in front of it. Immediately prior words were either 3–4 letters long (1.8A), or 5–6 letters long (1.8B). There was no control for the length of the current word.

The final analysis controlled for the length of both prior and current words. This was done with one of the most frequent pairs of word lengths in the present corpus of data: a current word of 6 letters preceded by a 3-letter word. Results presented in Fig. 1.10 confirm the observations reported above, although the data are a little noisier as n was strongly reduced in the present analysis. The whole set of data suggests the

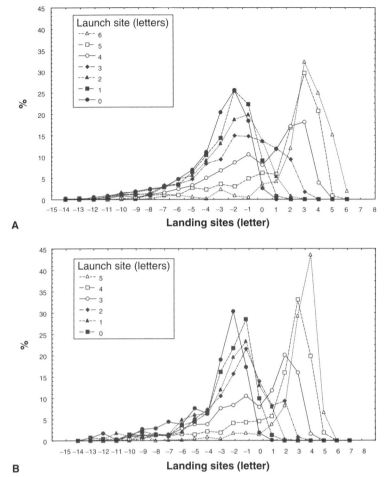

Figure 1.9 Distribution of regressive saccades' landing sites as a function of the launch site (or the position of the initial fixation on the current or launch word). Launch sites and landing sites are expressed in letters, with Letter 0 corresponding to the space in between both words. Positive values correspond to landing sites in the current word, while negative values correspond to landing sites in the prior word or one of the words in front of it. Current words were either 5–6 letters long (1.9A), or 7–8 letters long (1.9B). There was no control for the length of the immediately prior word.

existence of two separate populations of regressions, one that would direct the eyes to the prior word, and one that would aim at refixating the currently fixated word.

Discussion

In conclusion, it appears that the eyes are not sent randomly to the left when making a regressive saccade. Rather, they would be sent to precise word locations, suggesting

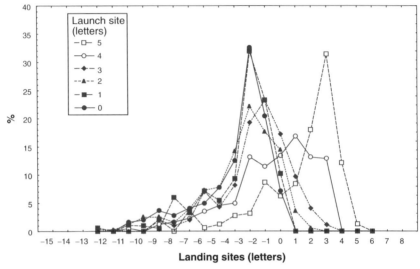

Figure 1.10 Distribution of regressive saccades' landing sites as a function of the launch site (or the position of the initial fixation on the current or launch word). Launch sites and landing sites are expressed in letters, with Letter 0 corresponding to the space in between both words. Positive values correspond to landing sites in the current word, while negative values correspond to landing sites in the prior word or one of the words in front of it. The current word was six letters long, and the immediately prior word three letters long.

the need to distinguish between inter- and intra-word regressions (see Radach and McConkie 1998). The former would mainly bring the eyes towards the center of the immediate prior word, while the latter would send the eyes somewhere to the left of the initial fixation. The respective roles of ongoing word identification and low-level visuomotor processes in determining the likelihood and the destination of a regressive saccade remains to be determined. Further research will also investigate the relationship between where and when decisions in the particular case of regressions. Given that the durations of the fixations that preceded regressions in the present data set were on average approximately 240 ms, the distinction between inter- and intra-word regressions does not seem to require long delays from fixation onset to emerge. This was actually confirmed in further analyses (not presented here), which revealed the possibility to obtain bimodal distributions around 150 ms from fixation onset. Thus, the system would not wait until 250 ms or longer to execute targeted regressions (see Yang and McConkie 2004), at least when those rely for a great part on prior oculomotor and processing events. The exact onset of targeted regressions, could not be determined here. However, a plot of the distribution of regressive saccade lengths (not presented here) reveals that regressions initiated under 150 ms are on average much longer and exhibit a greater variability than later regressions. Thus, it looks like regressions would be more accurately programmed when incoming information becomes available, although the possibility remains that the system sometimes makes recourse to internal representations for the planning of regressive eye movements (see chapter 2).

General conclusion

Research on regressive saccades in reading has focused on three main issues related to the determinants of regressions, and the spatial and temporal properties of regressions. This research has shown that regressive saccades are most often made in response to both low-level visuomotor and word identification processes, although they may also serve the needs of higher-level syntactic and semantic processes. When regressions are associated with immediately prior oculomotor and processing events, they start occurring at very short delays after fixation onset or even before new visual information comes in, but they are long-lasting, implying that their likelihood could also be influenced by incoming information. These regressions differ fundamentally from another set of regressions that occur in response to the processing of newly available information, and that result from process-related inhibition, although it is not clear at present how both sets of regressions articulate. The length of regressions is not randomly determined. Rather, the eyes are sent to specific word locations, suggesting therefore the need to distinguish between inter- and intra-word regressions.

Acknowledgements

I would first like to thank George W. McConkie and David Zola for letting me use the corpus of fifth grade eye movement reading data that was collected at the University of Illinois at Urbana-Champaign in collaboration with John Grimes. I would also like to mention that the motivation behind the present work came from long and fruitful interactions with George W. McConkie. These interactions were supported by a grant from a specific agreement between CNRS (France) and the University of Illinois at Urbana-Champaign (USA). I am also grateful to A. Inhoff, G.W. McConkie and an anonymous reviewer for their very helpful comments on an earlier version of the chapter.

References

Andriessen, J. J., and De Voogd, A. H. (1973). Analysis of eye movement patterns in silent reading. *IPO Annual Progress Report*, **8**, 29–34.

Balota, D. A., Pollastek, A. and Rayner, K. (1985) The interaction of contextual constraints and parafoveal visual information in reading. *Cognitive Psychology*, **17**, 364–390.

Bayle, E. (1942). The nature and causes of regressive movements in reading. *Journal of Experimental Education*, **11**, 16–36.

Becker, W. (1989). Metrics. In: R.H. Wurzt and M.E. Goldberg (ed.) *The neurobiology of saccadic eye movements*. Asterdam, New York: Elsevier, pp. 13–67.

Becker, W., and Jurgens, R. (1979). An analysis of the saccadic system by means of double-step stimuli. *Vision Research*, **19**, 967–983.

Bouma, H. (1978). Visual search and reading: Eye movements and functional visual field: A tutorial review. In: J. Requin (ed.) *Attention and performance VII*. Hillsdale, NJ: Erlbaum, pp. 115–145.

Bouma, H., and De Voogd, A. H. (1974) On the control of eye saccades in reading. *Vision Research* **14,** 273–284.

Brysbaert, M., and Vitu, F. (1998). Word skipping: Implications for theories of eye movement control in reading. In: G. Underwood (ed.). *Eye guidance in reading, driving, and scene Perception.* Oxford: Elsevier, pp. 125–147.

Buswell, G. T. (1920). An experimental study of the eye-voice span in reading. *Supplementary Educational Monographs, 17,* Chicago, University of Chicago.

Carpenter, P.A., and Just, M. A. (1977). Integrative processes in comprehension. In: D. Laberge and S.J. Samuels (ed.) *Basic processes in reading: Perception and comprehension.* Hillsdale, NJ: Erlbaum.

Carroll, J. B., Davies, P., and Richman, B. (1971). *The American Heritage word frequency book.* New York: Houghton Mifflin Company.

Coëffé, C. (1985). La visée du regard sur un mot isolé. *L'Année Psychologique,* **85,** 169–184.

Cunitz, R. J., and Steinman, R. M. (1969). Comparison of saccadic eye movements during fixation and reading, *Vision Research,* **9,** 683–693.

Engbert, R., Longtin, A., and Kliegl, R. (2002). A dynamical model of saccade generation in reading based on spatially distributed lexical processing. *Vision Research,* **42,** 621–636.

Findlay, J. M. (1982). Global visual processing for saccadic eye movements. *Vision Research,* **22,** 1033–1045.

Henderson, J. M., and Ferreira, F. (1990). Effects of foveal processing difficulty on the perceptual span in reading: Implications for attention and eye movement control. *Journal of Experimental Psychology: Learning, Memory and Cognition,* **16,** 417–429.

Hochberg, J. (1976). Toward a speech-plan eye-movement model of reading. In: R.A. Monty and J.W. Senders (ed.) *Eye movements and psychological processes.* Hillsdale, New Jersey: Erlbaum, pp. 397–416.

Huestegge, L., Radach, R., Vorstius, C., and Wade, N. (2003). On the metrics of refixation saccades in normal reading. Paper held at the 12th European Conference on Eye Movements, 20–24 August 2003, Dundee, Scotland.

Inhoff, A. W., and Radach, R. (1998). Definition and computation of oculomotor measures in the study of cognitive processes. In: G. Underwood (ed.) *Eye Guidance in Reading and Scene Perception.* Oxford: Elsevier, pp. 29–53.

Just, M. A., and Carpenter, P.A. (1980). A theory of reading: from eye fixations to comprehension. *Psychological Review,* **87,** 329–354.

Kapoula, Z. (1985). Evidence for a range effect in the saccadic system. *Vision Research,* **25,** 1155–1157.

Kennison, S. M., and Clifton, C. C. (1995). Determinants of parafoveal preview benefit in high and low working memory capacity readers: Implications for eye movement control. *Journal of Experimental Psychology: Learning, Memory, and Cognition,* **21,** 68–81.

Klein, G. A., and Kurlowski, F. (1974). Effect of task demands on relationship between eye movements and sentence complexity. *Perceptual and Motor Skills,* **39,** 463–466.

Lesèvre, N. (1964). Les mouvements oculaires d'exploration. Etude électro-oculographique comparée d'enfants normaux et d'enfants dyslexiques. Thèse, Paris.

McConkie, G. W., Kerr, P. W., Reddix, M. D., and Zola D. (1988). Eye movement control during reading: I. The location of initial eye fixations on words. *Vision Research,* **28,** 1107–1118.

McConkie, G. W., Kerr, P. W., Reddix, M. D., Zola, D., and Jacobs, A. M. (1989). Eye movement control during reading: II. Frequency of refixating a word. *Perception and Psychophysics*, **46,** 245–253.

Morrison, R. E. (1984). Manipulation of stimulus onset delay in reading: Evidence for parallel programming of saccades. *Journal of Experimental Psychology: Human Perception and Performance*, **10,** 667–682.

Nazir, T., O'Regan, J. K., and Jacobs, A.M. (1991). On words and their letters. *Bulletin of the Psychonomic Society*, **29,** 171–174.

O'Regan, J. K. (1990). Eye movements and reading. In: E. Kowler (ed.) *Eye movements and their role in visual and cognitive processes.* Amsterdam, Oxford: Elsevier, pp. 395–453.

O'Regan, J. K. (1992). Optimal viewing position in words and the Strategy-Tactics theory of eye movements in reading. In: K. Rayner (ed.) *Eye movements and visual cognition: Scene perception and reading.* New York: Springer-Verlag, pp. 333–354.

O'Regan, J. K., and Lévy-Schoen, A. (1987). Eye movement strategy and tactics in word recognition and reading. In: M. Coltheart (ed.) *Attention and Performance XII: The psychology of reading.* Hillsdale, NJ: Erlbaum, pp. 363–383.

Pollatsek, A., and Rayner, K. (1990). Eye movements and lexical access in reading. In: D. A. Balota, G. B. Flores d'Arcais, and K. Rayner (ed.) *Comprehension processes in reading.* Hillsdale, NJ: Erlbaum, pp. 143–163.

Pynte, J. (1996). Lexical control of within-word eye movements. *Journal of Experimental Psychology: Human Perception and Performance*, **22(4),** 958–969.

Radach, R., and McConkie, G. W. (1998). Determinants of fixation positions in words during reading. In: G. Underwood (ed.) *Eye guidance in reading and scene perception.* Oxford: Elsevier, pp. 77–100.

Rayner, K. (1979). Eye guidance in reading: fixation location within words. *Perception*, **8,** 21–30.

Rayner, K., and Pollatsek, S. (1989). *The psychology of reading.* London: Prentice-Hall.

Rayner, K., Sereno, S. C., and Raney, G. E. (1996). Eye movement control in reading: A comparison of two types of models. *Journal of Experimental Psychology: Human Perception and Performance*, **22,** 1188–1200.

Reichle, E. D., Pollatsek, A., Fisher, D. L., and Rayner, K. (1998). Toward a model of eye movement control in reading. *Psychological Review*, **105,** 125–157.

Reichle, E. D., Rayner, K., and Pollatsek, A. (2003). The E-Z Reader model of eye movement control in reading: comparisons to other models. *Behavioral and Brain Sciences*, **26,** 445 – 526.

Reilly, R., and O'Regan, J. K. (1998). Eye movement control in reading: A simulation of some word-targeting strategies. *Vision Research*, **38,** 303 – 317.

Reilly, R., and Radach, R. (2003). Foundations of an interactive model of eye movement control in reading. In: J. Hyönä, R. Radach, and H. Deubel, (ed.) *Cognitive and applied aspects of eye movement research.* Amsterdam: Elsevier, pp. 429–455.

Schroyens, W., Vitu, F., Brysbaert, M., and d'Ydewalle., G. (1999). Eye movement control during reading: foveal load and parafoveal processing. *Quarterly Journal of Experimental Psychology*, **52A,** 1021–1046.

Shebilske, W. (1975) Reading eye movements from an information-processing point of view. In: D. Massaro (ed.) *Understanding language.* New York: Academic Press, pp. 291–311.

Shebilske, W. L., and Fisher, D. F. (1983). Eye movements and context effects during reading of extended discourse. In: K. Rayner (ed.) *Eye movements in reading: Perceptual and language processes.* New York: Academic Press, pp. 153–179.

Taylor, E. (1971). The dynamic activity of reading: A model of the process. *Research information bulletin No. 9*. New York: Educational Developmental Laboratories.

Trueswell, J. C., Tanenhaus, M. K., and Kello, C. (1993). Verb-specific constraints in sentence processing: Separating effects of lexical preference from garden-paths. *Journal of Experimental Psychology: Learning, Memory and Cognition*, **19**, 528–553.

Vitu, F. (1991a). The influence of parafoveal preprocessing and linguistic context on the optimal landing position effect. *Perception and Psychophysics*, **50**, 58–75.

Vitu, F. (1991b). Research Note: Against the existence of a range effect during reading, *Vision Research*, **31**, 2009–2015.

Vitu, F. (1991c). The existence of a center of gravity effect during reading, *Vision Research*, **31**, 1289–1313.

Vitu, F. (2003). The basic assumptions of E-Z Reader are not well-founded. *Behavioral and Brain Sciences*, **26**, 506–507.

Vitu, F., and McConkie, G. W. (2000). Regressive saccades and word perception in adult reading. In: A. Kennedy, R. Radach, D. Heller, and J. Pynte (ed.) *Reading as a perceptual process*, Oxford: Elsevier, pp. 301–326.

Vitu, F., and O'Regan, J. K. (1995). A challenge to current theories of eye movements in reading. In: J. Findlay, R. W. Kentridge, and R. Walker (ed.) *Eye movement research: Mechanisms, Processes and applications*. Amsterdam, Lausanne, NY, Oxford, Shannon, Tokyo: Elsevier, pp. 381–392.

Vitu, F., O'Regan J. K., and Mittau, M. (1990). Optimal landing position in reading isolated words and continuous text. *Perception and Psychophysics*, **47**, 583–600.

Vitu, F., O'Regan, J. K., Inhoff, A. W., Topolski, R. (1995). Mindless reading: Eye movement characteristics are similar in scanning strings and reading texts. *Perception and Psychophysics*.

Vitu, F., McConkie, G. W., and Zola, D. (1998). About regressive saccades in reading and their relation to word identification. In: G. Underwood, *Eye guidance in reading and scene perception*. Oxford: Elsevier, pp. 101–124.

Vitu, F., McConkie, G. W., Kerr, P., and O'Regan, J. K. (2001). Fixation location effects on fixation durations during reading : an inverted optimal viewing position effect. *Vision Research*, **41**, 3511–3531.

Vitu, F., McConkie, G. W. and Yang, S.-N. (2003). Readers' oculomotor responses to intra-saccadic text shifts. *Perception*, **32**, 24.

Vitu, F., Brysbaert, M., and Lancelin, D. (2004). A test of parafoveal-on-foveal effects with pairs of orthographically related words. *The European Journal of Cognitive Psychology*, **16**, 154–177.

Wanat, S.F. (1976). Language behind the eye: Some findings, speculations, and research strategies. In: R. A. Monty and J. W. Senders (ed.) *Eye movements and psychological processes*. Hillsdale, NJ: Erlbaum.

Yang, S.-N., and McConkie, G. W. (2001). Eye movements during reading: a theory of saccade initiation times. *Vision Research*, **41**, 3567–3585.

Yang, S.-N., and McConkie, G.W. (2004). Saccade generation during reading: Are words necessary? *The European Journal of Cognitive Psychology*, **16**(1/2), 226–261.

2

Sources of information for the programming of short- and long-range regressions during reading

Albrecht W. Inhoff, Ulrich W. Weger and Ralph Radach

Abstract

Readers execute regressions to move the eyes to a previously-read segment of text. Short-range regression and similar size forward directed saccades differ in that interword regressions are neither influenced by word length nor launch site. We propose that these regressions are controlled by relatively precise representations of word location. Longer-range regressions are relatively rare during reading. Recent results from our laboratory indicate that they are spatially inaccurate and that readers generally execute more than one regression to find the location of a relatively distant regression target. We propose that linguistic knowledge contributes to the guidance of these regressions.

Introduction

Written linguistic symbols need to be arranged according to spatial conventions so that their order can be determined. In English and other alphabetic writing systems, letters and words are ordered from left to right along lines of print and consecutive lines are ordered from top-to-bottom. Traditional Chinese uses more flexible convention, as a sequence of characters can be arranged from left to right, right to left, or top to bottom. Writing systems also differ in the spatial marking of constituent units. In English and other European scripts, words are spatially segmented by interword blank spaces, and large differences in word length give each word a distinct spatial appearance. Interword spaces are absent in Chinese (and in some other Asian languages) where text is composed of equal-sized and equal-spaced characters.

The spatial segmentation and ordering of linguistic symbols provides two sources of information: they define the location of to-be-read symbols, and they inform the reader where a previously-read segment of text can be found. Readers need to know the location of new information because effective vision is limited to a relatively small spatial segment of text during each fixation in reading. Rayner's (1975) and McConkie and Rayner's (1975) influential studies with English text, together with a large number of follow-up studies with English and other languages (see Rayner 1998, for a review), showed that the bulk of effective linguistic information is obtained from the directly fixated word and, to a lesser extent, from the adjacent (parafoveal) words in the text. To read further on, readers must thus execute a saccade so that a new segment of text can be viewed.

Left-to-right directed saccades, which typically extend across 7 to 10 letter spaces, account for the vast majority of eye movements in the reading of left-to-right ordered text. A much smaller proportion of eye movements, between 5–20 per cent, are directed to a location to the left of a current fixation (Huey 1908). Typically, the size of these regressions is relatively small. In Vitu and McConkie's (2000) corpus data, the modal amplitude was 2 letter spaces for within-word regressions, and 3–4 letter spaces for interword regressions, and 99 per cent of all regressions extended across fewer than 10 letter spaces. Though overall quite rare, longer-range regressions occur with increased frequency when text comprehension difficulties are encountered. For instance, regressions to a previously-read lexically ambiguous word occur more often than regressions to a matched control word when the text following the ambiguous word favors its subordinate meaning (Carpenter and Daneman 1981; Folk and Morris 1995).

The current chapter first examines differences in the programming of short-range progressive and of similar-size regressive saccades during reading. It then seeks to determine the source(s) of knowledge that guide readers' short- and long-range regressions.

The programming of short-range progressive and regressive saccades during reading

In normal reading, saccades going from left to right from one word to another (progressive interword saccades) tend to land between the beginning and the center of the target word. This basic phenomenon of eye movement control in reading is commonly referred to as the preferred viewing position (Rayner 1979). In a now classic paper, McConkie et al. (1988), provided the first detailed examination of the metrical properties of these saccades. They showed that the truncated Gaussian distributions of initial saccade landing positions can be partitioned into launch site and word length specific sub-distributions. Of particular importance is the influence of the distance between the launch site of the critical saccade and the position of the target word. If this distance is short, interword progressions tend to overshoot the intended target location, commonly assumed to be the center of the word. If saccades are launched from more distant positions, they tend to undershoot the target, which may even result in an increasing proportion of saccades landing left of the word boundary. There is a linear relation between launch site and landing position such that for every increment in launch distance (measured in character spaces) there is a leftward shift of the resulting mean landing position in the order of about 0.5 characters. This basic metrical property of progressive saccades in reading is often referred to as the 'saccade range' or 'launch distance' effect.

Using a similar methodology, Radach and McConkie (1998) examined the metrical properties of several types of reading saccades using a corpus of eye movement data collected at the University of Illinois. Four subjects ware asked to read the first half of the novel *Gulliver's Travels* in German, resulting in a corpus of about 220,000 fixations. Radach and McConkie first replicated and extended the original analyses by McConkie *et al.* (1988), showing that several visual low-level factors influence the landing positions of progressive interword saccades. Again, the most important variable was the launch distance with incoming progressive saccades from nearer previous fixation positions landing further to the right within the target word. Additional low-level factors like the length of the target word and its position on the line also influenced landing positions (see chapter 1 for a recent detailed analysis of line position effects).[1] Another powerful, more cognitively determined factor was the previous fixation pattern. For a given launch distance, the nonfixation (skipping) of the prior word shifted landing positions to the left, while a prior refixation shifted landing positions to the right (Radach and Kempe 1993).

Critically, Radach and McConkie found that the linear 'landing position function' between launch distance and mean landing site described above can also be extended to refixation saccades. This result suggests that refixations (including regressive refixations) have the same metrical properties and are hence likely to be guided by the same mechanism of control as progressive interword saccades. A strikingly different pattern of results emerged when short-range interword regressions were examined. As in the corpus used by Vitu and McConkie (2000), most of these regressions originated from positions relatively close to the target word. Of all regressive saccades made within the same line of text to words of length 5–10, 26.0 per cent were launched from within the same word (regressive refixations), 49.4 per cent came from the immediately following word and only 24.6 per cent originated from more distant locations. Looking at the distribution of landing positions for short-range regressive saccades, there was no longer any effect of launch site. Irrespective of whether interword regressions extended across one or ten letters, the landing site distribution always had a clear maximum at the word center (see also Vitu *et al.* 1998).

A reanalysis of Radach and McConkie's (1998) corpus, examining the effect of the length of the to-be-fixated word on progressive and regressive interword saccades,

---

[1] It could be claimed that factors like eccentricity and word length are not only visual-spatial in nature but do also provide constraints for linguistic processing. However, at least for the case of word length it has been shown that parafoveal word length information does not constrain orthographic and lexical processes (Inhoff *et al.* 2003).

reveals additional differences between both types of saccades. In agreement with McConkie *et al.* (1994), Radach (1996) had found a significant effect of word length on mean landing positions for progressive saccades. For the four German readers, the individual average increase (relative to the word beginning) in mean landing position was 0.16, 0.18, 0.14 and 0.11 letters for each one-character increase in word length. Radach and McConkie (1998) interpreted this finding as evidence for a 'center of gravity' phenomenon (Findlay 1982) that modulates the much stronger effect of launch distance. This followed O'Regan's (1990) idea that the landing position of saccades can be influenced by the presence of further elements in the critical visual configuration, in this particular case additional letters belonging to the same target word (see also Vitu 1991; chapter 1).

The influence of word length on progressive initial landing positions just described may appear to be relatively small, but looking at a range of word length, e.g. from 5 to 10 letters, it results in a substantial shift of the whole distribution. We were interested in whether this effect would also be present in the case of regressive interword saccades. Figure 2.1 shows the distribution of landing positions of interword regressions landing within words of length 5–10, using the aggregated data set from all readers in the German Gulliver corpus. Clearly, there is no systematic relation between word length and landing position. In all cases there is a peak at or very near to the center of the target word and the shapes of the distributions are nearly identical. Taken together, the missing launch site effect first shown by Radach and

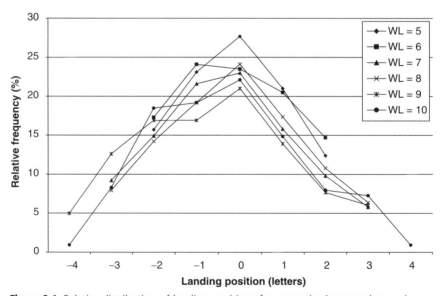

Figure 2.1 Relative distribution of landing positions for regressive interword saccades as a function of target word length. The ordinate, indicating mean landing position, is numbered with respect to the center of the word. Pooled data from four subjects.

McConkie (1998) and the missing word length effect reported here reveal that low-level factors that strongly influence landing positions of progressive interword saccades (and intraword refixations) have virtually no effect on short-range interword regressions. In her chapter in the present volume, Vitu presents a detailed analysis of regressive saccades based on a large corpus of reading data collected from fifth-grade children. With regard to the *question* of launch distance and word length effects on the metrics of regressions, she arrives at very similar conclusions, again underscoring the special status of interword regressive saccades in reading.

Form a theoretical point the distinct properties of interword regressions are quite intriguing. They represent a deviation from the normal routine pattern of 'automated scanning' during forward reading (see Findlay and Walker 1999, for a detailed discussion of automated oculomotor control). They may thus be based on a mode of visuomotor control as it is typical for single goal-directed saccades. As shown, for example by Lemij and Colleweijn (1989), the saccadic undershoot often reported in basic oculomotor research can be nearly eliminated in conditions where target positions remain stationary over several trials, as opposed to sudden peripheral onsets. In paradigms with saccade targets at varying eccentricities, conditions can be created in which the saccade range effect is diminished (Kapoula and Robinson 1986). Moreover, when subjects are instructed to delay the execution of an imminent saccade, accuracy can also be greatly increased by reducing the amount of under- and overshoot (Coëffé and O'Regan 1987). In essence, the key idea is that both interword progression and regressions are under direct visual control. The critical difference may be that in the case of regressions a more careful or effortful mode of preparation is used. This suggestion will be referred to as the *focused visual control hypothesis*. Given that many regressions are caused by interruptions in word or sentence processing, it appears reasonable to assume that saccade accuracy may profit from an exclusive focusing of both low and high spatial frequency vision on the target region or object immediately left of the currently fixated word.

An alternative explanation for the missing saccade distance effect could be that the coordinates for interword regressions are taken from a spatial representation in memory that serves as an index of previously fixated objects or locations (Kennedy 1987, 1992; Kennedy *et al.* 2003). Assuming that the spatial reference system is constant between successive saccades and that the current position within this reference frame is determined at fixation onset, this type of saccade preparation would not require substantial visual processing of the peripheral target region. We will present a detailed review of the relevant literature concerning this spatial indexing hypothesis in the second part of the present chapter.

Data from a recent series of experiments enable us to examine the alternative hypotheses introduced above. The original purpose of these studies was to test the idea put forward by Beauvillain *et al.* that within-word refixation saccades are planned as one package together with the intial interword saccade (e.g. Beauvillain *et al.* 2000; Vergilino and Beauvillain 2001). These authors suggest that, when (and only when) a refixation of the next word is imminent, a sequence of two saccades is pre-programmed.

To test this idea, we used a sentence reading paradigm where the entire line of text can be shifted to the left or to the right while subjects execute a progressive saccade into a critical word.[2] These critical words were 10 or 11 letters long with carefully controlled word frequency and morphological complexity and they were always preceded by a medium (5–9 letter) length adjective. The main result from various variations of the line shift technique is that refixation saccades are in fact under direct visual control and that there is no substantial difference in the mode of control for progressive interword vs. refixation saccades. Compelling evidence for this position comes from the finding that, depending on the shift condition, the visual configuration that is present when the eyes enter the target word determines both direction and target word of the following inter- or intraword saccades (Huestegge *et al.* 2003). As an example, when the eyes land in a target word that has been shifted to the right, significantly more progressive and less regressive refixations are made from a given absolute (pre-shift) landing position of the initial progressive saccade.

In the context of the present discussion the line shift paradigm provides a useful tool to examine whether regressive interword saccades are under direct visual control (Rayner and Pollatsek 1981) or based on a memory representation of visuo-spatial coordinates (Kennedy 1992). Two experiments were selected from Huestegge *et al.* with observations where readers made interword regressions immediately after the initial progressive saccade into the 10- or 11-letter critical word. In both experiments, subjects were asked to read single sentences in preparation for responses to comprehension questions. The line of text was either not shifted or it was shifted by one character position to the left or right as soon as the eyes crossed an invisible boundary immediately left of the target word. In a total of 8329 saccades originating from the initial fixation within the target word, 8.0 per cent were interword regressions, providing a sample of 668 observations for our analysis.

Figure 2.2(A) shows frequency distributions of regressive saccades going to the prior word (in identical pre-shift coordinates) on the same line of text. To minimize the number of saccades that correct an erroneous overshoot, regressions originating from the blank space before the target word or its first letter were removed from this data set.[3] Mean saccade amplitudes in letters were –8.85 (2.44) for the no-shift control condition, –8.86 (2.56) for the leftward shift condition and –8.73 (2.74) for the rightward shift condition. As indicated by a non-parametrical Kruskal-Wallis test, there was no significant effect of shifting the line on the amplitude of subsequent

---

[2]   The text shift was implemented using the boundary technique of saccade contingent display manipulations (Inhoff *et al.* 1998). Using an EyeLink II eye tracking system running at 500 Hz, the line shifts were executed within less than 12 ms, and readers never reported to have seen any display changes.

[3]   When interword regressions coming from the blank space and the first letter of the target word are included in the analysis, mean amplitudes (in letters) are –7.71 (3.04) for the leftward shift, –7.89 (2.85) for the no-shift control and –8.02 (3.09) for the rightward shift conditions. As indicated by a nonparametrical Kruskal-Wallis test, there is again no significant effect of the shift conditions ($chi^2 = 0.72$; $p = 0.70$). However, although far from compensating the two ±1 letter shifting of the target word, the numerical order of the means is in the appropriate direction. This may be taken to suggest that purely corrective regressions may in fact be sensitive to relative visual coordinates.

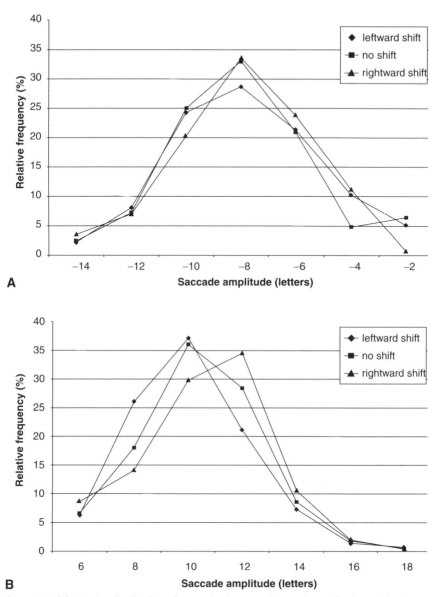

Figure 2.2 (A) Relative distribution of regressive interword saccade amplitudes originating form a 10- or 11-letter target word and going to the prior word in the sentence. The origin word was always a noun and the pretarget word was a contextually neutral adjective. During the initial progressive saccade to the target, the whole line was either shifted to the left or right by one letter or was not shifted. Pooled data from 64 subjects; (B) Relative distribution of progressive interword saccade amplitudes originating form a 10- or 11-letter target word. During the initial progressive saccade to the target, the whole line was either shifted to the left or right by one letter or was not shifted. Pooled data from 64 subjects.

regressive saccades ($chi^2 = 0.26$, $p = 0.88$). It is important to note that the interword regressions in the three-line shift conditions do not originate from different launch distances. The mean positions of the prior fixations in absolute pre-shift coordinates relative to the left boundary of the 10- or 11-letter origin word were 4.12 (1.67) for the control condition, 4.06 (1.64) for the left shift and 4.04 (1.44) for the right shift condition ($chi^2 = 0.18$; $p = 0.91$).

In contrast, the equivalent analyses for progressive interword saccades reveal significant effects of the shift conditions on both the initial landing sites from which they are launched ($chi^2 = 37.61$; $p < 0.00$) and the respective saccade amplitudes ($chi^2 = 32.38$; $p < 0.00$). When the within-word launch position is fixed at letter 4, creating a condition roughly equivalent to the launch positions of the interword regressions, the effect size on the interword progression amplitudes increases from 0.48 to 0.57 letters. The respective mean amplitudes are 11.05 (2.12) for the leftward shift condition, 11.38 (2.17) for the no shift condition and 11.62 (2.31) for the rightward shift condition ($chi^2 = 13.36$; $p = 0.01$). Figure 2.2(B) shows the corresponding frequency distributions of progressive interword saccade amplitudes.

These findings indicate that only in the planning of progressive interword saccades a substantial movement of the target immediately prior to the onset of the initial fixation is substantially compensated for by the visuomotor system. This compensation appears to be absent in the case of regressive interword saccades. This pattern of results supports a theoretical position according to which short-range interword regressions are guided by precise knowledge of the spatial location of words during and immediately after their identification. They are not in harmony with an account relying on extensive parafoveal processing of the target area as maintained by the focused visual control hypothesis. Whether the type of spatial knowledge that forms the base of spatial indexing persists long enough to be still available for the preparation of long-range regressions will be one of the central issues that will be discussed in the reminder of the present chapter.

Do readers have accurate spatial knowledge for previously-read text segments?

To execute a long-range regression to a relatively distant target word readers may use spatial knowledge of the spatial location of previously identified words. In the first examination of spatial working memory during reading, Rothkopf (1971) asked subjects to read extended passages (approximately 3000 words) and then to answer a series of comprehension questions. Each comprehension question was followed by a localization task in which was indicated the quarter of the page containing the relevant content-based information. The results showed that the success with which subjects answered comprehension and page location questions was better than chance, and that readers with a high level of recall for passage content were more likely to make correct spatial decisions. Similarly, Zechmeister et al. (1975) showed that accuracy for content- and location-based questions was above chance and significantly correlated. On occasion, readers could recall where on a page specific linguistic information was conveyed even when linguistic information itself could not be retrieved (Zechmeister et al. 1975; Zechmeister and McKillip 1972).

Relatively detailed knowledge of the location of previously-read words has been demonstrated with shorter passages of text. Baccino and Pynte (1994) had subjects read two types of paragraphs each of which contained approximately 80 words. One type was linguistically nondistinct, the other was distinct, containing a perspective shift from third to first person. The passage was erased after it was read and a probe word was presented at the bottom of the screen that was either identical to, or a synonym of, the target word in the previously-read passage. Readers were asked to move the cursor to the target and the angular degree of the pointing error was determined. Overall, readers' spatial selection was highly accurate. The results revealed a reliable effect of the linguistic manipulation, with smaller errors when the passage contained a perspective shift.

Readers also showed near perfect localization performance when the location of words in a previously-read sentence had to be determined. In one of the conditions of Fischer's (1999) Experiment 1, words of an eight-word sentence were presented sequentially, 500 ms each, from left to right on a computer screen. Subsequently, readers were asked to decide whether the sentence stated a true or false assertion and then to select the location of a target word, shown at the bottom of the screen, by moving a mouse cursor to its location in the previously-read sentence. The accuracy of spatial selection was very high, approximately 90 per cent, and reached 100 per cent when a queried word occupied a position at or near the onset of the previously-read sentence (Experiments 1 and 3).

Spatial memory may also guide regressions to a previously-read segment of text that is critical for sentence or passage comprehension. As noted before, these regressions occur with increased frequency when the meaning previously selected for an ambiguous word is inconsistent with subsequently read text (Carpenter and Daneman 1981; Folk 1998; Folk and Morris 1995), when the meaning of an identified word does not fit prior or subsequent sentence context (Ehrlich and Rayner 1983), or when the syntactic parsing of a sentence was garden pathed (Frazier and Rayner 1982; Rayner and Frazier 1987). Readers also tend to move the eyes to a previously-read passage segment for re-inspection when this segment helps answer a subsequent question (Christie and Just 1976). Kennedy and Murray's (1987; see also Kennedy et al. 2003) data suggest that long-range regressions reach their linguistic target via a single regression. Similar to short-range regressions, long-range regressions thus appear to be guided by precise spatial memory for word locations.

Kennedy and Murray's (1987) original study used single line materials that consisted of a sentence, shown for three seconds, and of a single probe word that was shown to the right of the last word of the sentence. The task was to decide whether the probe had appeared in the previously read (and still visible) sentence. The probe word shown to the right was either identical to a (target) word in the previously-read sentence or it was a synonym of it. For instance, the target word 'spade' in the sentence was followed either by the probe word 'spade' or 'shovel'. Under these conditions, readers executed a single long-range regression of up to 60 character spaces that moved the eyes onto the previously-read target. In a more recent study, readers executed precise regressions to the anaphoric referent of a subsequently encountered pronoun (Kennedy et al. 2003). These long-range regressions were spatially selective even when the target-containing sentence was removed from the screen before the regression to a target word could be initiated, although regression rate was relatively low in this condition (Kennedy *et al.* 2003, Experiment 3). Together, these findings indicate that regressions are spatially precise and that they can be guided by represented knowledge.

To account for the high spatial accuracy of long-range regressions, Kennedy and Murray (1987, 1992; Kennedy *et al.* 2003) proposed that recognized linguistic units (words, phrases) are spatially indexed and that spatial indexes become an integral part of an item's knowledge representation. Partial lexical knowledge of a linguistic unit, e.g. that a previously-read word denoted a garden tool, can thus be used to access its spatial index and, conversely, knowledge of where a word was located can assist the retrieval of linguistic information.

To be useful, a particular spatial index needs a general reference system which could be the page of print (Fischer 2000; Rothkopf 1971) or spatial landmarks (Kennedy *et al.* 2003). To distinguish between these alternatives, Kennedy *et al.* (2003) manipulated the location of frames that surrounded sentences and probes, while sentence location itself was left unchanged. Specifically, frames were slightly shifted to the right or left before a regression into the target-containing sentence was initiated. Under these conditions, shifts of the frame to the right increased targeting error in the form of undershoot, i.e. the landing position of the regression shifted with the frame to the right of the target. Conversely, a shift of the frame to the left increased targeting error in the form of overshoot, as the landing position shifted with the frame to a more leftward location.

The spatial indexing with reference to landmarks can explain a broad range of findings. It explains the correlation between linguistic knowledge and spatial localization performance (Baccino and Pynte 1998; Rothkopf 1971; Zechmeister *et al.* 1975) by assuming that some linguistic knowledge must be accessible before a unit's spatial index can be retrieved. It is also plausible to assume that spatial indexing is linguistically constrained (Kennedy 1992), so that indexes are primarily applied when processing difficulties arise during initial sentence reading. This explains why readers execute long-range regressions to a previously ambiguous word when its meaning was incorrectly determined (Carpenter and Daneman 1981; Folk and Morris 1995) or when subsequent text indicates that a previously encountered syntactic ambiguity was incorrectly resolved (Frazier and Rayner 1982; Rayner and Frazier 1987). Near perfect pointing performance for words near the sentence onset (Fischer 1999) can be explained by their proximity to a spatial landmark, the left-side page margin.

Do readers infer the spatial location of previously-read linguistic units?

Virtually all demonstrations of spatial memory for text location can also be explained, however, by assuming that knowledge of linguistic content, together with knowledge of word and line order, was used to reconstruct the likely location of relevant prior linguistic information. The localization tasks used by Rothkopf (1971) and

Zechmeister *et al.* (1975) required relatively global spatial decisions. Because the sequence of events in a passage is correlated with the relative spatial location of these events, knowledge of content can be used to estimate the approximate location of a queried text. The reconstruction hypothesis accounts for the better localization performance for linguistically distinct elements in the text by assuming that their content is remembered more effectively, and it can explain the relatively good localization performance for a sentence initial location by assuming that it benefits from the familiar primacy effect for verbal material, that is obtained irrespective of whether the material is visually or auditorily presented. To rule out a linguistic reconstruction account, it has to be shown that readers can determine the location of a previously-read linguistic unit with a high degree of accuracy, even when linguistic knowledge of sentence or passage content cannot be used to infer the location of constituent units.

One condition of Fischer's (1999) Experiment 1 sought to dissociate linguistic and spatial word order. In this condition, each consecutive word of an eight-word sentence was presented for 500 ms. Successive words were not displayed from left to right, however, but at randomly chosen locations at one of three short lines of text (each of which accommodated two to three words). Next, a probe word was shown at the bottom of the screen and readers had to indicate the location of the probe in the previously-read sentence. Under these conditions, correct localization performance was 13.5 per cent, which was virtually identical to the estimated accuracy level based on guessing alone (12.5 per cent).

Fischer's (1999) Experiment 3 indicated that memory for precise word location is relatively short lived, less than 2 s, and much shorter temporal spans of as little as 50 ms were obtained by Werner and Diedrichsen (2002) for the representation of precise line orientation. A rapid degradation of accurate spatial memory would limit the usefulness of integrated spatial-linguistic representations, and the precision of long-range regressions should rapidly decrease as an increasing number of words intervene between a fixation and a previously-read word.

Other findings are also consistent with an account according to which memory for prior word location is reconstructed rather than part of an integrated spatial-lexical representation. In Therriault and Raney's (2002) study of passage reading, memory for the location of information on a page was consistently lower than memory for the sequence of events in the text. In Christie and Just's (1976) study, requests for spatial information were answered more slowly than requests for linguistic information. As they point out, substantially longer latencies for the retrieval of location specific information suggest that it was less accessible than content-specific linguistic information.

Similar to this, it took readers a considerable amount of time to select the location of a probe word in Fischer's (1999) experiment – on average more than 3 s. Although it may well be the case that accessing of a previously-read segment's spatial index may be relatively time-consuming, it appears more plausible to assume that these long delays are the consequence of inference-based processes that exploit the redundancy that typically exists in the general progression of sentence and passage content and the relative spatial location of this content. Consistent with this, Rawson and Miyake (2002) found that readers' linguistic abilities, but not their visuospatial abilities, were correlated with word localization performance after passage reading.

In defense of integrated spatial-linguistic representations, as maintained by the spatial indexing hypothesis, it could be argued that key evidence against readers' precise memory for previously-read words was obtained under conditions that are exceedingly unfavorable to spatial indexing effects. Specifically, the dissociation of linguistic word order and spatial word order in Fischer's (1999) study created an exceedingly unfamiliar reading condition which eliminated all redundancy between consecutive spatial indexes. This may have increased the difficulty of the spatial task resulting in poor spatial memory. It is plausible to assume that an analogous dramatic decreases in linguistic redundancy would have led to a substantial decrease of verbal memory as well.

The pointing task also used a relatively strict criterion, in that an accurate response required that the readers point to the precise location of the previously-read word. A less stringent performance criterion could have revealed some spatial memory. That is, rather than pointing at random locations, readers may have pointed at locations in the vicinity of the target. Moreover, the experimental task in Fischer's (1999) experiments, and most other studies that provide evidence against memory for word spatial location (Raney *et al.* 2000; Rawson and Miyake 2002), examined *explicit* memory for word location that required the execution of a deliberate and time-consuming response after each trial. In reading, by contrast, *implicit* knowledge of prior word location may guide the programming of long-range regressions. These eye movements can be initiated at any point in time while the task is performed, and their programming and execution takes very little time, usually less than 300 ms.

In fact, Kennedy's (Kennedy and Murray 1987; Kennedy *et al.* 2003) results indicate that long-range regressions during reading are highly accurate when executed, with the mean deviations from the center of a targeted word ranging from two to five letter spaces. That is, the vast majority of regressions successfully positioned the eyes at the target, irrespective of the distance of the target from the probe word. The spatial reconstruction account has difficulty explaining this high level of accuracy as reconstruction of a previously-read word's spatial location should succeed in moving the eyes in the general vicinity of the target but rarely move the eyes directly at it. Over- and undershooting of the target location should be common and reaching the target should often require additional eye movements.

In view of the critical theoretical role of Kennedy's (2003; Kennedy and Murray 1987) studies, we (Inhoff and Weger, in press) recently examined the spatial accuracy of long-range regressions executed after sentence reading. In one of the experiments, each trial required that subjects read a sentence that asserted a particular factual relationship, e.g. 'my mother is younger than my father', and then a question, e.g. 'who was born earlier?' which probed the relationship between two of the previously-read candidate words, 'mother' and 'father' in the sample sentence. The fact-defining sentence and the question occupied a single line of text, and the question did not repeat any of the words used in the sentence so that each word on the line occupied a unique spatial location. The experimental task required that the reader articulated the correct candidate word (the target) during or after question reading.

Similar to one of Kennedy *et al.*'s (2003) experiments, two sentence-viewing conditions were created, one in which the fact-defining sentence was available for reinspection during question reading and one in which it was removed from the screen when the eyes moved from the sentence onto the question. In view of Kennedy *et al.*'s (2003) results, readers were expected to execute precise regressions to the target even when the fact-defining sentence was no longer visible in the periphery. Peripheral sentence visibility should primarily influence regression rate, with a much higher regression rate when the fact-defining sentence was visible in the periphery than when it was removed.

Readers answered the question correctly on more than 90 per cent of the trials, irrespective of the peripheral visibility of the sentence. Represented sentence content could thus be used to answer the question correctly, although response accuracy was higher when the target occurred earlier in the sentence. Readers also executed long-range regressions into the fact-defining sentence. This occurred on approximately 40 per cent of the trials when the sentence was visible in the periphery and on approximately 4 per cent of the trials when the sentence was removed, which affirms this particular finding of Kennedy *et al.*'s (2003) earlier study.

Mean regression size was 37 letter spaces in the sentence visible condition. Regressions were significantly larger (41 letter spaces) when the target word was relatively distant and occurred earlier in the sentence than when it was relatively near and occurred later in the sentence (32 letter spaces). In spite of their paucity, regressions also showed some spatial selectivity when the sentence was removed prior to the regression.

Although long-range regressions were spatially selective, they did not move the eyes directly onto the target. The regression error, comprising the distance between the landing position of the first regression into the fact-defining sentence and the center of the target word, was quite large, 31 letter spaces for left-side targets and 17 letter spaces for right-side targets. Still, readers eventually re-inspected the target, implying that additional eye movements were executed toward the target after the initial long-range regression had been executed.

These findings are difficult to reconcile with the spatial indexing hypothesis. It predicted that readers should have been able to use a target's spatial index to determine its precise spatial location and that a single saccade should have moved the eyes near or at the target center. Conversely, the results are in harmony with the reconstruction hypothesis. Knowledge of sentence content, together with knowledge of spatial ordering conventions, appears to have been used to determine the approximate location of the target. Knowledge of sentence content revealed whether a target occurred early or late in the sentence and knowledge of word order conventions could be used to infer roughly where the target would be located on the line of text. An initial regression thus moved the eyes in the vicinity of the target. Additional saccades then searched for – and homed in on – the target.

In defense of the spatial indexing hypothesis, it could be argued that the spatial selectivity of long-range regressions in the experiment revealed the use of spatial indexes and that readers moved the eyes accurately to destination words of their choice. If these destination words were not the designated target word on a considerable proportion of trials, then the discrepancy between the hypothesized goal of the regression and the designated goal could yield a relatively large regression error – not because regressions were inaccurate but because the hypothesized and actual regression targets were widely separated in the sentence.

Eye movements during reading are under the control of the reader. Consequently, it is *in principle* not possible to pre-determine the intended goal location of a spontaneously executed regression. We used a recently developed experimental method, the contingent-speech technique (Inhoff *et al.* 2002, 2004) to overcome this limitation. The technique was used to request the execution of regressions during question reading and, more critically, to control the location of the regression target (see Figure 2.3).

The same materials were used as in the previously described experiment. The fact-defining sentence was either visible in the periphery or removed from screen when the question was read. The novel aspect of the experiment was that the saccade that moved the eyes at one of the last 15 letters of the question also initiated the presentation of a spoken word (over headphones) that identified the regression target

Sample sentence with the invisible contingent speech boundary:

My mother is younger than my father. Who was born earlier?

The eyes' boundary crossing initiates articulation of the regression target:

My mother is younger than my father. Who was born earlier?

"MOTHER"

or

"FATHER"

Figure 2.3 An illustration of the contingent speech technique used to elicit mandatory regressions during question reading. Movements of the eyes to the right of an invisible boundary, which was 15 letter spaces from the end of the question, initiated the spoken presentation of the regression target.

word. For example, during the reading of the question 'who was born earlier?', a saccade to the right of the letter 'a' of the word 'was', initiated the presentation of the spoken word 'mother' over headphones. This instructed the reader to move the eyes to the corresponding word in the previously-read sentence either immediately or upon completion of question reading. The target word was spoken, rather than visually presented, so that the uniqueness of the spatial index of the target in the fact-defining sentence would not be compromised. The articulated word was the correct answer to the question in all instances and subjects were no longer required to articulate this word upon question reading. Instead, they were asked questions about sentence content at the end of a subset of trials. According to the spatial indexing hypothesis, long-range regressions to the visual target word should now be highly accurate and position the eyes at the center of the visual target.

Long-range regressions into the fact-defining sentence were once more spatially selective. As in the prior experiment, regressions were larger when the known regression target occupied a more distant left-side location near the sentence onset than when it occupied a more proximal location (42 vs. 31 letter spaces, respectively). Critically, as was the case with spontaneously executed regressions, experimentally elicited regressions rarely moved the eyes directly onto the target. The regression error was 16 letter spaces for distant targets and 11 letters for more proximal targets.

The experimental control over the location of the regression target, together with the availability of a relatively large pool of regression data, also provided the opportunity to trace the sequence of eye movements by which the target was eventually reached. For this, we defined several new measures that examined properties of consecutive regressions that readers executed toward the target. For instance, if a reader executed three consecutive regressions of 40, 10, and 5 letter spaces during re-inspection that moved the eyes onto the center of the target word which was 55 letter spaces from the location at which the regression was initiated, then the number of consecutive regressions would have been three, the consecutive regression size measure would have been 55 letter spaces, and the consecutive regression error would have been zero. If the reader executed a large regression of 40 letter spaces, then a small progressive saccade of two characters, and then, and then two additional regressions of 13 and 5 letter spaces, then the number of consecutive regressions would have been one, the consecutive regression size and regression size error would have been 40 and 15 letter spaces, respectively.

These additional analysis revealed that readers executed on average 2.25 consecutive regressions toward a distant (left side) target with a cumulated regression size of 60 letter spaces and 1.6 consecutive regressions toward a more proximal (right side) target with a cumulated regression size of 38 letter spaces. Critically, the regression error of consecutive regressions was 5 letter spaces for distant targets and 12 letter spaces for proximal targets when the target was visible during question reading. That is, the effect pattern for consecutive regressions was opposite to the effect pattern for initial long-range regressions (which positioned the eyes closer to a more proximal target). Strikingly, this occurred even when the sentence was no longer visible on the screen, which yielded consecutive regression errors of 6 and 13 letter spaces for distant and proximal targets.[4]

Why would consecutive regressions be more successfully directed at distant left-side targets? According to the spatial indexing hypothesis, this may occur because left-side targets are closer to a spatial landmark, the left-side page margin. According to the reconstruction hypothesis, left-side targets enjoyed an advantage because they were more effectively represented in verbal memory. This latter account is in harmony with the results of the target naming task, which showed a significantly higher target naming accuracy when the target had occupied a left-side location than when it occupied a right-side location. Moreover, the reconstruction hypothesis can also explain why readers typically executed more than one regression toward a target word. According to this view, readers could determine the approximate location of the target using knowledge of linguistic content and spatial order. This was used to launch a large regression that moved the eyes in the vicinity of the target. Additional eye movements were then executed to search and locate the target. Analyses of the landing position of the eye movement that eventually moved the eyes back to the target are also consistent with this view. In contrast to short-range regressions, the final landing position of consecutive regressions did not show a distinct preference for the target center. Instead, landing positions were roughly evenly distributed, when target words were partitioned in five equal-sized landing positions, with relative frequencies of 17, 18, 20, 23, and 21 per cent for landing positions 1–5, respectively.

In the absence of an explicit instruction to regress to the target, readers re-inspected the target on relatively few occasions when the fact-defining sentence was removed upon question reading (approximately 4 per cent). Since there is no incentive to re-construct the spatial location of a previously-read target that is no longer visible in the periphery it could be argued that the small number of these spatially selective regressions appear to provide prima facie evidence for the accessing of a previously-read target's spatial representation for regression planning.

A systematic examination of saccades toward the location of a previously read but no longer visible word did not support this view, however. In Experiment 2 of our study (Inhoff and Weger, in press), subjects read single line sentences, e.g. 'I'll take the lone puppy from the five boys who were teasing it'. Sentence reading was followed by the presentation of one of its words in the center of an otherwise blank screen, e.g. 'lone' or 'five'. The experimental task now required a decision whether the word had previously occupied a left- or right-side sentence location. Since the task tested spatial

---

[4] Fixation durations prior to the initiation of the initial regression toward the target were shorter in the sentence visible than the sentence absent condition, 319 ms vs. 375 ms, $F(1,31) = 9.91$, $p < 0.01$. Visibility of the fact-defining sentence also influenced the relationship between fixation durations and regression accuracy. Pre-regression fixation durations tended to increase as the regression error decreased when the fact-defining sentence was visible, $r = -0.23$ for single shoot regressions and $r = -0.17$ although neither effect was reliable, >0.2. The corresponding correlations were close to zero in the sentence absence condition.

knowledge, readers should be inclined to access a previously-read word's spatial index. On occasion, this should result in the execution of a regression toward the prior location of the target word, even though this word was no longer visible on the screen. Eye movements during the classification task never moved the eyes to the location of the previously-read target, however. Instead, there was a general tendency to move to the eyes toward the right during the decision task, irrespective of the location of the target within the previously-read sentence, which could be due to the general left-to-right viewing of text.

Manual classification of the probe word was influenced by target location, however. RTs were shorter and spatial decisions were more accurate when the target had occupied a left-side sentence location near the sentence onset (1472 ms and 97 per cent, respectively) than when it had occupied a right-side location (1658 ms; 91 per cent). The manual classification performance thus suggests that readers scanned the words of the represented sentence from beginning to end. A 'left' decision could be made when the word was encountered early in the scan and a 'right' decision when it was encountered relatively late. The analogue left-to-right ordering of words could have biased eye movements toward the right while the scanning of linguistic material was in progress. Again, this account assumes that spatial word location was determined by using specific knowledge of sentence content and general knowledge of word order.

Conclusion

The programming of progressive and regressive interword saccades uses functionally distinct types of information. In contrast to forward directed saccades, short-range regressions attain the center of the targeted word, irrespective of launch site and target word length. Moreover, the amplitudes of these short-range regressions appear to be programmed on the basis of a spatial index stored in memory. Long-range regressions are also guided by represented rather than visible information. They differ from short-range regressions in that they typically move the eyes in the general vicinity of a targeted word, often followed by additional eye movements towards the target location. These regressions do not appear to be guided by knowledge of the precise spatial location of previously-read words. Instead, spatial location appears to be inferred from specific knowledge of sentence or passage content and from general knowledge of word order. Taken together, our results support the idea that the retrieval of information from memory plays a key role in the re-inspection of previously scanned segments of text. Whether this retrieval takes the form of direct access to a spatially-indexed representation or is based on a more indirect route involving a reconstruction of text information appears to depend on the spatiotemporal distance between launch position and target.

References

Baccino, T. and Pynte, J. (1994). Spatial coding and discourse models during text reading. *Language and Cognitive Processes*, **9**, 143–155.

Baccino, T. and Pynte, J. (1998). Spatial encoding and referential processing during reading. *European Psychologist*, **3**, 51–61.

Beauvillain, C., Vergilino, D. and Dukic, T. (2000). Planning Two-Saccade Sequences in Reading. In: A. Kennedy, R. Radach, D. Heller and J. Pynte (ed.) *Reading as a perceptual process.* Oxford: Elsevier, pp. 327–354.

Carpenter, P. A. and Daneman, M. (1981). Lexical retrieval and error recovery in reading: A model based on eye fixations. *Journal of Learning and Verbal Behavior,* **20,** 137–160.

Christie, J. M. and Just, M. A. (1976). Remembering the location and content of sentences in a prose passage. *Journal of Educational Psychology,* **68,** 702–710.

Coëffé, C. and O'Regan, J. K. (1987). Reducing the influence of non-target stimuli on saccade accuracy: Predictability and latency effects. *Vision Research,* **27,** 227–240.

Ehrlich, K. and Rayner, K. (1983). Pronoun assignment and semantic integration during reading: Eye movements and immediacy of processing. *Journal of Verbal Learning and Verbal Behavior,* **22,** 75–87.

Findlay, J. M. (1982). Global processing for saccadic eye movements. *Vision Research,* **22,** 1033–1045.

Findlay, J. M. and Walker, R. (1999). A model of saccade generation based on parallel processing and competitive inhibition. *Behavioral and Brain Sciences,* **22,** 661–721.

Fischer, M. H. (1999). Memory for word locations in reading. *Memory,* **7,** 79–116.

Fischer, M. H. (2000). Perceiving spatial attributes of print. In: A. Kennedy, R. Radach, and J. Pynte (ed.) *Reading as a perceptual process.* Amsterdam: Elsevier, pp. 89–118.

Folk, J. R. and Morris, R. K. (1995). Multiple lexical codes in reading: Evidence from eye movements, naming time and oral reading. *Journal of Experimental Psychology: Learning, Memory, and Cognition,* **21,** 1412–1429.

Frazier, L. and Rayner, K. (1982). Making and correcting errors during sentence comprehension: Eye movements in the analysis of structurally ambiguous sentences. *Cognitive Psychology,* **14,** 178–210.

Huestegge, L., Radach, R., Vorstius, C. and Wade, N. (2003). On the metrics of refixation saccades in normal reading. Paper held at the 12th European Conference on Eye Movements, 20–24 August 2003, Dundee, Scotland.

Huey, E. B. (1908). *The psychology and pedagogy of reading.* New York: Macmillan.

Inhoff, A. W. and Weger, U. W. (in press). Memory for word location during reading: eye movements to previously read words are spatially selective but not precise. *Memory and Cognition.*

Inhoff, A., Starr, M., Liu, W. and Wang, J. (1998). Eye-movement-contingent display changes are not compromised by flicker and phosphor persistence. *Psychonomic Bulletin and Review,* **5,** 101–106.

Inhoff, A. W., Connine, C. and Radach, R. (2002). A contingent speech technique in eye movement research on reading. *Behavior Research Methods, Instruments and Computers,* **34,** 471–480.

Inhoff, A. W., Radach, R. Eiter, B. M. and Juhasz, B. (2003). Distinct subsystems for the parafoveal processing of spatial and linguistic information during eye fixations in reading. *Quarterly Journal of Experimental Psychology: Human Experimental Psychology,* **56A,** 803–827.

Inhoff, A. W., Connine, C., Eiter, B., Radach, R., and Heller, D. (2004). Phonological representation of words in working memory during sentence reading. *Psychonomic Bulletin and Review,* **11,** 320–325.

Kapoula, Z. and Robinson, D. A. (1986). Saccadic undershoot is not inevitable: Saccades can be accurate. *Vision Research,* **26,** 735–743.

Kennedy, A. (1987). Eye movements, reading skill and the spatial code. In: J. R. Beech, and A. M. Colley (ed.) *Cognitive approaches to reading*. London: John Wiley and Sons, pp. 169–186.

Kennedy, A. (1992). The spatial coding hypothesis. In: K. Rayner (ed.) *Eye movements and visual cognition: Scene perception and reading*. New York: Springer Verlag, pp. 379–396.

Kennedy, A. and Murray, W. S. (1987). Spatial coordinates and reading: Comments on Monk (1985). *Quarterly Journal of Experimental Psychology*, **39A**, 649–656.

Kennedy, A., Brooks, R., Flynn, L.-A., and Prophet, C. (2003). The reader's spatial code. In: J. Hyona, R. Radach, and H. Deubel (ed.) *The mind's eye: Cognitive and applied aspects of eye movement research*. North Holland, Amsterdam, The Netherlands, pp. 193–212.

Lemij H. G, and Collewijn H. (1989). Differences in accuracy of human saccades between stationary and jumping targets. *Vision Research*, **29**, 1737–48.

McConkie, G. W. and Rayner, K. (1975). The span of the effective stimulus during a fixation in reading. *Perception and Psychophysics*, **17**, 578–586.

McConkie, G. W., Kerr, P. W., Reddix, M. D. and Zola, D. (1988). Eye movement control during reading: I. The location of initial eye fixation on words. *Vision Research*, **28**, 1107–1118.

McConkie, G. W., Kerr, P. W. and Dyre, B. P. (1994). What are 'normal' eye movements during reading: Toward a mathematical description. In: J. Ygge and G. Lennerstrand (ed.) *Eye movements in reading*. Pergamon, Oxford, pp. 315–328.

Radach, R. (1996). *Blickbewegungen beim Lesen. Psychologische Aspekte der Determination von Fixationspositionen*. (Eye movements in reading. Psychological aspects of fixation position control). Münster/New York: Waxmann.

Radach, R. and Kempe, V. (1993). An individual analysis of fixation positions in reading. In: G. d'Ydevalle, and J. van Rensbergen. (ed.). *Perception and Cognition. Advances in eye movement research*. Amsterdam: Elsevier, pp. 213–225.

Radach, R. and McConkie, G. W. (1998). Determinants of fixation positions in words during reading. In: G. Underwood (ed.) *Eye guidance in reading and scene perception*. Elsevier, pp. 77–100.

Raney, G. E., Minkoff, S., and Therriault, D. (2000). Repetition effects from paraphrased text: Evidence for an integrated representation model of text representation. *Discourse Processes*, **29**, 222–238.

Rawson, K. A. and Miyake, A. (2002). Does relocating information in text depend on verbal or visuospatial abilities? *Psychonomic Bulletin and Review*, **9**, 801–806.

Rayner, K. (1975). Parafoveal identification during a fixation in reading. *Acta Psychologica*, **39**, 271–281.

Rayner, K. (1979). Eye guidance in reading: Fixation locations within words. *Perception*, **8**, 21–30.

Rayner, K. (1998). Eye movements in reading and information processing: 20 years of research. *Psychological Bulletin*, **124**, 372–422.

Rayner, K and Frazier, L. (1987). Parsing temporarily ambiguous complements. *Quarterly Journal of Experimental Psychology: Human Experimental Psychology*, **39**, 657–673.

Rayner, K. and Pollatsek, A. (1981). Eye movement control during reading: Evidence for direct control. *Quarterly Journal of Experimental Psychology*, **33A**, 351–373.

Rothkopf, E. Z. (1971). Incidental memory for location of information in text. *Journal of Verbal Learning and Verbal Behavior*, **10**, 608–613

Therriault, D. J. and Raney, G. E. (2002). The representation and comprehension of place-on-page and text-sequence memory. *Scientific Studies of Reading*, **6**, 117–134.

Vergilino, D. and Beauvillain, C. (2001). Reference frames in reading: evidence from visually and memory guided saccades. *Vision Research*, **41,** 25–26, 3547–3557.

Vitu, F. (1991). The existence of a center of gravity effect during reading. *Vision Research*, **31,** 1289–1313.

Vitu, F. M., and McConkie, G. W. (2000). Regressive saccades and word perception in adult perception. In: A. Kennedy, R. Radach, and J.Pynte (ed.) *Reading as a perceptual process.* Amsterdam: Elsevier, pp. 89–118.

Vitu, F., McConkie, G. W. and Zola, D. (1998). About regressive saccades in reading and their relation to word identification. In: G. Underwood (ed.) *Eye guidance in reading and scene perception.* Amsterdam, New York: Elsevier, pp. 101–124.

Werner, S. and Diedrichsen, J. (2002). The time course of spatial memory distortions. *Memory and Cognition*, **30,** 718–730.

Zechmeister, E. B., and McKillip, (1972). Recall of place on the page. *Journal of Educational Psychology*, **63,** 446–453.

Zechmeister, E. B., McKillip, J., Pasko, S., and Bespalec, D. (1975). Visual memory for place on the page. *Journal of General Psychology*, **92,** 43–52.

3

Word skipping: Implications for theories of eye movement control in reading

Marc Brysbaert, Denis Drieghe
and Françoise Vitu

Abstract

When skilled readers read English texts, about one-third of the words are skipped. In this chapter, we review the different explanations that have been proposed to explain this. We also take an in-depth look at the variables that influence word skipping. These are: errors in the programming and execution of a saccade, the length of the upcoming word $n+1$ in parafoveal vision, the distance from word $n+1$ relative to the current fixation location (also known as the launch site), and the difficulty of word $n+1$ within the sentence. We provide evidence that the effects of word length and distance cannot be explained by assuming that word $n+1$ is skipped only when it has been identified in parafoveal vision. Rather, readers often seem to make an educated guess about where to send the next forward saccade on the basis of incomplete information. If this guess turns out to be incorrect (and a difficult word has been skipped inappropriately), an immediate correction follows. This is either a regression to the skipped word or a longer fixation duration. In this manner, eye movements remain closely coupled with the ongoing processing of language.

Introduction

Eye movements in reading are characterized by short periods of steadiness (fixations) followed by fast movements (saccades). Saccades vary from 1 to 18 letter positions, and are needed to bring new information into the centre of the visual field where acuity is highest. Fixations take some 150–300 ms and are required to identify the words.

Assuming that the fixated word is recognized by the end of the fixation, it is tempting to think of eye movements in reading as a sequence of word-to-word movements, with the eyes starting from the first word of a line, going to the second word, the third, and so on until the end of the line is reached, at which point a return sweep is made to the first word of the next line and the whole cycle starts over again. Unfortunately, such a simple sequence of movements is rarely observed in empirical data. Many words are fixated more than once, or are initially not fixated but regressed to immediately afterwards, or are not fixated at all. Ever since the first measurements of eye movements in reading, researchers have been puzzled by this complicated pattern of activity and suggested various explanations. In this chapter, we will focus on one aspect, namely the fact that when proficient readers are reading an English text, their eyes are never directed at about one-third of the words.

Before we discuss the different explanations of word skipping and the existing empirical evidence, it may be worth explicitly stating that in eye movement control, two decisions have to be made: when to initiate an eye movement, and where to send the eyes to? There is substantial evidence indicating that these 'when' and 'where' decisions are largely independent of one another (e.g. Rayner and Sereno 1994; Rayner and Pollatsek 1989). The decision of *where* to fixate next is partly determined by the length of the words to the right of fixation and partly by the ongoing language processing. If word or text comprehension is experiencing difficulties, a decision is made either to refixate the currently fixated word or to regress to a previous part of the text (some 14 per cent of eye movements in text reading are regressions). If text comprehension is running smoothly, the eyes are sent to one of the words to the right of fixation, either to the first word or to a word further down the line (in which case one or more words will be skipped). When a forward saccade is made, it is generally assumed that the eyes are programmed so that they will land between the beginning and the middle of the target word. The actual landing position depends on a number of factors such as the launch site, the features of the first letters of the word, and the position of the word within a line of text. The landing position is closer to the word beginning when the eyes were launched from a long distance (see below), when the first three letters of a word form a rare combination (as in *awkward*; Underwood 2003, White and Liversedge 2004), and when the word is situated towards the end of a line of text (Vitu and McConkie 2003).

There are two different views about what drives the decision of *when* to move the eyes. The dominant view is that this depends entirely on the ongoing word processing: The decision to move the eyes is taken only when the processing of the currently fixated word has reached a certain level (Reichle *et al.* 2003; Reilly and Radach 2003). The alternative view is that a significant proportion of saccades are triggered autonomously after a certain time delay and that the influence of the ongoing text processing is limited to an inhibition of the automatic signal or to determining the place where the eyes are sent (Engbert *et al.* 2002; Yang and McConkie 2001).

Needless to say, the issue of word skipping deals with the *where* decision, and in particular with the *where* decision related to first-pass, forward, interword eye movements. These are saccades directed to words to the right of the current fixation location, that have not been yet read (i.e. that are not part of a line of text which is reread after a regression). Although this decision is an important component of eye movement control in reading, it is obvious that any explanation of it should be integrated within a larger, comprehensive model of eye movement control in reading. We will start this discussion with a short overview of the various ideas that have been proposed to explain why so many words are skipped in text reading.

Word skipping in different models

The loose relation between eye movements and text layout made many of the first researchers believe that eye movements were controlled by an autonomous oculomotor control centre (e.g. Buswell 1920; Erdman and Dodge 1898; Huey 1908). According to this view, saccade sizes were more or less constant and only changed as a function of the global difficulty of the materials being read. Variations in saccade size resulted from noise in the oculomotor system and adjustments to the difficulty of the text. As for word skipping, this implied that the probability of skipping a word depended on the overall difficulty of the text but not on the difficulty of the word itself.

The autonomous oculomotor control model remained the dominant model until the middle of the 1970s, although some refinements were added. For instance, Bouma and de Voogd (1974; see also Shebilske 1975) attributed changes in saccade size to the limited capacity of an input buffer which could contain but a few activated word units. When the buffer became overloaded, saccade sizes decreased. Gradually, however, the possibility of word-based influences on the probability of word skipping began to be taken into account. In his cognitive and peripheral search guidance theory, Hochberg (1975) still maintained that eye movements were primarily determined by pre-established scanning routines independent of the linguistic information extracted at each fixation, but these routines depended on both the readers' knowledge of the language constraints and on the task they set for themselves when reading. If the task required paying attention to the letters and the spelling of the words without paying attention to the meaning (proof-reading), readers were assumed to adopt a letter-by-letter or word-by-word scanning routine. If, however, the reading purpose was to extract meaning from the text, then larger saccades were made in order to reduce the number of samples per line. In such a case, the size of the saccades was controlled by peripheral search guidance mechanisms. At each fixation, readers anticipated what they would find next on the basis of the meaning and the grammatical status of the words read so far and on the basis of global visual information extracted from parafoveal vision (such as the next word's length). To test their predictions, readers directed their eyes to those parts of the text that seemed to be the most informative. Thus, according to Hochberg, the size of a saccade depended on the text difficulty and redundancy (which affected a word's predictability and the size of the perceptual span), and on the reader's ability to extrapolate upcoming information and to process parafoveal information.

A similar reasoning can be found in Shebilske (1975). Saccade sizes were mainly determined by the capacities of the input buffer (see above), but on some instances the ongoing text processing could intervene. If both the overall meaning of the words read on previous fixations and the visual information extracted from the parafovea (such as the next word's length) made the next word highly predictable, then the automatic oculomotor program could be interrupted and the word skipped. This could occur independently of the state of the internal buffer. So, discourse-based word skipping was possible when the word was highly predictable from prior context and when the parafoveal visual information was compatible with the prediction.

In the late 1970s, the idea that word skipping did not happen at random but was determined by the probability of the parafoveal word being identified on the previous fixation was promoted in a series of highly influential papers. Rayner (1978) and McConkie (1979) hypothesized that saccade lengths were determined by the size of the perceptual span. The perceptual span is a 16-letter region around the fixation location in which the letters are visible enough so that words can be identified. At each fixation, the upcoming saccade was directed to the word in the text that was not clearly visible from the current fixation location. The position of this word depended on visual acuity constraints, but also on the difficulty of the words involved (i.e. their predictability on the basis of the preceding text and their frequency of occurrence).

The word-identification account of word skipping was further developed in a series of papers by researchers from the University of Massachusetts (UMass), who put forth a sequential, attention-based model of eye movement control in reading (Henderson and Ferreira 1990; Morrison 1984; Pollatsek and Rayner 1990; Reichle *et al.* 1998, 2003). In the original version of this sequential attention-based model (Morrison 1984) it was assumed that at the beginning of the first fixation attention was focused on the word in foveal vision (called word n). As soon as this word was identified, the attention beam shifted towards the next word $n+1$ and that word started to be processed. The shift of attention triggered the programming of a saccade to word $n+1$, which could only be executed after a programming time of some 150 ms. If during this time, processing of the word $n+1$ was completed fast enough, the program of the original saccade to word $n+1$ could be cancelled and replaced by a saccade to word $n+2$, to which the attention beam had, meanwhile, shifted. If processing of word $n+1$ was not finished rapidly enough, then the saccade to word $n+1$ was executed and no word skipping took place. Because, in this view, word skipping depended on the speed with which word $n+1$ could be processed, the model predicted that more word skipping would be observed for easy words than for difficult words. Easy words are high-frequency words and/or words that are highly predictable from the preceding context. Difficult words are low-frequency words and/or words that are not expected on the basis of the text read thus far. Evidence in favour of this prediction was reported by Ehrlich and Rayner (1981) and Balota *et al.* (1985).

Morrison's (1984) sequential attention-based model was subsequently implemented in a computer model of eye movement control in reading, the so-called E-Z Reader model (Reichle *et al.* 1998, 2003). A major change introduced at this stage was that the programming of an eye movement started not when the fixated word n was fully identified (and the attention beam shifted to word $n+1$) but some 100 ms earlier when a familiarity check indicated that the fixated word was likely to be recognized shortly. This change was needed to finish the various processes within a normal fixation duration. The fact that the saccade programming and the shift of the attention beam were to some extent decoupled, also allowed the authors to account for the spill-over effect. This effect refers to the fact that the first fixation duration on word $n+1$ tends to be longer after a difficult word n than after an easy word n (presumably because there is less time between the shift of attention and the eye movement for a difficult word n than for an easy word n).

The various versions of the UMass model have dominated eye movement research over the last two decades, but in recent years other language-related models of eye movement control have gained impetus (Engbert *et al.* 2002; Reilly and Radach 2003). The origin of these contenders lay in some unease with the strong sequential assumption of the UMass model. In the UMass model, words are selected and identified one at a time by the attention beam. However, there is evidence that such early, attention-based selection may not be possible. When, in a visual word-recognition experiment, a foveally-presented target word is accompanied by a parafoveal flanker word, there are indications that the parafoveal word is processed even though the attention beam is never directed towards it. Fuentes and Tudela (1992), for instance, in a lexical decision task showed that the processing of a foveally-presented word is faster when it is semantically related to a parafoveally-presented word on the previous trial. This suggests that a parafoveal word may be processed in parallel with the foveal word, but with some time delay because of the lower visual acuity in the parafovea and the slower projection pathways from the parafoveal retina to the language centres in the brain. According to the new, parallel-processing view, three or four words become activated in parallel and compete as the target for the next saccade. Their strength of attraction increases up to a certain threshold level, and then decreases again (because the word is almost identified). The speed with which the attraction strength increases, and the threshold level it has to reach depend on the frequency of the word and its predictability from the context. Thus, high-frequency words and/or words that are highly expected on the basis of the preceding part of text, will exceed their threshold value and start to decrease in attraction strength sooner than words that are less easy to recognize. As a result, high-frequency words and/or highly-predicted words may have less pulling power to be the target than the word next to them by the time the next saccade is programmed and, thus, will be skipped. Engbert *et al.* (2002) wrote a computer model on the basis of these principles (the SWIFT model) and showed that it accounts for human eye-movement data in reading as accurately as the E-Z Reader model.

Although language-related views of word skipping are dominant nowadays, the idea that word skipping may be controlled by non-linguistic strategies has not completely vanished. For instance, Just and Carpenter (1980, 1987) argued that saccade sizes were independent of the ongoing discourse processing and were programmed so that the eyes fixated every word and landed between the beginning and the middle of these words. They hypothesized that the information that could be extracted from the parafovea was not detailed enough to identify an upcoming word and simply served to locate the target for the next saccade. The only exception occurred when the eyes were located at the very end of a word and the upcoming word was a short, high-frequency word (e.g. a function word). In such a case, the parafoveal word could be skipped because it had been recognized. Thus, according to Just and Carpenter, word skipping was largely independent of the difficulty of the parafoveal word, and the variability in saccade sizes mainly resulted from visual and oculomotor factors. Just and Carpenter's view on landing sites is surprising, if one considers how high-level the rest of their theory of eye movement control in reading was. This is a particularly clear example of how strongly the ideas about the *when* and the *where* decisions can differ within a theory.

Another prime example of a non-linguistic view of word skipping can be found in O'Regan's (1990, 1992) strategy-tactics theory. According to this view, forward inter-word saccades are always aimed at the centre of one of the upcoming parafoveal words. Which word is selected, depends on the length of the words and their distance from the current fixation position. The most detailed proposal of this selection process has been made by Reilly and O'Regan (1998). They tried to simulate McConkie *et al.*'s (1998) empirical findings of the landing site positions (see Figure 3.1) with four different computer models. The first computer model simulated a word-by-word reading strategy, in which the target word always was the first word to the right of the fixation location. The second computer model was based on a strategy in which the target word was the longest word in the 20-letter window to the right of the fixation location. The strategy of the third computer program consisted of skipping words as a function of their frequency. Finally, the fourth computer program was based on an implementation of Morrison's (1984) sequential attention model. Reilly and O'Regan (1998) observed that the second computer program yielded the best fit: the empirical data were best predicted by a strategy that consisted of simply choosing the longest word in the parafovea, without any further identification of the words involved. The computer program based on a word-by-word strategy performed poorly, because it predicted many more short saccades than were observed in the human data. The sequential attention model underestimated the skipping rates because there was not enough time to complete all the stages needed for word skipping.

Brysbaert and Vitu (1998) also pointed to the time constraints that seriously limit the possibility of language-related influences on word skipping. It is well-accepted that visual signals at the centre of the visual field require at least 50 ms before they can start to activate word representations in the brain (e.g. Pynte *et al.* 1991). In addition, saccade programming time is assumed to require some 100–150 ms, although there is evidence that a programmed saccade can be cancelled up to 70 ms before the initiation of the movement (Deubel *et al.* 2000). Given a fixation duration of 250 ms, this leaves a time interval between 50 and 100 ms (250–50–100/150) for a foveally-presented word to determine the target of the upcoming saccade, and a time interval of some 130 ms (250–50–70) to cancel an upcoming saccade. These are the time constraints for foveally-presented words. However, there is evidence that words presented in the parafovea require more time to activate word representations in the brain, partly because there are fewer receptors in parafoveal vision and partly because projection times from the retina to the brain are slower. One estimate of the extra time needed before parafoveal input can activate word representations in the brain is 90 ms per degree of eccentricity (Rayner and Morrison 1981). This means that a parafoveally-presented word at a distance of seven letter positions (2° of eccentricity) from the fixation location requires an extra 180 ms before it can be identified. This is more than the maximum time interval that is available within a fixation to influence the target of the upcoming saccade. Reichle *et al.*'s E-Z Reader model (1998, 2003) addressed this criticism by introducing the notion of a familiarity check in order to speed up the saccade programming, but even this model has been criticized because the information from a parafoveal word cannot reach the brain in time to cancel the saccade to word $n+1$ and replace it by a saccade to word $n+2$ (see the comments by Findlay and White 2003, Radach *et al.* 2003, and Sereno *et al.* 2003 to the Reichle *et al.* 2003 target article in *Behavioral and Brain Sciences*). The E-Z Reader model requires fixations that are on average 60 ms longer when word $n+1$ is skipped than when it is not skipped.

Because parafoveal word information requires a long time before it can influence the target of the next saccade, Brysbaert and Vitu (1998) proposed that within the first 100 ms of a fixation, an educated guess is made about the chances of recognizing the parafoveal word $n+1$ based on the length of the word and its distance from the fixation location (rather than on a familiarity check). This initial estimate is used to select the target of the next saccade. When a word (e.g. a three-letter word starting at a distance of three letters from the fixation location) on average has a 70 per cent chance of being identified by the end of the current fixation, it will be skipped with a probability of 70 per cent. As in the E-Z Reader model, the programming of the initial saccade can be cancelled up to 70 ms before execution, if the ongoing language processing indicates that the initial estimate was wrong.

Finally, it should be noted that McConkie in more recent publications (McConkie *et al.* 1994; Yang and McConkie 2001) also returned to the idea of independent oculo-motor strategies during reading. Having found that the probability of word skipping can be predicted rather well by equations that only involve word length and launch site (see below), he started to question the viability of linguistic control theories. Or to put it in his own words (McConkie *et al.* 1994, p. 325):

> We have briefly outlined the approach we are taking in our attempt to produce a mathe-matical model of the eye movements of normal, skilled readers. Our greatest surprise thus far has been to observe how much of the variance in the data can be accounted for with a relatively few parameters, and these often reflecting such low-level variables as word length, eye position in word and launch site.

In summary, there are two different views on word skipping. In the first view, which we will call the autonomous oculomotor scanning strategy, the decision where to move the eyes is based on the visual lay-out of the word blobs in a line of text. A word is skipped, because it is short and/or close to the current fixation location. In the second view, which we will call the language control view, a word is skipped because it has been identified on the previous fixation. Historically, the first view was dominant until the late 1970s, whereas the second view has received more attention in the last two decades.

Empirical data

In this section we will look carefully at the empirical evidence on which the above models are based. We will deal successively with (1) the existence of oculomotor error in the execution of eye movements, (2) the effects of word length and launch site, and (3) the contribution of language factors such as word frequency and the extent to which a word is predicted by the sentence context. In the last part of this section, we will attempt to determine the relative importance of visual and linguistic variables, in order to decide which should come first in an acceptable model of interword eye movement control.

Errors in the programming and execution of eye movements

A first factor that influences word skipping is the fact that the eyes do not always land exactly on the intended position. As is true for all biological processes, the programming and execution of eye movements is subject to a certain degree of error. This has been shown most convincingly by McConkie and his group (McConkie *et al.* 1988, 1994). A typical experiment involved a few participants reading a complete novel, so that analyses could be based on a large number of observations per person. One of the major analyses was the frequency distribution of the initial fixations on a word as a function of the launch site (i.e. the letter position relative to the target word centre, from which the eye movement started). Figure 3.1 depicts the prototypical findings. There are two main effects. First, the distribution of landing positions is well captured by a Gaussian curve, and second, the mean of the distribution is a function of the launch site. For each launch site one character position further to the left, the mean of the landing position distribution moves leftward by about one-third of a character position. McConkie attributed this to a range error, by which the system tends to overshoot near targets and undershoot far targets.

There is no doubt that any comprehensive model of word skipping has to take into account the existence of involuntary word skipping due to oculomotor error (as well as the fact that some words are involuntarily looked at because of a saccade undershoot).

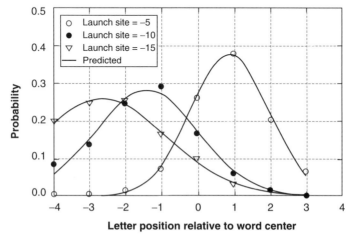

Figure 3.1 Frequency distributions of the initial fixations on seven-letter words, following saccades launched from 5, 10, and 15 letter positions to the left of the centre of the target word (reprinted from McConkie *et al.* 1994).

However, research (in particular, Reilly and O'Regan 1998) has indicated that not all word skipping can be explained by oculomotor error alone. Some words are skipped, not because the saccade was badly programmed and/or executed, but because there never was an intention to fixate the words. As indicated above, the autonomous oculomotor scanning view claims that such voluntary word skipping happens because a word is too short and/or too close to the fixation location. According to the language control view, such skipping happens because the word was easy enough to be identified in parafoveal vision. In the next part, we will look at the effects of word length and launch site.

Word length and launch site

One of the most conspicuous aspects of word skipping is that it happens more often with short words than with long words. For instance, Vitu *et al.* (1995) reported skipping probabilities of about 80 per cent for one-letter words, 60 per cent for three-letter words, 30 per cent for five-letter words, and 10 per cent for words of seven letters or longer. Interestingly, skipping rates were virtually the same when the stimulus materials were changed into meaningless z-strings with the same layout as the original text, and participants were asked to pretend they were reading these letter strings.

Kerr (1992) was the first to note that the average word length effect hides another, equally strong effect, that of the launch site. Figure 3.2 shows some typical data. They are drawn from a study in which 24 participants read 120 sentences (see Brysbaert and Mitchell 1996, Experiment 3 for further details), resulting in a total of more than 22,000 observations for words from two to nine letters. Skipping rate is plotted as a function of word length (2–9 letters) and launch site (1–15 letters, operationalized as

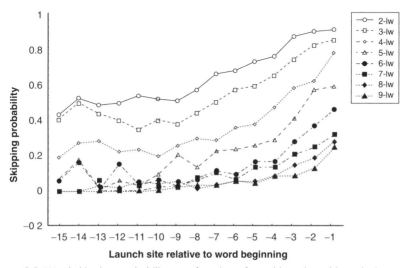

Figure 3.2 Word skipping probability as a function of word length and launch site (defined in letter positions relative to the blank space in front of the target word).

the distance in letter positions from the blank space in front of the word). Although a two-letter word on average was skipped in 69 per cent of the cases, this figure ranged from 90 per cent at launch site one (the last letter of the previous word) to some 50 per cent at launch site 15 (when the eyes already skipped one or two words). Similar data have been reported by Kerr (1992), Vitu *et al.* (1995), and Rayner *et al.* (1996). In addition, Vitu *et al.* (1995) showed that the effect of launch site on skipping rate also applies to meaningless z-strings.

It should be noted that the effects of word length and launch site are equally well explained by both models based on autonomous oculomotor scanning strategies, and models based on language control. According to the oculomotor control models, short words and words close to the launch site are skipped because they lie in the area of high visibility around the fixation location and/or because their length and their distance make them less probable targets for a saccade. According to the language control view, short words and words close to the launch site are skipped because they are more likely to be identified before saccade onset. This is again due to the drop of visibility outside the fixation position and, in the case of word length, to the fact that short words in general are easier than long words (e.g. they usually have a higher frequency). In order to decide between both types of theories, researchers have tried to disentangle length and processing difficulty by looking at skipping rates for carefully controlled stimulus words and sentences.

Language factors

The only way to find out whether parafoveal words are skipped because they were identified during the previous fixation is to examine the skipping rate for stimulus materials that are identical except for the difficulty of the target word. Otherwise, it is impossible to disentangle the effects of the oculomotor scanning strategy (which can be a function of the difficulty of the text up to the target word, and of the length of the words in front of the target word) from those of the language processing. Hence, the target words should be of equal length and be presented within the same text. The only variable on which they should differ is their identification difficulty. Target word difficulty has been manipulated in two different ways: either by manipulating the properties of the word itself, or by manipulating the extent to which the word was predicted by the previous words in the sentence. As not all models predict an equal effect size for both cases (e.g. Hochberg and Shebilske predict a larger effect of contextual constraints than of word difficulty), we will discuss them separately.

We were able to locate 10 studies in which skipping rates were compared for easy and difficult parafoveal words (see Table 3.1). In eight of these studies, the variable that was manipulated was the frequency of the word. For instance, Rayner and Fischer (1996) compared sentences like 'He invested his money to build a *store* and was soon bankrupt' with sentences like 'He invested his money to build a *wharf* and was soon bankrupt'. In the other two studies, the word was manipulated so that it was either visible in parafoveal vision or not visible until the moment the eyes crossed the blank space in front of the word. As can be seen, in all studies and for all word lengths, skipping rate was higher or equal in the easy condition than in the difficult condition.

Table 3.1 Word skipping probabilities as a function of word characteristics

Study	Manipulation	Word length	Easy	Difficult	Difference
Blanchard *et al.* (1989)	Parafoveal preview	1–3 (value used: 2)	0.56	0.43	0.13
exp 1 and 2		4–5 (value used: 4.5)	0.20	0.10	0.10
		6–10 (value used: 8)	0.06	0.04	0.02
Pollatsek *et al.* (1992)	Parafoveal preview	3–8 (value used: 5.5)	0.12	0.10	0.02
Henderson and Ferreira (1990)	Word frequency	4–7 (value used: 5.5)	0.18	0.18	0.01
Inhoff and Topolski (1994)	Word frequency	4–7 (value used: 5.5)	0.27	0.18	0.09
Rayner *et al.* (1996)	Word frequency	5	0.20	0.14	0.06
		6	0.19	0.16	0.03
		7	0.13	0.12	0.01
		8	0.09	0.08	0.01
		9	0.06	0.06	0.00
		10	0.08	0.07	0.01
Rayner and Raney (1996)	Word frequency	6–9 (value used: 7.5)	0.17	0.11	0.06
Rayner and Fisher (1996)	Word frequency	5	0.18	0.08	0.10
		6	0.12	0.05	0.07
		7	0.05	0.01	0.04
		8	0.02	0.02	0.00
		9	0.03	0.02	0.01
Altaribba *et al.* (1996)	Word frequency	5.8	0.15	0.12	0.03
Schilling *et al.* (1998)	Word frequency	6–9 (value used: 7.5)	0.11	0.07	0.04
Kliegl *et al.* (2004)	Word frequency	3	0.41	0.32	0.09
		4	0.30	0.20	0.10
		5	0.19	0.13	0.06
		6	0.21	0.11	0.10
		7	0.18	0.09	0.09
		8	0.06	0.04	0.02
		9	0.04	0.03	0.01
		Mean	0.16	0.11	0.05

This establishes beyond doubt that lexical variables do influence the probability of word skipping. However, it should be noted that the overall difference in skipping rate is rather small (5 per cent) and tends to be slightly larger for short words than for long words.

Fifteen other studies looked at the effects of contextual constraints on word skipping (see Table 3.2). Contextual constraints are usually measured by examining how many participants fill in a particular word in a cloze task. For instance, given the sentence 'The man decided to shave his _____', participants are much more likely to fill in 'beard' (83 per cent) than 'chest' (8 per cent) (Rayner and Well 1996). Thus, a language

Table 3.2 Word skipping probabilities as a function of context predictability

Study	Manipulation	Word length	Easy	Difficult	Difference
Ehrlich and Rayner (1981)	Context constraint	5	0.41	0.35	0.06
Balota et al. (1985)	Context constraint	4–8 (mean = 5.2)	0.11	0.02	0.09
Vonk (1984)	Pronoun prediction	3	0.40	0.17	0.23
Schustack et al. (1987)	Context constraint	3–8 (value used: 5.5)	0.28	0.16	0.12
Hyona (1993)	Context constraint	7–10 (value used: 8.5)	0.04	0.00	0.04
Inhoff and Topolski (1994) exp 1	Word consistency	4–7 (value used: 5.5)	0.13	0.07	0.06
Brysbaert and Vitu (1995)	Pronoun prediction	3	0.49	0.40	0.09
Rayner and Well (1996)	Context constraint	4–8 (value used: 6)	0.22	0.10	0.12
Altaribba et al. (1996)	Context constraint	5.8	0.17	0.11	0.06
Rayner et al. (2001) exp 1	Context constraint	4–8 (mean = 5.2)	0.30	0.18	0.12
Rayner et al. (2001) exp 2	Context constraint	4–8 (mean = 5.2)	0.23	0.13	0.10
Calvo et al. (2001)	Context constraint	4–10 (mean = 6.6)	0.09	0.09	0.00
Calvo and Meseguer (2002)	Context constraint	4–11 (mean = 7)	0.09	0.07	0.02
Drieghe et al. (2004)	Context constraint	2	0.79	0.74	0.05
		4	0.55	0.46	0.09
Kliegl et al. (2004)	Context constraint	3–4 (value used: 3.5)	0.35	0.29	0.06
		5–6 (value used: 5.5)	0.21	0.14	0.07
		7–9 (value used: 8)	0.07	0.07	0.00
		Mean	0.27	0.20	0.08

control view would predict more word skipping in the former case than in the latter. All studies also showed that predicted words were skipped more often than unpredicted words. The mean difference amounted to 8 per cent. The largest effect (of 23 per cent) was reported by Vonk (1984) who (in Dutch) compared sentences like 'Mary was envious of Helen because *she* never looked so good', where the pronoun had no disambiguating value, with sentences like 'Mary was envious of Albert because *she* never looked so good', where the pronoun did disambiguate (in an unexpected continuation of the sentence). Brysbaert and Vitu (1995) used the same materials, but compared sentences with an expected continuation 'Mary was envious of Marc because *he* always looked so good' and sentences with an unexpected continuation 'Mary was envious of Marc because *she* never looked so good'. They found a difference in skipping rate of 9 per cent.

Rayner and Well (1996) pointed out that the difference in contextual constraints between predicted and unpredicted words has to be rather large in order to obtain an effect on skipping rate. For example, in their first experiment Ehrlich and Rayner (1981) had a difference between 93 and 15 per cent continuations in the cloze task and reported skipping rates of 49 vs. 38 per cent. In their second experiment, however, continuations were only 60 and 0 per cent, and no difference in skipping rate was found (twice 32 per cent). Similarly, Hyönä (1993) compared conditions of 65 and 32 per cent continuation and found virtually no effect on word skipping (4 vs. 0 per cent). To test the effect of context constraints directly, Rayner and Well (1996) compared three conditions: one in which the target word had been given by 86 per cent of the raters in a cloze task, one in which the target word had been given by 41 per cent of the raters, and one in which the target word had been given by only 4 per cent of the raters. Skipping rates were 22, 12, and 10 per cent respectively; that is, virtually no difference was found between the 41 and the 4 per cent condition.

In a final test of the influence of language factors on skipping rates, Rayner *et al.* (2004) simultaneously manipulated the frequency of the target words and their predictability, to see what the combined effects of these two variables would be. The four conditions are listed below, together with the associated skipping rates:

High-frequency, predictable:

Before warming the milk the babysitter took the infant's *bottle* out of the travel bag.   23%

High-frequency, unpredictable:

To prevent a mess the caregiver checked the baby's *bottle* before leaving.   15%

Low-frequency, predictable:

To prevent a mess the caregiver checked the baby's *diaper* before leaving.   14%

Low-frequency, unpredictable:

Before warming the milk the babysitter took the infant's *diaper* out of the travel bag. 16%

The findings of this study are in line with those from the previous studies, because a predictability effect of 8 per cent was found. In addition, however, the Rayner *et al.* (2004) study suggests that the predictability effect summarized in Table 3.2 is limited to target words of a reasonably high frequency. When the frequency of the target words is low, predictability is not strong enough to influence the skipping rate.

The relative importance of visual and linguistic variables

Thus far, we have shown evidence for oculomotor, visual, and language-related influences on word skipping. However, it should be noted that much of this evidence is not fully conclusive. For instance, the effects of word length and launch site (Figure 3.2) are usually reported without reference to the frequency of the words in the different cells. An exception to this can be found in Rayner *et al.* (1996, Figure 3.2) who looked at the effects of launch site and word frequency on the skipping rate for five- and six-letter words. They reported independent effects of word length and launch site, together with a frequency effect at close launch sites (up to three letter positions in front of the target word). However, even in this study, the text fragments on which the data were based may have been quite different in the various conditions (e.g. it is reasonable to assume that certain sequences of word lengths resulted in near launch sites, and others in more distant launch sites; or that high-frequency and low-frequency words appeared in different sequences of word lengths).

Another question is how to interpret the language effects in Tables 3.1 and 3.2. Although these effects are undeniably and consistently apparent, they seem to be rather small (5–8 per cent), certainly if we compare them with the effects of word length and launch site as shown in Figure 3.2. Tables 3.1 and 3.2 show skipping rates for words that were controlled for their length, that were presented in identical sentences, and that were constructed in such a way as to maximize their difference in processing difficulty (e.g. by having a large difference in frequency or in contextual constraint). Thus, for these stimuli, any language control model that defines word difficulty primarily in terms of word frequency and predictability, would have to predict that the effect of processing difficulty will be stronger than the effect of word length, because we do not have the usual confound between word length and word difficulty here (as short words tend to be easier than long words). For these particular sentences, we would not predict that a difficult (low-frequency or unexpected) three-letter word is skipped more often than an easy (high-frequency or highly-expected) five-letter word, because, for these sentences, the processing difficulty has been manipulated independently of the word length.

The relative contribution of word length and processing difficulty can be determined on the basis of Tables 3.1 and 3.2 by running multiple regression analyses with these two variables as predictors and skipping rate as the dependent variable. This is straightforward as the predictors in Tables 3.1 and 3.2 are orthogonal.

Although we could have taken the raw values of word length, we opted for an exponential transformation. This has the advantage that more weight is given to differences between short words than between large words, and that the function asymptotes to 1 (for word length zero) and to 0 (for long words). As it turned out, only one free parameter was needed for a model based on word length (*wl*) alone. Below we list the equations for the four conditions (the high-frequency and low-frequency words from Table 3.1, and the predictable and unpredictable words from Table 3.2) together with the variance explained by the following model:

High-frequency words: $P(skip) = e^{-0.31wl}$ 88% variance explained (27 data)

Low-frequency words: $P(skip) = e^{-0.39wl}$ 82% variance explained (27 data)

Predictable words: $P(skip) = e^{-0.26wl}$ 75% variance explained (18 data)

Unpredictable words: $P(skip) = e^{-0.35wl}$ 55% variance explained (18 data)

These regression analyses teach us four things. First, when we want to predict the skipping rate of one of the studies listed in Table 3.1 or 3.2, knowing the length of the target word helps us a lot to improve our estimate. When the target word is short (e.g. two letters), the skipping rate will be high (e.g. $P(skip) = e^{-0.31*2} = e^{-0.62} = 0.54$ for the high-frequency words in Table 3.1). In contrast, when the target word is long (e.g. nine letters), the skipping rate will be low ($P(skip) = e^{-0.31*9} = e^{-2.79} = 0.06$ for the same type of words). Second, these regression analyses show that word length is a better predictor for the studies of Table 3.1 than for those of Table 3.2. The reason for this might be that in Table 3.1 several data came from the same studies, whereas in Table 3.2, there was more diversity in the origins of the data. Third, it can be seen that the difficult conditions resulted in a larger weight of the word length variable. As will be shown in Figures 3.3 and 3.4 below, this change in weight means that the skipping probability drops faster as a function of word length for difficult words than for easy words. Finally, the regression analyses show us that there is no major difference between the easy and the difficult condition, meaning that little prediction power is lost, if we fit a general model to all the data of Table 3.1 or 3.2. This is shown below:

High + low frequency words: $P(skip) = e^{-0.34wl}$ 80% variance explained (54 data)

Predicted+unpredicted words: $P(skip) = e^{-0.30wl}$ 62% variance explained (36 data)

When we run similar regression analyses with the difficulty of the words as a predictor (i.e. D, defined as 0 for the easy condition and 1 for the difficult condition), we get the following results:

High + low frequency words: $P(skip) = 0.16–0.05D$ 5% variance explained (54 data)

Predicted + unpredicted words: $P(skip) = 0.27–0.08D$ 5% variance explained (36 data)

The regression analyses on the basis of word difficulty show that for improving predictions, knowing the difficulty of the words is significantly less helpful than knowing the word length (5 per cent variance explained vs. 70 per cent variance explained). Basically, information about word difficulty forces us to predict that all cells in the high-frequency row of Table 3.1 should have a value of 0.16 and all cells of the low-frequency words should have a value of 0.11. Similarly, our predictions of the values in Table 3.2 are that all cells in the first column have a value of 0.27 and all those of the second column have a value of 0.19.

Because word length and word difficulty are orthogonal variables in Tables 3.1 and 3.2, we can combine them into a single regression analysis to further improve our predictions. This is shown below:

High + low frequency words: $P(skip) = e^{-(0.31+0.8D)wl}$ 87% variance explained (54 data)

Predicted + unpredicted words: $P(skip) = e^{-(0.26+0.8D)wl}$ 67% variance explained (36 data)

The lines in Figure 3.3 show the predicted values for Table 3.1 on the basis of the combined regression analysis with both word length and word difficulty as predictor variables. The figure also displays the observed data from Kliegl *et al.* (in press), Blanchard *et al.* (1989), Rayner *et al.* (1996), and Rayner and Fischer (1996). In this figure, we easily see that the predicted probability of skipping a high-frequency two-letter word (0.54 or 54 per cent) is quite close to the value obtained in the Blanchard *et al.* study (0.56). Similarly, we can compare the predicted probability of skipping a low-frequency five-letter word (0.14) with the empirical data reported by Kliegl *et al.* (0.13), Blanchard *et al.* (0.10), Rayner *et al.* (0.14), and Rayner and Fischer (0.08). Notice that in Figure 3.3 (and in Figure 3.4) skipping rates have been averaged over launch sites, as information about this variable was not available in the articles.

Figure 3.4 shows the information for Table 3.2. The empirical data that have been included here, are Drieghe *et al.* (2004), Ehrlich and Rayner (1981), Kliegl *et al.* (2004), Rayner *et al.* (2001), and Vonk (1984). The figure shows the larger scatter in these data. At the same time, it illustrates how both word length and word difficulty (predictability) influence the skipping probabilities.

The implications of our findings for theories of eye movement control

Making precise predictions about the impact of word length and processing difficulty

The main conclusion from Figures 3.3 and 3.4 is that even for studies which specifically looked at the effects of processing difficulty on skipping rate, word length was a

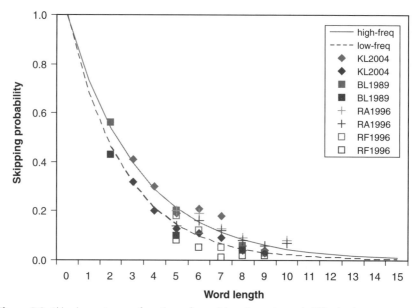

Figure 3.3 Skipping rate as a function of word length and word difficulty (gray = easy condition; black = difficult condition). Empirical data from Table 3.1. Fitted curve based on nonlinear regression with word length and word difficulty as predictors.

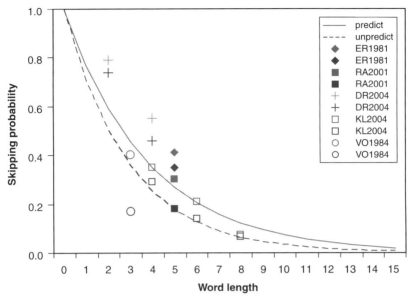

Figure 3.4 Skipping rate as a function of word length and context predictability (gray = easy condition; black = difficult condition). Empirical data from Table 3.2. Fitted curve based on nonlinear regression with word length and context predictability as predictors.

more important predictor of skipping rate than processing difficulty. That is, to predict how often a word was skipped, it was better to know how long the word was, than to know whether it was visible in the parafovea, of high frequency, or highly constrained by the preceding context. This is shown quite convincingly in a study reported by Drieghe *et al.* (2004). In this study, Dutch sentences of the following types were compared (presented together with their associated skipping rates):

(1) The robber pointed the gun to the policeman and ordered him
to put his hands *up* and face the wall.   79%

(2) The robber pointed the gun to the policeman and ordered him
to put his hands *in* and face the wall.   74%

(3) He was very disappointed in his friends because he felt they had
let him *down* when he was in trouble.   55%

(4) He was very disappointed in his friends because he felt they had
let him *stew* when he was in trouble.   46%

In one half of the sentences, a two-letter word was expected; in the other half, a four-letter word was expected (82 per cent continuation in the cloze-task; see sentences 1 and 3 for English counterparts of the type of stimulus materials used). In half of the trials, the expected words were replaced by an unexpected word of the same length (0.5 per cent continuation; see sentences 2 and 4). These four types of sentences were then presented to the participants as part of a short paragraph of text, describing a familiar situation. When we look at the skipping rates for the different types of sentence, we see that the effect of word predictability was 7 per cent, in line with the other studies of Table 3.2. At the same time, however, we see a massive 26 per cent difference between the two-letter words and the four-letter words. Because of this large effect, the totally unexpected two-letter word in sentence 2 was skipped more often (74 per cent) than the highly expected four-letter word in sentence 3 (55 per cent).

Our regression analyses not only establish the importance of word length and processing difficulty for explaining word skipping rates, they also allow us to make precise statements about the magnitudes of the effects that will be found. On the basis of Table 3.1 and Figure 3.3, we can predict that studies that manipulate the difficulty of the target words will find an average difference in skipping rate of 5 per cent. The effect is maximal for word lengths of 2–4 letters, where it can be as high as 8 per cent. For longer words, the effect is expected to be smaller. Similarly, Table 3.2 and Figure 3.4 inform us that a slightly larger difference of 8 per cent will be found when the sentence context is manipulated. The difference will be at its maximum (10–11 per cent) for word lengths of 3–5 letters, and slightly smaller for shorter and longer words. At the same time, the effect of word length can be estimated with the equation $P(skip) = e^{-0.32wl}$, implying that a two-letter word is expected to be skipped in 53 per cent of the instances, a four-letter words in 28 per cent, and an eight-letter word in 8 per cent (at least for the type of sentences and situations that have been used in the experiments reported in the tables, and averaged over different launch sites).

In search of the underlying mechanisms

Although Figures 3.3 and 3.4 quite elegantly demonstrate the importance of word length and processing load for the understanding of word skipping rates, we must not forget that they only provide us with a description of the data. They do not tell us which underlying mechanisms give rise to these patterns. On their own, they certainly do not constrain the space of possible models to one single candidate. For instance, it may be possible to produce the curves of Figures 3.3 and 3.4 with a computer model of eye movement control that is entirely based on the language control view. If visual acuity outside the fixation location drops steeply enough, chances of identifying words in the parafovea will be a function of the word length rather than the easiness of the word within the sentence. Reichle *et al.* (2003) claim (but have not shown explicitly yet) that their E-Z Reader model predicts a word length effect on skipping rate. The question, therefore, is whether the predicted word length effect is of the same size as the one found in the empirical studies listed in the present chapter. Similarly, one could imagine that a model of eye movement control based on the idea that multiple words become activated on each fixation and compete as the target of the next saccade, could come up with curves very similar to the ones shown in Figures 3.3 and 3.4. This may be possible by implementing a sufficiently strong decrease in the activation gradient (or pulling strength) as a function of the distance from the fixation location.

Alternatively, one can imagine that our data also fit well within an autonomous oculomotor scanning model of word skipping. Such models capitalize on the lengths of the upcoming word blobs and predict strong effects of word length (and launch site) in the absence of language-related influences. Thus, it may very well be that Reilly and O'Regan's (1998) strategy of targeting the longest word in the parafovea would result in a word length effect very similar to the one discovered here. Similarly, Brysbaert and Vitu (1998) showed that the word length effect (Figures 3.2–3.4) and the launch site effect (Figure 3.2) can easily be simulated by a simple scanning strategy that is based on the assumption of a normally distributed word recognition probability curve around the fixation location, and that uses this curve to quickly estimate the chances of recognizing a word of a particular length at a particular distance by the end of the current fixation. Finally, McConkie (personal communication) rightfully pointed out that the word length data may even be compatible with a much cruder autonomous oculomotor scanning model that simply consists of selecting saccades from a frequency distribution without any attention to the actual word blobs in the sentence. If the selected saccade lengths are sufficiently long, such a blind saccade selection strategy would also predict more skipping of short words than of long words.

Although Figures 3.3 and 3.4 on their own may not refute any of the current models of eye movement control, they put strong constraints on the weights that should be given to the different components in the model. As such, they form a benchmark against which the performance of models should be evaluated, in very much the same way as the frequency distributions of fixation durations and landing positions are currently used. A model of eye movement control that does not predict a strong effect of word length and launch site on skipping probability is clearly at odds with human performance. At the same time, a model that predicts a word length effect but no effect of processing load, is at odds with the human data as well. It is our suspicion that all current models will fail on this double requirement. For instance, we believe that both the E-Z Reader model and the SWIFT model overestimate the effects of word frequency and word predictability because these variables have been explicitly included in the model, whereas the word length variable has been considered as a confounding variable (e.g. the E-Z Reader model claims to 'successfully' simulate a 60 per cent difference in skipping rate between high-frequency and low-frequency words, when words are averaged over different word lengths; see Figure 6 in Reichle *et al.* 2003). Conversely, the word skipping models based on an autonomous scanning strategy readily explain the word length effect (and the fact that the same length effect is observed when participants 'read' meaningless z-strings), but face difficulties incorporating the processing load component. Neither Reilly and O'Regan (1998) nor Brysbaert and Vitu (1998) offer detailed proposals about how to implement the effects of word frequency and word predictability in their mathematical models of word skipping. The future will have to show which adaptations must be made to the current models, so that they can account for the exact pattern of data presented in Figures 3.3 and 3.4.

What happens after a word has been skipped?

More information about what guides word skipping can be gained from analysing the consequences of such skipping. In a simple model where words are only skipped when they have been recognized in parafoveal vision, the only consequence one would expect is a slightly longer fixation duration following a skip, because skipping a word usually results in a long saccade, meaning that less information from the parafovea could be sampled on the previous fixation. However, we have seen that this is unlikely to be a true account of human performance. Words are often skipped on the basis of incomplete information, because the initial decision to program a saccade needs to be taken at least 150 ms before the onset of the saccade. Thus, it may be worth having a detailed look at what happens when a word has been skipped.

An initial informative observation is that a number of eye movements resulting in word skipping are immediately followed by a regressive eye movement to the very same word $n+1$ that was skipped, sometimes after a short fixation on word $n+2$. Vitu and McConkie (2000) reported 19 per cent immediate regressions to skipped words, compared with 11 per cent immediate regressions to non-skipped words. Needless to say, such regressions are more common after a difficult word has been skipped than after an easy word has been skipped. Drieghe *et al.* (2004) reported 22 per cent immediate regressions for unexpected words compared with 14 per cent for expected words. This is a first indication that readers in a considerable number of cases immediately correct for word skipping, as if by the time the eyes landed, they realized the previous saccade was not what was needed.

Another observation is that the first fixation after a skipped word, when not followed by a regressive eye movement, is longer when a difficult word has been skipped than when an easy word has been skipped. Again, this is an indication that readers are able to rapidly assess the consequences of skipping a wrong word.

These two observations support the idea that as far as eye movements between words are concerned, the reader is regularly one saccade 'too far' and needs to correct an immediately prior decision. Interestingly, as far as we know, this correction happens instantaneously, on the first fixation after the premature skipping. This is a good example of the tight coupling between oculomotor behaviour and the ongoing language processing. Although the literature on word skipping presents a case where eye movement control and language processing often are one step out of phase, there is no evidence that they ever get two steps out of phase. Apparently, it is more economical for a reader sometimes to make a wrong forward saccade that is immediately corrected, than to adopt a cautious strategy of always targeting the next word unless this word has already been identified (or passed the familiarity check). The most probable reason for the decoupling between language processing and target selection is the time delay between the initiation of a saccade program and its execution. This requires the reader to make 'educated guesses' on the basis of incomplete information. The alternative, however, probably would be much slower reading.

Conclusion

It is tempting to think of eye movements during reading as an activity that is completely regulated by either a dumb oculomotor scanning strategy or by the ongoing text processing. In both cases, the pattern of fixations within a line of text seems needlessly complicated.

In this chapter we have reviewed the evidence for both positions with respect to word skipping, and we have noticed that some findings are more in line with the autonomous oculomotor view, and others with the language control view. This suggests that neither approach at present gives a complete account of the phenomenon. To summarize, it has been established beyond doubt that word skipping depends on four variables: the length of word $n+1$ in the parafovea, the launch site of the saccade, the existence of oculomotor error in the programming and execution of saccades, and the difficulty of word $n+1$ within the sentence. In addition, it has been shown that the effects of word length and launch site cannot be reduced to the probability of identifying word $n+1$ in parafoveal vision. Rather, it looks like the decision to skip word $n+1$ is often based on incomplete information related to the length of the word and its distance from the fixation location.

In our view, there are two reasons why words are regularly skipped without being recognized in parafoveal vision. The first is the long programming time (100–150 ms) of a saccade. This forces the oculomotor system to select the target of the next saccade within the first 100 ms of a fixation. The second factor is the delayed recognition of words in parafoveal vision relative to central vision. This means that verbal information about word $n+1$ is not available until reasonably late in the fixation.

At the same time, eye guidance in reading is closely linked to the ongoing language processing. Word frequency and word predictability have small but consistent effects on word skipping. In addition, when a word has been skipped without being fully recognized, remedial action follows immediately, either in the form of a regressive eye movement or in the form of a prolonged fixation on word $n+2$. These corrections ensure that eye movement control and language processing are never more than one step out of phase.

References

Altarriba, J., Kroll, J. F., Sholl, A., and Rayner, K. (1996). The influence of lexical and conceptual constraints on reading mixed-language sentences: Evidence from eye fixations and naming times. *Memory and Cognition*, **24**(4), 477–492.

Balota, D. A., Pollatsek, A., and Rayner, K. (1985). The interaction of contextual constraints and parafoveal visual information in reading. *Cognitive Psychology*, **17**(3), 364–390.

Blanchard, H. E., Pollatsek, A., and Rayner, K. (1989). The acquisition of parafoveal word information in reading. *Perception and Psychophysics*, **46**(1), 85–94.

Bouma, H., and De Voogd, A. H. (1974). On the control of eye saccades in reading. *Vision Research*, **14**, 273–284.

Brysbaert, M., and Mitchell, D. C. (1996). Modifier attachment in sentence parsing: Evidence from Dutch. *Quarterly Journal of Experimental Psychology*, **49A**, 664–695.

Brysbaert, M., and Vitu, F. (1995). Word skipping: Its implications for theories of eye movements in reading. Paper presented at the Eighth European Conference on Eye Movements. Derby, UK.

Brysbaert, M., and Vitu, F. (1998). Word skipping: Implications for theories of eye movement control in reading. In: G. Underwood (ed.) *Eye guidance in reading and scene perception*. Oxford: Elsevier, pp. 125–147. (available at http://cogprints.ecs.soton.ac.uk/).

Buswell, G.T. (1920). An experimental study of eye-voice span in reading. *Supplementary Educational Monographs*, **17**.

Calvo, M. G., and Meseguer, E. (2002). Eye movements and processing stages in reading: Relative contribution of visual, lexical and contextual factors. *Spanish Journal of Psychology*, **5**(1), 66–77.

Calvo, M. G., and Meseguer, E., and Carreiras, M. (2001). Inferences about predictable events: Eye movements during reading. *Psychological Research*, **65**, 158–169.

Deubel, H., O'Regan, J. K., and Radach, R. (2000). Attention, information processing, and eye movement control. In: A. Kennedy, R. Radach, D. Heller, and J. Pynte (ed.) *Reading as a perceptual process*. Oxford: Elsevier, pp. 701–719.

Drieghe, D., Brysbaert, M., Desmet, T., and Debaecke, C. (2004). Word skipping in reading: On the interplay of linguistic and visual factors. *European Journal of Cognitive Psychology*, **16**, 79–103.

Ehrlich, S. F., and Rayner, K. (1981). Contextual effects on word perception and eye movements during reading. *Journal of Verbal Learning and Verbal Behaviour*, **20**, 641–655.

Engbert, R., Longtin, A., and Kliegl, R. (2002). A dynamical model of saccade generation in reading based on spatially distributed lexical processing. *Vision Research*, **42**, 621–636.

Erdmann, B., and Dodge, R. (1898). *Psychologische Untersuchungen uber das Lesen auf experimenteller Grundlage*. Halle, Germany: N. Niemeyer.

Findlay, J. M., and White, S. J. (2003). Serial programming for saccades: Does it all add up? Open-peer commentary to Reichle, Rayner, and Pollatsek: 'The E-Z Reader model of eye-movement control in reading: Comparisons to other models'. *Behavioral and Brain Sciences*, **26**, 483–484.

Fuentes, L. J., and Tudela, P. (1992). Semantic processing of foveally and parafoveally presented words in a lexical decision task. *Quarterly Journal of Experimental Psychology*, **45A**, 299–322.

Henderson, J. M., and Ferreira, F. (1990). Effects of foveal processing difficulty on the perceptual span in reading: Implications for theories of reading eye movements. *Journal of Experimental Psychology: Learning, Memory, and Cognition*, **16**, 417–429.

Hochberg, J. (1975). On the control of eye saccades in reading. *Vision Research*, **15**, 620.

Huey, E. B. (1908). *The psychology and pedagogy of reading*. New York: MacMillan.

Hyönä, J. (1993). Effects of thematic and lexical priming on readers' eye movements. *Scandinavian Journal of Psychology*, **34**(4), 293–304.

Inhoff, A. W., and Topolski, R. (1994). The use of phonological codes during eye fixations in reading and in on-line and delayed naming tasks. *Journal of Memory and Language*, **33**, 689–713.

Just, M. A., and Carpenter, P. A. (1980). A theory of reading: From eye fixations to comprehension. *Psychological Review*, **87**, 329–354.

Just, M. A., and Carpenter, P. A. (1987). *The psychology of reading and language comprehension*. Newtown, MA: Allyn and Bacon.

Kerr, P. W. (1992). Eye movement control during reading: The selection of where to send the eyes. Doctoral dissertation, University of Illinois at Urbana-Champaign, Urbana, IL.

Kliegl, R., and Engbert, R. (in press). Fixation durations before word skipping in reading. *Psychonomic Bulletin and Review.* In press.

McConkie, G. W. (1979). On the role and control of eye movements in reading. In: P. A. Kolers, M. E. Wrolstad and H. Bouma (ed.) *Processing of visible language* (Vol. 1). New York: Plenum, pp. 37–48.

McConkie, G. W., Kerr, P. W., Reddix, M. D., and Zola, D. (1988). Eye movement control during reading: I. The location of initial eye fixations on words. *Vision Research*, **28**(10), 1107–1118.

McConkie, G. W., Kerr, P. W., and Dyre, B. P. (1994). What are 'normal' eye movements during reading: Toward a mathematical description. In: J. Ygge and G. Lennerstrand (ed.) *Eye movements in reading.* Oxford: Elsevier Science, pp. 315–327.

Morrison, R. E. (1984). Manipulation of stimulus onset delay in reading: Evidence for parallel programming of saccades. *Journal of Experimental Psychology: Human Perception and Performance*, **10**, 667–682.

O'Regan, J. K. (1990). Eye movements and reading. In: E. Kowler (ed.) *Eye movements and their role in visual and cognitive processes* (pp. 395–453). Amsterdam: Elsevier.

O'Regan, J. K. (1992). Optimal viewing position in words and the strategy-tactics theory of eye movements in reading. In: K. Rayner (ed.) *Eye movements and visual cognition: Scene perception and reading.* New York: Springer-Verlag, pp. 333–354.

Pollatsek, A., and Rayner, K. (1990). Eye movements and lexical access in reading. In: D. A. Balota, G.B. Flores d'Arcais, and K. Rayner (ed.) *Comprehension processes in reading.* Hillsdale, NJ: Erlbaum, pp. 143–163.

Pollatsek, A., Lesch, M., Morris, R. K., and Rayner, K. (1992). Phonological codes are used in the integration of information across saccades in word identification and reading. *Journal of Experimental Psychology: Human Perception and Performance*, **18**, 148–162.

Pynte, J., Kennedy, A., and Murray, W. S. (1991). Within-word inspection strategies in continuous reading – time course of perceptual, lexical and contextual processes. *Journal of Experimental Psychology: Human Perception and Performance*, **17**, 458–470.

Radach, R., Deubel, H., and Heller, D. (2003). Attention, saccade programming, and the timing of eye movement control. Open-peer commentary to Reichle, Rayner, and Pollatsek: 'The E-Z Reader model of eye-movement control in reading: Comparisons to other models'. *Behavioral and Brain Sciences*, **26**, 497–498.

Rayner, K. (1978). Eye movements in reading and information processing. *Psychological Bulletin*, **85**, 618–660.

Rayner, K., and Fischer, M. H. (1996). Mindless reading revisited: eye movements during reading and scanning are different. *Perception and Psychophysics*, **58**(5), 734–747.

Rayner, K., and Morrison, R. M. (1981). Eye movements and identifying words in parafoveal vision. *Bulletin of the Psychonomic Society*, **17**, 135–138.

Rayner, K., and Pollatsek, A. (1989). *The psychology of reading.* Englewood Cliffs, NJ: Prentice Hall.

Rayner, K., and Raney, G. E. (1996). Eye movement control in reading and visual search: Effects of word frequency. *Psychonomic Bulletin and Review*, **3**, 245–248.

Rayner, K., and Sereno, S. C. (1994). Eye movements in reading: Psycholinguistic studies. In: M. Gernsbacher (ed.) *Handbook of psycholinguistics.* New York: Academic Press, pp. 57–82.

Rayner, K., and Well, A. D. (1996). Effects of contextual constraint on eye movements during reading: a further examination. *Psychonomic Bulletin and Review*, **3**(4), 504–509.

Rayner, K., Sereno, S. C., and Raney, G. E. (1996). Eye movement control in reading: a comparison of two types of models. *Journal of Experimental Psychology: Human Perception and Performance*, **22**(5), 1188–1200.

Rayner, K., Binder, K. S., Ashby, J., and Pollatsek, A. (2001). Eye movement control in reading: word predictability has little influence on initial landing positions in words. *Vision Research*, **41**(7), 943–954.

Rayner, K., Ashby, J., Pollatsek, A., and Reichle, E. D. (2004). The effects of frequency and predictability on eye fixations in reading: Implications for the E-Z Reader model. *Journal of Experimental Psychology: Human Perception and Performance*, **30**, 720–732.

Reichle, E. D., Pollatsek, A., Fisher, D. L., and Rayner, K. (1998). Toward a model of eye movement control in reading. *Psychological Review*, **105**(1), 125–157.

Reichle, E. D., Rayner, K., and Pollatsek, A. (2003). The E-Z Reader model of eye movement control in reading: comparisons to other models. *Behavioral and Brain Sciences*, **26**, 445–526.

Reilly, R., and O'Regan, J. K. (1998). Eye movement control in reading: A simulation of some word-targeting strategies. *Vision Research*, **38**, 303–317.

Reilly, R., and Radach, R. (2003). Foundations of an interactive model of eye movement control in reading. In: J. Hyönä, R. Radach, and H. Deubel (ed.) *Cognitive and applied aspects of eye movement research*. Amsterdam: Elsevier, pp. 429–455.

Schilling, H. E. H., Rayner, K., and Chumbley, J. I. (1998). Comparing naming, lexical decision, and eye fixation times: Word frequency effects and individual differences. *Memory and Cognition*, **26**, 1270–1281.

Schustack, M. W., Ehrlich, S. F., and Rayner, K. (1987). Local and global sources of contextual constraint in reading. *Journal of Memory and Language*, **26**, 322–340.

Sereno, S. C., O'Donnell, P. J., and Sereno, A. B. (2003). Neural plausibility and validation may not be so E-Z. Open-peer commentary to Reichle, Rayner, and Pollatsek: 'The E-Z Reader model of eye-movement control in reading: Comparisons to other models'. *Behavioral and Brain Sciences*, **26**, 502.

Shebilske, W. (1975). Reading eye movements from an information-processing point of view. In: D. Massaro (ed.) *Understanding language*. New York: Academic Press, pp. 291–311.

Underwood, G. (2003). Where to look next? The missing landing position effect. Open-peer commentary to Reichle, Rayner, and Pollatsek: 'The E-Z Reader model of eye-movement control in reading: Comparisons to other models'. *Behavioral and Brain Sciences*, **26**, 505–506.

Vitu, F., and McConkie, G. W. (2000). Regressive saccades and word perception in adult reading. In: A. Kennedy, R. Radach, D. Heller, and J. Pynte (ed.) *Reading as a perceptual process*. Oxford: Elsevier, pp. 301–326.

Vitu, F., and McConkie, G. W. (2003). Visuo-motor influences on eye movements in reading: How word position on line affects landing positions in words. Paper presented at the XXIIth European Conference on eye movements, August 20–24, Dundee, (Scotland).

Vitu, F., O'Regan, J. K., Inhoff, A. W., and Topolski, R. (1995). Mindless reading: eye-movement characteristics are similar in scanning letter strings and reading texts. *Perception and Psychophysics*, **57**(3), 352–364.

Vonk, W. (1984). Eye movements during comprehension of pronouns. In: A. G. Gale and F. Johnson (ed.) *Theoretical and applied aspects of eye movement research.* Amsterdam: North-Holland.

White, S. J., and Liversedge, S. P. (2004). Orthographic familiarity influences initial eye fixation positions in reading. *European Journal of Cognitive Psychology,* **16,** 52–78.

Yang, S.-N., and McConkie, G. W. (2001). Eye movements during reading: a theory of saccade initiation times. *Vision Research,* **41,** 3567–3585.

4

Identifying compound words in reading: an overview and a model

Jukka Hyönä, Raymond Bertram
and Alexander Pollatsek

Abstract

In this chapter, we summarize our eye movement studies on reading
Finnish compound words in sentential context. Two advantages of
using Finnish are (a) that compounding is productive so that there are
a lot of compound words and (b) that compounds always appear in
the concatenated form (no spaces between components) so that they
are orthographically 'words'. Our results are consistent with a
processing model that assumes that a whole-word route and a
decomposition route operate in parallel. In the identification of long
compounds, the decomposition route dominates the early processing
stages because (due to visual acuity constraints) a compound word
constituent is easier to access on a single fixation than the whole-word
form. In the identification of shorter compounds, however, most of the
whole word form usually falls onto the fovea and the whole-word
route is able to dominate the identification process. We also discuss
studies that have demonstrated effects of segmentation cues, such as
spacing and 'vowel harmony', on compound word identification. In
the final part, we suggest avenues for future research, including studies
on the effects of morphological family size and on the computation of
the meaning multiple-constituent compounds.

Introduction

In this chapter, we review the work on compound word identification that we have
conducted over the past 6–7 years. We start out by presenting a descriptive model of
compound word processing in the form of 'a processing schema'. After giving a rough
sketch of the model, we flesh it out by discussing the data on which the model is
based. The model we propose is a parallel dual-route model, where the holistic route

and the decomposition route are assumed to be simultaneously active during compound word processing. For the decomposition route, we specify factors that are found to be influential during the identification of the first constituent. Note that we assume that many of the processes we specify can be in parallel.

As the name indicates, a compound word consists of two or more parts that we call *constituents*, which are lexical units that also appear as separate words in the language. An example of a multiple constituent Finnish compound is *lumipallosotatantere* (= snowball fight field), which has four constituents, *lumi, pallo, sota*, and *tantere*. The rightmost constituent in Finnish (and also in English) is the compound word *head*, which is modified by the leftward constituents. (The compound always has the same part of speech as the head.) In compounds comprising more than two constituents, however, the relationship among the constituents is not deducible from their order. In the above example, the relations may be depicted as a two-level hierarchy. At the lower level *sota* modifies *tantere* and *lumi* modifies *pallo;* at the higher level *lumipallo* modifies *sotatantere,* so that the compound would be parsed [(*lumi*)(*pallo*)][(*sota*) (*tantere*)], whereas other four constituent compounds could be parsed differently. At present, we have not yet tackled the issue of how more complex compounds are parsed, but have concentrated on two-constituent compounds, where the modifier-head relation is unambiguous. As the constituents in Finnish compounds are typically nouns, we have primarily restricted our studies to noun-noun compounds. In many two-noun compounds, the modifier noun (*lumi*) is simply attached to the head (*pallo* → *lumipallo* = snowball), but sometimes a genitive marker is attached to the modifier, as in *autonpesu* where *n* is the genitive inflection (its literal translation is car's wash). In most of our studies, we have used compounds with non-inflected constituents.

Compounding is very productive in Finnish. In fact, about 60 per cent of all the words in the dictionary of modern Finnish (*Nykysuomen sanakirja*) are compounds. Finnish is not an exception, as compounding is quite productive in many languages including English. However, this productivity is easier to see in Finnish, as all Finnish compounds always appear unspaced in writing whether or not a genitive inflection is added. (Compounds also always appear unspaced in many other languages such as German, Swedish, Dutch, and Chinese, whereas a majority of compounds in English have spaces between the constituents.) As novel compounds are easily created by attaching two nouns to each other, listeners and readers of Finnish are exposed to novel compounds every day. Thus, to fully understand the process of word identification in Finnish and other languages where compounding is productive, it is of great importance to understand how compound words are identified.

A key question in compound word processing is whether compounds are identified holistically via the whole-word form or whether the identification goes via the constituents (or both). To this end, we have applied an approach introduced by Taft (1979), where frequency is used as a tool to study the processing of morphologically complex words. By independently manipulating the frequency of the whole-word form and

---

[1] The constituent frequency is the frequency with which the constituent appears in the corpus as a separate word. All frequency values were computed using the WordMill program (Laine and Virtanen, 1999) to access a 22.7 million word newspaper corpus.

the frequencies of the constituents[1] (matching for the non-manipulated frequency characteristics), one is in the position to assess the extent to which identification of a compound occurs via the whole-word form vs. the constituents. The logic is as follows. When an effect of constituent frequency is observed in the absence of a whole-word frequency effect, the identification process is assumed to proceed via the parts. Conversely, when there is only a whole-word frequency effect, the identification process is assumed to be holistic in nature. The presence of both constituent frequency and whole-word frequency effects suggests a 'dual-route model' in which both processes are operative, although there are other possible explanations for such a pattern.

In all our studies, the target compounds were embedded in sentences. A compound from the high-frequency condition was paired with a compound from the low-frequency condition, and a sentence frame was created for each matched pair, which was identical up through the word following the target compound. The target compound appeared toward the beginning of the sentence preceded by a semantically neutral sentence fragment (e.g. *John was told that…*, *According to a common belief…*, etc.). The frequency characteristics that were not manipulated were closely matched. For example, when the frequency of the first constituent was manipulated, the frequency of the whole word and the frequency of the second constituent were matched for the sets of words that differed on first constituent frequency (other characteristics like word length, constituent length and average bigram frequency were also matched). Readers' eye fixation patterns were recorded when they silently read the target sentences for comprehension. Comprehension was periodically checked by asking the participants to paraphrase the sentence they just read. The recordings were made by an EyeLink eye-tracker (SR Research Mississauga, Canada).

A processing schema for compound word processing

Next, we provide a general outline designed to capture the main results of our studies. Each item is then discussed in more detail. The identification process is assumed to go as follows: the identification process starts when attention shifts to the yet non-fixated word in the parafovea (see chapter 6; Reichle *et al.* 2003), but complete identification of the word or any of its components is not achieved prior to the reader fixating the compound word. On the initial fixation on the compound word, most (if not all) of its letters are in foveal vision when the word is short (no longer than 8–9 letters) and holistic processing of it is possible and swamps componential processing; however, when the word is long (at least 12 letters), holistic processing on a single fixation is not possible (because of limitations due to visual acuity) and componential processing dominates processing and starts with identification of the left constituent. For long compounds, access of the second constituent is initiated after access of the first constituent is completed (or is nearly completed). A necessary step in a compositional process is 'parsing' or deciding where the boundary between the components is; if the first component is short, the parsing process is usually easily accomplished in the process of identifying the first constituent (again, largely for visual acuity reasons). In contrast, when the first constituent is hard to identify on a single fixation, the parsing process is difficult and certain kinds of orthographic segmentation cues help in the parsing process, which in turn aids in the identification of both constituents.

Significant effects of identification are observed only after the compound is fixated

Although compound word identification undoubtedly begins in the parafovea before the word is fixated, there is little evidence that enough lexical or morphological processing is done to influence the eye movement system prior to the initial fixation. Hyönä and Bertram (2004) examined whether the frequency of either the first constituent or the whole-word form has an effect on the eyes prior to fixating the compound word and found no consistent support for so-called 'parafoveal-on-foveal' effects of either constituent frequency or word frequency. They analysed the data of five compound word experiments: In three, the gaze duration on word $n-1$ was unaffected by the frequency manipulation; in one, there was an inverted frequency effect of first constituent frequency (i.e. gaze duration was longer on word $n-1$ when the first constituent was of high-frequency); in the fifth, there was a marginal parafoveal-on-foveal frequency effect in the orthodox direction (i.e. gaze duration on word $n-1$ was longer when the first constituent of compound word was of low-frequency). These data indicate that parafoveal morphological processing of compound words is at best negligible.

An unpublished study of Hyönä points to the same conclusion. Hyönä employed a gaze contingent display change paradigm to study the parafoveal processing of the first constituent of long compounds. There were two types of first constituents: short (3–4 letters) and long (7–9 letters). There was a display change condition, in which only the first three or four letters of the compound were intact prior to fixating the compound. This made the entire short first constituent, but only a portion of the long first constituent, parafoveally visible. If significant lexical (or morphological) parafoveal preprocessing occurred, the short first constituent compounds should have benefited more from the parafoveal preview than the long first constituent compounds. However, the parafoveal preview effect was of similar magnitude for the short and long first constituent compounds.

Another piece of evidence comes from a study by Hyönä and Pollatsek (1998) in which the length of the first constituent was varied (3–5 letters vs. 8–11 letters) with the length of the compound word held constant. If the first constituent had been processed up to the level that its length (or at least its approximate length) had been encoded, one would expect that the initial fixation would be drawn further into the word for long first constituent compounds than for short first constituent compounds. (This would be analogous to the 'length effect' on the initial landing position in words, where the initial landing position is further from the beginning of the word, the longer the word.) However, there was no difference in the initial landing position in the two conditions.

Decomposition versus holistic access

As indicated above, the major tool that we have employed in studying compound word identification is either to vary the frequency of one of the constituents of a compound word or to vary the frequency of the compound word (holding the other frequencies constant). The logic of this manipulation is clearest if one gets an effect of whole-word frequency but no effect of constituent frequency. In this case, the clear conclusion is that there is no evidence for componential processing. Inferences from the opposite case (constituent frequency effects but no whole-word frequency effect) appear to be about as clear: no evidence for holistic processing. In the case of getting both effects, however, the inference is less clear. Among other things, even if one assumes componential processing, it seems plausible that after the components are identified, a third stage would appear to be necessary to understand the meaning of the compound, especially in the case when the meaning of compound word is opaque (e.g. *strawberry*). That is, in such cases, one cannot deduce the meaning of the compound from the meanings of the constituents. Moreover, such a third stage may be used for all compounds, as Pollatsek and Hyönä (2005) have shown that there is no difference between the processing of transparent and opaque Finnish words, either in any processing time measure or in how the frequency of the initial constituent affects processing. However, if one observes a word frequency effect early in processing, in addition to constituent frequency effects, this seems like definite evidence for a parallel dual-route model.

Our results indicate that the identification of compound words is attempted via a holistic route and a decomposition route that work in parallel. The speed of the holistic route depends on the length of the compound to a much greater extent than does the speed of the decomposition route. If the compound is reasonably short (perhaps no more than eight characters), most (if not all) of its letters are in foveal vision, and the compound can be accessed as a single entity. Compositional processing may also occur, but there is little evidence of it from the eye movement record. In contrast, if the compound word is long (certainly for words that are 12 characters or more), poor visual acuity for the entire word renders holistic processing difficult, so that the decomposition route is more effective. In the decomposition route, the compound word is identified by first accessing the left constituent followed by the access of the right constituent, which in turn leads to access of the word.

Bertram and Hyönä (2003) provided convincing evidence that word length governs the way compounds are identified. They employed both short (7–9 letters) and long (12–15 letters) compounds in two experiments. In Experiment 1, they manipulated the first constituent frequency to look for effects of componential processing, and in Experiment 2, they manipulated whole-word frequency to look for effects of whole-word processing. The duration of first fixation made on the word was used to index early effects, and gaze duration (i.e. the summed duration of fixations made on the word before exiting it) was used as the primary index of the overall effect of the frequency manipulations.

The frequency of the first constituent frequency had a reliable effect on first fixation duration for long compounds. The mean first fixation duration was 16 ms longer when the initial constituent was a low-frequency constituent (replicating Hyönä and Pollatsek 1998, see below). However, there was no effect of first constituent frequency for the short compounds (there was a 3 ms trend in the opposite direction).[2] The pattern of results was similar in gaze duration. There was a highly significant effect (70 ms) of first constituent frequency for long compounds (also replicating Hyönä and Pollatsek 1998), but at best a small effect (11 ms) for short compounds (significant in the participant analysis but clearly non-significant in the item analysis). The observation that constituent frequency exerts a large effect for long compounds and a small effect for short compounds was confirmed by a reliable interaction observed in both the first fixation and gaze duration. These data support the view that the identification of long compounds is initiated by the access of the first constituent, while for short compounds, either the first constituent is not activated or its activation is too slow to have an effect on eye movement behaviour because successful activation of the word controls the eyes. It should be noted that the qualitative difference in processing of short versus long compounds was not due to a frequency difference, as they were closely matched for word frequency (the average frequency was about three per million).

In contrast, there was a reliable 10 ms effect of word frequency on first fixation duration for short compounds, whereas the 4 ms effect for long compounds was only marginally significant. For gaze duration, however, both the 79 ms word frequency effect for long compounds (replicating Pollatsek *et al.* 2000) and the 52 ms word frequency effect for short compounds were significant. The results of Experiment 2 demonstrated that the holistic route is quickly in operation for short compounds. The word frequency effect that appears later for long compounds could either be due to holistic processing or to word frequency effects that occur at late stages of compositional processing.

Converging evidence in support of the mediating role of word length in word identification was provided by Niswander-Klement and Pollatsek (in press). They examined the effects of word frequency and root frequency in reading English prefixed words (e.g. *remove* whose root is *move*). They observed a larger root frequency effect for longer words and a larger word frequency effect for shorter words. Niswander-Klement and Pollatsek interpreted their results in terms of a parallel dual-route model with competing whole-word access and compositional access routes that was similar to the model proposed by Bertram and Hyönä (2003).

Further support for the dual-route account is provided by Hyönä and Pollatsek (1998), Pollatsek *et al.* (2000), Hyönä *et al.* (2004), and Pollatsek and Hyönä (2005). In all these studies, reading of long compounds (an average of 12–13 letters) was examined (for a summary, see Table 4.1). In support of the early involvement of the first constituent, all but one experiment examining first constituent frequency observed an effect of first constituent frequency in first fixation duration.[3] Moreover, all five

----

[2] The readers skipped over the first constituent of the short compounds in about 40 per cent of the trials. However, this does not explain the lack of a first constituent effect, because there was no effect even for the trials in which the initial fixation landed on the first constituent.

[3] In the only experiment (Experiment 2 of Pollatsek and Hyönä, 2005) where the effect was not significant, the frequency manipulation was a 'between-item' variable in the sense that low- and high-frequency items appeared in different sentence frames.

Table 4.1 Summary of frequency effects in the first fixation duration and gaze duration

Study	Compound type	Frequency manipulation	First fixation duration	Gaze duration
Hyönä and Pollatsek (1998), Exp. 2.	Long	First constituent	Yes	Yes
Bertram and Hyönä (2003), Exp. 1	Long	First constituent	Yes	Yes
Bertram and Hyönä (2003), Exp. 1	Short	First constituent	No	Marginal[a]
Hyönä et al. (2004)	Long	First constituent	Yes	Yes
Pollatsek and Hyönä (2005), Exp. 1	Long, transparent and opaque	First constituent	Marginal[a]	Yes
Pollatsek and Hyönä (2005), Exp. 2	Long, transparent and opaque	First constituent	No	Marginal[a]
Pollatsek and Hyönä (2005), Exp. 3	Long, transparent and opaque	First constituent	Yes[b]	Yes
Pollatsek et al. (2000), Exp. 1	Long	Second constituent	No	Yes
Pollatsek et al. (2000), Exp. 2	Long	Whole word	Marginal[a]	Yes
Bertram and Hyönä (2003), Exp. 2	Long	Whole word	Marginal[c]	Yes
Bertram and Hyönä (2003), Exp. 2	Short	Whole word	Yes	Yes

[a]Not significant in the item analysis; [b]Subgaze on the first constituent was used as the measure of early processing; [c]Marginally significant in participant analysis, not significant in the item analysis

experiments demonstrated a first constituent frequency effect in gaze duration. Thus, it can be safely concluded that a decomposition route is an important component in the identification of long Finnish compounds, and that it starts early in processing. Two studies have examined the processing of English compounds during reading. In these studies, the privileged status of the first constituent in early stages of processing has not come out as strongly as it has for Finnish compounds. Andrews et al. (2004) and Juhasz et al. (2004) found only marginally significant effects of first constituent frequency in the first fixation duration. This might be due to the fact that both studies examined compounds that were shorter in length than those in our Finnish experiments (Andrews et al. used 6–11-letter compounds, and Juhasz et al. used 9-letter compounds).

As may be noted in Table 4.1, we have not studied the involvement of whole-word frequency in reading long compounds to the same extent as the involvement of the first constituent. In addition to Bertram and Hyönä (2003) discussed above, Experiment 2 of Pollatsek et al. (2000) was the only study in which the whole-word frequency of long compounds was manipulated. Consistent with Bertram and Hyönä (2003), Pollatsek *et al.* (2000) obtained evidence in support of the involvement of the whole word route in identifying long compounds: whole-word frequency effects were significant from the second fixation onwards and there was even a suggestion of an effect on the first fixation duration (the 5 ms word frequency effect did not reach significance in the item analysis).[4] All in all, the pattern of results was the same as in Bertram and Hyönä (2003) and indicates that both componential and holistic processes are involved early in processing and likely in parallel.

The simplest model consistent with the results summarized above is a version of a morphological 'race' model, which posits a parallel race between the whole-word route and the decomposition route. In the race model of Schreuder and Baayen (1995), the balance of holistic and decomposed processing is determined by factors such as word frequency and phonological and semantic transparency: for relatively low frequency compounds, the decomposition route dominates access, whereas for relatively high frequency compounds the holistic route is more dominant. Although their model can explain some of our compound word data, it faces difficulties in explaining the fact that long and short compounds with similar whole-word frequency are processed differently. This is because their model does not assume that word length significantly affects the balance of holistic and decompositional processing. Bertram and Hyönä (2003) proposed a modified version of the race model, in which visual acuity governs the relative speeds of the two processes. When all (or most) letters of the compound are in foveal vision, the whole-word route dominates the identification process, whereas when all the letters of the compound can not be identified during a single fixation, the whole-word route is significantly slowed down, and the decomposition route becomes at least equally important, particularly during initial processing.

Accessing the second constituent

When the identification takes place at least in part via the decomposition route, the access of the left constituent is followed by the access of the right constituent. In other words, the decomposition route operates serially so that the access of the first constituent is initiated prior to the access of the second constituent. However, the process is not necessarily completely serial in that full identification of the first constituent may not be completed before an access to the second constituent is initiated (e.g. its orthographic form may be accessed but not its meaning). One piece of evidence for this is that first constituent frequency effects are not only early, but also appear in the probability of making three or four fixations on the word. However, as previously discussed, the earliest effect of second constituent frequency is later than that of first constituent frequency. For example, in Experiment 1 of Pollatsek *et al.* (2000) the earliest eye movement measure that was affected by second constituent frequency

---

4 It may be argued that the early effect of word frequency for long compounds could be bigger when the first fixation lands further into the word (more letters would fall on the fovea). However, this did not appear to be the case (see Pollatsek *et al.* 2000).

was the duration of second fixation on the compound. It was 8 ms longer for low-frequency than high-frequency second constituents, which was only significant in the participant analysis. However, there was a sizeable (95 ms) second constituent frequency effect in gaze duration, most of which was due a greater probability of making a third fixation on the compound when the second constituent was of low-frequency. Thus, processing of the second component, as a component, was affecting identification of the word.

Andrews *et al.* (2004) and Juhasz *et al.* (2004) also investigated the effects of second constituent frequency in reading English compounds. The pattern of the results in both studies was similar to that observed by Pollatsek *et al.* (2000), but the effects were weaker, probably due to the fact that the compound words were shorter. In Experiment 1 of Andrews *et al.*, there was only a marginal effect (15 ms) of second constituent frequency in gaze duration, and as in Pollatsek *et al.* (2000), there was only a small (4 ms) and non-significant effect in first fixation duration. In Experiment 3 of Juhasz *et al.*, there was a significant second constituent frequency effect (27 ms) in gaze duration and a non-significant effect (7 ms) in first fixation duration. These results also indicate that the second constituent is accessed relatively late during compound word reading. Combined with the early effect of first constituent frequency, we conclude that the identification of long compounds takes place serially by first attempting the access of the first constituent followed by the access of the second constituent.

A more direct test of the serial nature of the decomposition route was conducted by Hyönä *et al.* (2004). They used a gaze-contingent display-change paradigm to examine the extent to which processing of the second constituent was having an effect when the eyes were still fixating on the first constituent. In the display change condition, all but the first two letters of the second constituent were replaced by visually similar letters until the eyes moved across an invisible boundary, which was set at the constituent boundary. When the eyes crossed the boundary, the second constituent was changed to its intended form (*joukkuehesdl→joukkuehenki*). Before the change, the second constituent was a non-word that was visually similar to the intended constituent. In the control condition, there was no display change. The major findings were: (1) The 'subgaze' time on the first constituent before crossing the boundary (i.e. what would have been the gaze duration on the first constituent, had it been a separate word) was strongly affected by the frequency of the first constituent (42 ms shorter for high-frequency than for low-frequency first constituent compounds), but was hardly affected by whether or not the second constituent was visible (the 8 ms difference between the display change and the no-change condition was non-significant). (2) The subsequent 'subgaze' time (the summed fixation time on the target compound subsequent to leaving the first constituent including intraword refixations to the first constituent) was strongly affected by the display change (80 ms longer when the last letters of the second constituent were initially replaced, in comparison to the no change condition). That is, the presence versus virtual absence of the second constituent did not influence the movement of the eyes when the first constituent was fixated; its effects only surfaced when the second constituent was fixated. These results are most parsimoniously explained by a serial access of the two constituents of these long compound words.

What is also notable is that the size of the parafoveal preview benefit was much greater (the difference in gaze duration between the full preview and the visually similar non-word preview was 101 ms) than has been previously observed for parafoveal words separated from the foveal word by a space (for a summary, see Hyönä *et al.* 2004; Rayner 1998). Interestingly, Inhoff, Starr *et al.* (2000) reported an effect of display change quite comparable to ours (91 ms). An examination of their materials indicates that almost all their changed words were the second halves of spaced compound words such as *garage door*. Thus, our large display change effect size may not be due to our display change being 'within a visual word' (i.e. the incorrect letters being part of a string of letters that is fixated). Instead, the crucial factor seems to be that our display change is within word in the linguistic sense of 'word'. It thus appears that the second constituent of a compound (whether physically joined to the first constituent or not) captures attention earlier and perhaps more extensively than a parafoveal word that stands by itself.

Segmentation cues aid in the identification of long compounds when the first constituent is long

As shown above, the identification of long compounds is initiated by first attempting to access the left constituent. In order to do so, the reader has to be able to separate the first constituent from the second constituent. Bertram *et al.* (2004) investigated this segmentation process by examining the effects of two segmentation cues, *vowel harmony*, and the *morphological ambiguity of the consonant* at the constituent boundary, on the ease of processing a compound word. Vowel harmony refers to a feature of Finnish: back vowels (a, o, u; pronounced toward the back of the mouth) and front vowels (ä, ö, y; pronounced toward the front of the mouth) cannot appear in the same lexeme. Thus, in *talo* (house) both vowels are back vowels, whereas in *pyörä* (wheel) all three vowels are front vowels. (The neutral vowels, *e* and *i*, can appear with either front or back vowels.) This vowel harmony principle does not apply to compound words, however, which can have vowels of different quality across the constituents (but not within the constituents). In *selkäongelma* (back problem), the first constituent ends with a front vowel *ä* and the second constituent begins with a back vowel *o*. In our first attempt to study this potential segmentation cue, we made it as salient as possible by using compounds in which the last letter of the first constituent was a front or back vowel as was the first letter of the second constituent. The key comparison was between compounds such as *selkäongelma*, which have vowels of different quality at the constituent boundary so that it is orthographically marked, and compounds such as *ryöstöyritys* (robbery attempt) which have two vowels of the same quality (*ö* and *y*) at the constituent boundary.

In Experiment 2 of Bertram *et al.* (2004) the first constituent length was also manipulated with word length controlled (on average, about 13 letters). The short first constituents were 3–5 letters and the long first constituents were 7–9 letters. Here we focus on the results concerning long first constituent compounds; the data for short first constituents are summarized in the next section. In fact, for the long first-constituent compounds, the vowel harmony cue had a large effect. Gaze duration was 114 ms longer when the two vowels at the constituent boundary were the same quality than when they were different quality. Somewhat surprisingly, the early effects of vowel harmony were very small. For example, there was only a 3 ms effect on the first fixation duration. There were some effects on later fixations; however, they appeared both in changes in the duration of the fixation and changes in the probability of refixating the word subsequent to that fixation, and the only one of these vowel harmony effects that was significant was the probability of a fourth fixation. Yet, the small differences in these measures added up to the highly significant gaze duration effect of 114 ms. This led us to think that in order to assess the time course of the effect, the probability and duration measures should be jointly considered. That is, on each fixation in the word, the reader makes two 'choices', one is how long to stay on a certain location, the other is whether or not a refixation should be made on the word. To assess the impact of a manipulated variable on each fixation, one should consider the difference in fixation duration on a given fixation between (two) conditions, but also consider the implications of a difference in refixation probability for the (two) conditions. In order to capture the impact of the manipulated variable on each individual fixation (in this case vowel harmony), we designed two measures that included a duration and probability component. The simpler measure is given in the following formula, where SVQ and DVQ refer to the same vowel quality and different vowel quality conditions, respectively, n is the ordinal number of the fixation, $FixDur_n$ is the mean fixation duration (conditional on the word receiving an nth fixation) and $ProbFix_n$ is the (unconditional) probability that the word receives an nth fixation.

$$\text{Effect size at Fix}_n = \text{ProbFixDVQ}_n * (\text{FixDurSVQ}_n - \text{FixDurDVQ}_n) +$$
$$\text{FixDurSVQ}_{n+1} * (\text{ProbFixSVQ}_{n+1} - \text{ProbFixDVQ}_{n+1})$$

This measure has the property that the sum of the effect sizes at the different fixation numbers add up to the gaze duration effect. The formula above tacitly assumes that the DVQ condition is the 'baseline' in the first part of the formula and the SVQ condition is the 'baseline' in the second part of the formula. The analogous formula that assumes the opposite arrives at quite similar values, so for simplicity, we will only present this one. The terms do have to be from different conditions to make the sum equal to the gaze duration difference – that is, if one chooses ProbFixSVQ_n in the first term, one has to choose FixDurDVQ_{n+1} for the second term. The meaning of first term is fairly transparent. It is the difference in fixation duration between the conditions on fixation n; however, this difference is multiplied by the probability of making an nth fixation in the baseline condition, as this would be the effect on gaze duration of increasing the duration of the fixation. Similarly, the second term attempts to capture how much gaze duration would be increased by an increase in the probability of making a subsequent fixation. That is, as mentioned above, we assume that the decision to make a refixation is made on the prior fixation and has a direct effect on the gaze duration by adding more fixation durations to the gaze duration calculation. This term, in particular, assumes that the difference in probability of fixation$_{n+1}$ is completely due to a decision on fixation$_n$ and the result of this effect is completely accounted for on fixation$_{n+1}$.

Table 4.2 Hypothetical results of a vowel quality experiment to illustrate the principles involved in calculating the time course of the effect

	Gaze	First fixation duration (ms)	Second fixation duration (ms)	Third fixation duration (ms)	First fixation (%)	Second fixation (%)	Third fixation (%)
SVQ	446	230	250	220	1	0.6	0.3
DVQ	332	210	200	210	1	0.4	0.2

SVQ: same vowel quality; DVQ: different vowel quality

The chief problem with this measure is that it does not give enough 'credit' to early fixations for refixation decisions. For example, the probability of making a third fixation depends not only on decisions made on the second fixation, but also decisions made on the first fixation. Consider the following example (see Table 4.2). Suppose that, at most, three fixations are made in both conditions, and for the same vowel quality condition, the mean fixation durations are 230 ms, 250 ms, and 220 ms and the probability of fixation is 1, 0.6, and 0.3, respectively, and for the different vowel quality condition, the data are 210 ms, 200 ms, and 210 ms, and 210 ms and 1, 0.4, and 0.2. The gaze durations would be $230 + 0.6 \times 250 + 0.3 \times 220 = 446$ ms for the SVQ condition and $210 + 0.4 \times 200 + 0.2 \times 210 = 332$ ms for a difference of 114 ms between the conditions. Given the above formula, the effect size on fixation 1 is $1(230 - 210) + 250(0.6 - 0.4) = 20 + 50 = 70$ ms, the effect size on fixation 2 is $0.4(250 - 200) + 220(0.3 - 0.2) = 20 + 22 = 42$ ms, and the effect size on fixation 3 is $0.2(220 - 210) = 2$ ms. However, in this example, it does not seem correct to ascribe the difference in fixation probability on fixation 3 to a decision on fixation 2. That is, for both the SVQ and DVQ conditions, the conditional probability of fixating a third time is equal to 0.5. Thus the difference in fixation probability on fixation 3 seems more logically ascribed to the decision on fixation 1 about whether to make a second fixation. Accordingly, our revised formulation would be identical to the one given by the above formula except it would 'give' the $220(0.3 - 0.2) = 22$ ms effect to fixation 1 rather than to fixation 2. More generally, it would give all subsequent effects due to the difference in fixation probability on fixation 2 to the decision on fixation 1. Unfortunately, this correction is not captured in a simple formula as it involves a complex correction that is applied recursively. Hopefully, this example gives the general logic of the correction. We calculated the effect size on each fixation with both the simple formula and the corrected version. The results of these calculations, as well as the results of the calculations for the two manipulated factors in Experiment 3 (vowel quality and consonant ambiguity) of Bertram *et al.* (2004), can be seen in Fig. 4.1.

Even though the picture from the two measures is somewhat different (the corrected version moves effects slightly earlier), they agree in general outline. The effect due to the vowel harmony cue begins to show up in the second fixation, peaks at the

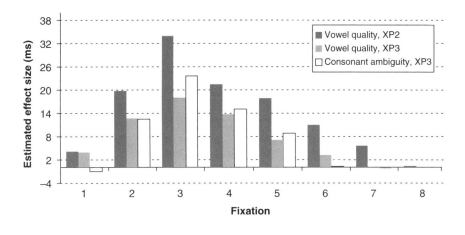

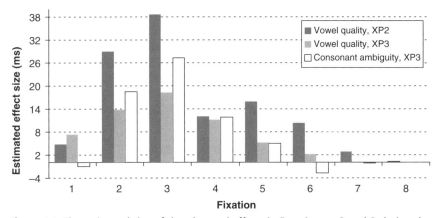

Figure 4.1 The estimated size of the observed effects in Experiment 2 and 3 during the course of processing (from Fixation 1 onwards). The effect size is estimated with two related methods (see the text for details). The upper panel represents the outcome of the simplified method. The lower panel represents the outcome of the more extended method.

third fixation, and it is still visible as late as in the fifth fixation. What is notable about this late effect is that it is at odds with morphological processing models, such as Schreuder and Baayen (1995), where the morphological segmentation stage is assumed to operate at the earliest possible stage of word processing. It is also at odds with Taft's (1979, 1994) theorizing; he assumes the morphological parser to operate at the prelexical stage. Our results suggest that vowel harmony functions as a segmentation cue at the lexical level by facilitating the access of a long first constituent in a long compound word (see Bertram *et al.* 2004, for more details). As will become clear in the following section, the first constituent has to be long (at least seven letters) for the segmentation cues to exert an effect.

Experiment 3 of Bertram *et al.* (2004) had several objectives. One was to uncon-found vowel quality from bigram frequency and a second was to test whether vowel quality has an effect when the two vowels of different quality are not positioned adja-cent to each other at the constituent boundary. Because vowels of different quality never appear next to each other in a lexeme, they must be low frequency bigrams. Thus, it is unclear whether the effect we observed was merely because the bigram at the boundary was low frequency, or whether it was a special property of the difference in vowel harmony because a bigram containing different quality vowels unambigu-ously signals a morpheme boundary. In Experiment 3, we tested this by having a consonant as the first letter of the second constituent, as in *pyörähuolto* (bike repair), where the two constituents contain vowels of different quality but where the vowels are not adjacent to each other. (As a result, we could match the bigram frequencies at the boundary in both conditions.) In addition, we examined whether the type of con-sonant beginning the second constituent could also function as a 'parsing' cue. We contrasted two types of consonants: (a) in the unambiguous consonant condition, the consonant beginning the second constituent can not end a first constituent; (b) in the ambiguous consonant condition, the consonant can either be the last letter of a first constituent, or the first letter of a second constituent. Thus, in (a) the constituent bound-ary is marked by the consonant if the boundary is assumed to be somewhere adjacent to the consonant, whereas in (b) it is not. (In the different vowel quality condition, the loca-tion of the boundary is exactly marked in the unambiguous consonant condition. This is because the consonant is between two vowels that have to be in different constituents so it must either be the end of the first constituent or the beginning of the second and because it is unambiguous it must be the beginning of the second constituent.)

In fact, in Experiment 3, there was a significant (60 ms) effect of vowel harmony on gaze duration, indicating that a vowel harmony effect does not depend on either the vowels being adjacent nor to having a low frequency bigram at the boundary. However, the size of the effect was only about half of that observed in Experiment 2, which suggests that part of the effect in Experiment 2 may have been due to the vowels being adjacent. There was also an effect of the ambiguity of the consonant in gaze duration (ambiguous consonants were slower than unambiguous consonants) that was similar in size (52 ms) to that of the vowel harmony effect. Curiously, the effects of the two segmentation cues were additive. That is, one might have expected that the presence of both the cues – disharmonious vowels with the unambiguous consonant in the middle – would have been much more facilitative than either in iso-lation because, together, they unambiguously indicated where the constituent boundary was. Another interesting finding was that post-hoc analyses indicated that the frequency of the trigram at the constituent boundary (i.e. the vowel-consonant-vowel trigram that included the consonant at the boundary) had no predictive effect on the gaze duration. The time course of the two cues was also assessed in a similar manner to that in Experiment 2, and both showed roughly the same (relatively delayed) time course as the vowel harmony cue did in Experiment 2: both functions peaked at the third fixation (see Fig. 4.1). In summary, Experiment 3 confirmed that the vowel harmony effect was more than a bigram frequency effect and it indicated that there are other segmentation cues that can facilitate the processing of compound words with a long first constituent.

These data raise the question of why these segmentation cues affect processing as late as they do. In fact, the majority of the effect is likely to occur after the eyes have moved from the first constituent to the second constituent (although there are some earlier effects). This may seem inconsistent with a sequential attention mechanism. However, remember that we have posited that this attentional shift occurs before processing of the first constituent is complete. (This seems like an optimal strategy not to get stuck on the first constituent, but to begin processing the second constituent once the first is reasonably close to identification.) Thus, in those cases where processing of the first constituent is very problematic (as with harmonious vowels at the constituent boundary), more processing time and effort is needed to try to recognise the second constituent as a unit and thus be able to parse the compound and thus completely identify the first constituent. With a good segmentation cue (such as disharmonious vowels at the constituent boundary), such additional processing is unnecessary.

Our results appear to contrast with those obtained by Inhoff, Radach *et al.* (2000) for processing three-constituent German compounds. They examined the effects of two types of linguistics markers of constituent boundaries in separate experiments, and neither had any noticeable effect on compound word processing. The first was the frequency of the bigram separating the compound head from the preceding constituent, and the second was the type of binding morpheme prior to the head: they compared the binding morpheme '-s' (the letter *s* is obviously not always a morpheme) with the nominalizing suffix '-ung' + the binding morpheme '-s' combination (as in *Augenbewe**gungs**analyse* = eye movement analysis) that is a reliable constituent boundary predictor.

There are many possible reasons for why we observed reliable effects for linguistic segmentation cues while Inhoff, Radach *et al.* (2000) were unable to do so. One possibility is that vowel harmony is not limited to a single bigram but it extends over the whole word so that it might be easier to pick up than a bigram when it is not the focus of attention. Related to this, the length of Inhoff, Radach *et al.*'s target words may have worked against their finding effects, as they were quite long (15–25 characters) and were also three-constituent compounds, so that a single bigram may not have stood out.

Easy access to the first constituent when it is short

In Experiment 2 of Bertram *et al.* (2004), a set of long compounds were included that had a short (3–5 letters) first constituent. This experiment showed that the vowel harmony cue had no impact on the identification process when the first constituent was short, in contrast to the large effect it had when the first constituent was long (see above). Thus, the presence of two disharmonious vowels at the constituent boundary, which unambiguously signalled the location of the constituent boundary had no positive effect over when there were two harmonious vowels so that both the constituent boundary and even the syllable boundary were ambiguous.

The most plausible explanation for this is that, when the first constituent is short, its identification is relatively immediate and this identification is sufficient to parse the compound word. Together with the late effect of the segmentation cues we observed for long compounds, it suggests that the process of segmenting the compound word is also a 'race' between two processes. One is the identification of the first constituent from its component letters and the other is a more complex process that probably involves partial identification of the first constituent from its component letters and the use of orthographic cues (especially those that unambiguously define morpheme boundaries). It is even possible that partial identification of the second constituent is involved in this latter process. The fact that the effect of the segmentation cues is delayed indicates that this second 'horse' in the race is relatively slow and may be largely a back-up when identification of the first constituent is taking time. It is also worth noting that the use of a segmentation cue such as the ambiguity of the consonant beginning the second constituent argues that these cues are likely working together with partial identification of the constituents. That is, in the case when the vowels of the two constituents are harmonious, our 'unambiguous consonant cue' is not really an unambiguous cue for the constituent boundary; it is only a useful cue if one knows from other sources of information that the constituent boundary is on one side of this consonant, or the other. Similarly, the disharmonious vowels, when separated by a consonant do not indicate the exact location of the boundary. We suspect a similar pattern would emerge if people read English text with the spaces removed: that is, for short words, orthographic cues signalling word boundaries would have little effect, whereas for long words, cues like low-frequency bigrams and trigrams would facilitate processing.

Saccade programming during compound word processing

In the study of eye guidance during reading, *when* decisions (i.e. when to terminate a fixation) are often distinguished from *where* (i.e. where to fixate next) decisions. Our discussion so far has focused on the *when* decisions. The results summarized above convincingly demonstrate that durations of individual fixations, as well as summed durations of fixations made on a word, faithfully reflect the ongoing mental processes – both holistic and componential – that are related to compound word identification. In this section we discuss what our compound word studies tell us about the *where* decisions.

In deciding where to fixate next, the reader has to make two types of decisions: (1) whether to refixate the currently fixated word or to go to the next word, and (2) where in a word (either the current word or the following word) to position the eyes. This distinction implies that there are two processes: saccade target selection and saccade amplitude computation. In our compound word experiments, all the frequency manipulations (whether related to word or constituent frequency) produced reliable effects on the probability of refixating the word. These data are summarized in Table 4.3. Given the length of our compound words, the effect typically did not show up in the probability of making a second fixation on the word, because the long compounds were almost always refixated once (i.e. it is likely that there was a 'ceiling effect'),

Table 4.3 Summary of frequency effects in the probability of making two or three fixations on the compound word

Study	Compound type	Frequency manipulation	Probability of two fixations	Probability of three fixations
Hyönä and Pollatsek (1998), Exp. 2.	Long	First constituent	No	Yes
Bertram and Hyönä (2003), Exp. 1	Long	First constituent	No	Yes
Bertram and Hyönä (2003), Exp. 1	Short	First constituent	No	No
Hyönä et al. (2004)	Long	First constituent	Marginal[a]	Yes
Pollatsek and Hyönä (2005), Exp. 1	Long, transparent and opaque	First constituent	Yes	Yes
Pollatsek and Hyönä (2005), Exp. 2	Long, transparent and opaque	First constituent	Marginal[b]	No
Pollatsek and Hyönä (2005), Exp. 3	Long, transparent and opaque	First constituent	No	Yes
Pollatsek et al. (2000), Exp. 1	Long	Second constituent	No	Yes
Pollatsek et al. (2000), Exp. 2	Long	Whole word	Marginal[b]	Yes
Bertram and Hyönä (2003), Exp. 2	Long	Whole word	Yes	Yes
Bertram and Hyönä (2003), Exp. 2	Short	Whole word	Yes	Yes

[a]Not significant in the participant analysis; [b]Not significant in the item analysis

but there were reliable frequency effects on the probability of making a third fixation on the compound (see Footnote 3 for one exception). Thus, it appears that the need for the first refixation is primarily because of visual acuity limitations (i.e. all letters of long compounds cannot be perceived during a single fixation), whereas the programming of the second refixation reflects lexical and/or constituent processing; a third fixation was made more frequently when the compound or one of its constituents was difficult to identify (i.e. when it was of low-frequency).

The computation of the amplitude of the first within-word saccade was also found to be affected by our constituent frequency manipulations but not by whole-word frequency (see also Hyönä and Pollatsek 2000). Table 4.4 summarizes these data. (We have used either the location of the second fixation or the length of the first within-word saccade as the measure of saccade amplitude computation in different studies.) The two studies that used saccade length as the measure showed a reliable effect of first constituent frequency: the within-word saccade length was shorter when

Table 4.4 Summary of the frequency effects in the second fixation location and in the length of the first within-word saccade

Study	Compound type	Frequency manipulation	Second fixation location	Within-word length saccade
Hyönä and Pollatsek (1998), Exp. 2.	Long	First constituent	Yes	–
Bertram and Hyönä (2003), Exp. 1	Long	First constituent	–	Yes
Hyönä et al. (2004)	Long	First constituent	–	Yes
Pollatsek and Hyönä (2005), Exp. 1	Long, transparent and opaque	First constituent	Marginal[a]	–
Pollatsek and Hyönä (2005), Exp. 2	Long, transparent and opaque	First constituent	No	–
Pollatsek and Hyönä (2005), Exp. 3	Long, transparent and opaque	First constituent	Marginal[a]	–
Pollatsek et al. (2000), Exp. 1	Long	Second constituent	No	–
Pollatsek et al. (2000), Exp. 2	Long	Whole word	No	–
Bertram and Hyönä (2003), Exp. 2	Long	Whole word	–	No

[a]Not significant in the item analysis

the first constituent was infrequent. A similar effect was observed in the location of second fixation, but as it becomes apparent from Table 4.4, it was not very reliable. However, neither of the studies examining word frequency effects nor the study where the frequency of the second constituent was manipulated showed such an effect. Finally, with one exception (Experiment 1 of Hyönä and Pollatsek 1998), the position of the initial fixation on the word was not influenced by the frequency manipulations, which suggests that no lexical information is picked up parafoveally of the compound prior to its fixation (or at least parafoveally available lexical information does not affect inter-word saccade computation).

To accommodate this pattern of results, Hyönä and Pollatsek (2000) put forth a processing difficulty hypothesis, according to which processing difficulty in the form of first constituent frequency is capable of influencing intra-word saccade computation. An increase in the foveal load shortens the saccade that is typically launched from the first to the second constituent. Word frequency and second constituent frequency did not affect the amplitude of the first within-word saccade because their effects appear later in the compound word processing (from the second fixation onwards). The fact that the frequency manipulations do not exert an effect on inter-word saccades (i.e. saccades exiting the word, see Hyönä and Pollatsek (2000) for further details) suggests that local processing difficulty does not spill over to the next word, at least in so far as saccade programming is concerned.

Additional issues related to compound word processing

The issue of spacing

As mentioned in the beginning of the chapter, Finnish compounds are always written without spaces between the constituents (as are compounds in German, Dutch, Swedish, and many other languages). English, on the other hand, shows much more flexibility, as in English compounds can be written in one of three ways: unspaced (e.g. *snowball*), hyphenated (e.g. *eye-tracker*), or spaced (e.g. *wedding cake*). To our knowledge, there are only two eye-tracking studies where the processing of spaced and unspaced compounds was systematically investigated. In the study of Inhoff, Radach *et al.* (2000) this question was studied using three-constituent German compounds. As noted above, in German the insertion of spaces between constituents is not permitted. In spite of this, Inhoff, *et al.* observed facilitation in processing due to spacing, as indexed by shorter gaze durations and total viewing times for spaced compounds than for unspaced compounds. Presumably the reason for this facilitation is that spacing speeds up the access to the constituents, as the spaces between constituents unambiguously and saliently delineate the constituent boundaries. Interestingly, spaces between constituents incurred a cost in later processing, as indexed by longer post-target viewing times and increased third and fourth fixation durations on the compound expressions. The later processing cost is assumed to reflect difficulties in meaning computation. This is because spacing obscures the constituent's relative position in the compound expression (whether it is the head or a modifier), which in turn hampers the specification of the compound meaning. In German (and Finnish) compounds the head is always the last (i.e. the right-most) constituent. In concatenated compounds (i.e. in all permitted German compounds) this is readily perceptible, whereas with spaces added between constituents this information is obscured.

Recently the results of Inhoff, Radach *et al.* (2000) were extended to English by Juhasz *et al.* (2005). These authors studied the processing of both unspaced (e.g. *bookcase*) and spaced (e.g. *rush hour*) two-constituent compounds (both noun-noun and adjective-noun compounds) when they appeared either in their 'correct' or 'incorrect' (*book case* vs. *rushhour*) form. (Here, correctness is defined by typical usage rather than by a grammatical rule.) The first fixation on a compound was shorter if the compound was shown with a space, irrespective of whether or not the compound was supposed to be spaced – indicating that providing a space between the two constituents facilitates the access to the first constituent by providing a salient segmentation cue. However, for gaze duration, which indexes both early and later processing, there was a somewhat different pattern of results than in Inhoff, Radach *et al.* (2000). When a space was added between the two constituents for compounds that are supposed to be unspaced, gaze duration was reliably longer than for the correct form. This finding is similar to what was observed by Inhoff, Radach *et al.* (2000) for the duration of third and fourth fixation and for the post-target viewing time, and it suggests that concatenation of the constituents facilitates the meaning computation. However, for compounds that were supposed to be spaced, it did not seem to matter whether they appeared in their correct form or unspaced, as gaze duration did not differ between these two versions.

Juhasz *et al.* (2005) interpreted the results for the concatenated compounds to support the dual route model described above. Specifically, they argued that providing a space between the constituents helps the decomposition route in early processing, as indexed by the first fixation duration. However, they posited that concatenation is beneficial to accessing the compound's meaning, because the whole-word route is able to begin to accessing the compound, whereas in the spaced condition the direct route may not begin until the second lexeme is identified. This is presumably indexed by the gaze duration data.

It is also interesting that spacing of the compound word constituents also has an impact on saccadic programming. Similar results were obtained by Inhoff and Radach (2002) and by Juhasz *et al.* (2005). If a compound word is presented without spaces between the constituents, the readers' initial fixation lands further into the word than when a space is inserted between the constituents. This occurs whether or not the insertion of a space is grammatically permitted. Moreover, readers are less likely to refixate the word when the compound has no spaces between constituents. This is plausibly because the first fixation lands further into the compound word when the entirety looks like a word than when the first constituent looks like a word, and thus it is more probable that the word can be identified with a single fixation.

Parafoveal-on-foveal effects

Recently, there has been an increased interest in the eye movement literature in what have been termed *parafoveal-on-foveal effects* (see Kennedy 2000). These are effects where features of the parafoveal word presumably influence fixation times on the foveal word. Such effects, particularly if lexical or semantic information is concerned, are theoretically interesting, because they not only suggest that the reader's attention is engaged in the processing of the parafoveal word, but that processing of the parafoveal word is sufficiently advanced to exert control over the eye movement system. Perhaps the strongest claim from this research is that such effects imply that processing of words in text goes on in parallel, which in turn is taken as evidence for eye guidance models that postulate an attentional gradient that can extend to the neighbouring words as well, and to be in conflict with models, such as E-Z Reader (Rayner *et al.*, this volume; Reichle *et al.* 2003), which assume that lexical processing of words in reading takes place serially, one word at a time (for an alternative view, see Yang and McConkie, this volume).

The display change study (Hyönä *et al.* 2004) discussed above allowed us to examine possible parafoveal-on-foveal effects in compound word processing (see also Hyönä and Bertram 2004, as previously discussed). Remember that in this experiment, the second constituent initially appeared as a non-word in the display change condition and during the saccade across the constituent boundary, the non-word was replaced with the intended lexical item. We observed that the fixation duration on the first constituent was not affected by the second constituent being initially a non-word. Thus, the lexical status of the second part of the word did not influence the processing time of the first part, which supports the serial view advocated by the E-Z Reader model (Reichle *et al.* 2003). Given a healthy 100-ms preview effect, we think this study provides strong evidence against the generality of the parafoveal-on-foveal effects. This finding was replicated in Experiment 3 of Pollatsek and Hyönä (2005).

Inhoff, Starr *et al.* (2000) examined parafoveal-on-foveal effects with materials that appear to be spaced compounds (with three exceptions) although this feature of the study is not made explicit in the article. Examples of their materials are spaced compounds such as *hockey puck*, *head ache*, and *traffic light*. They had four parafoveal preview conditions: the baseline (*traffic light*), the uppercase preview (*traffic LIGHT*), the dissimilar-letter preview (*traffic qvtqp*), and the inconsistent-context preview (*traffic smoke*) conditions. Gaze duration on the first constituent of these spaced compounds was found to be significantly inflated, compared with the baseline condition, for the uppercase preview condition (25 ms) and the dissimilar-letter preview condition (34 ms), but not for the inconsistent-context preview condition (3 ms). Thus, these results indicate that unusual orthographic stimuli in the parafovea can have an effect on fixation times, but that the meaning of the parafoveal word has little or no effect. The results of Hyönä *et al.* (2004) appear to contrast with these results, as our manipulation which was similar to the dissimilar-letter preview condition did not produce a significant parafoveal-on-foveal effect (8-ms). One difference between these two studies is that Inhoff, Starr *et al.* (2000) changed all the letters of the second constituent while we preserved the first two letters. However, we think the important result is that both studies are consistent with the view that the lexical or semantic information that may be picked up from the second constituent while fixating the first constituent of a two-constituent compound has no effect on the eyes until that constituent is fixated – regardless of whether the compound is spaced or unspaced. We also think the finding that there is no such parafoveal-on-foveal effect when the parafoveal information is part of the same word as the foveal information makes it unlikely that there are such effects when the parafoveal information is a different word.

Directions for future research

The race between whole-word access and constituent access

The general pattern of our results is consistent with a model that posits a parallel race between a holistic route and a decomposition route. It also indicates that for shorter compounds the holistic route is the dominant one and in operation right from the start. However, for longer compounds, there is no direct evidence that the holistic route is in operation from the start. It could either be that it starts later or that processing is not sufficiently advanced by the end of the first fixation to be able to have an effect on eye movements. It seems more plausible that there is no executive directing processing and that the holistic route always starts immediately. That we have twice observed a marginally significant effect of whole-word frequency on the first fixation duration supports this. More generally, getting a better understanding of the relative time course of the two routes needs further study. The eye-contingent display change technique may be one way to tap into the time course. As indicated above, we have started to examine this by looking at the effect of delaying the second constituent while varying the frequency of the first constituent. Varying the whole-word frequency and the frequency of the second constituent together with the display change manipulation should provide interesting new data about how the two routes are related.

The identification of multi-constituent compounds

An interesting topic for future research is how meaning is computed for compounds with more than two constituents. As indicated earlier, these multi-constituent compounds differ from two-constituent compounds in that the role of the constituents is not as straightforward as with two-constituent compounds, in which the left constituent is always the modifier and the right constituent the head (this is the case, for example, with Finnish, German, Dutch, and Swedish compounds). To date, the only eye-tracking experiment that has examined this issue is the one of Inhoff, Radach *et al.* (2000) summarized above.

Morphological family size

In the study of morphological processing, an issue that has recently emerged is whether *morphological family size* plays a role in the identification of morphologically complex words apart from the frequency of the constituent (e.g. Bertram *et al.* 2000; Moscoso del Prado Martín *et al.*, 2004; Schreuder and Baayen 1997). Morphological family refers to the set of derived and compound words that are constructed from a given 'simplex' word (e.g. for *think*, family members constitute, *thinker, thinkable, unthinkable, think tank,* etc.). De Jong *et al.* (2002) established an effect for the so-called positional family size in compound word processing. Positional family size refers to the number of compound words in the language that share the same constituent (e.g. the first constituent). De Jong *et al.* (2002) showed that a large family facilitates compound word processing in the lexical decision task. However, such an effect may not necessarily generalize to reading.

We have conducted some post-hoc analyses on the effect of positional family size (the number of compounds given the left constituent). These results should be considered cautiously as positional family size correlated significantly with first constituent frequency in these analyses. Hyönä *et al.* (2004) observed that the size of the preview benefit of the second constituent was bigger the smaller the family size. The most plausible explanation was that a small positional family size made the second constituent more predictable so that relatively more information may be parafoveally picked up of the second constituent. When the size of the parafoveal preview effect was regressed separately for the high- and low-frequency first constituent compounds, it was found that positional family size made a significant contribution for the low-frequency first constituent compounds, for which the positional family size was appreciably smaller. Thus, Hyönä *et al.* reasoned that family size may only matter when it is relatively small (that is, there is an upper threshold for family size to exert an effect on processing, see also Moscoso del Prado Martín *et al.*, 2004).

Pollatsek and Hyönä (2005) used positional family size to predict gaze duration on semantically transparent and opaque compounds that had either a high- or low-frequency first constituent. For opaque compounds, they found an inhibition effect due to the family size of the first constituent: the larger the morphological family, the longer the gaze duration. They hypothesized that the critical factor is whether or not the word that is seen is the most frequent member of the family. If the observed word is the most frequent, it may be 'predicted' and thus there would be little interference.

This would typically be the case when the family is small (e.g. only one or two compounds exist that begin with the given first constituent). However, if it is not the most frequent (as it would be more likely when the family size increases), another compound word (which is presumably usually transparent) will be predicted, and its activation will cause interference with obtaining the correct meaning for an opaque compound. However, we hasten to add that these post-hoc analyses should be considered speculative, and proper experiments need to be conducted to examine the possible effects of morphological family size in more detail. In terms of eye guidance in reading, studies on the effects of positional family size may also give clues about the amount of parafoveal lexical processing that can be done. How much of the second constituent can be lexically processed when it is strongly constrained by the first constituent? Will there be parafoveal-on-foveal effects of positional family size?

Conclusions

The eye movement studies discussed in the present chapter have demonstrated that there are two routes in operation in compound word processing, the morphological decomposition route and the holistic route, which are assumed to run in parallel. Visual acuity constrains the relative efficiency of these processes. With short compounds, with letters that all fall onto the fovea when the word is fixated, the whole-word route dominates the identification process from the very beginning, whereas with longer compounds that cannot be identified with a single eye fixation the decomposition route dominates the initial stages of processing.

The study of compound word processing also allows a good testing ground for theories of eye guidance and attentional processes in reading. Our studies have shown that foveal load, as indexed by lexical frequency, is capable of affecting saccadic programming within a spatially unified compound. Whether it can also do so for spaced compounds remains yet to be seen. If not, it would suggest that the *when* component of within-word saccadic programming (i.e. within the same visual object) is under the control of the lexical properties of the object, whereas the *when* component of inter-word saccades (i.e. saccades going from one visual object to the next) is primarily guided by lower level information, such as word length and orthographic information picked up from the parafovea. We also think that compound words are an ideal arena to understand and model the processes by which words are refixated, as refixations in compound words are clearly driven both by lexical factors and lower-level factors.

Finally, we believe our results provide a pretty strong case that parafoveal-on-foveal effects are not an important part of reading. That is, they indicate that even when there is evidence that what is in parafoveal vision has undergone substantial processing (as indicated by a substantial preview benefit for the second constituent), there was little evidence that this processing had any control over processing time on the prior, fixated, material (as indicated by little or no effect on gaze duration on the first constituent). As one would expect parallel processing to be more likely over a single (unspaced) compound word than over two consecutive words in text, this also casts doubt on whether there is any solid evidence for parallel processing of more than one word at a time in text.

Acknowledgements

Jukka Hyönä and Raymond Bertram acknowledge the support of Suomen Akatemia (the Academy of Finland) and Alexander Pollatsek acknowledges support from grant HD26765 of the National Institute of Health. We also thank Francoise Vitu and Ulrich Weger for their useful comments on a previous version of this chapter.

References

Andrews, S., Miller, B., and Rayner, K. (2004). Eye movements and morphological segmentation of compound words: There is a mouse in the mousetrap. *European Journal of Cognitive Psychology*, **16**, 285–311.

Bertram, R., and Hyönä, J. (2003). The length of a complex word modifies the role of morphological structure: Evidence from eye movements when reading short and long Finnish compounds. *Journal of Memory and Language*, **48**, 615–634.

Bertram, R., Baayen, R. H., and Schreuder, R. (2000). Effects of family size for complex words. *Journal of Memory and Language*, **42**, 390–405.

Bertram, R., Pollatsek, A., and Hyönä, J. (2004). Morphological parsing and the use of segmentation cues in reading Finnish compounds. *Journal of Memory and Language*, **51**, 325–345.

De Jong, N. H., Feldman, L. B., Schreuder, R., Pastizzo, M., and Baayen, R. H. (2002). The processing and representation of Dutch and English compounds: Peripheral morphological, and central orthographic effects. *Brain and Language*, **81**, 555–567.

Hyönä, J., and Bertram, R. (2004). Do frequency characteristics of non-fixated words influence the processing of non-fixated words during reading? *European Journal of Cognitive Psychology*, **16**, 104–127.

Hyönä, J. and Pollatsek, A. (1998). The role of component morphemes on eye fixations when reading Finnish compound words. *Journal of Experimental Psychology: Human Perception and Performance*, **24**, 1612–1627.

Hyönä, J. and Pollatsek, A. (2000). Morphological processing of Finnish compound words in reading. In: A. Kennedy, R. Radach, D. Heller and J. Pynte (ed.) *Reading as a perceptual process*. Oxford: Elsevier, pp. 65–87.

Hyönä, J., Bertram, R., and Pollatsek, A. (2004). Are long compound words identified serially via their constituents? Evidence from an eye-movement contingent display change study. *Memory and Cognition*, **32**, 523–532.

Inhoff, A.W., and Radach, R. (2002). The biology of reading: The use of spatial information in the reading of complex words. *Comments on Theoretical Biology*, **7**, 121–138.

Inhoff, A. W., Radach, R., and Heller, D. (2000). Complex compounds in German: Interword spaces facilitate segmentation but hinder assignment of meaning. *Journal of Memory and Language*, **42**, 23–50.

Inhoff, A. W., Starr, M., and Shindler, K. L. (2000). Is the processing of words during eye fixation in reading strictly serial? *Perception and Psychophysics*, **62**, 1474–1484.

Juhasz, B. J., Inhoff, A. W., and Rayner, K. (2005). The role of interword spaces in the processing of English compound words. *Language and Cognitive Processes*, **20**, 291–316.

Juhasz, B. J., Starr, M. and Inhoff, A. W., and Placke, L. (2004). The effects of morphology on the processing of compound words: Evidence from naming, lexical decisions, and eye fixations. *British Journal of Psychology*, **94**, 223–244.

Kennedy, A. (2000). Parafoveal processing in word recognition. *Quarterly Journal of Experimental Psychology*, **53A**, 429–455.

Moscoso del Prado Martín, F., Bertram, R., Häikiö, T., Schreuder, R., and Baayen, R. H. (2004). Morphologically family size in a morphologically rich language: the case of Finnish compared with Dutch and Hebrew. *JEP: Learning, Memory, and Cognition*, **30**, 1271–1278.

Niswander-Klement, E., and Pollatsek, A. (in press). The effects of root-frequency, word frequency, and length on the processing of prefixed English words during reading. *Memory and Cognition*.

Pollatsek, A., and Hyönä, J. (2005). The role of semantic transparency in the processing of Finnish compound words. *Language and Cognitive Processes*, **20**, 261–290.

Pollatsek, A. Hyönä, J., and Bertram, R. (2000). The role of morphological constituents in reading Finnish compound words. *Journal of Experimental Psychology: Human Perception and Performance*, **26**, 820–833.

Rayner, K. (1998). Eye movements in reading and information processing: 20 years of research. *Psychological Bulletin*, **124**, 372–422.

Reichle, E. D., Rayner, K., and Pollatsek, A. (2003). The E-Z Reader model of eye movement control in reading: Comparisons to other models. *Behavioral and Brain Sciences*, **26**, 445–526.

Schreuder, R., and Baayen, R. H. (1995). Modeling morphological processing. In: L. B. Feldman (ed.), *Morphological aspects of language processing*. Hillsdale, NJ: Erlbaum, pp. 131–154.

Schreuder, R., and Baayen, R. H. (1997). How complex simplex words can be. *Journal of Memory and Language*, **37**, 118–139.

Taft, M. (1979). Recognition of affixed words and the word frequency effect. *Memory and Cognition*, **7**, 263–272.

Taft, M. (1994). Interactive-activation as a framework for understanding morphological processing. *Language and Cognitive Processes*, **9**, 271–294.

5

New directions in theories of eye-movement control during reading

Shun-nan Yang and George W. McConkie

Abstract

Several recent models of eye-movement control during reading have relaxed or abandoned assumptions about direct cognitive control of saccades and/or sequential attention to, and processing of, individual words. In this chapter we briefly describe these models and explore the implications of such changes for the field. The Competition/Interaction, or C/I, model (Yang and McConkie 2001) is presented in some detail, illustrating how its perspective changes the issues of interest, interpretation of data and even vocabulary for discussing eye movements in reading.

Introduction

Eye movements are instrumental in visual exploration. In reading, the goal of visual exploration is to identify printed words and to comprehend the underlying linguistic information communicated by the text. Not surprisingly, in reading, relationships are observed between language characteristics and eye behavior. For example, longer eye fixations and gaze times occur for less common words, misspelled words, and words that are less predictable from their context, and it is more likely that the eyes will be directed at these words (Rayner 1998; Rayner and Pollatsek 1989). These relationships have been exploited by researchers interested in studying the on-line language processes taking place during reading, primarily by testing predictions about relative processing difficulty or load at different text locations, or at the same locations when occupied by different words, by comparing fixation and gaze times under the conditions studied. This work has proceeded very productively in spite of an incomplete understanding of the bases for these relationships or the mechanisms by which they occur. It has been sufficient to invoke the general observation that greater processing difficulty or load tends to increase fixation and gaze times and often to reduce the lengths of forward saccades and increase the frequency of regressing. Thus, a longer fixation or gaze time in one condition than in another serves as evidence for a difference in processing difficulty, and the region to which the eyes are directed when this difference is observed (often called the fixated region) indicates the approximate location in the text where the processing difference occurs.

At the same time there has been a continued interest in the nature of the mechanisms by which the relationships between language processing and eye behavior occur. To the psycholinguist, this work is relevant for two reasons: first, to justify current procedures for using eye-movement data in studying language processes and, second, to suggest new eye-movement measures or measurement procedures that might provide additional information about the processing taking place.

The purpose of the current chapter is to briefly examine the nature of the link between language processing and eye behavior during reading that is assumed in some of the most prominent theories or models over the past quarter century; to point out some new directions being taken in recent work with an emphasis on our own work; and to look at the implications of these new directions for the field.

Relating language processing and eye behavior

The simplest explanation of the relationship between language processes and eye behavior is to assume that these processes drive eye activity directly. Just and Carpenter (1980) proposed that the eyes go to a word when it is to be processed and remain directed at that word for the period of its processing. In essence, the eyes are assumed to be a pointer indicating which word is being processed and for how long. This assumes that words are processed sequentially. The total time spent reading a sentence or passage is sliced into segments by interword gaze shifts, with each time segment being assigned to a word based on gaze direction and being assumed to be the processing time required by that word. Thus, words are the base units for which processing time is calculated, and saccades are of significance only when they take the eyes to a different word. This position, which might be called the 'direct measurement position', leads to the interpretation of gaze duration as a direct measure of the processing time required or enabled by a word. While issues arise about what to do with time spent in making a saccade, how to handle situations such as when a word receives no direct fixation (i.e. is 'skipped') or when the eyes return to a previously fixated word, these are methodological issues rather than concerns about the position itself. This is the type of relationship between eye and mind that we wish existed, since it would make the interpretation of eye behavior data transparent. Unfortunately, there are lags in visual input and in motor control that make this an unlikely description of eye-movement control in reading. If eye behavior were controlled in this manner, with the processing of one word being completed before beginning the planning of a saccade to the next, the brain would spend nearly half its time just waiting for the required visual input (McConkie *et al.* 1985; Rayner and Pollatsek 1989), which would constitute a terribly inefficient mechanism. Thus, more recent theories assume that saccades in reading are usually or always initiated before the processing of information from the prior fixation has been completed.

Morrison (1984) proposed an alternative model of the relation of language processing and eye movements that still assumes a close link between word processing and eye movements. He proposed that the reader's attention moves from word to word along the line, and that each shift of attention triggers a saccade to the newly-attended word. Thus, both the Just and Carpenter (1980) and the Morrison (1984) models assume strict sequential processing of words, and assume that saccades are initiated by the occurrence of a cognitive event, the completion of word processing (Just and Carpenter) or word identification (Morrison). Morrison's proposal allows the time from the call for a saccade until the arrival of new visual information from the next fixation to be spent in higher levels of language processing, such as retrieving semantic information or completing structure integration, thus avoiding the above-noted inefficiency.

Defining the processing event that triggers a saccade is a critical issue for the psycholinguist, since this determines which processes are assumed to be measured by, or reflected in, fixation or gaze duration indices. Just and Carpenter's (1980) position allows the gaze time to include all, or nearly all, of the processing associated with a word, including syntactic and semantic processing; whereas Morrison's (1984) position suggests that only the time to recognize the word is included. Higher language processes would be reflected only to the degree that they affect word identification itself, at least in the initial fixation on a word. Morrison also proposed that under certain conditions the eyes would not go to a currently-attended word and the saccade to this word would be cancelled, resulting in the phenomenon of word skipping. Thus, the initially-assumed tight relation between processing and eye movements is relaxed somewhat in the Morrison model, adding complexities to a direct measurement position.

The University of Massachusetts group has built on the foundation of Morrison's (1984) work to create an impressive computational model, E-Z Reader, extending it to produce frequency distributions of fixation times and saccade lengths and to account for various observed characteristics of eye behavior in reading. To accomplish this, it was necessary to modify the processing events that are assumed to cause attention and the eyes to move to the next word (Reichle *et al.* 1998, 1999, 2003). In the current version of E-Z Reader, presented in one of the contributing chapters (see chapter 6), it is assumed that a saccade is initiated to the next word even before the current word is completely identified. This represents a further weakening of the direct measurement position and less direct relationship between eye behavior and language processing.

Other models that have been recently proposed (SWIFT, Glenmore and the Competition/Interaction model) have further reduced the degree to which eye fixations and gaze durations are assumed to indicate temporal characteristics of language processing. The SWIFT model (Engbert *et al.* 2002) accepts some characteristics of E-Z Reader, but assumes that all words in the perceptual span (i.e. fixated word plus one to the left and two to the right) are being processed simultaneously and gives up the assumption that a saccade is triggered by a specific processing event associated with the fixated word; rather, saccade onsets are planned at random times. Also, the word to which the eyes are sent is determined probabilistically, biased by the processing activity level of each of the words in the perceptual span. The relationship between language processing and eye behavior is obtained by allowing saccades to be delayed according to an indication of processing difficulty ('lexical activity'), and by having greater likelihood of sending the eyes to words with greater lexical activity.

The introduction of these probabilistic control functions explicitly reduces the proportion of the variance in fixation and gaze times, and in where the eyes are sent, that can be empirically associated with individual words in the manner assumed by the direct measurement position.

The Glenmore model (Reilly and Radach 2003) abandons the Morrison mechanism entirely, choosing instead a neural network implementation of the type of neurophysiologically-based saccade control described by Findlay and Walker (1999). Words within the perceptual span are activated in parallel, at rates that vary with word and language characteristics. Saccades occur when activation in the 'fixate center', which holds the eyes in a fixation state, falls below a threshold, taking the eyes to the word with the highest activity level in a two-dimensional saliency map, with that activation produced by word and language characteristics. The authors note that the time of executing a saccade does not bear any direct relationship to the processing of the currently fixated word, though it is influenced by it as well as by many other factors.

The Competition/Interaction (C/I) model (Yang and McConkie 2001, 2004), which is described in greater detail below, also assumes parallel processing of words, random saccade initiation times and a saccade targeting system that is competition-based and not typically guided by attention. Of three mechanisms by which language processing is assume to affect eye behavior, the two most common are a fast inhibition of saccades when processing difficulty is encountered, and a slower adjustment of parameters for general control of saccadic activity.

Thus, the simple direct measurement position has been largely abandoned in the development of recent models of eye-movement control in reading (see Boland 2004, for a counter-example). These current models have various means of keeping an influence of language processing in the control of eye movements, but the proportion of the variance in individual fixation and gaze times that is assumed to be attributable to these influences appears to be dropping substantially, though no one has yet directly assessed this.

Another research tradition has, for several decades, argued against a direct cognitive control of eye behavior in reading (O'Regan 1989; O'Regan and Levy-Schoen 1987; Vitu *et al.* 1995). While admitting the existence of some cognitive influence, these researchers have proposed that visuo-oculomotor factors are prominent in controlling the eyes during reading. Their primary focus has been to identify non-cognitive factors that influence when and where the eyes move, thus calling into question the assumption that the control is cognitively based. These factors include tendencies for the eyes to go to the center of words (O'Regan 1981), for fewer refixations of words to occur following fixations near their centers (O'Regan and Levy-Schoen 1987; McConkie *et al.* 1989), for fixations in the centers of words to be longer than those near the ends (Vitu *et al.* 2002), for saccade length to vary with eye position on the line (Vitu *et al.* 2004), and for regressions to be more likely following longer forward saccades (Vitu and McConkie 2000). While cognitive interpretations of such phenomena are possible, the existence of perceptuo-oculomotor explanations indicates that they are not necessary. Vitu *et al.*, (1995) demonstrated that several of these phenomena are observed when a person pretends to read a page in which all letters have been replaced by Zs, indicating that they do not arise from language-processing influences (but see Rayner and Fisher 1996).

In some sense, the recent models noted above represent a rapprochement between the cognitive and oculomotor traditions and include both types of influences in their models. Thus, most researchers now accept the existence of both; the primary issue concerns the nature of the mechanism that gives rise to these phenomena. However, a related issue that has not been sufficiently addressed concerns the proportion of variance in eye behavior during reading that can be attributed to cognitive aspects of control. There is still a tendency for the more cognitively-oriented researchers to assume that most of the variance reflects ongoing language processing, while perceptuo-oculomotor oriented researchers suspect that the cognitive influences are relatively small. As noted above, this is an issue in need of more attention.

Some effects of abandoning sequential word processing

SWIFT, Glenmore and C/I models, by giving up sequential word processing and assuming parallel processing of words, may have a deeper and more pervasive influence on the field than might initially be expected. Much of the language currently used to describe eye-movement data comes out of the sequential word processing perspective. For example, the use of the gaze duration on a word (i.e. the sum of fixation times of the initial run of fixations in which the eyes are directed at that word) as a basic measure of processing time seems intuitively obvious and well justified from the perspective of sequential word processing. That perspective makes a strong distinction between two fixations in which the eyes are directed at the same word, and two fixations in which they are directed at different, say, successive, words, and generally assumes that these two patterns indicate very different cognitive processes. From a parallel word processing perspective, however, this distinction is usually rather minor, resulting from only a small absolute or probabilistic difference in the degree or speed of processing of the various words that are within the perceptual span. From a parallel processing perspective, there seems to be no intuitive basis for using the word-based gaze duration as a fundamental dependent variable[1] (though a possible justification is suggested below).

The sequential word processing tradition in our field has led to the development of a vocabulary for describing eye movements in reading that is based on this word processing assumption. Strong distinctions are made between the word to which the eyes are directed during a fixation (W0), words to the left of it (W–1, W–2 ...), and words to the right (W+1, W+2 ...), assuming that the processing activities associated with

---

[1] It should be noted that the gaze duration, if considered to be the total time that the eyes are continuously directed within a given region of the text, can be better justified as a dependent variable when the text segments are large in relation to the size of the perceptual span, such as with multi-word phrases, clauses, sentences, etc. Even if words are perceived in parallel, these larger segments must be perceived sequentially, thus meeting the implicit sequential processing assumption that underlies the use of the gaze duration. Here, the gaze duration might be referred to simply as the reading time for the text segment.

these words during a fixation are qualitatively different. Evidence that information was acquired about W+1 during a fixation is referred to as a 'preview' of the word, as if the processing were different from that which occurred for W0. When characteristics of W–1 or W–2 are shown to affect eye behavior, this is referred to as a 'spillover effect', implying that the processing might have been expected to be completed previously, presumably when the eyes were directed at those words. If the eyes are never directed at a word in the text, this is noted as being an exceptional event by saying the word was 'skipped,' thus implying a non-normal processing situation.[2] If the eyes were directed at W0 on the last fixation, the current fixation is marked as exceptional by calling it a 'refixation'. Both Morrison (1984), on the cognitive theory side, and O'Regan (1989), on the oculomotor theory side, explicitly stated that the default eye-movement pattern is one in which the eyes move from one word to the next sequentially, with a single fixation directed at each; their models then attempted to explain the departures from this basic pattern: skipping, regressing and refixating. From the perspective of models such as SWIFT, Glenmore and C/I, observed preview and spillover effects are simply evidence that word processing is occurring in parallel and is not limited to the fixated word. Furthermore, the processing distinctions implied by these eye-movement categories tend to be lost; there is no longer a compelling reason to distinguish between a 6-letter forward saccade that crosses a word boundary vs. one that does not, nor between 10-letter forward saccades that cross one vs. two word boundaries. While these categories may prove useful for descriptive purposes in characterizing eye-movement patterns, within this new theoretical context, they tend to lose the meanings that initially motivated them.

Summary

The history of theorizing about the relation between language processing and eye behavior has two traditions: one claiming strong cognitive control, and the other stressing oculomotor control principles with varying degrees of cognitive influence. In the cognitive tradition, the direct measurement position has been weakened and sometimes abandoned, and there has been a gradual move toward assuming more indirect routes for cognitive influences on eye behavior during reading. Not only is the mechanism by which language-processing affects eye behavior in dispute, but we do not even have a well-justified estimate of how much of the variance in eye behavior can be accounted for on the basis of language processing. The sequential word processing position which has dominated thinking in this area is embedded within the vocabulary that has developed and the dependent variables commonly used in data analysis. Recent models that assume parallel processing of words reconfigure the theoretical context in ways that change the issues of interest, the meanings of terms and even what should be considered appropriate dependent variables for analysis. We now describe one recent model, the C/I model, in greater detail to give some sense of how it changes issues of interest and data analysis procedures.

---

[2] Kerr (1992) observed that, for four college students reading a novel, about half the words were 'skipped' in this sense, suggesting that this is not as exceptional event as is often believed.

The Competition/Interaction model of eye-movement control

After obtaining results in a series of studies that seem quite inconsistent with E-Z Reader and related models of eye-movement control during reading, we (Yang and McConkie 2001, 2004) have been developing a model to account for these results.[3] In the studies, a new method was used, referred to as the single fixation replacement method, to measure how much time elapses from the time the eyes land on a stimulus pattern of interest until that pattern begins to affect eye-movement decisions – both when and where to send the eyes. Participants were asked to read chapters from a novel displayed page-by-page on the computer screen while their eyes were monitored. During selected saccades the text was replaced by an alternative stimulus pattern, with the original text returning during the next saccade, as illustrated in Fig. 5.1. Thus, the alternative stimulus was present for an occasional single fixation, and the stimulus motion that necessarily accompanies such display changes was hidden because it occurred during the saccade. The rest of the time the normal text was present, allowing continuous reading.

Our interest was in how soon the alternative stimulus pattern would begin to modify saccade decisions regarding when and where to send the eyes next. Since cognitive control theories have generally assumed that saccades are triggered by some language-processing event, if that event is delayed or eliminated, the onsets of the saccades should be delayed. For example, if saccades are triggered when word identification is complete (Morrison 1984) but the alternative stimulus is composed of nonwords, saccades should be delayed by the lack of an indication of success in identifying words. If they are triggered when the familiarity of words has been checked, with this checking processing taking longer for unfamiliar words (Reichle *et al.* 2003), then the presence of illegal nonwords, which are definitely unfamiliar, should slow the checking process and thus delay the time at which the saccade is initiated. Finally, if the decision of which word to send the eyes to is part of the process of programming a saccade, and the alternative stimulus pattern is made up of solid strings of letters without word units, this lack of potential saccade targets should delay the saccade preparation process and probably change the lengths, and possibly the directions, of the saccades. Cognitive control theories predict that these delays in saccade onset time should occur for almost all saccades except for a few short latency saccades that are assumed to be preprogrammed during the previous fixation and to occur even in the absence of current stimulus information (Morrison 1984; Reichle *et al.* 1998). Thus, our studies were an attempt to test these predictions, as well as to determine which aspects of the text stimulus must be modified to produce delays

---

[3] A reviewer challenged our characterization of this model as being neurophysiologically based and as a model. The model is neurophysiological in the sense that it was initially developed from findings from oculomotor research at the neuronal and system level. We are currently formalizing it in a form that allows quantitative parameter estimates through model-fitting procedures. The current paper does not discuss these aspects of the model.

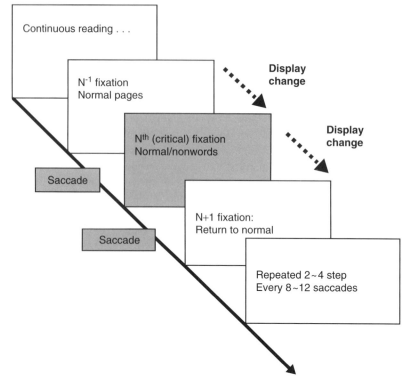

Figure 5.1 A diagram of the procedure used in the single fixation replacement method.

in saccade onset times (reflected as longer fixation durations) and how early in the fixation these delays begin.

Figure 5.2 presents data from Yang and McConkie (2001) showing the frequency distributions of saccade onset times (i.e. fixation durations) for the critical fixations in a control condition with no text replacement and an illegal nonword condition in which the text was replaced by random consonant strings of the same lengths as the words during that fixation. The delaying of saccades is indicated by the distribution for the experimental condition falling below that for the control condition in the earlier part of the distribution: any such delays simply push some saccades to a later part of the distribution, where the experimental distribution then rises above the control condition.

A comparison of these two distributions, moving with time from left to right, shows that most saccades were not delayed by this manipulation: all saccades that normally occurred before 200 ms apparently occurred at their normal time. These saccades, constituting 50 per cent of the entire set, apparently did not require any word identification or word familiarity check to trigger them. Further analysis of the remainder of the distribution suggested that once effects began to occur (i.e. once the frequency of the experimental condition dropped below that of the control condition), it was still

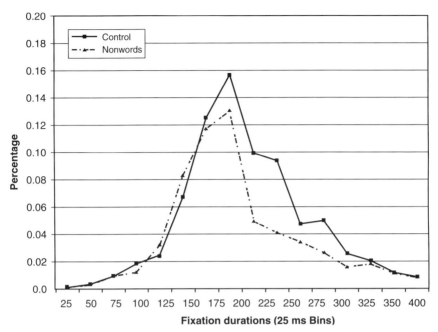

Figure 5.2 Frequency distributions of the durations of critical fixations that end with forward saccades, when the text is not changed (control condition) and when it is replaced for a single fixation by nonword letter strings.

the case that most saccades occurred at their normal times, again arguing against a language-processing event being critical in triggering the saccades. Thus, the onset times of most saccades were unaffected by whether or not word processing could be completed, a result that is inconsistent with the 'cognitive saccade triggering event' assumption. If delaying or eliminating the assumed critical triggering event fails to delay most of the saccades, then their onsets must not be dependent on this event.

Similar results were obtained when perceptible word units were removed by replacing the text with unbroken letter strings, such as replacing 'in the city' with 'inxthexcity' for a single fixation (where the letter x is a randomly selected letter): the onset times of saccades occurring before 200 ms appeared unaffected. Apparently the presence of visible word units is also not critical in determining the onset times of saccades, contrary to most current thinking[4] (McConkie *et al.* 1989). These results and others led to the

---

[4] The lack of a significant effect on saccade initiation times when the word segmentation is removed does not invalidate the idea that word units play a role in eye-movement control; rather, it indicates that the presence of visible word units is not critically involved in determining when a saccade is to occur. There is ample evidence that the locations and lengths of word units influence the decision of where to send the eyes.

development of an alternative model of eye-movement control during reading, in which saccade decisions are influenced, but not directly controlled by, language-processing activities (see descriptions in Yang and McConkie 2001, 2004; McConkie and Yang 2003). We have called it the Competition/Interaction, or C/I, model to reflect characteristics of the mechanism proposed. Here the 'competition' refers to the race between the neural signal triggering saccades and that suppressing them; the 'interaction' refers to the dynamic interface that determines the saccade direction and amplitude during eye fixations.

The C/I model begins with a mechanism that generates saccades with no 'direct' cognitive influence other than the arousal of a reading strategy that biases the direction and amplitude of saccades. The amplitude and latency of forward and regressive saccades are computed separately in the oculomotor system. The triggering signals for forward and regressive saccades race, or compete, toward separate predetermined thresholds and the winner triggers a saccade with an amplitude determined by the movement coding corresponding to the direction of movement. The model proposes three mechanisms, explained below, by which cognitive influences can produce their effect by modifying the ongoing saccadic activity.

The basic saccade-generating engine

The model builds on the neurophysiological observation that the saccadic system is an active system, in which saccades must be suppressed in order to maintain a steady eye fixation, rather than requiring a stimulating event to put the eyes into motion (Hikosaka and Wurtz 1983; Munoz and Wurtz 1995). Such saccade-enabling events as the appearance of a visual target, or even the anticipation of a target appearance, can excite saccade-related brain regions, causing a release of this suppression, resulting in the occurrence of a saccade of a particular direction and length. However, in reading there are no momentary stimulus or stimulus-related events to excite these brain regions, so this is assumed to be done on a strategic basis (Levy-Schoen 1981). The C/I model assumes that this oculomotor strategy is activated by the intent to read, which periodically disinhibits the eye-movement system, allowing a saccade to occur. The time of this disinhibition is variable but not directly related to the activity taking place in the language centers of the brain: its timing is considered to usually be independent of the timing of the language processes.

There are within-fixation dynamics that occur, with strong (though not complete) suppression of saccades at the beginning of each fixation, followed by a period during which the release of this suppression typically occurs and the likelihood of making a saccade rises rapidly. Once the suppression is released, a saccade occurs after a random waiting time, giving rise to the exponential characteristics of the latter part of the fixation duration frequency distribution (Harris *et al.* 1988; McConkie and Dyre 2000). As noted below, the general time of the release and properties of the waiting time are modulated by adjustable parameters.

Where the eyes go when a saccade occurs is determined by the pattern of activation in a retino-topic salience map related to movement coding. We propose an oculomotor reading strategy that includes an activation of a region in this map in each fixation, producing a bias of movement coding that increases the likelihood that the next saccade will take the eyes into this region. This is referred to as 'strategy-based activation'. The location of this region is largely determined by the directions and lengths of saccades made in past reading experience and especially of recent saccades, as observed in recent neurophysiological research (Carpenter and Williams 1995; Dorris *et al.* 1999). In reading European languages, this strategy-based activation typically occurs in the right visual field, centered about 6–12 letter positions to the right of the center of the fovea, though individual differences also affect the preferred letter locations.

Visual word units, or the strings of letters separated by spaces, also are assumed to produce activation at their locations in the saliency map, with their eccentricity, length, and possibly orthographic regularity affecting the activation levels in their regions (Hyona and Bertram 2004; Inhoff 1987, Inhoff *et al.* 2003). In the saliency map a location with the highest activation level tends to draw the eyes. As a result, saccades tend to be made to the location of a word unit, though with some error. In addition, the word unit regions in the near-right visual field are more likely to draw the eyes than those in other areas, due to the benefit from strategy-related activation. Furthermore, since the visual patterns of words take time to be encoded by the brain and to influence the saliency map, over time during a fixation the selection of saccade location is increasingly affected by the word units; early saccades are more likely to be dominated by the strategic bias. Thus, endogenous, spontaneous activity in the oculo-motor system, influenced by later activity resulting from the stimulus pattern, produces reading-like eye movements like those observed by Vitu *et al.* (1995) in the Z-string reading study.

The strategy-based bias also includes the adjustment of parameters related to the timing of triggering saccades, with the rightward saccades being more readily triggered then the leftward ones in English reading (McConkie and Dyre 2000). These parameters determine the time-related change in the readiness of saccade initiation, or saccade likelihood, effecting different reading speeds when the context or the material on hands requires such adjustment.

Influences from language processing

The first of three cognitive influences on this saccadic engine, as described by McConkie and Yang (2003), is illustrated in Fig. 5.2. Here, the presence of nonwords is seen to cause the cancellation or delay of some saccades, beginning 200 ms into the fixation. This is assumed to result from an inhibitory signal that arises from brain centers where processing difficulty is encountered, which has the effect of reducing the momentary likelihood of making a saccade. In Fig. 5.2, the signal likely results from the failure to categorize a string of letters as a word, which is a requirement for language processing to proceed, though it could result from encountering a different letter string than was present during the previous fixation, a possibility that we argue against below. The size of the effect can also be seen here: about 50 per cent of the saccades that would normally have occurred during the 225 ms period were suppressed.

A clearer picture of the effect of the nonwords on saccade onset times can be obtained by plotting the data in Fig. 5.2 as hazard curves, which show changes over time in the momentary likelihood of making a saccade. This is done by dividing the

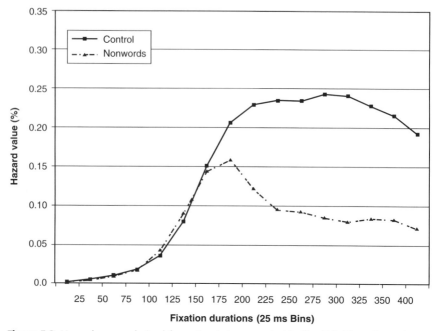

Figure 5.3 Hazard curves derived from the data presented in Fig. 5.2. These hazard values show the momentary likelihood of making a forward saccade for surviving fixations, thus indicating the momentary level of saccadic activity.

number (frequency) of saccades that occurred during each 25 ms time period by the number of fixations that still survived at the beginning of that period. This gives the proportion of surviving fixations that ended with a saccade during each time period in the distribution, as seen in Fig. 5.3, for control and nonword conditions.[5] Comparing the curves for these two conditions indicates that they are initially very similar, showing the saccadic hazard function pattern typically seen in reading

[5] A hazard curve is an alternative representation of the data in a frequency distribution, and either can be derived from the other. Percentage frequency distributions, like those in Fig. 5.2, are obtained by dividing the number of cases (here, the number of saccades that occurred) in each time bin by the total number of cases. Hazard curves are obtained in a similar way, except that the number of cases in each time bin is divided by the number of cases still remaining (here, the number of fixations for which a saccade has not yet occurred) at the beginning of that bin. Thus, instead of indicating the proportion of saccades that occurred in each time period, it indicates what proportion of the surviving fixations ended with a saccade during each period. This indicates the level of saccadic activity during each period. An inhibition of saccades results in a drop in the saccadic activity, or hazard, level relative to that of the appropriate control condition.

eye-movement data: very low at first and then rising rapidly. The presence of non-words produces an inhibitory effect on saccade initiation (that is, the experimental condition curve drops below the curve for the control condition) that begins about 200 ms into the fixation and continues through at least the next 200 ms. While both the frequency distribution and the hazard curve show the onset time of the inhibition, the hazard curve gives a clearer picture of the dynamics of the inhibitory influence over time. One limitation of the hazard curve is that, since the number of surviving fixations drops over time, the proportions based on these saccade frequencies become increasingly unstable, thus requiring a larger data set to reliably observe effects at later periods.

Since the momentary hazard values are proportions, it is possible to directly interpret them. For example, in the 350 ms time period of Fig. 5.3 the proportion of saccades that was suppressed can be calculated as the difference between the control and experimental hazard values divided by the hazard value for the control, for a suppression level of 35 per cent. This relation cannot be derived directly from the difference in frequency revealed in Fig. 5.2, which shows the same percentage of saccades occurring in both conditions during this time period. In addition, Fig. 5.3 indicates that both the hazard level (or momentary saccade likelihood, as shown by the control condition data) and the suppression level (as shown by a comparison between the experimental and control data) are dynamic, changing over the period of a fixation.

Previous studies have shown that both the onset time of the inhibition (the time at which the hazard level for the experimental condition drops in relation to that for the control condition), and the strength of that inhibition (i.e. the proportion of saccades that are suppressed at a given time) vary with the type of difficulty encountered in language processing (McConkie and Yang 2003; Yang and McConkie 2001). This point is further illustrated and supported below.

Thus, the C/I model proposes that the first type of cognitive influence on eye-movement decisions is in the form of inhibition of the saccadic system when a difficulty or anomaly is encountered in any aspect of visual or language processing. The onset time and degree of this inhibition varies with the type of difficulty encountered. The initiation times of saccades occurring prior to this inhibition onset time are unaffected by the inhibition. They occur at their normal time whether the text is normal or is a string of nonwords, so they cannot be initiated by any process that distinguishes between these. Saccades occurring later have some likelihood of being suppressed, depending on the degree of inhibition, thus delaying the onset of the next saccade. However, unlike SWIFT and Glenmore, there is no assumption that the amount of delay in the onset times of individual saccades varies in response to characteristics of the momentary language processing taking place. It is primarily the probability of suppression of saccades that is assumed to vary with degree of inhibition.

Note that when fixation durations are averaged across trials or subjects, since a suppressed saccade prolongs the fixation, increasing the number of suppressed saccades will increase the mean fixation duration in a way that looks like a graded effect on the mean. Thus, effects that are strictly probabilistic at the individual saccade level will produce changes in mean fixation duration that appear graded or continuous in nature. The existence of small changes in averaged measures, such as finding that an experimental condition increases the mean duration of a set of fixations by 15 ms as compared with a control condition, is not evidence that the durations of individual fixations are being increased by some small amount, or that the processing of the fixated word requires an additional 15 ms to be completed. Thus, the C/I model assumes probabilistic, rather than graded, effects of processing difficulty on fixation durations in reading, and is more concerned with the proportion of saccades that is being affected and when this effect occurs.

If our proposals are correct, this has two implications. First, such measures as mean fixation duration and mean gaze duration should be affected by changes in the proportion of saccades being suppressed, how early this inhibition occurs, and how much time passes after a saccade is suppressed before the suppressed saccade eventually occurs. Thus, they can be used in statistical tests to determine whether variables have produced significant effects on this aspect of eye behavior and may also indicate which of two variables produces the greatest effect. Second, if we are correct, however, then these average time measures are not the appropriate basis for model development, since they do not accurately represent the true nature of the effects on eye movements being produced by perceptual or language-processing difficulties encountered during reading. Given a case where a variable has no effect on the onset time of the 40 per cent of the fixations that occur before 200 ms, and then causes a suppression and 100 ms delay of 30 per cent of the fixations that occur after 200 ms, with the remaining saccades showing no delay, it is technically correct to represent this situation as showing an 18 ms increase in the mean fixation duration:

$$\frac{(0.40 \times 0 \text{ ms increase} + 0.18 \times 100 \text{ ms increase} + 0.42 \times 0 \text{ ms increase})}{100\%} = 18 \text{ ms}$$

However, we believe that a model that is designed to account for such mean time measures is problematic in successfully representing the true nature of the control processes taking place and the manner in which cognitive events affect them during reading.

The second type of cognitive influence on the basic saccade generating mechanism involves a slower and more continuous form of adjustment: the adjustment of parameters that control the general operation of the mechanism. For example, reading can be slowed by modifying the location of strategy-based activation, reducing its eccentricity, which increases the likelihood that the eyes will go to a nearer word, and by tuning parameters controlling the saccade initiation time directionally, which reduces the bias toward making rightward saccades, thereby resulting in a higher proportion of regressive movements. The latter also reduces the number of saccades that occur before the onset of inhibition when it occurs, thus increasing the number that are suppressed as a result of processing difficulties. Through such parametric adjustments, readers modify their oculomotor strategies to meet the needs of the language processing taking place in a global manner. An example of this type of adjustment is seen in a study (Fisher *et al.* in preparation) in which individuals read the same text with different instructions. They were told to read the text as prose or as poetry. We converted the frequency distributions of fixation duration into hazard values for these two conditions, and showed that there were differences in the frequency of regressing, and also in the maximum hazard levels for regressive saccades, with the poetry condition producing higher regression hazard values in general. Recent oculomotor research places the effected change of this parameter-adjusting mechanism in the superior colliculus, showing that the predictability of a target direction facilitates the neural activity associated with the predicted target location and affects the latency and bias of triggering saccades toward a given direction (Carpenter 2001; Dorris *et al.* 1999).

Third, it is possible for the cognitive system to override or exert direct control over the basic saccade generating mechanism. We obviously have the ability to direct our eyes to an intended target, and to voluntarily suppress saccades to some degree. This ability can also be employed during reading, directing the eyes to a particular part of the text or holding the gaze on a particular word (see chapter 2). However, this type of control is quite slow and resource-demanding. McConkie and Yang (2003) presented data from a study that was conducted to find out how much time it takes to redirect a saccade during reading. Using the single fixation replacement method, the text was replaced by strings of Fs or Rs on occasional fixations. The participants were instructed to read the text but when Rs appeared they were to immediately make a regressive saccade and when Fs appeared they were to make a forward saccade (which is what they would usually do, anyway). Hazard curves for forward and regressive saccades showed an initial and equal inhibition of saccades with both the F and R conditions relative to a control condition somewhat similar to that in Fig. 5.3, as a response to the non-textual stimulus pattern. The likelihood of making a regressive saccade in the R condition did not rise above that in the F condition until 475 ms after the fixation onset, indicating that the readers took this much time before being able to purposively produce a regressive saccade in response to a clear visual cue.

Thus, in this simple situation where the need to redirect a saccade is clearly signaled to the system by visual cues, at least 475 ms is needed to execute the response. It seems likely that more complex forms of direct cognitive control, such as making a regression based on language processing, may take even longer. Only are few fixations in normal reading long enough to allow this type of control to occur. Thus, in most cases, cognitively-directed saccades must occur on a later fixation. While it is possible for the direction of a saccade to be determined on the basis of visual information obtained during that fixation, most saccades are probably directed on some more automated basis.

The three types of cognitive influence on saccade control differ in the speed and precision of their effects on eye behavior. The first is a rapid, non-specific response to processing difficulty that suppresses saccades, and by reducing the influence of strategy-based biases, reduces the frequency of rightward saccades and often changes the lengths of saccades. The second is a more specific response that changes the configuration of saccadic activity, or the readiness of saccade initiation associated with it, in particular ways that develop across eye fixations. The third produces precise oculomotor acts but requires time to be achieved, typically more than a single fixation. However, the onset time of the cognitive influence also depends on when the difficulty or need for change is perceived, which undoubtedly varies with the nature of the problem encountered.

Finally, it should be noted that the time parameters that we have obtained in our work often deviate from observations made in previous studies. This is a natural result of the method we have used and the analyses that we have conducted so far. In our studies we wished to measure how much time elapses from the moment when the visual information leading to a processing difficulty of a particular type is encountered until saccade decisions begin to be affected. This requires a method in which the time of visually encountering the critical information is constrained; it could not have been encountered earlier than a specified moment, from which the measurement of time begins in determining how early the eye behavior is modified. This is not possible under normal reading conditions, since the critical information is constantly available peripherally, and the time at which it is encountered is not known. The single fixation replacement method that we have used assures that the critical stimulus patterns, such as nonwords, the lack of spaces between words, etc., are not encountered until the beginning of specified eye fixations on which these patterns occur, which are the points from which time can be measured.

This method has been very useful in indicating how much time elapses before certain types of textual abnormalities begin to produce effects on eye-movement decisions, thus yielding time parameter estimates needed in formalizing the C/I model. However, it is important to note that in normal reading, earlier effects will often be observed. For example, an effect that requires 200 ms to occur will produce a situation in which half of the fixations will have ended before this and, hence, will not show the effect. However, the factors, such as inhibition or the intention to move the eyes to a particular location, which would have produced an effect on the saccade had it not occurred so early, are still active and will likely affect the when and where decisions for the next saccade. Thus, on that saccade it will be possible to see early differences between experimental and control conditions, and earlier effects that are cognitively driven. Such early effects are not an embarrassment to the C/I model, nor a challenge to the time estimates obtained from our prior studies. They simply indicate that the oculomotor state is not reset with each saccade and that influences assumed by the C/I model can survive saccades. There is a need for further research on the time course of these influences that extend beyond the fixation on which the critical visual information is encountered.

Linguistic processing and saccade inhibition

Inhibition of the saccadic system when processing problems occur is the primary basis for local effects of language processing on eye behavior in the C/I model. While Yang and McConkie (2001, 2004) provide evidence for this inhibition, two concerns arise. First, since the single fixation replacement method used in these studies causes text to be different during one fixation than it had been during the last, it is possible that the inhibition observed in the experimental conditions is an artifact of the method: such intersaccadic stimulus discrepancies may, by themselves, cause the perceptual system to suppress saccadic activity. Second, the alternative stimulus patterns used in those studies were quite extreme, consisting of random letters, Xs, and filling in spaces between words, rather than being more normal language manipulations.

Thus, the suppression of saccades might result from one of these factors, rather than from encountering language-processing difficulties.

Results from a study reported briefly by McConkie *et al.* (1992) allay these concerns. This study was designed to find out how much time elapses between the moment a problem-causing word is foveated and the moment eye behavior begins to be changed by the problem. College students read chapters from a novel, in which words at selected critical word locations had been replaced by pseudowords of the same length. No display changes were made in the text during reading. A pseudoword was expected to produce processing difficulty at the word identification level. In other conditions the original word remained in the text, thus providing a control condition, or was replaced by errors of other types. Cases were then identified in which the first fixation on a critical word location was preceded by a saccade from a location 5–11 letter positions to the left of it. This data exclusion was done in an attempt to minimize the amount of processing of the stimulus in the critical word location prior to the first fixation directly on it. Figure 5.4 shows the hazard curves of fixation durations for the first fixation on the critical word location in the control and pseudoword conditions. In addition, Fig. 5.4 presents data for a third condition in the study, in which words in the same locations were replaced by other words that violated local semantic constraints, typically constraints established by a prior verb or adjective, thus producing processing problems at the semantic level. The lengths and frequencies of the alternate words matched those of the original words.

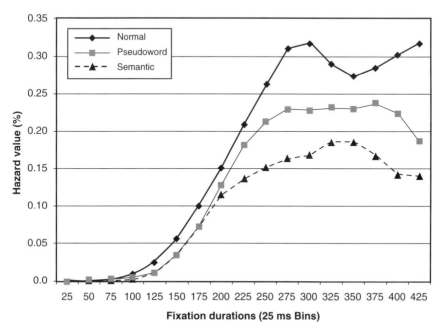

Figure 5.4 Hazard curves for the onset times of forward saccades that terminate the first fixations on the critical words in the control, pseudoword, and semantically incongruent conditions.

A comparison of the hazard curves for experimental and control conditions leads to several conclusions. First, the data show the characteristics observed by Yang and McConkie (2001): the curves are quite similar up to a particular point in time, at which point the experimental condition data drop below those of the control condition, thus showing the suppression of saccadic activity in that condition. The fact that this pattern is observed in a study having no display changes and with more normal language manipulations provides evidence that it is the result of processing difficulties rather than of abnormal stimulus patterns or changes in the display.

Second, the time of the separation point is earlier for the pseudoword condition (225 ms) than it is for the semantic violation condition (250–275 ms), thus showing the pattern that one would expect on the assumption that word identification occurs prior to semantic integration. In fact, the time difference between these two separation points provides an estimate of the minimum time that elapses between the initiations of these two levels of processing during reading.

Third, there is a difference between the curves in Fig. 5.4 and those presented by Yang and McConkie (2001): in Fig. 5.3, the curves are very similar up to the point of separation, whereas in Fig. 5.4 the experimental condition curves are consistently below that of the control condition, even at the shortest intervals. This is to be expected from the nature of the two studies. In the latter case, the erroneous stimuli were present during all fixations, thus making it possible for initial processing of the words in the critical locations to begin prior to the eyes landing on them and thereby leading to some inhibition of the saccadic system even before the first fixation on these words. The removal of cases in which the prior fixation was close to the critical word was an attempt to minimize this processing, but was obviously not sufficient to prevent it. This illustrates the fact noted above that early effects can be observed in studies where the time of visual encounter with critical information is not controlled.

Fourth, the effected inhibition of saccadic activity in the experimental conditions was not short-lived; that is, it was not just a short suppression of saccades, followed by a rebound of high saccadic activity once the nature of the problem was discovered. Rather, once the suppression occurs, it continues throughout the remainder of the fixation and perhaps into the following fixation.

Fifth, and finally, the fact that a severe semantic error begins the suppression of saccades so late in the fixation, and even then affects so few, provides an explanation for why mean fixation durations for first fixations on words often fail to show effects of syntactic and semantic processing (Rayner *et al.* 1986). Apparently, most saccades occur prior to the time at which they can be affected by the inhibition which results from encountering processing problems at higher language levels during the period of that fixation, so the effect only occurs on a small proportion of the longer fixations. Thus, the effects of higher language-processing variables on the durations of first fixations on a word are more likely to be observed in summary statistics related to the latter part of the frequency distribution, such as the third quartile or 90th percentile, than in the mean.

Figure 5.5, using data from the pseudoword condition describe above, shows the effect of processing difficulty of a not-yet-fixated word (W+1) on fixation duration. Cases were selected in which the eyes were directed at the word prior to fixating at the pseudoword, and a hazard curve plotted of their saccade onset times. The control

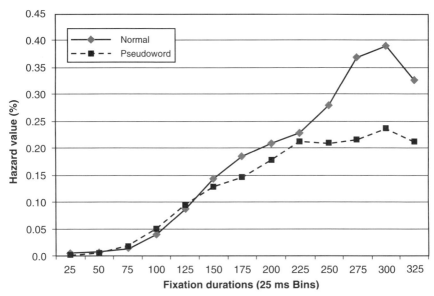

Figure 5.5 Hazard curves for the onset times of forward saccades that precede the first fixations on the critical words in the control and pseudoword conditions.

condition curve was obtained in the same way, for cases in which the words in the critical locations were not replaced. The onset time and suppressing effects of inhibition can be observed in the pseudoword condition, as compared with the control, though the inhibition does not begin until much later than in Fig. 5.4, when the eyes were directed at the critical word location, and is less severe. A similar parafoveal-to-foveal effect has been previously reported (Pynte *et al.* 2004; Rayner 1975). This is to be expected from a model assuming parallel processing of multiple words, if processing speed of words decreases with retinal eccentricity. This effect is difficult for sequential processing models to explain.

Many studies have found that increased fixation durations are often accompanied by an increase in the frequency of regressing, with a relatively short latency, which is often interpreted as a cognitive decision in response to the need for more processing time for that word. Figure 5.6 shows, for the pseudoword and control conditions, the proportion of regressive saccades made at each point in time. As can be seen, encountering the pseudoword and semantic errors produces an increase in the proportion of regressive saccades at each point in time. Although this effect appears to begin quite early, this may be artificial, since the number of saccades made at 150 and 175 ms is very small, thus producing unstable proportions. It is clear, however, that by 250 ms, the increase in the proportion of regressive saccades is reliable. Thus, the results appear to justify a conclusion that by at least 250 ms into a fixation a reader can intentionally redirect saccades when processing problems occur, in order to re-inspect the text and resolve the difficulty.

However, an examination of the hazard curves for regressive saccades, presented in Fig. 5.7, leads to a different interpretation: in fact, the saccadic activity level for regressive

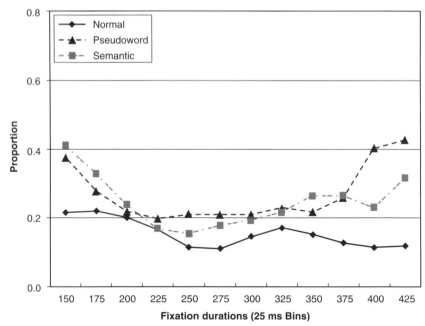

Figure 5.6 Momentary regression rates for saccades that terminate the initial fixations on the critical words in the control, pseudoword, and semantically incongruent conditions.

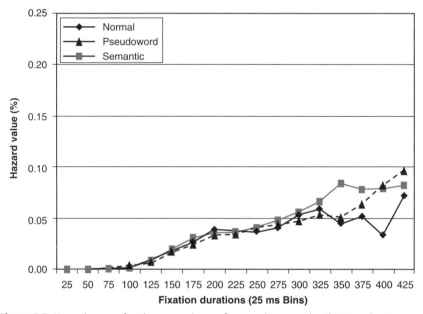

Figure 5.7 Hazard curves for the onset times of regressive saccades that terminate the initial fixations on the critical words in the control, pseudoword and semantically incongruent conditions.

saccades is very similar for the control, pseudoword and semantic error conditions until very late in the fixation. The erroneous words are not stirring up increased regressions; rather, they are suppressing the likelihood of making forward saccades, as shown in Fig. 5.4. Thus, the increased proportion of regressions comes mainly from a decreased number of forward saccades, not an increased number of regressive saccades, at each time interval. The delay of saccades sometimes increases the fixation time to the point where direct cognitive control can occur, as posited above (McConkie and Yang 2003). This is an instance in which an examination of the hazard curves indicating the momentary levels of forward and regressive saccadic activity actually leads to a different conclusion than examining only the proportion of saccades that are regressive.

Summary

The inhibition of the saccadic system, observed by Yang and McConkie (2001) and assumed in the C/I model, is not an artifact of display changes or un-text-like stimuli. Rather it is a prototypical response to processing difficulty, here observed in encountering both pseudowords and semantic errors with no display changes involved. This simple response, together with the assumption of parallel processing of words, is capable of accounting for phenomena that have previously been assumed to result from sequential processing of words and direct cognitive control of the eye-movement system. This includes processing-related variation in mean fixation durations, preview effect, spillover effect, and regressing in response to processing difficulty.

Summary and implications

There has been a strong tradition in eye-movement research in reading to assume that eye behavior is directly controlled by cognitive processing, and thus can be directly used to measure variables such as word processing time. In this chapter we have pointed out that in recent years, for several reasons, there has been a steady erosion of this position. Adopting an assumption of parallel processing of words, rather than sequential processing, in particular, undercuts the assumption that eye fixation times and gaze durations can be used as measures of processing time for individual words. It also leads to a new perspective on the meanings of eye-movement events such as refixations, word skipping and moving to the next word, in general reducing their significance.

At the same time, most current theories recognize the well-documented fact that eye-movement measures (typically summary statistics such as means) show variance that is predictable from language variables. We have argued that this results, not from language processes directly controlling eye movements, but from three types of influence that the language processes can have on the activity of a system that produces saccades on some other basis.

This may seem like a gloomy position to the psycholinguist who is looking to eye-movement data for measures of processing times for words during reading, similar to reaction time measures in discrete tasks. However, we would point out that the existence of cognitive influences on eye behavior makes it possible to use eye-movement data to detect differences in processing between conditions and to indicate the condition that produces the greatest difficulty, though not to indicate exactly how much more time is required. This is sufficient to test many hypotheses about the ongoing language-processing taking place during reading, and is a sufficient basis to justify the procedures used in much of the language-processing research that has been conducted using eye-movement recording.

In this regard, it should be noted that in psycholinguistic research, the word-based gaze duration has proved to be a useful and sensitive dependent variable. While we have argued against its interpretation as a measure of processing time for a word, there are reasons why it is such a useful indicator of processing differences and difficulties. Since processing differences can produce change in several independent aspects of eye behavior, including fixation durations, saccade lengths and frequencies of refixating, if one desires a single dependent variable that is sensitive to differences, it should be a composite variable that is affected by each of these. Gaze duration has this property: it can be increased by increasing the durations of eye fixations; by shortening forward saccades which increases the frequency with which the next fixation will remain on the same word; and by increasing the frequency of regressive saccades which, because regressions tend to be shorter, also have this same effect. Thus, even though the gaze duration may not be an actual measure of processing times for words, it serves as a composite measure that can be more sensitive to eye behavior change resulting from processing differences than are any of its component variables.

At the same time, it is important to make two points concerning the gaze duration. First, as with most composite variables, it is possible to fail to detect processing differences that lead to reciprocal changes in different component variables. Second, from the perspective of parallel word processing, there is no reason to believe that gaze durations are more sensitive to processing differences than are other composite measures that one might devise. We suggest that the general acceptance of this dependent variable has come from its apparent transparency, given the assumptions underlying the direct measurement position. With a change in those assumptions, this transparency vanishes, and the possibility is raised that a composite measure based on regions other than individual words, or with other combinations of components, or different weightings, could be more sensitive to language-processing differences. Research is needed to explore such possibilities. A bright note for the psycholinguist is that the new theoretical perspectives are likely to produce new indicators of language-processing characteristics. Our work with the single fixation replacement method indicates that if one is interested in knowing how early some aspect of language processing, for which language constraints can be violated in the text, occurs, it is possible to obtain a precise indication of this. We suspect that these perspectives will generate other new measures that can aid researchers in studying language processing, some of which are likely to appear in the form of parameters in models of language processing and eye-movement control that, when fit to data, indicate characteristics of different aspects of the processing taking place.

For researchers investigating the motor control of eye movements and how it is influenced by cognition, the new theories offer interesting enhancements of, and alternatives to, the traditional sequential word processing theories. There is an attempt, in both the Glenmore and C/I models, to base the modeling on established neurophysiological principles and findings, thus providing additional constraints on the models and raising the possibility that some issues may be resolved through brain research. This is also leading to a greater focus on the temporal dynamics of the eye-movement control system.

Finally, the coming decade should be an interesting one for research on eye-movement control during reading. It seems critical that we determine in which ways the processing of words is serial vs. parallel; the answer to this question could have profound effects on how eye-movement data are interpreted, both with respect to the nature of the control occurring, and to how cognitive activities can be inferred from eye-movement data. The rise in modeling that is taking place has the potential to provide new model-based measures of underlying processing and neurophysiological activities. It also demands specificity and quantification of results from studies, if those results are to be useful in furthering model development. The advancement of knowledge of oculomotor control and of language processing in the brain sciences provides new constraints on theorizing and, at the same time, gives useful concepts and mechanisms for explaining the nature of this control. Detailed analyses of eye-movement data are rapidly increasing the catalogue of phenomena that a theory of eye-movement control in reading should be able to predict or account for. We anticipate an exciting and challenging period for investigators in this area.

Acknowledgements

We thank Denis Drieghe and Keith Rayner for their thoughtful comments on an earlier draft of the chapter.

References

Boland, J. E. (2004). Linking eye movements to sentence processing in reading and listening. In: M. Carrieras and C. Clifton (ed.) *The on-line study of sentence comprehension: Eyetracking, ERP and beyond.* Brighton: Psychology Press, pp. 51–76.

Carpenter, R. H. S. (2001). Express saccades: Is bimodality a result of the order of stimulus presentation? *Vision Research*, **41**, 1145–1151.

Carpenter, R. H. S., and Williams, M. L. L. (1995). Neural computation of log likelihood in control of saccadic eye movements. *Nature*, **377**(6544), 59–62.

Dorris, M. C., Taylor, T. L., Klein, R. M., and Munoz, D. P. (1999). Influence of previous visual stimulus or saccade on saccadic reaction times in monkey. *Journal of Neurophysiology*, **81**(5), 2429–2436.

Engbert, R., Longtin, A. and Kliegl, R. (2002). A dynamical model of saccade generation in reading based on spatially distributed lexical processing. *Vision Research*, **42**, 621–636.

Findlay, J. M., and Walker, R. (1999). A model of saccade generation based on parallel processing and competitive inhibition. *Behavioral and Brain Sciences*, **22**, 661–721.

Fischer, M. H., Carminati, M. N., Stabler, J., and Roberts, A. (in preparation). *Eye movements during poetry and prose reading.*

Harris, C. M., Hainline, L., Abramov, L., Lemerise, E., and Camenzuli, C. (1988). The distribution of fixation durations in infants and naïve adults. *Vision Research*, **28**, 419–432.

Hikosaka, O., and Wurtz, R. H. (1983). Visual and oculomotor functions of monkey substantia nigra pars reticulata: II. Visual responses related to fixation of gaze. *Journal of Neurophysiology*, **49**(5), 1254–1267.

Hyona, J., and Bertram, R. (2004). Do frequency characteristics of non-fixated words influence the processing of non-fixated words during reading? *European Journal of Cognitive Psychology*, **16**, 104–127.

Inhoff, A. W. (1987). Parafoveal word perception during eye fixations in reading: Effects of visual salience and word structure. In: M. Coltheart (ed.) *Attention and performance 12*. London: Erlbaum, pp. 403–420.

Inhoff, A. W., Radach, R., Eiter, B., and Juhasz, B. (2003). Parafoveal processing: Distinct subsystems for spatial and linguistic information. *Quarterly Journal of Experimental Psychology: Human Experimental Psychology*, **56A**, 803–827.

Just, M. A., and Carpenter, P. A. (1980). A theory of reading: From eye fixations to comprehension. *Psychological Review*, **87**(4), 329–354.

Kerr, W. K. (1992). Eye movement control during reading: The selection of where to send the eyes. (Doctoral dissertation, University of Illinois at Urbana-Champaign 1992). *Dissertation Abstracts International* (UMI No. AAT 9305577)

Levy-Schoen, A. (1981). Flexible and/or rigid control of oculomotor scanning behavior. In: D. F. Fisher, R. A. Monty and J. W. Senders (ed.). *Eye movements: Cognition and visual perception*. Hillsdale, NY: Erlbaum, pp. 299–314.

McConkie, G.W., and Dyre, B.P. (2000). Eye fixation durations in reading: Models of frequency distributions. In A. Kennedy, D. Heller, and J. Pynte (eds.) *Reading as a perceptual process*. Oxford: Elsevier, pp. 683–700.

McConkie, G. W., and Yang, S.-N. (2003). How cognition affects eye movements during reading. In: J. Hyönä, R. Radach, and H. Deubel (ed.). *The mind's eye: Cognitive and applied aspects of eye movement research* . Oxford: Elsevier, pp. 413–427.

McConkie, G. W., Underwood, N. R., Zola, D., and Wolverton, G. S. (1985). Some temporal characteristics of processing during reading. *Journal of Experimental Psychology: Human Perception and Performance*, **11**, 168–186.

McConkie, G. W., Kerr, P. W., Reddix, M. D., and Zola, D. (1988). Eye movement control during reading: I. The locations of initial eye fixations in words. *Vision Research*, **28**(10), 1107–1118.

McConkie, G. W., Kerr, P. W., Reddix, M. D., Zola, D., and Jacobs, A. M. (1989). Eye movement control during reading: II. Frequency of refixating a word. *Perception and Psychophysics*, **46**(3), 245–253.

McConkie, G. W., Reddix, M. R., and Zola, D. (1992). Perception and cognition in reading: Where is the meeting point? In: K. Rayner (ed.) *Eye movement and visual cognition*. New York: Springer-Verlag, pp. 293–303.

Morrison, R. E. (1984). Manipulation of stimulus onset delay in reading: Evidence for parallel programming of saccades. *Journal of Experimental Psychology: Human Perception and Performance*, **10**(5), 667–682.

Munoz, D. P., and Wurtz, R. H. (1995). Saccade-related activity in monkey superior colliculus: I. Characteristics of burst and buildup cells. *Journal of Neurophysiology*, **73**(6), 2313–2333.

O'Regan, J. K. (1981). The 'convenient viewing position hypothesis'. In: D. F. Fisher, R. A. Monty and J. W. Senders (ed.) *Eye movements: Cognition and visual perception.* Hillsdale, NJ: Erlbaum, pp. 289–298.

O'Regan, J. K. (1989). Visual acuity, lexical structure, and eye movements in word recognition. In: B. G. Elsendoorn and H. Bouma (ed.) *Working models of human perception.* London: Academic Press, pp. 261–292.

O'Regan, J. K., and Levy-Shoen, A. (1987). Eye-movement strategy and tactics in word recognition and reading. In: M. Coltheart (ed.) *Attention and performance 12: The psychology of reading.* Hove: Erlbaum, pp. 363–383.

O'Regan, J. K., Levy-Schoen, A., Pynte, J., and Brugaillere, B. (1984). Convenient fixation location within isolated words of different length and structure. *Journal of Experimental Psychology: Human Perception and Performance,* **10,** 250–257.

Pynte, J., Kennedy, A., and Ducrot, S. (2004). The influence of parafoveal typographical errors on eye movements in reading. *European Journal of Cognitive Psychology,* **16,** 178–202.

Rayner, K. (1975). The perceptual span and peripheral cues in reading. *Cognitive Psychology,* **7,** 65–81.

Rayner, K. (1998). Eye movements in reading and information processing: 20 years of research. *Psychological Bulletin,* **128**(3), 372–422.

Rayner, K., and Fischer, M. H. (1996). Mindless reading revisited: Eye movements during reading and scanning are different. *Perception and Psychophysics,* **58**(5), 734–747.

Rayner, K., and Pollatsek, A. (1989). *The psychology of reading.* Englewood Cliffs, NJ: Prentice-Hall.

Rayner, K., Balota, D.A., and Pollatsek, A. (1986). Against parafoveal semantic preprocessing during eye fixations in reading. *Canadian Journal of Psychology,* **40,** 473–483.

Reichle, E. D., Pollatsek, A., Fisher, D. L., and Rayner, K. (1998). Toward a model of eye movement control in reading. *Psychological Review,* **105**(1), 125–157.

Reichle, E. D., Rayner, K., and Pollatsek, A. (1999). Eye movement control in reading: Accounting for initial fixation locations and refixations within the E-Z Reader model. *Vision Research,* **39**(26), 4403–4411.

Reichle, E. D., Rayner, K., and Pollatsek, A. (2003). The E-Z Reader model of eye movement control in reading: comparisons to other models. *Behavioral and Brain Sciences,* **26,** 445–526.

Reilly, R. G. and Radach, R. (2003). Foundations of an interactive activation model of eye movement control in reading. In: J. Hyönä, R. Radach, and H. Deubel (ed.) *The mind's eye: Cognitive and applied aspects of eye movement research.* Oxford: Elsevier, pp. 429–455.

Vitu, F., and McConkie, G. W. (2000). Regressive saccades and word perception in adult reading. In: Kennedy, A., Radach, R., Heller, D. and Pynte, J. (ed.) *Reading as a perceptual process.* Oxford: Elsevier, pp. 301–326.

Vitu, F., O'Regan, J. K., and Mittau, M. (1990). Optimal landing position in reading isolated words and continuous text. *Perception and Psychophysics,* **47**(6), 583–600.

Vitu, F., O'Regan, J. K., Inhoff, A. W., and Topolski, R. (1995). Mindless reading: Eye movement characteristics are similar in scanning strings and reading texts. *Perception and Psychophysics,* **57,** 352–364.

Vitu, F., McConkie, G. W., Kerr, P. W., and O'Regan, K. (2002). About the determinants of fixation times in reading: A possible influence of perceptuo-oculomotor strategies. *Vision Research,* **41,** 3513–3533.

Vitu, F., Kapoula, Z., Lancelin, D., and Lavigne, F. (2004). Eye movements in reading isolated words: Evidence for strong biases towards the center of the screen. *Vision Research*, **44**(3), 321–338.

Yang, S.-N., and McConkie, G. W. (2001). Eye movements during reading: a theory of saccade initiation times. *Vision Research*, **41**, 3567–3585.

Yang, S.-N., and McConkie, G. W. (2004). Saccade generation during reading: Are words necessary? *European Journal of Cognitive Psychology*, **16**(1/2), 226–261.

6

Eye movement control in reading and the E-Z Reader model

Keith Rayner, Erik D. Reichle and Alexander Pollatsek

Abstract

In this chapter, we first review the important empirical facts about eye-movement control in reading. In this first section of the chapter, we briefly describe the basic characteristics of eye movements during reading and then discuss the issue of the perceptual span (or span of effective vision). We then discuss relevant data concerning the issue of where to look next in reading, followed by the data on when to move the eyes. After discussing these two important eye-movement decisions, we discuss the issues of refixations and of word skipping (which both involve *where* and *when* decision components). Two controversial issues, one related to fixation durations prior to word skipping and one related to so-called *parafoveal-on-foveal* effects, are also discussed. In the remainder of the chapter, we describe the details of the E-Z Reader model and some of the controversies it has generated. We end by discussing some recent simulations dealing with preview effects.

Introduction

A few years ago, we (Rayner *et al.* 1998; Reichle *et al.* 1998) introduced a formal computational model of eye-movement control in reading, the E-Z Reader model, which has been rather influential in the field. The model makes clear predictions and has generated a considerable amount of further research and interest. These are the standards by which models are typically judged, so via these criteria the model has been quite successful. In reality, the 1998 model was more like a family of models. In the Reichle *et al.* article (1998), we developed five successive versions of the model, with each instantiation providing a better description of reading behavior while maintaining a very good fit of the observed data. With each subsequent version of the model (see Pollatsek *et al.* 2003; Rayner *et al.* 2004a; Reichle *et al.* 1999, 2003), we have striven to account for a wider range of data while still maintaining the overall psychological plausibility of the model.

One consequence of the development of the E-Z Reader model is that other models have been proposed as competitors to account for the same basic facts about reading. We have compared and contrasted these various models with the E-Z Reader model elsewhere (see Reichle *et al.* 2003), and we will briefly mention some of the competitors later in this chapter. The important point about these models is that they represent implemented simulations of eye movements in reading and as such they tend to be more precise than the class of models that preceded them.

Prior to the development of the E-Z Reader model, two general categories of model had been proposed. These were (a) *oculomotor* models, of which O'Regan's *strategy-tactics* model (1990, 1992) was the prototypical example, and (b) *cognitive/linguistic processing* models, of which Just and Carpenter's *Reader* model (1980) and Morrison's *attention shift* (1984) model were prime examples. Advocates of the former type of model maintained that eye movements are mainly controlled by oculomotor factors and are only indirectly related to ongoing language processing; advocates of the latter type of model maintained that lexical processing or ongoing comprehension processes play a major role in influencing eye movements. Importantly, the models in both classes were primarily qualitative verbal descriptions and not quantitative implemented models (though the Just and Carpenter (1980) model was an implemented model).

As we suggested above, the virtue of implemented models is that much greater precision is obtained than with verbal descriptive models. It is interesting then in this context that many of the implemented models have a linguistic processing component.[1] Indeed, some oculomotor models do survive (see Yang and McConkie 2004) but either they are not implemented or it is questionable if the actual implementations coincide with plausible time parameters. In the remainder of this chapter, we will first briefly review the important empirical facts about eye-movement control in reading, for which a model must account. We will then describe the E-Z Reader model and some of the controversies it has generated.

Empirical data

Understanding how eye movements are controlled in reading is central to developing an overall model of skilled reading (Rayner and Pollatsek 1989). Thus, it is not at all

---

[1] According to two of the more recently implemented models (SWIFT: Engbert *et al.* 2002; and Glenmore: Reilly and Radach, 2003), the decision about *where* to move the eyes is determined by ongoing lexical processing, whereas the decision about *when* to move the eyes is largely determined by a saccade generator that automatically moves the eyes at a fixed pace through the text. Although lexical processing can inhibit this saccade generator so as to increase fixation durations on difficult-to-process words, this inhibition happens very infrequently (e.g. in SWIFT, this happens on fewer than 15 per cent of the fixations on low-frequency words). Thus, although lexical processing plays a bigger role in these models than it does in pure oculomotor models, such as Yang and McConkie's (2004) Push-Pull model, lexical processing in these models plays only a minor role is deciding when to move the eyes.

surprising that there has been considerable research interest in this issue. Twenty-five years ago, there was much discussion over whether or not eye movements were controlled on a moment-to-moment basis (Bouma and deVoogd 1974; Hochberg 1975; O'Regan 1979; Rayner and McConkie 1976; Rayner and Pollatsek 1981). The general consensus that emerged from this early debate is that the decision about where to look next (fixation location) and when to move the eyes (fixation duration) are somewhat independent and influenced by different factors. A recent edited volume (Radach *et al.* 2004) provides a good overview of current views on many issues related to eye movements in reading (see also Rayner 1998).

In the present chapter, we will first briefly describe the basic characteristics of eye movements during reading and then we will discuss the issue of the perceptual span (or span of effective vision). We will then review relevant data concerning the issue of *where* to look next in reading, followed by the data on *when* to move the eyes. After discussing these two important eye-movement decisions, we will turn to the issue of refixations (which involves both *where* and *when* decision components). Finally, we will discuss the issue of word skipping (which also involves *where* and *when* decisions) and two controversial issues; one related to fixation durations prior to word skipping and one related to so-called *parafoveal-on-foveal* effects. After reviewing the data on these issues, we will provide an overview of the E-Z Reader model.

Eye movements in reading

Contrary to our subjective impressions, our eyes do not move smoothly across a line of text during reading. Rather, we make a series of short and rapid movements (saccades) that typically move the eyes forward about 6–9 character spaces. Because the distribution of saccade sizes, measured in number of character spaces, is pretty much independent of visual angle when the number of characters is held constant (Morrison and Rayner 1981), virtually all studies of reading use number of character spaces as the appropriate metric. The actual saccades typically take 20–50 ms to complete (depending on the size of the movement), and virtually no visual information is extracted during the saccade (Ishida and Ikeda 1989; Wolverton and Zola 1983). Between the saccades, the eyes remain relatively stationary for about 200–250 ms (these stationary periods are termed *fixations*). Because information is only extracted during these fixations, reading is similar to a slide show in which short segments of text are displayed for about a quarter of a second. However, it is important to note that there is considerable variability in the length of these fixations and the length of the saccades (Rayner 1978, 1998). Thus, some fixations are as short as 50 ms and some are longer than 500 ms. Likewise, some saccades only move the eyes a single character, while others are as large as 15–20 character spaces. However, these very large saccades typically follow regressions (or backwards movements in the text), and place the eyes beyond the point in the text from which the regression was launched.

Because of issues related to refixations (when readers make a second or third fixation on a word prior to moving to another word) and word skipping (when readers do not make a fixation on a word), both of which are discussed below, the most common eye-movement measures used to assess moment-to-moment processing are *first fixation duration, single fixation duration,* and *gaze duration*. First fixation duration is the mean duration of the first fixation on a word independent of the number of fixations on the word; single fixation duration is the mean fixation time when only a single fixation is made on the word; and gaze duration is the mean of the total fixation time on a word before a saccade is made off of the word. The latter measure is clearly a composite: a function of both the durations of the individual fixations and the number of fixations on a word. All three measures are conditional on the word being fixated on the first pass through the text (see Inhoff and Radach 1998; Liversedge *et al.* 1998; Rayner 1998 for further discussion of these measures).[2]

The perceptual span

One critical issue with respect to eye movements in reading is the question of how much information a reader processes on each fixation. Our phenomenological impression is that we can identify many words on a line of text. In reality, however, the evidence is pretty clear that the perceptual span is limited to a region extending from about 3–4 character spaces to the left of fixation to about 14–15 character spaces to the right of fixation for readers of English (as well as French, German, and other left-to-right alphabetic scripts). The evidence for this conclusion comes from a number of studies, originating with those of McConkie and Rayner (1975), Rayner (1975) and Rayner and Bertera (1979), using the gaze-contingent display change paradigm (wherein changes in the text are made contingent on the reader's eye movements). In particular, the moving window paradigm limits how much useful information is available to a reader on each fixation. Within the perceptual span region, different types of information are obtained, but information useful for identifying a word is restricted to a region extending about 7–8 character spaces to the right of fixation (see Rayner 1998 for a summary of this research).

The results of the research dealing with the perceptual span are important because they demonstrate that virtually all of the relevant processing in reading is going on

---

[2] This description of eye movements has focused entirely on first-pass measures, i.e. those measures used to describe the eye movements of readers who are presumably having no difficulty understanding what they are reading, and hence moving their eyes forward through the text. This is clearly an overly simplistic description of eye movements because approximately 10–15 per cent of the saccades that are executed during normal reading are regressions, i.e. saccades that move the eyes back to parts of the text that have already been read. The majority of these regressions are thought to reflect difficulty with whatever higher-level linguistic processes are necessary for comprehension, although some interword regressions may also stem from saccadic error (e.g. cases where a reader intends to move his or her eyes closer to the beginning of a word, but because of motor error the eyes overshoot their target). We will continue to focus of the first-pass measures in this chapter because our model does not provide an account of higher-level comprehension processes, but instead only describes those processes that guide the eye movements of readers when comprehension is proceeding smoothly. (We believe that our description of these lower-level processes is sufficient to account for most of the eye-movement behavior of skilled readers who are reading text within their reading ability.)

within a restricted region around the fixation point. Numerous experiments (see Rayner 1998) have verified the basic conclusions regarding the size of the perceptual span in English and other orthographic writing systems. Another interesting result is that experiments using the moving window paradigm have demonstrated that the perceptual span for Hebrew text is smaller than for English (because the information is more densely packed in Hebrew than English) and is asymmetric to the left of fixation (Pollatsek *et al.* 1981). Furthermore, experiments with the Japanese (Ikeda and Saida 1978; Osaka 1992) and Chinese (Chen and Tang 1998; Inhoff and Liu 1998) writing systems have demonstrated that the perceptual span is considerably smaller in terms of number of characters for these writing systems than English (because they have ideographic components and are even more densely packed than English).

There are a number of other interesting aspects to the research on the perceptual span that we do not have space here to discuss (see Rayner 1998; Reichle *et al.* 2003 for further discussion). For our discussion of eye guidance in reading, the main point to be gleaned from the various studies dealing with the perceptual span is that eye movements are programmed using information extracted from within a rather restricted region, except for when readers program either long range regressions (see chapter 2) back to earlier parts of a page (which do not occur very often) or when they program a return sweep of the eyes from the end of one line to the beginning of the next.

Where to fixate next

There is relatively widespread agreement among researchers from different theoretical viewpoints that low-level visual information obtained from parafoveal and peripheral vision is the most important factor determining where to fixate next in reading. Specifically, most researchers seem to agree that word boundaries, defined by the spaces surrounding the fixated word and the next word in the text, provide critical cues for guiding eye movements. The major evidence in support of this conclusion is that when low level visual information is not available (e.g. when spaces between words are removed), readers move their eyes a shorter distance (and reading is slowed down) than when this low level information is available (McConkie and Rayner 1975; Morris *et al.* 1990; Pollatsek and Rayner 1982; Rayner and Bertera 1979; Rayner and Pollatsek 1981; Rayner *et al.* 1998). Basically, the evidence suggests that when space information is not available, word recognition and eye guidance are both disrupted (Rayner *et al.* 1998).

The length of the word to the right of fixation has also been shown to have a large influence on how far the eyes move in the next saccade. When the next word is longer, the eyes tend to go further than when the next word is shorter (Blanchard *et al.* 1989; O'Regan 1979, 1980, 1981; Rayner 1979). However, it is not quite that simple because the issue of word skipping comes into play (see the section below). That is, if the next word is very short, the eyes will typically skip that word (leading to a somewhat longer saccade).

Another important finding is that there is a somewhat systematic landing position effect regarding where the eyes first fixate on a word. That is, the first fixation on a word tends to be about halfway between the beginning and middle of a word across a fairly wide range of word lengths (Dunn-Rankin 1978; McConkie *et al.* 1988; O'Regan 1981; Radach and Kempe 1993; Rayner 1979; Rayner and Fischer 1996; Rayner *et al.* 1996, 1998; Vitu *et al.* 1990, 1996). This finding is true not only for English, French, and German words which are printed (and read) from left to right, but also for Hebrew words (Deutsch and Rayner 1999) which are printed and read from right to left. Rayner (1979) called this prototypical location the *preferred viewing location*. It should be noted, however, that the preferred viewing location is a mean, and there is considerable variability in the initial landing position. Thus, the histograms of initial landing positions tend to look like truncated Gaussian distributions; moreover, readers fixate on the spaces between words about 10 per cent of the time (Rayner *et al.* 1998).

There has been much discussion in the literature regarding the difference between the preferred viewing location and the optimal viewing position (O'Regan and Lévy-Schoen 1987), which is the center of a word. There has been considerable research on what happens when the initial fixation is not at the optimal viewing position, but this work has primarily dealt with words in isolation. The main conclusion drawn from this work is that when readers initially land away from the center of a word in reading, they are more likely to make a refixation on the word than if they land near the middle of the word (see Rayner 1998; Rayner *et al.* 1998 for further discussion). Since refixations on a word (i.e. making another fixation on a word before moving to the next word) represent a special case of the decision regarding where to fixate next (which is related to the decision about when to move off of the fixated word), we will discuss refixations separately below.

Although the landing position effect is quite robust, an important additional factor in where the eyes land is the launch site effect. McConkie *et al.* (1988) made a detailed analysis of a large corpus of data (see also Radach and Kempe 1993; Rayner *et al.* 1996) which indicated that the further the launch site (i.e. the location of the prior fixation) was from the center of the next word to be fixated, the further to the left the mean landing position was (and the more variability there was in the landing position). Thus, the finding that the first fixation is typically between the beginning and the middle of the word is an average of the data from different launch sites, each of which has a somewhat different pattern (see Fig. 6.1). In addition, we need to stress that there is considerable inaccuracy in programming saccadic eye movements. As a result, it is often difficult to pinpoint the causes of a particular eye movement. For example, there are undoubtedly words skipped because the eyes overshot their target; this would most commonly occur for short words (Blanchard *et al.* 1989; Rayner 1979; Vitu *et al.* 1995). Likewise, there are undoubtedly words that do not receive a direct fixation because the eyes undershoot the target; this would also result in refixations on some words, particularly long words (Hyönä and Pollatsek 1998; Rayner and Morris 1992), where the next word was really the intended location of the fixation (and the word that was actually being processed).

Later in this chapter, we will document that decisions about whether or not to skip a word or to refixate a word are clearly influenced by cognitive factors. In contrast, the initial fixation location appears to be primarily influenced by a low-level oculomotor strategy – fixate the center of the word – though, as discussed above, there is systematic and random error in carrying out the motor program. Moreover, there is little

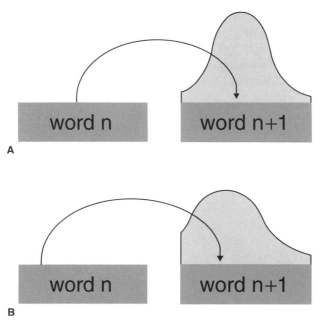

Figure 6.1 The effects of saccade length on the landing site distribution. Panel A shows a landing site distribution that follows an average size saccade from word *n* to word *n+1*. Panel B shows a landing site distribution which results from a long saccade.

evidence that cognitive variables influence where on a word the eyes land. One question is whether contextual constraint influences where the eyes fixate on a word. Even though predictability has a clear effect on word skipping (as will be documented below), it has very little effect on the actual landing site in the word when it is fixated (Rayner *et al.* 2001; Vonk *et al.* 2000). A second question is whether semantic information influences the initial landing position on a word. Several studies attempted to get at this issue by using long target words (10 letters or more) and varying whether the beginning or the end of the word was informative (i.e. the word part is infrequent in the language) or redundant (i.e. the word part is frequent). A number of these studies initially suggested that the eyes move farther into a word when the informative portion is located at the end rather than the beginning of the word (Everatt and Underwood 1992; Hyönä *et al.* 1989; Underwood *et al.* 1988, 1990). However, neither Rayner and Morris (1992) nor Hyönä (1995) replicated the effect. Both of these latter studies (along with all of the original studies) found that if the beginning of the word was redundant, readers quickly moved to the informative part of the word. However, there was no evidence that readers moved further into words when the informative information was at the end of the word. Given that the effect was either small or inconsistent in the original studies, it seems most appropriate to conclude that informativeness did not influence the initial fixation location. Furthermore, Hyönä and Pollatsek (1998) found that the length of the first constituent of a two-constituent

Finnish compound word (with the length of the word held constant) had no effect on the position of the initial fixation on the word. However, there is now fairly clear evidence that orthographic information (particularly the beginning letters of a word) does influence the initial landing position (Beauvillain *et al.* 1996; Hyönä 1995; Radach *et al.* 2004; White and Liversedge 2004).

When to move the eyes

The question of what determines *when* readers move their eyes in reading is central to the distinction between different models of eye-movement control. The early oculo-motor models assumed that cognitive operations are relatively slow and thus unlikely to play a major role in deciding when the eyes move. However, there is now so much evidence that various cognitive/lexical variables influence when the eyes move that the most successful implemented models of eye-movement control incorporate the assumption that the ease or difficulty associated with processing a fixated word influences when the eyes move away from that word.

A paradigm that has been used to address the issue of how long it takes to encode visual information involves either masking the text or making the text disappear at different intervals during reading (Ishida and Ikeda 1989; Liversedge *et al.* 2004; Rayner *et al.* 1981, 2003a; Slowiaczek and Rayner 1987). These studies have demonstrated that if text is exposed for 50–60 ms on each fixation before being masked (or before the fixated word disappears) that reading proceeds quite normally. If the mask appears earlier, reading is disrupted. As it is extremely unlikely that words are fully identified within the first 50–60 ms of a fixation, this finding means that sufficient visual information can be extracted during the first 50–60 ms of a fixation so that cognitive operations can proceed normally even when the visual information is removed after that.

The studies discussed above indicate that the completion of the early stages of visual processing is quite rapid. There is another reason to think that full word identification may be completed fairly rapidly after a word is initially fixated: word identification typically begins before a word is fixated. This phenomenon is called *preview benefit* and it has usually been assessed by examining the fixation time on a word. The typical finding is that processing time is sped up by 20–50 ms by seeing a preview of the word before it is fixated (Balota *et al.* 1985; Binder *et al.* 1999; Rayner *et al.* 1982). Moreover, a preview of a word that is either orthographically similar (Balota *et al.* 1985; Rayner *et al.* 1980) or phonologically identical (Pollatsek *et al.* 1992; Miellet and Sparrow 2004) to the target word also produces preview benefit. These latter findings suggest that preview benefit is not merely due to full processing of the parafoveal word prior to fixating it. Rather, the results suggest that preview benefit is largely due to some sort of integration of the processing of the word prior to fixating it (in parafoveal vision) combined with processing of the word when it is later fixated (in foveal vision).

These data clearly indicate that the cognitive operations in reading are fast enough to guide the decision of when to move the eyes. They are part of a large body of evidence collected over the past 25 years that has demonstrated that a number of lexical, syntactic, and discourse factors influence fixation times on words (see Rayner 1998 for a review).

Specifically, there is now clear evidence that word frequency (Inhoff and Rayner 1986; Rayner and Duffy 1986; Rayner *et al.* 1996, 2004a; Schilling *et al.* 1998), word predictability (Balota *et al.* 1985; Ehrlich and Rayner 1981; Rayner *et al.* 2004a; Rayner and Well 1996), age of acquisition (Juhasz and Rayner 2003, 2005), and various other variables influence fixation time on a word (see Rayner 1998 for a complete listing).

Thus, the conclusion that linguistic variables are very much involved in the decision to move the eyes seems beyond controversy at this point. Nevertheless, there are still assertions that low-level oculomotor effects are important determinants of fixation time on a word. The most recent striking example of this claim is that Vitu *et al.* (2001) reported a counter-intuitive inverted v-shaped function dependent on where readers landed in a word. Specifically, they found that single fixations were actually longer on a word when the eyes landed in the middle of the word (near the optimal viewing position) than when they landed on the ends of a word. Exactly what this means is not fully clear. Furthermore, the result is not predicted either by models that account for the *when* component of eye-movement control via cognitive processes or by models in which oculomotor processes are central. And, finally, and perhaps more critically as far as we are concerned, even with the unusual inverted v-shaped function that they obtained, Vitu *et al.* still found frequency effects independent of where the eyes landed (see also Rayner *et al.* 1996).

One recent demonstration of the importance of linguistic influences on fixation times comes from 'disappearing text' experiments (Liversedge *et al.* 2004; Rayner *et al.* 2003a). In these experiments, to which we briefly alluded earlier, the fixated word disappeared 60 ms after the beginning of the first fixation on the target word. Embedded in these experiments was a frequency manipulation such that certain target words were either high- or low-frequency words. The interesting finding from this research is that the frequency effect was identical under normal reading situations and the disappearing text condition. That is, even though the fixated word had disappeared after 60 ms, readers still left their eyes in place longer when the target word was a low-frequency word than when it was a high-frequency word. This is very compelling evidence for lexical factors driving the eyes in reading and it is inconsistent with claims (Yang and McConkie 2001, 2004) that lexical variables only have an effect late in an eye fixation.

At this point, let us make our biases clear. We believe that the bulk of the evidence suggests that variables that are related to lexical processing have the strongest (and most immediate) effects on when the eyes move and which word is fixated. As a result, it seems most parsimonious to us to assume that lexical processing drives the eyes through the text, and only when lexical processing breaks down, as when there are syntactic parsing difficulties, will 'higher-order' language processes intervene in the process of controlling the eyes. Admittedly, these processes will sometimes have an immediate effect, as with some syntactic 'garden path' effects or when a semantically anomalous word is encountered (Rayner *et al.* 2004). However, the effects of these 'higher-order' processes are delayed, such as with plausibility violations that are not as severe as anomaly (Rayner *et al.* 2004b. Thus, in the E-Z Reader model, lexical variables are assumed to drive the eyes through the text (as a first approximation).

In summary, it has been shown that lexical/cognitive variables have definite effects on both the time spent processing a word and the duration of individual fixations.

This indicates that at least some cognitive operations are fast enough to influence the decision of when to move the eyes. Moreover, a parafoveal preview of a target word reduces fixation time on the word. Thus, one factor helping to allow cognitive operations to be fast enough to guide fixations off of a word is that processing for most words starts before they are fixated. There are some data, however, that indicate that lower-level factors, such as the initial landing position, can effect the duration of fixations.

Refixations

Refixations are influenced by both low-level variables and linguistic/cognitive variables. The fact that the location of the initial fixation on a word influences whether or not a refixation will be made (with more refixations the further the eyes are away from the center of the word) stands as clear evidence that low-level factors affect refixations. Conversely, the fact that low-frequency 5–6 letter words are refixated more than high-frequency words that are matched in length (Rayner *et al.* 1996; Rayner *et al.* 2003a) is clear evidence that linguistic processing also affects refixations.

   A more interesting question is whether or not refixations are automatically preprogrammed before the reader fixates on a word. This is of particular interest to us because in the early versions of E-Z Reader the decision to refixate on a long word was assumed to be preprogrammed (i.e. a decision is made to refixate the word when it was fixated). Indeed, there is some evidence (from tasks that are not reading, but which try to mimic the sequence of eye fixations in reading) that such preprogramming of refixations occurs for long words (Vergilino and Beauvillain 2000, 2001; Vergilino-Perez *et al.* 2004). In more recent versions of the model, however, we (Reichle *et al.* 2003) modified our assumptions about automatic refixations. A refixation program is now assumed to be initiated with a probability that increases as the length of the word increases, rather than a refixation being programmed by default upon fixating a given word. As we shall see later, the model correctly predicts that long words are more often the recipients of multiple fixations than short words. It also correctly predicts that there will be more refixations on low-frequency words than on high-frequency words. The reasons for this will become more clear after we discuss the model.

Word skipping

Word skipping (the phenomenon that readers do not fixate on each word in the text) is very interesting because it does not fit in neatly with the convenient when/where dichotomy with respect to eye-movement control (see chapter 3). To be precise, about 30 per cent of the words in text are skipped during reading (Rayner 1998). While word skipping is clearly closer to the question of where to move the eyes, influences of both low-level visual factors and high-level linguistic factors have been shown to affect skipping behavior. One of the most striking findings in word skipping is that short words are skipped more often than long words (Brysbaert and Vitu 1998; Drieghe *et al.* 2004; Rayner 1979; Rayner and McConkie 1976; Vitu *et al.* 1995). However, words that are predictable from the preceding context are skipped more often than words that are not predictable (Altaribba *et al.* 1996; Balota *et al.* 1985; Drieghe *et al.* 2004; Ehrlich and Rayner 1981; Rayner and Well 1996; Rayner *et al.* 2001, 2004a; Schustack *et al.* 1987). Furthermore, high-frequency words are more likely to be skipped than low-frequency words (even when their lengths are matched), especially when the eyes are close to the target word on the preceding fixation (Henderson and Ferreira 1993; Radach and Kempe 1993; Rayner and Fischer 1996; Rayner *et al.* 1996). Thus, it is clear that visual and lexical/linguistic variables both affect whether a word is skipped. But arguably the most convincing piece of evidence that word skipping is not easily placed in the classic when/where dichotomy is (as we noted earlier) that even though predictability has a clear effect on skipping, it has little effect on the actual landing site in the word when it is fixated (Rayner *et al.* 2001; Vonk *et al.* 2000). This clearly indicates that a distinction needs to be made between the mechanisms that determine the saccade target (which word to fixate) and the ones that determine the actual landing site (where to fixate on the word), a distinction we believe should be present in the architecture of any comprehensive model of eye movements in reading (Radach and McConkie 1998).

As predictability and frequency both influence word skipping, it must be the case that some words that are skipped have been identified, at least to a certain extent. It is this processing component that sets word skipping apart from all the other *where* decisions. The extent to which a word that is skipped was processed during the prior fixation remains an issue of some debate in the literature (e.g. Radach and Kennedy 2004; Rayner and Juhasz 2004; Reichle *et al.* 2003). Views on this matter differ rather dramatically. At one extreme, it is claimed that a word is skipped based on an educated guess taking into account only coarse information about the target word (Brysbaert and Vitu 1998; Drieghe *et al.* 2004), and at the other extreme, it is claimed that a word is usually skipped because it was identified in parafoveal vision (e.g. Reichle *et al.* 2003). While a broad consensus exists among researchers in the field on the determinants of the where/when decision, the debate on word skipping continues.

Perhaps the most controversial issue with respect to skipping follows from the prediction of the E-Z Reader model that the fixation duration prior to skipping should be somewhat inflated. Indeed, such inflated fixation durations have been reported in several studies (Drieghe *et al.* 2005; Pollatsek *et al.* 1986; Pynte *et al.* 2004; Rayner *et al.* 2004). However, other studies (generally using corpus analyses) have found it difficult to replicate this finding (Drieghe *et al.* 2004; Engbert *et al.* 2002; Radach and Heller 2000). Recently, Kliegl and Engbert (2005), in an attempt to resolve the controversy between the replications and failures to replicate, reported an extensive study, using a large corpus, where they attempted to control the regions where skipping and non-skipping occurred (and also control the participants) and found that fixations before skipped words were shorter before short or highly-frequent words and longer before long or low-frequency words. However, this issue is complex, as assessing this effect depends on what are essentially correlational analyses. That is, whether or not the reader skips a word is determined by the reader, so that one can never achieve stimulus or participant control over the situations in which readers skip and the situations in which they do not. Furthermore, the likely confounds here (e.g. good readers will skip more and have shorter fixation durations) work against finding an inflated fixation duration prior to skipping. This issue regarding fixations prior to skipping is one of the two main motivations that led to alternative models of eye-movement control, such as the SWIFT model in which words are processed in parallel.

Parafoveal-on-foveal effects

While the dispute about the duration of the fixation prior to skipping constitutes one important reason why some models adopt a parallel view on the time course of foveal and parafoveal processing, the main reason for adopting such a view is probably because of the claim that there are pervasive parafoveal-on-foveal effects, or that parafoveal information obtained from word $n +1$ influences the fixation duration of the currently fixated word. However, there is considerable controversy over the extent to which parafoveal processing on a fixation influences the duration of that fixation. While a model that holds a parallel view on the processing of two adjacent words appears to be harmonious with such a phenomenon, it has been considered to be very damaging to a model such as the E-Z Reader model that, due to its serial nature, apparently cannot explain parafoveal-on-foveal effects. That is, in the E-Z Reader model, it does not seem plausible that the processing of a parafoveal word can influence the fixation time on the foveal word because it is the completion of the processing of the foveal word that (a) enables processing of the parafoveal word to begin and (b) is actually after the signal to move the eyes to the next word (see below). However, this argument assumes that all fixations are accurately guided and that fixation locations are always recorded accurately. In fact, there are data indicating that eye movements, like other motor movements are not always sent to the target location. Thus, the E-Z Reader model (and similar models) would predict that one can get apparent parafoveal-on-foveal effects when an eye movement falls short of the target so that that word $n +1$ was intended to be fixated but word n was fixated instead (McConkie *et al.* 1988).

Moreover, the data on parafoveal-on-foveal effects are somewhat mixed. A number of studies have indicated that the foveal viewing time can be altered by the words presented in the parafovea (e.g. Inhoff *et al.* 2000; Kennedy 2000; Kennedy *et al.* 2002, 2004; Schroyens *et al.* 1999; Starr and Inhoff 2004; Underwood *et al.* 2000; Vitu *et al.* 2004), but the strength of the argument is weakened by methodological problems associated with some of these studies, as well as failures to obtain consistent effects across experiments (Hyönä and Bertram 2004). The finding that does seem to be fairly consistent is that an unusual beginning of the word $n +1$ can result in longer fixations on word n (Inhoff *et al.* 2000; Underwood *et al.* 2000). However, it is far less clear whether the meaning of word $n +1$ influences the fixation time on word n (for a review see Rayner *et al.* 2003b). In a recent study, Kennedy and Pynte (2005) used a large corpus of eye-movement data and claimed to find further evidence of the meaning of the word to the right of fixation influencing the current fixation (particularly when word $n+1$ was a short word). However, there are problems with corpus analyses in that there is no control over how difficult the text was in the region from which the two consecutive words were drawn. Furthermore, as we just noted, there is good reason to think that some of these effects are due to target mislocation or undershoots in reading (Rayner *et al.* 2004b).

The E-Z Reader model

E-Z Reader is a model of eye-movement control during reading. As such, it provides a quantitative account of some of the most important cognitive and non-cognitive processes that determine when and where a reader's eyes will move while reading text. The earliest version of the model (Rayner *et al.* 1998) was described in the precursor to the present volume on eye guidance (Underwood 1998). Since then, we have continued to refine the model (Pollatsek *et al.* 2003; Reichle *et al.* 1999, 2003), changing specific details about the model and adding complexity as it became necessary to make the model more plausible or account for additional phenomena outside of the scope of the original model (Rayner *et al.* 1998; Reichle *et al.* 1998). Given this, it seems appropriate that the current volume on eye guidance should introduce the latest version of the model – E-Z Reader 8 (see also Pollatsek *et al.* 2005). We believe that this version of our model is a significant advancement over its predecessors and we will provide reasons for this assertion in this chapter.

E-Z Reader 8, like both its predecessors and other cognitive-control models, shares the assumption that word identification is the 'engine' that drives the eyes forward during reading.[3] It also retains two other assumptions that were central to all previous versions of our model: (a) that attention is allocated serially, one word at a time; and (b) that the signal to shift attention is decoupled from the initiating of saccadic programming. Figure 6.2 indicates how word identification, attention, and the oculomotor system are coordinated in the E-Z Reader model to guide the eyes during reading.

Word identification is assumed to be completed in three stages. The first is a pre-attentive stage of visual processing (labeled 'V' in Fig. 6.2): Visual information on the printed page is propagated from the retina to those areas of the brain that mediate vision, lexical processing, and oculomotor control. This stage is pre-attentive because the visual features that define a given word are not bound into a single unified representation (Wolfe 1994; Wolfe and Bennett 1996). The low-spatial frequency information that is available from this stage of processing is also useful in that it demarcates word boundaries and therefore can be used to identify the targets of upcoming saccades – the centers (i.e. optimal viewing positions) of words. The high-spatial frequency information is used in subsequent lexical processing. In our model, the subsequent stages of lexical processing are dependent upon attention, so that a small portion of the visual field is selected for further (lexical) processing. (Our conceptualization for how this might happen is discussed below.)

In the most recent version of our model (Reichle *et al.* 2003), we had assumed that pre-attentive processing required 90 ms to complete, but that the rate of this processing was modulated by visual acuity so that the processing of words that are far from

---

[3] In Underwood's (1998) first volume on eye guidance, we devoted a considerable portion of our chapter reviewing the different models of eye-movement control. For the sake of brevity we will not provide such a review in this chapter. For such a recent review of models of eye-movement control during reading, see Reichle *et al.* (2003).

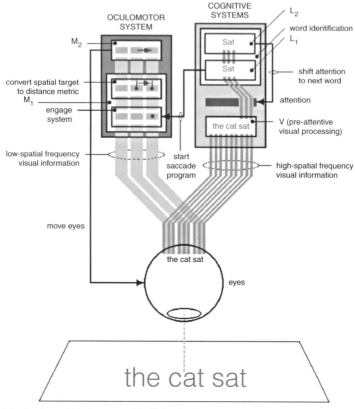

Figure 6.2 A schematic diagram of E-Z Reader 8.

the fovea takes longer than the processing of words in the fovea. Unfortunately, both of these assumptions are probably wrong. There is a considerable amount of evidence that our previous estimate of the 'eye-to-mind' lag was too conservative, and that the effects of retinal stimulation can be detected in the visual cortex in as little as 45–55 ms post-stimulus onset (Clarke *et al.* 1995; Foxe and Simpson 2002; Mouchetant-Rostaing *et al.* 2000; Van Rullen and Thorpe 2001). There is also evidence suggesting that, although lexical processing may be slower and less accurate in peripheral vision, the rate of visual processing per se does not decrease with visual acuity (Lee *et al.* 2003; Rayner and Morrison 1981). These results led us to shorten our model's pre-attentive stage to 50 ms and to reject the assumption that the rate of pre-attentive processing is affected by visual acuity. (We instead reverted to the assumption used in earlier versions of our model that visual acuity modulates the rate of lexical processing; see Equation 2, below).

As already mentioned, a subset of the available pre-attentive visual information is selected for further lexical processing via attention. In our model, attention is allocated to one word at a time. This assumption is important because it minimizes any potential 'cross-talk' between the orthographic, phonological, and semantic codes of adjacent words (making it easier to identify the words) and because it allows the reader to maintain the order of the words (which is an important source of syntactic information in languages like English; Pollatsek and Rayner 1999). This assumption also provides a clear point of contrast between our model and several alternative models in which attention is allocated across a spatial gradient or 'window,' allowing several words to be processed in parallel (e.g. *Glenmore:* Reilly and Radach 2003; *Mr. Chips:* Legge *et al.* 1997, 2002; *SWIFT:* Engbert *et al.* 2002; Kliegl and Engbert 2003). We suspect that whether attention is allocated serially or in parallel during reading is an important issue that modeling will help to decide.

Turning now to the latter stages of word identification, Fig. 6.2 shows that lexical processing in E-Z Reader is completed in two successive stages: The first (labeled 'L_1' in Fig. 6.2) causes the oculomotor system to begin programming a saccade to move the eyes to the next word, whereas the second (labeled 'L_2') causes attention to shift to the next word. (Some portion of the time that is allotted to L_2 in the model probably includes the time that is necessary to disengage attention from one word and shift it to the next.) The programming of eye movements is thus de-coupled from the shifting of attention. It is also important to point out that L_1 and L_2 also correspond to functionally distinct stages of word identification. As we have noted elsewhere (Rayner *et al.* 2003c), the distinction between L_1 and L_2 can be conceptualized in at least two different ways, and at this point we prefer to remain agnostic about which of these conceptualizations is correct. By one interpretation, L_1 may correspond to a rapidly available sense of a word's overall familiarity, while L_2 corresponds to lexical access. This view is suggested in our earlier papers (Rayner *et al.* 1998; Reichle *et al.* 1998, 1999), where we referred to L_1 as being the 'familiarity check' and L_2 as being the 'completion of lexical access'. (For an example of how this could be implemented in a model of word identification, see Reichle and Perfetti 2003.) By an alternative interpretation, L_1 may correspond to the processing of a word's orthography and/or phonology, while L_2 corresponds to the processing of its meaning. Of course, these two interpretations of the L_1 vs. L_2 distinction are neither mutually exclusive nor exhaustive. For example, a rapidly available sense of word familiarity may be more heavily weighted by word-form information than meaning.[4] Our decision to adopt the neutral L_1 and L_2 nomenclature reflects our belief that that the L_1 vs. L_2 distinction is open to interpretation. Although many details of the L_1 vs. L_2 distinction are admittedly underspecified, the fact that L_1 and L_2 play functionally distinct roles means that they may be influenced by different variables (e.g. see Hanes and McCollum 2003; Raney 2003; Reingold 2003). Future research may take advantage of this fact to rule out various interpretations of L_1 and L_2.

---

[4] Another interpretation is that L_1 and L_2 distinction corresponds to passing two discrete thresholds in one continuous word-identification process. This interpretation is seems less harmonious with the spirit of the model because L_1 and L_2 play different functional roles in the model and are affected by different variables, e.g. visual acuity affects L_1, but not L_2.

The time that is required to identify a word in E-Z Reader is a function of the word's frequency of occurrence in printed text[5] and its predictability within a given sentence (as determined by separate cloze-task experiments). In earlier versions of our model, word frequency and predictability were combined in a multiplicative fashion to give the mean times needed to complete L_1 and L_2 on a word. Unfortunately, this assumption also proved to be incorrect; a recent experiment by Rayner *et al.* (2004a) orthogonally manipulated the frequency and predictability of targets words and found that these variables contributed additively to the fixation durations on these words. This result forced us to modify our model. Thus, in E-Z Reader 8, the time that is necessary to complete L_1 on the word that is being processed (i.e. word *n*) is given by Equation 1.

$$(1) \quad L_1 \begin{cases} 0 & \text{if } p \leq \text{pred}_n \\ L_1 = \alpha_1 - [\alpha_2 \ln(\text{freq}_n)] - (\alpha_3 \text{pred}_n) & \text{if } p > \text{pred}_n \end{cases}$$

Equation 1 can be interpreted as follows: upon shifting attention to word *n*, there is a probability (p) equal to a word *n*'s predictability (pred_n), that the reader will not use whatever bottom-up information about the word would otherwise be available after completing L_1, and will instead use whatever top-down information is available about the word from its context (i.e. its predictability) to immediately begin L_2. In these cases, L_1 is equal to 0 ms (as given by the top part of Equation 1). This assumption is consistent with the finding that readers sometimes skip words under conditions where they are not visible (e.g. a one-word moving window) but highly constrained by their context (Rayner *et al.* 1982).[6] Because word *n* is usually unpredictable, however, the reader usually uses the information about the word that is available from L_1. The time that is required for this information to become available is given by the bottom part of Equation 1, and is the sum of: (1) a maximum amount of time, α_1 (= 136 ms), that is needed to process completely unpredictable words of minimal frequency; (2) an amount by which this maximal time is reduced that is a function of the natural logarithm of word *n*'s frequency (freq_n) weighted by α_2 (= 3 ms); and (3) some amount by which the maximal time is reduced by word *n*'s predictability weighted by α_3 (= 20 ms). Although Equation 1 gives the mean time to complete L_1 for word *n*, the actual time that is needed to complete L_1 for a given encounter with the word, $t(L_1)$, is a random deviate that is sampled from a gamma distribution[7] with $\mu = L_1$ and $\sigma = 0.18\mu$.

---

[5] We have used the Francis and Kučera (1982) values in our modeling because they were handy. However, there may be better norms (e.g. CELEX) that may improve the performance of the model.

[6] The assumption that this takes 0 ms is roughly consistent with a model in which the computation involving the top-down information takes little time and occurs in parallel with lexical processing. It is probably an over simplification that this takes no additional time and that the time is independent of the predictability value, but we wanted to minimize the number of parameters.

As we have previously mentioned, several recent findings forced us to abandon the assumption that visual acuity modulates the pre-attentive stage of visual processing. We instead assume that decreasing visual acuity attenuates the rate at which L_1 completes by positing that increasing the distance from the fixation point increases the duration of L_1, and this assumption is formalized by Equation 2. Here, the duration of $t(L_1)$ (i.e. the random deviate that is sampled from the gamma distribution with a mean given by Equation 1) is modulated by visual acuity, resulting in $t(L_1)'$. The amount by which $t(L_1)$ increases is a exponential function of the mean distance (i.e. the mean number of character spaces) between each of the letters in word n and the center of the fixation location (i.e. the fovea). In Equation 2, ε (= 1.09) is a free parameter that modulates the effect of visual acuity, and N is the number of letters in word n. The duration of $t(L_1)'$ thus increases as both the length of the word n increases and as the distance between the center of word n and the fovea increases. The value of ε that was used in the simulations below is sufficient to slow L_1 by factors of 1.09, 1.19, and 1.30 when 3-, 5-, and 7-letter words (respectively) are viewed from their first letter positions.

$$(2) \quad t(L_1)' = t(L_1)\varepsilon^{\left(\left|\Sigma \text{ letter} - \text{fixation}\right|/N\right)}$$

The mean time to complete the last stage of word identification, L_2, is determined using Equation 3, where the value of L_1 is that given by the bottom part of Equation 1 (i.e. the non-zero value of L_1, prior to sampling a random deviate from a gamma distribution *and* prior to the value of this deviate being modulated by visual acuity). As with L_1, the actual time needed to complete L_2 on a given word is a random deviate sampled from a gamma distribution with $\mu = L_2$ and $\sigma = 0.18\ \mu$. Note that L_2 is a fixed proportion of L_1 (as determined by the free parameter $\Delta = 0.5$). One implication of this is that the amount of time between when L_1 completes and when L_2 subsequently completes increases as word n becomes more difficult to process. Because saccadic programming is initiated by the completion of L_1, and because the time needed to complete a saccadic program is (on average) constant, the amount of time between when L_2 completes on word n (causing attention to shift to word $n+1$) and when the eyes move from word n to word $n+1$ decreases as the processing difficulty of word n increases. This is significant because the model predicts that the amount of parafoveal processing of word $n+1$ that is completed while word n is fixated will decrease as the processing difficulty of word n increases. Consequently, the model predicts less preview benefit from difficult-to-process words, which is consistent with empirical results (Henderson and Ferreira 1990; Inhoff *et al.* 1989; Kennison and Clifton 1995; White *et al.* 2005). This also causes the model to predicts a 'spillover'

---

[7] We introduced stochasticity into our simulations by setting the durations of L_1 (and the durations of several other processes in our model) equal to values that were sampled from gamma distributions. Gamma distributions are a family of positively skewed distributions having variances that are positively correlated to their means. Our decision to use them was based on the fact that the durations of motor processes tend to be distributed like gamma distributions.

effect on word $n + 1$ because, if word n is difficult to process, then there will be less parafoveal processing of word $n + 1$, which will consequently lengthen the duration of the subsequent fixation on word $n + 1$. Such spillover effects have also been reported in the literature (Rayner and Duffy 1986). Also note that, because L_2 is *not* a function of visual acuity, $t(L_2)$ is *not* affected by retinal eccentricity. This is consistent with the assumption that the visual processing is largely finished in L_1 and that L_2 processing is on a more abstract representation of the information.

$$(3) \quad L_2 = \Delta L_1$$

Our assumptions regarding the programming and execution of saccades are based on the research of Becker and Jürgens (1979; see also Leff *et al.* 2001; McPeek *et al.* 2000; Mokler and Fischer 1999; Vergilino and Beauvillain 2000) suggesting that saccades are programmed in two successive stages: an initial, labile stage of programming (M_1) that can be canceled by a subsequent saccadic program, followed by a non-labile stage (M_2) that is not subject to cancellation. As Fig. 6.2 indicates, M_1 is divided into two sub-stages, each of which takes exactly half of the total M_1 duration to complete. During the first of these sub-stages, the oculomotor system is 'engaged' to move the eyes to a new spatial location. When a labile program is canceled by a subsequent program, whatever portion of the first sub-stage happens to have been completed is 'saved' and is applied to the time of the first sub-stage of the subsequent program (i.e. the time needed to ready the oculomotor system). The second stage then converts the spatial target into a distance metric so that the amount of muscle force that is necessary to move the eyes to the target can be calibrated. Because different spatial targets require a different amount of muscle force, there is no savings from this sub-stage across successive saccades; that is, if one saccade cancels another, then whatever amount of time had been spent converting the first spatial target into a distance metric will have to be completely re-done (see Findlay and Walker 1999).

Our estimates of the times that are needed to complete the two stages of saccadic programming are based upon – and congruent with – estimates from prior research; the means time are $M_1 = 100$ ms and $M_2 = 25$ ms, respectively, and the actual time are sampled from gamma distributions with $\sigma = 0.18 \mu$. Given the values of M_1 and M_2, the mean saccadic latency in a task in which subjects are asked to rapidly move their eyes to unpredictable target locations would be at least 175 ms (i.e. saccadic latency = $V + M_1 + M_2 = 175$ ms), which agrees with observed saccadic latencies (Becker and Jürgens 1979; Rayner *et al.* 1983). Finally, for convenience, saccade durations in the model are fixed equal to 25 ms even though they do vary depending on their length. In our model, lexical processing continues during the saccades, at the same rate (due to visual acuity) as during the fixation prior to the saccade. Lexical processing then continues at this same rate until the pre-attentive stage of processing can complete and thereby provide visual information from the new viewing location. Thus, in E-Z Reader 8, we have explicitly assumed that the information processing continues on the attended word during saccades.

Our assumptions about the way saccade targets are selected and saccades are executed are based on the work of McConkie, O'Regan and their colleagues (McConkie *et al.* 1988; McConkie *et al.* 1991; O'Regan 1990, 1992; O'Regan and Lévy-Schoen 1987).

Our starting assumption is that saccades are always directed toward to optimal viewing position, but that the actual saccades are prone to two types of error: systematic and random. Equation 4 thus gives the length of the saccade that is actually executed (in terms of character spaces) as a function of the intended saccade length and the two sources of saccadic error. The systematic error reflects both the degree to which the intended saccade length deviated from the 'preferred' distance (which for readers of English is equal to 7 character spaces; McConkie *et al.* 1988, 1991) and the time that is allotted to program the movement. However, the random error is simply a function of the saccade length, with longer saccades being more prone to Gaussian error. These ideas are reflected in Equations 5 and 6. In Equation 5, the systematic error is a function of the difference between the intended and preferred ($\Psi = 7$ character spaces) saccade lengths, scaled by the logarithm of the fixation duration on the launch site. Ω_1 ($= 7.3$) and Ω_2 ($= 4$) are free parameters that modulate the effect of the latter. Equation 6 specifies how the variability of the random error component increases with saccade length; this error is sampled from a Gaussian distribution with $\mu = 0$ and σ given by Equation 6. η_1 ($= 1.2$) and η_2 ($= 0.15$) are free parameters that modulate the effect of the intended saccade length.

(4)   actual saccade = intended saccade + systematic error + random error

(5)   systematic error = $(\Psi - \text{intended length})\{[\Omega_1 - \ln(\text{fixation duration})]/\Omega_2\}$

(6) $\sigma = \eta_1 + \eta_2 (\text{intended length})$

Our final assumption about saccades concerns refixations. As with human readers, our model generates some refixations whenever saccades from word *n* to word *n* +1 are too short and the eyes undershoot their intended targets. However, we also believe that some refixation saccades are adaptively programmed so that longer words (which take longer to identify than shorter words due to visual acuity limitations) can be viewed from more than one location, and hence can be identified more rapidly than would otherwise be the case. These refixations may also reflect the fact that longer words tend to be more difficult to process than shorter words (e.g. word length and frequency are negatively correlated), and readers may learn to initiate refixation saccades on a long word if they anticipate that the word will be difficult to process (Reichle and Laurent 2005). As Fig. 6.2 shows, low-spatial frequency information about word length is rapidly available from peripheral vision and can be used to make decisions about whether or not a word, upon first being fixated, should be the recipient of another fixation. In our model, a word is refixated with a probability that is a function of its length (in character spaces) scaled by a free parameter ($\lambda = 0.01$). This assumption is specified in Equation 7. The refixation program is assumed to be programmed the instant the word is fixated.

(7) $p = \begin{cases} \text{length } \lambda & \text{if (length } \lambda) < 1 \\ 1 & \text{if (length } \lambda) \geq 1 \end{cases}$

The preceding overview provides a complete description of E-Z Reader 8. The model, as described, was used in several simulations, the results of which will be reported next. Before doing this, however, it is important to mention that each simulation was completed using 1000 statistical subjects using a corpus of 8–14 word sentences from Schilling *et al.* (1998). Furthermore, because E-Z Reader is a model of skilled readers who are reading material well within their reading ability, we did not include trials (simulated or observed) containing interword regressions because such regressions often stem from difficulty with higher-level language processing and are hence outside of the scope of our model. (For a discussion of how the model's best-fitting parameter values were estimated, see the appendix of Reichle *et al.* 1998.)

The first simulation was necessary to evaluate the model's capacity to generate the mean values of six commonly reported word-based measures: the first-fixation duration, single-fixation duration, and gaze duration, and the probabilities of skipping, fixating once, or making two or more fixations. We calculated each of these measures for five frequency classes of words in our sentence corpus: (1) 1–10 per million; (2) 11–100 per million; (3) 101–1000 per million; (4) 1001–10 000 per million; and (5) >10 001 per million. The observed and simulated word-based means for each of these frequency classes are shown in Fig. 6.3; the top panel shows the fixation-duration measures, and the bottom panel shows the fixation-probability measures. The distributions (using 50-ms bins) of the observed and simulated first-fixation and gaze durations are shown in Fig. 6.4.

Based upon these simulation results, we conclude that E-Z Reader 8 does as well as its predecessors at reproducing the aggregate data from the Schilling *et al.* (1998) experiment.[8] It is also worth mentioning that, according to the model and its parameter values, the predicted minimum amount of time that is needed to identify the most frequent English word, 'the', when it is very predictable (0.9) but not 'guessed' (i.e. $L_1 \neq 0$ ms; see Equation 1) is approximately 175 ms ($V + L_1 + L_2 = 50$ ms + 86 ms + 40 ms).[9] The model likewise predicts that rare three-letter words in completely unpredictable contexts should take about 269 ms to identify (= 50 ms +145 ms + 67 ms). We would argue that these predicted minimum and maximum word identification times are 'just right,' and are neither too short nor too long (Rayner and Pollatsek 1989). This is important because it shows that a serial word identification process can be the engine driving eye movements with the constraint that the times posited by the model for identifying words and for programming saccades are plausible. We believe that E-Z Reader 8, with its parameter values, provides a clear demonstration that this is in fact possible – it shows how a system in which saccades to the simplest visual events take 175 ms to program, and word identification is both slow (175–300 ms) and serial,

---

[8] In prior papers, we have always used a goodness-of-fit measure (RMSD) to evaluate our model's capacity to fit the observed data. Our previous 'best fits' (where smaller values indicate better model fits) were: (1) E-Z Reader 5, RMSD = 0.198 (Reichle *et al.* 1998); (2) E-Z Reader 6, RMSD = 0.218 (Reichle *et al.* 1999); and (3) E-Z Reader 7, RMSD = 0.088 (Reichle *et al.* 2003). By comparison, the current model gives an overall goodness-of-fit measure of RMSD = 0.109.

[9] This calculation assumes that the word 'the' is being processed from the letter 'h', so that the 86 ms that is needed to complete L_1 has been increased by a factor of 1.06 due to visual acuity constraints (see Equation 2).

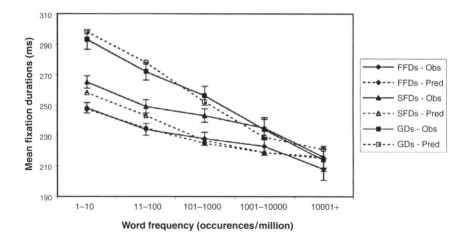

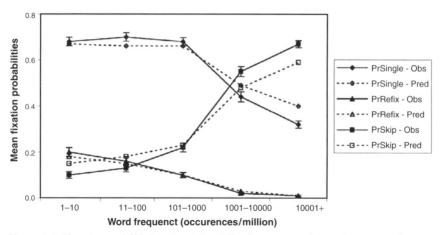

Figure 6.3 The observed (Obs) and predicted (Pred) mean word-based measures for five frequency classes of words. The top panel shows the first-fixation durations (FFDs), single-fixation durations (SFDs), and gaze durations (GDs). The bottom panel shows the probabilities of making a single fixation (PrSingle), making two or more fixations (PrRefix), and skipping (PrSkip). (Note: The bars show the standard errors of the observed means.)

can nevertheless make moment-to-moment decisions about when and where to move the eyes during reading.

This claim that E-Z Reader 8 provides more realistic estimates (in comparison with earlier versions of the model) of the times necessary to identify words and program saccades is also supported by the results of several new simulations that were undertaken to examine the model's capacity to account for the results of experiments that involve gaze-contingent display changes, such as the moving-window and boundary paradigms that were discussed in the first part of this chapter. These paradigms are important because they provide clear limits on the time course of various processes

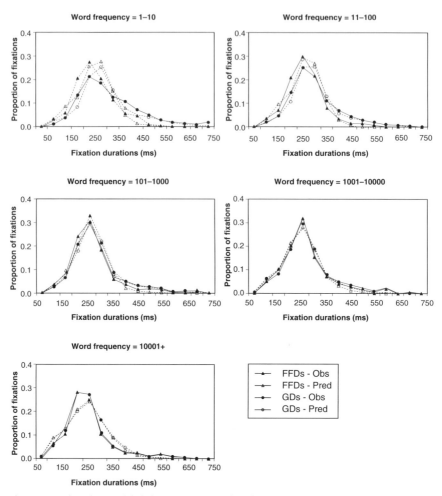

Figure 6.4 The observed (Obs) and predicted (Pred) distributions of the first-fixation durations (FFDs) and gaze durations (GDs) for five frequency classes of words.

that are operational during reading, and thus provide important benchmarks against which to evaluate our model. The results of one of these tests (one involving the boundary paradigm) are reported below.

In the boundary paradigm (Rayner 1975), the parafoveal processing that is normally done on word n +1 while fixating word n can be prevented by simply replacing all of the letters in word n +1 with Xs (or random letters) until the word is actually fixated. By comparing the fixation duration on words in this condition (where they receive no parafoveal processing) to fixation durations on the same words during normal reading (where they do receive parafoveal processing), one can ascertain how much of the visual and lexical processing necessary to identify a word is done in the parafovea. In a recent review of published boundary-paradigm experiments, Hyönä *et al.* (2004)

found a sizeable benefit associated with parafoveal processing: Across seven studies, the preview benefit – the difference between normal reading and the no-preview condition – ranged from 18 to 54 ms, with a mean preview benefit of 42 ms.

To simulate this paradigm (see Pollatsek *et al.* 2005), E-Z Reader 8 was used to predict the first-fixation and gaze durations on target words from the Schilling *et al.* (1998) corpus in two conditions: (1) a normal reading condition in which parafoveal processing of the target words was allowed; and (2) a no-preview condition in which parafoveal processing of the target words was prevented. Thus, in the latter condition, both pre-attentive visual processing and lexical processing of the target words were not allowed to begin until the model's 'eyes' were either on or to the right of the character space immediately before the target words. The results of this simulation support our contention that the model's parameter values provide reasonable estimates of the times needed to identify words: The model predicted a mean preview benefit of 42 ms on the first-fixation durations, and a mean preview benefit of 50 ms on the gaze durations. Both of these predicted values are within the range of values that were reported by Hyönä *et al.* (2004). Other simulations using our prior 90 ms value for the duration of the visual processing stage predicted preview effects that were far too large. We also suspect that models that assume parallel processing of words in the fovea and parafovea (such as SWIFT and Glenmore) will predict preview effects that are too large.

General discussion

In this chapter, we first summarized certain key data and phenomena that models of eye-movement control in reading were trying to deal with, and then outlined the current version of our E-Z Reader model. In the discussion of the data, we made a distinction between the decision of *when* to move the eyes and *where* to move the eyes. We believe there is general agreement that such a distinction is meaningful and that the latter decision is largely based on relatively low-level features such as word length and the position of spaces between words. Of course, the decisions about whether to refixate a word and whether to skip a word are, in some sense, *where* decisions, but most researchers would agree that such decisions are importantly influenced by higher-level variables such a word frequency and predictability. We think this consensus also extends to quantitative models of reading, although there may be some disagreement about the extent to which cognitive variables play any role. We also think that there may be some general agreement among the models about how the *where* decisions are programmed, although there may be some disagreement about details.

We suspect that the major area of disagreement is about the *when* decisions. As indicated above, E-Z Reader makes what we believe is the simplest possible assumption (if one allows processes like word identification to have any significant role in eye-movement control): the identification of individual words is serial and identification of a word (up to some level) is the signal to move the eyes. Other models either (a) give word identification a minor role in controlling eye movements (Yang and McConkie 2004) or (b) posit more parallel processing of words (Kliegl and Engbert 2003; Reilly and Radach 2003) and there is a complex 'push-pull' relationship between the identification of words that determines when the reader abandons word n for word $n+1$ (or word $n+2$). We think that enough data about the influence of cognitive variables on reading has accumulated to indicate that models that posit purely low-level visual control of where decisions are not viable. In contrast, we think that the question of which of the competing cognitive models is 'correct' (if any are) is still an open question.

One of our guiding principles in developing E-Z Reader was to make it as simple as possible, and, from our perspective, we feel that the assumptions of seriality and the direct relationship between word identification and eye movements make it an attractive heuristic model for considering eye movements in reading. As a result, we are reluctant to abandon these assumptions without convincing data to the contrary. As indicated earlier, parafoveal-on-foveal effects (i.e. that properties of word $n+1$ affect fixation time on word n) are often cited as strong evidence against a model such as E-Z Reader. However, we think this judgment is premature. First, there is little evidence for such parafoveal effects based on lexical properties of word $n+1$ in reading. Second, the existence of effects due to unusual orthographic properties of word $n+1$ can be explained by E-Z Reader because eye movements do not always go to the intended word and thus word $n+1$ is actually the attended word on a non-trivial number of fixations. Indeed, some recent results suggest that semantic parafoveal-on-foveal effects may be due to mislocalized fixations (Rayner *et al.* 2004b). Whether E-Z Reader can adequately model such effects, however, is an open question.

We think that the arena that we touched on at the end of the last section – explaining display change experiments – may prove important, as in these experiments, one is manipulating the time course of processing events, and thus assumptions about the time course of processing become even more critical. We think that the simulations we have embarked on indicate that E-Z Reader is on the right track and appears to give a good account of such data. We wonder whether more parallel models will do so. For example, if deciding to move the eyes from word n to word $n+1$ is a 'push-pull' process, we wonder what these models will predict when word $n+1$ is a string of Xs or random letters and thus is generating little or no signal that significant word processing is occurring.

In summary, we would suggest that the development of the E-Z Reader model has been very successful for two reasons. First, the development of the model has stimulated others to produce competitor models that attempt to account for the basic data on eye movements in reading via different principles. Second, E-Z Reader has stimulated a fair amount of research that otherwise might not have been realized without its development. We anticipate that the next few years will reveal interesting data related both to the model and to furthering our understanding of eye-movement control in reading.

Acknowledgments

Preparation of this chapter was supported by Grant HD26765 from the National Institute of Health and by Grant R305G020006 from the Department of Education, Institute of Education Sciences. We thank Marc Brysbaert and Ralph Radach for helpful comments on an earlier draft.

References

Altarriba, J. Kroll, J. F., Sholl, A., and Rayner, K. (1996). The influence of lexical and conceptual constraints on reading mixed language sentences: Evidence from eye fixation and naming times. *Memory and Cognition*, **24**, 477–492.

Balota, D.A., Pollatsek, A., and Rayner, K. (1985). The interaction of contextual constraints and parafoveal visual information in reading. *Cognitive Psychology*, **17**, 364–390.

Beauvillain, C., Doré, K., and Baudouin, V. (1996). The 'center of gravity' of words: Evidence for an effect of the word-initial letters. *Vision Research*, **36**, 589–603.

Becker, W., and Jürgens, R. (1979). An analysis of the saccadic system by means of double step stimuli. *Vision Research*, **19**, 967–983.

Binder, K. S., Pollatsek, A., and Rayner, K. (1999). Extraction of information to the left of the fixated word in reading. *Journal of Experimental Psychology: Human Perception and Performance*, **25**, 1162–1172.

Blanchard, H. E., Pollatsek, A., and Rayner, K. (1989). The acquisition of parafoveal word information in reading. *Perception and Psychophysics*, **46**, 85–94.

Bouma, H., and de Voogd, A. H. (1974). On the control of eye saccades in reading. *Vision Research*, **14**, 273–284.

Brysbaert, M., and Vitu, F. (1998). Word skipping: Implications for theories of eye movement control in reading. In: G. Underwood (ed.) *Eye guidance in reading and scene perception.* Oxford: Elsevier, pp. 125–148.

Chen, H.-C., and Tang, C.-K. (1998). The effective visual field in Chinese. *Reading and Writing*, **10**, 245–254.

Clark, V. P., Fan, S., and Hillyard, S. A. (1995). Identification of early visual evoked potential generators by retinotopic and topographic analyses. *Human Brain Mapping*, **2**, 170–187.

Deutsch, A., and Rayner, K. (1999). Initial fixation location effects in reading Hebrew words. *Language and Cognitive Processes*, **14**, 393–421.

Drieghe, D., Brysbaert, M., and Desmet, T., and De Baecke, G. (2004). Word skipping in reading: On the interplay of linguistic and visual factors. *European Journal of Cognitive Psychology*, **16**, 79–103.

Drieghe, D., Rayner, K. and Pollatsek, A. (2005). Eye movements and word skipping during reading revisited. *Journal of Experimental Psychology: Human Perception and Performance*, in press.

Dunn-Rankin, P. (1978). The visual characteristics of words. *Scientific American*, **238**, 122–130.

Ehrlich, S. F., and Rayner, K. (1981). Contextual effects on word perception and eye movements during reading. *Journal of Verbal Learning and Verbal Behavior*, **20**, 641–655.

Engbert, R., Longtin, A., and Kliegl, R. (2002). A dynamical model of saccade generation in reading based on spatially distributed lexical processing. *Vision Research*, **42**, 621–636.

Everatt, J., and Underwood, G. (1992). Parafoveal guidance and priming effects during reading: A special case of the mind being ahead of the eye. *Consciousness and Cognition*, **1**, 186–197.

Findlay, J. M., and Walker, R. (1999). A model of saccade generation based on parallel processing and competitive inhibition. *Behavioral and Brain Sciences*, **22**, 661–674.

Foxe, J. J. and Simpson, G. V. (2002). Flow of activation from V1 to frontal cortex in humans: A framework for defining 'early' visual processing. *Experimental Brain Research*, **142**, 139–150.

Francis, W. N. and Kuĉera, H. (1982). *Frequency analysis of English usage: Lexicon and grammar.* Boston: Houghton Mifflin.

Hanes, D., and McCollum, G. (2003). Dimensionality and explanatory power of reading models. *Behavioral and Brain Sciences*, **26**, 486.

Henderson, J. M., and Ferreira, F. (1990). Effects of foveal processing difficulty on the perceptual span in reading: Implications for attention and eye movement control. *Journal of Experimental Psychology: Learning, Memory, and Cognition*, **16**, 417–429.

Henderson, J. M., and Ferreira, F. (1993). Eye movement control during reading: Fixation measures reflect foveal but not parafoveal processing. *Canadian Journal of Experimental Psychology*, **47**, 201–221.

Hochberg, J. (1975). On the control of eye saccades in reading. *Vision Research*, **15**, 620.

Hyönä, J. (1995). Do irregular letter combinations attract readers' attention? Evidence from fixation locations in words. *Journal of Experimental Psychology: Human Perception and Performance*, **21**, 68–81.

Hyönä, J., and Bertram, R. (2004). Do frequency characteristics of nonfixated words influence the processing of fixated words? *European Journal of Cognitive Psychology*, **16**, 104–127.

Hyönä, J., and Pollatsek, A. (1998). Reading Finnish compound words: Eye fixations are affected by component morphemes. *Journal of Experimental Psychology: Human Perception and Performance*, **24**, 1612–1627.

Hyönä, J., Bertram, R., and Pollatsek, A. (2004). Are long compound words identified serially via their constituents? Evidence from an eye-movement contingent display change study. *Memory and Cognition*, **32**, 523–532.

Hyönä, J., Niemi, P., and Underwood, G. (1989). Reading long words embedded in sentences: Informativeness of word halves affects eye movements. *Journal of Experimental Psychology: Human Perception and Performance*, **15**, 145–152.

Ikeda, M., and Saida, S. (1978). Span of recognition in reading. *Vision Research*, **18**, 83–88.

Inhoff, A. W., and Liu, W. (1998). The perceptual span and oculomotor activity during the reading of Chinese sentences. *Journal of Experimental Psychology: Human Perception and Performance*, **24**, 20–34.

Inhoff, A. W., and Radach, R. (1998). Definition and computation of oculomotor measures in the study of cognitive processes. In: G. Underwood (ed.) *Eye guidance in reading and scene perception*. Oxford: Elsevier, pp. 29–54.

Inhoff, A. W., and Rayner, K. (1986). Parafoveal word processing during eye fixations in reading: Effects of word frequency. *Perception and Psychophysics*, **40**, 431–439.

Inhoff, A. W., Pollatsek, A., Posner, M. I., and Rayner, K. (1989). Covert attention and eye movements during reading. *Quarterly Journal of Experimental Psychology*, **41A**, 63–89.

Inhoff, A. W., Radach, R., Starr, M., and Greenberg, S. (2000). Allocation of visuo-spatial attention and saccade programming during reading. In: A. Kennedy, R. Radach, D. Heller, and J. Pynte (ed.) *Reading as a perceptual process*. Amsterdam: North Holland, pp. 221–246.

Inhoff, A. W., Starr, M., and Shindler, K.L. (2000). Is the processing of words during eye fixations in reading strictly serial? *Perception and Psychophysics*, **62**, 1474–1484.

Ishida, T. and Ikeda, M. (1989). Temporal properties of information extraction in reading studied by a text-mask replacement technique. *Journal of the Optical Society A: Optics and Image Science*, **6**, 1624–1632.

Juhasz, B. J., and Rayner, K. (2003). Investigating the effects of a set of intercorrelated variables on eye fixation durations during reading. *Journal of Experimental Psychology: Learning, Memory, and Cognition*, **6**, 1312–1318

Juhasz, B. J., and Rayner, K. (2005). The role of age-of-acquisition and word frequency in reading: evidence from eye fixation durations. *Visual Cognition*. in press.

Just, M. A., and Carpenter, P.A. (1980). A theory of reading: From eye fixations to comprehension. *Psychological Review*, **87**, 329–354.

Kennedy, A. (2000). Parafoveal processing in word recognition. *Quarterly Journal of Experimental Psychology*, **53A**, 429–456.

Kennedy, A., and Pynte, J. (2005). Parafoveal-on-foveal effects in normal reading. *Vision Research*, **45**, 153–168.

Kennedy, A., Pynte, J., and Ducrot, S. (2002). Parafoveal-on-foveal interactions in word recognition. *Quarterly Journal of Experimental Psychology*, **55A**, 1307–1338.

Kennedy, A., Murray, W.S., and Boissiere, C. (2004). Parafoveal pragmatics revisited. *European Journal of Cognitive Psychology*, **16**, 128–153.

Kennison, S. M., and Clifton, C. (1995). Determinants of parafoveal preview benefit in high and low working memory capacity readers: Implications for eye movement control. *Journal of Experimental Psychology: Learning, Memory, and Cognition*, **21**, 68–81.

Kliegl, R., and Engbert, R. (2003). SWIFT explorations. In: J. Hyönä, R. Radach, and H. Deubel (ed.). *The mind's eyes: Cognitive and applied aspects of eye movement research*. Amsterdam: Elsevier, pp. 391–412.

Kliegl, R., and Engbert, R. (2005). Fixation durations before word skipping in reading. *Psychonomic Bulletin and Review*, in press.

Lee, H.-W., Legge, G. E., and Ortiz, A. (2003). Is word recognition different in central and peripheral vision? *Vision Research*, **43**, 2837–2846.

Leff, A. P., Scott, S. K., Rothwell, J. C., and Wise, R. J. S. (2001). The planning and guiding of reading saccades: A repetitive transcranial magnetic stimulation study. *Cerebral Cortex*, **11**, 918–923.

Legge, G. E., Klitz, T. S., and Tjan, B. S. (1997). Mr. Chips: An ideal-observer model of reading. *Psychological Review*, **104**, 524–553.

Legge, G. E., Hooven, T. A., Klitz, T. S., Mansfield, J. S., and Tjan, B. S. (2002). Mr. Chips 2002: New insights from an ideal-observer model of reading. *Vision Research*, **42**, 2219–2234.

Liversedge, S. P., Paterson, K. B., and Pickering, M. J. (1998). Eye movements and measures of reading time. In: G. Underwood (ed.) *Eye guidance in reading and scene perception*. Oxford: Elsevier, pp. 55–76.

Liversedge, S. P., Rayner, K., White, S. J., Vergilino-Perez, D., Findlay, J. M., and Kentridge, R. W. (2004). Eye movements when reading disappearing text: is there a gap effect in reading? *Vision Research*, **44**, 1013–1024.

McConkie, G. W., and Rayner, K. (1975). The span of the effective stimulus during a fixation in reading. *Perception and Psychophysics*, **17**, 578–586.

McConkie, G. W., Kerr, P. W., Reddix, M. D., and Zola, D. (1988). Eye movement control during reading: I. The location of initial eye fixations in words. *Vision Research*, **28**, 1107–1118.

McConkie, G. W., Zola, D., Kerr, P. W., Bryant, N. R., and Wolff, P. M. (1991). Children's eye movements during reading. In. J. F. Stein (ed.) *Vision and Visual Dyslexia 13*. MacMillan: London.

McPeek, R. M., Skavenski, A. A., and Nakayama, K. (2000). Concurrent processing of saccades in visual search. *Vision Research*, **40**, 2499–2516.

Miellet, S., and Sparrow, L. (2004). Phonological codes are assembled before word fixation: Evidence from boundary paradigm in sentence reading. *Brain and Language*, **90**, 299–310.

Mokler, A., and Fischer, B. (1999). The recognition and correction of involuntary prosaccades in an antisaccade task. *Experimental Brain Research*, **125**, 511–516.

Morris, R. K., Rayner, K., and Pollatsek, A. (1990). Eye movement guidance in reading: The role of parafoveal letter and space information. *Journal of Experimental Psychology: Human Perception and Performance*, **16**, 268–281.

Morrison, R. E. (1984). Manipulation of stimulus onset delay in reading: Evidence for parallel programming of saccades. *Journal of Experimental Psychology: Human Perception and Performance*, **10**, 667–682.

Morrison, R. E., and Rayner, K. (1981). Saccade size in reading depends upon character spaces and not visual angle. *Perception and Psychophysics*, **30**, 395–396.

Mouchetant-Rostaing, Y., Giard, M.-H., Bentin, S., Aguera, P.-E., and Pernier, J. (2000). Neurophysiological correlates of face gender processing in humans. *European Journal of Neuroscience*, **12**, 303–310.

O'Regan, J. K. (1979). Eye guidance in reading: Evidence for linguistic control hypothesis. *Perception and Psychophysics*, **25**, 501–509.

O'Regan, J. K. (1980). The control of saccade size and fixation duration in reading: The limits of linguistic control. *Perception and Psychophysics*, **28**, 112–117.

O'Regan, J. K. (1981). The convenient viewing position hypothesis. In: D. F. Fisher, R. A. Monty, and J. W. Senders (ed.) *Eye movements: Cognition and visual perception.* Hillsdale, NJ: Erlbaum, pp. 289–298.

O'Regan, J. K. (1990). Eye movements and reading. In: E. Kowler (ed.) *Eye movements and their role in visual and cognitive processes.* Amsterdam: Elsevier, pp. 395–453.

O'Regan, J. K. (1992). Optimal viewing position in words and the strategy-tactics theory of eye movements in reading. In: K. Rayner (ed.) *Eye movements and visual cognition: Scene perception and reading.* New York: Springer-Verlag, pp. 333–354.

O'Regan, J. K., and Lévy-Schoen, A. (1987). Eye movement strategy and tactics in word recognition and reading. In: M. Coltheart (ed.), *Attention and performance XII: The psychology of reading.* Erlbaum, pp. 363–383.

Osaka, N. (1992). Size of saccade and fixation duration of eye movements during reading: Comparison of English and Japanese text processing. *Journal of the Optical Society of America A*, **9**, 5–13.

Pollatsek, A., and Rayner, K. (1982). Eye movement control in reading: The role of word boundaries. *Journal of Experimental Psychology: Human Perception and Performance*, **8**, 817–833.

Pollatsek, A., and Rayner, K. (1999). Is covert attention really unnecessary? *Behavioral and Brain Sciences*, **22**, 695–696.

Pollatsek, A., Bolozky, S., Well, A. D., and Rayner, K. (1981). Asymmetries in the perceptual span for Israeli readers. *Brain and Language*, **14**, 174–180.

Pollatsek, A., Rayner, K., and Balota, D. A. (1986). Inferences about eye movement control from the perceptual span in reading. *Perception and Psychophysics*, **40**, 123–130.

Pollatsek, A., Lesch, M., Morris, R. K., and Rayner, K. (1992). Phonological codes are used in integrating information across saccades in word identification and reading. *Journal of Experimental Psychology: Human Perception and Performance*, **18**, 148–162.

Pollatsek, A., Reichle, E. D., and Rayner, K. (2003). Modeling eye movements in reading. In: J. Hyönä, R. Radach, and H. Deubel (ed.). *The mind's eyes: Cognitive and applied aspects of eye movement research.* Amsterdam: Elsevier, pp. 361–390.

Pollatsek, A., Reichle, E. D., and Rayner, K. (2005). Tests of the E-Z Reader Model: Exploring the interface between cognition and eye-movement control. Submitted.

Pynte, J., Kennedy, A., and Ducrot, S. (2004). The influence of parafoveal typographical errors on eye movements in reading. *European Journal of Cognitive Psychology*, **16**, 178–202.

Radach, R., and Heller, D. (2000). Relations between spatial and temporal aspects of eye movement control. In: A. Kennedy, R. Radach, D. Heller, and J. Pynte (ed.) *Reading as a perceptual process*. Amsterdam: North Holland, pp. 165–192.

Radach, R., and Kempe, V. (1993). An individual analysis of initial fixation positions in reading. In: G. d'Ydewalle and J. Van Rensbergen (ed.) *Perception and cognition: Advances in eye movement research*. Amsterdam: North Holland, pp. 213–226.

Radach, R., and Kennedy, A. (2004). Theoretical perspectives on eye movements in reading: Past controversies, current issues, and an agenda for future research. *European Journal of Cognitive Psychology*, **16**, 3–26.

Radach, R., and McConkie, G. W. (1998). Determinants of fixation positions in words during reading. In: G. Underwood (ed.) *Eye guidance in reading and scene perception*. Oxford: Elsevier, pp. 77–101.

Radach, R., Inhoff, A., and Heller, D. (2004). Orthographic regularity gradually modulates saccade amplitudes in reading. *European Journal of Cognitive Psychology*, **16**, 27–51.

Radach, R., Kennedy, A., and Rayner, K. (2004). *Eye movements and information processing during reading*. Hove: Psychology Press.

Raney, G. E. (2003). E-Z Reader 7 provides a platform for explaining how low- and high-level linguistic processes influence eye movements. *Behavioral and Brain Sciences*, **26**, 498–499.

Rayner, K. (1975). The perceptual span and peripheral cues in reading. *Cognitive Psychology*, **7**, 65–81.

Rayner, K. (1978). Eye movements in reading and information processing. *Psychological Bulletin*, **85**, 618–660.

Rayner, K. (1979). Eye guidance in reading: Fixation locations within words. *Perception*, **8**, 21–30.

Rayner, K. (1998). Eye movements in reading and information processing: 20 years of research. *Psychological Bulletin*, **124**, 372–422.

Rayner, K., and Bertera, J. H. (1979). Reading without a fovea. *Science*, **206**, 468–469.

Rayner, K., and Duffy, S. A. (1986). Lexical complexity and fixation times in reading: ffects of word frequency, verb complexity, and lexical ambiguity. *Memory and Cognition*, **14**, 191–201.

Rayner, K., and Fischer, M. H. (1996). Mindless reading revisited: Eye movements during reading and scanning are different. *Perception and Psychophysics*, **58**, 734–747.

Rayner, K., and Juhasz, B. J. (2004). Eye movements in reading: Old questions and new directions. *European Journal of Cognitive Psychology*, **16**, 340–352.

Rayner, K., and McConkie, G. W. (1976). What guides a reader's eye movements. *Vision Research*, **16**, 829–837.

Rayner, K., and Morris, R. K. (1992). Eye movement control in reading: Evidence against semantic preprocessing. *Journal of Experimental Psychology: Human Perception and Performance*, **18**, 163–172.

Rayner, K., and Morrison, R. M. (1981). Eye movements and identifying words in parafoveal vision. *Bulletin of the Psychonomic Society*, **17**, 135–138.

Rayner, K., and Pollatsek, A. (1981). Eye movement control during reading: Evidence for direct control. *Quarterly Journal of Experimental Psychology*, **33A**, 351–373.

Rayner, K., and Pollatsek, A. (1989). *The psychology of reading*. Englewood Cliffs, NJ: Prentice Hall.

Rayner, K., and Well, A. D. (1996). Effects of contextual constraint on eye movements in reading: A further examination. *Psychonomic Bulletin and Review*, **3**, 504–509.

Rayner, K., McConkie, G. W., and Zola, D. (1980). Integrating information across eye movements. *Cognitive Psychology*, **12**, 206–226.

Rayner, K., Inhoff, A. W., Morrison, R., Slowiaczek, M. L., and Bertera, J. H. (1981). Masking of foveal and parafoveal vision during eye fixations in reading. *Journal of Experimental Psychology: Human Perception and Performance*, **7**, 167–179.

Rayner, K., Well, A.D., Pollatsek, A. and Bertera, J.H. (1982). The availability of useful information to the right of fixation in reading. *Perception and Psychophysics*, **31**, 537–550.

Rayner, K., Slowiaczek, M. L., Clifton, C.,and Bertera, J. H. (1983). Latency of sequential eye movements: Implications for reading. *Journal of Experimental Psychology: Human Perception and Performance*, **9**, 912–922.

Rayner, K., Sereno, S. C., and Raney, G. E. (1996). Eye movement control in reading: A comparison of two types of models. *Journal of Experimental Psychology: Human Perception and Performance*, **22**, 1188–1200.

Rayner, K., Reichle, E. D., and Pollatsek, A. (1998). Eye movement control in reading: An overview and a model. In: G. Underwood (ed.) *Eye guidance in reading and scene perception*. Oxford: Elsevier, pp. 243–268.

Rayner, K., Fischer, M. H., and Pollatsek, A. (1998). Unspaced text interferes with both word identification and eye movement control. *Vision Research*, **38**, 1129–1144.

Rayner, K., Binder, K. S., Ashby, J., and Pollatsek, A. (2001). Eye movement control in reading: Word predictability has little influence on initial landing positions in words. *Vision Research*, **41**, 943–954.

Rayner, K., Liversedge, S. P., White, S. J., and Vergilino-Perez, D. (2003a). Reading disappearing text: Cognitive control of eye movements. *Psychological Science*, **14**, 385–389.

Rayner, K., White, S. J., Kambe, G., Miller, B., and Liversedge, S. P. (2003b). On the processing of meaning from parafoveal vision during eye fixations in reading. In: J. Hyona, R. Radach, and H. Deubel (ed.) *The mind's eye: Cognitive and applied aspects of eye movement research*. Amsterdam: North Holland, pp. 213–234.

Rayner, K., Pollatsek, A. and Reichle, E. D. (2003c). Eye movements in reading: Models and data. *Brain and Behavioral Sciences*, **26**, 507–526.

Rayner, K., Ashby, J., Pollatsek, A., and Reichle, E. (2004a). The effects of frequency and predictability on eye fixations in reading: Implications for the E-Z Reader model. *Journal of Experimental Psychology: Human Perception and Performance*, **30**, 720–732.

Rayner, K., Warren, T., Juhasz, B. J., and Liversedge, S. P. (2004b). The effect of plausibility on eye movements in reading. *Journal of Experimental Psychology: Learning, Memory, and Cognition*, **30**, 1290–1301.

Reichle, E. D., and Laurent, P. A. (2005). The emergence of 'intelligent' eye-movementcontrol during reading: A reinforcement learning approach. Submitted.

Reichle, E. D. and Perfetti, C. A. (2003). Morphology in word identification: A word experience model that accounts for morpheme frequency effects. *Scientific Studies of Reading*, **7**, 219–237.

Reichle, E., Pollatsek, A., Fisher, D. L., and Rayner, K. (1998). Toward a model of eye movement control in reading. *Psychological Review*, **105**, 125–157.

Reichle, E. D., Rayner, K., and Pollatsek, A. (1999). Eye movement control in reading: Accounting for initial fixation locations and refixations within the E-Z Reader model. *Vision Research*, **39**, 4403–4411

Reichle, E. D., Rayner, K., and Pollatsek, A. (2003). The E-Z Reader model of eye movement control in reading: Comparison to other models. *Brain and Behavioral Sciences*, **26,** 445–476.

Reilly, R.G., and Radach, R. (2003). Foundations of an interactive activation model of eye movement control in reading. In: J. Hyönä, R. Radach, and H. Deubel (ed.). *The mind's eyes: Cognitive and applied aspects of eye movement research.* Amsterdam: Elsevier, pp. 429–456.

Reingold, E. M. (2003). Eye-movement control in reading: Models and predictions. *Behavioral and Brain Sciences*, **26,** 500–501.

Schilling, H. E. H., Rayner, K., and Chumbley, J. I. (1998). Comparing naming, lexical decision, and eye fixation times: Word frequency effects and individual differences. *Memory and Cognition*, **26,** 1270–1281.

Schroyens, W., Vitu, F., Brysbaert, M., and d'Ydewalle, G. (1999). Eye movement control during reading: Foveal load and parafoveal processing. *Quarterly Journal of Experimental Psychology*, **52A,** 1021–1046.

Schustack, M. W., Ehrlich, S. F., and Rayner, K. (1987). The complexity of contextual facilitation in reading: Local and global influences. *Journal of Memory and Language*, **26,** 322–340.

Slowiaczek, M. L., and Rayner, K. (1987). Sequential masking during eye fixations in reading. *Bulletin of the Psychonomic Society*, **25,** 175–178.

Starr, M. S., and Inhoff, A. W. (2004). Attention allocation to the right and left of a fixated word: Use of orthographic information from multiple words during reading. *European Journal of Cognitive Psychology*, **16,** 203–225.

Underwood, G. (1998). *Eye guidance in reading and scene perception.* Oxford: Elsevier.

Underwood, G., Bloomfield, R., and Clews, S. (1988). Information influences the pattern of eye fixations during sentence comprehension. *Perception*, **17,** 267–278.

Underwood, G., Clews, S., and Everatt, J. (1990). How do readers know where to look next? Local information distributions influence eye fixations. *Quarterly Journal of Experimental Psychology*, **42A,** 39–65.

Underwood, G., Binns, A., and Walker, S. (2000). Attentional demands on the processing of neighbouring words. In: A. Kennedy, R. Radach, D. Heller, and J. Pynte (ed.), *Reading as a perceptual process.* Amsterdam: North Holland, pp. 247–268.

Van Rullen, R., and Thorpe, S. (2001). The time course of visual processing: From early perception to decision-making. *Journal of Cognitive Neuroscience*, **13,** 454–461.

Vergilino, D., and Beauvillain, C. (2000). The planning of refixation saccades in reading. *Vision Research*, **40,** 3527–3538.

Vergilino, D., and Beauvillain, C. (2001). Reference frames in reading: evidence from visually guided and memory-guided saccades. *Vision Research*, **41,** 3547–3557.

Vergilino-Perez, D., Collins, T., and Dore-Mazars, K. (2004). Decision and metrics of refixations in reading isolated words. *Vision Research*, **44,** 2009–2017.

Vitu, F., O'Regan, J. K., and Mittau, M. (1990). Optimal landing position in reading isolated words and continuous text. *Perception and Psychophysics*, **47,** 583–600.

Vitu, F., O'Regan, J. K., Inhoff, A. W., and Topolski, R. (1995). Mindless reading: Eye movement characteristics are similar in scanning letter strings and reading text. *Perception and Psychophysics*, **57,** 352–364.

Vitu, F., McConkie, G. W., Kerr, P., and O'Regan, J. K. (2001). Fixation location effects on fixation durations during reading: an inverted optimal viewing position effect. *Vision Research*, **41,** 3513–3533.

Vitu, F., Brysbaert, M., and Lancelin, D. (2004). At test of parafoveal-on-foveal effects with pairs of orthographically related words. *European Journal of Cognitive Psychology*, **16**, 154–177.

Vonk, W., Radach, R., and van Rijn, H. (2000). Eye guidance and the saliency of word beginnings in reading text. In: A. Kennedy, R. Radach, D. Heller, and J. Pynte (ed.), *Reading as a perceptual process*. Amsterdam: North Holland, pp. 269–300.

White, S. J., and Liversedge, S. P. (2004). Orthographic familiarity influences initial eye positions in reading. *European Journal of Cognitive Psychology*, **16**, 52–78.

White, S. J., Rayner, K., and Liversedge, S. P. (2005). Eye movements and the modulation of parafoveal processing by foveal processing difficulty: A re-examination. *Psychonomic Bulletin and Review*, in press.

Wolfe, J. M. (1994). Guided Search 2.0: A revised model of visual search. *Psychonomic Bulletin and Review*, **1**, 202–238.

Wolfe, J. M., and Bennett, S. C. (1996). Preattentive object files: Shapeless bundles of basic features. *Vision Research*, **37**, 25–43.

Wolverton, G. S., and Zola, D. (1983). The temporal characteristics of visual information extraction during reading. In: K. Rayner (ed.) *Eye movements in reading: Perceptual and language processes*. New York: Academic Press, pp. 41–52.

Yang, S.-N., and McConkie, G. W. (2001). Eye movements during reading: A theory of saccade initiation time. *Vision Research*, **41**, 3567–3568.

Yang, S.-N., and McConkie, G. W. (2004). Saccade generation during reading: Are words necessary? *European Journal of Cognitive Psychology*, **16**, 226–261.

7

Eye fixations on pictures of natural scenes: Getting the gist and identifying the components

Geoffrey Underwood

Abstract

Newspapers, magazines and textbooks frequently present pictures accompanied by captions, but in contrast to our studies of text reading and picture perception, we know relatively little about the inspection of these picture-text combinations. Eye-fixation studies indicate that viewers characteristically look briefly at the picture, then read the text, and then, if necessary, they look more carefully at the picture. When viewers look at these presentations in preparation for a sentence verification decision, their inspection of the sentence does not show sensitivity to its accuracy, suggesting that insufficient detail has been extracted from the picture during the initial inspection. The gist of a picture can be acquired with a very brief glimpse, and can help or hinder in the identification of objects in the picture, but it cannot support a decision about the accuracy of a statement. The gist, or scene schema, is a very general overall impression of the setting of a scene that does not capture the detail of its components.

Introduction

Using the justification of the well-voiced maxim of 'a picture is worth a thousand words', many publications feature photographs and other graphics prominently. Newspapers and magazines use pictures on almost every page, in addition to commercial advertisements that also usually contain images. Academic publications such as journals are less profligate in their use of pictures, but college textbooks do contain an abundance of graphs and flowcharts as well as photographs of scenes depicting the subject of the discussion, and pictures of well-known scientists whose work is being described. In the modern era even humorous cartoons are used to lighten the treatise, with the work of Charles Schultz and Gary Larson being particularly popular with psychology textbook publishers. A common feature of all of these uses of pictures in the printed media is that they invariably contain a mix of graphics and text. In the case of advertisements the two may be superimposed, but more usually a photograph, drawing or graph will be accompanied by a caption printed next to it. The caption may simply be a label (e.g. 'Graph showing change of recall over time') or it may add content to the picture. Typically, a newspaper photograph of a sports scene will name the principal actor and describe the effects of the depicted action. Using an example from my personal collection, a newspaper report of the 1979 European Cup Final, between the Nottingham Forest and Malmö soccer teams, has a picture showing four players foregrounded near the goal. The accompanying caption reads: 'Trevor Francis heads home John Robertson's cross to win the cup'. In this case a highly informative caption names the principal actors, and describes both the action and its eventual consequence. The question to be discussed here is that of how readers distribute their attention between the text and the picture – how does the information collected from the picture and text interact, and how does one source of information drive the collection of information from the other source? We now know a great deal about how readers move their eyes over uninterrupted text, and also about how pictures are inspected, but we know relatively little about we look at pictures and their captions. What we do know is that, characteristically, a reader will take a very brief look at the picture, then read the caption carefully, and then look more extensively at the picture. The question addressed in this chapter concerns the purpose of the initial glance at the picture, and specifically whether it is sufficient for the reader to acquire the gist, or overall meaning, of the picture. This will lead us to examine the definition of gist, and to reconsider some well-established studies that have been interpreted as suggesting that we can acquire the gist of a photograph within the time that we allocate to a single fixation when looking at pictures.

Scanpaths on picture-text displays

When viewers inspect a picture-text combination, the typically observed scanpath consists of two or three fixations on the picture prior to reading of the caption. This pattern has been observed with a number of different graphics. In one of the earliest investigations Carroll *et al.* (1992) had viewers look at Gary Larson's *Far Side* cartoons with the task of rating each one on a number of dimensions as part of an investigation of humour. The cartoons were line drawings enclosed in a frame, with a sentence or two printed directly below. The characteristic scanpath was that after very few fixations on the drawing viewers shifted their gaze to read the text, and then they looked at the cartoon again. This pattern of a brief inspection of the illustration, followed by detailed reading of the text, and then re-inspection of the picture, will be a recurring pattern. In some studies the reading of the text is interrupted at specific points to check the detail of the illustration that has been described, but with short texts it is common to see viewers read the text entirely, and then spend time looking at the picture.

Hegarty (1992) used pictures of simple mechanical diagrams of pulley systems accompanied by explanatory captions, to demonstrate that the text was dominant in determining the shift of gaze between the two parts of the display. The task was to understand how the pulley system worked, in preparation for comprehension questions that asked about the direction of movement of specific components, or about the configuration of the components. Her viewers would characteristically read part of the text, which might be several sentences of description, and then inspect part of the diagram. Fixation would then return to the next part of the text, and then the corresponding part of the diagram. Shifts of fixations between text and diagram occurred at the ends of sentences or clauses, and would be re-located on the part of the diagram corresponding to a referent in the part of the text recently read. Hegarty concluded that the viewer's mental model of the pulley system was being constructed part by part, with the order of construction being determined by the order of referents described in the sentences. As with the Carroll *et al.* (1992) experiment, inspection of the picture was dependent upon reading the text, and it is this order of inspections that will become important as the present discussion progresses.

A study of children's eye movements as they read an illustrated biology textbook has been reported by Hannus and Hyönä (1999), finding considerably greater visual attention to the text and to figure captions than to the figures themselves. Inspection of the figures was minimal, and tended to be driven by the content of the text, especially for higher-ability children. Each figure (e.g. a detailed drawing of a fly) was accompanied by a text of around 200 words appearing on the same 'page' of a virtual textbook, and while the children spent around 4 min reading the text, they spent less than half a minute inspecting the diagram. An analysis of differences between children of differing ability found that high-ability was associated with more attention both to sections of text and to parts of the illustration that were judged to be more pertinent. Hannus and Hyönä also found that high-ability children switched their gaze between text and figure more than other children, suggesting that their learning style was more interactive, with switches of fixation prompted by the text, as Hegarty (1992) reported. The switch of gaze from picture to text will be a prominent characteristic of the scanpaths described, and will be used to identify changes in the knowledge of the viewer.

The dominance of the text was also demonstrated in a study of magazine advertisements reported by Rayner *et al.* (2001) in which participants were told to pretend that they were interested in purchasing one type of product that featured in some of the advertisements that were displayed. In the two advertisements of interest (a skincare product, and a car) there were simple images and several lines of text (more than 100 words in each of them). Although the arrangements of images and texts varied between advertisements, Rayner *et al.* noted a consistent scanpath pattern, with a tendency for inspection of the text in large font size early in the sequence of fixations on the page. The viewers then looked either at the picture, or at smaller sized text and then the picture. Prior to the initial fixation of the large text, however, there was a cursory inspection of the picture, with the text being inspected with the third fixation on average.

The final demonstration of brief initial inspections of pictures comes from a recent study using a version of the sentence verification task. We had viewers make judgements about the accuracy of textual statements about colour photographs of natural scenes while their eye movements were recorded (Underwood *et al.* 2004). The characteristic scanpath found in the previous studies was also apparent here. Viewers made two or three fixations on the picture, then read the sentence fully, and then inspected the picture more closely. This pattern is indicated in Fig. 7.1, which shows one viewer's fixations on the picture and sentence. The picture appeared on the computer screen while the viewer fixated near to the centre of the picture (in this case, near the horse-rider's head), and one further fixation was made on the picture before the sentence was fixated and read completely. There were then four further fixations on the picture. In all of these experiments, the preference was for the text to take primary importance, and to use this information to direct attention within the picture.

The minimal initial inspection of the images in these studies of eye fixations on text-image displays suggests either that images are of little value, in these particular tasks, until at least part of the text has been understood, or alternatively that the important aspect of the image can be captured with a very brief inspection.

The car ahead is passing a cyclist.

Figure 7.1 A sample picture-text stimulus from the sentence verification task used by Underwood *et al.* (2004, Experiment 1). The task was to judge whether or not the sentence (in this example, 'The car ahead is passing a cyclist') accurately described the events shown in the picture, and to make a yes/no keyboard response when the decision was made. The fixations of one viewer are superimposed on the stimulus here, with yellow lines indicating the movements between fixations that are themselves shown as red circles. (The yellow lines join successive fixations here, rather than showing saccadic paths.) Fixation durations are represented by the size of the circles. Taken from *Quarterly Journal of Experimental Psychology,* **57A,** p. 171 (http://www.psypress.co.uk/journals.asp), and is reprinted by permission of The Experimental Psychology Society.

The answer to which of these alternatives is driving the scanpath may well depend upon the task itself. In Hegarty's (1992) experiments with mechanical pulley systems, a brief glance will only confirm what the viewer already knows – there is a picture of a pulley system – and so even brief inspections are of little value. The task required comprehension of the diagram, and this is facilitated by the descriptive caption. In this task, each part of the picture was inspected only after reading a description of it. In the Carroll *et al.* (1992) study using *Far Side* cartoons the humour is usually created by an incongruity between the picture and the caption. There is relatively little humour in a drawing of two cows looking at the lock on the gate to their field, and the force of the cartoon resides in a dialogue caption that reveals a discussion between the cows on the advantages of opposable thumbs. In this case, inspection of the picture would deliver the overall gist, to indicate that it is a drawing of cows, and detailed scrutiny would offer nothing further until the caption has been read. Inspection of the simple pictures in the Rayner *et al.* (2001) study using advertisements would similarly produce relatively sparse information. In the two critical advertisements the images are a car and a side view of a face. The useful information is in the text. In at least some of these studies using combinations of graphics and text, there is little information to be gained from the image until the text has been understood. This may account for the brief glance at the image prior to detailed inspection of the text.

In contrast with studies using relatively sparse images, in the Underwood *et al.* (2004) sentence verification task the picture was rich in detail, and the sentence was relatively simple (an example is shown in Fig. 7.1). The same pattern of textual dominance was observed, however. Brief initial glances at pictures are made whether they are detailed or sparse, and whether the accompanying text is a simple sentence or a detailed paragraph. What is the purpose of this initial inspection of the picture, and what information is extracted? When the image has little added value, as in Hegarty's (1992) experiments, then little attention is given to the diagram, if any, prior to understanding of the text. Reading the description acts to determine the order of inspection of the components in the diagram. The value of the pictorial information in cartoons and advertisements will vary from example to example, and generalizations may be premature. In our sentence verification experiment with photographs the pictorial image was rich, and there were many potential statements that could have been made about each of them. An indication of this richness came from a study in which viewers did not know the focus of the statement until the picture was no longer available. When viewers did not see the sentence until after display of the picture had been terminated (Underwood *et al.* 2004, Experiment 2), they made a large number of fixations in order to encode as many salient features as possible in preparation for the sentence that was to verified or denied. In each case the display was available until the viewer pressed a space bar to indicate their response (Experiment 1) or their being ready to see the sentence (Experiment 2). Comparison of Figs. 1 and 2 shows an increase in the number of fixations in Experiment 2, and also a modest increase in the durations of fixations between experiments (the size of a red circle again represents the duration of the fixation). Experiment 2 used both orders of presentation, and when viewers read the sentence first, before the picture was available, their fixations on the picture were very selective and focused on the subject of the sentence.

Figure 7.2 A sample picture-text stimulus from the sentence verification task used by Underwood *et al.* (2004, Experiment 2, Picture-Sentence condition). The task was to inspect the picture in preparation for a sentence that appeared only when the picture was removed from display. Unknown to the viewer at the point when the picture was available for inspection, the sentence would ask about the place name on the road sign. The large number of fixations and the longer fixations (in comparison with those shown in Figure 7.1) indicate an attempt to encode the salient features of picture prior to appearance of the sentence. In the example shown in Figure 7.1 the viewer was able to search the relevant parts of the picture selectively.

In these cases when the pictures were shown after a sentence, they typically attracted 6 or 7 fixations in contrast with 14 or 15 fixations when shown first. Figure 7.2 shows detailed inspection pattern, with fixations on a number of objects, but this does not tell the whole story, because fixation on the car ahead does not indicate whether the viewer was encoding the car's position on the road, its relationship to other road users, the colour or type of car it was, whether it was signalling or braking, etc. The pictures were information-rich and comprehension of the events depicted required detailed and lengthy inspection. An initial brief inspection of the picture may have been sufficient to determine the gist of the scene, however, and this idea is supported by a series of studies by Biederman, Potter and others, using briefly presented displays. Before considering the purpose of the initial glance at a picture further, the evidence in favour of the early capture of gist will be reviewed.

Capturing the gist with very brief displays

The gist or schema of a scene is a representation of what the scene is about, and may be described in a brief title or simple phrase. Pictures might show vehicles in a street, rows of well-stacked shelves in a supermarket, people sitting in a restaurant, an ancient building, a rocky coastline, or a group of footballers in a goal-mouth scramble. These phrases describe the gist of different pictures and are characterized by being relatively high-level descriptors, in contrast with detailed lists of the objects that are shown. Gist is related to holistic, as opposed to local or configural processing, and captures the essential concern of the picture. Our main question concerns the information that can be acquired with a very brief glance – can the gist be captured in the first couple of fixations, and what is the extent of this processing? By suggesting that the gist can be acquired prior to an analysis of the detailed components of a scene, we raise an interesting question about the roles of top-down and bottom-up processing. If a viewer must judge whether a person in a street scene is to the left or to the right of a traffic sign, for example, they would need to inspect these objects and then identify the relationship between the person and sign. Long before they have made the necessary eye fixations, they would know that they were looking at a street scene. One very pertinent question here is how we can know about the meaning of the whole picture without having identified its individual components. The issue to be addressed here, however, concerns the extent of early processing. In the eye monitoring studies already mentioned, viewers looked at pictures for less than 1 s before transferring their gaze to the text, and studies of gist have simulated this by showing the pictures for less than 1 s.

A simple and ingenious way of separating gist information from featural information was devised by Biederman (1972). Photographs of natural scenes such as kitchens, streets and desktops were presented for 1 s in a task in which the viewer was to say which of four objects had appeared in a specified location. Viewers either saw the photograph in a conventional format, or jumbled. A jumbled picture was one cut up into six parts, and the part containing the target object was the only segment to remain in its original position. Understanding the gist of the scene is impaired with the jumbled pictures even though all of the featural components are still present. If acquiring the gist helps identification of the individual objects, then it should be easier to select a target from four candidate objects with coherent scenes, and this is what Biederman found. This is a case of holistic processing facilitating local processing. Furthermore, jumbling remained effective even when viewers knew what to look for (target cued before the picture), and where to look (location cued before the picture). These effects have been interpreted to suggest that we understand the gist of scene early, and that it aids recognition of the scene's components. This hypothesis requires that some features of the scene are identified earlier than the target and can aid in its identification, even when the target object is cued in advance.

Support for the idea of the early understanding of gist comes from a series of studies using jumbled scenes. Biederman *et al.* (1973) found that jumbling a scene had a greater effect on trials when the target was not present but was likely to be present than when it was unlikely. For example, when showing a street scene with a target of a car, jumbling would be more disruptive than if the target had been a cup. Unlikely objects were always associated with fast negative decisions, and jumbling the picture impaired these decisions, but the effect of jumbling was greater in the case of target objects that were plausible. Scene coherence enables the gist to be established, and this in turn makes it easier to search for objects that are concordant with the gist and to decide that an implausible object is absent. Biederman *et al.* (1974) looked at the time course of gist acquisition by varying the exposure duration of jumbled and coherent pictures with the task of deciding which of two labels is the most appropriate. The labels, which approximate to the gist of the scene, were either similar (and therefore required more detailed processing of the scene) or were dissimilar. For example, for a picture of a shopping plaza the pair of similar labels were 'busy road and stores' vs. 'shopping plaza' and the pair of dissimilar labels were 'kitchen' vs. 'shopping plaza'. With a 20 ms exposure, performance was barely above chance except for coherent pictures with dissimilar alternatives, but there was good separation of the four conditions with a 100 ms exposure. By this point the effect of jumbling was strong, and dissimilar labels provided a robust advantage. This study is an important development, because it demonstrates that the advantages of gist, as represented in a non-jumbled picture, are apparent with a display seen for only 100 ms. A second experiment confirmed this timing, using an object identification task similar to that introduced by Biederman (1972). At 20 ms there was no difference between jumbled and coherent pictures, but by 100 ms it was easier to identify an object in a coherent picture than in a jumbled picture. In the sentence verification task used by Underwood *et al.* (2004) we found that fixation durations on photographs were in the range 250–300 ms, and Rayner *et al.* (2001) report similar values. An effect of the overall scene schema is apparent well within this range, at exposures of 100 ms.

A different procedure has been used by Potter (1976) and her colleagues, but with a similar conclusion emerging (Potter and Levy 1969; Potter *et al.* 2002). These studies have presented a sequence of pictures in rapid succession, with the task being to look for one particular picture that is named in advance. A typical version of this rapid serial visual presentation (RSVP) task showed a sequence of 16 photographs with presentation times of 113–333 ms, with instructions to identify a target picture shown in advance, or a target picture that corresponded to a verbal label. If naming is equivalent to presenting the gist – and this will depend upon how appropriate the label is, and on the similarity of the non-targets to the label of course – then the task can be thought of as requiring the rapid capture of the gist. The number of pictures shown varied from study to study, together with the exposure duration of each picture, as well as the nature of the search task and the subsequent recognition task, but the general conclusion from Potter's studies is that rapidly presented scenes can be understood even when subsequent recognition memory is poor. Even at the 113-ms/picture rate of presentation, viewers performed at better than 60 per cent accuracy on the detection task when given a verbal label (with instructions to look for the picture of a boat or a picnic, for example), suggesting that the gist was available under these speeded viewing conditions. The Potter RSVP studies and the Biederman jumbled picture studies have been criticized by Rayner and Pollatsek (1992) on the grounds that the essential information can be extracted from the point of fixation, and that selection of the correct response alternative does not necessarily mean that the object has been identified. By analysing the fixation patterns made during scene inspection we can take a more sensitive measure of processing difficulty.

The final set of studies to be reviewed here addresses the question of how quickly we can recognize violations of the gist within a picture. Mackworth and Morandi (1967) reported an eye-tracking result that has subsequently become the subject of debate. Viewers tended to look first at those parts of a picture that were rated as being highly informative, suggesting that salient meanings could be captured sufficiently early to direct eye movements during the first few seconds of viewing. Instead of having a panel of judges rate the information values of zones within a picture, Loftus and Mackworth (1978) created line drawings of scenes with a recognizable gist (e.g. a farmyard scene, with a barn, farmhouse, fencing and a cart), and placed an object in the drawing that was congruous (a tractor) or incongruous (an octopus). Incongruous objects were fixated before their congruous counterparts (and this early fixation was also longer in duration, a result confirmed by Friedman 1979), leading to the suggestions that gist and violations of gist are detected in time to drive the first few fixations, if not the very first movement to an object in the scene.

Louise Humphreys and I have recently confirmed this result, using photographs of natural scenes onto which objects have been copied using digital images. Software packages now allow the creation of composite pictures, and having taken photographs of scenes and objects we first extracted target objects from their backgrounds, and then copied them into new scenes that were congruent, in that the object did not violate the gist, or were incongruent, or were neutral. Examples of these pictures are shown in Fig. 7.3, in which the same background scene has had a congruent object (a vacuum cleaner) and an incongruent object (a lawnmower) pasted into it. In a third condition the objects were pasted onto a photograph of a wall that could be indoors or outdoors, in an attempt to create a neutral baseline condition that would indicate how quickly an object would be fixated without distracters and without a constraining gist. Eighteen participants each saw 20 pictures with congruent objects, 20 with incongruent, and 20 neutral scenes, and with the same object appearing in a congruent, incongruent or neutral picture for different viewers. Eye movements were observed with an SMI EyeLink system that recorded eye position every 4 ms. The viewer's task was to inspect the picture in preparation for a memory test, and the preliminary results from the experiment suggest that the scanpath is sensitive to the violation of gist.

Viewers in this experiment found the incongruous objects with fewer fixations than their congruous equivalents, with incongruous objects found in 2.8 fixations (taking 0.97 s from onset of the display) while congruous objects were found with an average of 3.4 fixations (1.11 s from onset). The first fixation on the photograph was always in the centre of the display, on a fixation marker that was replaced by the picture. This first fixation did not require a saccade to bring the picture into the line of sight, but started with a stationary eye in the location of the centre of the screen. Classification of the first fixation therefore started with onset of the display, and continued until the first saccade was detected. A more appropriate way of describing the fixation data might be to say that the incongruous objects were fixated with an average of 1.8 saccadic eye movements in comparison with the 2.4 saccades that were required for fixation of a congruous object. Once fixated, the total gaze on incongruous targets was longer than that on congruous objects (1.39 s vs. 1.07 sec).[1] As expected, objects set against

---

[1] Both the comparison of gaze durations and the comparison of the number of fixations prior to target fixation were statistically reliable, and each of these conditions differed from the neutral condition on both measures.

Figure 7.3 Congruous (upper) and incongruous (lower) objects as they were digitally pasted onto a scene, with the eye movements of viewers recorded as they inspected the photograph in preparation for a memory test. In pictures for equivalent conditions, the lawn mower and the vacuum were copied into a garden scene.

neutral backgrounds were fixated very early (after 1.4 fixations, or 0.48 s from onset of the picture), and as there were no other objects to look at, viewers inspected them for longer (2.30 sec). These results are consistent with those from Loftus and Mackworth's (1978) study in that an object that violates the gist of the picture is inspected earlier than one that is consistent with the scene. On this basis of these experiments we can conclude that objects that violate the gist attract attention, and that the formation of the scene schema must be completed in the first fixation or two, in order to initiate an eye movement that results in the inspection of the inconsistent object.

Other studies using line drawings of scenes have not always confirmed the attractive effect of incongruity on the first fixation (De Graef *et al.* 1990; Henderson *et al.* 1999), and so we must regard the effect cautiously. It is possible that these studies with detailed line drawings required inspection strategies that did not facilitate the rapid detection of incongruity (e.g. see Fig. 8.2 in chapter 8), but the explanation of the inconsistent pattern of results is unclear. Further, the problem of explaining inconsistent results as a product of using line-drawings is exacerbated by Gordon's (2004) experiments using the same library of line-drawings as Henderson, De Graef, and their colleagues, and which demonstrated that attention was attracted to incongruous objects soon after onset of the display. In these studies the viewers looked at the drawing for a very brief period, and then made a decision as to which of two possible symbols had appeared after the display of the drawing was terminated. Faster responses were made to symbols appearing in the same location as an incongruous object (a fire hydrant in a bedroom scene, for example), suggesting that viewers had given more attention to these locations. The explanation of the inconsistent incongruity effect is therefore not grounded in whether or not line-drawings are used, although this may be a factor. The objects in the line-drawing experiments are smaller and less obvious or less salient than the incongruous objects used in our study with photographs (see Fig. 7.3, for example). De Graef (1998; see also chapter 8) suggests that incongruous objects may be fixated sooner because they are more difficult to identify with peripheral vision. The decrement associated with eccentricity of location would be smaller with our relatively large objects, but this does not solve the problem why the incongruity effect should appear in Gordon's experiments but not in other studies using similar line drawings. Perhaps the task used by Gordon encouraged the viewers to broaden their attention at the point that the picture was presented, in anticipation of a probe appearing in an uncertain location. Object recognition would then have been facilitated by attention being given to all parts of the scene. In the Henderson and De Graef studies attention was more focused and may have excluded the detailed processing of specific objects. Clearly, the task used and the viewer's engagement with the picture are implicated, and this effect is sure to be the subject of further investigation in the near future.

Our own study with digitally edited photographs did not find an effect on the first fixation, of course, only that incongruous objects were fixated earlier than objects that did not violate the gist of the scene. The first fixation of this target object took approximately 1 s, during which time the viewer (on average) fixated the centre of the picture, made another fixation on a non-target area of the picture, and then looked at the target object. In all of the studies looking at the attractiveness of incongruous objects, incongruity is associated with longer initial inspection of an improbable object, but this is a simple reflection of the violation of expectancy once the gist has been captured. There is an interesting correspondence here with a study of gist violations by Biederman *et al.* (1982). Line drawings of scenes such as a living room were presented in this study, with the task of detecting whether a named object (such as a sofa) was present or absent. Having read the name of the target object, viewers then initiated onset of the drawing, which was displayed for 150 ms and followed immediately by a location cue in a mask of lines. The exposure duration was set to allow a single fixation on the drawing, and a central marker determined this fixation. The cue that appeared after the drawing indicated the location of the target object on half the trials (it would be in the same location as the sofa, in this example), and at a location occupied by another object on the other trials. The task was to say yes or no according to whether the named target had appeared in the cued location. The important feature of this experiment was that the cued objects were either drawn in normal locations as they might in a natural scene, or their placement violated the expected relationships between objects and their environments. Violations that were investigated were (a) *support* – an object that does not rest on a surface (a sofa floating in the air in a street scene); (b) *interposition* – objects appear to be superimposed, or pass through one another (the drawing of the sofa and the background do not occlude each other, but pass through each other); (c) *probability* – an object that is unlikely to appear in that location (a fire hydrant in a living room); (d) *position* – an object that is plausible in the scene, but not in that position (a fire hydrant on top of a mailbox in a street scene); (e) *size* – a violation of perspective in which one object is too small or too large relative to the other objects. When cued objects were drawn with a violation, there could be combinations of violations, with, for example, a very small sofa (size violation) floating above (support violation) a garage forecourt (probability violation). The more an object violated the natural laws governing the relationships with its context, the more difficult was the decision about its presence or absence. A second experiment answered the question of how incongruous objects were inhibited. Non-violating objects were sometimes probed in drawings containing a non-probed violating object. Biederman *et al.* called these objects 'innocent bystanders', and the experiment asked whether their recognition would be impeded by the presence of a violation. They were unaffected, suggesting that the inhibition of violating objects was not due to a failure in evoking the scene schema but that the schema interfered with the identification of an object that was incongruous.

A series of studies with photographs of natural scenes has also found a recognition advantage for congruent objects, using very brief displays (Davenport and Potter 2004). After seeing a masked 80 ms display, viewers named either a foregrounded object or the background scene by typing a response into a dialogue box that appeared immediately after the mask. More accurate identification was found for objects that fitted the contexts (e.g. a ballerina on a stage) than for objects that were edited into incongruent contexts (the same ballerina in a roadway scene). Viewers reported either the foregrounded object, the background scene, or both, and the pattern of results supports an interactive model of scene perception in which the context and the component objects provide mutual facilitation.

On the basis of studies claiming that incongruous objects capture attention, and attract early fixations in the sequence of inspection, we might predict that the violating objects in the Biederman *et al.* (1982) study should also attract attention and be detected more easily than non-violating, congruous objects. Further, we might predict that the more incongruous an object, the more attractive and detectable it should be. Biederman *et al.* (1982) presented data for accuracy and for response time, and the measures told a similar story: non-violating objects were easiest to detect, and increasing the number of violations increased the difficulty of detection. The results do not support the idea that incongruous objects are detected easily – quite the opposite – and the result is consistent with the easier recognition of congruent objects in the studies with colour photographs reported by Davenport and Potter (2004). We are left with the apparent paradox of incongruous objects being salient in that they attract early fixations, but are more difficult to identify. In the fixation studies the early capture of objects is perhaps initiated without full analysis, and hence the longer gazes when they are first fixated. Prior to detailed inspection the viewer may know that some aspect of the incongruous object is unexpected without knowing what the object is. If the observer knows only that there is a mismatch between an object and its context, then its perceptual recognition in the Biederman *et al.* task may be impeded, in comparison with the same object in a congruent context. Alternatively, the slow and inaccurate identification responses in their task may be a product of cautious responding after adequate recognition, with viewers needing to double check when they think that they have seen something odd in that it is not drawn in accord with their knowledge of how objects behave in the natural world. The Biederman *et al.* (1982) results do, however, confirm that the relationship between a picture and an object within it can be processed with a single fixation, and that the congruity of the object can influence its detectability. The less the object matched the gist of the scene, the more difficult it was to say whether a named object was present in a cued location.

In an important development of the investigation of incongruous objects Boyce *et al.* (1989) asked whether it is the identification of gist that determines recognition difficulty, or the identification of other specific objects. If gist is simply the sum of the components in a scene, then recognition of one object is equivalent to the extraction of partial gist, and two objects would be an increased amount of gist, and so on. This componential model holds no specific role for scene schema or gist, and would attribute the effects of congruity and scene violation to the relationship between specific objects and the target object. In the Boyce *et al.* (1989) experiment a drawing of several objects was shown, with the task being to decide whether an object that was named in advance was present at a location indicated after the display was terminated. This is the task used by Biederman *et al.* (1982). A set of objects appeared against a congruent scene (e.g. a group of food products in a refrigerator) or an incongruent scene (the same products in a bedroom), and the experiment asked whether it is the related objects or the congruent scene that facilitates recognition. Objects were identified more often when the background was congruent, suggesting that it is not the diagnostic value of the individual objects that is responsible for the effect. Boyce *et al.* (1989) argued in favour of the global gist of scenes as an influence rather than the incremental identification of the component objects of a scene. This conclusion was supported by a subsequent experiment in which objects in a drawing had to be named (Boyce and Pollatsek 1992). The target object was identified to the viewer by having it 'wiggle' – it moved a short distance and then moved back to its original location. Wiggling objects attracted eye fixations very effectively, and the important result is that the naming responses were faster when the object was congruent with its background. In one of the experiments, using a display that changed according to the viewer's point of fixation, the effects of congruity were apparent when the background was only available during the first fixation on the display. If the background was also available during the second fixation, the congruity effect increased slightly, suggesting that the gist was available on the first fixation and that it built during the second fixation.

With brief displays of pictures – brief enough to be sure that only one fixation has been made – the results indicate that (a) viewers can identify a named picture in an RSVP sequence, (b) in a task requiring identification of one of the objects in the picture, viewers are adversely influenced by jumbling the components of the picture, and (c) the detection of an object in a picture is increasingly impaired as the object becomes less congruous. The results considered so far suggest that with a single fixation that (a) we can acquire enough information about a picture to be able to say whether it matches a simple label, (b) we can say whether it matches a previously shown picture, and (c) we will be influenced by whether the objects in the scene are congruous with the general setting or gist. Supporting data also comes from experiments by Intraub (1980), Antes *et al.* (1981), and Schyns and Oliva (1994), and the case for rapid gist recognition is reviewed further by Potter (1999) and by Intraub (1999). The accumulating evidence favours a model of scene perception in which the gist is acquired on the first fixation, and that the gist can then influence the detectability of the component objects in a top-down or conceptual process, and that the identification of individual objects within the scene is the subject of processing after the early acquisition of the gist. This account is inconsistent with Hollingworth and Henderson's (1998) conclusion that object perception is not facilitated by the context provided by the scene, but it does agree with the theoretical positions on contextual facilitation taken by investigators such as Bar (2004), Boyce and Pollatsek (1992), Davenport and Potter (2004) and De Graef (1992). We now return to the studies of picture-text combinations, in which the picture is characteristically inspected very briefly, and scrutinized only after the text has been read carefully.

What do viewers see during the early inspection of a picture?

The evidence from studies of picture recognition, using RSVP, jumbled displays, very briefly presented pictures, and pictures containing incongruous objects, points to the acquisition of gist with just one fixation. We can see what the picture is about and know whether it shows a kitchen scene or a harbour or cars on a busy road, for example, in less time than is taken by an average fixation on a photograph. The studies reviewed in the previous section allowed viewing of the picture long enough for one fixation, or found effects of congruity during the first few fixations. Discrimination of a target from a set of pictures will depend upon the similarity of the pictures in the set, and upon the similarity of the names used, of course, and the label that best describes the gist of a picture will vary according to the other pictures being inspected. The conventional account of picture perception, however, is that the general meaning of a picture can be understood within the time taken for a single fixation. When we look at combined displays of pictures and captions we look briefly at the picture and then read the text carefully (Carroll *et al.* 1992; Hegarty 1992; Rayner *et al.* 2001; Underwood *et al.* 2004), and so we might conclude that during the first glance at the picture the gist is acquired and the overall meaning of the picture understood. However, our picture-text studies with a sentence verification task suggest that limited information is acquired from the picture during the first few fixations, and these studies will now be described in more detail, so that this contrary conclusion can be justified.

Underwood *et al.* (2004, Experiment 1) presented photographs of road scenes accompanied by simple active declarative sentences that were true or false descriptions of the scenes. An example is shown in Fig. 7.1, with the sentence declaring that the car is passing a horse or a cyclist. All 24 participants were drivers and had no difficulties in understanding the events depicted, with response accuracy being greater than 95 per cent. The task was to judge whether the sentence was a true or false description of the scene, and to indicate this judgement by pressing one of two response keys. The picture and sentence were shown together in this experiment, and remained on screen until a response key was pressed. Eye fixations were recorded with an SMI EyeLink system, and measures taken included the locations and durations of fixations, as well as sentence verification times. Viewers characteristically looked at the picture for two or three fixations (including the first fixation on the picture when it appeared on the screen near the centre of the viewer's gaze), then read the sentence, and only then looked extensively at the picture, making their decision about the sentence while looking at the picture.

Decisions that the sentence was false took longer than those to declare that the sentence was true, in accord with linguistic-propositional models of the sentence verification task (Clark and Chase 1972; Carpenter and Just 1975). To understand the requirements of the task it is first necessary to consider these conventional accounts of the verification task, and to attribute variations in decision times to stages of processing. The established pattern of results from these earlier studies is that sentences gain the fastest responses when they are true and affirmative (TA), such as 'The star is above the plus' next to a picture of a star printed directly above a plus sign; the next fastest are false affirmatives (FA) such as 'The plus is above the star', followed by false negatives (FN) such as 'The star is not above the plus'; and the slowest decisions are for true negatives (TN) such as 'The plus is not above the star'. The linguistic-propositional models account for this pattern by arguing that what determines the point at which a comparison can be made is the number of steps required to generate equivalent propositional representations of the sentence and the picture. False affirmative sentences require one extra comparison step relative to TA sentences, FN sentences require four extra steps, and TN sentences require five extra steps, according to Clark and Chase (1972). The constituent comparison model proposed by Carpenter and Just (1975) has sentences requiring k, $k+1$, $k+2$, and $k+3$ comparisons for TA, FA, FN and TN sentences respectively. The common feature of the models is that performance is determined by converting both the picture and the sentence into a propositional representation, and the decision being made on the basis of comparing one representation against the other.

The propositional comparison models provide a good account of performance when the pictures are simple and are predictable, and when the picture and sentence are presented together. Difficulties arise when the pictures are not simple geometric displays, and when the participants prefer to use a non-propositional strategy (or when they are encouraged to do so by the instructions in an experiment). Difficulties also arise when the sentence and picture are presented separately, as we shall see shortly (Underwood *et al.* 2004, Experiment 2), and when less simple pictures are used (Goolkasian 1996, 2000; Feeney *et al.* 2000). Participants may use a non-propositional imagery strategy to perform the task, by first converting the sentence into an image of what the display would look like, and then comparing that image with the actual picture (MacLeod *et al.* 1978; Tversky 1975). The strategy is encouraged by the repeated use of the same two stimuli – a star (*) and a plus sign (+), one above the other – as the only stimuli presented to the participants. Such a strategy was preferred by a subset of the MacLeod *et al.* (1978) sample of participants, and was used under instruction by those in the Mathews *et al.* (1980) experiment. Use of the imagery strategy leads to a changed pattern of results, with false statements having slower responses than their true equivalents, but with negatives no longer causing delays. MacLeod *et al.* found of a pattern of (TA = TN) < (FA = FN) for participants with high spatial ability. Kroll and Corrigan (1981) confirmed this pattern in a study that identified two subsets of participants, and then encouraged those who preferred the imagery strategy to abandon it in favour of a linguistic-propositional strategy by presenting displays that were less predictable. In some blocks of trials the star and the plus sign were presented side by side as well as one above the other, but with the same set of statements to be verified. The imagined forms of unpredictable displays were more difficult to generate because there were more possible configurations that could appear after the sentence, and so the most effective strategy was to perform a propositional comparison. There is some doubt, therefore, over the generality of the linguistic-propositional models suggested by Clark and Chase (1972) and by Carpenter and Just (1975), but one result that appears to be robust is what we might call the falsification effect – slower responses to false statements than to those that are true. The point at which the falsification effect appears can be taken as an indication that both the picture and the sentence have been understood. Whichever strategy is used – propositional or imagery – it is only when both picture and sentence have been understood that they can be compared, and only then can the falsification effect appear. By looking at the eye-fixation records in the Underwood *et al.* (2004) experiment we can see that viewers do not arrive at this point until they have completed reading the sentence and have relocated their gaze to give detailed scrutiny of the picture. This distinction is shown in Fig. 7.4, where sensitivity to the validity of the statement appears only when viewing the picture. There is no difference between true and false statements in the number of fixations made on the sentence, whereas more fixations were made on pictures that did not agree with the sentence. The effect is also shown in Fig. 7.5, which presents the total inspection time on the picture and on the

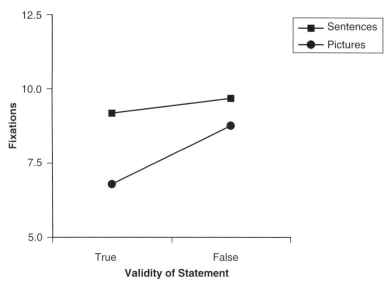

Figure 7.4 Number of fixations on the two parts of the picture-text display in Underwood *et al.* (2004, Experiment 1). This interaction shows the total amount time viewers spent looking as the picture and at the sentence, with the distinction between a true and false statement only becoming apparent after careful reading of the sentence and when looking at the picture.

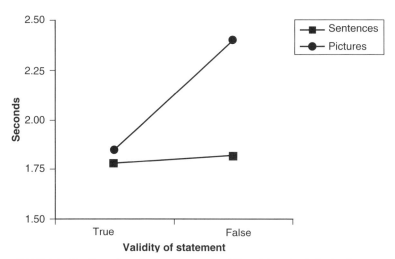

Figure 7.5 Total attention given to the two parts of the picture-text display from Underwood *et al.* (2004, Experiment 1). This indicates the total amount time viewers spent looking as the picture and at the sentence, with the distinction between a true and false statement failing to appear.

sentence. The falsification effect only appears during re-inspection of the picture, after the sentence has been understood.

Viewers showed sensitivity to the true-false distinction after they had made the initial glance at the picture and after, not during, their reading of the sentence. An analysis using the total inspection time (total of all fixations) on each part of the display presents the same conclusion, with a falsification effect appearing only in the inspection of the picture. Only after they moved their eyes away from the sentence and looked again at the picture did they recognize that the sentence was or was not accurate. While reading the sentence they did not know this because their reading times are equivalent. At this point they had glanced at the picture, making one or two fixations on it in addition to the initial fixation at the onset of the display, and then they had read the sentence. But they were unable to make a decision about the sentence, and their fixation behaviour showed no sensitivity to the accuracy of the sentence. Their initial fixations on the picture did not allow them to acquire sufficient information to make a decision after reading the sentence, and they had to look again at the picture. Their initial fixations on the picture, therefore, did not deliver the detailed representation necessary for a decision. The viewers knew about the type of statements that appeared in the experiment and they had unconstrained viewing, i.e. they could look at any part of the display for as long as they wished before making their decision. The viewers' preferred strategy was to look only briefly at the picture before reading the sentence, and then look selectively at the part of the display described by the sentence. During the initial glance we must assume that viewers acquire the gist of the scene, but we must also conclude that knowing the gist is insufficient to be able to answer a question about the relationships between objects in the scene.

In Underwood *et al.* (2004) Experiment 2, pictures and sentences appeared consecutively, and the picture-sentence order provides a possible explanation for the brevity of the initial glance at the picture. Figure 7.2 is taken from the record of one of the viewers in this experiment, and shows the large number of fixations that are necessary on a picture when there is uncertainty about the content of the sentence that is to be verified. The time spent looking at the picture is doubled relative to Experiment 1 but the sentence reading time increased by only one third. If the picture is to be sufficiently well encoded as to be able to respond to the sentence, then it must be inspected thoroughly and all salient objects recognized and their relationships identified. With a concurrent display it is simpler to read the sentence and then inspect the most relevant part of the picture, rather than attempting to encode all objects and their relationships. A notable feature of the results from the second experiment is the absence of the falsification effect in the decision times indicated by the true/false keyboard response or in any of the eye-fixation measures. The formal models of sentence verification performance have no explanation for the absence of true-false differences in judgements about the accuracy of sentences.

The information collected in two or three fixations is not sufficiently rich to support decisions about the accuracy of statements made about a picture. This is the conclusion from Underwood *et al.* (2004, Experiment 1), and is based on the appearance of a falsification effect only after the picture has been inspected briefly and the sentence read completely. Until the picture was re-inspected, there was no sensitivity

The car ahead is passing a cyclist.

Plate 1 A sample picture-text stimulus from the sentence verification task used by Underwood *et al.* (2004, Experiment 1). The task was to judge whether or not the sentence (in this example, 'The car ahead is passing a cyclist') accurately described the events shown in the picture, and to make a yes/no keyboard response when the decision was made. The fixations of one viewer are superimposed on the stimulus here, with yellow lines indicating the movements between fixations that are themselves shown as red circles. (The yellow lines join successive fixations here, rather than showing saccadic paths.) Fixation durations are represented by the size of the circles. Taken from *Quarterly Journal of Experimental Psychology*, **57A,** p. 171 (http://www.psypress.co.uk/journals.asp), and is reprinted by permission of The Experimental Psychology Society.

Plate 2 A sample picture-text stimulus from the sentence verification task used by Underwood *et al.* (2004, Experiment 2, Picture-Sentence condition). The task was to inspect the picture in preparation for a sentence that appeared only when the picture was removed from display. Unknown to the viewer at the point when the picture was available for inspection, the sentence would ask about the place name on the road sign. The large number of fixations and the longer fixations (in comparison with those shown in Figure 7.1) indicate an attempt to encode the salient features of picture prior to appearance of the sentence. In the example shown in Figure 7.1 the viewer was able to search the relevant parts of the picture selectively.

Plate 3 Congruous (upper) and incongruous (lower) objects as they were digitally pasted onto a scene, with the eye movements of viewers recorded as they inspected the photograph in preparation for a memory test. In pictures for equivalent conditions, the lawn mower and the vacuum were copied into a garden scene.

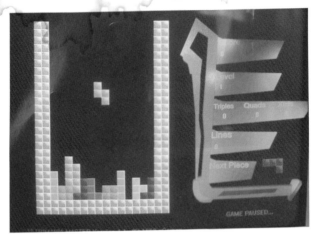

Plate 4 Screen dump of the Tetris playing area with a game in progress (after Gustafsson 1988).

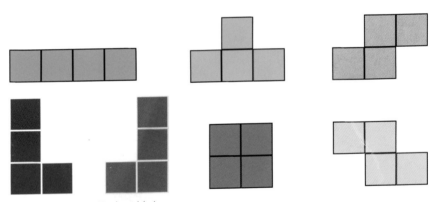

Plate 5 The seven Tetris zoid shapes.

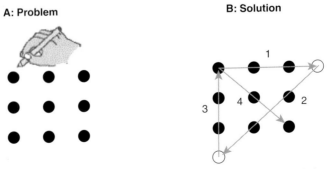

A: Problem

B: Solution

te 6 The nine-dot problem (Scheerer 1963): connect the nine dots with four straight
  without lifting the pen. Panel B shows the solution.

to the accuracy of the sentence. If the initial inspection had delivered a rich representation of the picture, then a falsification effect would have emerged during the reading of the sentence, as the inaccuracy was uncovered. Gist can be captured within the time taken by this initial inspection, according to the studies by Biederman, Potter and others, and so it seems that gist does not include featural detail of the kind probed in the sentence verification task. If we had used statements such as 'The cars are on the road' or 'A pedestrian is crossing the road' then perhaps a falsification would have been seen immediately upon completion of reading the sentence. The statements used in the Underwood *et al.* (2004) experiments all required recognition of the relationship between objects or identification of detail, rather than the overall setting or schema of the scene or the presence of a single object.

Underwood and Green (2003) simulated the early brief inspection of a photograph, again with a sentence verification task, in an attempt to encourage viewers to make use of the pre-sentence sight of the picture. In this experiment the picture was available for a short period, prior to the combined presentation of the picture and sentence. If viewers could make use of this early sight of a picture, then they should be able to acquire the gist prior to the sentence appearing. The experiment also varied the type of question being asked, with some statements being more holistic and related to the gist, and others referring to more detailed, local features. Viewers saw a preview of the picture for 750 ms or 2250 ms, with the short preview simulating approximately three fixations, and the long preview being three times this duration, and sufficient for the viewers to look extensively around the picture. We also had a no-preview condition for comparison, and this was essentially the same picture-sentence display as used by Underwood *et al.* (2004, Experiment 1). Preview was a between-groups variable, and statements were randomized for each viewer, with a total of 24 participants. The extrinsic or gist-related sentences were statements about the relationship between fore-grounded objects (e.g. with a photograph of a man standing next to a child's pushchair, in a park the accompanying sentence was 'The person is standing beside an empty pushchair') and the intrinsic or featural statements concerned the properties of fore-grounded figures (e.g. 'The person is wearing a pair of black shoes').

The falsification effect was not reliable in this experiment, but more notable was the difference between judgments about extrinsic and intrinsic statements. There was a main effect of extrinsic statements being more difficult to verify than intrinsic statements, but also no interaction with picture preview. Faster decisions were associated with increasing amounts of preview, but the simulated three fixations with the 750 ms preview did not differentiate in facilitating gist-related rather than feature-related statements. This pattern of results is shown in Fig. 7.6. If gist is always acquired with the first fixation or two, then we must conclude that the extrinsic statements about the relationship of objects in the scene did not question the gist of the picture. Preview provided a similar advantage to both types of sentence judgment. This would suggest that gist does not contain this level of detail, and that it perhaps only concerns the overall setting of the scene such as that which could be described with a single word (e.g. 'garden') or short phrase (e.g. 'cars on a busy road').

In a recent attempt to influence the viewers' inspection strategies, Underwood *et al.* (2005) allowed 12 participants to know the focus of interest of the sentence that was

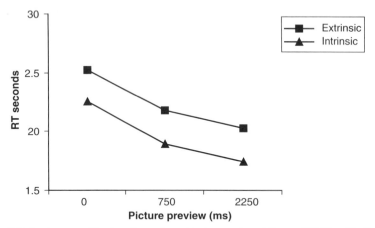

Figure 7.6 Sentence verification times from Underwood and Green (2003), with three picture preview conditions, and extrinsic (gist-related) and intrinsic (feature-related) sentences.

to be verified, while for another 12 viewers the sentence could concern any aspect of the photograph. No instructions were given about the likely focus of the sentence, but throughout practice and with all experimental trials, one group of viewers were consistently asked about a foregrounded person. The picture and sentence appeared together in this eye-tracking experiment, and viewers were unconstrained in their inspection strategies. We expected that with predictable sentences the early fixations on the picture would focus upon the foregrounded person and their immediate surroundings in anticipation of the sentence. Cueing was predicted to encourage the acquisition of gist from the early fixations on the picture, and facilitate the decision about the validity of the sentence. The picture-sentence display remained in view until the viewer made a key-press response to indicate that the sentence was true or false. The photographs in this experiment were similar in composition to those used by Underwood and Green (2003), with individuals performing a range of actions in indoor and outdoor settings. The sentences for the cued group addressed some aspect of the foregrounded person (e.g. with a picture of a girl standing near to a construction site with a wire-mesh fence supporting a yellow warning light, the sentence was 'The girl is wearing a white jacket'). For the uncued group the sentence sometimes addressed the person, and sometimes addressed another aspect of the scene (e.g. with the example of the girl standing next to the fence, the sentence was 'A yellow light is attached to the fence').

There were several effects of cueing in this experiment, and the locus of the falsification effect changed from our previous studies. The number of early fixations on the picture increased reliably for the cued participants, indicating that these viewers were giving more attention to the picture prior to reading the sentence. Cueing also reduced the duration of fixations, but only for fixations on the pictures. As in previous experiments, fixations on pictures were considerably longer than those

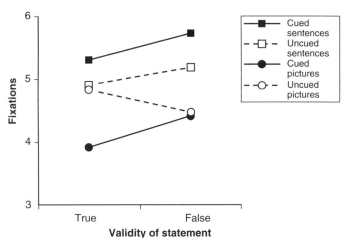

Figure 7.7 Number of fixations on the two components of the picture-sentence display from Underwood *et al.* (2005). The subject of the sentence, which was to be judged as true or false, was predictable for some participants (cued), but not for other (uncued).

on sentences. There was also an effect of cueing on the overall number of fixations on the two parts of the display, as shown in Fig. 7.7. Cueing influenced the distribution of fixations, with more fixations on sentences than pictures only in the cued conditions, and a notable reduction in the attention given to pictures for the cued viewers. There was also an effect of sentence validity in this experiment, with the cued viewers showing an increase in the amount of attention when the sentence was false. This increase held for fixations on the sentence as well as the picture, suggesting that the cued viewers were sensitive to the accuracy of the sentence as they were reading it. This is in contrast to the uncued viewers here and in the Underwood *et al.* (2004) experiment, in which sentence validity only had an effect on inspection behaviour when the picture was re-inspected. The initial reading of the sentence was not sensitive to its accuracy for the uncued participants, indicating that they had not encoded the picture in sufficient detail for them to know whether the sentence was true or false. Cueing the viewers enabled them to acquire information about the subject of the sentence prior to reading it.

Getting the gist: Some conclusions based on studies of eye fixations

In an experiment with a sentence verification task and photographs of natural scenes, we found that the characteristic inspection pattern or scanpath was to look briefly at the picture, then read the sentence, then look more closely at the picture, and then make the decision about the accuracy of the sentence (Underwood *et al.* 2004). This pattern of a brief inspection of the picture prior to reading the accompanying text has also found with a range of other graphic materials, by Carroll *et al.* (1992), Hegarty (1992), and Rayner, *et al.* (2001). The present discussion has concerned the purpose of this initial glance at the picture.

Well-established studies using a range of methods have shown that viewers can recognize the scene schema or gist of a picture with a very brief glimpse, and so we can assume that the scene gist is acquired during the initial inspection of the graphical component of a picture-text display. These studies have used very brief presentations – sufficiently brief for us to be sure that only one fixation is made on the picture. Biederman and his colleagues have demonstrated the recognition of gist using jumbled pictures (e.g. Biederman 1972; Biederman *et al.* 1973, 1974), on the basis that jumbling a picture makes extracting the gist more difficult, while leaving the component objects largely unchanged. When jumbling makes object identification difficult, then we can conclude that the scene schema contributes to the recognition of the components of the scene – a case of recognition of the parts by the whole, rather than analysis-by-synthesis. This view here is that scene perception involves the general gist influencing object recognition, rather than the piecemeal identification of components that in turn would prime the to-be-identified object. This position is also supported by Boyce *et al.* (1989) and by Boyce and Pollatsek (1992), who varied the background scene and the component objects independently.

A second series of experiments, conducted by Potter and her colleagues, used an RSVP technique with a set of pictures being shown very briefly one after the other (e.g. Potter 1976; Potter, and Levy 1969; Potter *et al.* 2002). Viewers could correctly detect the presence or absence of one of these pictures, on the basis of being shown the target in advance or being told to look for a picture on the basis of a name.

The third series of experiments concerned the detectability of objects that do not match the scene schema, although there are some apparent contradictions in the pattern of results here, and some inconsistencies in the results between experiments. Biederman *et al.* (1982) presented line drawings very briefly, with the task being to say whether a previously named object had been present in the location indicated by a post-exposure marker. Objects that violated environmental constraints, by being too small for their position, or that did not rest on a horizontal surface, for example, were detected with more difficulty than those that were congruous. This study also supports the notion that gist helps with object identification because it was objects that violated the scene schema which were more difficult to recognize. A similar pattern of results, with more difficult recognition of incongruous objects in photographs, has been reported by Davenport and Potter (2004). Eye-tracking studies have pointed to an inconsistent story about the detectability of objects that violate the gist of the picture, and where they do find an effect, it is the *faster* detection of incongruous objects rather than *impaired* detection. Loftus and Mackworth (1978) found that incongruous objects (an octopus drawn in a farmyard scene) were fixated earlier than congruous objects drawn in the same location, and we have found a similar result by digitally pasting objects in photographs (Fig. 7.3). De Graef *et al.* (1990) and Henderson *et al.* (1999) did not find an effect of incongruity on the probability of an early fixation, however, and this relationship between gist and detectability remains in need of clarification.

The scene schema or gist can be acquired very rapidly, well within the time required for a single fixation on a picture, and influences the identification of objects within the scene. The brief initial inspection of a picture might serve the purpose of identifying the gist of the picture, so that before reading the caption we know what the picture is about and what we might expect from the text. The gist may be acquired very early, but the information represented by the gist is insufficient to support the sentence verification decision, and we must conclude that it contains only a very general impression of the setting of the scene. Perhaps if the sentence to be verified had been a very general, high-level description (for example, 'This is a harbour' accompanying a picture of a harbour or an airport runway) a falsification effect would have been seen following a brief, early inspection of the picture. This conclusion comes from the locus of the effect of sentence accuracy in Underwood *et al.* (2004, Experiment 1), in which there was an effect of accuracy while making a detailed inspection of the picture, but not while reading the sentence. During the initial brief inspection, insufficient detailed information had been extracted from the picture to enable the decision about sentence accuracy to be made when the sentence was read. There was no difference between the reading of true and false sentences at this point. The effect of sentence accuracy was apparent only when the picture was re-inspected for detail. Our subsequent studies have confirmed that detailed information is not available from the initial inspection (Underwood and Green 2003), and that by cueing viewers with advance knowledge of the subject of the sentence to be verified, enough information can be extracted from the picture for sentence accuracy to be detected when the sentence is first read (Underwood *et al.* 2005). These results leave us with the conclusions that the scene schema or gist is a very general overview of the setting of the picture that can be used to detect objects that are congruent with the schema, but that the schema is a representation that contains insufficient detail to support consideration of the components of the picture.

Acknowledgements

Peter De Graef, Jukka Hyönä, and Sandy Pollatsek provided invaluable comments on the first draft of this chapter. In addition I would like to thank colleagues at Nottingham for their comments during discussion of the issues raised here, particularly Peter Chapman, David Crundall, Jean Underwood, Adam Galpin and Louise Humphreys.

References

Antes, J. R., Penland, J. G., and Metzger, R. L. (1981). Processing global information in briefly presented pictures. *Psychological Research*, **43**, 277–292.

Bar, M. (2004). Visual objects in context. *Nature Reviews Neuroscience*, **5**, 617–629.

Biederman, I. (1972). Perceiving real-world scenes. *Science*, **177**, 77–80.

Biederman, I., Glass A. L., and Stacy, E. W. (1973). On the information extracted from a glance at a scene. *Journal of Experimental Psychology*, **103**, 597–600.

Biederman, I., Rabinowitz, J. C., Glass, A. L., and Stacy, E. W. (1974). On the information extracted from a glance at a scene. *Journal of Experimental Psychology*, **103**, 597–600.

Biederman, I., Mezzanotte, R. J., and Rabinowitz, J. C. (1982). Scene perception: Detecting and judging objects undergoing relational violations. *Cognitive Psychology*, **14**, 143–177.

Boyce, S. J., and Pollatsek, A. (1992). Identification of objects in scenes: the role of scene background in object naming *Journal of Experimental Psychology: Learning, Memory and Cognition*, **18**, 531–543.

Boyce, S. J., Pollatsek, A., and Rayner, K. (1989). Effect of background information on object recognition. *Journal of Experimental Psychology: Human Perception and Performance*, **15**, 556–566.

Carpenter, P. A., and Just, M. A. (1975). Sentence comprehension: A psycholinguistic processing model of verification. *Psychological Review*, **82**, 45–73.

Carroll, P. J., Young, J. R., and Guertin, M. S. (1992). Visual analysis of cartoons: A view from the far side. In: K. Rayner (ed.) *Eye movements and visual cognition: Scene perception and reading*. New York: Springer Verlag, pp 444–461.

Clark, H. H., and Chase, W. G. (1972). On the process of comparing sentences against pictures. *Cognitive Psychology*, **3**, 472–517.

Davenport, J. L., and Potter, M. C. (2004). Scene consistency in object and background perception. *Psychological Science*, **15**, 559–564.

De Graef, P. (1992). Scene-context effects and models of real-world perception. In: K. Rayner (ed.) *Eye movements and visual cognition: Scene perception and reading*. New York: Springer Verlag, pp 243–259.

De Graef, P. (1998). Prefixational object perception in scenes: Objects popping out of schemas. In: G. Underwood (ed.) *Eye guidance in reading and scene perception*. Oxford: Elsevier, pp. 315–338.

De Graef, P., Christiaens, D., and d'Ydewalle, G. (1990). Perceptual effect of scene context on object identification. *Psychological Research*, **52**, 317–329.

Feeney, A., Hola, A. K. W., Liversedge, S. P., Findlay, J. M., and Metcalfe, R. (2000). How people extract information from graphs: Evidence from a sentence graph verification paradigm. In: M. Anderson, P. Cheng and V. Haarslev (ed), *Theory and applications of diagrams: First international conference, Diagrams 2000*. Berlin: Springer-Verlag, pp. 149–161.

Friedman, A. (1979). Framing pictures: The role of knowledge in automatised encoding and memory for gist. *Journal of Experimental Psychology: General*, **108**, 316–355.

Goolkasian, P. (1996). Picture-word differences in a sentence verification task. *Memory and Cognition*, **24**, 589–594.

Goolkasian, P. (2000). Pictures, words and sounds: From which format are we best able to reason? *The Journal of General Psychology*, **127**, 439–459.

Gordon, R. D. (2004). Attentional allocation during the perception of scenes. *Journal of Experimental Psychology: Human Perception and Performance*, **30**, 760–777.

Hannus, M., and Hyönä, J. (1999). Utilization of illustrations during learning of science textbook passages among low- and high-ability children. *Contemporary Educational Psychology*, **24**, 95–123.

Hegarty, M. (1992). The mechanics of comprehension and the comprehension of mechanics. In: K. Rayner (ed.) *Eye movements and visual cognition: Scene perception and reading*. New York: Springer Verlag, pp 428–443.

Henderson, J. M., Weeks, P. A., and Hollingworth, A. (1999). The effect of semantic consistency on eye movements during complex scene viewing. *Journal of Experimental Psychology: Human Perception and Performance*, **25**, 210–228.

Hollingworth, A., and Henderson, J.M. (1998). Does consistent scene context facilitate object perception? *Journal of Experimental Psychology: General*, **127**, 398–415.

Intraub, H. (1980). Presentation rate and the representation of briefly glimpsed pictures in memory. *Journal of Experimental Psychology: Human Learning and Memory*, **6**, 1–12.

Intraub, H. (1999). Understanding and remembering briefly glimpsed pictures: implications for visual scanning and memory. In: V. Coltheart (ed.) *Fleeting memories: Cognition of brief visual stimuli*. Cambridge, MA: MIT Press, pp. 47–70.

Kroll, J. F., and Corrigan, A. (1981). Strategies in sentence-picture verification: The effect of an unexpected picture. *Journal of Verbal Learning and Verbal Behavior*, **20**, 515–531.

Loftus, G. R., and Mackworth, N. H. (1978). Cognitive determinants of fixation location during picture viewing. *Journal of Experimental Psychology: Human Perception and Performance*, **4**, 565–572.

Mackworth, N. H., and Morandi, A. J. (1967). The gaze selects informative details within pictures. *Perception and Psychophysics*, **2**, 547–552.

MacLeod, C. M., Hunt, E. B., and Mathews, N. N. (1978). Individual differences in the verification of sentence-picture relationships. *Journal of Verbal Learning and Verbal Behavior*, **17**, 493–507.

Mathews, N. N., Hunt, E. B., and MacLeod, C. M. (1980). Strategy choice and strategy training in sentence-picture verification. *Journal of Verbal Learning and Verbal Behavior*, **19**, 531–548.

Potter, M. C. (1976). Short-term conceptual memory for pictures. *Journal of Experimental Psychology: Human Learning and Memory*, **2**, 509–522.

Potter, M. C. (1999). Understanding sentences and scenes: The role of conceptual short-term memory. In: V. Coltheart (ed.) *Fleeting memories: Cognition of brief visual stimuli*. Cambridge, MA: MIT Press, pp. 13–46.

Potter, M. C., and Levy, E. I. (1969). Recognition memory for a rapid sequence of pictures. *Journal of Experimental Psychology*, **81**, 10–15.

Potter, M. C., Staub, A., Rado J., and O'Connor D. H. (2002). Recognition memory for briefly presented pictures: The time course of rapid forgetting. *Journal of Experimental Psychology: Human Perception and Performance*, **28**, 1163–1175.

Rayner, K., and Pollatsek, A. (1992). Eye movements and scene perception. *Canadian Journal of Psychology*, **46**, 342–376.

Rayner, K., Rotello, C. M., Stewart, A. J., Keir, J., and Duffy, S. A. (2001). Integrating text and pictorial information: Eye movements when looking at print advertisements. *Journal of Experimental Psychology: Applied*, **7**, 219–227.

Schyns, P. G., and Oliva, A. (1994) From blobs to boundary edges: Evidence for time and spatial scale dependent scene recognition. *Psychological Science*, **5**, 195–200.

Tversky, B. (1975). Pictorial encoding of sentences in sentence-picture comparison. *Quarterly Journal of Experimental Psychology*, **27**, 405–410.

Underwood, G., and Green, A. (2003). Processing the gist of natural scenes: Sentence verification with intrinsic and extrinsic configurations of objects. *Cognitive Processing*, **4**, 119–136.

Underwood, G., Jebbett, L., and Roberts, K. (2004). Inspecting pictures for information to verify a sentence: Eye movements in general encoding and in focused search. *Quarterly Journal of Experimental Psychology*, **57A,** 165–182.

Underwood, G., Crundall, D., and Hodson, K. (2005). Confirming statements about pictures of natural scenes. *Perception*, in press.

8

Semantic effects on object selection in real-world scene perception

Peter De Graef

Abstract

When trying to predict where the eyes will go next in the free exploration of real-world scenes, recent models have focused on the analysis of visual stimulus properties in order to compute the priority that will be assigned to a given scene component or object. Possible influences on gaze control that are rooted in the meaning of the scene and the semantic relation of the scene to the objects in it, have been regarded as elusive and mostly relevant to later stages of scene exploration. In the present chapter, I will review recent theoretical developments that provide a more acceptable framework to consider influences of object-in-scene semantics on gaze control. In addition, I will present eye-tracking data recorded in intentional search and exogenous cueing paradigms, which demonstrate reliable and immediate context effects on eye guidance in meaningful scenes.

Introduction

In a recent review of research on human gaze control during real-world scene-perception, Henderson (2003) presents a simple, yet comprehensive taxonomy of factors influencing where a viewer will send the eyes in a meaningful, realistic scene. First, there are low-level, observer-independent stimulus properties such as spatial frequency, contrast, color, intensity, and edge orientation which can all be used to identify discontinuities in the visual stimulus. Because discontinuity is more informative than continuity these stimulus regions will carry the highest weights in a stimulus-based saliency map that determines where the eyes will go next. Second, there are various sources of observer-dependent knowledge that can guide the observer's gaze: personal, episodic knowledge of the specific scene that is viewed (e.g. *my* kitchen); generic, schematic knowledge of the scene category instantiated in the current view (e.g. *a* kitchen); and task-related knowledge stipulating the best visual foraging strategy given the current task goal and visual environment (e.g. finding a glass in someone else's kitchen).

Having distinguished stimulus-based and knowledge-driven determinants of gaze control, Henderson (2003) poses the logical question whether and how these two should be combined in a single saliency measure for a given stimulus region. So far, the prevailing view appears to be that a stimulus-based saliency map provides the primary input to the gaze control system. On this view, knowledge works as a secondary filter modulating the stimulus-based saliency weights when required by the task at hand.

The stimulus-based account of gaze control in scene perception seems to be quite successful. Detailed, biologically motivated models of saliency computation have been outlined and the saliency maps computed by the models were found to correlate with fixation patterns of subjects engaged in free viewing (Parkhurst et al. 2002) or in visual search (see chapter 11; Rao et al. 2002). Admittedly, there are limits to this correlation. Specifically, when scenes become more meaningful (e.g. pictures of real buildings and interiors rather than computer-generated fractals) the correlation between the models' predictions and the human observers' performance decreases (Parkhurst et al. 2002). In addition, when the correlation is examined as a function of scene viewing time, the stimulus-based saliency map loses its impact on gaze control after the first few saccades (Mannan et al. 1995, 1997).

The above discrepancies between actual fixation patterns and stimulus-based predictions of fixation placement have been regarded as a reflection of untractable, knowledge-driven viewing strategies that introduce noise in what would normally be an orderly stimulus-based scanpath (Mannan et al. 1997; Parkhurst et al. 2002). However, one might also argue that purely stimulus-based scanning is the deviation, explaining fixation placement only for nonsensical stimuli which are very rare in our everyday perception. From this perspective, we might want to invest more energy in uncovering knowledge-driven rather than stimulus-based regularities in the selection of saccade targets in real-world scenes.

Of course, this is precisely the approach taken in a rapidly growing body of research on task-dependent eye movement behavior. Saccade target selection has been shown to predictably reflect the acquisition of specific information relevant to the goals and stages of execution of even very complex tasks such as block copying (Ballard et al. 1997; Hayhoe et al. 1998), driving in the real world (Chapman and Underwood 1998; chapter 12) or in a simulator (Shinoda, et al. 2001), playing chess (see chapter 14), or playing ping pong (Land and Furneaux 1997). However, what happens when the observer is not engaged in a specific task that more or less stringently dictates where and what piece of relevant information should be sampled next from the visual stimulus?

Exploring a scene for meaning is exactly that kind of ill-defined task. What guides the eyes when a viewer is looking at a scene with the (often implicit) intention to identify background and objects, to grasp the scene's spatial and functional layout, to determine how the depicted situation came about and what may happen next? Can one still identify knowledge-driven regularities in saccade target selection under these viewing conditions? Or do scanpaths reflect nothing but idiosyncratic viewing strategies driven by the viewer's personal style of scene exploration and/or experience with the viewed stimulus? Although the answer is bound to be complex, this still seems to be a worthwhile question given the fact that a considerable portion of our waking time is devoted to explicitly or implicitly exploring visual scenes for understanding.

Schema-driven eye guidance in scene perception

I have previously argued that real-world scene semantics might play a role in determining where the eye will go next in a free viewing situation (De Graef 1998). The basic assumption underlying this argument is that long experience with different instances of a limited number of environmental settings causes human observers to develop categorical scene representations or *schemas*. These schemas stipulate the background, objects, and spatial relations that are characteristic for a particular setting (Biederman 1981; Friedman 1979; Hess and Slaughter 1990; Rumelhart *et al.* 1986). It is further assumed that access to the correct schema representing the currently viewed scene is accomplished during the first scene fixation. In the earlier stages of scene perception research there was quite a bit of controversy on what the exact scene information could be, which underlies immediate scene schema activation: diagnostic objects (Antes *et al.* 1981); the scene background (Boyce *et al.* 1989); or clusters of volumetric object representations (Biederman 1988). Recently, however, a number of more precise mechanisms for rapid scene identification have been outlined on the basis of a detailed analysis of scene image statistics (Oliva and Torralba 2001; Torralba and Oliva 2003), or inspired by functional and neuroanatomical study of the visual system (Epstein and Kanwisher 1998; Steeves *et al.* 2004; Rasche and Koch 2002). These studies all support the notion that the overall identity or gist of a scene can be acquired from very brief scene exposures (Potter *et al.* 2002; chapter 7) that are well below the modal duration of a fixation on a realistic scene (about 220 ms, as reported by Henderson and Hollingworth 1998).

Concerning what happens once the schema has been activated, a host of more or less detailed accounts have been suggested. The central notion is that subsequent peripheral and/or foveal processing of objects in the scene will vary as a function of whether the object is represented in the schema, i.e. whether or not the object can be expected to be present in the scene. Proposed theories about processing differences between scene-consistent and scene-inconsistent objects refer to the general distinction between concept-driven and data-driven processing (De Graef 1998; Johnston and Hawley 1994), to the difference between object-diagnostic features that are defined by the object's internal structure versus those defined by the object's relation to the scene (Torralba and Sinha 2001), or to the difference between strictly feedforward analysis of a visual object and top-down modulation by re-entrant processes activated by a preliminary low spatial-frequency representation of the object (Bar 2003; Rao *et al.* 2002).

Regardless of the precise description of the schema influence on object perception, all these accounts predict that scene-consistent objects will be processed and recognized more quickly than scene-inconsistent objects. Translating this prediction to the process of gaze control in scene perception, this implies that a peripheral object's saliency as a future saccade target during scene exploration might be influenced by the object's semantic plausibility in the scene. The remainder of this chapter will be devoted to two illustrations of how scene semantics may influence which objects in the scene are selected as saccade targets.

Context-guided object search in scenes

That scene semantics may modulate object selection is not a new suggestion. Scene perception research has known a long-standing controversy on whether or not covert attention and overt gaze shifts preferentially go to objects that have a low semantic plausibility in the scene (e.g. a dumptruck on top of a building, De Graef 1992). Early work with realistic scenes has often been cited as evidence for this notion of semantic pop-out (Loftus and Mackworth 1978). Later research, however, with better controlled stimuli and more sophisticated eye-tracking equipment failed to replicate a saccadic preference for semantic oddballs (De Graef *et al.* 1990; Henderson *et al.* 1999; but see chapter 7, for a recent report of saccadic preference for inconsistent objects). In their review of high-level scene perception, Henderson and Hollingworth (1999) therefore concluded that there is no solid evidence for the claim that the semantics of peripherally located objects play a role in gaze control during free scene viewing.

However, they did point out that scenes can provide an efficient framework for searching for a particular object, given that the object belongs in that scene. Specifically, Henderson *et al.* (1999) had viewers scan line drawings of scenes in search for a predesignated object which could be highly plausible or highly implausible given the viewed scene. Plausible target objects were reached by a saccade more quickly and from greater distances than implausible target objects. This advantage was attributed to a search strategy that exploits knowledge about the usual location in which particular objects could be found in particular scenes, a strategy that can only work for objects that are frequently encountered in the viewed scene and that have a prototypical location in that scene.

Context-guided object search has also been invoked as a possible explanation of the greater detectability of scene-consistent target objects in briefly presented scenes (e.g. Biederman *et al.* 1982). Specifically, it has been argued that guided by a target object's name, viewers may selectively allocate attention to that part of the scene which according to everyday experience is most likely to contain the target (Boyce and Pollatsek 1992a; Davidoff and Donnelly 1990; De Graef 1992; Henderson 1992a). Such context-guided attention shifts can be executed prior to or during the brief scene presentation. For instance, when 'truck' is the target, the physical properties of a truck suggest to be on the lookout for a large, freestanding object located at the scene's ground level. Thus, prior to scene exposure the viewer could already allocate attention to the bottom half of the display and selectively tune to a coarse spatial scale suitable for capturing information about large objects (Oliva and Schyns 1997). Alternatively, attention shifts may be guided by contextual information processed from the scene itself and executed during the scene presentation. For instance, the target 'toaster' could suggest a medium-sized, box-like object, placed on top of another large box (kitchen counter) which is lined along the kitchen wall. Viewers could use the brief scene exposure to 'home in' on the location and form which most closely fits this relational description.

Since perceptual discriminability is higher at the center of attention (e.g. Downing 1988; Hawkins *et al.* 1990) either type of expectation-based attention shift would enhance the identifiability of objects that conform to these expectations. It is clear, however, that a priori attention shifts are not a very reliable basis for a perceptual advantage: many objects have similar general properties and they allow only coarse predictions about the target's most likely location. Moreover, the general area in which an object can be expected in a given scene depends on the depicted perspective on the scene which cannot be predicted by participants.[1] Thus, it seems that if attention shifts are to account for the enhanced detection of scene-consistent objects in 150 ms scene exposures, these shifts must be planned and executed on-line, during the scene's presentation.

To determine whether such a fast context-guided search mechanism might be operating, we designed a modified version of the object detection task (Biederman *et al.* 1982) taking into account earlier demonstrations of flaws in the original construction of the catch trials (De Graef 1992; Hollingworth and Henderson 1998). Figure 8.1 illustrates the course of a trial in the object detection task. Participants are required to first read an object name and then look at a tachistoscopically flashed scene, which is subsequently masked. They then have to determine whether a specific object in that scene, marked by a position cue in the post-exposure mask, was the target object named before scene presentation. Cued objects appeared at unpredictable locations (average eccentricity of 4.75°) and for only 150 ms thus preventing the execution of deliberate visually-guided eye movements. The cued object either appeared as it normally would in a real-world version of the scene, or it appeared in a scene in which it normally would not be encountered. To ensure that speed and accuracy of responses reflected the perceptibility of the cued object, the named target appeared at the cued position on only half of the trials (target trials) while some other object appeared at that location on the other half (catch trials). In this manner, hits and false alarms could be computed and measures of sensitivity as well as response bias could be derived. A detailed discussion of the experimental design and detection data can be found elsewhere (De Graef 2004). For now, I will focus on the question whether fast context-guided search could be demonstrated.

According to the search hypothesis, participants will attempt to quickly shift attention to the first peripheral form that has a size and location that, given the overall setting, would be consistent with the previously named target. If only the object at the cued position fits this relational description of the target, then context-guided attention shifts can be an efficient mechanism for enhancing discriminability of the cued object. However, if several forms in the scene have a size and position that would be consistent with the target in that setting (i.e. target decoys) attention is more likely to be turned to an object other than the one at the cued location and discriminability at the cued location will be reduced.

---

[1] Thanks to David Crundall for suggesting this argument.

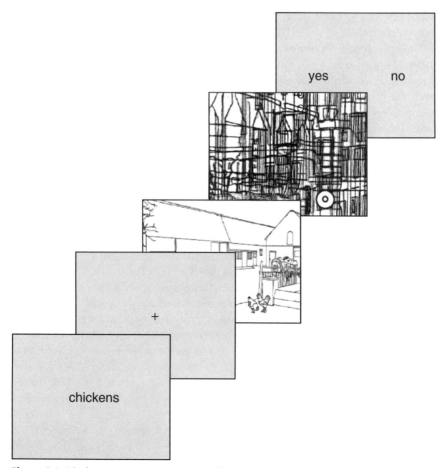

Figure 8.1 Display sequence on a typical object detection trial is shown from left to right. Reading of the target name is self-terminated, followed by a central fixation cross, a brief scene exposure (values have ranged between 100 and 250 ms), a pattern mask with embedded position cue, and a self-terminated reminder of the response alternatives: 'yes' if the target did appear at the cued position, 'no' if it did not.

To test this prediction, a new object detection study was conducted in which the number of decoys was manipulated. Figure 8.2 shows four displays, which preceded by the target name 'laundry basket', provided an orthogonal combination of setting (expected vs. unexpected) × decoys (0 vs. 2). To identify possible attention shifts while looking at these displays, eye movements were recorded on every trial. Voluntary saccades and attention shifts are intimately linked in the sense that saccade execution only occurs after a preceding attention shift to the saccade target (e.g. Cavegn and d'Ydewalle 1996; Henderson 1992b; Mackeben and Nakayama 1993; Schneider 1995;

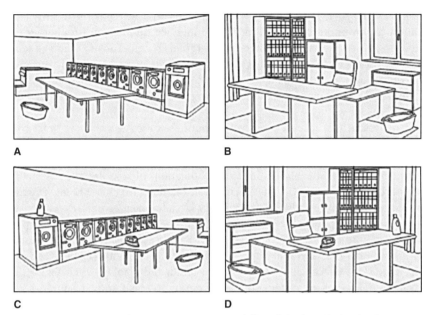

Figure 8.2 Target stimuli for determining perceptibility of the laundry basket in an expected setting (A and C) vs. an unexpected setting (B and D), and in the presence of two decoys (C and D) vs. no decoys (A and B).

Zelinsky 1996; Zelinsky and Sheinberg 1997). By this rationale, the target of the first saccade after scene onset can reveal where in the scene attention was sent. If attention is indeed systematically shifted to the form that most closely fits a relational description of the target's usual real-world appearance, then we should find that when there are no decoys present, the cued object receives more saccades in the expected settings than in the unexpected settings. In addition, adding decoys should have a more adverse effect in the expected than in the unexpected settings: Because there is no prior real-world experience with the target in the unexpected settings, viewers have no clue as to which briefly glimpsed form is most likely to be the target. It can therefore be predicted that adding decoys should decrease the frequency of saccades to the cued object more in the expected settings than in the unexpected settings. Finally, the frequency of saccades to the decoys should be higher in the expected than in the unexpected settings.

It may of course seem pointless to formulate predictions with respect to saccade targets in scenes that are only shown for 150 ms. Indeed, there is sufficient evidence that voluntary saccades across line drawings of scenes generally have latencies longer than this (De Graef 1998; Henderson *et al.* 1999; van Diepen *et al.* 1995). Thus, while a voluntary saccade can be planned before the end of the scene, its execution may well be cancelled because the target has disappeared (McConkie *et al.* 1985). To explore this possible problem, participants first completed the experiment with 150 ms scene exposures, and then repeated it with 300 ms exposures which is sufficiently long to allow for voluntary saccades. In this manner, we could examine whether the memory-guided saccades executed *after* a 150 ms scene exposure had the same characteristics as the visually guided saccades executed *during* the 300 ms exposures. This would indicate that the memory-guided saccades were in fact visually-guided saccades that were planned during the 150 ms exposure and executed in the absence of the scene.

An analysis of first saccade latency distributions at the two exposure times confirmed that a 150 ms scene flash is enough to select a saccade target in the scene and to submit the saccade program for execution. As can be seen in Fig. 8.3, the distribution for the 150 ms exposures shows three sub-populations of saccades: the first before 150 ms, the second in the 150–300 ms interval, and the third after 300 ms. The first population primarily consists of anticipatory saccades planned before scene onset. Visually guided, voluntary saccades take 70–80 ms neural transmission time to plan and execute, and the fastest subpopulation of human saccadic reactions (so-called *express saccades*) has a modal latency between 90 and 120 ms (e.g. Cavegn and d'Ydewalle 1996; Gezeck *et al.* 1997; Wenban-Smith and Findlay 1991). Taking this into account, most of the saccades registered during 150 ms scene exposures were in fact too fast to be aimed at targets encoded from the scene. By the same rationale,

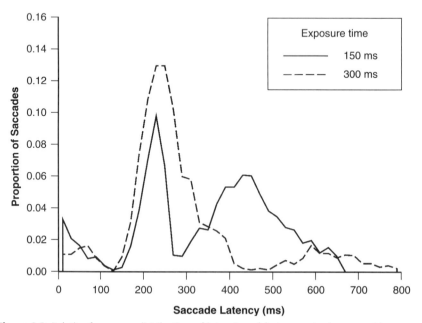

Figure 8.3 Relative frequency distribution of latencies of first saccades (measured in ms from scene onset). Distributions are constructed with 20 ms bins and plotted as a function of scene exposure time.

most of the saccades in the second population, based around 230 ms, are too fast to be responses to elements in the post-scene mask which appeared at 150 ms. Thus, it is reasonable to assume that the 230-population consists of saccades to targets selected during the 150 ms scene presentation. This conclusion is supported by the fact that the same 230-population emerges regardless whether the saccade is executed *after* a 150 ms scene exposure or *during* a 300 ms scene exposure. Finally, the third saccade population based around 430 ms, contains saccades aimed at the position cue in the mask.

To determine whether the observed saccades did indeed reflect fast, context-guided attention shifts, landing sites of the saccades were determined and the proportion of saccades ending on the cued object or on one of the decoys was computed. These proportions were entered in a repeated-measures analysis of variance, which showed that, as predicted, cue-directed saccades were most frequent in expected settings with no decoys present. In addition, cue-directed saccades were reliably less frequent in the presence of decoys and this effect was more outspoken in the expected settings, as illustrated in Fig. 8.4. Finally, decoy-directed saccades were reliably more frequent in the expected than in the unexpected settings. We can therefore conclude that a 150 ms scene exposure can be used by viewers in order to locate and attend to objects that are likely to appear in the depicted scene. Thus, gaze control in this speeded object detection task is influenced by prior schematic knowledge about the viewed setting.

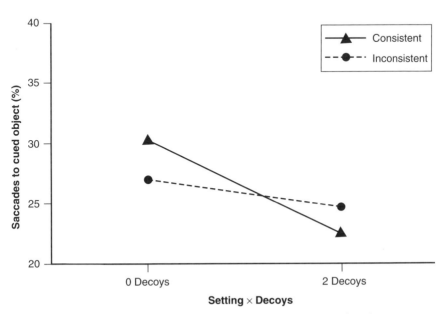

Figure 8.4 Proportion of saccades directed towards the cued object's location as a function of whether the scene could be expected to contain the target, and as a function of the presence of decoys.

Effects of scene context on attentional orienting to object onsets

In the preceding section, I presented evidence for the very rapid operation of schema-driven eye guidance in the context of an object search task. But can scene semantics also direct gaze when the scene cannot be used as a framework for quickly locating a meaningful, expected object? As already mentioned above the presently available evidence is mixed. Loftus and Mackworth (1978) had viewers scan scenes in preparation for a memory test and found a fixation precedence for semantically anomalous objects. Henderson *et al.* (1999) used the same task and found no fixation precedence effect, but Underwood (chapter 7) did observe a fixation precedence for anomalous objects during scene inspection for a memory task. De Graef *et al.* (1990) registered scanpaths during the search of a scene for non-objects (Kroll and Potter 1984) and failed to find a precedence effect. However, when the same search task was slightly modified to control the viewer's first saccade in the scene, the selection of an object as target for that first saccade was affected by the object's semantic consistency with the surrounding scene (De Graef *et al.* 1992).

In this last paradigm we borrowed a technique from Boyce and Pollatsek (1992b): as soon as a steady first fixation on the scene was detected by the eye tracker, a peripherally located object (average eccentricity of 6°) briefly jumped up and down (*wiggled*), thus creating a transient that attracted attention and gaze. Importantly, the wiggling object could be either semantically consistent with the scene or semantically inconsistent. Two studies were conducted: one with an SOA of 140 ms between scene and wiggle onset, and one with an SOA of 160 ms.

An analysis of gaze shift reactions to the peripherally wiggling object, as a function of the object's semantic consistency with the surrounding scene, revealed three things (De Graef 1998). First, consistent objects drew reliably fewer saccades and were fixated later (if at all) in the course of scene exploration than inconsistent objects. Second, when consistent objects were skipped by the viewer's gaze, the fixations preceding that skip were reliably longer than fixations preceding a saccade to a consistent object. No such effect was found for inconsistent objects. Third, as illustrated in Fig. 8.5, latency distributions of saccades in response to the wiggling object indicated the presence of three subpopulations of saccades: reflexive, normal voluntary saccades, and delayed voluntary. This last subpopulation only surfaced in response to the wiggle of consistent objects, but could not be taken to simply signal a slower reactivity to objects that fit in the scene. As can be seen for the short wiggle onsets (top panel), consistent objects also attracted more reflexive saccades than inconsistent objects. Note that this early preference for consistent objects dissolves for the longer wiggle onset delay (bottom panel). This is consistent with the notion that in visual scenes conceptually activated objects or words exert an early pull on attention which gradually reverts to an attentional preference for objects or words that are not activated (Christie and Klein 1995; Gordon 2004; Hoffmann 1987).

Based on these data, I speculated that due to their incorporation in the currently active scene schema, scene-consistent objects can be processed at greater eccentricities reducing the need to actually fixate the objects in order to recognize them (De Graef 1998).

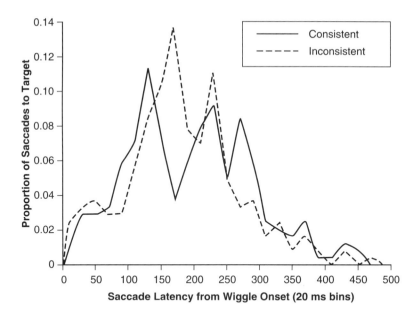

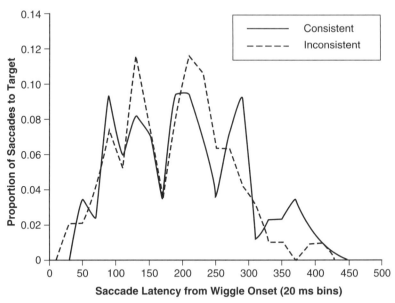

Figure 8.5 Relative frequency distribution of latencies of first saccades towards the wiggled object (measured in ms from wiggle onset). Distributions are plotted with 20 ms bins as a function of the semantic consistency between the wiggled object and the scene. Top panel presents the data obtained with a 140 ms SOA between scene and wiggle onset, bottom panel presents the data obtained with a 160 ms SOA.

This would explain the more frequent skipping and greater delays before a consistent object is finally fixated. In agreement with similar findings in reading research (Balota *et al.* 1985; chapter 6; Rayner and Well 1996), it would also account for the longer durations of fixations preceding a skip or a delayed voluntary saccade to the object. Specifically, in those cases the saccade is delayed or ultimately even cancelled because peripheral processing of a consistent object is sufficiently efficient to allow the visual system to maintain fixation without falling below a criterion level of information intake per unit of time.

Having suggested that the useful field of view may be larger for semantically consistent than inconsistent objects, it remains to be established what mechanism underlies this advantage. Earlier, I suggested two possibilities (De Graef 1998). First, top-down stimulation from the activated schema may enhance the diagnosticity of object features derived from a bottom-up image analysis of peripheral stimulus regions. This view was recently defended in neurophysiological and computational models which propose that low spatial-frequency, iconic object representations play a central role in quickly finding and recognizing objects (Bar 2003; Rao *et al.* 2002). Second, because consistent objects in a scene resonate with object representations contained in the activated scene schema, figure-ground segregation will be faster and the object will be more likely to become a salient attentional and fixation target. This because the visual foraging system has a natural inclination to be on the look-out for objects (Henderson 2003).

Obviously, enhanced bottom-up processing of a segregated object and facilitated figure-ground segregation of that object are not mutually exclusive and can in fact be subserved by the same visual architecture and image analysis algorithms (e.g. Lamme and Roelfsema 2000). However, the two mechanisms are functionally distinct: It is quite possible that scene context affects object processing once the object has received attention, but that it has no effect whatsoever on the initial allocation of attention (Henderson, *et al.* 1999). In fact, given the mixed evidence reviewed above, there seems to be little reason to maintain that semantic scene context may systematically affect attentional orienting to objects. Before we conclusively reject this hypothesis, however, there is one methodological problem in the reviewed studies that needs to be addressed. Specifically, in all but one of these studies attentional orienting is indirectly inferred from incidental saccades to one particular predesignated object which the viewer does not know to be the target. Hence, an actual advantage for consistent objects may always be underestimated because every realistic scene contains a number of consistent objects that all may be contextually facilitated saccade targets. In fact, as illustrated in Fig. 8.5, when a short wiggle singles out the target object from all other potential saccade targets, we do observe a tendency for consistent objects to elicit more reflexive orienting responses than inconsistent objects (De Graef 1998).

To address this issue we conducted a series of experiments (De Graef *et al.* 2000) built around a standard exogenous cueing paradigm (e.g. Posner 1980). In this paradigm, participants were told that they would have to perform a simple discrimination between a percentage symbol (%) and an ampersand symbol (&), as quickly and as accurately as possible. To complicate the task, each target symbol would appear in an unpredictable position on the screen and would be preceded by briefly flashed line-drawings of everyday scenes. As illustrated in Fig. 8.6, each trial started with a central

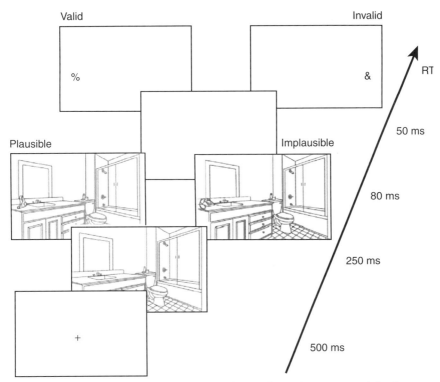

Figure 8.6 Trial in the exogenous-cueing paradigm. After 500 ms, a central fixation cross is replaced by a 250 ms scene exposure, followed by an 80 ms onset of a plausible or implausible object in the scene. Subsequently, a blank screen is shown for 50 ms and followed by a discrimination target which is presented at the validly cued location or in the opposite hemifield.

fixation cross. Participants were told to fixate the cross and press a button to initiate the trial. After 500 ms, the fixation cross was replaced with a black-on-white line drawing of a scene background. Following 250 ms of scene exposure, a peripherally located cue object was added to the scene for an 80 ms period. The screen was then blanked for 50 ms prior to the appearance of the target symbol against a white background. The target symbol stayed on the screen until the participant responded with a button press. The target symbol either appeared at the location previously occupied by the cue object (valid trials) or at the same location in the opposite half of the screen (invalid trials). Reaction times were measured from the onset of the target symbol and eye movements were recorded throughout the trial.

To directly determine whether the attentional saliency of an object is modulated by that object's semantic consistency with the surrounding scene, we varied the cue object's real-world plausibility in the scene. As outlined above, we hypothesized that schema-contained scene-consistent objects are more easily segregated from the scene background than objects for which no contextual activation of object representations has occurred. In line with earlier work demonstrating that the onset of a new object is a powerful signal for an attention shift (Yantis and Hillstrom 1994), we expected that the onset of a consistent object would be a more salient cue for attentional and subsequent gaze shifts. Specifically, we predicted that an analysis of response times to the target symbols should show the standard cueing effect (i.e. faster responses when the cue object and target symbol appeared in the same rather than in opposite locations), and that this effect should be stronger for the consistent objects. In addition, we expected that the greater attentional saliency of the consistent objects would also produce more and faster saccades in the direction of consistent objects than of inconsistent objects.

The analysis of manual response times confirmed that this object-in-scene cueing paradigm elicits the standard advantage of valid trials over invalid trials: the brief object onset in the scene draws attention to its location and reliably speeds subsequent target discrimination at that location by about 24 ms (De Graef *et al.* 2000). In addition, response times showed a spatial stimulus-response compatibility effect: Reponses were a reliable 26 ms faster when the position of the target symbol and the required manual response overlapped in space (e.g. a right-handed response to a target appearing on the right) than when they did not (e.g. a right-handed response to a target appearing on the left). This classic Simon effect (for a review, see Lu and Proctor 1995) is not directly relevant to our current discussion but needs to be mentioned in order to evaluate our second prediction that the cueing effect should be stronger for consistent objects. Specifically, we found that this was indeed the case but only for responses that were spatially incompatible with the location of the target symbol. This three-way interaction between cueing effect, consistency effect, and Simon effect can be interpreted as indirect support for the greater attentional saliency of consistent objects (De Graef *et al.* 2000). Specifically, earlier studies showed that the Simon effect decreases when the target location is validly precued (Stoffer and Yakin 1994). In the current experiment, this decrease of the Simon effect was reliably stronger when consistent objects were used as valid cues, suggesting that they were more efficient than inconsistent objects. However, a more direct indication of this greater attentional saliency would be more compelling.

Such an indication was found in the analysis of saccade characteristics recorded during the task. For all trials with correct responses, we determined target and latency of the first saccade following the onset of the cue object. Saccade latencies were measured from cue onset, saccade targets were determined by examining whether the saccade landed inside or within 0.5° of the smallest rectangle enveloping the cue object and/or target symbol. As predicted, we observed that consistent cue objects were targeted on a reliably greater proportion of the trials than inconsistent cue objects. This conclusion may at first seem puzzling given the fact that the cue object only appears for 80 ms, and that participants can hardly be expected to make visually-guided saccades in such a short time. However, as already argued above, saccades can be planned in the presence of a stimulus and accurately executed even if the stimulus has disappeared before the saccade actually started.

For the present set of data this can be easily illustrated by plotting the distribution of recorded latencies of saccades that landed at the location of the cue and/or target. As can be seen in Fig. 8.7, there were two saccade populations. The first population

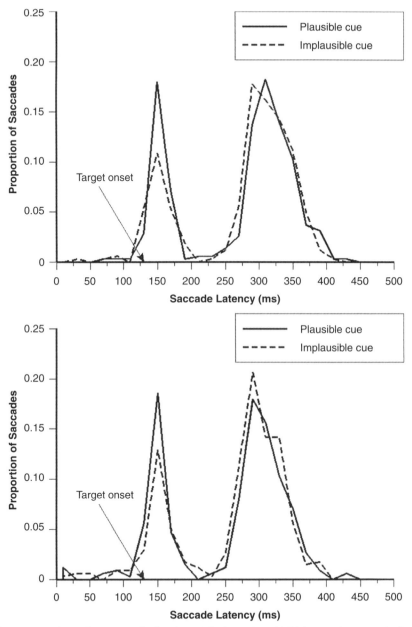

Figure 8.7 Relative frequency distribution of the latencies of initial saccades towards the cued location. Bin-size is 20 ms and distributions are plotted as a function of cue validity and semantic plausibility of the cue object in the scene.

had a modal latency of 150 ms from cue onset and contained saccades that were executed in response to the onset of the cue object. These saccades did not reflect orienting responses to the onset of the target symbol because this only appeared 130 ms after cue onset, as marked on the graphs. In contrast, the second population of saccades had a modal latency of 290–310 ms, i.e. 160–180 ms after target onset. This population reflected orienting responses to the target symbol instead of the cue object.

Inspection of the first population for both valid and invalid trials confirmed our final prediction: Fast saccadic responses to cue onset were most frequent when the cue was a semantically consistent object, as statistically confirmed in a repeated-measures analysis of the proportion of saccades that fell in the 130–170 ms range. That this effect did not change as a function of cue validity again underlines that the effect is caused by characteristics of the cue, not of the target nor of the combination of cue and target. Contrary to what was observed for the saccadic responses to the cue, saccadic responses to the target symbol's onset were somewhat faster when preceded by an inconsistent cue. Note that this effect is most evident on valid trials, where we see a shift in the peak for the consistent objects (310 ms) relative to the inconsistent objects (270 ms). On invalid trials, both peaks fall at 270 ms. That only target-directed saccades preceded by consistent cue objects are affected by cue validity could possibly reflect an inhibition-of-return effect preventing attention to return to a recently attended location (e.g. Klein and MacInnes 1999; Fuentes et al. 1999). Because early allocation of attention is more likely in the case of a consistent cue object than of an inconsistent cue object, later allocation of attention to a target symbol appearing in that same location (i.e. on valid trials) is more likely to be hindered by the inhibition-of-return mechanism for consistent cue objects than for inconsistent cue objects.

To conclude this section on attentional and saccadic orienting in scenes, I should briefly discuss an apparent discrepancy between the results obtained with the wiggling paradigm and with the cueing paradigm. Specifically, in the cueing studies we observed that a sudden object onset in a scene drew more saccades when the object was semantically consistent with the scene than when it was inconsistent. In the wiggling studies, however, a sudden object wiggle in a scene drew more saccades when the object was inconsistent than when it was consistent. These results may seem to be contradictory, but they are not. First, in the cueing studies the saccadic preference for consistent objects is observed in a population of short-latency saccades (130–170 ms). In the wiggling studies, the same population of saccades shows the same preference (see Fig. 8.5) indicating the same initial high salience for scene-consistent objects in both types of studies.

Second, whether or not a peripheral transient will exogenously elicit a saccade is also a function of the degree to which endogenous control systems have disengaged from the current fixation point (see chapter 11; Findlay and Walker 1999). In the cueing studies, viewers had been fixating the center of the scene 250 ms prior to the cue onset, and their fixation point rarely contained an object. In the wiggling studies, the viewers were always fixating an object at the time of the peripheral wiggle and this fixation had only been going on for 140–160 ms. This implies that in the wiggling study, the fixation system was always more likely to be engaged at the time of the peripheral transient. Thus, while a saccadic program will be set up to respond to the peripheral transient, execution of the saccade is delayed. In line with recent models of gaze control in reading (Reichle *et al.* 1998) this creates a moratorium during which an initial familiarity check can be performed on the peripherally signaled object. If this check is successful (i.e. object identification is deemed to be imminent) a second saccade program can be set up and the peripheral object will be skipped. Because context facilitates the familiarity check for consistent objects, they will be skipped more often than inconsistent objects.

The current case for scene-context effects on object selection in scenes

In the preceding sections, I reviewed theories and presented new evidence concerning the notion of schema-driven eye guidance in real-world scene perception. In doing so, I hope to have conveyed two main points. First, although it is significantly easier to coherently and transparently model an object's saliency in terms of stimulus-based characteristics than in terms of knowledge-based characteristics, we should not automatically assume that the latter cannot exert a systematic and traceable influence on gaze control. Both the context-guided search data and the analysis of rapid saccadic responses to contextually manipulated objects show that object-in-scene semantics are available at the very first stages of scene exploration. In addition, the results of the cueing experiments show that this contextual influence is automatic: even when scene and object identity are entirely irrelevant to task performance, they do influence where attention is allocated. Also note that, in contrast to models of stimulus-based saliency, we have not employed sophisticated techniques for determining the precise strength of semantic object-scene associations and thus predicting the saliency of that object in that scene. Instead we have used common sense or independent ratings as a basis for deciding whether or not an object is consistent with a scene. The fact that even under these conditions we can observe reliable semantic effects, illustrates that these effects are quite robust.

Second, there is constant progress in the sophistication of our methods to detect contextual influences on gaze control and in the detail of our accounts of these influences. In terms of methodology, fast and accurate eye-trackers have provided us with the opportunity to look at saccade latency distributions instead of averages and thus use the precise chronometry of stimulus presentation as an anchor to functionally interpret the presence and frequency of various subpopulations of saccades. In terms of theoretical frameworks, we have come a very long way since scene-specific schemas were invoked in a *deus ex machina* fashion to explain how scene context could affect object perception (e.g. Friedman 1979). We now have working computational accounts of how an activated object representation may guide gaze (Rao *et al.* 2002; Torralba and Sinha 2001) as well as neurophysiologically plausible accounts of how scene schemas, object templates and their influence on gaze control can be implemented in the human visual system (Bar 2003; Ganis and Kutas 2003; Hochstein and Ahissar 2002; Rasche and Koch 2002; Sheinberg and Logothetis 2001).

Of course, methodological and theoretical progress in observing and explaining eventual effects does not discharge us from the responsibility to actually show the effects in a convincing manner. With respect to the first of the two context effects presented in this chapter, there seems to be a consensus that fast and efficient context-guided search for a specific target object is indeed a reliable and robust phenomenon (Henderson 2003). In contrast, the idea that attentional orienting to objects is modulated by context effects remains a point of discussion. As already mentioned earlier, the main argument against this type of context effect has been that scanpath recording during scene exploration has shown no consistent fixation precedence effect for objects that do or do not fit in with the scene semantics (De Graef *et al.* 1990; Henderson *et al.* 1999). However, with the wiggling and cueing studies discussed in the present chapter I hope to have demonstrated that a reliable attention and fixation precedence can be found for scene-consistent objects when the target object is not just one of many equally consistent and equally salient objects.

Nevertheless, in line with criticisms launched against earlier claims of a fixation precedence (Loftus and Mackworth 1978) one could point out that stimulus-based object saliency was not controlled for. Therefore, semantic consistency and stimulus-based object saliency may have been inadvertently confounded, and scene-consistent objects may have been visually more salient. To refute this possibility, we recently completed a replication of the cueing studies with vertically inverted scenes and objects (De Graef 2001). Stimulus inversion makes it more difficult to rapidly access the meaning of the scene but does not affect any possible differences in visual saliency (Kelley *et al.* 2003). In our control study, the observed saccadic response precedence for consistent objects disappeared completely with the inverted stimuli. We are therefore confident that the effect can be attributed to access to the semantics of the scene rather than to an incidental difference in stimulus-based saliency.

Finally, one might wonder (Gordon 2004) whether our finding of a context-based preference in saccades with latencies as short as 130 ms is compatible with recent studies on the time course of object recognition (Thorpe *et al.* 1996; Fabre-Thorpe *et al.* 2001; VanRullen and Thorpe 2001). Specifically, in a task requiring participants to quickly detect the presence of an animal in peripherally flashed natural scenes, manual response times and ERP-signals indicated that about 150 ms of stimulus processing time is required to classify a peripheral visual form as animal. If this is the case, how can our participants determine the semantic fit of an object in a scene and plan and execute a saccade to that object in less time than is required to make a simple categorization? The answer is quite simply that the rapid access to object-in-scene semantics evidenced in our saccadic response data does not logically require recognition of the object, nor conscious identification of the scene. Instead, activation of a scene-specific schema and of the coarse scale representations of likely objects that can signal the potential presence of objects in peripheral vision, is likely to be a fully automatic, pre-attentive and implicit process based on associations learned during our extensive experience with the semantic structure of the world (Bar 2003; Rasche and Koch 2002). In this sense, the initial computation of knowledge-based and stimulus-based saliency values for objects in real-world scenes may very well occur in the same time frame and yield a single, integrated saliency value for any given object in the scene.

Conclusion

Recent accounts of gaze control in scene perception have, implicitly or explicitly, assigned great importance to the analysis of image characteristics in order to derive saliency values for different scene components. These values are then used as input to control attention and gaze shifts towards various objects in the scene. Knowledge-based control of shifts in processing focus is assigned a modulating role at best and this only in later stages of scene exploration. In this chapter, I have presented data on schema-guided attention and gaze shifts during intentional search and exogenously cued exploration of real-world scenes. In both cases, the viewer's experience with what objects can typically be expected in a given setting was found to exert a systematic influence on where the eye would go next and this during the very first fixation on a scene. It is therefore proposed that any complete model of gaze control in meaningful scenes should integrate the computation of stimulus-based and schema-based saliency values for the individual objects in the scene.

Acknowledgements

This chapter benefited greatly from the revision of an earlier version by Peter Chapman and David Crundall. This work was supported by conventions GOA 98/01 and GOA 2005/03 of the Research Fund K.U. Leuven and convention G.0583.05 of the Fund for Scientific Research-Flanders.

References

Antes, J. R., Mann, S. M., and Penland, J. G. (1981). *Local precedence in picture naming: The importance of obligatory objects*. Paper presented at the 22nd meeting of the Psychonomic Society, Philadelphia, PA.

Ballard, D. H., Hayhoe, M. M., Pook, P. K., and Rao, R. P. N. (1997). Deictic codes for the embodiment of cognition. *Behavioral and Brain Sciences*, **20**, 723–767.

Balota, D. A., Pollatsek, A., and Rayner, K. (1985). The interaction of contextual constraints and parafoveal visual information in reading. *Cognitive Psychology*, **17**, 364–390.

Bar, M. (2003). A cortical mechanism for triggering top-down facilitation in visual object recognition. *Journal of Cognitive Neuroscience*, **15**, 600–609.

Biederman, I. (1981). On the semantics of a glance at a scene. In: M. Kubovy, and J. R. Pomerantz (ed.) *Perceptual organization*. Hillsdale, NJ: Erlbaum, pp. 213–263.

Biederman, I. (1988). Aspects and extensions of a theory of human image understanding. In: Z. Pylyshyn (ed.) *Computational processes in human vision: An interdisicplinary perspective*. Norwood, NJ: Ablex, pp. 370–428.

Biederman, I., Mezzanotte, R. J., and Rabinowitz, J. C. (1982). Scene perception: Detecting and judging objects undergoing relational violations. *Cognitive Psychology*, **14**, 143–177.

Boyce, S. J., and Pollatsek, A. (1992a). An exploration of the effects of scene context on object identification. In: K. Rayner (ed.) *Eye movements and visual cognition: Scene perception and reading*. New York: Springer Verlag, pp. 227–242.

Boyce, S. J., and Pollatsek, A. (1992b). Identification of objects in scenes: The role of scene background in object naming. *Journal of Experimental Psychology: Learning, Memory, and Cognition*, **18**, 531–543.

Boyce, S. J., Pollatsek, A., and Rayner, K. (1989). Effect of background information on object identification. *Journal of Experimental Psychology: Human Perception and Performance*, **15**, 556–566.

Cavegn, D., and d'Ydewalle, G. (1996). Presaccadic attention allocation and express saccades. *Psychological Research*, **59**, 157–175.

Chapman, P. R., and Underwood, G. (1998). Visual search of dynamic scenes: Event types and the role of experience in viewing driving situations. In: G. Underwood (ed.) *Eye guidance in reading and scene perception*. Oxford, UK: Elsevier, pp. 369–393.

Christie, J., and Klein, R. (1995). Familiarity and attention: Does what we know affect what we notice? *Memory and Cognition*, **23**, 547–550.

Davidoff, J., and Donnelly, N. (1990). Object superiority: A comparison of complete and part probes. *Acta Psychologica*, **73**, 225–243.

De Graef, P. (1992). Scene-context effects and models of real-world perception. In: K. Rayner (ed.) *Eye movements and visual cognition: Scene perception and reading*. New York: Springer, pp. 243–259.

De Graef, P. (1998). Prefixational object perception in scenes: Objects popping out of schemas. In: G. Underwood (ed.) *Eye guidance in reading and scene perception*. Oxford: Elsevier, pp. 315–338.

De Graef, P. (2001). Peripheral processing of objects in real-world scenes. *Journal of Vision*, **1**, 417a, http://journalofvision.org/1–3/417, DOI 10.1167/1.3.417.

De Graef, P. (2004). Speeded object verification in real-world scenes: Perceptual, decisional, and attentional components. Manuscript submitted for publication.

De Graef, P., Christiaens, D., and d'Ydewalle, G. (1990). Perceptual effects of scene context on object identification. *Psychological Research*, **52**, 317–329.

De Graef, P., De Troy, A., and d'Ydewalle G. (1992). Local and global contextual constraints on the identification of objects in scenes. *Canadian Journal of Psychology*, **46**, 489–508.

De Graef, P., Lauwereyns, J., and Verfaillie, K. (2000). *Attentional orienting and scene semantics* (Psyc. Rep. No. 268). Leuven: University of Leuven, Laboratory of Experimental Psychology.

Downing, C. J. (1988). Expectancy and visual-spatial attention: Effects on perceptual quality. *Journal of Experimental Psychology: Human Perception and Performance*, **14**, 188–202.

Epstein, R., and Kanwisher, N. (1998). A cortical representation for the local visual environment. *Nature*, **392**, 598–601.

Fabre-Thorpe, M., Delorme, A., Marlot, C., and Thorpe, S. (2001). A limit to the speed of processing in ultra-rapid visual categorization of novel natural scenes. *Journal of Cognitive Neuroscience*, **13**, 171–180.

Findlay, J.M., and Walker, R. (1999). A model of saccade generation based on parallel processing and competitive inhibition. *Behavioural and Brain Sciences*, **22**, 661–721.

Friedman, A. (1979). Framing pictures: The role of knowledge in automatized encoding and memory for gist. *Journal of Experimental Psychology: General*, **108**, 316–355.

Fuentes, L. J., Vivas, A. B., and Humphreys, G. W. (1999). Inhibitory mechanisms of attentional networks: Spatial and semantic inhibitory processing. *Journal of Experimental Psychology: Human Perception and Performance*, **25**, 1114–1126.

Ganis, G., and Kutas, M. (2003). An electrophysiological study of scene effects on object identification. *Cognitive Brain Research*, **16**, 123–144.

Gezeck, S., Fischer, B., and Timmer, J. (1997). Saccadic reaction times: A statistical analysis of multimodal distributions. *Vision Research*, **37**, 2119–2131.

Gordon, R. D. (2004). Attentional allocation during the perception of scenes. *Journal of Experimental Psychology: Human Perception and Performance*, **30**, 760–777.

Hawkins, H. L., Hillyard, S. A., Luck, S. J., Mouloua, M., Downing, C. J., and Woodward, D. P. (1990). Visual attention modulates signal detectability. *Journal of Experimental Psychology: Human Perception and Performance*, **16**, 802–811.

Hayhoe, M. M., Bensinger, D. G., and Ballard, D. H. (1998). Task constraints in visual working memory. *Vision Research*, **38**, 125–137.

Henderson, J. M. (1992a). Object identification in context: The visual processing of natural scenes. *Canadian Journal of Psychology*, **46**, 319–341.

Henderson, J. M. (1992b). Visual attention and eye movement control during reading and picture viewing. In: K. Rayner (ed.) *Eye movements and visual cognition: Scene perception and reading*. New York: Springer, pp. 260–283.

Henderson, J. M. (2003). Human gaze control during real-world scene perception. *Trends in Cognitive Sciences*, **7**, 498–504.

Henderson, J. M., and Hollingworth, A. (1998). Eye movements during scene viewing: An overview. In: G. Underwood (ed.) *Eye guidance in reading and scene perception*. Oxford: Elsevier, pp. 269–298.

Henderson, J. M., and Hollingworth, A. (1999). High-level scene perception. *Annual Review of Psychology*, **50**, 243–271.

Henderson, J. M., Weeks, P. A. Jr., and Hollingworth, A. (1999). The effects of semantic consistency on eye movements during complex scene viewing. *Journal of Experimental Psychology: Human Perception and Performance*, **25**, 210–228.

Hess, T. M., and Slaughter, J. S. (1990). Schematic knowledge influences on memory for scene information in young and older adults. *Developmental Psychology*, **26**, 855–865.

Hochstein, S., and Ahissar, M. (2002). View from the top: Hierarchies and reverse hierarchies in the visual system. *Neuron*, **36**, 791–804.

Hoffmann, J. (1987). Semantic control of selective attention. *Psychological Research*, **49**, 123–129.

Hollingworth, A., and Henderson, J. M. (1998). Does consistent scene context facilitate object perception? *Journal of Experimental Psychology: General*, **127**, 398–415.

Johnston, W. A., and Hawley, K. J. (1994). Perceptual inhibition of expected inputs: The key that opens closed minds. *Psychonomic Bulletin and Review*, **1**, 56–72.

Kelley, T. A., Chun, M. M., and Chua, K.-P. (2003). Effects of scene inversion on change detection of targets matched for visual salience. *Journal of Vision*, **2**, 1–5.

Klein, R. M., and MacInnes, J. W. (1999). Inhibition of return is a foraging facilitator in visual search. *Psychological Science*, **10**, 346–352.

Kroll, J. F., and Potter, M. C. (1984). Recognizing words, pictures, and concepts: A comparison of lexical, object, and reality decisions. *Journal of Verbal Learning and Verbal Behavior*, **23**, 39–66.

Lamme, V. A. F., and Roelfsema, P. R. (2000). The distinct modes of vision offered by feedforward and recurrent processing. *Trends in Neurosciences*, **23**, 571–579.

Land, M. F., and Furneaux, S. (1997). The knowledge base of the oculomotor system. *Philosophical Transactions of the Royal Society of London, Series B: Biological Sciences*, **352**, 1231–1239.

Loftus, G. R., and Mackworth, N. H. (1978). Cognitive determinants of fixation location during picture viewing. *Journal of Experimental Psychology: Human Perception and Performance*, **4**, 565–572.

Lu, C.-H., and Proctor, R. W. (1995). The influence of irrelevant location information on performance: A review of the Simon and spatial Stroop effects. *Psychonomic Bulletin and Review*, **2,** 174–207.

Mackeben, M., and Nakayama, K. (1993). Express attentional shifts. *Vision Research*, **33,** 85–90.

Mannan, S., Ruddock, K. H., and Wooding, D. S. (1995). Automatic control of saccadic eye movements made in visual inspection of briefly presented 2-D images. *Spatial Vision*, **9,** 363–386.

Mannan, S., Ruddock, K. H., and Wooding, D. S. (1997). Fixation patterns made during brief examination of two-dimensional images. *Perception*, **26,** 1059–1072.

McConkie, G. W., Underwood, N. R., Zola, D., and Wolverton, G. S. (1985). Some temporal characteristics of processing during reading. *Journal of Experimental Psychology: Human Perception and Performance*, **11,** 168–186.

Oliva, A., and Schyns, P. G. (1997). Coarse blobs or fine edges? Evidence that information diagnosticity changes the perception of complex visual stimuli. *Cognitive Psychology*, **34,** 72–107.

Oliva, A., and Torralba, A. (2001). Modeling the shape of the scene: A holistic representation of the spatial envelope. *International Journal of Computer Vision*, **42,** 145–175.

Parkhurst, D., Law, K., and Niebur, E. (2002). Modeling the role of salience in the allocation of overt visual attention. *Vision Research*, **42,** 107–123.

Posner, M. I. (1980). Orienting of attention. *Quarterly Journal of Experimental Psychology*, **32A,** 3–25.

Potter, M. C., Staub, A., Rado, J., and O'Connor, D. H. (2002). Recognition memory for briefly presented pictures: The time course of rapid forgetting. *Journal of Experimental Psychology: Human Perception and Performance*, **28,** 1163–1175.

Rao, R. P. N., Zelinsky, G. J., Hayhoe, M. M., and Ballard, D. H. (2002). Eye movements in iconic visual search. *Vision Research*, **42,** 1447–1463.

Rasche, C., and Koch, C. (2002). Recognizing the gist of a visual scene: possible perceptual and neural mechanisms. *Neurocomputing*, **44–46,** 979–984.

Rayner, K., and Well, A. D. (1996). Effects of contextual constraint on eye movements in reading. *Psychonomic Bulletin and Review*, **3,** 504–509.

Reichle, E. D., Pollatsek, A., Fisher, D. L., and Rayner, K. (1998). Toward a model of eye movement control in reading. *Psychological Review*, **105,** 125–157.

Rumelhart, D. E., Smolensky, P., McClelland, J. L., and Hinton, G. E. (1986). Schemata and sequential thought processes in PDP models. In: J. McClelland, and D. Rumelhart (ed.) *Parallel distributed processing: Explorations in the microstructure of cognition. Vol. 2. Psychological and biological models.* Cambridge, MA: MIT Press, pp. 7–57.

Schneider, W. X. (1995). VAM: A neuro-cognitive model for visual attention, control of segmentation, object recognition, and space-based motor action. *Visual Cognition*, **2,** 331–375.

Sheinberg, D. L., and Logothetis, N. K. (2001). Noticing familiar objects in real world scenes: The role of temporal cortical neurons in natural vision. *The Journal of Neuroscience*, **21,** 1340–1350.

Shinoda, H., Hayhoe, M. M., and Shrivastava, A. (2001). What controls attention in natural environments? *Vision Research*, **41,** 3535–3545.

Steeves, J. K. E., Humphrey, K. G., Culham, J. C., Menon, R. S., Milner, D. A., and Goodale, M. A. (2004). Behavioral and neuroimaging evidence for a contribution of color and texture information to scene classification in a patient with visual form agnosia. *Journal of Cognitive Neuroscience*, **16,** 955–965.

Stoffer, T. H., and Yakin, A. R. (1994). The functional role of attention for spatial coding in the Simon effect. *Psychological Research*, **56**, 151–162.

Thorpe, S., Fize, D., and Marlot, C. (1996). Speed of processing in the human visual system. *Nature*, **381**, 520–522.

Torralba, A., and Oliva, A. (2003). Statistics of natural image categories. *Network: Computation in Neural Systems*, **14**, 391–412.

Torralba, A., and Sinha, P. (2001). Statistical context priming for object detection. *Proceedings of the International Conference on Computer Vision, ICCV01.* Vancouver, Canada, pp. 763–770.

van Diepen, P. M. J., De Graef, P., and d'Ydewalle, G. (1995). Chronometry of foveal information extraction during scene perception. In: J. M. Findlay, R. Walker, and R. W. Kentridge (ed.) *Eye movement research: Mechanisms, processes and applications.* Amsterdam: North-Holland, pp. 349–362.

VanRullen, R., and Thorpe, S. J. (2001). Is it a bird? Is it a plane? Ultra-rapid visual categorisation of natural and artifactual objects. *Perception*, **30**, 655–668.

Wenban-Smith, M. G., and Findlay, J. M. (1991). Express saccades: Is there a separate population in humans? *Experimental Brain Research*, **87**, 218–222.

Yantis, S., and Hillstrom, A. P. (1994). Stimulus-driven attentional capture: Evidence from equiluminant visual objects. *Journal of Experimental Psychology: Human Perception and Performance*, **20**, 95–107.

Zelinsky, G. J. (1996). Using eye saccades to assess the selectivity of search movements. *Vision Research*, **36**, 2177–2187.

Zelinsky, G. J., and Sheinberg, D. L. (1997). Eye movements during parallel-serial visual search. *Journal of Experimental Psychology: Human Perception and Performance*, **23**, 244–262.

9

Eye movements and visual memory for scenes

John M. Henderson and Monica S. Castelhano

Abstract

In this chapter we discuss three types of memory that are relevant for understanding how scene representations are generated over the course of scene viewing. We focus particularly on scene memory generated dynamically across eye movements, and we highlight studies that record eye movements. We argue that the results of studies focusing on transsaccadic memory, active on-line scene memory, and long-term scene memory converge on the conclusion that relatively detailed visual scene representations are retained both over the short and long term, and that these representations are generated incidentally as a consequence of scene viewing.

Introduction

During natural scene viewing, the eyes move to a new fixation location about three times each second (Henderson and Hollingworth 1998; Henderson 2003; see Fig. 9.1), yet we do not experience the tens of milliseconds that transpire during the saccadic movements as blank periods or 'holes' in our visual experience, nor do we experience the visual world as the series of discrete snapshots. Instead, we have the perceptual experience of a complete, full color, highly detailed, and stable visual world. That is, our perceptual experience suggests to us that the visual system in some sense creates a high-resolution internal copy of the external world. Indeed, this phenomenology has historically motivated much of the theoretical work in human and computer vision, and the experience of a complete and detailed visual world has been a major consideration in recent theoretical treatments of scene representation, visual memory, and the nature of consciousness (e.g. Dennett 1991; O'Regan 1992; Rensink 2000a; Wolfe 1999).

Reductions in visual acuity and color sensitivity as a function of distance from the center of fixation place severe constraints on the generation of a detailed internal visual representation of the external scene, so creation of such a representation would require the storage of visual information across each saccade, with representations from consecutive fixations integrated in some way. Furthermore, such representations

Figure 9.1 During scene viewing, the eyes move to a new fixation location about three times per second on average. In this figure, a participant was viewing the scene while searching for people. Lines represent saccades and circles represent fixations (circle size is scaled to fixation duration). Note that the original images were presented in color.

would have to be retained in active on-line memory over multiple-fixation saccade cycles if they were to be integrated over the entire course of scene viewing. Finally, once constructed, such representations would need to be stored in longer-term memory so that they would be available to support future viewing, perceptual learning, and other cognitive activities such as visual thinking and reasoning, as well as language use (see Henderson and Ferreira 2004). In the following sections we briefly review the evidence for retention and integration of visual representations over a single saccade (transsaccadic memory), over multiple-fixation saccade cycles (active on-line scene memory), and over the longer term (long-term scene memory). We use these categories as an expository device to help organize the literature, and make no claim that retention and integration over these different time scales requires separate structural memory stores. We do not attempt an exhaustive review, but rather try to highlight some of the critical studies as we see them, with an emphasis on eye-movement research and specifically on recent experiments from our laboratory. Our conclusion is that relatively detailed (though not sensory or iconic) visual representations are generated and retained in memory as a natural consequence of active, dynamic scene perception.

Transsaccadic memory

What is the nature of the representation that is retained and integrated across saccades? A proposal with a venerable history is that high-resolution sensory images are stored across saccades, with images from consecutive fixations integrated to form a composite sensory image (for reviews see Bridgeman *et al.* 1994; McConkie and Currie 1996). Traditionally, this spatiotopic fusion hypothesis (Irwin 1992a) has been instantiated by models in which a sensory image (i.e. a precise, highly detailed, metrically organized, pre-categorical image) is generated during each fixation and stored in a temporary buffer, with sensory images from consecutive fixations spatially aligned and fused in a system that maps a retinal reference frame onto a spatiotopic frame (Breitmeyer *et al.* 1982; Davidson *et al.* 1973; Duhamel *et al.* 1992; Feldman 1985; Jonides *et al.* 1982; McConkie and Rayner 1976; O'Regan and Lévy-Schoen 1983; Pouget *et al.* 1993; Trehub 1977). In such models, the composite image formed during consecutive fixations is aligned by tracking the extent of the saccade (via afferent or efferent pathways) or by comparing the similarity of the individual images.

Although many versions of the sensory fusion hypothesis have been proposed, the vast majority of psychophysical and behavioral evidence from the vision and cognition literatures has failed to support it. Perhaps the most convincing evidence arises from direct demonstrations that viewers are unable to fuse simple visual patterns across saccades. In these studies, viewers are required to integrate a pre-saccade and post-saccade pattern in order to accomplish the task successfully. If visual patterns can be fused in a spatiotopically-based sensory memory system, then performance should be similar in a transsaccadic condition in which the environmental spatial position of the patterns is maintained but retinal position is displaced due to a saccade, and a condition in which position in both retinal and environmental spatial reference frames is maintained within a fixation. For example, when two dot patterns forming a matrix of dots are presented in rapid succession at the same retinal and spatial position within an eye fixation, a single fused pattern is perceived and performance (e.g. identification of a missing dot from the matrix) can be based upon this percept (Di Lollo 1980; Eriksen and Collins 1967; Irwin 1991). However, when the two patterns are viewed with similar timing parameters at the same external spatial position but different retinal positions across a saccade, no such fused percept is experienced and performance is dramatically reduced (Bridgeman and Mayer 1983; Irwin 1991; Irwin *et al.* 1988, 1983, 1990; Jonides *et al.* 1983; O'Regan and Lévy-Schoen 1983; Rayner and Pollatsek 1983). In the latter case, overall performance is limited to and constrained by the capacity of short-term memory (Irwin *et al.* 1988). Other effects which might be expected based on the formation of a composite image via sensory fusion, such as spatiotopically-based visual masking, are also not observed (Irwin *et al.* 1988; Irwin *et al.* 1990). For other reviews of this work, see Irwin (1992b), Irwin and Andrews (1996), Pollatsek and Rayner (1992), and Rayner (1998).

If the visual information acquired from successive fixations is fused into a single composite sensory image, then displacements of the viewed world during a saccade should be highly noticeable and troublesome because fusion should be disrupted. Contrary to this prediction, Bridgeman *et al.* (1975) demonstrated that a scene could be spatially displaced during a saccade with no conscious experience that the stimulus had shifted position, and with little or no disruption to the performance of a visual task. This insensitivity to spatial displacement across saccades has subsequently been replicated many times (e.g. Bridgeman and Stark 1979; Currie *et al.* 2000; Henderson 1997; Irwin 1991; Mack 1970; McConkie and Currie 1996; Verfaillie *et al.* 1994; Whipple and Wallach 1978). An interesting exception to these findings was reported by Deubel *et al.* (1996, 2002; Gysen *et al.* 2002). In these experiments, participants were found to be sensitive to spatial displacements of a target during a saccade when a blank interval was inserted following the saccade and prior to the reappearance of the spatially shifted target. This is an intriguing finding regarding the retention of information across saccades and suggests that sensory memory may persist during the saccade. However, given that there is typically no blank period at the beginning of each new fixation, it is not clear how this retained information would be functional in the transsaccadic integration process.

Changes to other visual properties are similarly difficult to detect across a saccade. For example, readers are insensitive to changes in the visual properties of text from fixation to fixation (McConkie and Zola 1979). In these experiments, participants read text made up of characters of alternating case. During a given saccade, the case of all characters was exchanged. These case changes were not noticed by readers and had very little if any effect on reading rate or comprehension. Similar insensitivity to changes in visual features of an image across a saccade has been shown with pictures of objects and scenes. For example, Henderson (1997) found that it was very difficult for observers to detect a change to the specific contours of an object from fixation to fixation (see Fig. 9.2). In this study, participants were asked to fixate a point on a computer screen. A line drawing of an object was then presented to the right of fixation. About half of the contours of the object were presented; the other contours were occluded by black stripes. The participant executed a saccade to the object as soon as it appeared. During the saccade, the object remained exactly the same; changed to reveal the complementary set of contours; shifted one stripe width in position; or changed to a different object. The participant was asked to indicate if any change occurred. Participants failed to detect the majority of contour changes or position shifts. In a control condition in which the changes took place at the same retinal and spatial position (and at the same visual eccentricity as the preview had appeared) within a fixation, change detection was quite good. This latter result ensured that the contours and positions could be discriminated at the visual eccentricity used in the transsaccadic change experiment. Henderson and Hollingworth (2003a) reported similar results for full scenes. Other visual changes such as enlargements and reductions of object size often go unnoticed when they take place during a saccade (Henderson *et al.* 1987; Pollatsek *et al.* 1984).

What is retained across saccades?

Irwin and colleagues have demonstrated in a transsaccadic partial report task that the perceptual properties of up to four visual patterns can be retained across saccades in visual short-term memory (Irwin and Andrews 1996). Carlson-Radvansky (Carlson-Radvansky 1999; Carlson-Radvansky and Irwin 1995) found that structural descriptions of simple visual patterns can be retained across saccades. In transsaccadic

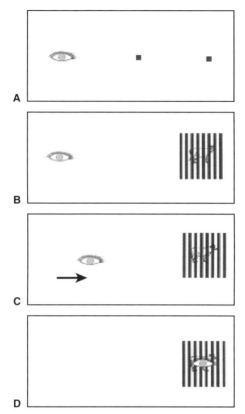

Figure 9.2 Illustration of the study reported by Henderson (1997). Participants began by fixating a point (Panel A). An image of a line drawing of an object was presented to the right of fixation, with about half of the contours occluded by black stripes (Panel B). The participant executed a saccade to the object, and during the saccade the object remained the same, changed to reveal the complementary set of contours, shifted one stripe width in position, or changed to a different object (Panel C). Following fixation, the participant indicated if any change occurred or named the object (Panel D). Contour changes and position shifts were very difficult to detect and did not affect naming latencies.

object identification studies, participants are quicker to identify an object when a preview of the object is available prior to the saccade than when no preview is available (e.g. Henderson 1992a, 1994, 1997; Henderson and Siefert 1999, 2001; Henderson *et al.* 1987, 1989; Pollatsek *et al.* 1984, 1990). Furthermore, preview benefits for objects can be affected by visual changes such as replacement of one visual token with another token of the same conceptual type (Henderson and Siefert 2001) and mirror reflections (Henderson and Siefert 1999, 2001). The influence of visual change on preview benefit is more pronounced when the spatial location of the target object remains constant compared with when the location changes (Henderson 1994; Henderson and Anes 1994; Henderson and Siefert 2001).

The transsaccadic integration results strongly suggest that visual properties are preserved in the representations that are retained across saccades, and furthermore that such representations are at least partially tied to spatial position. It is important to note, however, that visual representations need not be sensory. That is, representation of detailed visual information does not imply the preservation of an iconic image. For example, in the study reported in Henderson (1997) and shown in Fig. 9.2, replacement of the specific contours present in the image from preview to fixation had no effect on preview benefit as assessed by naming latency. We take sensory representation to refer to a complete, precise, pre-categorical, maskable, and metrically organized image of the visual scene (Irwin 1992b; Neisser 1967; Sperling 1960). In contrast, a post-sensory visual representation is an imprecise, post-categorical, non-maskable, and non-iconic visual description encoded in the vocabulary of visual computation. This same distinction maps onto the distinction in the 'iconic memory' literature between visual and informational persistence on the one hand, and visual short-term memory on the other (Irwin 1992b; see also Coltheart 1980). Based on explorations of integration of visual patterns across saccades, Irwin has argued that transsaccadic memory is in fact visual short-term memory (e.g. Irwin 1991, 1992b). Importantly, however, abstract visual representations are still visual in the sense that they represent visual properties such as object shape and viewpoint, albeit in a non-sensory format. An example of a non-sensory representation of shape is a structural description; as noted above, recent evidence suggests that shape may be encoded and retained across saccades in this representational format (Carlson-Radvansky and Irwin 1995; Carlson-Radvansky 1999). In our view, abstract visual representations are neither sensory, nor are they equivalent to conceptual representations (which encode semantic properties) or linguistic descriptions. Examples of abstract visual representations are structural descriptions (e.g. Biederman 1987; Marr 1982; Palmer 1977) and hierarchical feature representations (e.g. Riesenhuber and Poggio 1999).

Active memory: On-line scene representations

Transsaccadic memory as it is traditionally studied concerns the retention of scene information for the very short period of time that transpires from one fixation to the next during saccadic eye movements – durations typically on the order of 20–80 ms. In this section we consider on-line scene representations that are kept active in visual (working) memory over the course of the current perceptual episode lasting several seconds and multiple-fixation saccade cycles. Much of the recent change detection research in scene perception has tapped into active scene memory in this sense. For example, in a classic initial demonstration of 'change blindness', McConkie and Grimes (McConkie 1990, 1991; see Grimes 1996) had viewers study full-color photographs of scenes in preparation for a relatively difficult memory test. The viewers were told that something in a scene might occasionally change and that they should press a button if and when they noticed such a change. Eye movements were monitored with a dual-Purkinje-image eyetracker so that part of each scene could be changed quickly during a saccade. The changes took place during the nth saccade, where n was predetermined prior to the onset of the scene. The decisive result was that viewers often failed to detect what would seem to be very obvious visual changes. For example, none of the participants detected that the hats on two central men in a scene switched heads (Grimes, 1996). Unlike the transsaccadic integration experiments described in the preceding section, scene viewing took place over multiple fixations both before and after the change, so the opportunity was available for constructing an on-line representation over extended viewing time both prior to and after the change.

Reduced sensitivity to visual changes in scenes across saccades has been shown for changes to spatial orientation, color, and object presence (Grimes, 1996; Henderson and Hollingworth 1999a; McConkie 1991; McConkie and Currie 1996). Reduced sensitivity is also observed in paradigms that simulate saccades, such as when a blank field is inserted between two scene images (Rensink *et al.* 1997). In general, it appears that when the local transient motion signals that usually accompany a visual change are unavailable, as is the case during a saccade, sensitivity to what would otherwise be a highly-visible change becomes reduced, and in the extreme case eliminated. These results were initially taken to call into question the view that a detailed visual scene representation is constructed on-line in memory during scene viewing (e.g. O'Regan 1992; Rensink 2000a, 2000b; Wolfe 1999).

In the past few years it has become clear that the original interpretation of 'change blindness' was incorrect and that relatively detailed on-line visual memory representations of scenes can be observed in change detection experiments. Two general sources of evidence converge on this conclusion (for more extensive review, see Henderson and Hollingworth 2003b). In one set of experiments, a change detection paradigm was used in which a target object was changed during a saccade within the scene (Henderson and Hollingworth 1999a; Hollingworth and Henderson 2002; Hollingworth *et al.* 2001). As in the original saccade-contingent scene change experiments (McConkie 1990, 1991; see Grimes 1996) participants viewed pictures of scenes to prepare for a difficult memory test, and in addition were asked to monitor for changes. A target object changed during a saccade toward the object (toward condition); away from the object after it had been fixated the first time (away condition); or during a saccade to a different non-target object elsewhere in the scene (other object condition). In several experiments, the change to the other object region was only activated after the object had received at least one fixation (e.g. Hollingworth and Henderson 2002; Hollingworth *et al.* 2001). Thus, in the away and other object conditions, the target object was attended at some point prior to the scene change but visual attention was directed away from the target object and to a different object in the visual field prior to the saccade that triggered the change (visual attention must be allocated to the target of the next saccadic eye movement prior to the saccade's execution, Henderson 1992b, 1993, 1996; Hoffman and Subramanian 1995; Kowler *et al.* 1995; Shepherd *et al.* 1986). A viewer's ability to detect changes in these conditions provides evidence about whether visual object representations are preserved after the withdrawal of attention and can accumulate during extended visual exploration of a scene.

Four change manipulations have been tested using the on-line saccade-contingent change paradigm: deletion of the target object from the scene (Henderson and Hollingworth 1999a; 2003c); type changes in which the target object is replaced with another object from a different basic-level category (Henderson and Hollingworth 2003c;

Hollingworth and Henderson 2002); token changes in which the target object is replaced with another object from the same basic-level category (Henderson and Hollingworth 2003c; Hollingworth and Henderson 2002; Hollingworth *et al.* 2001), and rotations in which the target object is rotated 90° around its vertical axis (Henderson and Hollingworth 1999a; Hollingworth and Henderson 2002). In each of these conditions, change detection for previously attended objects was significantly above the false alarm rate (which is typically very low). These results suggest that a memory representation is generated and available during on-line scene viewing. It is possible that deletions and type changes could be detected based on semantic information (e.g. deletions and type changes could alter scene meaning), but token changes and rotations as implemented in these experiments did not alter the gist of the scenes in which they appeared.

In the studies described above, object changes were sometimes not detected in the away and other object conditions when they first occurred, but were then detected when the changed object was fixated later in the course of scene viewing. Viewers typically fixated many intervening scene regions and objects over the course of the several seconds that transpired between the initial fixation on the target, the target change, and the first refixation of the (now changed) target object in these cases. The observed delayed change detection following target refixation establishes that the on-line visual scene representation survived over time and potential interference from other fixated objects, and suggests that refixating the changed object provided a cue to retrieve and compare the stored visual object representation to current perceptual information. Hollingworth (2003) has provided additional evidence supporting the hypothesis that change detection failure is often a retrieval problem.

A second source of evidence that change detection in the saccade-contingent change experiments is based on an on-line memory system that lasts longer than a single saccade comes from a manipulation of the semantic consistency of the target object in the scene (Hollingworth *et al.* 2001). In this study, participants viewed line drawings of scenes in which the target object was either semantically consistent or inconsistent with the scene. The target object was replaced by another token of the same basic-level category (e.g. one chicken was replaced by a different chicken in a farm scene) during a saccade away from that object. Scene memory research has demonstrated that the memory representation of a semantically inconsistent object in a scene is more detailed and/or complete compared with a semantically consistent object (e.g. Friedman 1979). Based on these prior results, if visual representations accumulate on-line in memory during scene viewing, then changes to semantically inconsistent objects (which should be represented more completely) should be detected more accurately than changes to semantically consistent objects. The results confirmed this prediction. Furthermore, because the change occurred during the saccade away from the target object, the change was not always detected immediately (see also Henderson and Hollingworth 1999b; Hollingworth and Henderson 2002). Overall, 41 per cent of the detection responses took place more than 1.5 s after the change, and of these responses, 94 per cent occurred only after the target object was refixated. Again, these results suggest that visual object representations are maintained on-line over the course of scene viewing and across extended time and multiple-fixation saccade cycles.

The use of change detection to study the nature of the representations generated during scene perception assumes that the experience of change directly reflects the underlying representation. However, contrary to this assumption, we have found that overt change detection often significantly underestimates the degree to which on-line visual representations are retained in memory. Specifically, gaze duration (the sum of the durations of all fixations from the initial fixation on an object region to the first saccade taking the eyes away from that object) is elevated for trials in which a change occurred but was not reported, compared with no-change control trials (Henderson and Hollingworth 2003c; Hollingworth and Henderson 2002; Hollingworth *et al.* 2001). For example, in one study we found that when a token change was not explicitly detected, mean gaze duration on that object after the change was 749 ms, whereas mean gaze duration was 499 ms when no change occurred (Hollingworth *et al.* 2001). As found for delayed explicit detection, this 'implicit' or covert detection effect was observed despite several intervening seconds and many fixations on other objects between the object change and the first refixation of the target (when gaze durations were found to be elevated). These results provide strong evidence that visual object representations were available in on-line scene memory over the course of viewing even when they were not easily reportable. Thus, the failure to report a change does not provide unambiguous evidence that the information needed to detect that change is unavailable in on-line memory (see also Fernandez-Duque and Thornton 2000; Hayhoe *et al.* 1998; Williams and Simons 2000). In summary, despite the failure of participants to report scene changes taking place during saccades, it is clear that when fixation duration is used to assess the underlying visual representation, robust evidence of visual representation is obtained.

Given the potential difficulty of interpreting overt change detection failure, Andrew Hollingworth (Hollingworth and Henderson 2002) developed a forced-choice memory test to directly investigate viewers' on-line memory for objects in scenes (see Fig. 9.3).

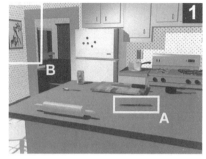 

Figure 9.3 Illustration of the paradigm developed by Hollingworth and Henderson (2002). Participants freely viewed each scene, and after the target object (region A) had been fixated, a saccade to another pre-defined object in the scene (region B) triggered masking of the target object. A forced-choice memory test was then presented for the target object. Note that the boxes surrounding regions A and B were not visible to the participants, and the original images were presented in color.

Participants viewed images of common environments while their eye movements were monitored. Following the start of each trial, the computer waited until the target object (indicated by Region A in Fig. 9.3) had been fixated at least once, assuring that it had been attended prior to the test. Then, during a saccade to another object on the other side of the scene (Region B in Fig. 9.3), the target object was obscured by a pattern mask. The onset of the mask coincided with a saccade to a different object in the scene, so the target object was not attended at the time the mask appeared. Following the appearance of the mask, a forced-choice memory test was presented in which two object alternatives were displayed sequentially within the scene: the original target and a distractor object. The distractor was either a different token from the same basic-level category (token discrimination) or a version of the target object rotated 90° in depth around the vertical axis (orientation discrimination).

Performance in this memory test was very good: token discrimination was 87 per cent correct and orientation discrimination was 82 per cent correct. Again, on many trials viewers fixated multiple objects between the last fixation on the target object and the onset of the mask (and the initiation of the forced-choice test), but performance did not differ statistically as a function of the number of intervening fixations; when nine or more fixations intervened between the last fixation on the target object and the onset of the memory test, performance in the token discrimination test was 85 per cent correct and performance in the orientation discrimination test was 92 per cent correct. These results suggest that on-line scene representations are relatively stable in memory. These data, along with the change detection results reviewed above, provide very strong evidence that visual representations from previously attended objects accumulate on-line in memory, forming a relatively detailed scene representation.

Contrary to proposals based on change blindness, visual object representations are not lost upon the withdrawal of attention. At the same time, change blindness clearly is mediated by attention, presumably because attention is needed to encode the pre-change and post-change regions as well as to facilitate retrieval of the pre-change representation from memory following the change. In the transsaccadic change detection paradigm, the same change is much more easily detected when it occurs during a saccade toward the changing object (Currie *et al.* 2000; Hayhoe *et al.* 1998; Henderson and Hollingworth 1999a, 2003c) than during a saccade away from that object (Henderson and Hollingworth 1999a, 2003c; Hollingworth *et al.* 2001). Similarly, transsaccadic integration is heavily weighted toward the saccade target (Henderson 1994; Henderson and Anes 1994; Irwin and Andrews 1996), at least partly due to the fact that the allocation of attention to the saccade target is mandatory prior to a saccade (Deubel and Schneider 1996; Henderson 1992b, 1993, 1996; Henderson *et al.* 1989; Hoffman and Subramanian 1995; Irwin and Gordon 1998; Kowler *et al.* 1995; Rayner *et al.* 1978; Shepherd *et al.* 1986). In the change blindness literature, detection of change is better in the flicker paradigm for scene regions rated to be of higher interest (Rensink *et al.* 1997), for semantically unexpected objects (Hollingworth and Henderson 2000), at locations to which attention has been explicitly directed (Scholl 2000), and at locations near fixation (Hollingworth *et al.* 2001).

Long-term scene memory

In this section, we briefly consider the evidence concerning eye movements, scene representations, and long-term memory. We take long-term scene memory to involve the representations that linger once the current perceptual episode is over. For example, if the current perceptual episode involves working at your desk, in which an active visual representation of the desktop may be generated and maintained, what continues to reside in memory about your desk if you go to another room to watch the Red Sox win the World Series on television? This issue is typically operationalized by studying long-term memory for pictures of scenes.

Classic scene memory research has demonstrated very good long-term memory for scene detail. For example, Nickerson (1965) had participants view 200 black-and-white photographs for 5 s each; on an old-new recognition test, participants correctly recognized 92 per cent of the pictures (controlling for false alarm rate). Shepard (1967) similarly demonstrated 97 per cent correct recognition for 612 color pictures when tested immediately and 99.7 per cent when tested 2 h later. Standing *et al.* (1970) showed participants 2560 pictures for 10 s each over several days. Memory for the entire set of pictures was well over 90 per cent correct. Furthermore, memory for a subset of 280 thematically similar scenes, which required remembering more details about the pictures than general category or gist, was 90 per cent correct. Standing *et al.* (1970) also manipulated the left–right orientation of the scene at study and test, and showed that participants could recognize the studied picture orientation 86 per cent of the time after a 30 s retention interval and 72 per cent of the time after 24 h.

Hollingworth and Henderson (2002) tested long-term memory for individual objects in scenes. A difficult forced-choice discrimination memory test was given for specific target objects after the scenes were removed from view for between 5–30 min. Similar to the on-line memory test described in the previous section, for each studied scene, participants viewed two versions of the scene in the test session: one that was identical to the studied scene and a distractor scene that differed only in the target object. The distractor object was a different type, different token, or the same object rotated in depth. This longer retention interval did not cause a significant decrement in discrimination performance compared with online discrimination. Mean type-discrimination performance was 93 per cent correct, mean token-discrimination performance was 80.6 per cent correct, and mean orientation-discrimination performance was 82 per cent correct. The similarity between discrimination performance in the on-line and long-term tests suggests that visual object representations are stable after attention is removed, at least over the retention intervals we tested. These long-term memory results are consistent with evidence from the picture memory literature cited above suggesting very good memory for the visual form of whole scenes (Standing *et al.* 1970) and for the visual form of individual objects within scenes (Friedman 1979; Parker 1978).

Results from other scene memory studies also support the notion that visual details of objects are encoded in memory (Bahrick and Boucher 1968; Mandler and Ritchey 1977; Mandler and Parker 1976). Although relatively simpler 'scene sketches' (Henderson and Ferreira 2004) were used in these earlier studies (line drawings of 6–9 objects in each), participants were able to distinguish between the target object and similar distractors of the same basic-level category (Bahrick and Boucher 1968) and were able to recall different types of visual details (Mandler and Ritchey 1977). Several studies have also demonstrated that over the long term, participants are able to recognize object types (Goodman 1980; Friedman 1979; Henderson *et al.* 2003; Hock, Romanski *et al.* 1978); visual details (Mandler and Parker 1976; Friedman 1979; Pezdek *et al.* 1988, 1989); and verbally recall and recognize object descriptions (Brewer and Treyens 1981).

Incidental scene representation and memory

The evidence described in the previous sections appears to provide compelling support for the idea that detailed visual representations are generated and retained in memory during scene perception. A lingering concern from these studies, however, is the possibility that these results arise from scene processing strategies tied to the use of viewing instructions that stress scene memorization. That is, it is possible that detailed visual scene representations can be generated and retained in memory when viewers engage in intentional memory encoding, but that these representations are not typically generated incidentally during natural scene perception. If this view were correct, then the evidence for good visual memory performance obtained in prior studies might be dismissed as irrelevant to normal scene perception.

If detailed visual memory is only generated under intentional memorization instructions, then evidence for the preservation of the visual details of previously viewed objects should only be observed in intentional memorization tasks. Conversely, viewing tasks for which intentional memory encoding is unnecessary should produce no visual representation in memory. On the other hand, if detailed visual representations are typically generated and stored in memory as a natural consequence of scene perception, then evidence for the long-term preservation of visual detail should be found in both intentional and incidental memorization conditions. To investigate this issue, we have recently conducted two sets of experiments to examine the nature of the visual representations of objects generated incidentally over the course of viewing (Castelhano and Henderson 2005; Williams *et al.* 2005).

As part of his doctoral dissertation work, Carrick Williams investigated the nature of the visual memory representations that are generated for real-world objects during visual search through object arrays (Williams *et al.* 2005). Participants searched through these arrays while their eye movements were recorded. Each array contained 12 unique full-color photographs of objects from a wide variety of categories (see Fig. 9.4, top panel). In each trial, participants were asked to search for and count the number of exemplars of a specific target object, such as a green drill. Arrays contained three types of distractors: category distractors (drills that were not green), color distractors (green objects that were not drills), and unrelated distractors (objects that were neither green nor drills). After all of the arrays had been searched, participants were given a surprise forced-choice visual memory test in which they had to discriminate objects that had appeared in the arrays from memory foils that were different tokens of the same object class. Memory test items were of all three types: search targets,

Figure 9.4 Illustration of the paradigm developed by Williams *et al.* (2005). Participants searched for a specific target (e.g. yellow bird) through object arrays containing 12 unique full-color photographs of objects (top panel). Arrays contained targets, category distractors, color distractors, and unrelated distractors. After all of the arrays had been searched, a surprise forced-choice visual memory test for all types of items was given (bottom panel). Note that the original images were presented in color.

distractors sharing either color or category with the search target, and distractors sharing neither color nor category. For example, if the test object from an array were a yellow bird, the foil would be another yellow bird (see Fig. 9.4, bottom panel). This test therefore required that relatively detailed visual information be preserved in memory. The memory task was designed to eliminate the contribution of context and semantic information to performance by presenting targets and foils that fit the same semantic description. Due to the surprise nature of the visual memory test, any learning that occurred during the search portion of the experiment was incidental.

There were three main findings in this study. First, preserved visual memory was observed for all three types of objects. This finding is remarkable because participants did not anticipate a memory test during the search task (so learning was completely incidental), and because the memory test was very stringent (test objects were presented without the context within which they were initially viewed and the foils were very similar to the targets). Second, memory was graded, with best visual memory for the search targets, intermediate memory for the related distractors, and poorest memory for the unrelated distractors. Third, this pattern was mirrored in the eye-movement data; search targets received the greatest number of fixations and the most fixation time, followed by related (color or category) distractors, followed by unrelated distractors. These last results suggest that fixation during encoding is related to the strength of the resulting memory representation. This finding is reminiscent of Friedman's (1979) observation that expected objects in scenes receive less fixation time than unexpected objects and show poorer memory when tested later. However, the results here were a bit more complex. When eye-movement behavior was directly compared with memory performance via linear regression, it became clear that search targets were remembered better than would be expected only on the basis of number of looks or total fixation time. Specifically, although there was a relationship between fixation time and memory performance for all types of objects, memory for search targets was better than memory for distractors when fixation time was equated. Thus, while eye fixations and the consequent opportunity for memory encoding was highly related to later memory performance, it was not the only factor at work. In summary, this study clearly demonstrated that visual representations for objects are generated and retained incidentally during search.

In a related study, we investigated the nature of the visual memory representation that is generated during scene perception by examining memory performance for visual information obtained either intentionally or incidentally from objects (Castelhano and Henderson 2005). In three experiments, participants viewed scenes while engaged in an incidental-learning visual search task or an intentional-learning memorization task. After both viewing tasks had been completed, a memory test for a critical object in each scene was administered, although no memory test was anticipated by the participant during the visual search task. In the memorization task, participants were instructed to view the scenes in preparation for a difficult memory test that would require knowledge of details of specific objects. In the visual search task, participants were instructed to find a specific target object in each scene, and were not told that they would receive a memory test. The top panel of Fig. 9.5 shows an example of a scene used in the experiment.

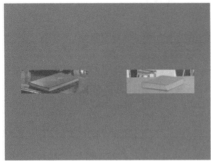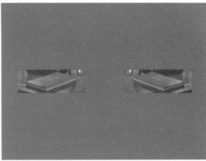

Figure 9.5 Illustration of the study reported by Castelhano and Henderson (2005). Participants searched for a specific target (e.g. ashtray) through photographs of real-world scenes (top panel). After all of the arrays had been searched, a surprise forced-choice visual memory test for the detail or the orientation of a non-target was given (bottom panels). Note that the original images were presented in color.

The test always focused on the visual properties of a specific critical object drawn from each scene. Unlike the Williams *et al.* (2005) study, the critical test objects for the search scenes were never the search targets. In the first experiment, the memory test involved discriminating between a previously seen critical object drawn from each scene and a matched foil object of the same basic-level category type (e.g. two different books, as shown in the bottom left panel of Fig. 9.5). In the second experiment, participants had to discriminate between the previously viewed orientation of the critical object and a mirror-reversed distractor version of the same object (see bottom right panel of Fig. 9.5). In both experiments, all participants took part in both the memorization and visual search tasks. In the third experiment, each participant was given only one of the two initial viewing conditions (memorization or search) from Experiment 1. This between-subjects design ensured that there was no contamination from the memorization condition to the visual search condition. The main question in the three experiments was whether long-term visual memory would be observed for objects that were incidentally encoded during scene viewing.

In all three experiments, participants showed above-chance memory for the tested objects. Furthermore, there was no evidence that memory was better in the intentional than in the incidental learning condition. As Castelhano and Henderson (2005) noted, the study involved a relatively stringent test of visual memory. Memory performance was based on a total of only 10 s of viewing time per scene and an average of <1 s of total fixation time during learning for each critical object. During the memory test, the tested objects (and their matched foils) were presented alone on a blank screen without any indication of which scene they had come from. In addition, memory performance in this study had to rely on long-term storage rather than active on-line scene representations. The retention interval varied between approximately 4–20 min between initial scene viewing and object test depending on where in the randomized sequence each scene and memory test appeared. Furthermore, the total number of objects likely to have been encoded across all of the scenes was relatively large. Using conservative estimates of object encoding (e.g. assuming that only fixated objects were encoded), Castelhano and Henderson (2005) estimated that between 373 and 440 objects were fixated and processed on average by each participant in the three experiments. All of these factors would work against finding evidence for memory of visual detail, yet such evidence was clearly obtained. Together, these results strongly suggest that visual representations are generated and stored in long-term memory as a natural consequence of scene viewing.

Scene representation, visual memory, and perceptual experience

Given the clear evidence, both historically and recently, for the creation and storage of visual object and scene representations, we might ask what leads theorists to posit the lack of such representations (e.g. O'Regan and Nöe 2001). From our perspective, this proposal has its roots in the fact that there are two traditions in vision science. The first tradition is tied to approaches that are largely concerned with attempting to explain the phenomenology of perception. Why do we experience red in the way we do? How is it that we experience a stable visual world despite the presence of saccadic eye movements? And most relevant to the topic of the current chapter, why and how do we experience a complete, detailed, full color visual world despite the fact that (a) the retinas cannot deliver this high-fidelity input within a given fixation, and (b) the visual system cannot fuse together discrete retinotopic images to generate a composite internal picture?

The second tradition, which derives from cognitive psychology and is reflected in current theoretical approaches in visual cognition as well as computer vision, is concerned with the visual representations that are available for visual and cognitive computations (and implemented in the brain in the case of human cognition) without concern for whether they give rise to perceptual experience or are open to awareness. Instead of asking what gives rise to the experience of stability across saccades (for example), those studying vision within this tradition have tended to ask about the nature of the internal representation generated across saccades, regardless of whether this representation is functional in generating experience. In the present case, the issue from a cognitive perspective revolves around the nature of the scene representation(s) that is (potentially) generated over the course of multiple fixations and (potentially) stored in memory, again without regard for which of, or even whether, these representations give rise to perceptual experience.

In our view, a problem arises when the interpretation of data generated within the first tradition that is centered on the issue of visual experience bleeds into the second tradition, which focuses on internal representation and computation. In the case of scene perception, the problem revolves around claims about the nature of visual representation made purely on the basis of reported experience. As stated most recently and forcefully by O'Regan and Noë (2001) based on the change blindness phenomenon (though others have made similar strong statements based on change blindness in the past), 'Indeed there is no '*re*'-presentation of the world inside the brain …'. (O'Regan and Nöe 2001). But we know, and have known for a very long time in cognitive psychology, that what people experience (or can report) is not necessarily a very good indication of what the brain represents. Cognitive science is rife with examples of this, but a couple of examples here should suffice to illustrate the point. First, in the study of memory, it is common place that people do not experience and cannot report memories that nonetheless exist. This sort of finding can be shown in myriad behavioral and neuro-cognitive tasks, as well as in careful assessment in the neuropsychology of amnesia. In the memory literature, the dissociation between report and representation is sometimes captured by the theoretical distinction between explicit and implicit memory. The degree to which explicit and implicit memories are supported by separate memory systems is controversial, but the dissociation between the two types of memories is not.

More directly relevant to the issue of scene representation and memory, the change blindness phenomenon similarly suggests that viewers can be unaware (or unable to report) what would otherwise appear to be salient changes to a viewed scene when those changes take place across a saccade or other visual disruption. At the same time, however, as described in an earlier section of this chapter, we have demonstrated that behavioral consequences of those changes can be observed in the absence of awareness (or at least, in the absence of report). The clearest example is increased fixation time on a changed visual region in the absence of explicit report (e.g. Henderson and Hollingworth 2003c; Hollingworth and Henderson 2002; Hollingworth *et al.* 2001). The increased fixation times, which can be in the order of a couple of hundred milliseconds, are themselves neither under conscious control nor consciously experienced, and they clearly indicate that there is more to an internal representation than conscious experience would lead one to believe. The implication is that one cannot draw any kind of strong conclusion about internal visual representation or computation based solely on perceptual phenomenology.

Conclusion

In this chapter we reviewed the literature concerned with the types of memory systems relevant for understanding the nature of the object and scene representations generated during scene viewing. We specifically focused on three memory epochs important for understanding how scene representations are generated dynamically across multiple eye movements: transsaccadic memory, active on-line scene memory, and long-term scene memory. We argued that the evidence supports the conclusion that relatively detailed visual scene representations are retained over the short and long term. Furthermore, we presented recent evidence strongly suggesting that these representations are generated incidentally as a natural consequence of scene viewing. Finally, we discussed the implications of these studies and how they relate to the findings from change detection research. We conclude that the evidence strongly supports the view that relatively detailed visual representations are generated and stored in memory during active, dynamic scene perception.

Acknowledgements

Preparation of this chapter was supported by funding from the National Science Foundation (BCS-0094433 and IGERT grant ECS-9873531) and the Army Research Office (W911NF-04–1–0078; the opinions expressed in this article are those of the authors and do not necessarily represent the views of the Department of the Army or any other governmental organization). We thank Peter De Graef and Iain Gilchrist for helpful comments on an earlier draft of this chapter, and the other members of the MSU Visual Cognition Lab, James Brockmole, Daniel Gajewski, Michael Mack, Aaron Pearson, and Graham Pierce, for their spirited discussion of many of the issues raised here.

References

Bahrick, H. P., and Boucher, B. (1968). Retention of visual and verbal codes of the same stimuli. *Journal of Experimental Psychology*, **78**, 417–422.

Biederman, I. (1987). Recognition-by-components: A theory of human image understanding. *Psychological Review*, **94**, 115–147.

Breitmeyer, B. G., Kopft, W., and Julesz, B. (1982). The existence and role of retinotopic and spatiotopic forms of visual persistence. *Acta Psychologica*, **52**, 175–196.

Brewer, W. F., and Treyens, J. C. (1981). Role of schemata in memory for places. *Cognitive Psychology*, **13**, 207–230.

Bridgeman, B., and Mayer, M. (1983). Failure to integrate visual information from successive fixations. *Bulletin of the Psychonomic Society*, **21**, 285–286.

Bridgeman, B., and Stark, L. (1979). Omnidirectional increase in threshold for image shifts during saccadic eye movements. *Perception and Psychophysics*, **25**, 241–243.

Bridgeman, B., Hendry, D., and Stark, L. (1975). Failure to detect displacements of the visual world during saccadic eye movements. *Vision Research*, **15**, 719–722.

Bridgeman, B., Van der Hejiden, and Velichkovsky (1994). A theory of visual stability across saccadic eye movements. *Behavioral and Brain Science*, **17**, 247–292.

Carlson-Radvansky, L. A. (1999). Memory for relational information across eye movements. *Perception and Psychophysics*, **61**, 919–934.

Carlson-Radvansky, L. A., and Irwin, D. E. (1995). Memory for structural information across eye movements.

Castelhano, M. S., and Henderson, J. M. (2005). Incidental visual memory for objects in scenes. *Visual Cognition: Special Issue on Scene Perception*.

Coltheart, M. (1980). Iconic memory and visible persistence. *Perception and Psychophysics*, **27,** 183–228.

Currie, C., McConkie, G., Carlson-Radvansky, L. A., and Irwin, D. E. (2000). The role of the saccade target object in the perception of a visually stable world. *Perception and Psychophysics*, **62,** 673–683.

Davidson, M. L., Fox, M. J., and Dick, A. O. (1973). Effect of eye movements on backward masking and perceived location. *Perception and Psychophyics*, 14,110–116.

Dennett, D.C. (1991). *Consciousness explained.* Boston: Little, Brown.

Deubel, H., and Schneider, W. X. (1996). Saccade target selection and object recognition: Evidence for a common attentional mechanism. *Vision Research*, **36,** 1827–1837.

Deubel, H., Schneider, W. X., and Bridgeman, B. (1996). Postsaccadic target blanking prevents saccadic suppression of image displacement. *Vision Research*, **36,** 985–996.

Di Lollo, V. (1980). Temporal integration in visual memory. *Journal of Experimental Psychology: General*, **109,** 75–97.

Duhamel, J. R., Colby, C. L., and Goldberg, M. E. (1992). The updating of the representation of visual space in parietal cortex by intended eye movements. *Science*, **255,** 90–92.

Eriksen, C. W., and Collins, J. F. (1967). Some temporal characteristics of visual pattern recognition. *Journal of Experimental Psychology*, **74,** 476–484.

Feldman, J. A. (1985). Four frames suffice: a provisional model of vision and space. *Behavioral and Brain Sciences*, **8,** 265–289.

Fernandez-Duque, D., and Thornton, I. M. (2000). Change detection without awareness: Do explicit reports underestimate the representation of change in the visual system? *Visual Cognition*, **7,** 323–344.

Friedman, A. (1979). Framing pictures: The role of knowledge in automatized encoding and memory for gist. *Journal of Experimental Psychology: General*, **108.** 316–355.

Goodman, G. (1980). Picture memory: How the action schema affects retention. *Cognitive Psychology*, **12,** 473–495.

Grimes, J. (1996). On the failure to detect changes in scenes across saccades. In: K. Akins (ed.) *Perception: Vancouver studies in cognitive science.* Oxford: Oxford University Press, pp. 89–110.

Gysen, V., Verfaillie, K., and De Graef, P. (2002). The effect of stimulus blanking on the detection of intrasaccadic displacements of translating objects. *Vision Research*, **42,** 2021–2030.

Hayhoe, M. M., Bensinger, D. G., and Ballard, D. H. (1998). Task constraints in visual working memory. *Vision Research*, **38,** 125–137.

Henderson, J. M. (1992a). Identifying objects across eye fixations: Effects of extrafoveal preview and flanker object context. *Journal of Experimental Psychology: Learning, Memory, and Cognition*, **18,** 521–530.

Henderson, J. M. (1992b). Visual attention and eye movement control during reading and picture viewing. In: K. Rayner (ed.) *Eye movements and visual cognition: scene perception and reading.* New York: Springer-Verlag, pp. 260–283.

Henderson, J. M. (1993). Visual attention and saccadic eye movements. In: G. d'Ydewalle and J. Rensbergen (ed.), *Perception and cognition: Advances in eye movement research.* Amsterdam: Netherland Science Publishers, pp. 37–50.

Henderson, J. M. (1994). Two representational systems in dynamic visual identification. *Journal of Experimental Psychology: General*, **123,** 410–426.

Henderson, J. M. (1996). Visual attention and the attention-action interface. In: K. Aikens (ed.) *Perception: Vancouver studies in cognitive science.* Oxford: Oxford University Press, pp. 290–316.

Henderson, J. M. (1997). Transsaccadic memory and integration during real-world object perception. *Psychological Science*, **8**, 51–55.

Henderson, J. M. (2003). Human gaze control in real-world scene perception. *Trends in Cognitive Sciences*, **7**, 498–504.

Henderson, J. M., and Anes, M. D. (1994). Effects of object-file review and type priming on visual identification within and across eye fixations. *Journal of Experimental Psychology: Human Perception and Performance*, **20**, 826–839.

Henderson, J. M., and Ferreira, F. (2004). *The interface of language, vision, and action: Eye movements and the visual world.* New York: Psychology Press.

Henderson, J. M., and Hollingworth, A. (1998). Eye movements during scene viewing: An overview. In: G. Underwood (ed.) *Eye guidance in reading and scene perception.* Oxford: Elsevier, pp. 269–283.

Henderson, J. M., and Hollingworth, A. (1999a). High-level scene perception. *Annual Review of Psychology*, **50**, 243–271.

Henderson, J. M., and Hollingworth, A. (1999b). The role of fixation position in detecting scene changes across saccades. *Psychological Science*, **10**, 438–443.

Henderson, J. M., and Hollingworth, A. (2003a). Global transsaccadic change blindness during scene perception. *Psychological Science*, **14**, 493–497.

Henderson, J. M., and Hollingworth, A. (2003b). Eye movements, visual memory, and scene representation. In: M. A. Peterson and G. Rhodes (ed.), *Analytic and holistic processes in the perception of faces, objects, and scenes.* New York: Oxford University Press, pp. 356–383.

Henderson, J. M., and Hollingworth, A. (2003c). Eye movements and visual memory: Detecting changes to saccade targets in scenes. *Perception and Psychophysics*, **65**, 58–71.

Henderson, J. M., Pollatsek, A., and Rayner, K. (1987). The effects of foveal priming and extrafoveal preview on object identification. *Journal of Experimental Psychology: Human Perception and Performance*, **13**, 449–463.

Henderson, J. M., Pollatsek, A., and Rayner, K. (1989). Covert visual attention and extrafoveal information use during object identification. *Perception and Psychophysics*, **45**, 196–208.

Henderson, J. M., and Siefert, A. B. (1999). The influence of enantiomorphic transformation on transsaccadic object integration. *Journal of Experimental Psychology: Human Perception and Performance*, **25**, 243–255.

Henderson, J. M., and Siefert, A. B. C. (2001). Types and tokens in transsaccadic object identification: Effects of spatial position and left-right orientation. *Psychonomic Bulletin and Review*, **8**, 753–760.

Henderson, J. M., Williams, C. C., Castelhano, M. S., and Falk, R. J. (2003). Eye movements and picture processing during recognition. *Perception and Psychophysics*, **65**, 725–734.

Hock, H. S., Romanski, L., Galie, A., and Williams, C. S. (1978). Real-world schemata and scene recognition in adults and children. *Memory and Cognition*, **6**, 423–431.

Hoffman, J. R., and Subramanian, B. (1995). The role of visual attention in saccadic eye movements. *Perception and Psychophysics*, **57**, 787–795.

Hollingworth, A. (2003). Failures of retrieval and comparison constrain change detection in natural scenes. *Journal of Experimental Psychology: Human Perception and Performance*, **29**, 388–403.

Hollingworth, A., and Henderson, J. M. (2000). Semantic informativeness mediates the detection of changes in natural scenes. *Visual Cognition (Special Issue on Change Blindness and Visual Memory)*, **7**, 213–235.

Hollingworth, A., and Henderson, J. M. (2002). Accurate visual memory for previously attended objects in natural scenes. *Journal of Experimental Psychology: Human Perception and Performance*, **28**, 113–136.

Hollingworth, A., Schrock, G., and Henderson, J. M. (2001). Change detection in the flicker paradigm: The role of fixation position within the scene. *Memory and Cognition*, **29**, 296–304.

Hollingworth, A., Williams, C. C., and Henderson, J. M. (2001). To see and remember: Visually specific information is retained in memory from previously attended objects in natural scenes. *Psychonomic Bulletin and Review*, **8**, 761–768.

Irwin, D. E. (1991). Information integration across saccadic eye movements. *Cognitive Psychology*, **23**, 420–456.

Irwin, D. E. (1992a). Memory for position and identity across eye movements. *Journal of Experimental Psychology: Learning, Memory, and Cognition*, **18**, 307–317.

Irwin, D. E. (1992b). Visual memory within and across fixations. In: K. Rayner (ed.) *Eye movements and visual cognition: Scene perception and reading.* New York: Springer-Verlag, pp. 146–165.

Irwin, D. E., and Andrews, R. (1996). Integration and accumulation of information across saccadic eye movements. In: T. Inui and J. L. McClelland (ed.), *Attention and performance XVI: Information integration in perception and communication.* Cambridge, MA: MIT Press, pp. 125–155.

Irwin, D. E., and Gordon, R. (1998). Eye movements, attention and trans-saccadic memory. *Visual Cognition*, **5**, 127–155.

Irwin, D. E., Brown, J. S., and Sun, J. (1988). Visual masking and visual integration across saccadic eye movements. *Journal of Experimental Psychology: General*, **117**, 276–287.

Irwin, D. E., Yantis, S., and Jonides, J. (1983). Evidence against visual integration across saccadic eye movements. *Perception and Psychophysics*, **34**, 49–57.

Irwin, D. E., Zacks, J.L., and Brown, J.S. (1990). Visual memory and the perception of a stable visual environment. *Perception and Psychophysics*, **47**, 35–46.

Jonides, J., Irwin, D. E., and Yantis, S. (1982). Integrating visual information from successive fixations. *Science*, **215**, 192–194.

Jonides, J., Irwin, D. E., and Yantis, S. (1983). Failure to integrate information from successive fixations. *Science*, **222**, 188.

Kowler, E., Anderson, E., Dosher, B., and Blaser, E. (1995). The role of attention in the programming of saccades. *Vision Research*, **35**, 1897–1916.

Mack, A. (1970). An investigation of the relationship between eye and retinal image movements in the perception of movement. *Perception and Psychophysics*, **8**, 291–298.

Mandler, J. M., and Parker, R. E. (1976). Memory for descriptive and spatial information in complex pictures. *Journal of Experimental Psychology: Human Learning and Memory*, **2**, 38–48.

Mandler, J. M., and Ritchey, G. H. (1977). Long-term memory for pictures. *Journal of Experimental Psychology: Human Learning and Memory*, **3**, 386–396.

Marr, D. (1982). *Vision.* San Francisco: Freeman

McConkie, G. W. (1990). *Where vision and cognition meet.* Paper presented at the Human Frontier Science Program Workshop on Object and Scene Perception, Leuven, Belgium.

McConkie, G. W. (1991). Perceiving a stable visual world. In: J. Van Resnbergen, M. Devijver, and G. d'Ydewalle (ed.), *Proceedings of the sixth European conference on eye movements.* Leuven, Belgium: Laboratory of Experimental Psychology, pp. 5–7.

McConkie, G. W., and Currie, C. B. (1996). Visual stability while viewing complex pictures. *Journal of Experimental Psychology: Human Perception and Performance*, **22**, 563–581.

McConkie, G. W., and Rayner, K. (1976). Identifying the span of the effective stimulus in reading: Literature review and theories of reading. In: H. Singer and R. B. Ruddell (ed.), *Theoretical models and processes in reading*. Newark, DE: International Reading Institute, pp. 137–162.

McConkie, G. W., and Zola, D. (1979). Is visual information integrated across successive fixations in reading? *Perception and Psychophysics*, **25**, 221–224.

Neisser, U. (1967). *Cognitive psychology*. East Norwalk, CT: Appleton-Century-Crofts.

Nickerson, R. S. (1965). Short-term memory for complex meaningful visual configurations: A demonstration of capacity. *Canadian Journal of Psychology*, **19**, 155–160.

O'Regan, J. K. (1992). Solving the 'real' mysteries of visual perception: The world as an outside memory. *Canadian Journal of Psychology Special Issue: Object perception and scene analysis*, **46**, 461–488.

O'Regan, J. K., and Lévy-Schoen, A. (1983). Integrating visual information from successive fixations: Does trans-saccadic fusion exist? *Vision Research*, **23**, 765–768.

O'Regan, J. K., and Noë, A. (2001). A sensorimotor account of vision and visual consciousness. *Behavioral and Brain Sciences*, **24**, 939–1031.

Parker, R. E. (1978). Picture processing during recognition. *Journal of Experimental Psychology: Human Perception and Performance*, **4**, 284–293.

Palmer, S. E. (1977). Hierarchical structure in perceptual representation. *Cognitive Psychology*, **9**, 441–474.

Pezdek, K., Maki, R., Valencia-Laver, D., Whetstone, T., Stockert, J. and Dougherty, T. (1988). Picture memory: Recognizing added and deleted details. *Journal of Experimental Psychology: Learning, Memory, and Cognition*, **14**, 468–476.

Pezdek, K., Whetstone, T., Reynolds, K., Askari, N., and Dougherty, T. (1989). Memory for real-world scenes: The role of consistency with schema expectation. *Journal of Experimental Psychology: Learning, Memory, and Cognition*, **15**, 587–595.

Pollatsek, A., and Rayner, K. (1992). What is integrated across fixations? In: K. Rayner (ed.) *Eye movements and visual cognition: Scene perception and reading*. New York: Springer-Verlag, pp. 166–191.

Pollatsek, A., Rayner, K., and Collins, W. E. (1984). Integrating pictorial information across eye movements. *Journal of Experimental Psychology: General*, **113**, 426–442.

Pollatsek, A., Rayner, K., and Henderson, J. M. (1990). Role of spatial location in integration of pictorial information across saccades. *Journal of Experimental Psychology: Human Perception and Performance*, **16**, 199–210.

Pouget, A., Fisher, S. A., and Sejnowski, T. J. (1993). Egocentric spatial representation in early vision. *Journal of Cognitive Neuroscience*, **5**, 150–161.

Rayner, K. (1998). Eye movements in reading and information processing: 20 years of research. *Psychological Bulletin*, **124**, 372–422.

Rayner, K., McConkie, G. W., and Ehrlich, S. (1978). Eye movements and integrating information across fixations. *Journal of Experimental Psychology: Human Perception and Performance*, **4**, 529–544.

Rayner, K., and Pollatsek, A. (1983). Is visual information integrated across saccades? *Perception and Psychophysics*, **34**, 39–48.

Rensink, R. A. (2000a). Seeing, sensing, and scrutinizing. *Vision Research*, **40**, 1469–1487.

Rensink, R. A. (2000b). The dynamic representation of scenes. *Visual Cognition Special Issue: Change blindness and visual memory*, **7**, 17–42.

Rensink, R. A., O'Regan, J. K., and Clark, J. J. (1997). To see or not to see: The need for attention to perceive changes in scenes. *Psychological Science*, **8**, 368–373.

Riesenhuber, M., and Poggio, T. (1999). Hierarchical models of object recognition in cortex. *Nature Neuroscience*, **2**, 1019–1025.

Scholl, B. J. (2000). Attenuated change blindness for exogenously attended items in a flicker paradigm. *Visual Cognition Special Issue: Change blindness and visual memory*, **7**, 377–396.

Shepard, R.N. (1967). Recognition memory for words, sentences, and pictures. *Journal of Verbal Learning and Verbal Behavior*, **6**, 156–163.

Shepherd, M., Findlay, J. M., and Hockey, R. J. (1986). The relationship between eye movements and spatial attention. *The Quarterly Journal of Experimental Psychology*, **38A**, 475–491.

Sperling, G. (1960). The information available in brief visual presentation. *Psychological Monographs*, **74**, 29.

Standing, L., Conezio, J., and Haber, R. N. (1970). Perception and memory for pictures: Single-trial learning of 2500 visual stimuli. *Psychonomic Science*, **19**, 73–74.

Trehub, A. (1977). Neuronal models for cognitive processes: Networks for learning, perception and imagination. *Journal of Theoretical Biology* , **65**, 141–169.

Verfaillie, K., De Troy, A., and Van Rensbergen, J. (1994). Transsaccadic integration of biological motion. *Journal of Experimental Psychology: Learning, Memory, and Cognition*, **20**, 649–670.

Whipple, W.R., and Wallach, H. (1978). Direction-specific motion thresholds for abnormal image shifts during saccadic eye movement. *Perception and Psychophysics*, **24**, 349–355.

Williams, C. C., Henderson, J. M., and Zacks, R. T. (2005). Incidental visual memory for targets and distractors in visual search. *Perception and Psychophysics*.

Williams, P., and Simons, D. J. (2000). Detecting changes in novel, complex three-dimensional objects. *Visual Cognition Special Issue: Change blindness and visual memory*, **7**, 297–322.

Wolfe, J. M. (1999). Inattentional amnesia. In: V. Coltheart (ed.) *Fleeting memories*. Cambridge, MA: MIT Press, pp. 71–94.

10

Remembering what we've seen: Predicting recollective experience from eye movements when viewing everyday scenes

Peter Chapman

Abstract

Most people have the impression of forming a complete visual representation of the world they look at, and traditional studies have suggested that visual scene recognition is extremely good even in situations where verbal memory is relatively poor. However, recent research into change-blindness, memory-free visual search and related phenomena have led some researchers to suggest that virtually no visual information is retained from individual fixations. This chapter reviews a number of studies that have recorded eye movements and subsequent visual memory in both laboratory and field settings. It concludes that while visual memory is sometimes quite poor, it is by no means absent in most situations. In most applied settings, records of people's eye movements will prove highly predictive of later memory performance. Factors such as emotional stress and danger which have been found to systematically distort people's memory for situations generally do so because they also distort people's eye movements. Nonetheless there is clear evidence that long-term memories are formed for items that have never been fixated directly, and there is also evidence for important differences in memory amongst different items that have been fixated. The chapter goes on to argue is that it may be necessary to separate out visual memory based on familiarity from that based on recollection. Items or scenes which have only been briefly fixated may be recognized at levels greater than chance based on processes of familiarity, while more extended fixations may be necessary to produce full recollection.

Introduction

In real-world situations people are often required to remember visual information to which they have only paid brief attention. A car driver may be questioned about the vehicles present just before an accident. A party guest may have to recognize a person to whom they have previously been introduced. An eyewitness may have to identify items from a crime scene. A walker may have to identify a path down which they have previously travelled. Such tasks vary dramatically in difficulty, however, most people would assume that we possess a visual memory system that is sufficient for performing these and a variety of related tasks. However, a number of recent experiments have caused some theorists to query whether visual memory for scenes is available even for short-term tasks such as visual search and change detection. Simple visual search tasks are sometimes performed in a way that suggests people do not actually remember the distractor locations that they have already viewed. When changes to a scene are masked by a brief flicker, a saccade, or an everyday interruption such as an occluding object passing them, people are sometimes even unable to report changes as substantial as the identity of the person with whom they were talking. Such failures to use visual memory in short-term tasks raises questions about the quality of long-term visual memory in everyday situations and the degree to which it can be predicted by knowing what items a person initially looked at. Many of the theoretical issues related to eye guidance and very short-term representations of visual space are explored in chapter 11, while evidence that longer-term memory representations are formed after visual search is described in chapter 9. The present chapter first explores the applied issue of whether records of people's eye movements when viewing everyday situations are good predictors of their subsequent memory. It focuses initially on evidence from people's memory for driving videos and goes on to explore the way in which other variables, specifically the experience of emotional stress or danger, can influence both visual search and memory. The second part of the chapter explores the general issue in predicting memory from eye movements, specifically the question of how best to assess memory in such situations, with particular reference to the possibility that eye movements may prove good predictors of memory based on recollection, but are less effective when considering recognition performance based solely on familiarity.

Remembering pictures

Classic studies in picture memory seem to indicate that memory for pictures that people have viewed briefly just once is extremely good – of immense capacity and highly resistant to decay. Thus Shepard (1967) presented participants with 612 slides showing coloured pictures on a blank background. He then tested their memory by asking them to identify a subset of 68 pictures when paired with completely new pictures. Immediate recognition performance was around 97 per cent, and remained at 87 per cent even after a week's delay. Increasing the number of items does not seem to greatly impair performance in such tasks – Standing *et al.* (1970) found that with a memory set of 2560 different slides, subsequent recognition performance for a subset of 280 pictures was around 90 per cent correct even when the mean retention interval was 1.5 days. Standing (1973) even went on to demonstrate that when participants spent 5 days viewing photographs (such that they viewed a total of 10 000 pictures for 5 s per item, 2000 pictures per day), 'immediate' recognition performance (because of the time spent learning, this gives a mean delay of over 2 days) was 83 per cent correct. Standing (1973) estimated that his participants had successfully memorized 6600 pictures in the 5 days of encoding.

The initial demonstrations of excellent memory for pictures were based on selecting the previously viewed item from a pair (two alternative forced choice). Although participants' performance in such tasks is extremely impressive, it is not at all clear exactly what aspect of picture memory is used to support such high levels of performance. Shepard (1967) and Standing both used pictures differing widely on many dimensions. As the distractor items become more similar to the target items in recognition tests, memory performance becomes poorer. For example Goldstein and Chance (1971) showed people 14 photographs of one of three types of items – photographed women's faces, snow crystals, or ink blots. After viewing each picture for 2–3 s they were tested immediately or after a 48 h delay by attempting to select the 14 previously viewed items from among 70 distractor items of the same type. Performance was 71 per cent correct for faces, 48 per cent for ink blots, and 33 per cent for snowflakes (chance performance in this task would be around 14 per cent). Although this is notably lower than the 97 per cent performance reported by Shepard (1967), performance is still well above chance and proved to be relatively constant across the two delay conditions.

Of course, just because visual memory for some items seems to be extremely good does not imply that this is always the case. Studies of people's memory for the visual appearance of coins (Nickerson and Adams 1979; Jones 1990) or stamps (Jones and Martin 1992) show that our memory for the visual details of some frequently encountered objects can be extremely poor. They find a number of dramatic failures in memory, with some aspects (such as the direction in which the 'head' is facing on a British coin) actually being recognized at levels that are systematically lower than chance performance (Richardson 1992). Similarly, although recognition of individual pictures tends to be good, recognition of specific details within a picture is not always equally reliable. For example, Friedman (1979) showed pictures of typical everyday scenes, such as kitchens or farms. In some cases the picture contained objects that did not fit in with the viewers' expectations. Participants were later required to identify modified pictures as either old or new. In some cases the modification involved a change of one typical kitchen object to another typical kitchen object (e.g. a toaster changed to a radio) and in these cases participants were extremely poor at recognizing that the scene had been changed, although performance was much better when schema-atypical items (Friedman 1979 uses the example of a fireplace in a kitchen) had been changed. This provides one example of superior memory for schema-atypical items, though not all testing procedures produce such effects (cf. Alba and Hasher 1983; Brewer and Nakamura 1984; Brewer and Treyens 1981; Locksley et al. 1984). In this case the recordings of participants' eye movements provide a simple explanation for this effect – viewers' first fixation durations on atypical objects were more than twice their first fixation durations on schema-typical objects – the longer you look at something, the more likely you are to remember it.

Relating eye movements to memory performance

It feels like a truism to say that people will remember items that they look at and be unable to remember items that they have not looked at, however, a brief survey of the recent psychological literatures on visual attention and memory might lead one to conclude exactly the opposite. Research showing memory-free visual search and change blindness could lead one to suspect that much of what we feel we have looked at is not available for later memory. Similarly research on the covert orientation of attention, rapid processing of gist from scenes, incidental learning and implicit memory might suggest that we may gain a great deal of information about items that we have never directly fixated. Of course, the reason that researchers have focused on such findings is precisely because they are surprising, however, it is worth stressing that in the overwhelming majority of real-world situations the longer we look at an item, the more likely we are to subsequently remember it. A clear applied example of this is provided by recent work with David Crundall, Geoffrey Underwood, and Nicola Phelps. In one study a group of police drivers viewed films of dangerous driving situations (these stimuli were a subset of those used by Crundall *et al.* 2003). The drivers' eye movements were recorded while they viewed the films and they subsequently performed a recognition memory test. In the memory test they were presented with details selected from a variety of locations from within the films and were required to say whether they had seen the details or not. Correct details were mixed with an equal number of similar distractors and presented in turn to the drivers. Figure 10.1 shows a typical spatial distribution of fixations across these driving videos, and Fig. 10.2 shows the probability of correctly recognizing a driving-related item (e.g. car, pedestrian, road-sign etc.) as a function of its spatial location from within the original scene. It is clear from such plots that in driving situations, the regions of a scene that we are most likely to look at are the same regions for which our memory is likely to be best. However, from Fig. 10.2 it is also clear that highly memorable individual items may appear in other regions, and that certain central items, though likely to be fixated, are still poorly remembered.

The spread of fixations shown in Fig. 10.1 is typical of that found in driving with a central bias, wide horizontal spread, and limited vertical spread (see Chapman and Underwood 1998a, 1998b; Recarte and Nunes 2000, 2003; and chapter 12). Few people would be surprised to find that these patterns of search turn out to be closely related to subsequent memory performance. The natural tendency when one views such plots is to conclude that fixating an item in a driving scene directly improves our chances of remembering it later, however, the relationship may not be a simple as this. One problem with the data in Fig. 10.2 is that the distribution of relevant information in driving scenes appears to closely mirror the standard patterns of drivers' eye movements. Creating test items for truly peripheral information (particularly from the vertical axis) is extremely difficult; hence the absence of recognition data from the far periphery of the field of view in Fig. 10.2. In fact, when a similar calculation is made

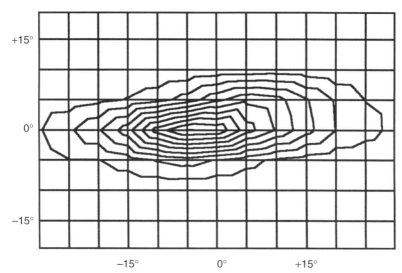

Figure 10.1 Fixation density plot for typical drivers averaged over all films. Regions in the outer area received less than 0.1 per cent of this participant's total gaze duration, while the very central region received approximately 10 per cent of total gaze duration.

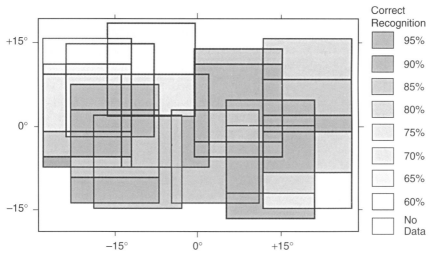

Figure 10.2 The probability of correctly recognizing a detail from a video as a function of its location on the viewing screen. Data come from 24 regions on the screen that contained driving-related recognition test items and are aggregated across all participants. Chance performance is 50 per cent in this task assuming unbiased responding.

using recognition data from driving-unrelated material (e.g. advertisements, roadside shops, passing planes etc.) the relationship between location and recognition probability becomes even less clear, with many such objects being poorly recognized irrespective of their locations. To directly test the relationship between fixation and memory we need to record each participant's full patterns of eye movements and relate these directly to his or her memory performance on an object-by-object basis. This has been done in a study by Underwood *et al.* (2003). In that study novices or experienced drivers viewed videos of driving scenes as described by Chapman and Underwood (1998a, 1998b), but the video was frequently stopped and the drivers were required to answer questions about items that had been on the screen either centrally or peripherally. Each test item was scored as to whether it had been fixated prior the question being asked. As would be expected given Fig. 10.1 above, 74.9 per cent of central items had been fixated and 49.8 per cent of peripheral items had been, and these proportions were roughly the same whatever the experience level of the drivers. In turn, 80.3 per cent of questions relating to central items were answered correctly, compared with 59.6 per cent of questions about peripheral items – though in this case there was a group difference, with experienced drivers correctly answering significantly more questions about peripheral items than novice drivers did.

Some participants in the study fixated virtually all the central items, and generally went on to remember them correctly; however, when these high performing participants were removed from the analysis it was possible to conduct a systematic analysis of how memory for items depended on having fixated them. In these cases correct recall for fixated objects was at 50.8 per cent, while correct recall for unfixated objects was dramatically poorer at 20.8 per cent. These effects interacted with whether items appeared centrally or peripherally such that for fixated objects performance was better for central than peripheral items (64.8 vs. 36.7 per cent) while for unfixated objects performance was extremely poor for both central and peripheral items (18.1 and 23.4 per cent respectively). In a driving context one of the most important manipulations is the level of danger present in a situation, and there is good reason to predict that changes in the danger experienced in a situation will affect both eye movements and subsequent memory. In an applied context it is important to discover whether drivers adopt appropriate visual search strategies in dangerous situations, and also potentially valuable to uncover distortions in memory that can be expected after dangerous events have been experienced. Theoretically this also provides an interesting opportunity to investigate the way a third variable might independently effect eye movements and memory and the degree to which memory is mediated by visual behaviour at the time of encoding.

Effects of emotional stress on eye movements and memory

In some cases visual search appears to be more clearly influenced by factors such as arousal than subsequent memory is. One commonly described pattern of memory results is that in stressful situations memory is particularly good for central information and impaired for peripheral information (e.g. Berntsen 2002; Burke *et al.* 1992;

Christianson and Loftus 1987, 1991). One simple explanation for such an effect might be that people look more at central information in stressful situations (cf. Easterbrook 1959), however, some theorists have suggested that such memory effects cannot be simply predicted by records of eye movements. Christianson (1992) suggests that effects of emotional stress on memory involve both early perceptual processing (e.g. emotional priming) and late conceptual processing (e.g. post-stimulus elaboration). This kind of theory predicts that effects of emotional stress on memory will be only tangentially related to simple measures of gaze at the time of experiencing the stimulus. Safer *et al.* (1998) specifically introduce the idea of 'tunnel memory' to describe the possibility that memories for stressful events will change over time to become more and more spatially focused on central information. Here it should be noted that studies showing tunnel memory for emotional pictures have proved hard to replicate (Candel *et al.* 2003; King 2004) and that there is evidence that even if such effects do occur, they may only be present for particularly anxiety-prone participants (Mathews and Mackintosh 2004).

Christianson (1992) used a study by Christianson *et al.* (1991) to support the contention that typical memory biases in stressful situations are not dependent on attentional biases. In a series of three studies Christianson *et al.* (1991) found that controlling for eye movements, either by using brief stimulus durations or equating the number of fixations in a less constrained viewing environment, does not prevent enhanced memory for central information in emotional situations. Although Christianson *et al.* (1991) do find advantages for central emotional information, these experiments remain slightly ambiguous in that they did not show any impairment for peripheral information in such circumstances. As such, it is always possible that the central aspects of the emotional scenes are simply more memorable than control conditions irrespective of any attentional bias. Even if enhanced memory for central information is detectable when eye movements are controlled for, in more typical situations it seems likely that eye movements will show the same pattern of focusing in stressful conditions that is evident in memory results. If anything, changes to eye movements brought about by emotion may be easier to observe than any resulting distortions in memory.

A study by Wessel *et al.* (2000) describes three experiments attempting to replicate standard findings of enhanced memory for central information and impaired memory for peripheral information from emotional scenes. Although they fail to find clear evidence for the memory effect in any of their experiments, they do record eye-movement measures in one of their experiments. Here they find clear evidence for longer total gaze durations on central details from emotional slides than on unusual or neutral comparison details. Indeed it is arguable that in the free viewing condition from Christianson *et al.* (1991), the pattern of focusing is clearer in the unmatched eye-movement data than it is in the memory results. In summary, emotional stress seems to have very clear influences on patterns of eye movements, and these influences are often easier to detect than the more subtle effects on memory. This is not to suggest that changes in eye movements are not related to subsequent memory in these circumstances, merely that memory biases are far more sensitive to the precise form of memory test used. In general the less constrained the viewing situations are, the more closely memory results seem to accord with measures of visual attention at the time of encoding.

In driving contexts it is easy to find similar effects of danger on visual search (see chapter 12) and on subsequent memory. Comparisons of visual search in dangerous and safer situations are generally consistent with the idea that total gaze time on central information is greater in dangerous situations than in safer ones (Chapman and Underwood 1998a) and recognition memory results appear to show the same pattern (e.g. Chapman and Groeger, 2004). The study previously described by Underwood *et al.* (2003) also allows this comparison to be made, although here the data come from tests of cued recall rather than recognition. In Fig. 10.3 fixation data and recall data are split by whether the situations being shown depict hazardous events or more normal driving situations. In Fig. 10.4, data is presented from the subset of participants for whom it was possible to systematically compare recall for fixated and unfixated items in all categories.

From Fig. 10.3 it is clear that there is an advantage for central information over peripheral information in both fixation data and in recall data, and that in both cases this advantage is more marked in videos showing hazardous driving situations than those showing normal ones. Thus far the story seems clear, in hazardous situations we are more likely to look at central information and more likely to subsequently remember it. However, Fig. 10.4 makes it clear that this is not the full story. For non-fixated information, memory is generally extremely poor, but better in normal situations than hazardous ones. When information has been fixated, memory is actually better in hazardous situations, but only when it was central. As well as the basic tendency to remember what we see, there is also evidence that the chance of remembering something that we did not fixate is affected by the level of hazard present, and that some types of fixated item are more memorable than others.

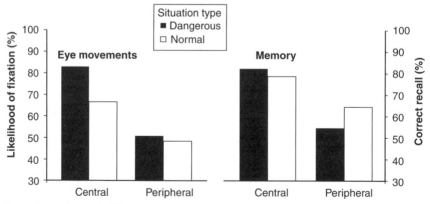

Figure 10.3 The probability of correctly fixating and recalling a detail from a video as a function of its location on the viewing screen and whether the video showed a hazardous or normal driving situation.

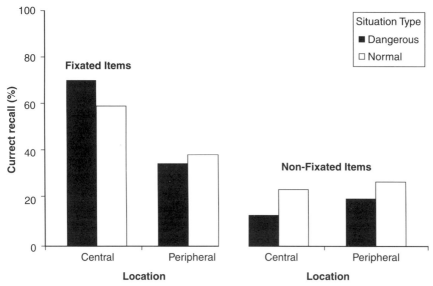

Figure 10.4 The probability of correctly recalling a detail from a video as a function of its location on the viewing screen, whether or not it was fixated, and whether the video showed a dangerous or normal driving situation.

The fact that we are less likely to remember non-fixated peripheral information in hazardous situations is of course completely consistent with work showing a decrement in peripheral target detection in high demand situations (Crundall *et al.* 1999, 2002; see also chapter 12). The fact that the enhanced memory for central information in stressful situations is not purely a function of what we looked at is also expected. In the Underwood *et al.* (2003) study the data are simply broken down by whether or not an item was fixated, however, Chapman and Underwood (1998a) have previously found that in stressful situations items are likely receive longer individual fixation times and overall gaze durations. It is thus likely that the central items from hazardous situations in the Underwood *et al.* (2003) study were not only more likely to be fixated, they are also likely to have received significantly longer total gaze times, and to be closer to other fixated objects within the scene.

One problem with using free recall as a measure is that it is hard to know exactly what level of performance would be expected by chance, and it is also clear that this level will differ between participants and between different types of information. This is particularly problematic when one tries to make assumptions about memory for objects that were not fixated at the time of encoding. Viewers' ability to correctly guess details about such objects may be influenced by all sorts of other information from the scene even if the target object is not fixated. One way around this is to use recognition testing. Recognition tests are traditionally thought of a being easier than recall tests (though see Tulving and Thomson 1973). However, the difficulty of recognition tests depends critically on the nature of the distractor items used. We have found that delayed recognition tests of visual memory for driving videos can sometimes prove surprisingly difficult for participants, particularly when they are limited in the amount of time they are able to spend looking at the developing road situation. In one study that I have conducted with Kate Roberts and Geoffrey Underwood we limited participants' time for information acquisition by showing them a series of 24 very brief (2 s per clip) videos of driving situations. The aim in this experiment had been to discriminate between informative and visually conspicuous items so one detail of each type had been identified in each clip (e.g. an important road-sign vs. a prominent advertisement). After viewing all 24 clips drivers then attempted to identify the 48 details that had appeared in the clips from among 48 distractor items. We found that drivers were more likely to fixate the informative items than the visually conspicuous ones, however, to our surprise overall recognition sensitivity as measured by d' did not prove to be better than chance for either type of material. Dynamic images previously have been found to produce memory performance comparable with or slightly superior to that observed with static images (Goldstein *et al.* 1982). However, in our experiment we found that isolated items in driving scenes were simply too hard for participants to discriminate in memory. This is partly because the distractor items were taken from extremely similar driving situations, and partly because of the very limited time that participants had to view the scenes. Nonetheless, the extremely poor performance on visual memory tests, even for fixated items, in this study was surprising, and it is reminiscent of the failure of Wessel *et al.*, (2000) to find memory differences even when differences in eye-movements had been observed.

A key distinction here is between memory for complete scenes and memory for specific items from within scenes. Loftus and Bell (1975) have argued that memory for pictorial details is predictable from participants' eye movements, while memory for general visual information is not. This general visual information is similar to the idea of gist discussed in chapter 7, and there is evidence that gist and detail information from visual scenes may be relatively independent in both content and longevity (e.g. Bahrick and Boucher 1968; Mandler and Ritchey 1977). In the recognition task described above, the fact that gist information was of no use to participants, and the fact that all the individual details were extremely plausible (cf. Friedman 1979) may explain very poor levels of performance. Although there are potential problems using recognition memory tests to assess visual memory, there are also potential advantages. A key gain from the use of recognition tests is the ability to potentially discriminate between different forms of memory.

Recollection and familiarity in recognition

Researchers have long suspected that there are two separate ways in which a person can recognize an item as having been previously experienced. Sometimes participants report that they have recognized the item on the basis of its general familiarity, but on other occasions a fuller feeling of recollection is experienced in which the person is able to recall specific episodic details about the occasion on which the item was originally encountered. This distinction between recollection and familiarity arises from work using three different paradigms to explore recognition memory. The first and most common paradigm is to ask participants about the subjective experience of recognizing an item (Tulving 1985). In a wide variety of studies participants are able to meaningfully distinguish between 'remember' and 'know' responses depending on whether they can fully recollect their previous encounter with the test item, or just feel that it is familiar without being able to uniquely identify the source of the familiarity (Gardiner and Richardson-Klavehn 2000). A second approach is the process dissociation procedure developed by Jacoby (1991) while a third approach involves collecting confidence ratings and estimating the form of the derived receiver operating characteristic (ROC) curves (Yonelinas 2001, 2002a, 2002b). Using a variety of traditional manipulations such as level and type of processing, and retention interval, these three methodologies have provided converging evidence that recognition based on recollection can be fully dissociated from that based on familiarity. Based on patterns of recognition memory in patients with selective brain damage, and on fMRI and ERP studies there is also evidence that separate brain regions are involved in these two aspects of memory (e.g. Düzel *et al.* 1997; Henson *et al.* 1999; Rugg and Yonelinas 2003; Yonelinas 2002b), with the hippocampus and anterior medial temporal lobe being separately involved in recognition judgments based on recollection (remember responses) and familiarity (knowing). Although the majority of studies that have dissociated recollection and familiarity have used words as targets, there are studies showing the distinction in just as important in memory for visual stimuli (e.g. Mäntylä 1997; Srinivas and Verfaellie 2000). Given the importance of this distinction in current memory research, it is interesting to see whether it can be related to records of eye movements at the time of encoding.

A series of studies that I have recently been carrying out with Lauren Burns, Geoffrey Underwood and Timothy Harrison have explored the relationship between initial patterns of eye movements during a search task and subsequent recollective experience in recognition tests for rejected distractors. The basic task involves searching for pictures or pictured objects from among an array of other items, though we have also extended this to searching arrays of photographs of emotional scenes, and simply watching videos of people walking through busy street scenes. In the standard version of the task we explore participants' memory for pictures that served as distractor items in an original search task. Fig. 10.5 shows a typical array from one experiment conducted with Lauren Burns. This version used displays containing 16 photographed objects on blank backgrounds (cf. Shepard 1967). Participants view a series of 16 such arrays in a speeded search task where they have to indicate whether a particular named item is present in the array.

In this task, approximately half the items are typically fixated by participants, and the gaze duration on fixated items varies widely. The second phase of the task is a surprise memory test in which a series of items are presented in turn and participants were required to identify whether they had appeared in one of the arrays shown in the earlier part of the experiment. Each item is shown at its original size, centred on the screen and participants have to initially respond 'yes' or 'no' as to whether they have seen the object in the arrays. If they make a 'yes' response, participants are subsequently asked to clarify the subjective experience associated with their memory using detailed instructions adapted from Gardiner and Richardson-Klavehn (2000). One difficulty

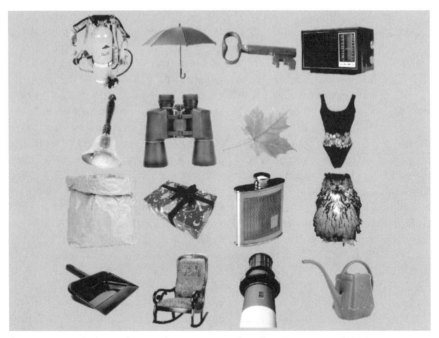

Figure 10.5 Typical search array: images were taken from Hemera's *50 000 Photo-objects premium image collection* vols I and II. Original stimuli as used in the experiments were in full colour on a grey background.

with the traditional remember–know distinction is that participants may be tempted to guess in some cases where no memory is actually present, and that such guesses may particularly distort the know category and consequently bias estimates of familiarity. Gardiner *et al.* (2002) have found that the giving participants the opportunity to explicitly mark a proportion of old responses as guesses clarifies the remember–know distinction, and that such guess responses do not themselves yield recognition performance above chance levels. The recognition test thus employed an initial old/new judgment followed by a remember/know/guess judgment to be made for items that were judged to have been previously viewed. Participants had thus viewed a total of 256 objects, and they then have to identify a subset of 72 of the items presented among 72 distractors. Such a task proves to be extremely difficult for participants. Overall performance was only around 56 per cent correct for items that served as distractors during the original search task.

A key issue in assessing recognition performance in such an experiment is deciding which model of recognition should be used to estimate separate contributions of familiarity and recollection, and of the potential influence of response bias in each case. Yonelinas *et al.* (1998) find support for a dual-process signal detection model of recognition. In this model recollection is assumed to be a discrete all-or-none process assessed as a proportion of remember responses (R) while familiarity is assumed to

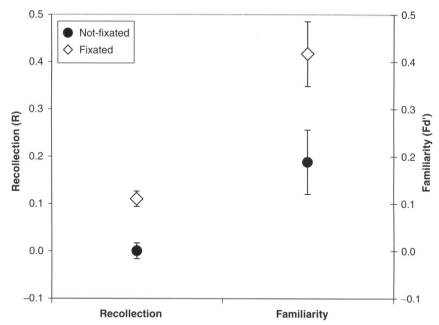

Figure 10.6 Estimates of the contribution of recollection and familiarity to the recognition of fixated and non-fixated items. Chance responding would produce estimates of zero for both recollection and familiarity, though it is important to note that the two scales (R and Fd') are not directly comparable.

rely on an underlying signal detection process that can provide an estimates of recognition sensitivity – Fd'. These data provide a clear distinction between recollection and familiarity based on whether or not individual items were fixated during the encoding phase of the experiment, see Fig. 10.6.

As can be seen from these data, recognition performance for non-fixated items is above chance, however, this contribution comes entirely from familiarity, there is no evidence for recollection of non-fixated items. To explore this pattern in more detail we can look individually at the total gaze times on items and plot the probability of an item receiving each type of response. Since the potentially fixated items all serve as targets in the recognition test, the possible responses are: no (miss), or yes (hit – remember, know, or guess).

Figure 10.7 shows the results from an experiment conducted with Timothy Harrison in which 36 participants were initially searching arrays that each contained six emotional pictures. Ochsner (2000) has reported that negative stimuli tend to be remembered, while positive stimuli tend to be known. We therefore used photographs from the International Affective Picture System (Lang *et al.* 2001) to explore the possibility that differences in recollective experience can also be predicted by eye-movement measures at the time of encoding. Memory performance in this version of the task is still extremely poor, though slightly better than that observed with search arrays

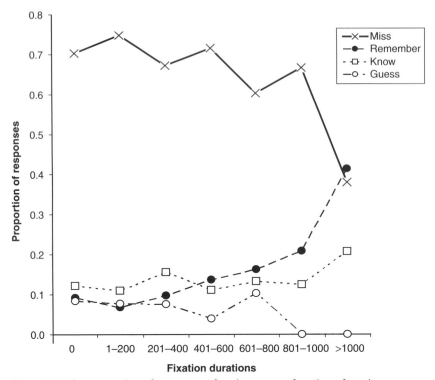

Figure 10.7 The proportion of responses of each type as a function of total gaze duration on the target picture at the time of encoding. Remember, know and guess responses are correct 'yes' responses, while misses are incorrect 'no' responses.

of 16 pictures. Overall correct recognition here was 59.9 per cent (chance performance in this task is again 50 per cent).

It is interesting to note from Fig. 10.7 that, while the probability of missing an item in the recognition test steadily declines with increasing gaze duration at the time of encoding, this increase is almost entirely accounted for by remember responses (recollection). The probability of recognizing an item through knowing (familiarity) is low, and relatively unaffected by fixation duration. As predicted by Gardiner *et al.* (2002) guess responses do not discriminate between seen and unseen items, and appear to be relatively insensitive to fixation duration except in the sense that they are absent for very long fixation durations. Only when an item has received a full second of gaze during the search part of the experiment is it more likely than chance to be correctly identified as having been previously presented, and in this case it is likely to be recognized with recollection rather than just familiarity.

It is interesting to note that there are similarities between the distinction between recollection and familiarity in recognition memory and distinctions that have made in models of reading and of visual search. For example Rayner's E-Z Reader model (e.g. Rayner *et al.* 1998) distinguishes between conducting a rapid familiarity check on a word and obtaining full lexical access – though see chapter 6 for alternative interpretations of L_1 and L_2. Another interesting comparison is with implicit and explicit memory for scenes – see also Shore and Klein (2000) and chapter 6. It is tempting to think that familiarity might be served by some implicit learning mechanism, while recollection required an explicit recognition of the content and context of a previous learning episode. In simple visual search tasks Chun and Jiang (1998, 2003) have demonstrated implicit contextual cueing – improved performance in visual search tasks based on learned associations between targets and surrounding visual context, that they propose is dependent on an intact medial temporal lobe system including the hippocampus (e.g. Chun and Phelps 1999). Chun and Jiang propose that this conceptual cueing exists without explicit recognition of the location of targets relative to backgrounds. Of course, all recognition is traditionally thought of as a test of explicit memory, even when such explicit recognition is based on familiarity. To the degree that the contextual cueing task requires the integration of objects with context it might be thought to be more closely related to recollection. Moreover, in this case it is not initially clear how familiarity might cause the contextual cueing result. Nonetheless it is clear that some form of long-term representation is being formed in these tasks which is not detected in traditional memory tests.

The possibility that much of our ability to recognize items that we have previously viewed is based on familiarity without recollection may also help us to understand studies implying that visual memory is extremely poor. An intuitive description of the process of visual search would suggest that as we look around we build a detailed representation of the world in some form of visual memory that can be used to guide subsequent search and action. However, recent research has caused a number of researchers to suggest that this view of visual memory may not be accurate. For example Horowitz and Wolfe (1998, 2003) employed a randomized visual search paradigm in which participants searched for an item in an array. In one condition this is a standard static search task in which the target appears among a constant set of distractors. In a second condition the search items are dynamically changed every 111 ms. Intuitively most people would expect the dynamic task to be much harder than the static one (memory for rejected distractor locations should mean that participants would rapidly detect the target in the static task, but might not detect it even after long delays in the dynamic task). Horowitz and Wolfe tested this assumption by measuring the slope of average reaction times as a function of the size of the search set. They find that this slope is almost exactly the same in static and dynamic conditions and conclude that static visual search is typically conducted without the use of memory for rejected distractors. Their suggestion that visual search has no memory is striking, but it should be noted that important caveats apply. A more limited conclusion might be that the process of visual search in arrays containing moderate numbers of targets does not always rely on memory for the location of previously rejected distractors. It remains possible that such a memory is formed but not used in the search process, or that memory for distractors is good but memory for their locations is absent.

Horowitz and Wolfe's findings have attracted much interest, and more recent studies suggest that their findings may reflect unusual strategic influences in their specific task (e.g. von Mühlenen *et al.* 2003), and that with minor variations to the task the expected reliance on memory for previous locations returns (e.g. Kristjánsson 2000). Moreover, it is possible that relatively low-level mechanisms such as inhibition of return (see discussion in chapter 11) may be sufficient to account for much of the simple components of visual memory demonstrated in visual search tasks. Such a mechanism is explicitly a relatively short-term form of memory, as are some other demonstrations of memory in visual search, such as priming of popout (Maljkovic and Nakayama 2000). Consequently such mechanisms, while potentially useful in visual search tasks, are unlikely to facilitate long-term visual memory for pictures or scenes.

Another area of research that has caused researchers to doubt the quality of visual memory is people's relatively poor performance in detecting changes to visual scenes (e.g. Simons and Levin 2002). In a typical 'change blindness' demonstration participants find it extremely difficult to identify even quite major changes made to a picture if the moment of change is hidden by a masking stimulus or saccade. Such findings have even been extended to real-world situations such as conversations with people whose identity is changed during a brief interruption (Levin *et al.* 2002). These findings, and related findings with respect to 'inattentional blindness' and 'repetition blindness' (e.g. Mack and Rock 1998; Kanwisher 1987) have caused some researchers to conclude that the whole idea that we see by building up an internal representation of the external scene is misplaced, suggesting instead that the outside world itself is all the representation that is necessary (O'Regan and Noë 2001). Other, more moderate current theories still abandon the idea that we maintain a global visual representation of our environment in favour of local transient scene representations which are limited almost entirely to the object being currently attended (e.g. Rensink 2000; Wolfe 1999). Although these proposals are striking, they may require us to specify more carefully the nature of the memories formed by everyday visual search tasks, rather than concluding that no such memory exists.

Why do most people feel that they have a detailed internal visual representation of their environment if such a representation does not exist? One possibility is that much of our processing of visual scenes is sufficient to support familiarity, without enabling recollection. This might be enough information to allow us to close our eyes and reopen them without being surprised by the scene we see. Because we feel familiarity with the scene in front of us, and indeed may be able to perform recognition tests at above chance levels, people may develop the assumption that what we have is a detailed and complete internal representation of the visual world with all visible items stored in a way the resembles the original scene. However, this is clearly not the case – we still do not necessarily have detailed information about the spatial context of every item in the scene. Nonetheless, familiarity alone should be sufficient for many demonstrations of scene memory after visual search and may even be sufficient for examples of excellent long-term visual memory such as those provided by Standing (1973). However, because item familiarity lacks contextual information it may be insufficient for use in paradigms where remembering the context in which an item was encountered is important. Successful performance in a change detection paradigm is often about realizing that an item at a particular location in one picture is different from an item in the same location in a second picture. This requires memory for the identity of an object to be integrated with information about its location, something that may be characteristic of recollection, but not of familiarity. In fact, a number of recent studies of change detection do show relatively good overall recognition performance for items whose change was not detected. Angelone *et al.* (2003) report that observers who fail to detect a change in objects presented in a short video still subsequently performed above chance in four alternative forced choice recognition memory tests; however, they do not distinguish between recollection and familiarity in their recognition tests, and they use recognition tests which can be performed successfully without the need to integrate items into the appropriate scene context.

Hollingworth and Henderson (2002; see also chapter 9) also provide evidence that fixating objects in a change detection task leads to relatively good memory performance. They used a saccade-contingent change paradigm to test short- and long-term recognition memory for items that had been fixated, but were not within the focus of attention at the time a change was made to the scene. They found that if the changing object had been fixated earlier in a trial, the observer had an approximately 40 per cent chance of detecting the change when it was made, but that this chance did not depend on how long elapsed between the initial fixation and the change. Rather, the actual fixation duration on the object seemed to determine the probability of change detection. Their participants were also good at making two alternative forced choice recognition discriminations that showed that they had encoded type, token, and orientation information about objects, and that these discriminations were still above 80 per cent correct after a delay of between 5–30 min. One interpretation of these results is that longer fixations are indicative of more detailed processing that supports subsequent recollection and change detection, while briefer fixations may be insufficient for change detection. while still allowing a chance of later recognition based on familiarity.

A number of other researchers have also found evidence showing that some information is integrated over a series of visual fixation in a scene, thus Hayhoe *et al.* (2003) extend a study by Land *et al.* (1999) to show that patterns of eye and hand movements in natural tasks imply the development of a spatial representation of scene structure over a series of fixations. These studies are particularly interesting as they suggest that in everyday tasks we may routinely construct complex visual representations and hold them in memory for extended periods. This raises the possibility that some of the deficits that have been observed in laboratory search tasks may not be present when visual search is observed in realistic contexts.

There are a wide variety of models of both memory and attention, many of which would be compatible with the results and distinctions made in this chapter. One particular model that links eye-guidance, scene perception and memory and that may be helpful for understanding recollection-familiarity differences is proposed by Hollingworth and Henderson (2002). This model is one of the few models of eye-guidance which explicitly allow for the development of long-term visual memory. It proposes a series of stages in which fixation of an object in a scene initially leads to a relatively high-level representation of the object being formed. This representation is subsequently integrated into a map coding the spatial layout of the scene to form an object file. These object files are then consolidated in long-term memory in a more abstract form, but one that still contains much contextual information. Short-term visual memory would still decay quite rapidly in this model once attention was withdrawn from an object. On the face of it, Hollingworth and Henderson's (2002) model seems to assume that all long-term visual memory will be recollective, since the object files are indexed to particular spatial locations. However it is clear that this model could be adapted to support the distinction between recollection and familiarity. Familiarity could arise by object files being transferred to long-term memory without including the full spatial context for objects. Alternatively, such long-term object files could themselves suffer from decay or interference over time, with the loss of contextual information.

Conclusions

Most people have the impression of forming a complete visual representation of the world they look at. The default assumption for the layperson is thus that visual memory should be relatively complete and anything less than perfect eidetic recall represents some form of failure in long-term memory. However, recent research into change-blindness, memory-free visual search and related phenomena have led some researchers to suggest that virtually no visual information is retained from individual fixations. As might be expected, the truth lies somewhere between these two accounts. There is plenty of evidence that in applied contexts visual memory is relatively good, at least for items that have been fixated by the viewer previously. In general people's patterns of memory performance are closely related to recordings of their eye movements at the time of encoding. Factors such as workload, danger, or arousal that systematically alter patterns of eye movements will generally produce similar alterations in later memory performance. With the increasing availability of low-cost eyetrackers, researchers now have the ability to record participants' eye movements in a much wider range of applied situations than ever before. Driving is a particular example of a domain where there has been an upsurge of interest in patterns of visual search. The pattern of results described in the present paper suggests that in many cases recording eye-movements will provide a more sensitive measure of attentional processes than later memory tests. Nonetheless, there will be cases where it is hard to predict subsequent memory from basic records of eye movements. Although the general pattern is for memory to follow eye movements, there is clear evidence that long-term memory for some non-fixated objects is still above chance. One specific proposal made in this chapter is that it may be necessary to separate out visual memory based on familiarity from that based on recollection. Items or scenes that have only been briefly fixated or never fixated at all may still be recognized at levels greater than chance based on processes of familiarity, while items that have received longer total gaze durations are the ones which are likely to be remembered with a full recollective experience of the context in which they were previously encountered.

Acknowledgements

I would like to thank Michael Öllinger for his helpful comments on an earlier version of this chapter, and to thank Geoffrey Underwood, David Crundall, Nicola Phelps, Lauren Burns, and Timothy Harrison for their assistance in the design, conduct, and interpretation of the studies.

References

Alba, J., and Hasher, L. (1983). Is memory schematic? *Psychological Bulletin*, **93**, 203–231.

Angelone, B. L., Levin, D. T., and Simons, D. J. (2003). The relationship between change detection and recognition of centrally attended objects in motion pictures. *Perception*, **32**, 947–962.

Bahrick, H. P., and Boucher, B. (1968). Retention of visual and verbal codes of the same stimuli. *Journal of Experimental Psychology*, **78**, 417–422.

Berntsen, D. (2002). Tunnel memories for autobiographical events: Central details are remembered more frequently from shocking than from happy experiences. *Memory and Cognition*, **30**, 1010–1020.

Brewer, W. F., and Nakamura, G. (1984). The nature and functions of schemas. In: R. S. Wyer, and T. K. Srull (ed.) *Handbook of social cognition (Vol. 1)*, Hillsdale, NJ: Lawrence Erlbaum Associates Ltd, pp. 119-160.

Brewer, W. F., and Treyens, J. C. (1981). Role of schemata in memory for places. *Cognitive Psychology*, **13**, 207–230.

Burke, A., Heuer, F., and Reisberg, D. (1992). Remembering emotional events. *Memory and Cognition*, **20**, 277–290.

Candel, I. Merckelbach, H., and Zandbergen, M. (2003). Boundary distortions for neutral and emotional pictures. *Psychonomic Bulletin and Review*, **10**, 691–695.

Chapman, P., and Groeger, J. A. (2004). Risk and the recognition of driving situations. *Applied Cognitive Psychology*, **18**, 1231–1249.

Chapman, P., and Underwood, G. (1998a). Visual search of driving situations: Danger and experience. *Perception*, **27**, 951–964.

Chapman, P., and Underwood, G. (1998b). Visual search of dynamic scenes: Event types and the role of experience in viewing driving situations. In: G. Underwood (ed.) *Eye guidance in reading and scene perception*. Oxford: Elsevier, pp. 371–396.

Christianson, S.-Å. (1992). Emotional stress and eyewitness memory: A critical review. *Psychological Bulletin*, **112**, 284–309.

Christianson, S.-Å., and Loftus, E. F. (1987). Memory for traumatic events. *Applied Cognitive Psychology*, **1**, 225–239.

Christianson, S.-Å., and Loftus, E. F. (1991). Remembering emotional events: The fate of detailed information. *Cognition and Emotion*, **5**, 81–108.

Christianson, S.-Å., Loftus, E. F., Hoffman, H., and Loftus, G. R. (1991). Eye fixations and memory for emotional events. *Journal of Experimental Psychology: Learning, Memory and Cognition*, **17**, 693–701.

Crundall, D., Underwood, G., and Chapman, P. (1999). Driving experience and the functional field of view. *Perception*, **28**, 1075–1087.

Chun, M. M., and Jiang, Y. (1998). Contextual cueing: implicit learning and memory of visual context guides spatial attention. *Cognitive Psychology*, **36**, 28–71.

Chun, M. M., and Jiang, Y. (2003). Implicit, long-term spatial contextual memory. *Journal of Experimental Psychology: Learning, Memory, and Cognition*, **29**, 224–234.

Chun, M. M., and Phelps, E. A. (1999). Memory deficits for implicit contextual information in amnesiac subjects with hippocampal damage. *Nature Neuroscience*, **2**, 844–847.

Crundall,, D., Underwood, G., and Chapman, P. (2002). Attending to the peripheral world while driving. *Applied Cognitive Psychology*, **16**, 459–475.

Crundall, D., Chapman, P., Phelps, N., and Underwood, G. (2003). Eye movements and hazard perception in police pursuit and emergency response driving. *Journal of Experimental Psychology: Applied*, **9**, 163–174.

Düzel, E., Yonelinas, A. P., Mangun, G. R., Heinze, H.-J., and Tulving, E. (1997). Event-related brain potential correlates of two states of conscious awareness in memory. *Proceedings of the National Academy of Science*, **94**, 5973–5978.

Easterbrook, J. A. (1959). The effect of emotion on cue utilization and the organization of behaviour. *Psychological Review*, **66**, 183–201.

Friedman, A. (1979). Framing pictures: The role of knowledge in automatized encoding and memory for gist. *Journal of Experimental Psychology: General*, **108**, 316–355.

Gardiner, J. M., and Richardson-Klavehn, A. (2000). Remembering and Knowing. In: E. Tulving and F. I. M. Craik (ed.), *The Oxford handbook of memory*. Oxford: Oxford University Press, pp. 229–244.

Gardiner, J. M., Ramponi, C., and Richardson-Klavehn, A. (2002). Recognition memory and decision processes: a meta-analysis of remember, know, and guess responses. *Memory*, **10**, 83–98.

Goldstein, A. G., and Chance, J. E. (1971). Recognition of complex visual stimuli. *Perception and Psychophysics*, **9**, 237–241.

Goldstein, A. G., Chance, J. E., Hoisington, M., and Buescher, K. (1982). Recognition memory for pictures: Dynamic versus static stimuli. *Bulletin of the Psychonomic Society*, **20**, 37–40.

Hayhoe, M. M., Shrivastava, A., Mruczek, R., and Pelz, J. B. (2003). Visual memory and motor planning in a natural task. *Journal of Vision*, **3**, 49–63.

Henson, R. N. A., Rugg, M. D., Shallice, T., Josephs, O., and Dolan, R. J. (1999). Recollection and familiarity in recognition memory: An event-related functional magnetic resonance imaging study. *Journal of Neuroscience*, **19**, 3962–3972.

Hollingworth, A., and Henderson, J.M. (2002). Accurate visual memory for previously attended objects in natural scenes. *Journal of Experimental Psychology: Human Perception and Performance*, **28**, 113–136.

Horowitz, T. S., and Wolfe, J. M. (1998). Visual search has no memory. *Nature*, **394**, 575–577.

Horowitz, T. S., and Wolfe, J. M. (2003). Memory for rejected distractors in visual search? *Visual Cognition*, **10**, 257–298.

Jacoby, L. L. (1991). A process dissociation framework: Separating automatic from intentional uses of memory. *Journal of Memory and Language*, **30**, 513–541.

Jones, G. V. (1990). Misremembering a common object: When left is not right. *Memory and Cognition*, **18**, 174–182.

Jones, G. V., and Martin, M. (1992). Misremembering a common object: Mnemonic illusion, not drawing bias. *Memory and Cognition*, **20**, 211–213.

Kanwisher, N. (1987). Repetition blindness: Type recognition without token individuation. *Cognition*, **27**, 117–143.

King, S. (2004). Visual memory and emotion: Investigating the phenomenon of boundary extension. Unpublished PhD thesis, University of Nottingham.

Kristjánsson, Á. (2000). In search of remembrance: Evidence for memory in visual search. *Psychological Science*, **11,** 328–332.

Land, M., Mennie, N., and Rusted, J. (1999). Eye movements and the roles of vision in activities of daily living: making a cup of tea. *Perception*, **28,** 1311–1328.

Lang, P. J., Bradley, M. M., and Cuthbert, B. N. (2001). International affective picture system (IAPS): Instruction manual and affective ratings. *Technical Report A-5*. Florida: The Center for Research in Psychophysiology, University of Florida.

Levin, D. T., Simons, D. J., Angelone, B., and Chabris, C. F. (2002). Memory for centrally attended changing objects in an incidental real-world change detection paradigm. *British Journal of Psychology*, **93,** 289–302.

Locksley, A., Stangor, C., Hepburn, C., Grosovsky, E., and Hochstrasser, M. (1984). The ambiguity of recognition memory tests of schema theories. *Cognitive Psychology*, **16,** 421–448.

Loftus, G. R., and Bell, S. M. (1975). Two types of information in picture memory. *Journal of Experimental Psychology: Human Learning and Perception*, **104,** 103–113.

Mack, A., and Rock, I. (1998). *Inattentional blindness*. Cambridge, MA: MIT Press.

Maljkovic, V., and Nakayama, K. (2000). Priming of popout: III. A short-term implicit memory system beneficial for rapid target selection. *Visual Cognition*, **7,** 571–595.

Mandler, J. M., and Ritchey, G. H. (1977). Long-term memory for pictures. *Journal of Experimental Psychology: Human Learning and Memory*, **3,** 386–396.

Mäntylä, T. (1997). Recollection of faces: Remembering differences and knowing similarities. *Journal of Experimental Psychology: Learning, Memory, and Cognition*, **23,** 1203–1216.

Mathews, A., and Mackintosh, B. (2004). Take a closer look: Emotion modifies the boundary extension effect. *Emotion*, **4,** 36–45.

Nickerson, R. S., and Adams, M. J. (1979). Long-term memory for a common object. *Cognitive Psychology*, **11,** 187–307.

Ochsner, K. N. (2000). Are affective experiences richly recollected of simply familiar? The experience and process of recognizing feelings past. *Journal of Experimental Psychology: General*, **129,** 242–261.

O'Regan, J. K., and Noë, A. (2001). A sensorimotor account of vision and visual consciousness. *Behavioral and Brain Sciences*, **24,** 939–1011

Rayner, K., Reichle, E.D., and Pollatsek, A. (1998). Eye movement control in reading: An overview and model. In G. Underwood (ed.) *Eye guidance in reading and sense perception*. Oxford: Elsevier, pp. 269–293.

Recarte, M. A., and Nunes, L. M. (2000). Effects of verbal and spatial-imagery tasks on eye fixations while driving. *Journal of Experimental Psychology: Applied*, **6,** 31–43.

Recarte, M. A., and Nunes, L. M. (2003). Mental workload while driving: Effects on visual search, discrimination, and decision making. *Journal of Experimental Psychology: Applied*, **9,** 119–137.

Rensink, R. A. (2000). The dynamic representation of scenes. *Visual Cognition*, **7,** 17–42.

Richardson, J. T. E. (1992). Remembering the appearance of familiar objects: A study of monarchic memory. *Bulletin of the Psychonomic Society*, **30,** 389–392.

Rugg, M. D., and Yonelinas, A. P. (2003). Human recognition memory: A cognitive neuroscience perspective. *Trends in Cognitive Neuroscience*, **7,** 313–319.

Safer, M. A, Christianson, S.-Å, Autry, M. W., and Österlund, K. (1998). Tunnel memory for traumatic events. *Applied Cognitive Psychology*, **12,** 99–117.

Shepard, R. N. (1967). Recognition memory for words, sentences, and pictures. *Journal of Verbal Learning and Verbal Behavior*, **6,** 156–163.

Shore, D.I., and Klein, R.M. (2000). On the manifestations of memory in visual search. *Spatial Vision*, **14**, 59–75.

Simons, D. J., and Levin, D. T. (2002). Change blindness. *Trends in Cognitive Neuroscience*, **1**, 261–267.

Srinivas, K., and Verfaellie, M. (2000) Orientation effects in amnesiacs' recognition memory: Familiarity based access to object attributes. *Journal of Memory and Language*, **43**, 274–290.

Standing, L. (1973). Learning 10,000 pictures. *Quarterly Journal of Experimental Psychology*, **25**, 207–222.

Standing, L., Conezio, J., and Haber, R. (1970). Perception and memory for pictures: Single-trial learning of 2500 visual stimuli. *Psychonomic Science*, **19**, 73–74.

Tulving, E. (1985). Memory and consciousness. *Canadian Psychologist*, **26**, 1–12.

Tulving, E., and Thomson, D.M. (1973). Encoding specificity and retrieval processes in episodic memory. *Psychological Review*, **80**, 352–373.

Underwood, G., Chapman, P. Berger, Z., and Crundall, D. (2003). Driving experience, attentional focusing, and the recall of recently inspected events. *Transportation Research F: Psychology and Behaviour*, **6**, 289–304.

von Mühlenen, A., Müller, H. J., and Müller, D. (2003). Sit-and-wait strategies in dynamic visual search. *Psychological Science*, **14**, 309–314.

Wessel, I., van der Kooy, P., and Merckelbach, H. (2000). Differential recall of central and peripheral details of emotional slides is not a stable phenomenon. *Memory*, **8**, 95–109.

Wolfe, J. M. (1999). Inattentional amnesia. In: V. Coltheart (ed.) *Fleeting memories*. Cambridge MA: MIT Press, pp. 71–94.

Yonelinas, A. P. (2001). Consciousness, control, and confidence: The 3 Cs of recognition memory. *Journal of Experimental Psychology: General*, **130**, 361–379.

Yonelinas, A. P. (2002a). Components of episodic memory: the contributions of recollection and familiarity. In: A. Baddeley, M. Conway, and J. Aggleton (ed.), *Episodic memory: New directions in research*, Oxford: Oxford University Press, pp. 31–52.

Yonelinas, A. P. (2002b). The nature of recollection and familiarity: A review of 30 years of research. *Journal of Memory and Language*, **46**, 441–517.

Yonelinas, A. P., Kroll, N. E. A., Dobbins, I., Lazzara, M., and Knight, R. T. (1998). Recollection and familiarity deficits in amnesia: Convergence of remember–know, process dissociation, and receiver operating characteristic data. *Neuropsychology*, **12**, 323–339.

11

Eye guidance and visual search

John M. Findlay and Iain D. Gilchrist

Abstract

This chapter presents an account of eye control during visual search. The primary mechanism for selection of the destination for each saccade involves the generation of an oculomotor salience map, in which processes of biased competition boost the salience signal at locations containing visual material that is similar to the search target. Generation of the salience map is a dynamic process. This is most clearly seen in the statistical properties of saccades in a task. Individual saccades appear generally to be ballistic, with the end point determined in advance, although the trajectory can reflect the dynamic activity. Additional forward planning mechanisms that allow saccade destinations to be 'pipelined' in some circumstances supplement the salience map. Further processes involving visual memory, such as inhibition of return, operate to allow saccades to be distributed over different regions of the search area.

Introduction

In our chapter for the first edition of this compendium (Findlay and Gilchrist 1998), we argued that active eye scanning is ubiquitous in visual search, and so understanding eye scanning must be integral to any theory of search. We proposed an account, based around the concept of a salience map, of how the eyes might be guided during this process. We contrasted that active account with a more passive one in which covert attention 'scanned' some mental image and eye movements were incidental. The passive tradition was, at the time, the dominant one in studies of visual search and so we felt our proposal was quite radical. Since then there has been increasing support for an active model of visual search, in part reflecting an increasing realization of the limitations of accounts based solely on covert attention. There has indeed been widening interest more generally in eye scanning and we have even been prepared to suggest that a fundamental theoretical shift is in the process of occurring (Findlay and Gilchrist 2003). We commence the present chapter with a brief recapitulation of our earlier arguments. This is followed by sections describing more recent experimental work that supports and elaborates the basic account.

Salience maps

A salience map is simply a means of representing information spatially. In its most abstract form, it consists of a set of values of a scalar parameter (i.e. a single-valued one) defined at each point in a two-dimensional space. It can be conveniently envisaged as a contoured landscape of hills and troughs where the scalar parameter corresponds to the height at each location. Peaks represent locations of high salience and troughs the converse. In the case of visual salience maps, the two-dimensional space corresponds to space in the visual field and the salience parameter that is represented by the values at locations in the map corresponds to the significance of the visual information at that location. In this chapter, we shall use salience in this general sense that only partially corresponds with the everyday meaning of the term. In particular, it is important to recognize that salience can be modulated by the current task. The approach entails no commitment to the idea that salience is an intrinsic aspect of the visual environment. It seems plausible to suppose this might be the case, as recognized by the inclusion of an 'intrinsic salience' route in the framework for saccade generation postulated by Findlay and Walker (1999). However, whether particular visual properties are intrinsically eye-catching should be regarded as an open question, amenable to empirical investigation (see discussion in chapter 12).

The concept of a salience map has its roots in the physiological properties of the visual brain. It is well known that visual processing in the brain occurs in a large number of anatomically distinct visual areas, in each of which the visual field (or strictly hemifield) is represented in a retinotopic mapping. Different visual properties are processed differentially in these different areas. Moreover, these areas also connect in a retinotopically mapped way, to oculomotor areas such as the frontal eye fields and superior colliculus. There are multiple cross-connections, both forward and backward, but spatiotopic organization is maintained (Felleman and Van Essen 1991; Stuphorn and Schall 2002). This architecture enables visual information to be transmitted between brain areas in the form of two-dimensional maps.

We propose that at some key stage, probably the superior colliculus, there is an oculomotor salience map that is the location at which a unique saccade destination is selected (Findlay and Walker 1999; Trappenberg et al. 2001). At this stage, the current point of maximum salience in the oculomotor salience map is selected as the destination for the saccade target. Note that, on this account, selection of a particular spatial location occurs late in the process. This emphasis on late selection differentiates the salience map account from accounts that involve earlier spatial selection, for example by a covert attentional spotlight. In the remainder of the paper we shall first argue the case for late selection and subsequently consider ways in which some forms of earlier selection might also contribute.

Early work on the visual system emphasized that its architecture and organization showed evidence of hard wiring, but more recent thinking has developed the idea that neural networks possess immense potential for flexible information processing. A neural architecture consisting of a set of interconnected map representations offers the potential for a process which may be termed 'search selection'. This can be seen as a manifestation of the 'biased competition' postulated by Desimone and Duncan (1995).

In their account of biased competition, a short-term description of the relevant search target controls the competitive biases between maps in the visual system, such that inputs matching the description are assigned greater weight. In this way, at least in principle, salience maps may be created in which similarity to the search target in part determines the level of neural activity. Detailed computational accounts have substantiated the idea (Hamker 2004; Itti and Koch 2000). The first neurophysiological demonstrations that such maps actually occurred in the visual system during search were made in the early 1990s (Chelazzi *et al.* 1993; Schall and Hanes 1993). Both studies reported measurement of single-cell activity in visual areas of the primate brain (respectively inferotemporal cortex, IT and the frontal eye fields, FEF) and showed that the activity possessed the expected properties if the visual areas coded a representation of salience.

The formation of salience maps implies that visual information from all locations in the visual field is processed in parallel. Parallel processing of simple features, such as colour, formed one facet of the well-known Feature Integration Theory (FIT) of visual search (Treisman and Gelade 1980). However a second facet of FIT proposed that for more complex search tasks, such as feature conjunction searches, an alternative serial process came into play. For complex tasks, the search function, which describes the relationship between response time and display size, increases linearly. FIT proposed that this linear increase came about because of a serial item-by-item scan. The slope of the search function allowed an estimate of the speed of this scanning and values of around 50 ms per item were typically obtained. Such a rate is clearly too fast to reflect overt eye scanning and so scanning by a covert attentional pointer was invoked as an alternative.

Several difficulties subsequently emerged for this account. As studies measuring visual search speeds accumulated (Wolfe 1998), it became evident that different search tasks generated a wide range of search functions with no obvious discontinuity between those showing parallel properties and those showing serial ones. Duncan and Humphreys (1989) had already pointed to findings in visual search that implicated parallel processing of the search array. Indeed, Wolfe *et al.* (1989) had developed a 'guided search' proposal in which the attentional pointer was itself guided by something resembling a salience map. Nevertheless the idea of a rapidly moving pointer was retained in this account (Wolfe *et al.* 2000) even though more direct measurements of the scanning rate of covert attention gave much slower estimates than those derived from feature integration theory (Egeth and Yantis 1997; Ward *et al.* 1996).

It also proved difficult to integrate the idea of a rapid covert attentional scan with studies of eye movements during search. For large arrays, the number of saccades made before the target is located shows a close parallel to the search time (Binello *et al.* 1995; Motter and Belky 1998a; Williams *et al.* 1997; Zelinsky and Sheinberg 1997). Could a rapid attentional scan be operative within each fixation to seek out candidate locations for the next saccade destination? As Findlay and Gilchrist (2001) discuss in detail, the most plausible prediction would then be that saccades directed to the search target would have shorter latency than those directed elsewhere. Two studies (Findlay 1997; Motter and Belky 1998b) both found that saccades to the search target had equal, or longer, latency than those to distractors and both concluded that covert attentional movements were not involved in saccadic selection.

A resolution of these problems requires a hybrid account of visual search that combines parallel processing within each fixation with serial saccadic scanning. The parallel processing through biased competition leads to an oculomotor salience map in which similarity to the search target contributes to salience. Items that are similar to the target will tend to have a higher salience level and thus are more likely to be selected as the target for the next saccade. This approach can readily account for an observed property of the saccades made to distractors before the target is located. Such saccades are directed predominantly to distractors having some similarity to the target (e.g. sharing a common feature; Findlay 1997; Motter and Belky 1998a). If it is assumed that the processes creating the salience map possess some intrinsic noise variability, then it is possible for the location with the highest salience to correspond to a distractor, particularly if the distractor is close to the current fixation and so gains additional weighting from the proximity factor discussed next.

The second important factor that has an influence on salience is proximity to the fixation location. Studies of saccade selection during visual search clearly show the importance of proximity: items that are closer to the current fixation are more likely to be selected as the target for the next fixation (Findlay 1997; Motter and Belky 1998a). This may be ascribed in part to the anisotropy of the visual pathways. Items presented further into the periphery will be less well represented in cortical brain areas and so more difficult to discriminate.

To summarize, the approach proposes that during visual search, saccade destinations are determined by selection of the point of highest salience in an oculomotor salience map formed through the process of biased competition. The two most important determinants of salience are similarity to the search target and proximity to the current fixation location. We propose that this basic account provides the key to understanding saccade generation in visual search but the account requires supplementation in at least three different ways. First, it is too simple to consider salience maps as static. Computational processes of vision are time consuming and so it is more realistic to envisage each salience map as a dynamically changing landscape. Second, there is evidence that forward planning mechanisms allow saccades to be 'pipelined' and supplement the saccade selection process. Finally, other forms of short- and longer-term storage processes serve to render particular locations or regions either more likely or less likely as the saccade destination. In the following sections we consider each of these points in turn.

Dynamic salience maps: Endogenous and exogenous activity combine to shape a complex dynamic landscape

Generation of a saccade requires selection of a unique single location for the saccade destination. The account given so far has emphasized that this selection occurs at a late stage, and prior to this late stage selection, information is carried in two-dimensional maps. Thus in the earlier visual stages, information about multiple potential saccade goals is encoded. We first consider experimental studies using the 'oculomotor capture' paradigm, a paradigm in which two competing saccade goals are generated. This work supports the salience map approach and also allows rejection, as inconsistent with the experimental evidence, of the stronger position that independent saccade programs are generated concurrently. The studies also show how the representations for the goals develop dynamically. Following this, we consider some of our own studies that show the consequences for visual search of such dynamic representations.

In the 'oculomotor capture' paradigm, introduced by Theeuwes *et al.* (1998), an observer views a display consisting of six grey discs (see Fig. 11.1a). The observer is told that five of these discs will change colour to red and the task is to saccade to the disc that remains grey. This is a simple form of search task that observers can carry out without difficulty. The interest comes when a seventh, new, red disc appears at the time of the colour change. Theeuwes *et al.* found that saccades were frequently directed to the newly-appearing disk rather than the search target. Their report was entitled 'Our eyes do not always go where we want them to'. In this situation there are two potential saccade goals, one provided by the search target and the other provided by the onset stimulus. There are strong grounds for thinking that any newly appearing stimulus activates the mechanisms that produce an orienting response towards it. Whether or not an overt orienting movement is actually made depends on the balance between activity in brain centres controlling fixation and those promoting movement (Findlay and Walker 1999). In the oculomotor capture situation, the system is already predisposed to break fixation and make an eye movement.

Could it be the case that programs for the two saccade goals are processed and stored independently, as indeed suggested by the terminology of 'exogeneous saccades' and 'endogenous saccades' adopted by Theeuwes *et al.* (1998)? We discuss in a subsequent section how multiple saccadic goals can be 'pipelined'. If so, it might then be expected that the saccade for which the programming is completed first would be executed first. On this 'horse race' account, with two potential saccadic goals, saccades would be directed to either one or the other. Most of the time, that outcome was found. However, when the onset target was reasonably close to the search target, a new phenomenon was found. In this situation many intermediate saccades landed at a location in the space between the two target locations (Godijn and Theeuwes 2002). Intermediate saccades would not be expected if each potential saccade goal fully specified a motor program for the movement. Rather the result suggests a shared late stage with both goals represented on a single salience map. The result additionally shows that this representation has low resolution so that the peaks of activity coalesce. This result is similar to the 'global effect' finding of averaging saccades directed to intermediate regions when orienting to a display consisting of two neighbouring elements (Chou *et al.* 1999; Findlay 1982; Walker *et al.* 1997). The result is usually attributed to broad spatial coding as associated with large receptive fields, such as those found in the superior colliculus (McIlwain 1975). Averaging saccades are also found in visual search tasks when two identical target elements are present with humans and monkeys showing a remarkably similar pattern (Arai *et al.* 2004; Findlay 1997). It has been argued that this averaging can contribute to search by allowing a strategy of homing in to the target (Zelinsky *et al.* 1997).

In comparison with the latency for a single target, a strict horse-race model would also predict a decrease in latency when there are two potential targets. In fact, Godijn and Theeuwes (2002) found that latencies were *increased* when the oculomotor distractor was presented in comparison with control trials where no distractor was presented (see also Leach and Carpenter 2001). Godijn and Theeuwes (2002) further demonstrated that the saccade destination varied systematically with saccade latency. They were able to analyse this by taking advantage of the natural variability found in the onset timing for saccades. Figure 11.1a,b shows the results from the case where the distractor was close to the search target. The fastest saccades (quartile 1: latencies less than 200 ms) were most likely to be directed to the onset distractor or to an inter-mediate location between onset distractor and search target. The majority of saccades had intermediate values of latency (200–230 ms) and were most likely to be directed to the intermediate location or to the search target. For the slowest quartile of saccades (with latencies greater than about 230 ms), saccades were often directed to the search target, and inaccurate saccades were more likely to be directed on the *opposite* side of the search target to the onset distractor than to the intermediate region between target and distractor.

The account given by Godijn and Theeuwes (2002) rejects the horse-race model in favour of a salience map account. However the salience map changes dynamically as illustrated diagrammatically in Fig. 11.1c. Initially (A), there is an activity peak in the fixation region. Following the display change (B), activity develops rapidly at the loca-tion of the onset distractor and the fixation activity decreases. The decrease in fixation activity comes about through competitive inhibition with the onset activity (see Findlay and Walker 1999) and would occur more rapidly if the fixation target were removed. At the time shown by (C), activity from the target starts to build up, activity from the abrupt onset now begins to decline, and activity at fixation continues to decline. Finally at (D) the activity at the target location has built up to the level neces-sary to trigger the saccade. This illustrates neatly the processes that can contribute to the dynamics of the salience map. Activity builds up over a finite time, dependent on the speed of the biased competition processes. The activity from the distractor onset is transient and is followed by a reversal in polarity so that excitation is followed by a phase of inhibition. These themes will recur as we discuss further empirical studies.

Subsequent work by Ludwig and Gilchrist (2002, 2003a) using an adapted capture paradigm demonstrated that if the sudden onset also shared a visual property with the target (in this case colour) then the capture effect was even more pronounced. They used a display in which the search array appeared when four grey placeholders changed colour. One changed to the target colour (e.g. red) and the other three to a different colour (e.g. green). Capture by a distractor having the target colour occurred more often (49 per cent of trials) than for a distractor in the alternative colour (7 per cent). These results show that capture is not simply a stimulus-driven phenomenon. Task-based effects, for example the characteristics of the target being searched for, influence capture. These results provide further evidence against a simple horse-race model between 'exogeneous saccades' and 'endogenous saccades'. Instead the results are consistent with the interactive model in which biased competition leads to prefer-ential processing of display items that share features with the target. This has an influence on the salience map and the selection of the next saccade. While signals that result from onsets may themselves be processed more quickly in such a system, onsets appear not to have a qualitatively different status.

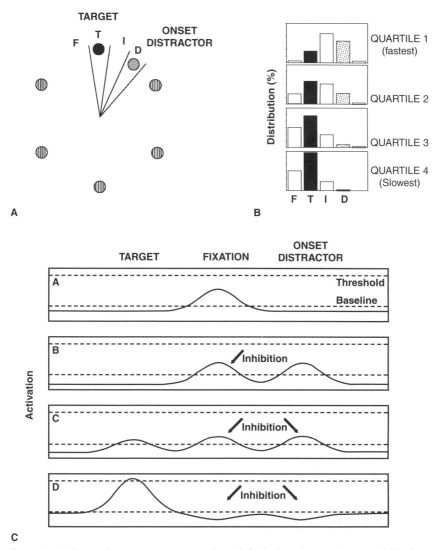

Figure 11.1 The oculomotor capture paradigm. [A] Display. The search target (T) is the only disc in the stimulus hexagon not to undergo a colour change. The onset distractor (D) may appear at an unpredictable location. The distractor is shown here in the 30° location. Saccades were classified as directed to the target (T) sector, distractor (D) sector, to the intermediate sector (I) or the far sector (F); [B] Distribution of saccade directions for the four quartiles of the latency distribution; [C] Schematic representation of the development of the hypothesized salience map landscape in the oculomotor distractor paradigm when target and distractor are in remote locations. Successive rows show the time sequence. Reproduced from Godijn and Theeuwes (2002). Copyright © 2002 by the American Psychological Association. Adapted with permission.

Even in a very straightforward search task, the transient activity generated by distractors at display onset may occasionally be adequate to promote oculomotor capture and these erroneous saccades can be highly informative. Figure 11.2 shows an example of the displays used in a study by Gilchrist *et al.* (1999). The task was to saccade to the vertical Gabor patch target, which could be in any of the eight locations, in the presence of horizontal Gabor patch distractors. The right-hand plot of Fig. 11.2 shows the distribution of erroneous saccades. Erroneous saccades were directed predominantly to distractor locations, located at 45° intervals around the angular axis. This again shows that sudden onsets have a high salience regardless of whether these onsets are task relevant.

An interesting and unpredicted feature revealed by the plot was the gradual decrease shown in both peaks and troughs with increasing angular deviation from the target axis. This effect could be attributed to long-range interaction between aligned Gabor patches, as previously demonstrated psychophysically by Polat and Sagi (1993). We suggested (Gilchrist *et al.* 1999) that the orientation-specific long-range interactions operate to enhance the horizontal feature signal at a distractor location when there are other adjacent horizontal distractors. This leads to a gradient in the strength of this signal amongst the set of distractors, with the distractor diametrically opposite to the target showing the maximum enhancement. These enhanced signals feed into the salience map through inhibitory connections and thus result in the presence of an oppositely-directed gradient in the salience map. As there is intrinsic noise in the

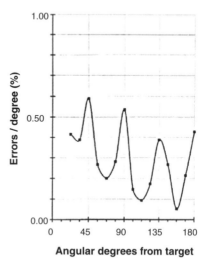

Figure 11.2 The left hand panel shows the type of display used in the study of Gilchrist *et al.* (1999). The search target was the Gabor patch containing vertical bars, which could occur in any of the eight possible locations. The right-hand panel shows the distribution of saccade directions, plotted relative to the axis to the target. The plot shows the distribution on the 317 (37.0 per cent) of trials classified as errors, hence the very large peak of correct saccades at the 0° and 11.25° points is not shown.

salience map, the point of maximum salience can on some trials be at a distractor location rather than the target. Because of the enhancement of the distractor signal and the resultant reduction in salience, such a distractor directed saccade is less likely to occur for a distractor further removed from the target.

The studies so far have shown that visual onset transients generate a bottom-up signal that peaks more rapidly than the top-down signal generated by search selection. Bottom-up signals may also be generated by an oddball element in a display (sometimes called 'intrinsic salience'). However, these signals do not appear to be processed as rapidly. In the studies reported by Findlay (1997), the general design was that a display appeared consisting of eight items, equispaced around a ring and equidistant from the point of fixation. In most cases, one item was the designated target and the others were distractors. The measure of interest was the proportion of first saccades directed to the target. Using the terminology that we have introduced, this measure should be influenced by the speed at which the search selection processes can generate a distinctive peak in the salience map in relation to the activity bursts generated by the onset transients arising from the distractors.

One experiment compared the influence of task factors with stimulus factors in saccade selection by comparing two alternative tasks for the same search displays. The displays contained one unique colour item and seven distractors of a different colour. When the observer had advance knowledge of the target colour, then search was highly efficient (90 per cent of first saccades landed precisely on target, with the majority of the remainder only slightly inaccurate). However, when the same displays were used without advance knowledge and the task was to locate the oddball (e.g. a single red item amongst seven green distractors), efficiency was considerably reduced (75 per cent of first saccades were on target). This result shows that the task-based processes (the *bias* in biased competition) can be brought into play rapidly. The relatively poor performance in the oddball condition might seem surprising in the light of 'pop-out' accounts of intrinsic salience. However the displays used were quite sparse, and as pointed out by Bravo and Nakayama (1992), oddity pop-out signals increase in effectiveness as displays become more dense.

As a final example in this section, we consider a study by McSorley and Findlay (2003) in which an explanation involving the dynamics of the salience map was invoked to explain a paradoxical result in which search apparently became easier as the number of distractors was increased. The search task involved detection of a target with a particular spatial frequency. This is normally considered to be an easy search task, supporting the notion that spatial frequency channels are involved in early vision (Carrasco *et al.* 1998; Sagi 1990). An example of our displays is shown in Fig. 11.3. The target for these displays was the low spatial frequency Gabor patch, described to observers as 'fat lines'. The task was to move the eyes as rapidly as possible to look at the target. In the two-element displays (Fig. 11.3a) the elements could appear on the left or the right and the target could appear in the near (3°) or the far (6°) position. In the 16-element displays, the target could appear in any of the 16 positions. The 16-element display had a slightly smaller size (83.3 per cent) because of screen size limitations but was otherwise identical.

There was a dramatic difference between the ease with which a first saccade could be directed to the target in the two cases. In the two-element displays with the target

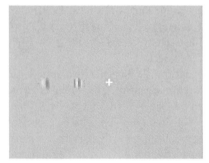 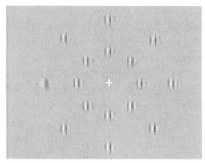

Figure 11.3 Stimulus displays used by McSorley and Findlay (2003). The task required subjects to search for a low spatial frequency Gabor target (fat lines) with high spatial frequency Gabors as distractors. With the right hand (16 element) display, many more first saccades were directed to the target than with the left hand (two element) display.

in the more distant position (as illustrated) only about 10 per cent of first saccades landed close to the target, even though a generous margin of spatial error was allowed (saccades landing between 4–7.5° were coded as correct). Instead, the great majority of saccades landed close to the near distractor element, although their amplitude was greater than those in control trials with a single target at 3°, showing that the far target exerted a small 'pull' effect on the calculation of amplitude. Conversely, with the 16-element displays, the task presented little difficulty and around 90 per cent of first saccades were directed to the target. In the displays with the target in the far position on the horizontal axis, as illustrated in Fig. 11.3a, the visual stimulation in the region near the target was identical in the two displays. Yet the presence of the additional distractors in the 16-item display resulted in a dramatic performance improvement.

We considered three possible explanations for the result. First, as found in the study by Gilchrist *et al.* (1999) discussed above, the regularity of the distractor elements in Fig 11.3b might promote perceptual grouping amongst the distractors, in some way facilitating the task. We carried out further experiments in which the distractor elements were subject to random variations in position, orientation, spatial frequency and contrast. In all cases, the high level of performance was maintained and thus we rejected perceptual grouping as an explanation. The other possibilities we considered arose from the observation that the latencies of the saccades in the two-element case were around 200 ms whereas those in the 16-element case were 250 ms. This might point to a strategic difference, with observers in the two-element case deciding in advance to make a rapid inaccurate movement because little time would be lost in fixating the wrong item. We ran an experiment in which two-item trials were intermixed with four-item trials where the search displays had two further distractors on the opposite side of the fixation point. Latency and accuracy differences were still found and thus we rejected the strategic explanation, at least as a full explanation of the result. Our final explanation brought in the concept of a dynamic salience map. We attributed the latency difference to the 'remote distractor effect' studied by Walker *et al.* (1997) whereby the onset of a distractor simultaneous with a saccade target results in a slowing of the saccadic orienting response to the target. Thus we proposed that the short latency saccades in the two-element case were generated from a salience map dominated by the activity from visual transients in which activity from targets and distractors were not well differentiated. The longer latency saccades in the 16-element case on the other hand were generated from a salience map in which the transient activity had dissipated and the predominating activity was from the biased competition of the search selection.

In summary, this section has provided evidence that the salience map involved in the generation of search saccades has a dynamic character. If visual onset transients are present, they appear to generate an automatic wave of activity. This activity is in the form of a time-limited burst, and there is evidence that it may dissipate rapidly to be followed by a reverse, inhibitory, effect. A second, more sustained, signal progressively dominates the choice of saccade destination. It should be noted that most of the evidence for a dynamic salience map (and indeed also for the related concept of pipelined saccades discussed in a subsequent section) comes from saccades made in displays with abrupt visual onsets. A challenge for future work is to determine whether these concepts can be usefully applied to the scanning saccades of extended searches.

From the salience map to the saccade

The previous section has emphasized that salience maps must be considered to be in a state of dynamic flux. Why is it that the resultant saccades do not reflect this dynamic activity but instead are ballistic and stereotyped? In fact, some saccades are occasionally found that do seem to 'change their minds' in mid-flight and change direction towards a new goal. This was found regularly for large (40°) saccades in a step-tracking task by Van Gisbergen *et al.* (1987) and examples also occurred in the study of McPeek *et al.* (2000) discussed in a subsequent section. Nevertheless these instances are rare and the majority of small amplitude saccades are directed to the goal that was selected before the saccade was initiated. However, although the landing position of smaller saccades appears to be predefined before the movement, the precise trajectory of the movement can, under some circumstances, be influenced by higher-level factors as first demonstrated by Sheliga *et al.* (1994). A number of groups have reported a subtle tendency for saccades to curve away from an irrelevant distractor (e.g. Doyle and Walker 2001, 2002, Ludwig and Gilchrist 2003b). In these studies, in what is a simplified capture paradigm, participants had to saccade to a target on the vertical meridian, and ignore abrupt distractors presented on the horizontal.

Could this result from on-line dynamic changes in the salience map so that, if the salience of a location rises during the programming of the saccade, the eyes are drawn towards that location? This is very unlikely to be the case. The variability affects saccade trajectory rather than the saccade end-point (as noted in the case of normal saccades by Jürgens *et al.* 1981). Instead saccade curvature almost certainly reflects the activity in the oculomotor salience map *prior* to the generation of the saccade by the burst cell firing. Saccade triggering in the colliculus occurs via a gradual increase in activity in the build-up cells followed by rapid and sudden firing of the burst cells prior and during the saccade. When the burst cell system in the colliculus triggers, it starts a very rapid and rate-limited process (Munoz and Wurtz 1995). This activity is self-sustaining and probably uninfluenced by visual events. The curvature corresponds to the correct programming of the end point position without a full determination of the saccade trajectory. There are two possible sources for the end-point correction. First, the correction might consist of the continued evolution of a target-related signal within the motor map (Keller and McPeek 2002). Alternatively, an active correction mechanism may be occurring via an alternative system. For example, Quaia *et al.* (1999) suggest that the cerebellum may be involved in the online directional control of saccades.

Ludwig and Gilchrist (2003b) showed how the saccade curvature measure could illustrate the different time courses of signals on the salience map. In their experiments, two items were presented: one above and one below fixation. Participants had to saccade to the target in the pair that was defined by the colour of the items. Participants also had to ignore abrupt onset distractors presented on the horizontal meridian. The study focused on the curvature of the correctly directed vertical saccades to the target.

In their first experiment they compared onset distractors that were the same colour as the target or the same colour as the distractor (cf. Ludwig and Gilchrist 2002; 2003a). In both cases the saccades curved away from the onset distractor but there was no evidence of a difference in the amount of curvature in the two conditions. This initial experiment suggested that the colour of the onset distractor did not affect the extent of interference. However, Ludwig and Gilchrist (2003b) reported two further experiments in which there was an increased curvature when the onset distractor was the same colour as the target. In the first experiment, the only change in the paradigm was that the onset distractor was presented slightly (78 ms) before the target. In the second of these experiments the only change to the paradigm was that the fixation point was present throughout the trial – a manipulation that increases the saccade latency to the target. In both cases the curvature metric now showed the influence of the colour of the onset distractor. In both experiments, curvature increased when the onset distractor was the same colour as the target. Both manipulations, in different ways, gave the similarity signal more time to influence the salience map before the generation of the saccade. This additional time was clearly required for the similarity of the onset distractor to the target to influence curvature. One way to interpret the finding is that the sudden visual onset results in a rapidly emerging peak in the salience map and that if the onset shares properties of the target then the salience is further enhanced by the similarity processes that emerge slightly later.

Forward planning mechanisms: Covert attention and preview

In one respect, our 1998 account requires supplementation. The active vision system contains a component devoted to forward planning. Humans and primates can follow instructions to memorize locations as future saccadic targets. Recent work with 'triple-step' sequences (Tian *et al.* 2000) shows that at least two memorized locations can be stored following instructions, although the memorized saccades are never as accurate as those made to a visible target (Gnadt *et al.* 1991; White *et al.* 1994). It seems likely that the process of storing a future saccade goal also occurs on a more automatic basis so that the process of planning the saccadic destination does not necessarily have to start from scratch on every new fixation. Such a process has been clearly demonstrated in studies of the initial saccades made when a new display is first presented, as discussed next.

The terminology of a 'pipeline' in which future saccade goals can be stored was used by McPeek *et al.* (2000) who demonstrated its presence with a simple and elegant experimental design. Their subjects were presented with a search display consisting of three items, either two red and one green, or two green and one red, arranged in a triangle with all items equidistant from fixation. The subjects' task was to make a saccade to the oddball item. This is a surprisingly difficult task and generates a large number of errors (e.g. Findlay 1997). Erroneous saccades are followed by a second saccade locating the oddball target. Quite frequently, such saccades occur after an extremely short intermediate fixation, suggesting that their goal had been selected during the initial fixation and stored 'in the pipeline'. McPeek *et al.* (2000) confirmed this with a manipulation whereby, on some trials, the display was changed during the execution of the first saccade so that the oddball appeared at a different location. This provided a test of whether the destination of the second saccade was based on a stored goal or on new analysis. If the second saccade goes to the previous target location, it shows it to have been pre-programmed. Such an outcome occurred on the great majority of occasions in McPeek *et al.*'s (2000) study. Only when the second saccade followed a fixation of 250 ms or more was the second saccade directed to the location at which the search target was actually present during the prior fixation. A recent paper by Caspi *et al.* (2004) further elucidates how visual information is accumulated for the first and second saccades in the pipeline situation.

In our own work (Findlay *et al.* 2001), we also studied initial saccade sequences using a more complex search display consisting of 16 items. We also found that second saccades often occurred with very short latencies following an erroneous first saccade to a distractor, suggesting that their goal had been selected and held in the pipeline. Additionally, we were able to show that the likelihood that the second saccade would locate the target depended not on the proximity of the target to the *initial* fixation location, but rather on the proximity of the target to the location fixated *after* the first saccade. Moreover, this likelihood was independent of the duration of the intermediate fixation following the erroneous first saccade. This points to a remarkable conclusion. Clearly, the second saccade target was selected during the penultimate fixation (the initial fixation) and stored in the pipeline. However, the selection was made taking into account the outcome of the first saccade in a way that gave increased weighting to locations near the saccade end-point even though the saccade had not been executed.

Direct measurements have shown that visual processing at the saccade goal is enhanced in the period before the saccade is made (Deubel and Schneider 1996; Kowler *et al.* 1995). The concept of preferential analysis for material at or near the saccade goal is one that has long been familiar in studies of eye control during reading. The phenomenon is termed 'preview advantage' and it has been shown that preview allows shorter fixation durations when the material is subsequently fixated foveally. As discussed in more detail elsewhere (Rayner 1998; chapter 6) reading ability deteriorates if upcoming material in the parafovea ahead of the current fixation position is rendered unavailable, for example using a gaze-contingent display. Preview advantage has also been implicated in saccade planning through the phenomenon of word skipping. During reading, short words are not always fixated and common short words are particularly likely to be skipped (Gautier *et al.* 2000; chapter 3).

These findings also provoke a reinterpretation of the role of covert attention. Covert attention describes the well-known finding that it is possible to attend to a location in peripheral vision while fixating elsewhere. Much of the early thinking about covert attention was based on the idea that covert attention could substitute for overt attention shifts, i.e. eye movements. The postulation of a rapidly shifting covert attentional spotlight, as discussed above, is one example of this approach. We believe it is more appropriate to regard covert attention as a process that acts to supplement the overt eye shifts of active vision through the phenomena of peripheral preview and pipelined saccades described in this section.

Two commonly encountered statements about the relation between covert attention and saccades are 'attention selects the goal of the saccadic movement' and 'attention shifts to the saccade goal prior to the actual movement'. The latter statement is underpinned by the finding of peripheral preview. However these formulations are problematic in several ways. First, unless we can define precisely the properties of attention, the statements lack explanatory power. Second, they imply that there is an identifiable attentional process, separable from the orienting control system, which exerts tight control over that system. Third, they often implicitly carry the further assumption that the attentional process must have a single localized focus. The spotlight metaphor has been widely used in studies of covert attention but, as Cave and Bichot (1999) noted, its popularity probably derives largely from its similarity to overt orienting. Cave and Bichot show that there is in fact surprisingly little evidence for a sharply localized spotlight-like process of covert attention. Finally, physiological studies are increasingly finding that attentional process are driven from brain regions, such as the frontal eye fields, that are generally assumed to be oculomotor (Moore *et al.* 2003). We believe that it is more satisfactory to adopt a position close to the pre-motor view of covert attention (Rizzolatti *et al.* 1994) that places primary emphasis on an integrated system that is designed to perceive actively through continual eye scanning.

To summarize the findings from this section, it has been shown that, following a display onset, it is possible for two saccadic goals to be pipelined so that a second saccade can be generated, often after a very brief fixation interval. The second saccade is largely based on information sampled during the penultimate fixation, with some evidence that a preview mechanism weights visual information at and around the goal of the first saccade.

Short-term storage mechanisms for distributing fixations

The account given so far assigns control of saccades to properties of the prior visual stimulation sampled either during the immediately preceding fixation or the penultimate one.

The factors introduced can account for many properties of saccades during visual search. How are these bottom-up processes combined with more high-level cognitive control mechanisms? One problem immediately shows the need to supplement the bottom-up account. A search driven solely by the bottom-up factors of similarity and proximity would show a strong tendency to be confined to a local restricted region. Suppose two items, A and B, are in close proximity and each have similarity to the target and thus an elevated level of salience. B may be the most salient element when A is fixated, and vice versa, so that a alternating sequence A-B-A-B ... is predicted if saccades are driven purely by immediate salience. How should the salience account be supplemented to avoid being trapped into such loops? It would appear necessary for information to be retained in some way about locations that have been visited and/or processed. Retention of information requires some memorial representation. In this section we shall discuss the wide variety of memory mechanisms that have been involved in visual search. As well as the basic studies discussed, this area is providing fertile ground for investigation of neurological conditions (Hodgson *et al.* 2002; Husain *et al.* 2001).

The issue has provoked considerable recent interest following a provocative claim by Horowitz and Wolfe (1998) that 'visual search has no memory'. Their concern was 'passive' visual search without eye movements and it is possible that they would have been ready to concede that when individuals used eye movements, they were able in some way to distribute their fixations over an array. Their claim provoked several rebuttals showing that various forms of memory influence visual search. Our discussion follows the excellent treatment by Shore and Klein (2000), who discuss evidence for at least three separate processes, all of which potentially affect eye control.

According to Shore and Klein (2000), the most rapidly operating form of memory is an inhibitory process discouraging immediate re-inspection. The term 'inhibition of return' (IOR) has become familiar in describing the phenomenon, first noted by Posner and Cohen (1984), of a reversal in the short-lived perceptual advantages found after visual stimulation at a peripheral location. Immediately following stimulation, reaction times to a probe are faster and visual discriminations are improved. However, if, as in the standard covert orienting paradigm, overt eye orienting does not occur, and also if no voluntary covert orienting to the location occurs, then these 'benefit' effects are short-lasting and followed by converse 'cost' effects of slower probe reaction times and poorer discriminations. In early work, the reversal was found to occur around 300 ms following stimulation, and for a while the effect was held to be automatic, straightforward, having a fixed time course, and restricted to one location. However it soon became clear that IOR was complex, with a time course that was dependent on the cognitive task carried out by the observer and could extend over more than one locus of stimulation (Klein 2000; Snyder and Kingstone 2000).

Klein proposed that IOR assists visual search by acting as a 'foraging facilitator' to avoid refixation of previously attended locations (Klein 1988). Klein and MacInnes (1999) developed this idea further and demonstrated an IOR effect during eye scanning. Subjects were slower to respond to visual probes presented in locations at or near the previous fixation than to those in control locations. However, when eye scans during search are analysed, there is evidence that in fact the eyes do quite frequently make an immediate refixation to the location just previously visited, whereas refixations with more than one intervening fixation are much rarer. This pattern may be seen in the data of Motter and Belky (1998b, Fig. 7) and was demonstrated clearly by Peterson *et al.* (2001). A possible interpretation is that IOR only comes into play after an item is fully processed, and immediate refixations occur to complete processing of an item that has not been fully processed (as indeed common sense might suggest). The idea that visual processing might itself exert an initial excitatory and subsequent inhibitory influence on the oculomotor salience map was proposed in a perceptive commentary by Crundall and Underwood (1999). It appears worth exploring further.

Leaving aside the issue of immediate refixations, the avoidance of refixations on already scanned items potentially allows an estimate of the size of the memory store for search. The key measure here has been the extent of refixation of distractors. The logic is that when no refixation occurs then the items have been remembered. A number of groups have modelled search scan data to obtain an estimate of the capacity (Gilchrist and Harvey 2000; Peterson *et al.* 2001). However the interpretation of refixations as a failure of memory is far from straightforward (Gilchrist and Harvey 2000, in press). It is clear from these results that locations are not simply being selected at random as predicted by a model in which there is no memory. McCarley *et al.* (2003) argue for a memory buffer with a search history comprising 3–4 items.

A similar conclusion had been reached less directly in earlier work (Ellis and Stark 1986; Engel 1977). These studies showed that in some search tasks, following the first few fixations on a display, subsequent fixations can be modelled by a process of random sampling with replacement. Figure 11.4, derived from Engel (1977), plots data from a search task for a small circular disk in a field of slightly larger distractor discs. The data points show how the probability of finding the target increases with search time. The thick lines show two models for sampling. The 'no replace' model scans regions until the target is found but never returns to a region previously visited. The 'replace' model chooses new regions on a purely random basis and revisits can occur. For the first second of search, the systematic model fits the data best but following this, search appears to become random.

Long-term and strategic mechanisms for distributing fixations

Shore and Klein (2000) discuss two more long-term forms of memory that might be interpreted as influencing the salience weighting of particular search targets. First, the phenomenon of 'priming of pop-out' has been demonstrated (Maljkovic and Nakayama 1994, 1996, 2000). This term describes the finding that the altered salience weightings of the biased competition process are found to show long-term persistence even when the higher-level voluntary processes have switched to a new search target. Saccades to targets where pop-out priming has occurred subsequently have shorter latency and improved accuracy (McPeek *et al.* 1999). This serves as a timely reminder

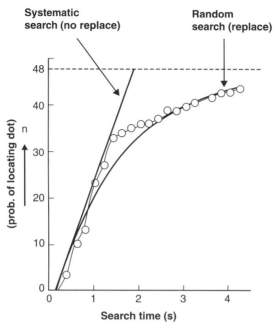

Figure 11.4 Plot showing data from a search experiment (Engel 1977). The task involved search for a small disc target in a large array of slightly larger, but otherwise identical, distractors. The observer viewed 48 displays, each with a different target location (chosen from an 8×6 grid to distribute the locations evenly across the display area). The displays were each presented for 4 s and the time to locate the target noted. The data points (from one observer) show the number of displays in which the target was located plotted cumulatively against the search time. The solid lines represent two search models as described in the text. Adapted with permission from Engel (1977).

that the settings of the biased competition network are affected not only by voluntary processes, but also through more automatic implicit mechanisms that are subject to learning.

The final learning mechanism considered by Shore and Klein (2000) is more long-term perceptual learning of contingencies. Visual search has been widely studied by presenting subjects with multiple trials in which similar displays are presented, with the location of the target and distractors changing from trial to trial. If, under these conditions, the target is more likely to occur in a particular location, this contingency is learned to permit faster search (Miller 1988). A somewhat more complex form of learning has been demonstrated by Chun (Chun 2000, Chun and Jiang 1998). If, during the course of a search experiment, certain specific displays are repeated, faster search times occur for these displays. This speeding can occur whether or not subjects show any awareness of the repetition. The process has been termed 'contextual cueing' and has been shown to depend upon the local configuration of distractors around the target element (Olson and Chun 2002). Peterson and Kramer (2001) drew the following conclusions from a study in which eye fixations were recorded in a contextual cueing paradigm. First, cueing occurs sufficiently rapidly so that the very first saccade, made when the repeated display is viewed, is slightly more likely to reach the search target. Initial saccades were directed to the target more often in repeated displays (11.3 per cent) than in control trials with novel displays (7.1 per cent). An increased probability was also found over the subsequent 4–5 fixations, suggesting that the process detecting the local configuration can occur at any time during the scanning sequence. Second, when the cueing effect was operative, saccades were directed precisely. There was no tendency for neighbouring distractors to receive increased numbers of fixations as would have been expected if the cueing gave low resolution spatial information.

Shore and Klein consider that the processes just discussed reflect implicit memory, describing this as 'the countless automatic and uneventful aspects of our everyday lives, which are affected by previous experience without our necessarily linking the present episode to the past learning environment' (Shore and Klein 2000, p. 61). Implicit memory processes are generally considered to operate automatically and below the level of conscious awareness, contrasting with the more explicit processes involved in conscious cognition. Shore and Klein note that more explicit memory is involved for such things as memory of the nature of the search target and the response that is required. More explicit strategies can also be used to distribute fixations over the whole of the search display. A number of authors have suggested that there may be a bias in the direction of saccades in search and that these biases reflect a systematic process rather than the action of a random process (Gilchrist and Harvey in press; Hooge and Erkelens 1996; Williams 1966). This systematic behaviour coincides with the intuition that when search becomes very difficult we tend to start in one place and work systematically through the display. The deployment of such a systematic process may have an additional consequence, namely that it reduces the need to remember each and every location visited. Instead subjects simply have to remember the order in which they searched the display (Gilchrist and Harvey in press). When systematic scanning of this type occurs, this has serious implication for the use of refixations as a measure for memory capacity as discussed above. Participants may fail to refixate items not because they remember that location as visited, but instead because they are following some fixed route through the display (see Gilchrist and Harvey in press, for a fuller discussion of these issues).

We have thus identified a number of ways that memory process can provide additional guidance to the saccadic selection process. Some of these, for example the inhibition of return mechanism, appear appropriate for the task of preventing the capture by local loops. Others, particularly those involving directional strategies, may contribute to local loop avoidance but potentially also serve the purpose of distributing fixations across different regions of an extended display. The more high-level strategies may require more conscious involvement to implement.

Summary

In this chapter we have presented an account of eye guidance during visual search. We have argued that the eyes are guided from an oculomotor salience map, shaped by the process of biased competition to form a representation in which similarity to the target controls salience. In addition to this basic mechanism, saccades can be planned ahead in a pipelined manner and further mechanisms such as inhibition of return prevent return to items that have been scanned in the very recent past.

Acknowledgements

Part of the work on this chapter was carried out while the first author was on research leave from the University of Durham, working at the University of Auckland. JMF is grateful to both institutions and to the Royal Society for a travel grant. We are also most grateful for the very constructive reviewing comments of Adam Galpin and Eyal Reingold.

References

Arai, K., McPeek, R. M., and Keller, E. (2004). Properties of saccadic responses in monkeys when competing visual stimuli are present. *Journal of Neurophysiology*, **91**, 890–900.

Binello, A., Mannan, S., and Ruddock, K. H. (1995). The characteristics of eye movements made during visual search with multi-element stimuli. *Spatial Vision*, **9**, 343–362.

Bravo, M. J. and Nakayama, K. (1992). The role of attention in different visual search tasks. *Perception and Psychophysics*, **51**, 465–472.

Carrasco, M., McLean, T. L., Katz, S. M., and Frieder, K. S. (1998). Feature asymmetries in visual search: Effects of display duration, orientation and spatial frequency. *Vision Research*, **38**, 347–374.

Caspi, A., Beutter, B. R., and Eckstein, M. (2004). The time course of visual information accrual guiding eye movement decisions. *Proceedings of the National Academy of Science*, **101**, 13086–13090.

Cave, K. R., and Bichot, N. P. (1999). Visuospatial attention: beyond the spotlight model. *Psychonomic Bulletin and Review*, **6**, 204–223.

Chelazzi, L., Miller, E. K., Duncan, J., and Desimone, R. (1993). A neural basis for visual search in inferior temporal cortex. *Nature*, **363**, 345–347.

Chou, I.-H., Sommer, M. A., and Schiller, P. H. (1999). Express averaging saccades in the monkey. *Vision Research*, **39**, 4200–4216.

Chun, M. M. (2000). Contextual cueing of visual attention. *Trends in Cognitive Sciences*, **4**, 170–178.

Chun, M. M., and Jiang, Y. (1998). Contextual cueing: implicit learning and memory of visual context guides spatial attention. *Cognitive Psychology*, **36**, 28–71.

Crundall, D., and Underwood, G. (1999). Is attention required in a model of saccade generation? *Behavioral and Brain Sciences*, **22**, 679–680.

Desimone, R., and Duncan, J. (1995). Neural mechanisms of selective attention. *Annual Review of Neuroscience*, **18**, 193–222.

Deubel, H., and Schneider, W. X. (1996). Saccade target selection and object recognition: Evidence for a common attentional mechanism. *Vision Research*, **36**, 1827–1837.

Doyle, M. C., and Walker, R. (2001). Curved saccade trajectories: voluntary and reflexive saccades curve away from irrelevant distractors. *Experimental Brain Research*, **139**, 333–344.

Doyle, M. C., and Walker, R. (2002). Multisensory interactions in saccade target selection: curved saccade trajectories. *Experimental Brain Research*, **142**, 116–130.

Duncan, J., and Humphreys, G. W. (1989). Visual search and stimulus similarity. *Psychological Review*, **96**, 433–458.

Ellis, S. R., and Stark, L. (1986). Statistical dependency in visual scanning. *Human Factors*, **28**, 421–438.

Engel, F. R. (1977). Visual conspicuity, visual search and fixation tendencies of the eye. *Vision Research*, **17**, 95–108.

Felleman, D. J., and Van Essen, D. C. (1991). Distributed hierarchical processing in the primate cerebral cortex. *Cerebral Cortex*, **1**, 1–47.

Findlay, J. M. (1982). Global processing for saccadic eye movements. *Vision Research*, **22**, 1033–1045.

Findlay, J. M. (1997). Saccade target selection in visual search. *Vision Research*, **37**, 617–631.

Findlay, J. M., and Gilchrist, I. D. (1998). Eye guidance and visual search. In: G. Underwood (ed). *Eye guidance in reading and scene perception*, Amsterdam: Elsevier, pp. 295–312.

Findlay, J. M., and Gilchrist, I. D. (2001). Visual attention: the active vision perspective. In: M. Jenkin and L. R. Harris (ed.) *Vision and attention*. New York: Springer-Verlag, pp. 83–103.

Findlay, J. M., and Gilchrist, I. D. (2003). *Active vision: The psychology of looking and seeing.* Oxford: Oxford University Press, pp. xiii+220.

Findlay, J. M., and Walker, R. (1999). A model of saccadic eye movement generation based on parallel processing and competitive inhibition. *Behavioral and Brain Sciences*, **22**, 661–721.

Findlay, J. M., Brown, V., and Gilchrist, I. D. (2001). Saccade target selection in visual search: the effect of information from the previous fixation. *Vision Research*, **41**, 87–95.

Gautier, V, O'Regan, J. K., and Le Gargasson, J. F. (2000). 'The-skipping' revisited in French: Programming saccades to skip the article 'les'. *Vision Research*, **40**, 2517–2531.

Gilchrist, I. D., and Harvey, M. (2000). Refixation frequency and memory mechanisms in visual search. *Current Biology*, **10**, 1209–1212.

Gilchrist, I. D., and Harvey, M. (in press). Evidence for a systematic component within scanpaths in visual search. *Visual Cognition*.

Gilchrist, I. D., Heywood, C. A. and Findlay, J. M. (1999). Saccade selection in visual search: evidence for spatial frequency specific between-item interactions. *Vision Research*, **39**. 1373–1383.

Gnadt, J. W., Bracewell, M., and Andersen, R. A. (1991). Sensorimotor transformation during eye movements to remembered visual targets. *Vision Research*, **31**, 693–715.

Godijn, R., and Theeuwes, J. (2002). Programming of endogenous and exogenous saccades: Evidence for a competitive integration model. *Journal of Experimental Psychology: Human Perception and Performance*, **28**, 1039–1054.

Hamker, F. H. (2004). A dynamic model of how feature cues guide spatial attention. *Vision Research*, **44**, 501–521.

Hodgson, T. L., Mort, D., Chamberlain M. M., Hutton S. B., O'Neill K. S., and Kennard C. (2002). Orbitofrontal cortex mediates inhibition of return. *Neuropsychologia*, **40**, 1891–1901.

Hooge, I. T. C., and Erkelens, C. J. (1996). Control of fixation duration in a simple search task. *Perception and Psychophysics*, **58**, 969–976.

Horowitz, T. S., and Wolfe, J. M. (1998). Visual search has no memory. *Nature*, **394**, 575–577.

Husain, M., Mannan, S., Hodgson, T., Wojculik, E., Driver J., and Kennard C. (2001). Impaired spatial working memory across saccades contributes to abnormal search in parietal neglect. *Brain*, **124**, 941–952.

Itti, L., and Koch, C. (2000). A saliency-based search mechanism for overt and covert shifts of attention. *Vision Research*, **40**, 1489–1506.

Jürgens, R., Becker, W., and Kornhuber, H. H. (1981). Natural and drug-induced variations of velocity and duration of human saccadic eye movements: evidence for a control of the neural pulse generator by local feedback. *Biological Cybernetics*, **39**, 87–96.

Keller, E. L., and McPeek, R. M. (2002). Neural discharge in the superior colliculus during target search paradigms. *Annals of the New York Academy of Sciences*, **956**, 130–142.

Klein, R. (1988). Inhibitory tagging facilitates visual search. *Nature*, **324**, 430–431.

Klein, R. M. (2000). Inhibition of return. *Trends in Cognitive Sciences*, **4**, 138–147.

Klein, R. M., and MacInnes, W. J. (1999). Inhibition of return is a foraging facilitator in visual search. *Psychological Science*, **10**, 346–352.

Kowler, E., Anderson, E., Dosher B., and Blaser E. (1995). The role of attention in the programming of saccades. *Vision Research*, **35**, 1897–1916.

Leach, J. C. D., and Carpenter, R. H. S. (2001). Saccadic choice with asynchronous target: evidence for independent randomisation. *Vision Research*, **41**, 3437–3445.

Ludwig, C. J. H., and Gilchrist, I. D. (2002). Stimulus-driven and goal-driven control over visual selection. *Journal of Experimental Psychology: Human Perception and Performance*, **28**, 902–912.

Ludwig, C. J. H., and Gilchrist, I. D. (2003a). Goal-driven modulation of oculomotor capture. *Perception and Psychophysics*, **65**, 1243–1251.

Ludwig, C. J. H., and Gilchrist, I. D. (2003b). Target similarity affects saccade curvature away from irrelevant onsets. *Experimental Brain Research*, **152**, 60–69.

Maljkovic, V., and Nakayama, K. (1994). Priming of pop-out 1. Role of features. *Memory and Cognition*, **22**, 657–672.

Maljkovic, V., and Nakayama, K. (1996). Priming of pop-out. 2. The role of position. *Perception and Psychophysics*, **58**, 977–991.

Maljkovic, V., and Nakayama, K. (2000). Priming of pop-out: III. A short-term implicit memory system beneficial for rapid target selection. *Visual Cognition*, **7**, 571–595.

McCarley, J. S., Wang R. F. Kramer, A. F., Irwin, D. E., and Peterson, M. S. (2003). How much memory does oculomotor search have? *Psychological Science*, **14**, 422–426.

McIlwain, J. T. (1975). Visual receptive fields and their images in the superior colliculus of the cat. *Journal of Neurophysiology*, **38**, 219–230.

McPeek, R. M., Maljkovic, V., and Nakayama, K. (1999). Saccades require focal attention and are facilitated by a short-term memory system. *Vision Research*, **39**, 1555–1566.

McPeek, R. M., Skavenski, A. A., and Nakayama, K. (2000). Concurrent processing of saccades in visual search. *Vision Research*, **40**, 2499–2516.

McSorley, E., and Findlay, J. M. (2003). Saccade target selection in visual search: Accuracy improves when more distractors are present. *Journal of Vision*, **3**, 877–892, http://journalofvision. org/3/11/20/

Miller, J. (1988). Components of the location probability effect in visual search tasks. *Journal of Experimental Psychology: Human Perception and Performance*, **14**, 453–471.

Moore, T., Armstrong, K. M., and Fallah, M. (2003). Visuomotor origins of covert spatial attention. *Neuron*, **40**, 671–683.

Motter, B. C., and Belky, E. J. (1998a). The guidance of eye movements during active visual search. *Vision Research*, **38**, 1805–1818.

Motter, B. C., and Belky, E. J. (1998b). The zone of focal attention during active visual search. *Vision Research*, **38**, 1007–1022.

Munoz, D.P., and Wurtz, R.H. (1995). Saccade-related activity in monkey superior colliculus. I. Characteristics of cell discharge. *Journal of Neurophysiology*, **73**, 2313–2333.

Olson, I., and Chun, M. M. (2002). Perceptual constraints on implicit learning of spatial context. *Visual Cognition*, **9**, 273–302

Peterson, M. S., and Kramer, A. F. (2001). Attentional guidance of the eyes by contextual information and abrupt onsets. *Perception and Psychophysics*, **63**, 1239–1249.

Peterson, M. S., Kramer, A. F., Wang, R. F., Irwin D. E., and McCarley J. S. (2001). Visual search has memory. *Psychological Science*, **12**, 287–292.

Polat, U., and Sagi, D. (1993). Lateral interactions between spatial channels: suppression and facilitation revealed by lateral masking experiments. *Vision Research*, **33**, 993–999.

Posner, M. I., and Cohen, Y. (1984). Components of visual orienting. In: H. Bouma and D. G. Bowhuis (ed.) *Attention and Performance X*. Hillsdale NJ: Erlbaum, pp. 531–556.

Quaia, C., Lefevre, P., and Optican, L. M. (1999). Model of the control of saccades by superior colliculus and cerebellum. *Journal of Neurophysiology*, **82**, 999–1018.

Rayner, K. (1998). Eye movements in reading and information processing. 20 years of research. *Psychological Bulletin*, **124**, 372–422.

Rizzolatti, G., Riggio, L., and Sheliga, B. M. (1994). Space and selective attention. In: C. Umiltà and M. Moscovitch (ed.). *Attention and Performance XV*. Cambridge, MA: MIT Press, pp. 231–265.

Sagi, D. (1990). Detection of an orientation singularity in Gabor textures: effect of signal density and spatial-frequency. *Vision Research*, **30**, 1377–1388.

Schall, J. D., and Hanes, D. P. (1993). Neural basis of target selection in frontal eye field during visual search. *Nature*, **366**, 467–469.

Sheliga, B. M., Riggio L., and Rizzolatti, G. (1994). Orienting of attention and eye movements. *Experimental Brain Research*, **98**, 507–522.

Shore, D. I., and Klein, R. M. (2000). On the manifestations of memory in visual search. *Spatial Vision*, **14**, 59–75.

Snyder, J. J., and Kingstone, A. (2000). Inhibition of return and visual search: how many separate loci are inhibited? *Perception and Psychophysics*, **62**, 452–458.

Stuphorn, V., and Schall, J. D. (2002). Neural control and monitoring of initiation of movements. *Muscle and Nerve*, **26**, 326–339.

Theeuwes, J., Kramer, A. F., Hahn S., and Irwin, D. E. (1998). Our eyes do not always go where we want them to go: Capture of the eyes by new objects. *Psychological Science*, **9**, 379–385.

Tian, J., Schlag, J., and Schlag-Rey, M. (2000). Testing quasi-visual neurons in the monkey's frontal eye field with the triple-saccade paradigm. *Experimental Brain Research*, **130**, 433–440.

Trappenberg, T. P., Dorris, M. C., Munoz, D. P., and Klein, R. M. (2001). A model of saccade initiation based on the competitive integration of exogenous and endogenous signals in the superior colliculus. *Journal of Cognitive Neuroscience*, **13**, 256–271.

Treisman, A. M., and Gelade, G. (1980). A feature integration theory of attention. *Cognitive Psychology*, **12**, 97–136.

Van Gisbergen, J. A. M., Van Opstal, A. J,. and Roebroek, J. G. H. (1987). Stimulus induced midflight modification of saccade trajectories. In: J. K. O'Regan and A. Lévy-Schoen (ed.) *Eye movements: from physiology to cognition.* Amsterdam: North-Holland, pp. 27–36.

Walker, R., Deubel, H., Schneider, W. X., and Findlay, J. M. (1997). The effect of remote distractors on saccade programming: evidence for an extended fixation zone. *Journal of Neurophysiology*, **78**, 1108–1119.

Ward, R., Duncan, J., and Shapiro, K. (1996). The slow time course of visual attention. *Cognitive Psychology*, **30**, 79–109.

White, J. M., Sparks, D. L., and Stanford, T. R. (1994). Saccades to remembered target locations: an analysis of systematic and variable errors. *Vision Research*, **34**, 79–92.

Williams, D. E., Reingold, E. M., Moscovitch, M., and Behrmann, M. (1997). Patterns of eye movements during parallel and serial visual search tasks. *Canadian Journal of Experimental Psychology–Revue Canadienne de Psychologie Experimentale*, **51**, 151–164.

Williams, L. G. (1966). The effect of target specification on objects fixated during visual search. *Perception and Psychophysics*, **1**, 315–318.

Wolfe, J. M. (1998). What can 1 million trials tell us about visual search? *Psychological Science*, **9**, 33–40.

Wolfe, J. M., Cave, K. R., and Franzel, S. L. (1989). Guided search: an alternative to the feature integration model for visual search. *Journal of Experimental Psychology: Human Perception and Performance*, **15**, 419–433.

Wolfe, J. M., Alvarez, G. A., and Horowitz, T. S. (2000). Attention is fast but volition is slow. *Nature*, **406**, 691.

Zelinsky, G. J., and Sheinberg, D. L. (1997). Eye movements during parallel-serial visual search. *Journal of Experimental Psychology: Human Perception and Performance*, **23**, 244–262.

Zelinsky, G. J., Rao, R. P. N., Hayhoe, M. M., and Ballard, D. H. (1997). Eye movements reveal the spatiotemporal dynamics of visual search. *Psychological Science*, **8**, 448–453.

12

The integration of top-down and bottom-up factors in visual search during driving

David Crundall

Abstract

What processes guide our eye movements when driving?
This chapter considers the interplay of bottom-up and top-down factors in deciding where the eyes should move next during various driving tasks. Although there is concern that bottom-up influences can distract as well as attract attention (such as with roadside advertising), it appears that top-down factors can inhibit or override these low level factors. Top-down strategies must, however, be developed over time, through practice and the accretion of experience. This has lead to the suggestion that accident rates in less experienced drivers could be reduced by training them to emulate the eye-movement patterns of more experienced drivers. Although several researchers have attempted this, any successful and transferable training intervention must take into account the subtle interplay of top-down and bottom-up factors in understanding *why* we look *where* we look when driving.

Introduction

Where do we look when we drive? Considering the large amount of visual information presented to drivers (Sivak 1996) and the limited capacity that one has to process visual information (e.g. Kahneman 1973), this question is very pertinent to driver safety. With modern advances in portable eye-tracking technology, and increasingly sophisticated simulators, it is becoming relatively easy to identify where people look when driving. However, despite the increase in the number of studies devoted to this topic over the past 20 years, we have been unable to find the simple, general answers that our colleagues in human factors desire. We do have certain suggestions as to the percentage of time that drivers spend fixating certain categories of environmental stimuli.

For instance, as early as 1969, Mourant *et al.* noted that about 40 per cent of all fixations fall on the vehicle ahead when actively engaged in a car-following task. However, interpretation of these values is fraught with problems. The difficulty of generalizing from an on-road study lies with any peculiarities of the test road and driving conditions (cf. Land and Lee 1994), while attempting to control for such differences through the use of simulated roads will inevitably lead to a less realistic experience. Furthermore, comparisons of such percentage terms across studies are difficult as methodologies tend to differ in terms of their participants' level of experience and age, the types of roads that are used, the nature of the task (particular manoeuvres, maintaining speed or headway, etc.), and the definition of object categories and oculomotor parameters (Brackston and Waterson 2004). Thus, while several important findings have been published that link vision in driving to major theoretical issues (e.g. Wann and Land 2000), it seems that normative gaze durations for different road types may still be some way off (Green 2002).

A more productive question might be 'why do we look where we do when driving?'. Initially this may seem a more daunting question than asking where we look. Surely, we need to know *where* we look, before exploring the reasons *why*? This is true to a certain extent, though this question no longer requires absolute or normative figures for where we look. Instead, we only need relative values spread across levels of a factor of interest. Relative differences between variables affecting visual search on roadways are potentially more stable, and through careful choice of variables one can detect patterns of visual search that are consistently influenced by specific events.

It is this second question that this chapter will address. There are two main contenders for why we look where we look: bottom-up and top-down influences. Bottom-up influences are generally discussed in terms of peaks on a saliency map (Henderson *et al.* 1999; Logan 1996), whereby the largest peak is the sum of all the attention-grabbing features at that point in space. The larger the peak, the more likely that particular location will be fixated next (see chapter 11).

Top-down processes are often referred to as directions of attention in response to expectations that pertinent information will be found in a particular location (Recarte and Nunes 2000; see also chapter 8). For instance, an experienced driver will check the front edge of a parked lorry while passing by, as this is an obscured location from which a pedestrian could appear (Fisher *et al.* 2003). This suggests conscious, controlled orientation of overt attention, though top-down influences could also manifest through automatic behaviours that develop from conscious controlled behaviours (e.g. mirror checking).

This chapter will consider the potential contributions of both bottom-up and top-down influences on eye movements in driving, whether distinctive oculomotor measures distinguish between these influences, and how they interact. The implications of this interaction will be discussed in regard to the potential benefits of training eye-movement strategies in drivers.

Bottom-up influences on drivers' visual search

Bottom-up influences on visual search have been repeatedly reported in laboratory studies of feature singletons, though as Egeth and Yantis (1997) point out, many of these studies do not provide direct evidence that low-level features capture attention, because the salient singleton is often the target of the visual search. Some researchers have, however, demonstrated that task-irrelevant feature singletons can still capture attention (e.g. Olivers and Humphreys 2003; Theeuwes 1991), although some studies have failed to demonstrate the effect of singleton capture under certain conditions (e.g. Hillstrom and Yantis 1994; Irwin *et al.* 2000; Olivers and Humphreys 2003). This has lead some to suggest that singletons can only capture attention inadvertently when a singleton detection strategy is activated (i.e. if one is simply searching for the odd-one-out in a collection of features such as colour or shape; Bacon and Egeth 1994). If an alternative strategy is employed (for instance, if one is searching for a particular feature), then irrelevant singletons are less likely to capture attention. This suggests that even the lowest levels of stimulus influence upon visual search can still be modified by the use of top-down strategies.

Abrupt onsets can also capture attention, such as the sudden appearance of a cue in a visual search task (e.g. Hillstrom and Yantis 1994; Irwin *et al.* 2000) though the appearance of a new object has a greater effect than a sudden change in luminance. Whether or not these abrupt onsets capture covert or overt attention (i.e. do the eyes move to fixate an abrupt onset?) is still debated (Irwin, *et al.* 2000; Tse *et al.* 2002), though it likely that in conditions where there is no requirement to inhibit eye movements, then a reflexive saccade will occur.

How do these laboratory experiments translate to the driving scenario? The ability of abrupt onsets, or salient objects to capture attention is of great importance to researchers in driver safety. For instance, what effect might the abrupt onset of an electronic speed warning sign have on eye movements? And how distracting might a particular advertisement be when placed at the side of the road? In order to answer these questions we must look for evidence to suggest that attentional capture might be triggered by such low level features during driving.

In regard to the salience of singletons, Cole and Hughes (1984; Hughes and Cole 1986) undertook a number of studies both on the road and in the laboratory, where participants were presented with a series of single-colour reflective discs at the side of the road (in locations where road signs may be typically found in Australia). They found that neither the reflectance of the signs or the size of the signs were dominant factors in making drivers look at them (assessed by verbal report). The major factor that determined whether the signs were reported was the visual angle at which the sign appeared from the line of sight, although the context was also influential. Targets were spotted more readily in a suburban area, than when passing through a shopping area.

One possible reason that the level of reflectance was not significant, acknowledged by Cole and Hughes (1984), is that salience due to luminance tends to depend on contrast, rather than luminance per se. As their signs were rotated through all the locations, both a bright white reflective sign and a less reflective black sign were placed on both light and dark backgrounds. This would equate contrast across the reflectivity condition.

Attempts to gauge attention to more realistic road signs have been conducted by Helmut Zwahlen and colleagues. Although, as we shall see later, the acquisition of information from traffic signs does receive input from top-down processes (Shinoda *et al.* 2001), Zwahlen's results have demonstrated some interesting effects of bottom-up capture. For instance, during night-time trials, Zwahlen *et al.* (2003) noticed that drivers tend to give a diagrammatic guide sign between two and three fixations, with the first fixation (attentional capture and information acquisition) being consistently longer than the last fixation (confirmation). Between fixations on these signs, drivers tend to fixate the road ahead. Zwahlen (1981) has also reported that certain signs are fixated sooner and for longer during the night-time than they are during the day. If top-down factors were responsible for the early fixation of signs during the night-time (perhaps because the driver prefers a greater preview time for upcoming road events during the hours of darkness) then one would imagine that the time spent processing the sign would be the same as in the daytime. Alternatively, one might argue that the reduced legibility of a sign during the night requires longer to process, hence the need to fixate it early. However, assuming that drivers fixate road signs in the daytime when they become legible, it is unlikely that fixating night-time signs sooner will provide any legible information. Instead, it seems that the increased salience of a reflective sign at night attracts attention sooner than required, perhaps even before the sign can actually be read, which may be the cause of longer fixation durations.

Such bottom-up factors are of especial importance if one considers the potential for driver distraction by billboards or other outdoor media. Several studies have attempted, with mixed success, to link the presence of advertising to accident rates (see Wallace 2003, for a review), though there are only a few examples that suggest such distraction may actually play a part in increasing accident liability. For instance, Ady (1967) collected accident data before and after the erection of a number of billboards and advertisements on a highway in America. Although several of these advertisements did not show any difference in terms of accident statistics, one particular sign did show a significant increase in the number of accidents at its location. This sign was large, illuminated by bright lights, and was positioned on a sharp bend in the road. Several other studies reviewed by Wallace (2003) tend to show an influence of advertisements on accident statistics but only in specific situations such as junctions (controlled for traffic exposure in some cases), in highly cluttered areas, or, in the case of Ady (1967), on a bend. As the great majority of such studies are retrospective and did not use eye trackers, it is impossible to say whether the advertisements were fixated in all conditions, yet this is most likely the case. The reason that some advertisements were more related to accidents than others is probably not because advertisements at junctions are more eye catching, or even that drivers are more likely to spend time looking at advertisements on an approach to a junction than when driving along an otherwise uninteresting road. Instead it is likely that if advertisements do have a causal role to play in accidents at specific locations it is because these locations place higher demands on the driver (Crundall *et al.* submitted). In these situations devoting attention to advertisements is no longer using up spare capacity, but is instead redirecting resources away from vital driving tasks.

Certainly the conditions under which Wallace (2003) reports that advertisements may cause a problem are all linked to increased visual demands placed on the driver. We know that curves, for instance, place a very specific demand on the driver for acquiring visual information, distinct from the demands incurred whilst driving along a straight road. Fixation durations tend to become shorter as drivers increase their sampling rate, and they foveate the lane markers and road edges more often (Shinar *et al.* 1977), particularly the tangent point (Land and Lee 1994; Land and Tatler 2001). Mike Land and colleagues have conducted a series of studies demonstrating that the tangent point of a curve (the apex of the curve as one approaches the bend) tends to be fixated about 0.8–0.9 s before the steering movement. This suggests that important information is extracted from the tangent point which is fed into the steering calculation. If attention is redirected away from the tangent point at a vital moment before an adjustment to the steering wheel angle is required, this could increase the possibility of an accident occurring. Indeed, Land (1998) reports that steering performance is increasingly impaired as the distance from between fixation and roadway markers increases. When participants were required to maintain fixation on a target away from the road in a simulator, he reported an almost linear decrease in steering performance with an increase in the eccentricity of the target.

In his review, Wallace (2003) concludes that bottom-up factors do play a role in distraction by outdoor media, although as most authors agree that, under normal conditions, experienced drivers can safely spend a proportion of time looking at driving irrelevant features (between 20–50 per cent according to different researchers – e.g. Hughes and Cole 1986; Land and Lee 1994; Renge 1980), the danger of this distraction is not readily apparent until the road begins to demand more attention. Incidentally, it should be pointed out that some ostensibly top-down influences could be partially explained by bottom-up features. For instance, though the tangent point is seemingly fixated during cornering, because it provides an excellent source of curvature information, it is not the only point on the bend that could provide this input. However, the tangent point is relatively stable in regard to the optic flow. Normally, if a driver fixates any nearby point while driving, other than the focus of expansion or the tangent point, the forward movement of the vehicle will result in the point moving to the peripheral edges of the scene within the optic flow field. When this occurs there is a tendency for eyes to move with a fixated object, producing a smooth pursuit eye movement. The tangent point has, however, limited movement within the optic flow field, and as such it provides a stable point for the eyes to rest upon without being dragged away (Land 1998; Wann and Land 2000; though see also Miles and Kawano 1987). Thus, there is a possibility that this bottom-up feature may contribute to the choice of the tangent point as the preferential guide to curvature.

One final bottom-up feature that should be considered is movement. Movement has been used as a singleton for capturing attention in simple laboratory-based experiments (e.g. Rauschenberger 2003). If one object is moving while everything else in the scene remains static, then this will result in attentional capture by the moving target. When one is driving, however, the observer is also moving, which generates an optic flow field and requires the visual system to make calculations extrapolating local movement from global movement. This tends to be easiest when the local movement goes against the optic flow. For instance, a car travelling down a side road, away from the current path of the driver will move in the same direction as the optic flow. While this movement may still be detectable (as it may be faster than the rate of optic flow), its salience will be less than that of movement which goes against the flow. Fortunately, this means that a car approaching a junction that will intersect with a driver's path will attract more attention than a car moving away from the junction. The angle at which an intersecting vehicle approaches a junction, and the distance of the car from the junction when it is first fixated are also vital sources of information when judging whether the intersecting vehicle will reach the junction before or after the driver's vehicle has passed (van Loon and Underwood 2004).

One recent study, conducted by Underwood *et al.* (2003a), was, in part, concerned with the nature of dynamic driving events and whether they captured attention. The study compared fixation behaviour across a number of different object features as participants watched video clips of driving whilst having their eye movements recorded. During the presentation of each clip, the video was stopped at a particular point and the participants were asked a question about an object that had been present in the scene for between 4–8 s before the trial stopped. The focus of the questions was on either central, driving-relevant objects or incidental, peripheral objects. In addition, these objects were either moving or static, relative to their local context, and could appear during a hazardous event in the driving clip (such as the sudden braking of a lead vehicle) or during a relatively safe period of driving. As one might expect, the eye-movement records showed that central objects and dynamic objects both received more fixations, and these objects tended to be remembered better when probed by the subsequent question. There was also an interaction between whether the object was involved in a hazardous event and whether or not the object was moving. This showed that hazardous, dynamic objects (usually those objects that threaten to collide with the observer's vehicle) received the most fixations. Underwood *et al.* (2003a) suggested that there might even be some form of *time to collision* (TTC) calculation that contributes to a low-level saliency map.

On the basis of the studies considered in this section, we must conclude that certain low-level features may capture attention in driving, though this is highly dependent upon other factors. The following two sections will consider (a) when bottom-up factors fail to attract attention or influence eye movements; and (b) when top-down factors modify the influence of these bottom-up factors.

When bottom-up influences fail to attract attention

The relatively recently reported phenomenon of change blindness (e.g. Simons 2000) has challenged our conceptions of visual representations of the world. A typical study demonstrates that participants find it very difficult to detect a change (e.g. the disappearance or movement of an object in the visual display) between two pictures, which are presented alternately in a repeating cycle. The key to inducing change blindness is to precede each new presentation of a picture with some form of unrelated transient which swamps any transient produced by the change between the two pictures. For instance, in one study we conducted (Crundall *et al.* 2005a), participants had to spot a change (such as the disappearance of road markings) between two otherwise identical road scenes. Each image was available for 1 s before the alternate image was presented. In order to hide the transient created by the abrupt offset and onset of the road markings as the cycle repeated, a short-duration blue screen was inserted after every image. This made it very difficult for participants to identify the change.

The results of nearly a decade of change-blindness research have had far reaching implications for our understanding of visual memory, but in regard to our current discussion they are important in the fact that they acknowledge the influence of local transients (abrupt onsets, sudden movement, etc.) in capturing attention. There is, however, a series of related studies, often termed studies of inattentional blindness (e.g. Mack and Rock 1998), which shows that sometimes even abrupt onsets and other similar transients are not sufficient to capture attention, and therefore do not need to be masked by a global flicker or 'mudsplashes' (an alternative method of masking local transients in change-blindness studies). Inattention blindness occurs when attention is tightly focused upon a localized visual stimulus, thus reducing the amount of attention that can be devoted to other objects or features in the visual field. The extent of inattentional blindness depends on how demanding the stimulus under scrutiny is. In general the more demanding the foveal stimulus is, the more attention it requires, therefore reducing spare capacity. This is often referred to in spatial terms, such that as one increases attention on a foveal stimulus, so attention to peripheral and parafoveal regions are reduced, as if a zoom lens of attention is refocused on a narrow beam (Eriksen and Murphy 1987). Although the true nature of the spatial decrement in attention has been under debate (Crundall *et al.* 1999, 2002; Williams 1982, 1985), there is evidence from a wide range of simple lab-based studies that increased foveal demand does decrease peripheral attention (e.g. Lavie 1995). Can these findings be generalized to driving?

In order to test the theory of demand-induced degradation of peripheral attention, we conducted a number of studies looking at the ability of drivers to report the presence of (or discriminate) peripheral targets while watching digital video clips of driving (Crundall *et al.* 1999, 2002, 2005b). The video clips were taken from a hazard perception test, and all of them included at least one event that was considered to be hazardous (such as a pedestrian stepping out into the road from the pavement). From previous research (Chapman and Underwood 1998), we knew that hazardous segments of video clips produce longer fixation durations and a smaller spread of visual scanning, as the appearance of a localized hazard (such as the foolhardy pedestrian) captures attention. This suggested that during those few seconds when a hazard was available for inspection, the demands in the visual scene increased appreciably, requiring more in-depth processing on the driver's part in order to assess the impact of the hazardous event. We speculated as to whether the increased demands present in the hazard perception clips would have the same effect as the foveal stimuli in studies of inattentional blindness. In other words, when a driver has to especially concentrate on an object in the visual scene, is the ability to spot transients such as abrupt onsets impaired?

In an initial study (Crundall *et al.* 1999), we partitioned the hazard clips into 5-s windows, and on the basis of the hazard perception responses of participants in the previous Chapman and Underwood (1998) study, we labelled each of these windows as either high or low demand. Participants were asked to watch the hazard perception clips and assess how dangerous the clips were. At the end of each clip they were asked to rate the clip (on a scale from 1 to 7) according to perceived danger and difficulty to drive. As a secondary task while watching the clips, participants were asked to press a mouse button whenever they saw a peripheral light appear in one of four placeholders at the edges of the screen. Analyses focused upon how many of these targets were spotted within the high- and low-demand time windows. In addition the location of the participants' eyes were recorded so that the distance from the point of fixation to the target location could be calculated to give an indication of target eccentricity from the fovea at the moment of target onset. The results demonstrated that fewer peripheral targets were spotted in the high demand windows (compared with low demand windows), suggesting that the increased processing required by hazardous events in these windows reduced the ability of participants to spot the abrupt onset of the peripheral lights. In other words, increased processing demand induced inattentional blindness in these participants such that bottom-up attentional capture by local transients was not always possible. In addition it was noted that the more eccentric the targets were from the point of fixation at the time of onset, the greater the reduction in peripheral target responses. This fits with Hughes and Cole's (1986) results that demonstrated eccentricity to be one of the most important factors in attracting attention.

One of our later studies (Crundall *et al.* 2002) went somewhat further and demonstrated that there is a time course to this degradation of peripheral attention that varies with driving experience. In this study, participants were required to watch the same films, but instead of producing a rating at the end of each clip they were required to press a foot pedal whenever they perceived a hazard. In addition they were asked to press a mouse button whenever they saw a peripheral light. With the addition of a discrete response for the detection of a hazard, we were able to assess the point leading up to the hazard response at which peripheral attention began to degrade. In experienced drivers, detection of peripheral targets dropped off suddenly with the appearance of the hazard at around 1.5 s prior to them pushing the foot pedal. As soon as the hazard response had been made, however, peripheral target detection rapidly returned to the levels that were seen prior to the onset of the hazard. Learner drivers spotted fewer targets overall, and after the drop in performance just before a hazard response, it took longer for their peripheral detection rates to return to a normal level compared with the experienced drivers (Fig. 12.1A). Additionally, with a greater temporal resolution (Fig. 12.1B), one can see that learner drivers' ability to spot peripheral targets degraded sooner than the experienced drivers. Not only do experienced drivers recover faster from the appearance of a hazard, but they also appear to keep their field of attention as wide as possible for as long as possible. When they finally succumb to the hazard, their foveal investment appears to be considerable (with peripheral detection rates even dipping below those of the learner drivers), but they rapidly redeploy attention to peripheral regions as soon as possible.

Ball *et al.* (1988) have also demonstrated that increased age tends to correspond with a general decline in peripheral attention, which is similarly due to a mismatch between processing demands and available resources. There have, however, been suggestions that top-down compensatory strategies may be employed by older, more experienced drivers to offset this deterioration, such as increased visual scanning of the driving scene (Fisher *et al.* 2003).

These studies suggest that though abrupt onsets may capture attention during driving under normal conditions, increased processing demands tend to make such capture less likely. Although one might equate abrupt onsets with the change in traffic lights, or the sudden activation of a variable message sign, many peripheral hazardous elements that occur during driving are more complex in form and appearance. Future research must, therefore, also address the ability of realistic peripheral stimuli to capture (or fail to capture) attention during driving.

One particular simulator study assessed the number of fixations that drivers made on passing pedestrians as a reflection of their attention to more realistic peripheral

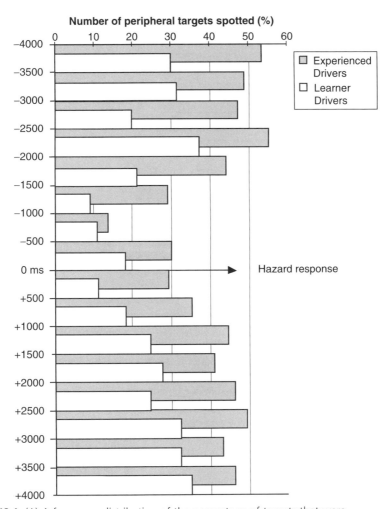

Figure 12.1 (A) A frequency distribution of the percentage of targets that were detected, split across 500 ms bins around the hazard response (at 0 ms) for both experienced and learner drivers; *Continued*

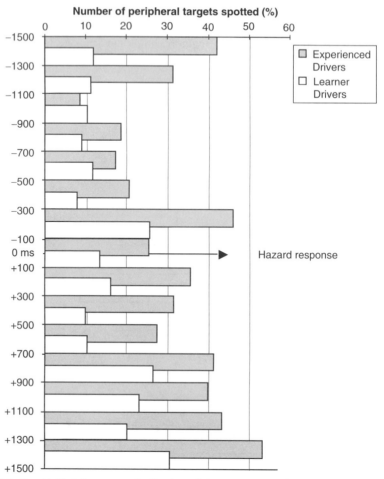

Figure 12.1 Cont'd (B) A frequency distribution of the percentage of targets that were detected, split across 500 ms bins around the hazard response (at 0 ms) for both experienced and learner drivers.

stimuli (Crundall *et al.* 2004). In this study drivers were required either to follow verbal directions through a simulated cityscape, or to follow a lead vehicle. In the latter condition participants were given the cover story that they were 'tailing a suspected criminal'. It was predicted that in the car-following condition, participants would spend more time looking at the vehicle ahead (which they did, even after exposure to a lead vehicle was accounted for). The lead vehicle thus became a more important source of information in the car-following condition, analogous to the increase in demand noted with hazardous objects in hazard perception studies (e.g. Chapman and

Underwood 1998). During the non-following trials, spread of search in the horizontal meridian was sensitive to the presence or absence of pedestrians, with wider search occurring when they were on-screen. However, in the car-following trials, horizontal search was reduced overall and was no longer influenced by pedestrians. This suggests that the drivers were either less aware that there were pedestrians to look at (because of a reduction in peripheral attention) or that the drivers prioritized attention away from the pedestrians and focused on the car ahead. Whichever explanation is correct, the drivers' performance deteriorated. When focusing on the car in the car-following condition (with increased fixation durations and decreased spread of horizontal search), the participants were more prone to accidents such as clipping the edge or mounting the pavement. Land and Horwood (1995) argue that lane maintenance is primarily achieved through peripheral vision. As such, the impairment in lane maintenance supports the hypothesis that the increased demands of the lead vehicle degraded peripheral attention. Furthermore, these drivers committed more give-way violations and were involved in more give-way accidents. The implications for driving safety are considerable if one accepts that increased foveal loads may impair any driving behaviour that requires an extensive spread of either covert or overt attention.

The moderation of bottom-up influences by top-down control

In addition to the failure of bottom-up features to attract attention in cases of demand-induced attentional blindness, there are several examples in the driving literature of the influence of bottom-up factors being limited by top-down attentional strategies. I will argue in this section that the reported studies represent the driving equivalent of Bacon and Egeth's (1994) singleton detection strategy.

An innovative study was undertaken by Shinoda *et al.* (2001) in order to investigate top-down influences upon attentional capture. Participants were asked to drive through a series of city blocks in a driving simulator. During the drive a number of road signs would change from a parking sign to a stop sign. In order to mask the transient of the road signs changing in the middle of a drive, they inserted a blank screen just before the change. This screen acted like a global flicker in change-blindness studies, and prevented the local transient created by the changing sign from attracting attention. Other flickers were inserted randomly into the drive, so that the participants did not associate the flicker with a changed sign. Participants were instructed to either follow a lead vehicle while obeying all instructional road signs (i.e. stopping when then saw a stop sign), or they were simply told to follow the lead vehicle without any reference to the traffic signs. The additional instructions affected the probability that the drivers would fixate the changed road signs, with drivers who received the instructions to obey the road signs increasing the amount of time they spent looking to the side of the road (where the signs were located) from 1 per cent of the time to 6 per cent. Thus drivers' information needs promoted a specific search strategy that increased the likelihood of the traffic signs catching their attention.

In addition to this manipulation, the target signs could change at one of two locations; either at an intersection (highly predictable on the basis of the context), or while driving along a straight road without a junction (unpredictable on the basis of location). Drivers who were instructed to heed traffic signs spotted the changed sign 100 per cent of the time if it was located at a junction, but only 33 per cent if the change occurred during a straight road. Shinoda *et al.* suggest that these effects occur because drivers employ specific search strategies on the basis of 'learned regularities in the environment'. In other words, experienced drivers adjust their search strategy according to the situation, on the basis of being in this type of situation previously. This is supported by eye-movement data collected from on-road driving by Crundall and Underwood (1998). In that study we found that experienced drivers adopted different search strategies that were specific to the context. For instance, on a demanding stretch of dual carriageway, these drivers increased their spread of horizontal search to deal with merging traffic. Novice drivers, however, had yet to learn the optimum search strategy for that particular situation (at the time of the study, learner drivers in the UK were not required to practise on dual carriageways in order to pass their driving test). The novices, therefore, maintained the same visual strategy that they had employed on both rural and suburban roads.

Fisher *et al.* (2003) found similar benefits of driving experience in fixating specific sources of potential hazards in a number of simulated scenarios. For instance, one particular scenario involved the participant driving through a junction that had a crossing marked on the road (and also indicated by a traffic sign). As they approached the crossing, a large hedge obscured the pavement near to the crossing, potentially hiding a pedestrian who could have stepped into the road at any point. Fisher *et al.* (2003) found that as experience increased across the drivers, so the likelihood of the participants fixating these potential sources of hazards increased. They suggest that experienced drivers build up schemas from experience in specific situations. These schemas can then be generalized to new, similar contexts, which will provide guidance for their visual search.

We too have found that, even in the face of extreme driving demands, highly-experienced drivers tend to fixate potential sources of hazards (Crundall *et al.* 2005c). This study reported the category analysis of what police drivers looked at while watching video clips of pursuit and emergency response driving (the general eye-movement data was reported earlier by Crundall *et al.* 2003). In the pursuit clips it was found that the fleeing car tended to attract the majority of the drivers' attention (as happened in Crundall, *et al.* 2004), yet when police drivers' eye movements were compared with the visual search of novice drivers, and age- and experience-matched control drivers, the trained police drivers still managed to redirect some attention from the fleeing vehicle so that they could monitor other potential sources of hazards such as side roads and parked vehicles.

The evidence reported so far suggests that whether a sudden onset or movement (e.g. a potential hazard) is spotted is dependent to some extent on the bottom-up processes of salience and attentional capture. However, top-down strategies can be learned, which will improve the likelihood of spotting certain objects and features in the driving scene, by positioning the eyes in the most likely places where these things might occur. The following section continues this argument, discussing the development of driving schema and mental models of driving.

The development of driving schemas

What is the nature of a visual search schema for driving, and how is it developed? There are at least two potential types of driving schema, which can perhaps be distinguished by their reliance on perceptual and motor factors, respectively. The first is concerned with specific contexts, where priority is given to specific items in the visual field (as reported at the end of the previous section). The second is related to scan paths, which generalize beyond fixations on specific objects in the visual scene. For instance, when approaching a junction, driving instructors encourage learner drivers to look both left and right as they pass through the junction, even if they have the right of way. Other scan paths that are explicitly taught include patterns for pulling out into the main carriageway from a parked position at the side of the road. This usually involves a mirror check, followed by a blind spot check. Even a simple nearside turn at a T-junction requires a specific scanning strategy: one cannot simply look in the offside direction to make sure there is no passing traffic. The driver must also rapidly reorient attention to the direction of heading once the turn begins to ensure that the road is still clear to enter. Many such scan paths show forward planning on the part of the driver, as they acquire information before deciding to make a manoeuvre. For instance, Salvucci and Liu (2002) found that drivers' eye movements shift to the adjacent lane before they announce their intention to overtake a vehicle in their own lane. Liu (1998) has also identified a number of scan paths of fixation transitions from one area of the visual scene to another that occur more often that chance would predict. He analysed strings of fixations during driving in a simulator and used Markov matrices to identify significant scan paths. Two particular patterns revealed themselves on straight roads: a preview pattern (where drivers would tend to look straight ahead, varying the distance of fixation from the car) and a horizontal scanning pattern (where drivers tend to look from side to side). On curved roads, the preview pattern disappeared, though the horizontal pattern remained.

If these scan patterns truly represent learned schemas, then we should also be able to see these schemas develop over time as the driver gains experience. Underwood *et al.* (2003b) looked at the development of schemas using Liu's methodology to look for significant scan paths in a comparison of experienced and novice drivers. It was initially thought that if these scan paths are learned, then the experienced drivers should show more of them. Using on-road eye movements (recorded by Crundall and Underwood 1998), a frame-by-frame analysis revealed a number of two and three fixation scan paths. Some of these scan paths were used by all drivers, such as the tendency to look at a middle distance in the road ahead, then to the far distance, before returning to the middle distance (similar to the preview pattern found by Liu). Other scan paths were used predominantly by experienced drivers, such as a pattern of rear view mirror, followed by the far distance on the road, followed by a mid distance on the road. Yet other scan paths were favoured by the novices, such as fixating a middle distance in the road, before fixating the right hand (offside) edge of the lane, followed by a fixation on the far distance directly ahead. Although there are many potential post hoc explanations that one could use for these scan paths, there are some common themes that fit with the literature. For instance, the novices appear to fixate the lane markings (as predicted by Land and Horwood 1995), and then move the eyes to the furthest distance in the road. This could suggest that they are aware of the dangers of looking away from the road, and therefore try to compensate by gaining the maximum preview of the road ahead once they have finished obtaining information from the lane markings. It is interesting to note the predominance of fixations on the middle distance of the road ahead in these scan patterns. The actual area that accrued the most foveal attention was the far distance of the road ahead (as is usually found with the focus of expansion). However the middle distance seems to provide a vital cog in linking fixation transitions between different areas. The surprising result of this study is that the experienced drivers demonstrated the fewest consistent scan paths on the demanding section of dual carriageway with merging traffic. This was interpreted as increased flexibility of experienced drivers' search strategies to the specific road conditions. This implicitly argues for a greater reliance upon bottom-up factors to attract attention (though again, these are moderated by the fact that visual search is restricted to a very flat and wide window of inspection).

Thus it seems that experienced drivers do develop certain scan paths, but at least under certain conditions their visual search is distinguished by an absence of consistent two- and three-fixation patterns (though they still restrict their visual search to specific areas of the scene). Novice drivers also display consistent scan paths, though it is more likely that these are generated by the limitations of their attentional resources. The scan path that makes extensive use of the offside edge of the road may be employed to make up for the resource limitations that they have for taking in lane maintenance information through peripheral vision (Land and Horwood 1995). The scan paths that both novice and experienced drivers share are more likely to be guided by low-level features, as they are patterns that occur without experience, yet they are not extinguished as experience increases. The results suggest that there is still a potential for bottom-up features feeding into consistent scan paths.

The possibility that inexperienced drivers employ different search strategies to more experienced drivers because their limited attentional resources require them to monitor different sources of information was addressed by Underwood *et al.* (2002, 2005). It was assumed that if resource limitations dictated the visual search of novice drivers, then reducing the demands on novice drivers (by removing the need to control a car) should allow them to adopt search strategies more akin to those of experienced drivers. If, however, reducing the demands placed on the novice drivers did not improve their search strategies it would instead lend credence to the hypothesis that they have an impoverished mental model of driving and visual search. In both studies, the visual search of novice and experienced drivers was compared while watching video clips of the same sort of roads that produced the experiential differences noted in our studies that used on-road data (Crundall and Underwood 1998; Underwood *et al.* 2003b). The two laboratory studies using this methodology found somewhat different results. Underwood *et al.* (2005) found that scanning did not differ between novice and experienced drivers if an undemanding stretch of dual carriageway was used, whereas Underwood *et al.* (2002) found that novice drivers still had a reduced spread of search on more demanding dual carriageway segments. The results suggest that although removing the demands of car control can improve the visual search of novices, it does not allow novices to emulate experienced visual search on the most demanding of roadways. This suggests that there is indeed a problem with the mental model of novice drivers, at least in the most demanding of conditions.

This proposition is supported by a number of studies which have looked at hazard perception tests as a method for distinguishing between drivers of varying experience. When applied as a diagnostic test for driver awareness (rather than merely as a tool for investigating eye movements in dangerous situations, as the studies that have been reported in previous sections have used it), the test usually comprises a series of short driving clips, with each clip containing at least one (usually staged) hazardous event. Participants are required to make a discrete response to the onset of the hazard. Their response times, and the number of hazards to which they respond are combined to give a measure that is said to reflect the stage of development in the participant's mental model of driving. Several studies have demonstrated differences between drivers' responses to these hazards that vary according to experience (McKenna and Crick 1994; Renge 1998). There is even evidence to suggest that newly licensed drivers who score poorly on these tests are more likely to have a fatal accident in their first year of qualified driving (Drummond 2000).[1]

The hazard perception test has now become part of the licensing procedure in the UK and several other countries (Horswill and McKenna 2004). As a result, driver training has adapted to the challenge, with a proliferation of self-help tutorials in hazard perception that claim to improve visual search for hazards, by improving the learner driver's mental model of driving. This brings us to the final section of this chapter, which looks at whether top-down strategies of eye-movement control during driving can be successfully taught.

Can we teach drivers where to look?

The evidence suggests that though bottom-up factors may play a role in guiding eye movements during driving, top-down factors are also important. These factors are interesting from a driving safety point of view because it is generally assumed that the expectancies, strategies and knowledge that influence an experienced driver's visual search are learned through experience. The final question we must then ask is whether we can circumvent the slow experiential development of these skills and strategies, and teach visual skills directly. This is certainly an aim of many driver training books (e.g. Coyne 1997), which offer insightful suggestions to keep the eyes moving, not to dwell

---

[1] There are other studies, including those conducted in our laboratory, which have failed to discriminate between drivers of different experience on the basis of simple behavioural responses to hazard onsets in these type of tests. The arguments concerning the validity of hazard perception are insightfully summarized from several different viewpoints in a review by Horswill and McKenna (2004).

in one place too long, and to sample the mirrors on a regular basis. Unfortunately we have seen that inexperienced drivers' visual search may be a result of both resource limitations and a poor mental model. In the latter case, improving the mental models of inexperienced drivers may well produce benefits in visual search but those inexperienced search patterns which occur due to resource limitations (e.g. when novices foveate lane markings instead of using peripheral vision for lane maintenance) cannot be overcome by simply telling drivers where to look. If, for instance, learner drivers are discouraged from fixating lane markers, they may not obtain vital information to help keep the car in the centre of the lane. In this scenario, teaching eye-movement strategies may actually be detrimental to driving performance.

Several studies have attempted to improve the mental models of inexperienced drivers, with the explicit aim of improving visual strategies and subsequent processing, though these studies have had mixed results. McKenna and Crick (1994) trained a group of inexperienced drivers in hazard detection by stopping videos of driving clips at crucial moments and asking the participants to predict what happened next. This training improved hazard perception scores on a subsequent test. Similar success stories in the training of hazard perception can be found in Horswill and McKenna (2004) though none of these studies investigated whether the training changed actual oculomotor behaviour. Chapman et al. (2002) undertook a wide ranging training intervention on novice drivers in an attempt to improve their visual search. Importantly, they were looking for changes to novices' visual search when driving on the road, as a result of a video-based training aid that was presented to the participants in the laboratory.

The training intervention required participants to watch a series of hazard perception clips with commentaries and with blue and red ellipses superimposed on the video clips representing areas that they should be monitoring (blue) and the appearance of potential hazards (red). The locations of the ellipses on the film actually reflected the locations of fixations made by experienced drivers when they had viewed the clips in a previous experiment (Chapman and Underwood 1998). The size of the ellipses varied as the circles moved around the visual scene. This reflected the amount of agreement in the experienced drivers' visual search when watching the clips. Ellipses on actual hazards tended to be tightly focused, as all experienced drivers in the previous study tended to fixate these areas. In less-demanding segments of the clip, the blue ellipse would increase in size as there was less consistency in the experienced drivers' fixation locations at these points in the film clips. When the ellipses were large, the novice drivers were told that this represented the area of the scene they should tend to scan the most.

Before and after training, participants were given a hazard perception test in the laboratory, and were also taken out on the road in an instrumented vehicle. Wider horizontal scanning was found on the post-training hazard perception test, and also when they were taken out in the instrumented vehicle. This suggested that the benefits of the training intervention had transferred to the real world. Unfortunately, when participants were tested 3–6 months later, only the increased scanning in the laboratory-based hazard perception test remained significant. Although real world scanning was affected, it appeared the result was short-lived.

Pollatsek *et al.* (submitted) also found effects of training upon subsequent eye movements in a simulator. They gave participants plan views of roads and asked them to mark on the pictures hazards which were obscured from the view of the driver, and which areas of the scene which they believed the driver should constantly monitor. Twenty-four novices were trained up on this task in an attempt to induce a more sophisticated mental model of hazardous driving situations. Eye movements of the trained participants were then compared with the eye movements of 24 untrained novices while driving through the three-dimensional versions of the plan views in a driving simulator. They found that the trained participants had a better visual search for the potential hazards than the untrained group, on those scenarios that were structurally the same as the plan views with which they had been trained. More importantly, there was also evidence that eye movements on new scenarios had been affected by the training, suggesting transference of skill between driving situations, similar to the results of Chapman *et al.* (2002). There was, however, no information on whether the effect of training persisted over the subsequent months, or whether eye movements during real-world driving were similarly affected.

These tentative forays into training eye movements of drivers are encouraging, but at the moment are still very far away from producing the effects that driving safety experts would like to see. In order to develop more successful training interventions, we do not just need to know *where* drivers look, but we need to know *why* they look at certain things at certain times. If we encourage learner drivers to emulate the visual search strategies of experienced drivers without first understanding why they cannot, or do not, use the same strategies, then we risk asking drivers to run before they can walk. Hopefully this review of some of the recent literature in this area will help to draw attention to some of the underlying issues that influence why we look where we look when driving. Both top-down and bottom-up factors can have an influence on visual search in driving, and exploring the interface between the two is the challenge for future research.

Acknowledgements

I would like to thank Alexander Pollatsek, John Findlay and Günther Knoblich for their comments on an earlier version of this chapter.

References

Ady, R. (1967). An investigation of the relationship between illuminated advertising signs and expressway accidents. *Traffic Safety Research Review*, **3**, 9–11.

Bacon, W. F., and Egeth, H. E. (1994). Overriding stimulus driven attentional capture. *Perception and Psychophysics*, **55**, 485–496.

Ball, K. K., Beard, B. L., Roenker, D. L., Miller, R. L., and Griggs, D. S. (1988). Age and visual search: expanding the useful field of view. *Journal of the Optical Society of America*, **5**, 2210–2219.

Brackstone, M., and Waterson, B. (2004). Are we looking where we are going? An exploratory examination of eye movement in high speed driving. *Proceedings of the 83rd Transportation Research Board Annual Meeting*. Paper 04–2602, CD-ROM. Washington, DC: Transportation Research Board.

Chapman, P. R., and Underwood, G. (1998). Visual search of driving situations: Danger and experience. *Perception*, **27**, 951–964.

Chapman, P., Underwood, G., and Roberts, K. (2002). Visual search patterns in trained and untrained novice drivers. *Transportation Research Part F*, **5**, 157–167.

Cole, B. L., and Hughes, P. K. (1984). A field trial of attention and search conspicuity. *Human Factors*, **26**, 299–313.

Coyne, P. (1997). *Roadcraft: The essential police driver's handbook*. London: The Stationery Office.

Crundall, D. E. and Underwood, G. (1998).The effects of experience and processing demands on visual information acquisition in drivers. *Ergonomics*, **41, 4,** 448–458.

Crundall, D., Underwood, G., and Chapman, P. (1999). Driving experience and the functional field of view. *Perception*, **28**, 1075–1087.

Crundall, D., Underwood, G., and Chapman, P. (2002). Attending to the peripheral world while driving. *Applied Cognitive Psychology*, **16**, 459–475.

Crundall, D., Chapman, P., Phelps, N., and Underwood, G. (2003). Eye movements and hazard perception in police pursuit and emergency response driving. *Journal of Experimental Psychology: Applied*, **9**(3), 163–174.

Crundall, D., Shenton, C., and Underwood, G. (2004). Eye movements during intentional car following. *Perception*, **33**, 975–986.

Crundall, D., Galpin, A., and Underwood, G. (2005a, in press). Driving experience and visual memory. In: A. Gale (ed.) *Vision in vehicles IX*. North Holland: Elsevier.

Crundall, D., Stacy, P., Underwood, G. and Chapman, P. (2005b, in press). Discrimination in the peripheral field while hazard spotting. In: A. Gale (ed.) *Vision in Vehicles VIII*. North Holland: Elsevier.

Crundall, D., Chapman, P., France, E., Underwood, G., and Phelps, N. (2005c, in press). What attracts attention during police pursuit driving? *Applied Cognitive Psychology*.

Crundall, D., van Loon, E., and Underwood, G. (submitted). Attraction and distraction of attention with outdoor media.

Drummond, A. E. (2000). Paradigm lost! Paradigm gained? An Australian's perspective on the novice driver problem. *Paper presented at the Novice Driver Conference*, Bristol.

Egeth, H. E., and Yantis, S. (1997). Visual attention: control, representation, and time course. *Annual Review of Psychology*, **48**, 269–297.

Eriksen, C. W., and Murphy, T. D. (1987). Movement of attentional focus across the visual field: A critical look at the evidence. *Perception and Psychophysics*, **42**, 299–305.

Fisher, D. L., Pradhan, A. K., Hammel, K. R., DeRamus, R., Noyce, D. A., and Pollatsek, A. (2003). Are younger drivers less able than older drivers to recognize risks on the road? *Injury Insights*, **1**, 2–7.

Green, P. (2002). Where do drivers look while driving (and for how long)? In: R. E. Dewar and P. L. Olson (ed.) *Human factors in traffic safety*. Tucson, AZ: Lawyers and Judges Publishing, pp. 77–110.

Henderson, J. M., Weeks, P. A. Jr., and Hollingworth, A. (1999). The effects of semantic consistency on eye movements during complex scene viewing. *Journal of Experimental Psychology: Human Perception and Performance*, **25**, 210–228.

Hillstrom, A. P., and Yantis, S. (1994). Visual motion and attentional capture. *Perception and Psychophysics*, **55**, 399–411.

Horswill, M. S., and McKenna, F. P. (2004). Drivers' hazard perception ability: Situation awareness on the road. In: S. Banbury and S. Tremblay (ed.). *A Cognitive Approach to Situation Awareness*. Aldershot, UK: Ashgate, pp. 155–175.

Hughes, P. K., and Cole, B. L. (1986). What attracts attention when driving? *Ergonomics*, **29**, 377–391.

Irwin, D. E., Colombe, A. M., Kramer, A. F., and Hahn, S. (2000). Attentional and oculomotor capture by onset, luminance and color singletons. *Vision Research*, **40**, 1443–1458.

Kahneman, D. (1973). *Attention and effort*. New Jersey: Prentice Hall.

Land, M. F., (1998). The visual control of steering. In: L. R. Harris and M. Jenkin (ed.), *Vision and Action*. Cambridge: Cambridge University Press, 163–180.

Land, M. F., and Horwood, J. (1995). Which parts of the road guide steering? *Nature*, **377**, 339–340.

Land, M. F., and Lee, D. N. (1994). Where we look when we steer. *Nature*, **369**, 742–744.

Land, M. F., and Tatler, B. W. (2001). Steering with the head: The visual strategy of a racing driver. *Current Biology*, **11**, 1215–1220.

Lavie, N. (1995). Perceptual load as a necessary condition for selective attention. *Journal of Experimental Psychology: Human Perception and Performance*, **21**, 451–468.

Logan, G. D. (1996). The CODE theory of visual attention: an integration of space-based and object-based attention. *Psychological Review*, **103**, 603–649.

Liu, A. (1998). What the driver's eye tells the car's brain. In: G. Underwood (ed.) *Eye guidance in reading and scene perception*. Oxford: Elsevier, pp. 431–452.

Mack, A., and Rock, I. (1998). *Inattentional blindness*. Cambridge, MA: MIT Press.

McKenna, F. P., and Crick, J. L. (1994). Hazard perception in drivers: A methodology for testing and training. *Transport Research Laboratory Report, 313*. Crowthorne: Transport Research Laboratory.

Miles, F. A., and Kawano, K. (1987). Visual stabilization of the eyes. *Trends in Neurosciences*, **10**, 4, 153–158.

Mourant, R. R., Rockwell, T. H., and Rackoff, N. J. (1969). Drivers' eye movements and visual workload. *Highway Research Record*, **292**, 1–10.

Olivers, C. N. L., and Humphreys, G. W. (2003). Visual marking inhibits singleton capture. *Cognitive Psychology*, **47**, 1–42.

Pollatsek, A., Narayanaan, V., Pradhan, A., and Fisher, D. L. (submitted). The use of eye movements to evaluate the effect of a PC-based Risk Awareness and Perception Training (RAPT) program on an advanced driving simulator. *Human Factors*.

Rauschenberger, R. (2003). Attentional capture by auto- and allo-cues. *Psychonomic Bulletin and Review*, **10**, 814–842.

Recarte, M. A., and Nunes, L. M. (2000). Effects of verbal and spatial-imagery tasks on eye fixations while driving. *Journal of Experimental Psychology: Applied*, 31–43.

Renge, K. (1980). The effects of driving experience on a driver's visual attention. An analysis of objects looked at using the 'verbal report' method. *International Association of Traffic Safety Sciences Research*, **4**, 95–106.

Renge, K. (1998). Drivers' hazard and risk perception, confidence in safe driving, and choice of speed. *Journal of the International Association of Traffic and Safety Sciences*, **22**, 103–110.

Salvucci, D. D., and Liu, A. (2002). The time course of a lane change: Driver control and eye-movement behaviour. *Transportation Research Part F*, **5**, 123–132.

Sivak, M. (1996). The information that drivers use: Is it indeed 90% visual? *Perception*, **25**, 1081–1089.

Shinar, D., McDowell, E. D., and Rockwell, T. H. (1977). Eye-movements in curve negotiation. *Human Factors*, **19**, 63–71.

Shinoda, H, Hayhoe, M. M., and Shrivastava, A. (2001). What controls attention in natural environments? *Vision Research*, **41**, 3535–3545.

Simons, D. J. (2000). Current approaches to change blindness. *Visual Cognition*, **7**, 1–15.

Theeuwes, J. (1991). Cross-dimensional perceptual selectivity. *Perception and Psychophysics*, **50**, 184–193.

Tse, P. U., Sheinberg, D. L., and Logothetis, N. K. (2002). Fixational eye movements are not affected by abrupt onsets that capture attention. *Vision Research*, **42**, 1663–1999.

Underwood, G., Chapman, P., Bowden, K., and Crundall, D. (2002). Visual search while driving: Skill and awareness during inspection of the scene. *Transportation Research Part F*, **5**, 87–97.

Underwood, G., Chapman, P., Berger, Z., and Crundall, D. (2003a) Attending and remembering events in a scene: The relationship between eye fixations and recall. *Transportation Research, Part F*, **6**(4), 289–304.

Underwood, G., Chapman, P., Brocklehurst, N., Underwood, J., and Crundall, D. (2003b). Visual attention while driving: Sequences of eye fixations made by experienced and novice drivers. *Ergonomics*, **46**, 629–646.

Underwood, G., Dobson, H., Chapman, P. and Crundall, D. (2005, in press). Eye movements during the inspection of dynamic traffic scenes. In: A. Gale (ed.) *Vision in Vehicles VIII*. North Holland: Elsevier.

van Loon, E. M., and Underwood, G. (2004). Visual strategies used for timing judgments in driving. Poster presented at the International Conference of Traffic and Transport Psychology, Nottingham, UK.

Wann, J., and Land, M. F. (2000). Steering with or without the flow: is the retrieval of heading necessary? *Trends in Cognitive Sciences*, **4**(8), 319–324.

Wallace, B. (2003). Driver distraction by advertising: genuine risk or urban myth? *Proceedings of the Institute of Civil Engineers: Municipal Engineer*, **156**, 185–190.

Williams, L. J. (1982). Cognitive load and the functional field of view. *Human Factors*, **24**, 683–692.

Williams, L. J. (1985). Tunnel vision induced by a foveal load manipulation. *Human Factors*, **27**, 221–227.

Zwahlen, H. T. (1981). Driver eye scanning of warning signs on rural highways. *Proceedings of the 25th Annual Meeting of the Human Factors Society*. Rochester, NY: Human Factors Society, pp. 33–37.

Zwahlen, H. T., Russ, A., and Schnell, T. (2003). Driver eye scanning behavior while viewing ground-mounted diagrammatic guide signs before entrance ramps at night. Paper presented at the 82nd Annual Meeting of the Transportation Research Board, January 12–16, Washington, DC.

13

Novice and expert performance with a dynamic control task: Scanpaths during a computer game

Jean Underwood

Abstract

Investigations into computer game playing stem from the search to elucidate the conditions under which transfer of expertise from one task to another novel task can and will take place. The research is predicated on the argument that such games provide best-case opportunities to identify that all elusive transfer. How is success with a complex dynamic control task reflected in the ongoing acquisition of information? The present study observed the performance of successful and less-successful individuals playing the computer game *Tetris*, asking whether successful game players exhibit different playing strategies or are simply more efficient than their less successful peers in the strategies they use. Twenty-two undergraduate psychologists were observed. They had an age range of 19–22 years, and they were all competent computer users and active game players. They played one practice and one experimental trial of the game Tetris extending over a number of levels of the game depending on the skill of the game player. Scanpath analyses of the locations of the eye movements of the participants showed that there were differences in game-playing strategies between less successful and more successful game players; with the latter making more lateral eye-movements. There were no differences in the frequencies of vertical eye movements, or fixation durations. These lateral movements can be seen as an attempt to create a modified representation of the screen world, allowing the player to acquire vital information; that is, lateral movements serve an epistemic function.

Introduction

The key question for learning theorists centres on the issue of how an individual moves from being a novice performer to an expert performer on any given task. Subsumed under this question are issues of individual differences in knowledge and skills acquisition; the level and extent of transfer of expertise; the nature and context of the task; and the interactions between requisite abilities and task. Psychological research, as opposed to that engendered by educational theorists, has focused on the nature and development of cognitive abilities and in particular on problem-solving behaviour. Classic investigations of problem-solving behaviour include the extensive research into implicit learning as exemplified by the Sugar Factory problem (Berry and Broadbent 1984) and insight problem solving typically seen in Maier's (1931) 'two string' or 'pendulum' problem, or Duncker's (1945) 'candle, matchbox and pin' problem.

The focus of this chapter is on expertise in problem solving, but the task chosen, a dynamic control task presented through the computer game *Tetris* (Gustafsson 1988), at first sight appears very different from traditional problem-solving tasks. Further discussion of the typology of problems is provided in chapter 15. Here only a brief outline of the types of cognitive problems which have been a focus of empirical research are presented to provide a context for the Tetris task.

Jones (2003) describes three main categories of problem: one-stop problems (Knoblich *et al.* 1999, 2001); limited-move problems (Scheerer 1963) and unlimited-moves problems (Jones 2003). One-stop problems are exemplified by the balancing of the roman numerals equation laid out in matchsticks through the action of moving one matchstick only. Limited-move problems are exemplified by Scheerer's (1963) nine-dot problem. This problem, in which nine dots are arranged in a 3×3 grid with the task being to bisect all of the dots using four straight lines only, has proved to be very difficult for participants to solve even when given a generous time-frame (Burnham and Davis 1969) or multiple trials (Weisberg and Alba 1981).

Investigations of unlimited move problems are sparse in the literature but the car park game (Jones 2003) is a current example. This is a relatively simple problem in which the goal is to manoeuvre a target car out of the car park. The exit route for the target car is blocked by other vehicles, and the objective is to move these other cars to free up the exit route. The cars, as in real life, can only move forwards and backwards. The problem is similar to classic children's games in which tiles (numbered 1–8) are moved around a 3×3 grid until they are in numerical order (see for example O'Hara and Payne 1998).

The problem facing players of Tetris is most closely aligned with Jones's car park problem in that it has some elements of the unlimited moves problems but it differs in that it lacks a final definitive solution. Suboptimal solutions will still be rewarded, albeit less generously in terms of number of points scored or prolongation of the game, than would an optimal solution. In an optimal solution, each new piece effectively contributes to a completed row, which results in points being awarded and the removal of the line from the screen, buying playing time for the game player.

Cognitive processes in computer game playing

The second half of this chapter presents a comparative study of novice and expert performance on a dynamic control task, the computer game Tetris. The purpose of this research was to explore the nature of expertise and asked whether successful game players exhibited different playing strategies from their less successful peers or whether they were simply more efficient in the strategies they used. The use of a computer game rather than a more conventional problem-solving task is in part a response to Ericsson's (2003) argument that many laboratory studies of expertise fail to capture the superior performance of experts because of their artificiality. Such fixed tasks, he argues, may constrain the expert performer. However, to be sat in front of a computer screen is the natural environment for the computer game player and this allows the study of expertise in context.

Investigations into computer game playing by educational and cognitive psychologists stems from the search to identify the occurrence of, and the conditions controlling, the transfer of expertise from a previously mastered task to another novel task; occurrences, which throughout the learning literature, have proved to be elusive and often insubstantial (Chi *et al.* 1988; Mayer and Wittrock 1996; Sims and Mayer 2002). Termed technological artefacts by Greenfield (1994) computer games present cognitive problem solving in highly-motivating environments, that is, in environments in which participants are eager to perform and from which it should be possible to achieve something approaching optimal performance (Thornburg and Pea 1991). Gee (2003) argues that games solve the motivation problem through the biological effect of manipulating objects or characters at a distance, much like operating a robot at a distance, but in a much more fine-grained way. This makes humans feel that their bodies and minds have actually been expanded into or entered that distant space. The argument here is that such games provide best-case opportunities to identify that so-elusive transfer of training, the 'golden fleece' of educational endeavours.

Computer games are highly varied and difficult to classify with any precision. Some games focus on hand-eye co-ordination and spatial representation; others focus on social communication; while others are tests of logical problem solving. Such games have proved to be a fertile ground for exploring a range of cognitive skills and it has been argued that they can be a powerful agent of the development and organization of thought (DiSessa 2000; Herz 1997), stimulating an individual's ability to operate strategically as shown by Rabbitt *et al.*'s (1989) investigations with the game *Space Fortress*. Indeed, Gee (2003) has asserted that such games create a 'cycle of expertise' as players develop strategies to cope with well-designed problems, and with sufficient practice, automaticity of skill develops. He argues that good games repeat this cycle again and again, and that this is how expertise is produced in any domain.

An important question here relates to whether the expertise acquired in the computer game is based on automaticity of skill and the use of subroutines of performance, or whether this expertise is more general, and hence can be flexibly used across a range of tasks. In the former case when specific routinized skills have been acquired, often implicitly, then transfer of skill may prove difficult, but where explicit knowledge has been acquired, transfer of skills to other situations should be enhanced (Pirolli and Recker 1994; Volet 1991).

The transfer of problem-solving skills can be at a variety of levels: transfer of general skills, transfer of specific skills, and transfer of specific skills in context (Mayer and Wittrock 1996). Those proposing general skills transfer argue that learning to problem solve in a domain such as computer gaming acts as a mental work-out, improving the mind in general. Many computer games have a strong spatial component, as is true for Tetris. The focus of the empirical work presented here, and from the general skills perspective performance on such games, should not only be on tests of spatial ability, but also whether growing expertise on such games should also lead to improvement in overall spatial competence. The argument for the transfer of specific skills suggests that only those skills inherent in the problem-solving situation – in the case of Tetris, skills such as mental rotation (Shepard and Cooper 1982) and visualization (Carroll 1993) – will be honed and therefore transferred to other situations. The more limited view of transfer, that of specific skills in context, suggests that component skills such as mental rotation are not altered in any global sense, but are used more efficiently when the stimuli are the same, or near equivalent, because of stored mental representations of those familiar stimuli (Sims and Mayer 2002).

Much of the research on the cognitive benefits of game playing has focused on the honing of general spatial abilities. However, the evidence of the efficacy of game playing is mixed. Gagnon (1985) found no post-test gains in general spatial skills of adults, although Dorval and Pepin (1986) reported such skills gains for adults but not children, all of whom had had extended game-playing exposure. Subrahmanyam and Greenfield (1994) have shown differential gains in spatial skills for game-playing children over peer controls, when the pre-post test tasks were closely related to game-playing task. To add confusion to the debate, Okagaki and Frensch (1994) have recorded gender effects after extensive playing of Tetris, with gains on two out of four spatial ability tests by male undergraduates, but no gains for females. These differences in male and female performance were not apparent in a follow-up task when gains in speed of mental rotation were apparent for both sexes.

McClurg and Chaille (1987) have shown gains in children's ability to mentally rotate shapes after playing a spatial computer game. While Sims and Mayer (2002) have shown that skilled undergraduate Tetris players outperformed non-Tetris players on mental rotation of shapes, these gains were confined to the manipulation of shapes which were identical or very similar to Tetris shapes. The undergraduates did not outperform peer controls on other tests of spatial ability. Tetris expertise proved to be related only to performance on spatial ability tasks involving mental rotation of Tetris-like shapes (termed 'zoids'), i.e. Tetris is a game where component skills are somewhat separate from other spatial skills. These results suggest that spatial expertise is highly domain-specific and does not transfer generally to other domains.

Despite extensive research and the highly-motivating nature of computer games, significant transfer of skills has not been identified. Sims and Mayer (2002) conclude that 'a domain-specific theory of problem-solving transfer in which skills learned in one domain are not generally transferred to other domains' (p. 113) is emerging from current research. The answers as to why this should be so are as yet unclear. It may be that transfer is domain-limited and skills are context-specific as Sims and Mayer argue. However, Scaife and Rogers (1996) present a radically different argument based on our ability to read and interpret external representations as a partial explanation of the failure to transfer in such highly dynamic and motivating environments. They argue that specifying how people interact with any representations, when learning, solving problems and making inferences, is complex since it will involve not only a specification of the cognitive mechanisms alluded to above, but also some sense of the behavioural aspects. They point out that students prefer to mark diagrams as they work, actively laying down cognitive traces and conducting a personal discourse with the representation. However the potential significance of such activity will vary with experience with the representation and knowledge domain, the nature of the task and abstractness of information being represented. It could be argued that many of the benefits of old-fashioned representations such as static diagrams emanate from years of practice of perceptual processing of visual stimuli and the learning of graphical conventions. This may in part explain why more advanced graphical technologies are yet to demonstrate comparable learning benefits. They also argue that computational offloading in such dynamic environments is poorly understood.

Tetris

Tetris is a real-time interactive computer game of which there are several different versions available. Versions differ in the number, shape and position of the elements of the game but the core problem remains true to the draft game invented in 1985 by Alexey Pazhitnov, then working for the Academy of Sciences, Moscow. The case for using game-playing software to investigate expertise has been argued on the grounds that the thorny issues such as maintenance of and variations in motivation which plague many empirical investigations are ruled out, or at least reduced when participants are asked to play such games. That Tetris is motivating is attested to by the longevity of the game and by sales figures; 30 million 'Gameboy' copies were sold in 1998 and computer copies continue to be sold (Antonietti *et al.* 2002). In addition, Tetris is relatively simple, with limited moves and available strategies, which should be accessible to both the player and the researcher. Finally, Tetris is a game of relatively short duration and so it is possible for players to be involved in many rounds of the game without experiencing fatigue effects.

Tetris consists of a playing area, and in the version used here, it is located off-centre towards the left of the screen, with an area of feedback information on performance located on the right of the screen (see Fig. 13.1). The game starts with an empty playing field, and on each trial or event, one of seven possible zoids, each composed of four squares or bricks (Fig. 13.2), appears at the top of the screen and descends to the bottom, at a regular speed which increases as the game proceeds. The target of the game is to stack the descending shapes in order to complete a horizontal line across the playing field. When such a line is constructed it will disappear and the zoids above will drop down to the lower level. The completion of a line results in points being added to the score but it also serves the function of providing the player with more

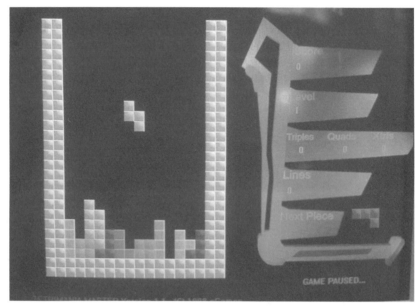

Figure 13.1 Screen dump of the Tetris playing area with a game in progress (after Gustafsson 1988).

playing time. The game continues until the zoids pile up to reach the top of the playing field. The player can take four actions in order to align zoids to build the point-winning wall. They are to move the target zoid left; to move the target zoid right; to rotate the zoid clockwise and to vertically drop the zoid.

Playing Tetris requires the abilities to recognize shapes, to mentally rotate those shapes and to place those shapes in a point-winning position (Sims and Mayer 2002). In addition the player may selectively choose to access peripherally-presented information on upcoming objects and on personal performance. All actions are undertaken under increasing time pressure as the presentation of new target zoids is accelerated.

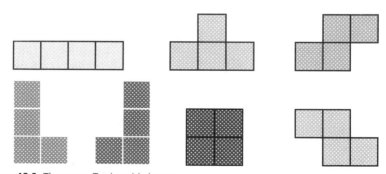

Figure 13.2 The seven Tetris zoid shapes.

Kirsh and Maglio (1994) divide the game-playing episode into a set of actions which form a pre-identification, an identification and a post-identification phase in which both epistemic and pragmatic actions occur. Pragmatic actions are clearly goal-directed, i.e. they move the zoid towards the end state, which is to place the zoid in a position that adds to, or completes the point-winning line. They argue that epistemic or knowledge-seeking actions such as rotating a zoid to help to disambiguate it from all other shapes, serve the function of reducing spatial and temporal complexity thus reducing the burden of the mental computation the player must make. They have shown that in the pre-identification phase, players often rotate zoids seemingly in this non-goal directed way. Players may also move the zoid sideways (lateral translations) in a way that seemingly takes the zoid away from the end-goal state. They argue that as all actions move the zoid to the right or left, every action by a player places the current target either closer to or further from its final resting place. The pace of the game necessarily means that first actions are undertaken without knowing where to place the current piece, so these actions should be viewed as knowledge-seeking. Lateral translations may also occur in the post-identification phase as players seemingly check the columnar placement before final dropping the zoid. They point out that actions in the identification phase are often more difficult to classify, as any action might simultaneously serve both an epistemic and a pragmatic function.

A theory of action must include the gathering of information as a prominent and natural part of the planning and action cycle (Kirsh and Maglio 1994). The transforming actions in the Tetris game, as described here, are best understood from this viewpoint as serving an epistemic rather than pragmatic function. Although an act may appear to be goal-seeking, the real point of the action may be to increase the reliability of judgment, or to reduce the spatial and temporal resources required for the necessary mental computations.

The current study

The current study is a partial replication of Kirsh and Maglio (1994) in that the study sought to identify the occurrence of such epistemic activity. The study is an extension in that it sought to identify how such strategies might vary with level of expertise. Specifically, the study asked the question whether successful game players exhibit different playing strategies, or are they simply more efficient in their strategies than less successful game players? In addition, the study questioned whether or not successful game players use the same strategies as they move up game levels and come under increasing time pressure? Based on Kirsh and Maglio's (1994) findings, one prediction would be that more expert players will perform more epistemic actions in the form of non-goal specific translations across the playing field than their less expert counterparts. Their theory also allows a prediction of strategy change with increasing cognitive load, such as occurs with increasing time pressure as the game accelerates. It could be argued that as the epistemic function is a partial compensation for spatial and temporal complexity, such functions will be all the more important as the game progresses. Equally, it could be argued that there will be a tipping point at which increasing time pressure overwhelms the search for information, and epistemic functions lapse, leading to failure. In the former case, one would predict the maintenance of the lateral translations, while in the latter case such translations will largely disappear.

The theoretical position espoused by Kirsh and Maglio (1994) was generated by using the keystroke data from 30 game players from which an expert system model was created. Their purpose was to test of the theory that certain cognitive and perceptual problems, such as those posed by Tetris, are more readily resolved by performing actions in the world rather than by performing mental computations alone. In the current study eye-movement measures were used to investigate whether such epistemic functions could be identified during active game-playing.

Eye-movement measures and problem solving

The use of eye-movement measures to identify impasses in problem solving, with a view to directing attention to core aspects of a problem and thus resolving the impasse, is a growing phenomenon in the problem-solving literature (see for example Grant and Spivey 2003; Knoblich *et al.* 2001). Eye movements allow the researcher to capture overt visual attention during diagram-based problem-solving events and to identify critical aspects of the thinking process not available though more traditional measures of accuracy and solution time (Grant and Spivey 2003). Jones (2003) argues that defining what constitutes an impasse is critical as the re-representation of the problem at the point of impasse is essential to resolution of that problem. For example, Grant and Spivey (2003), working with Duncker's (1945) 'tumour-and-lasers radiation' problem, found that successful solvers of this problem were more likely to direct their gaze to the boundary skin area of the tumour than their non-successful peers. When attention was drawn to this critical zone of the problem representation in a second experiment there was a significant increase in success rates. Eye movements are a functional way of examining effective strategies in problem solving.

In his review of current approaches and empirical findings in human gaze control during real-world scene perception, Henderson (2003) points out that visual information is required only from a limited spatial region surrounding the centre of gaze. Citing Buswell's (1936) pioneering work, he notes that fixations are not randomly placed in a scene, rather, fixations cluster on informative aspects of the scene with eye-movement adjustments being a response to the attentional demands of the visual image. So studies of gaze control have demonstrated that empty, uniform and uninformative scene regions are often not fixated. When viewing a scene, individuals focus on interesting and informative regions of the scene both for their first and subsequent fixations. Regions worthy of note are defined by two disparate sets of data: bottom-up stimulus-based data generated from the image, and top-down memory-based knowledge generated from the individual's internal visual and cognitive systems (see chapter 12). The low-level information is best exhibited through 'saliency mapping'. Shifts of attention are determined according to such maps, which are explicit two-dimensional representations of the saliency or conspicuity of objects in the visual environment. Saliency is determined according to local changes in brightness, colour, and the orientation of contours. Competition between localized regions in this map gives rise to a single winning region that corresponds to the next attended object.

Once attention (and an eye fixation) has moved to this location, its saliency is reduced and a return of attention inhibited. (for an expanded description of saliency mapping see Itti and Koch 2000; Parkhurst *et al.* 2002).

However, the match between the predicted pattern of eye movements and actual human eye movements varies from scene to scene, and real-world scenes produce only a partial match (see for example chapter 7). Henderson (2003, p. 500) concludes that

> human eye-movement control is 'smart' in that it draws not only on currently available visual input, but also on several cognitive systems, including short-term memory for previously attended information in the current scene, stored long-term visual, spatial and semantic information about other similar scenes, and the goals and plans of the viewer.

The link between low-level saliency and fixations is less strong when meaningful scenes are viewed during active tasks. The argument here is that visual saliency has reduced impact as knowledge-driven control increases, and this move to high-level direction of processing becomes more significant the longer a scene is viewed, and the greater the knowledge that is acquired about previously fixated objects and their relationships within the scene. Even the very first saccade in a scene may take the eye in the likely direction of a search target, whether or not the target is present. This targeting is a result of an understanding of the global scene gist (the whole game area) and the spatial layout acquired at first fixation, providing the viewer with relevant information about where an object is to be found. Scenes can be identified and their gist apprehended very rapidly within the duration of a single fixation (Biederman *et al.* 1982; Thorpe 1996; see also chapter 7). Such top-level processing should be apparent in successful Tetris game players.

The participants

Initially, the study presented here involved 22 undergraduate psychologists, ranging in age from 19 to 22 years. They were selected to take part in the study on the basis of self-report data that showed that they were all competent computer users and all active game players. Indeed, all but one of the 22 were familiar with the target game for this study (i.e. Tetris in one its many guises) leaving only one game player who had not previously played Tetris.

The procedure

The students played a familiarizing practice trial and then an experimental trial of Tetris. The experimental trial extended over a number of levels of game difficulty, depending only on the skill of the game player. The game continued until the player failed to progress to the next level. The three most advanced players reached Level 6 out the possible 10 levels of the game. The formal trial sessions varied from 10 to 40 min in length depending on the level achieved by the individual player.

Initial findings

Each player's individual performance was measured using three scores: a points score generated from the number of blocks placed appropriately; the number of lines completed and the level of game difficulty achieved, which for these trials varied across players from level 1 to level 6. These scores were all logged automatically by the system. In addition, in post-trial interviews each player reported the strategies they had used to achieve the goals of the game.

The first-level analyses from the 22 participants, which have been previously reported in Antonietti *et al.* (2002), showed that the majority of players were aware of the strategic aspects of Tetris, but that the extent of such awareness varied. Significantly better performance was accompanied by greater declarative knowledge, with those who best articulated their game-playing strategies performing at higher levels of the game, while those players who exhibited less well-developed metacognition were less successful. This indicates that the more successful game players developed explicit expertise, a finding at odds with the extensively cited findings of Berry and Broadbent's (1984) on implicit learning from their computer-based 'Sugar Factory Task'. In this game-like task, participants had to control output from a virtual factory by manipulating key variables. Unsurprisingly, performance improved with practice; i.e. effective control of production improved as the task progressed. However, the performance of participants on the task had no significant effect on the ability to answer post-task questions about the nature of the task. Indeed, people who were better at controlling the tasks were significantly worse at answering the post-task questions and Berry and Broadbent concluded that there were no benefits to performance of increased declarative knowledge, which led them to argue that successful completion of the task invoked implicit rather than explicit knowledge. This is in stark contrast to the findings from our computer game study, which clearly showed that the level of explicit knowledge of the game is positively correlated with performance gains.

Eye movements

In addition to the performance measures outlined above, participants' eye movements were monitored using an SMI EyeLink eye-tracker recording at 250 Hz. Although participants used both eyes for viewing, data from the right eye only were used in the following analyses. Three of the original 22 participants were removed from the analyses because of poor eye-tracker recordings, leaving 19 players in all. As for Sims and Mayer (2003), the sample was divided into two groups on the basis of level of performance in the trial. Low performers were defined as those achieving level 3 or lower in the game; high performers were defined as those achieving level 4 or more. This produced two groups: one of ten low performers and one of nine high performers.

Preliminary analyses of the eye-movement data for all of the players showed that the mean number of fixations per player declined with game level (Table 13.1). This is an artefact of the game. The higher levels are played at a faster pace than the lower levels, and so the players have less time available at the higher levels. However, mean fixation durations remained more or less constant across the levels of the game. The process of directing fixations to an important aspect of a scene – the control of *where* to look – has a key function of facilitating perceptual, cognitive and behavioural activity (Henderson 2003), and the control of fixation location is not necessarily linked to the control of fixation duration (the *when* to move decision). Fixation duration is often an indicator of depth of processing, and the invariant length of the fixation durations over levels for the total sample would suggest that the cognitive demand of the

Table 13.1 Mean number of fixations and mean fixation duration by player and game level

Players reaching ≥ level	Mean number of fixations per player duration (ms)	Mean fixation
1: $n = 19$	41.9 ± 36.1	170.7 ± 31.7
2: $n = 18$	26.0 ± 22.2	164.7 ± 24.5
3: $n = 16$	24.4 ± 17.3	156.3 ± 30.3
4: $n = 9$	22.2 ± 6.4	157.5 ± 20.7
5: $n = 6$	19.5 ± 13.8	148.7 ± 21.7
6: $n = 3$	14.7 ± 5.0	165.8 ± 16.9

problem remains more or less constant while the increasing game difficulty is due to increasing speed demands which eventually result in cognitive overload

However, there were two skill effects. While the low performers showed an albeit weak bimodal distribution of fixation durations, suggestive of strategy change, this was not apparent for the high performers at any level of the game (Fig. 13.3).

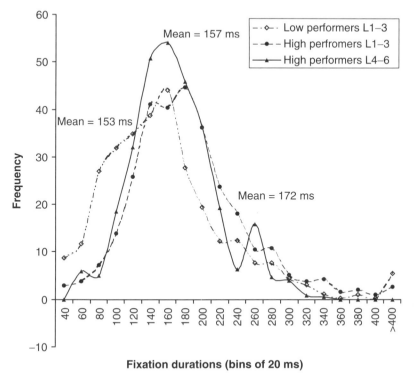

Figure 13.3 Distributions of fixation durations for the low performers (levels 1–3 only), and for the high performers (levels 1–3 and 4–6).

Secondly, the mean fixation durations were reliably longer for those players who were categorized as high performers compared with those deemed to be low performers at levels 1–3 of the game (Fig. 13.3). This finding is replicated in other domains; for example, studies of experienced players of ball sports have shown that they fixate on the hypothesized informative areas and employ fewer fixations of longer duration (Helsen and Pauwels 1993; Williams and Davids 1998). For example, experienced soccer players fixated on the position of the sweeper and the potential areas of free space whereas novices focused on the ball and the goal and their eye movements moved between these critical areas of information.

There is support in the literature to show that length of fixation durations varies according to whether a task is internally or externally paced (Henderson 2003). Internally paced tasks such as reading (Rayner 1998) and problem solving (Ballard *et al.* 1997; Knoblich *et al.* 2001) record longer fixation durations with increasing task difficulty. That is, the individual will devote additional processing time to extract information from more complex texts or problems.

However, in an externally paced task such as driving, as the road situation becomes more complex and dangerous, demanding time-controlled actions from the driver, time to reflect or to gather information is reduced by the very necessity of coping with other road users and obstacles. In such situations fixation durations will be longer for simple environments but will decrease with complex scenes that require greater depth of processing as drivers rapidly scan for information (Crundall and Underwood 1998; Crundall *et al.* 2004). In such driving studies, the longest fixation durations were seen when the processing load was at its easiest. However, other increases in demand can have the opposite effect. When the demands become severe, as in the case of an abrupt appearance of a hazard such as a pedestrian stepping out onto the road, then increased fixation durations occur (Chapman and Underwood 1998).

As the timing of Tetris events are largely externally paced, it was predicted that mean fixation durations would decrease as the difficulty of the levels increased. The overall figures suggest that this was not the case (Table 13.1), a finding that is supported from the studies of expertise in sport (see James and Patrick 2004). However, when a comparison of fixation durations for levels 1– vs. levels 4–6 was made for the high-performers group only (i.e. using only the players who succeeded in getting to beyond level 3), then the expected decrease in mean fixation durations was apparent (Fig. 13.3). The game's increasing speed demanded shorter fixation durations and provided an external control of attention and information gathering.

Eye-movement data show a general consensus that more skilled protagonists have search strategies relevant to the task, i.e. they fixate on the hypothesized informative areas and employ fewer fixations of longer duration. It is these movements between critical information that form the basis of the scanpath analysis below.

Identifying two-fixation scanpaths

In addition to the data on number and duration of fixations, an analysis was conducted to establish whether there was any pattern in the sequences of fixations as Kirsh and Maglio (1994) had predicted through their computer simulation of Tetris game playing. The question here was concerned with whether successful players looked at different parts of the display and whether they moved their eyes regularly from one part of the screen to another in a predictable sequence? The procedure to identify scanpaths was similar to one that we have used previously to distinguish between the patterns of visual search shown by novice and experienced drivers (Underwood *et al.* 2003). A first-order Markov transition matrix was calculated for each game-level/game-player combination using the fixation data, to indicate the location of the next fixation given that the current fixation is in a specified area of the scene. Twelve such matrices were calculated to reflect the two-factor design, with players (novice/experienced) and levels (1–6) as the factors. The transition probabilities within each matrix were evaluated by using a binomial test to calculate the z-score associated with each possible transition. This assumes that each part of the scene has an *a priori* equal probability of being inspected. The probability of each transition was determined as a proportion of all fixations within each area, and the expected probability of inspecting each part should be 0.14, given that there are seven areas (Fig. 13.4) available when refixations within the same zone are excluded. The four game-playing areas were the upper left and right quadrants (ULQ and URQ) and the lower left and right quadrants (LLQ and LRQ). There were also three information zones available, showing the next piece, itemized score, including two sets of information of how the score is being calculated, and score which included the overall points score and the game level. The z-score describes the difference between this expected probability of fixation and the observed probability. Only the reliable transitions (two-tailed) will be

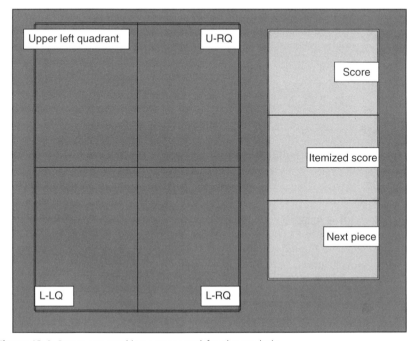

Figure 13.4 Seven eye-tracking zones used for the analysis.

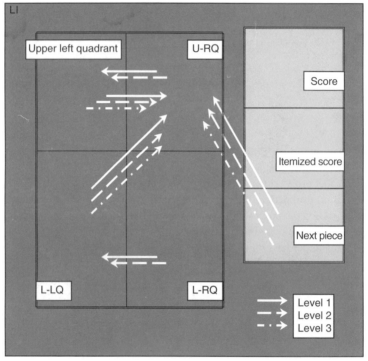

Figure 13.5 Two-fixation scanpaths for game levels 1–3 by players of all levels of expertise (Note: all scanpaths shown are significant at $p < 0.05$ or greater).

mentioned here, and they are shown in Figs 13.5–13.7. Transitions that are significant at the $p < 0.05$ level or better are shown by arrows between the first and second fixation locations.

Scanpath patterns across levels for all participants

An analysis of the scanpath patterns for all players at levels 1 and 2 of the game showed that there was considerable activity centred on the URQ which is a central location on the screen (Fig. 13.5). Surprisingly, given the nature of the game, which has an overall movement of targets from the top of the screen to the bottom of the screen, there were no strong vertical scanpaths. However, players exhibited strong lateral movements, or transitions in Kirsh and Maglio's terminology (URQ to ULQ; ULQ to URQ and LRQ to LLQ) and diagonals (LLQ to URQ; Next Piece to URQ). At level 3, two lateral movements (URQ to ULQ and LRQ to LLQ) are no longer significant. The loss of laterals at level 3 suggests that epistemic functions are being curtailed as game difficulty increases and players have reduced time in which to make decisions.

There were several strategies that players of all levels appeared to share, for example all players looked ahead at the incoming shape (new piece). MacGregor *et al.* (2001) point out that problem solvers who look several moves ahead anticipate problems and

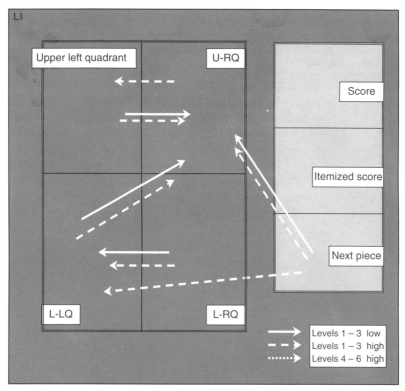

Figure 13.6 Two-fixation scanpaths for game levels 1–3 by low performers vs. high performers group. (Note: all scanpaths shown are significant at $p < 0.05$ or greater).

initiate retrieval strategies sooner, and early sight of the zoid is an obvious and clearly useful piece of information for any game player to collect. In this study no specific measures of mental rotation were taken, although Sims and Mayer (2002) have shown that both high- and low-skilled Tetris players used a mental rotation strategy to align the zoids, finding no support for Tarr and Pinker's (1989) assertion that familiar shapes are stored in multiple orientations.

Comparison of low and high performers

The combined analysis for all players obscured significant differences between low- and high-performing game players (Fig. 13.6). High-performing players made more lateral eye movements than the overall sample and the lateral movement from new piece to LLQ was only consistently present for the better performing players. In addition, the loss of lateral movements from the URQ to ULQ at level 3 recorded by the overall sample, occurred only for the low-performing players. The findings from these scanpath patterns are confirmed by the data on fixation durations (Fig. 13.3). The occurrence and maintenance of lateral movements by high performers supports Kirsh and

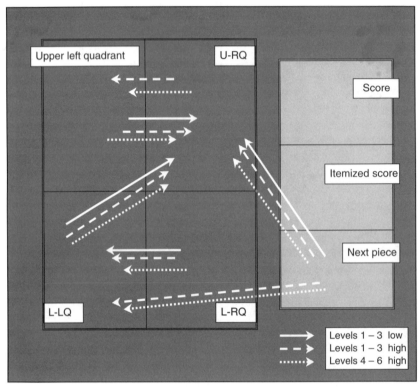

Figure 13.7 Two-fixation scanpaths for game levels 1 to 3 for low and high performers vs. game levels 4–6 for high performers only. (Note: all scanpaths shown are significant at $p < 0.05$ or greater).

Maglio's (1994) argument that such movements serve an information-gathering purpose that is necessary for good performance. They are an attempt to create a modified representation of the screen world allowing the player to acquire vital information, i.e. these movements have an epistemic function. The scanpath analyses of the locations of the eye movements of these game players showed that there were differences in game-playing strategies between less successful and more successful game players; with the latter making more lateral eye-movements.

The trade-off between expert performance, cognitive load and strategy

Figures 13.5 and 13.6 collectively show that for game levels 1–3 there is a loss of lateral scans, but that this loss is confined to the low performers who are having increasing difficulty with the game. For the better game players, no loss of laterals was apparent and it can be argued that this is because they were coping well with the task in hand. As these high-performing players moved to level 4 and beyond, they came under increasing time-pressure, and eventually they too reached a point at which they were no longer performing effectively. It could be argued that, if the loss of laterals was a function of time pressure leading to reduced decision-making time, then as the high performers moved to a point of failure, they too would reduce the use of lateral scans. However, if the strategy had reached a level of automaticity then one would expect the laterals to remain present even though performance was declining. The question here was then do successful game players use the same strategies as they move up game levels? Comparison of inspection patterns on the lower game levels (1–3) with those for the higher levels (4–6) for the high performers indicated no change in the scan-path patterns (Fig. 13.7). Lateral movements continued to be significantly above chance at the more advanced levels of the game, suggesting that they were not only strategically important but well-rehearsed actions for the better players.

Why might lateral movements be important?

There are only four actions a player can make when playing Tetris: laterally translate the zoid right; translate left; rotate the shape; and drop the shape vertically. As Kirsh and Maglio (1994) point out, every action moves the current zoid either closer or further away from its final resting position. They argue that as the as the game is played at speed, it is not surprising that first moves may lead away from final goal point and that in the early phases of the game the player is unlikely to know where to move the zoid. The player must first identify the piece, then compute where it would best fit into the target wall, and how to move the piece to that identified resting place within the limited timeframe available. They therefore argue that the early moves, i.e. the non-goal directed lateral movements, are in effect an attempt by the player to acquire vital information early on, i.e. they serve an epistemic function. Although the data presented here provide inferential rather than direct causal proof, the fact that the more successful game players use such lateral movements is supportive of the Kirsh and Maglio (1994) thesis. Further, Henderson states that 'task-related knowledge can involve a general "gaze-control policy" or strategy relevant to a given task ... producing specific sequences of fixations' (2003, p. 501) such as the use of the rear-view mirror by drivers (Underwood *et al.* 2003) or, as here in Tetris, the use of lateral translations of the zoid. These strategies, based as they are on top-down factors such as gist of the scene and task-related knowledge, support, if only indirectly, the argument that the lateral movements are critical acts, which as has been shown here, lead to better performance or more expert performance.

Late stage laterals such as those shown by scanpaths may appear more problematic under the Kirsh and Maglio (1994) thesis. These occur in the late stages of the game and so do they perform the same epistemic function at decision-making? New piece to LLQ moves are, of course, attempts to identify the new piece, as, of course, is new piece to URQ, and these are clearly epistemic in that the individual is beginning the identification process for the new target. Kirsh and Maglio (1994) recorded the equivalent move to LRQ to LLQ in the post-identification phase, when some players moved zoids to the nearest outer wall of the playing frame before translating the zoid back to the drop point. This they argued was an act of verification before finally dropping the zoid and occurred post the identification and decision-making stage.

Conclusions

This chapter has examined the strength of claims that the investigation of computer game playing will aid our understanding of cognition and particularly add to our understanding of transfer of training and the nature of expertise. The high level of player motivation recognized in the literature does make game-playing a fertile ground for such research; although the findings to date are mixed and more supportive of development and transfer of sub-skills than a more general and hence more flexible skills that transcend individual tasks. However, in the current study, as in studies by Pirolli and Recker (1994) and Volet (1991), it is clear that explicit knowledge has been acquired and that the strength of such knowledge is related to expert performance. Successful players show more lateral inspections of the board and they articulate a more detailed strategy for playing the game. They also use these same strategies as they move up game levels, showing a well-honed skill. While less-successful game players in this study initially used similar strategies to the high performers, albeit exhibiting a less extensive use of lateral transitions, the strategies changed with increasing difficulty of the task. Specifically, transitional movements were lost as these less-successful players moved up through the levels of the game. This suggests that for this group of players, skills were not well embedded and routinized. In addition to establishing that more successful game players exhibit more stable strategies than less-successful game players. The successful game players could articulate the strategies used, and they had acquired explicit knowledge, suggesting that some degree of transfer of training could be possible.

What skill is actually being learnt, and whether it is transferable to other situations remains to be answered. Kirsh and Maglio (1994) argue that success in Tetris is built upon strategic actions, encompassed in the use of lateral transitions that allow successful players to increase the reliability of a judgment of the space-time resources needed to compute a solution. Theories of action must incorporate not only planning and action themselves, but also information gathering. Kirsh and Maglio (1994) argue that epistemic activity encompasses far more than sensor-related activity. In achieving expertise in playing Tetris, the individual relies on this epistemic function, the top-down processing that Henderson (2003) points out needs to go hand-in-hand with low-level processing for any individual to operate intelligently in any problem-based scenario. This top-down processing, from a situated cognition perspective, allows environmentally-controlled perceptual properties to guide attention and eye movements in ways that assist in developing problem-solving insights that dramatically improve reasoned action (Grant and Spivey 2003).

Acknowledgements

I would like to thank David Crundall and Michael Spivey for their thoughtful, occasionally provocative but always supportive criticisms of the first draft of this chapter.

References

Antoinetti, A., Rasi, C., and Underwood, J. (2002) I videogiochi: Una palestra per il pensiero stratgico? Do video games enhance strategic thinking? *Ricerche di Psicologia*, **25**, 125–144.

Ballard, D. H., Hayhoe, M. M., Pook, P. K., and Rao, R. P. N. (1997). Deictic codes for the embodiment of cognition. *Behavior and Brain Sciences*, **20**, 723–767.

Berry, D. C. and Broadbent, D. E. (1984). On the relationship between task performance and associated verbalisable knowledge. *Quarterly Journal of Experimental Psychology*, **36**, 209–231.

Biederman, I., Mezzanotte, R. J., and Rabinowitz, J. C. (1982). Scene perception: Detecting and judging objects undergoing violation. *Cognitive Psychology*, **14**, 143–177.

Burnham, C. A., and Davis, K. G. (1969). The nine-dot problem: Beyond perceptual organisation. *Psychonomic Science*, **17**, 321–323.

Buswell, G. T. (1935). *How People Look at Pictures*. Chicago: University of Chicago Press.

Carroll, J. B. (1993). *Human Cognitive Abilities*. Cambridge: Cambridge University Press.

Chapman, P. R. and Underwood, G. (1998). Visual search of driving situations: Danger and experience. *Perception*, **27**, 965–976.

Chi, M. T., Glaser, R., and Farr, M. J. (1988). *The Nature of Expertise*. Hillsdale, NJ: Laurence Erlbaum.

Crundall, D. E., and Underwood, G. (1998). The effects of experience and processing demands on visual information acquisition in drivers. *Ergonomics*, **41**, 448–458.

Crundall, D., Shenton, C., and Underwood, G. (2004). Eye movements during intentional car following. *Perception*, **33**, 975–986.

DiSessa, A. A. (2000). *Changing minds: Computers, learning and literacy*. Cambridge, MA: MIT Press.

Dorval, M., and Pepin, M. (1986). Effects of playing a video game on a measure of spatial visualisation. *Perceptual and Motor Skills*, **62**, 159–162.

Duncker, K. (1945). On problem solving. *Psychological Monographs*, **58** No. 270.

Ericsson, K. A. (2003). How the expert performance approach differs form traditional approaches in sport: In: search of a shared theoretical framework for studying expert performance. In: J. L. Starkes and K. A. Ericsson (ed.) *Expert performance in Sport: Advances in Research on Sport Expertise*. Champagne, IL: Human Kinetics, pp. 371–402.

Gagnon, D. (1985) Videogames and spatial skills: An exploratory study. *Educational Communication and Technology Journal*, **33**, 263–275.

Gee, J. P. (2003). *What video games have to teach us about learning and literacy?* London: Palgrave Macmillan.

Grant, E. R., and Spivey, M. J. (2003). Eye-movements and problem solving: Guiding attention guides thought. *Psychological Science*, **14**, 462–466.

Greenfield, P. M. (1994). Videogames as cultural artefacts. *Journal of Applied Developmental Psychology*, **15**, 3–12.

Gustafsson, R. (1988). *Tetris*. Aledema, CA: Spectrum Holobyte Software.

Helsen, W. F., and Pauwels, J. M. (1993). The relationship between expertise and visual information processing in sport. In: J. L. Starkes and F. Allard (ed.) *Cognitive issues in motor expertise*. Amsterdam: Elsevier, pp. 109–34.

Henderson, J. M. (2003). Human gaze control during real-world scene perception. *Trends in Cognitive Science*, **7**, 498–504.

Herz, J. C. (1997). *Joystick nation: How videogames ate our quarters, won our hearts and rewired our minds*. Boston: Little Brown.

Itti, L., and Koch, C. (2000). A saliency-based search mechanism for overt and covert shifts of visual attention. *Vision Research*, **40**, 1489–1506.

James. N., and Patrick, J. (2004). The role of situation awareness in sport. In: S. Banbury and S. Tremblay (ed.) *A cognitive approach to situation awareness.* Aldershot: Ashgate Publishing, pp. 297–316.

Jones, G. (2003). Testing two cognitive theories of insight. *Journal of Experimental Psychology: Learning, Memory and Cognition,* **29,** 1017–1027.

Kirsh, D., and Maglio P. (1994). On distinguishing epistemic from pragmatic actions. *Cognitive Science,* **18,** 513–549.

Knoblich, G., Ohlsson, S., Haider, H., and Rhenius, D. (1999). Constraint relaxation and chunk decomposition in insight problem solving. *Journal of Experimental Psychology: Learning, Memory and Cognition,* **25,** 1534–1555.

Knoblich, G., Ohlsson, S., and Raney, G. E. (2001). An eye movement study of insight problem solving. *Memory and Cognition.* **29,** 1000–1009.

MacGregor, J. N., Ormerod. T. C., and Chronicle, E. P. (2001). Information processing and insight: A process model of performance on the nine-dot and related problems. *Journal of Experimental Psychology: Learning, Memory and Cognition,* **27,** 176–201.

Maier, N. R. F. (1931). Reasoning in humans II: The solution of a problem and its appearance in consciousness. *Journal of Comparative Psychology,* **12,** 181–194.

Mayer, R. E., and Wittrock, M. C. (1996). Problem-solving transfer. In: D. Berliner and R. Calfee (ed.), *Handbook of educational psychology.* New York: Macmillan, pp. 47–62.

McClurg, P.A., and Chaille, C. (1987). Computer games: Environments for developing spatial cognition? *Journal of Educational Computing Research,* **3,** 95–111.

O'Hara, K. P., and Payne, S. J. (1998). The effects of operator implementation cost on planfulness of problem solving and learning. *Cognitive Psychology,* **35,** 34–70.

Okagaki, L., and Frensch, P. A. (1994). Effects of video game playing on measures of spatial performance: gender effects in later adolescence. *Journal of Applied Developmental Psychology,* **15,** 33–58.

Parkhurst, D., Law, K., and Niebur, E. (2002). Modeling the role of salience in the allocation of overt visual attention. *Vision Research,* **42,** 107–123.

Pirolli, P., and Recker, M. (1994). Learning strategies and transfer in the domain of programming. *Cognition and Instruction,* **12,** 235–275.

Rabbitt, P., Banerji, N., and Szymanski, A. (1989). Space Fortress as an IQ Test: predictions of learning and of practiced performance in a complex interactive video-game. *Acta Psychologica,* **71,** 243–257.

Rayner, K. (1998). Eye movements in reading and information processing: 20 years of research. *Psychological Bulletin,* **124,** 372–422.

Scaife, M., and Rogers, Y. (1996). External cognition : how do graphical representations work? *International Journal of Human-Computer Studies* **45,** 185 – 213.

Scheerer, M. (1963). Problem Solving. *Scientific American,* **208,** 118–128.

Shepard, R. N., and Cooper, L. A. (1982). *Mental images and their transformations.* Cambridge, MA: MIT Press.

Sims, V. K., and Mayer, R. E. (2002). Domain specificity of spatial expertise: the case of video game players. *Applied Cognitive Psychology,* **16,** 97–115.

Subrahmanyam, K., and Greenfield, P. M. (1994). Effect of video game practice on spatial skills in girls and boys. *Journal of Applied Developmental Psychology,* **15,** 13–32.

Tarr, M. J., and Pinker, S. (1989) Mental rotation and orientation dependence in shape recognition. *Cognitive Psychology,* **21,** 233–282.

Thornburg, D. G., and Pea, R. D. (1991). Synthesising instructional technologies and educational culture: exploring cognition and metacognition in the social studies. *Journal of Educational Computing Research*, **7**, 121–164.

Thorpe, S. J., Fize, D., and Marlot, C. (1996). Speed of processing in the human visual system. *Nature*, **381**, 520–522.

Volet, S. E. (1991) Modelling and coaching of relevant metacognitive strategies for enhancing university students' learning. *Learning and Instruction*, **1**, 319–336.

Underwood, G., Chapman, P., Brocklehurst, N., Underwood, J., and Crundall, D. (2003). Visual attention while driving: Sequences of eye fixations made by experienced and novice drivers. *Ergonomics*, **46**, 629–646.

Weisberg, R. W., and Alba, J. W. (1981). An examination of the alleged role of 'fixation' in the solution of several 'insight' problems. *Journal of Experimental Psychology: General*, **110**, 169–192.

Williams, A. M., and Davids, K. (1998). Visual search strategy, selective attention and expertise in soccer. *Research Quarterly for Exercise and Sport*, **69**, 111–128.

14

Perception in chess: Evidence from eye movements

Eyal M. Reingold and Neil Charness

Abstract

We review and report findings from a research program by Reingold, Charness and their colleagues (Charness *et al* 2001; Reingold *et al.* 2001a, 2001b) that employed eye-movement paradigms and provided strong support for the suggestion of de Groot (1946, 1965) and Chase and Simon (1973a, 1973b) that a perceptual advantage is a fundamental component of chess skill. We demonstrated dramatically larger visual spans for experts while processing structured, but not random, chess positions. In addition, consistent with the encoding of chunks rather than individual pieces, experts made fewer fixations, and fixated between related pieces, rather than on pieces. It was also shown that chess piece saliency influenced the selection of experts' saccadic endpoints, and that experts completed the perceptual encoding phase and started the problem-solving phase sooner than intermediates. Finally, we demonstrated that experts, but not less-skilled players, extract chess relations using automatic and parallel procedures.

Introduction

Chess research dates back to the beginning of modern experimental psychology during the late 1800s and early 1900s (e.g. Binet 1894; Cleveland 1907; Djakow *et al.* 1927). Since the initiation of the field of artificial intelligence (AI), the pioneers of this discipline considered chess an ideal model domain for exploring search and evaluation processes in their attempt to construct skillful chess programs (see Berliner 1978 for a review). Indeed, during the last century, chess research has proven to be very instrumental in enhancing our understanding of human expertise and in contributing to the study of AI (for reviews see Charness 1992; Ericsson and Charness 1994; Gobet and Charness in press; Gobet *et al.* 2004). The usefulness of chess for the study of cognitive science is strongly advocated in the proposal by Simon and Chase (1973) that similar to the use of *Drosophila* (the fruit fly) as a model organism for the study of genetics, chess offers cognitive scientists an ideal task environment for the study of cognitive processes in general, and skilled performance in particular. Consistent with this idea, Newell and Simon (1972) selected chess as one of the three model tasks that they used in developing their highly influential information processing theory of human problem solving.

Chess research is appealing in part because it offers a rich, ecologically valid environment, which at the same time permits rigorous experimental control. One key methodological advantage in this area is the existence of an interval-level chess rating scale that is based on the outcome of competitions between players (Elo 1965, 1986), and which provides a true gold standard for the measurement of skill. In the vast majority of other areas of expertise, identifying true experts and quantifying the difference in skill across individuals is often a very complex and difficult methodological hurdle. In order to illustrate the chess ratings scale, Fig. 14.1 shows a distribution of ratings provided by the United States Chess Federation. Note that currently, the

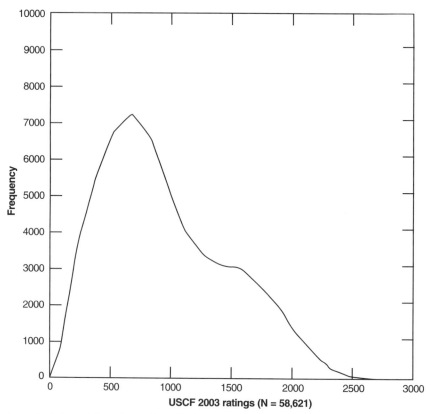

Figure 14.1 The United States Chess Federation (USCF) 2003 rating distribution (*n* = 58,621).

world's best players achieve ratings just above 2800 rating points. In addition, Grandmaster, International Master and Master levels of performance approximately correspond to 2500, 2400, and 2200 rating points respectively. As well, Expert and Class A levels are often defined as corresponding to the ranges 2000–2199 rating points and 1800–1999 rating points respectively.

Other characteristics of chess, including an efficient and extensive documentation of domain specific knowledge, and the prevalence of formalized symbolic representations, greatly facilitate using chess as a task environment for cognitive research and modeling, and for AI investigations. Chess is also ideal for studying nonverbal spatial problem solving. Furthermore, given that chess is played across the lifespan (4- or 5-year-old children to elderly adults) it offers a rare opportunity for studying the relation between age and skill.

Arguably, the most important contribution of chess research is in producing a major theoretical shift in the conceptualization of expertise in cognitive science, away from viewing skilled performance as the product of superior general intelligence and innate talent, toward the recognition that expertise largely reflects domain-specific knowledge acquired through extensive deliberate practice (for a review see Ericsson and Charness 1994). This dramatic change in perspective originated from pioneering work on chess by de Groot (1946, 1965) and Chase and Simon (1973a, 1973b). Prior to the publication of this research the prevailing view was that chess grandmasters were vastly superior to their less-able opponents, in terms of their general intelligence and thinking skills, and in terms of their ability to plan and consider long sequences of chess moves and countermoves. However, de Groot's research challenged some of these assumptions.

In his research de Groot (1946, 1965) instructed two groups of players (experts vs. grandmasters) to think aloud as they identified the best move for chess positions. From his analysis of the players' verbal protocols de Groot determined that although grandmasters were better than expert players in selectively exploring the most promising moves, they did not search further ahead through the sequences of moves as compared with their less-skilled counterparts. Thus, de Groot failed to document the expected difference between experts and grandmasters in the depth and breadth of the serial search through the space of possible moves. More recent research confirmed that depth-of-search effects as a function of skill are relatively small, and are only found when weaker players than those in de Groot's sample are included in the study (Charness 1981; Gobet 1998a; Holding and Reynolds 1982), for instance, those rated up to about 2000 rating points (Elo 1986). (In the Elo system, players are rated on an interval level scale, based on tournament performance, that starts at approximately 0 points and extends upwards. Grandmasters typically are rated about 2500 Elo points or higher; masters are about 2200–2399 points; experts are those between 2000 and 2199 points.) In contrast, performance on another task introduced by de Groot was shown to vary markedly as a function of chess skill. In this task players were briefly shown chess positions (2–15 s). Following this brief exposure, grandmasters were able to reproduce the locations of the chess pieces almost perfectly (about 93 per cent correct for positions containing about 25 pieces) and substantially better than expert players.

In a classic study, Chase and Simon (1973a, 1973b) replicated and extended de Groot's findings, demonstrating that after viewing valid (game) chess positions for 5 s, chess masters were able to reproduce these positions much more accurately than less-skilled players. However, there was little difference as a function of expertise when random board configurations were used instead of game positions. More recently, a very small but reliable advantage in recall for random configurations has been shown for expert players, although this is probably attributable to the occasional presence of familiar configurations in random positions (Gobet and Simon 1996a, 2000). Chase and Simon's (1973a, 1973b) finding that a master was only superior in the 5-s recall task when structured positions, rather than randomized positions, were presented, challenged the view that chess masters are superior in terms of their cognitive apparatus or processes (e.g. hardware aspects of perception, attention or memory). Rather, Chase and Simon (1973a, 1973b) postulated that knowledge of patterns specific to the domain of chess supported effective search for good moves. Soon, similar findings were reported for experts in other domains including bridge players (Charness 1979), music students (Beal 1985), electronics technicians (Egan and Schwartz 1979), and basketball players (Allard *et al.* 1980). Further illustrating the critical importance of knowledge structures for performance, work by Chi (1978) comparing skilled child chess players with novice adults, showed an advantage for children on chess recall but an adult advantage for digit recall. Furthermore, Simon and Chase (1973) reported that a 10-year period of intense preparation is necessary to reach the level of an international chess master strongly refuting the view that chess mastery can be achieved effortlessly in some individuals with superior general intelligence (see Ericsson *et al.* 1993 for a review).

As should be clear from the above discussion, research on chess by de Groot (1946, 1965) and Chase and Simon (1973a, 1973b) fundamentally transformed the study of expertise by highlighting the importance of domain-specific knowledge acquired through practice, and by de-emphasizing the role of innate talent and general ability in underlying skilled performance. In addition, these researchers introduced important investigative tools that have proven invaluable in subsequent studies of expertise such as the 5-s recall task employing domain-related and randomized patterns (see Ericsson and Smith 1991 for a review), and the think-aloud protocol analysis (see Ericsson and Simon 1993 for a review).

A thorough review of the contributions of chess research to the study of cognitive processes in general, and expertise in particular, is beyond the scope of the present chapter (for reviews see Charness 1992; Ericsson and Charness 1994; Gobet and Charness, in press). Rather, we will focus on an important argument advanced by de Groot (1946, 1965) and Chase and Simon (1973a, 1973b), which is best understood by considering the juxtaposition of the two key results reported by these investigators:

1) de Groot's (1946, 1965) finding that grandmasters select better moves than their less-able counterparts despite the absence of a difference across groups in the depth or breadth of the search.

2) Chase and Simon's (1973a, 1973b) finding that the master's advantage in encoding and recalling structured chess positions does not generalize to a condition in

which chess-related patterns are obliterated by randomly rearranging pieces on the chessboard.

Taken together, these findings suggest that chess grandmasters use efficient perceptual encoding of chess configurations to generate the most promising candidate moves and to restrict their reliance on the effortful and slow serial search through the space of possible moves. According to this view the efficiency of these pattern recognition processes in encoding chess configurations and the quality of the moves triggered by the extracted patterns is strongly correlated with chess expertise. However, the knowledge of chess experts concerning familiar chess-related patterns is rendered largely ineffective during the perceptual organization and internal representation of the randomized chess configurations.

Consistent with the above argument both de Groot (1946, 1965) and Chase and Simon (1973a, 1973b) highlight the importance of perceptual encoding of chess configurations as the key determinant of chess skill. For example, in a seminal paper entitled 'Perception in Chess', Chase and Simon (1973a) introduced their chunking theory of skilled performance in chess, stressing the role of perceptual encoding. Echoing an earlier conclusion by de Groot (1946, 1965) that the efficiency of perceptual encoding processes was a more important differentiator of chess expertise than was the ability to think ahead in the search for good moves, Chase and Simon (1973a) argued 'that the most important processes underlying chess mastery are these immediate visual-perceptual processes rather than the subsequent logical-deductive thinking processes' (p. 215). Chase and Simon (1973a, 1973b) postulated that the link between the initial *perceptual phase* and a subsequent *search phase* of the problem-solving process was to be found in the associations between perceptual chunks and plausible move generation. Through extensive study and practice, expert players build up associations between perceptually recognizable chunks (i.e. groups of chess pieces related by type, color, or role) and long-term memory structures that trigger the generation of plausible moves for use by a search mechanism. Search is thereby constrained to the more promising branches in the space of possible moves from a given chess position. The size of an expert's vocabulary of chess-related configurations (chunks) was initially estimated to be between 10 000–100 000 chunks (Simon and Gilmartin 1973) with 50 000 taken as the best estimate (Simon and Chase 1973). However, a more recent estimate puts the number of chunks at approximately 300 000 (Gobet and Simon 2000). In addition, small perceptual chunks are most likely supplemented by larger structures termed templates (Gobet and Simon 1996b; Gobet and Simon 1998).

In the remainder of this chapter we review the available empirical evidence pertaining to the suggestion of Chase and Simon (1973a, 1973b) and de Groot (1946, 1965) that a perceptual advantage is a fundamental component of chess skill. In particular, the present review is predominantly focused on key findings obtained from studies employing eye-movement monitoring methodology. Accordingly, we begin with a brief review of evidence concerning perceptual encoding in chess based on early studies employing eye-movement measurement. We then provide a detailed summary and review of a research program by Reingold, Charness and their colleagues (Charness *et al.* 2001;

Reingold *et al.* 2001a, 2001b) that employed more modern eye-movement paradigms and provided strong support for enhanced perceptual encoding as a function of chess expertise.

Predictions and early studies

An important goal of the present review is to illustrate the potential role of eye-movement measurement in supplementing traditional measures of performance such as reaction time (RT), accuracy, and verbal reports as a means for investigating the perceptual aspects of skilled performance in general, and chess skill in particular. Given the pivotal role played by eye-movement paradigms in the study of reading skill (see Rayner 1998 for a review) it is surprising that there are very few empirical studies which have employed these techniques in chess. One facilitating factor for using eye-movement measurement in chess is that just like words and sentences, the chess board is easily, visually segmentable. In addition, if as suggested by Chase and Simon (1973a, 1973b) and de Groot (1946, 1965), chess masters perceptually encode chess positions more efficiently by relying upon larger patterns of related pieces (i.e. chunks), then several predictions concerning differences in eye-movement patterns between expert and intermediate players can be made. For example, encoding of chunks rather than individual pieces may mean fewer fixations, and fixations between related pieces, rather than on pieces. This may also imply that in any given fixation experts process information about a larger segment of the chessboard than less-skilled players, con-stituting an increase in the perceptual or visual span as a function of expertise. That is, experts are expected to make greater use of parafoveal processing than intermediate players. In addition, experts may make greater use of automatic and parallel extraction of chess relations relative to intermediate players.

Several early studies employing eye-movement measurement provided weak sup-port for the idea that perception of chess-related configurations improves with skill. Tikhomirov and Poznyanskaya (1966) and Winikoff (1967) both found evidence that when chess players fixate on a chess piece, they also extract information about other pieces near the point of gaze and often move to fixate a related piece. Based on this general process, Simon and Barenfeld (1969) devised a computer model to simulate the initial scanning patterns chess players might use when encoding a chess position. Their simulation, PERCEIVER, produced eye-movement patterns that resembled those of chess players. Reynolds (1982) and Holding (1985) re-examined the eye-movement data collected by Tikhomirov and Poznyanskaya (1966), and noted that many fixations did not fall on pieces, but on empty squares. However, because these studies were not focused on individual differences, there was no report of systematic variation in the proportion of fixations on empty squares as a function of skill.

Re-analyzing the work of Jongman (1968), de Groot and Gobet (1996) reported no significant difference in the proportion of fixations on empty squares as a function of skill. These authors cautioned, however, that the negative results do not necessarily refute the chunking hypothesis. They pointed out that the crude frame-by-frame analysis of film records of eye movements and the transformation of gaze positions from a three-dimensional chessboard viewed by the players to a two-dimensional co-ordinate system may have resulted in the introduction of noise making it difficult to estimate the accuracy of the computed gaze position. Furthermore, de Groot and Gobet (1996) demonstrated that skilled players made more fixations along the edges of squares (28.7 per cent of fixations) as compared with novices (13.7 per cent), providing some indication that the skilled players may be able to encode two or more pieces in a single fixation. In addition, on the basis of their analysis of retrospective verbal reports, de Groot and Gobet (1996) concluded that the best players tended to perceive groups of pieces, rather than individual pieces. Finally, they developed a successful computer simulation that depended heavily on chunk differences to simulate eye-movement patterns differences between novices and experts.

Recent studies

In this section of the chapter we provide an extensive review of the findings we reported in several previous publications (Charness *et al.* 2001; Reingold *et al.* 2001a, 2001b). In addition, we report new data from several additional experiments, which we conducted, that replicate and extend the published findings. We also include re-analysis of published data in order to facilitate the integration of results across papers.

Visual span and chess expertise

In Reingold *et al.* (2001a) we predicted that the perceptual advantage demonstrated by chess experts is mediated by a larger visual span for chess-related, but not for chess-unrelated, visual patterns. Such an increase in the visual span as a function of skill would indicate that while examining structured but not random chess configurations, experts extract information from a larger portion of the chessboard during an eye fixation (hence the term visual span, also referred to in the literature as the perceptual span or the span of effective vision, see Jacobs 1986; Rayner 1998). We tested this prediction by employing two different tasks: 1) A 'change blindness' flicker paradigm, and 2) A check detection paradigm. The tasks and results are described below.

The participants in the flicker paradigm were 16 novices who reported playing no games of chess in the past year and very few games over their lifetime, 8 intermediates and 8 experts. Mean Chess Federation of Canada (CFC) ratings were 1483 (range = 1300–1700) and 2278 (range = 2200–2400) for the intermediates and experts respectively. Another group of 20 novices, 10 intermediates, and 10 experts participated in the check detection task. CFC ratings for the expert players ranged between 1950–2352 (mean = 2117) and CFC ratings for the intermediates ranged between 962–1387 (mean = 1226). Eye movements were measured with an SR Research Ltd. EyeLink system.

The change blindness flicker paradigm

The flicker paradigm was introduced by Rensink *et al.* (1997). In the present application of this paradigm, two types of configurations were used: chess configurations (with 20 chess pieces in each) selected from a large database of chess games, and random configurations, which were created by repeatedly and randomly exchanging pieces in the chess configurations. Thus, random positions maintained the same spatial configuration but destroyed the chess relation information. Each random or chess configuration was modified by changing the identity but not the color of a single piece to create a modified display (see the two diagrams in the top row of Fig. 14.2 for an illustration of an original and a modified display of a chess configuration). In each trial, images of the original and modified board configurations were displayed sequentially and alternated repeatedly with a blank interval between each pair of configurations (i.e. original, blank, modified, blank, original ...). Each variant of the configuration (i.e. original, modified) was presented for 1000 ms, with the display blanking for 100 ms between each alternation. As soon as participants detected the changing piece (the target), they ended the trial by pressing a button and naming the alternating pieces. Previous research indicated that participants are surprisingly poor

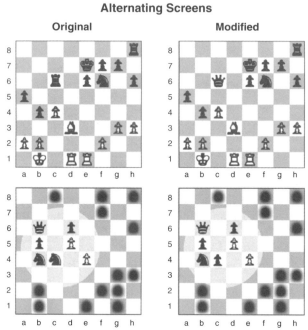

Figure 14.2 Illustration of the gaze-contingent flicker paradigm. The top row displays an original (left) and a modified (right) chess configuration taken from an actual game (the changed piece is in square c6). The top row also illustrates a no-window baseline trial in which the entire display was visible. The bottom row displays an original (left) and a modified (right) chess configuration (the changed piece is in square c4) in a gaze-contingent window condition, with chess pieces outside the window being replaced by blobs masking their identity and color (note that the difference in luminance between the regions inside and outside the window was not present in actual experimental displays and was added here for illustrative purposes). From Reingold *et al.* (2001a).

at change detection in the flicker paradigm, a phenomenon termed 'change blindness' (Rensink *et al.* 1997; see Simons and Levin 1997 for a review). We predicted that when processing chess configurations, but not random configurations, chess experts would demonstrate larger visual spans and better change detection than less-skilled players.

In this task the visual span as a function of chess skill (novice vs. intermediate vs. expert) and configuration type (chess configuration vs. random configuration) was measured using a gaze-contingent window technique (e.g. McConkie and Rayner 1975; see Rayner 1998, for a review). As shown in Fig. 14.2 (bottom row), a gaze-contingent window requires obscuring the identity of all chess pieces except those within a certain 'window' that is continually centered on the participant's gaze position. The pieces outside a circular, gaze-centered window were replaced with gray blobs masking the actual colors and shapes. The participant's visual span was measured by varying the size of the window over successive trials and determining the smallest possible window that did not significantly differ from the participant's normative RT criteria. These criteria were established separately for chess configuration and random configuration by using baseline trials in which the entire display was visible (i.e. no-window trials; see top row of Fig. 14.2). Note that change detection in the present task required no chess knowledge and consequently we were able to explore visual span across a broad range of chess skill stretching from novice to master.

For each skill group by configuration type, Fig. 14.3, Panel A displays the average median RTs obtained in the no-window baseline trials that were used to compute the normative RT criteria. As can be clearly seen in this figure, the difference between RTs in chess vs. random configuration trials was only significant in the expert group. Furthermore, for random configuration trials RTs did not differ significantly across skill groups. In contrast, on chess configuration trials RTs were significantly different across groups, with experts being significantly faster than both intermediates and novices. The visual span results shown in Fig. 14.3, Panel B follow the same pattern as the RT results. Specifically, experts' span area for chess configurations was dramatically larger than all other skill groups by configuration type cells, which in turn did not differ from each other. Thus, consistent with Chase and Simon's hypothesis (1973a, 1973b), the increase in visual span area and speed of responding which characterizes expert performance on trials with chess, but not random configurations, clearly indicates an encoding advantage attributable to chess experience, rather than to a general perceptual or memory superiority.

The check detection task

To examine differences in the spatial distribution of fixations between experts and novices, we monitored eye movements of another sample of chess players in a check detection task. Saariluoma (1985) has shown that master players can rapidly and accurately decide whether a chess piece is attacked, and do so more quickly than their less-skilled counterparts. The rather simple chess relation of check detection (attack of a king) is highly salient and presents a good model for the extraction of chess-relevant relations among pieces. As shown in Fig. 14.4 (top 2 rows), in the present study check detection was performed using a minimized 3×3 chessboard containing a black king and one or two potentially checking pieces. At the beginning of each trial, participants

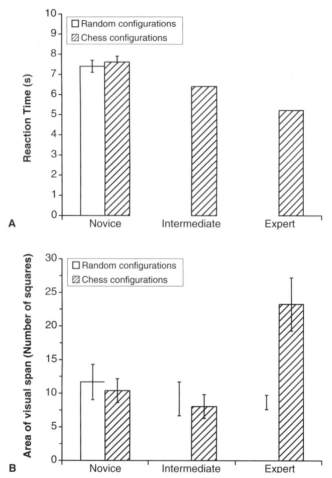

Figure 14.3 Median reaction times in the no-window baseline trials (Panel A) and area of visual span (number of squares) (Panel B) in the flicker paradigm by skill and configuration type. Data from Reingold *et al.* (2001a).

fixated the center square of the board, a square that was always empty. A large visual span in this task may result in few, if any, saccades, during a trial and in fixations between, rather than on individual pieces. To demonstrate that the encoding advantage of experts is related at least in part to their chess experience, rather than to a general perceptual superiority, we manipulated the familiarity of the notation (symbol vs. letter) used to represent the chess pieces. The symbol and letter notations (row 1 vs. 2 in Fig. 14.4) were used to represent identical chess problems. However, the symbol representation is much more familiar than the letter representation. Consequently, if encoding efficiency is related to chess experience, any skill advantage should be more pronounced in the symbol than in the letter trials (i.e. a skill by notation interaction).

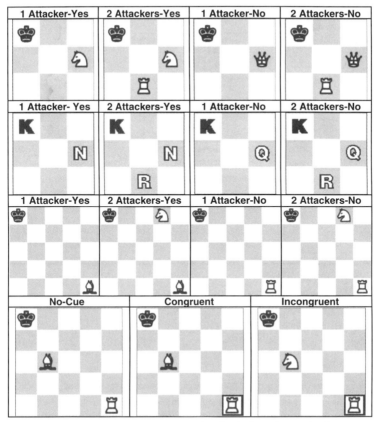

Figure 14.4 Illustration of the stimuli used in the check detection task. The top two rows illustrate the notation manipulation (row 1 – symbol vs. row 2 – letter) in Reingold *et al.* (2001a). The third row illustrates the manipulation of check status (present/'yes' vs. absent/'no' trials) by number of attackers (one vs. two) in Reingold *et al.* (2001b). The bottom row illustrates the Stroop manipulation in Reingold *et al.* (2001b) and in a replication study (see text for details). Three conditions are shown, the no-cue condition that consisted of 'no' trials with two attackers and two conditions in which a cued non-checking attacker (shown surrounded by a frame) appeared together with an attacker that was either congruent (i.e. non-checking) or incongruent (i.e. checking). In the latter two conditions the task was to determine if the cued attacker was checking the king while ignoring the other attacker.

In order to compare the spatial distributions of gaze positions in the check detection task across the novice, intermediate and expert groups, Fig. 14.5 shows scattergrams with each dot representing an individual gaze position. An inspection of the scattergrams collapsing across all trial types (i.e. the spatial layout of chess pieces, check status, and notation), with initial gaze positions included (the top row of Fig. 14.5), reveals a greater concentration of black pixels in the center of the scattergram

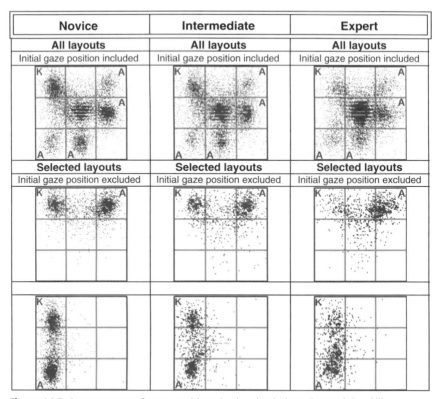

Figure 14.5 Scattergrams of gaze positions in the check detection task by skill. The capital letter 'A' represents the position of an attacker piece and 'K' represents the position of the king. Data from Reingold *et al.* (2001a).

for the experts as compared with the intermediates and novices. This center of gravity effect reflects a large disparity between skill groups in the proportion of trials without an eye-movement (i.e. no-saccade trials). In such trials the gaze position remained in the center square of the chessboard throughout the duration of the trial. For each skill group by notation type, Panel A of Fig. 14.6 displays the proportion of no-saccade trials. As can be clearly seen in this figure, only the expert group demonstrated a substantial proportion of no-saccade trials and the proportion of such trials was greater for the symbol notation than the letter notation in this group of players.

As shown in Fig. 14.6 Panel B, in trials in which eye movements occurred, experts made fewer fixations than intermediates and novices. More importantly, for both experts and intermediates, but not for novices, the symbol notation resulted in fewer fixations than the letter notation. In order to compare the spatial distribution of fixation positions across groups we computed the proportion of fixations landing on squares containing chess pieces (henceforth proportion on pieces). Examining scattergrams with initial gaze positions excluded (the middle and bottom rows of Fig. 14.5) clearly indicates that experts made proportionately fewer fixations on pieces

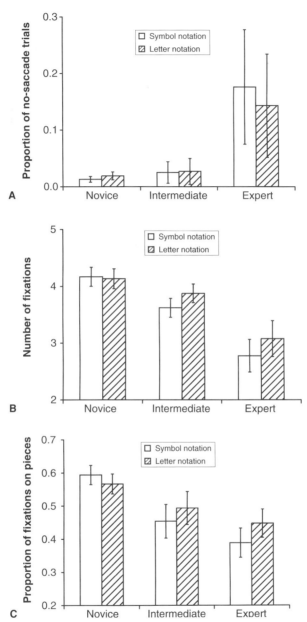

Figure 14.6 Proportion of no-saccade trials (Panel A), number of fixations (Panel B) and the proportion of fixations on pieces (Panel C) in the check detection task by skill and notation. Data from Reingold *et al.* (2001a).

than did intermediates and novices. As shown in Fig. 14.6, Panel C, for both experts and intermediates, the symbol notation resulted in fewer fixations on pieces than the letter notation, with the opposite being the case for novices.

Thus, consistent with Chase and Simon's (1973a, 1973b) chunking hypothesis, in the check detection task, chess experts made fewer fixations and placed a greater proportion of fixations *between* individual pieces, rather than *on* pieces. The magnitude of these effects was stronger for the more familiar symbol notation than for the letter notation, demonstrating that the experts' encoding advantage is related at least in part to their chess experience, rather than to a general perceptual superiority.

Automatic and parallel extraction of chess relations as a function of expertise

Based in part on the dramatic demonstration of larger visual span in chess experts, Reingold *et al.* (2001b) proposed that one possible mechanism that may allow chess masters to process chess configurations more efficiently is automatic and parallel extraction of several chess relations that together constitute a meaningful chunk. A prerequisite for the encoding of chess relations is the identification of pieces and locations. Thus, we envision a two-phase process underlying the encoding of meaningful chess positions. In the first phase, players encode the identity (type and color) and location of chess pieces (the locations of pieces are encoded via absolute location coding rather than relative location coding; Gobet and Simon 1996b; Saariluoma 1994). It is important to note that identification of pieces and locations is likely to involve multiple processes, some of which are serial in nature (e.g. directing or focusing of spatial attention that is often accompanied by eye movements) and consequently, total encoding time will be sensitive to the number of pieces in a configuration. In the second phase, which may partially overlap (i.e. cascade) with the first phase (see McClelland 1979 for a framework for analyzing processes in cascade), players process internal representations that contain piece identity and location information to extract or compute chess relations. This process can be seen as binding pieces into chess chunks.

Based on the results reviewed above, it is likely that the main perceptual advantage for experts is not in the identification of single chess pieces and board locations (i.e. phase 1 processes), but rather in the extraction of relational information between pieces (i.e. phase 2 processes). This is powerfully demonstrated by the strong skill effects on the area of the visual span obtained with actual chess configurations (i.e. where relational information is intact), coupled with the absence of skill effects on span size obtained with random configurations (i.e. where relational information is broken down). Accordingly, the research described in this section was specifically designed to test the hypothesis of automatic and parallel extraction of chess relations by experts.

We employed a check detection task in a minimized 5×5 section of the chessboard, containing a king and one or two potentially checking pieces. In the first part of the experiment we manipulated checking status (i.e. the presence or absence of a checking piece for 'yes' and 'no' trials respectively) and the number of attackers (one or two). As shown in the four diagrams in the third row of Fig. 14.4, adding a distractor (i.e. a non-checking piece) created trials with two attackers. We reasoned that if the chess relations between each of the attackers and the king are processed in a serial self-terminating manner, the RT cost of adding a distractor should be differentially greater in 'no' trials than in 'yes' trials. This is the case because an accurate response in 'no' trials requires considering both potentially checking relations, whereas, by chance, on half of the 'yes' trials the checking relation is examined first, permitting an accurate termination of the trial without considering the second attacker. In contrast, parallel processing of chess relations will manifest as comparable RT costs for adding a distractor across both types of trials. See Treisman and Gelade (1980) and Wolfe (1998) for a similar methodology aimed at documenting parallel visual search.

Note that we are predicting a reaction time cost for adding an attacker (i.e. one vs. two attackers), even for expert players, due to the prerequisite encoding of piece identity and location prior to the extraction of chess relations. The cost should occur because serial processing in phase 1 is assumed to be sensitive to the number of pieces in the configuration. Although the same prediction applies also to the check detection task in Reingold *et al.* (2001a) (see the four diagrams in the top row of Fig. 14.4) it was not tested in the published paper. We therefore present the results of an identical analysis for both papers (Reingold *et al.* 2001a, 2001b).

Given our interest in documenting automatic extraction of chess relations by experts, we also attempted to demonstrate a skill-related interference effect. The vast majority of studies investigating expertise in general, and chess skill in particular, have documented facilitation effects as a function of skill. That is, experts always outperformed their less-skilled counterparts. However, theories of attention and automaticity have long recognized that interference, such as that in the Stroop paradigm (Stroop 1935; see MacLeod 1992 for a review), is a much more compelling demonstration of automaticity relative to facilitation paradigms (for a related methodology in unconscious memory research see Jacoby 1991; Jacoby *et al.* 1993; Reingold 1995; Reingold and Toth 1996; Toth *et al.* 1994). This is the case because despite a strong incentive to consciously oppose automatic influences, such automatic influences are nevertheless manifested. In a typical demonstration of the Stroop effect, the irrelevant meaning of a color word interferes with the naming of an incongruent ink color in which it is written. Thus, skilled readers cannot strategically avoid the automatic encoding of word meanings despite its detrimental effects on performance.

Accordingly, in the second part of the experiment reported in Reingold *et al.* (2001b) we contrasted the standard check detection trials with two attackers, with trials in which one of two attackers was cued (colored). In this condition, the task was to determine if the cued attacker was checking the king while ignoring the other attacker. In order to avoid any predictability in the stimulus set, the checking status of the cued and uncued attackers were manipulated separately (i.e. yes/yes, yes/no, no/yes and no/no). However, as shown in the bottom row of Fig. 14.4, our predictions focus exclusively on contrasting three conditions: a no-cue condition (i.e. no cueing) which consisted of the standard check detection 'no' trials with two attackers, and two conditions in which a cued non-checking attacker appeared together with an attacker that was either congruent (i.e. non-checking, no/no) or incongruent (i.e. checking, no/yes) (henceforth the congruent and incongruent conditions). Note that all of these trials are 'no' trials even though the incongruent condition contains a checking attacker. That is, in the incongruent condition, the semantics of the cued chess relation (i.e. no check) is inconsistent with the semantics of the configuration as a whole (i.e. check). Serial processing of chess relations will manifest as faster RTs in the congruent condition, than in the no-cue condition, as the cueing constrains the search space. In contrast, parallel processing of chess relations should result in no benefit from cueing in the congruent condition. In addition, if parallel processing of chess relations occurs, cueing should produce slower RTs in the incongruent, than in the congruent condition, demonstrating Stroop-like interference.

We also conducted a replication study to the Stroop condition reported in Reingold et al. (2001b). The main difference across these two studies was that eye-movement measurement was added in the replication experiment. A more minor difference concerns the method used across studies to cue an attacker in the congruent and incongruent conditions. Specifically, in the published study, the cued attacker was colored, whereas in the replication study, a colored bold frame surrounded the cued attacker (see bottom row of Fig. 14.4).

In both Reingold et al. (2001b) and the replication study, three groups of 14 participants were included (14 novices, 14 intermediates and 14 experts). In Reingold et al. (2001b) CFC ratings for expert players ranged between 2100–2351 (mean = 2218) and CFC ratings for the intermediates ranged between 1401–2000 (mean = 1799). In the replication study CFC ratings for expert players ranged between 2053–2317 (mean = 2171) and CFC ratings for the intermediates ranged between 1436–1995 (mean = 1738).

Results

The differential cost of adding an attacker in a 'yes' vs. a 'no' trial

Figure 14.7 shows the results from the check status by number of attackers manipulation in both Reingold et al. (2001b) (see Fig. 14.7, Panel A for results; see third row in Fig. 14.4 for an illustration of the stimulus displays and conditions) and in the symbol notation condition in Reingold et al. (2001a) (see Fig. 14.7, Panel B for results; see top row in Fig. 14.4 for an illustration of the stimulus displays and conditions). As shown in Fig. 14.7 the results are extremely similar across studies and are therefore discussed together. Average median RTs were computed for each group and condition (trials on which participants responded incorrectly were excluded). As can be seen in Fig. 14.7, the group by check status by number of attackers interaction was significant. This interaction is best understood by considering the differences in the increase in RTs from one to two attackers for 'yes' vs. 'no' trials. For experts, there was a comparable cost for adding an attacker in both 'yes' trials (Reingold et al. 2001b = 171 ms; Reingold et al. 2001a = 131 ms) and 'no' trials (Reingold et al. 2001b = 167 ms; Reingold et al. 2001a = 123 ms). For intermediates, the corresponding increase for 'yes' trials (Reingold et al; 2001b = 203 ms; Reingold et al. 2001a = 258 ms) was numerically, but not significantly, smaller than 'no' trials (Reingold et al. 2001b = 262 ms; Reingold et al. 2001a = 291 ms). Finally for novices, the increase for 'yes' trials (Reingold et al. 2001b = 330 ms; Reingold et al. 2001a = 299 ms) was substantially and significantly smaller than 'no' trials (Reingold et al. 2001b = 458 ms; Reingold et al. 2001a = 422 ms). Analyzing error rates across the same conditions revealed no evidence of a speed-accuracy trade-off. Thus, in both studies, we documented a greater increase in RT cost for adding a

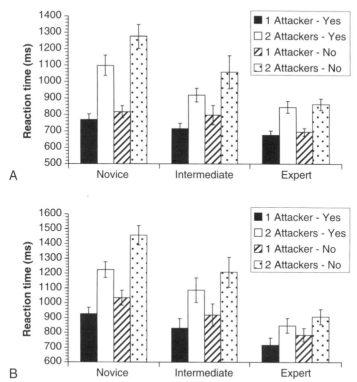

Figure 14.7 Average median reaction times (ms) in the check detection task by skill (expert vs. intermediate vs. novice) by check status (present/'Yes' vs. absent/'no' trials) and by number of attackers (1 vs. 2) in Reingold *et al.* (2001b) (Panel A) and Reingold *et al.* (2001a) (Panel B).

distractor (i.e. one vs. two attackers) in 'no' vs. 'yes' trials for weaker players, but not for experts. This is consistent with the hypothesis that chess experts can extract some chess relations in an automatic and parallel manner.

The chess Stroop condition

As discussed above, with respect to the Stroop manipulation there are two sets of critical contrasts: the no-cue and congruent conditions, and the congruent and incongruent conditions (see bottom row of Fig. 14.4). Figure 14.8, Panel A shows the pattern of RTs across these conditions in Reingold *et al.* (2001b). In addition, Fig. 14.8, Panels B–D present the results of the eye-movement measures for these conditions in the replication experiment.

The no-cue condition included 'no' trials with two uncued attackers. This condition was compared with the congruent condition which was identical to the no-cue condition in all respects except that one of the two attackers was cued and participants were asked to decide whether the cued attacker was checking, disregarding the other attacker.

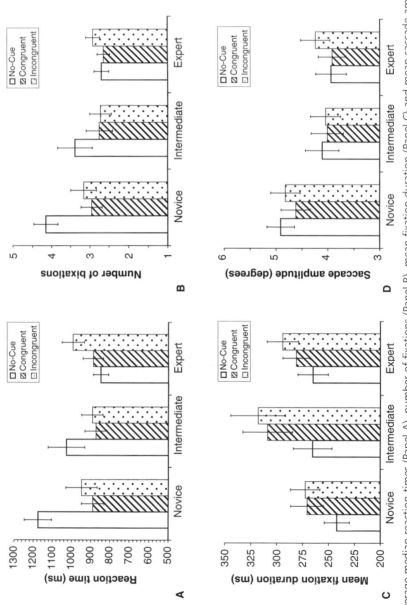

Figure 14.8 Average median reaction times (Panel A), number of fixations (Panel B), mean fixation duration (Panel C) and mean saccade amplitude (Panel D) in the check detection task by skill and condition (no-cue vs. congruent vs. incongruent). Data from Reingold et al. (2001b) and a replication study (see text for details).

If processing of chess relations is serial, the cueing in the congruent condition should improve performance compared with the no-cue condition because it eliminates the necessity to examine one of two potentially checking relations. On the other hand, in the case of parallel extraction of chess relations, cueing should not produce such facilitation. In addition, if parallel processing of chess relations occurs, cueing should produce worse performance in the incongruent, than in the congruent condition, demonstrating Stroop-like interference.

When comparing the congruent and the no-cue conditions in Fig. 14.8, Panel A, it is clear that experts derived no benefit from cueing (there was a non-significant trend in the opposite direction: 24 ms). In marked contrast, for both the intermediates and novices, the cueing in the congruent condition produced substantial facilitation relative to the no-cue condition (intermediates: 187 ms, novices: 386 ms). A very similar pattern was obtained in the replication experiment. Figure 14.8, Panel B shows that for intermediates and novices, cueing in the congruent condition produced facilitation in the form of fewer fixations relative to the no-cue condition. In contrast, for experts there was no significant difference in the number of fixations across these conditions.

When comparing the congruent and the incongruent conditions in Fig. 14.8, Panel A, it is evident that the experts demonstrated Stroop-like interference (a significant 105 ms slowing). Intermediates demonstrated no significant interference (19 ms slowing) and novices demonstrated marginally significant interference (58 ms slowing). Note, however, that for both the intermediates and novices, but not for the experts, the beneficial effects of cueing (i.e. constraining the search space) far outweighed any disruption caused by the uncued checking attacker, resulting in a net facilitation effect (incongruent vs. no-cue: intermediates: 136 ms facilitation; novices: 228 ms facilitation; experts: 144 ms interference). Similarly, as shown in Fig. 14.8, experts demonstrated Stroop-like interference effects on the eye movements measures producing significantly more fixations (Panel B), longer mean fixation duration (Panel C) and larger amplitude saccades (Panel D) in the incongruent condition as compared with the congruent condition.

Summary

Across all of the experiments employing the check detection paradigm (Reingold *et al.* 2001a, 2001b; and the eye-movement replication study reported here), there are three convergent findings demonstrating parallel extraction of chess relations by experts. First, we documented a greater increase in RT cost for adding a distractor (i.e. one vs. two attackers) in 'no' vs. 'yes' trials for weaker players, but not for experts. Second, when contrasting the no-cue condition with the congruent condition, it is clear that, unlike weaker players, experts do not benefit from cueing. Note that these two conditions are identical in terms of pieces and locations (both require the same 'no' response) and consequently this contrast provides a particularly powerful way for isolating the chess relation extraction processes. Finally, although parallel extraction of features normally facilitates performance, in the case of the artificial incongruent condition, it produced Stroop-like interference in skilled performers because they could not prevent the generation of a positive response (check present) to the configuration as a whole, even though the cued attacker was non-checking and the correct response was 'no'.

The move-choice task and the issue of ecological validity

Given the strong support for enhanced perceptual encoding as a function of chess expertise obtained in the studies reviewed above (i.e. Reingold *et al.* 2001a, 2001b), in Charness *et al.* (2001) we attempted to extend these findings to the more ecologically valid task of choosing the best move with full chessboard displays (henceforth, the move-choice task). We chose to investigate the move-choice task for several reasons. First, eye-movement studies have long shown that the nature of the task set for the observer can result in very different patterns of fixations for the same visual configuration (e.g. Yarbus 1967). The fixation patterns for memorizing a chess position (de Groot and Gobet 1996) or performing simple check detection (Reingold *et al.* 2001a) may not be representative of those in problem solving situations. Second, de Groot (1946, 1965) demonstrated that performance on the move-choice task (quality of move chosen) discriminates well between chess players at different levels of skill.

In this section of the paper we review the findings from two experiments that recorded eye movements of players during the performance of the move-choice task. An experiment by Charness *et al.* (2001) and an unpublished follow-up experiment. Twelve intermediate and 12 expert chess players participated in the experiment by Charness *et al.* (2001). CFC ratings for the expert players ranged between 2100–2350 (mean = 2238). CFC ratings for the intermediates ranged between 1400–1923 (mean = 1786). Ten intermediates, and ten experts participated in the follow-up experiment. CFC ratings for the expert players ranged between 1912–2332 (mean = 2105). CFC ratings for the intermediates ranged between 968–1355 (mean = 1245). In each study five experimental chess positions were used. All positions had a clear best move. Prior to the presentation of each position, players were told who was to move (white or black). Players were asked to choose and announce the best move as quickly and as accurately as possible.

Charness *et al.* (2001)

Given our interest in documenting the influence of expertise on perceptual encoding, in Charness *et al.* (2001) we focused on the first 1–2 s of eye fixations in each trial. This was considered important in order to attribute any potential skill differences to the perceptual, rather than the problem-solving phase. In other words, given that experts encode positions more quickly than intermediate players, going much beyond five fixations might lead to a skill-related confound of fixations used to encode the initial representation vs. fixations that promote problem-solving processes (e.g. search through the space of possible moves). Hence, we investigated the spatial distribution of the first five fixations produced by players who attempt to choose the best move for a given position.

We tested two specific predictions. First, on the basis of the chunking hypothesis and the results of Reingold *et al.* (2001a, 2001b), we predicted that a greater proportion of fixations would occur on empty squares for experts, as compared with intermediates. Second, among fixations occurring on individual pieces, we predicted that a greater proportion of fixations would occur on salient pieces (i.e. tactically active pieces) for experts, as compared with intermediates. The latter prediction is based on a finding by de Groot and Gobet (1996) that the number and total duration of fixations landing on chess pieces during a memorization task were at least partially correlated with the degree of importance or relevance of these pieces in a given position, and that the magnitude of this correlation increased as a function of skill. Similarly, based on their simulation of eye-movement data collected by Tikhomirov and Poznyanskaya (1966), Simon and Barenfeld (1969) argued that fixations fell on what they defined as the salient pieces for the position. In Charness *et al.* (2001) we determined piece saliency for the five positions used in the experiment by asking two international masters to classify pieces as salient or non-salient.

The top panel of Fig. 14.9 illustrates one of the positions used in the experiment. Pieces that were classified as salient are shown in this panel surrounded by a bold frame.

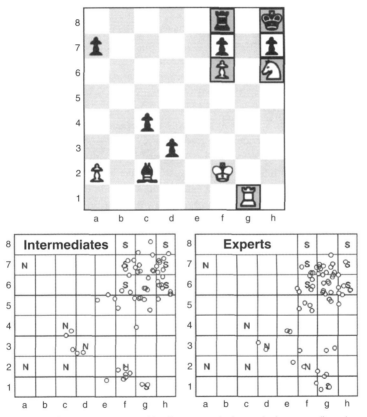

Figure 14.9 One of the positions used in the move choice task; (top panel) and scattergrams of gaze positions corresponding to the first five fixations produced by intermediates (bottom left panel) and experts (bottom right panel) while attempting to choose the best move in this position. Note: chess pieces surrounded by a bold frame in the top panel were judged to be salient (important) in the position by two international masters. In the bottom panels – S = Salient piece; N = Non-salient piece. Best move for this position = white rook moves to g8 check, black rook takes white rook, White knight takes pawn at f7 mate. Data from Charness *et al.* (2001).

The bottom panels in this figure show scattergrams aggregating the first five fixations for this position across intermediates (bottom left) and experts (bottom right). Each circle represents an individual fixation, and fixations were classified as falling on an empty square, or on a square occupied by a salient or a non-salient piece. To facilitate visual comparison across scattergrams, the letter S replaces salient pieces and the letter N replaces pieces that are not salient. As can be clearly seen by comparing the scattergrams, consistent with the chunking hypothesis, experts produced a greater proportion of fixations on empty squares than intermediates (experts: mean = 0.52; intermediates: mean = 0.41). In addition, consistent with de Groot and Gobet (1996), among fixations on pieces, experts produced a greater proportion of fixations on salient pieces than intermediates (experts: mean = 0.80; intermediates: mean = 0.64).

Follow-up experiment

Whereas in Charness *et al.* (2001) the focus was on the first five eye fixations (approximately the first 1–2 s) during the performance of the move-choice task, in the follow-up experiment we recorded fixations during the first 10 s in each trial. We hypothesized that an examination of changes in the number and duration of fixations, which may occur as the trial progresses, would be potentially useful in distinguishing between perceptual encoding and problem solving, or solution retrieval and evaluation. Specifically, perceptual encoding was expected to involve shorter fixations and consequently a greater number of fixations in a given time interval than problem solving. We were also interested in the proportion of fixations with durations greater than 500 ms. Such fixations have been previously identified as reflecting visual problem solving and evaluation (e.g. Nodine *et al.* 1978).

Figure 14.10 shows scattergrams aggregating all fixations in the first 10 s across intermediates (left panel) and experts (right panel) for one of the positions used in

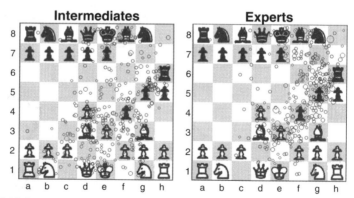

Figure 14.10 Scattergrams aggregating all fixations in the first 10 seconds across intermediates (left panel) and experts (right panel) for one of the positions used in the move choice task in follow-up experiment. Each circle represents an individual fixation, and the diameter of the circle increases as a function of an increase in fixation duration. Best move for this position = white queen takes pawn at h5 check, black rook takes white queen, white bishop moves to g6 mate.

the experiment. Each circle represents an individual fixation, and the diameter of the circle increases as a function of an increase in fixation duration. As can be clearly seen by comparing the scattergrams, consistent with the chunking hypothesis and the findings of Charness *et al.* (2001), experts produced a greater proportion of fixations on empty squares than intermediates (experts: mean = 0.55; intermediates: mean = 0.43). In addition, as indicated by a comparison of the relative size of circles across scattergrams, experts clearly produced a higher proportion of longer fixations than intermediates.

To analyze this issue more formally, we divided the 10-s period of eye-movement recording in the beginning of each trial into two 5-s intervals. We then computed the mean number of fixations and the proportion of fixations with durations > 500 ms in the first and second 5-s intervals across all trials for each player. Figure 14.11 displays these two dependent variables by skill group and interval. As can be seen in this figure, the pattern of performance is qualitatively different across experts and intermediates. Specifically, for intermediates there was no difference across intervals in the number of fixations and in the proportion of long fixations (i.e. > 500 ms).

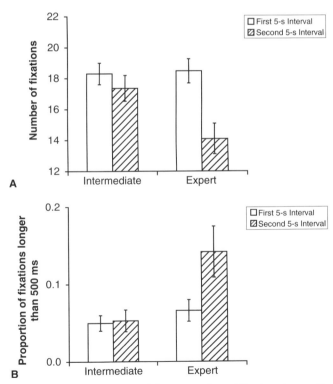

Figure 14.11 Number of fixations (Panel A), and the proportion of fixations longer than 500 ms. (Panel B) in the move choice task by skill and interval (first 5-s interval vs. second 5-s interval).

In marked contrast, experts produced substantially fewer fixations and a much greater proportion of long fixations as the trial progressed. This indicates that during the second 5-s interval in a trial, experts started engaging in problem solving, whereas intermediates were still perceptually encoding the chess configurations. This provides further support for the hypothesis of enhanced efficiency of pattern recognition processes in encoding chess configurations as a function of chess expertise.

Conclusions

The present review illustrates that eye-movement paradigms may prove invaluable in supplementing traditional measures of performance such as RT, accuracy, and verbal reports as a means for understanding human expertise in general, and chess skill in particular. Specifically, by employing eye-movement methodology, the research reviewed and reported here provided powerful and direct evidence for the suggestion of de Groot (1946, 1965) and Chase and Simon (1973a, 1973b) that a perceptual advantage is a fundamental component of chess skill.

The use of the gaze contingent window paradigm demonstrated that advanced chess skill attenuates change blindness by improving target detection in meaningful, but not scrambled chess configurations, and that this is due to a larger visual span size in the former, but not in the latter condition. The methodology reviewed here provided compelling evidence that in the case of check detection, a task that is well defined and for which positional uncertainty is minimized, experts, but not less-skilled players, extract chess relations using automatic and parallel procedures. Such procedures may help explain the greater reliance on parafoveal processing and the larger visual spans demonstrated by experts while examining chess configurations. In addition, the demonstration of a Stroop-like interference effect in experts, but not in intermediates, highlights the fact that expert–novice differences are qualitative, rather than just quantitative in nature. By examining the spatial distribution of fixations in both the simplified check detection task and the ecologically valid move-choice task it was demonstrated that consistent with the encoding of chunks rather than individual pieces, experts made fewer fixations, and fixations between related pieces, rather than on pieces. Furthermore, in the move-choice task the finding that piece saliency influences the selection of experts' saccadic endpoints during the first 1–2 s following display onset clearly supports the role of parafoveal or peripheral processing of chess configurations in guiding their eye movements. This is the case because random or systematic region-by-region scanning patterns (e.g. a reading like pattern from the top-left to the bottom-right section of the chessboard) would not be expected to result in similar findings of saccadic selectivity by piece salience. Finally, in the move-choice task, the comparison of the number and duration of fixations across the first and second 5-s intervals indicated that experts completed the perceptual encoding phase and started the problem solving or search phase sooner than intermediates.

The results of the eye-movement and chess studies reviewed and reported here are consistent with other demonstrations of superior perceptual encoding of chess-related material by experts in immediate recall tasks (see Gobet 1998b for a review), check detection tasks (Church and Church 1983; Milojkovic 1982; Saariluoma 1984), enumeration tasks (e.g. count the number of bishops – Saariluoma 1985, 1990), and a same-different task for side-by-side quarter-board positions (Ellis 1973). The present results are also consistent with another line of research investigating the importance of perceptual pattern recognition processes in mediating expertise in chess. Recently, convergent evidence for the critical role of perceptual encoding processes is emerging from studies that investigate the influence of extreme time pressure on chess performance (Burns 2004; Calderwood *et al.*1988; Chabris and Hearst 2003; Gobet and Simon 1996c).

Time pressure would be expected to be very detrimental to the slow and effortful problem solving or search and evaluation processes. In contrast, the fast perceptual pattern recognition processes should be much less impacted by time pressure. Based on this logic, Burns (2004) conducted a very extensive investigation of archival data on blitz chess. In blitz chess tournaments players are afforded less than 5 per cent of the time available during regular chess tournaments. Burns (2004) demonstrated that up to 81 per cent of variance in chess skill was accounted for by how players performed under the tremendous time pressure characteristic of blitz chess. More importantly, by computing for each player a score that quantified the degree to which their relative performance was influenced by time pressure associated with blitz chess, Burns (2004) was able to document that among weaker players skill differences were attenuated by playing blitz chess thereby demonstrating the importance of problem solving and search processes for less-skilled performers. In contrast, this effect all but disappeared for top players (with ratings > 2200).

Consistent with the findings of Burns (2004), Gobet and Simon (1996c) used ratings to analyze simultaneous exhibition matches played by world champion Gary Kasparov. Despite having substantially less time than his opponents, the decline in Kasparov's performance in such matches was rather modest (his rating in simultaneous matches was 2646 whereas his regular tournament rating at that time was 2750). Similarly, although in regular chess tournaments players are allowed on average about 3 min per move, Calderwood *et al.* (1988) demonstrated that chess masters generate promising moves even when allowed only about 5 s per move, and Chabris and Hearst (2003) showed that when world-class grandmasters are allowed on average less than 30 s per move, there was only a slight increase in the number of errors per 1000 moves (5.02 in regular games vs. 6.85 in speeded games). Thus, consistent with the findings of the eye-movement research reviewed and reported here, the results from investigations of the influence of severe time pressure on chess performance suggest a greater reliance on fast perceptual pattern recognition processes by top chess experts than by their less-skilled counterparts.

Finally, the studies reviewed and reported here provide a powerful illustration that in addition to the seminal contribution of chess research to the study of expertise, chess offers cognitive scientists a valuable model task environment for the study of complex cognitive processes such as perception, problem solving, and memory. For example, a fundamental research question in cognitive science concerns the effects of stimulus familiarity on perception in general (e.g. word, letter, object, face and scene superiority effects; see Reingold and Jolicoeur 1993), and visual search in particular (see Shen and Reingold 2001). As shown in Fig. 14.12, chess ratings are highly

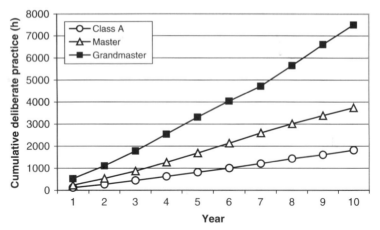

Figure 14.12 Cumulative deliberate practice for the first 10 years by Class A players (mean rating = 1903; n = 71–86), Masters (mean rating = 2321; n = 27) and Grandmasters (mean rating = 2542; n = 5). Data from Charness *et al.* (1996).

correlated with the degree of familiarity and experience with chess specific knowledge and materials. Consequently, skill effects reviewed here, such as ones obtained with the manipulation of notation in the check detection task, which kept the semantics constant while changing the familiarity of the surface representation of a chess problem, and with the manipulation of configuration type (i.e. chess vs. random) in the gaze contingent flicker paradigm, provided powerful demonstrations of the effects of familiarity on perception. Thus, similar to other visual context effects, for experts, but not novices, the coherent and familiar context of a chess configuration enhances the perception of constituent chess relations.

Acknowledgements

Preparation of this paper was supported by a grant to Eyal Reingold from the Natural Science and Engineering Research Council of Canada and NIA grant 5R01 AG13969 to Neil Charness. We are grateful for the helpful reviews of an earlier draft of this manuscript by Fernand Gobet and Jean Underwood. We also thank Elizabeth Bosman and Ava Elahipanah for their assistance.

References

Allard, F., Graham, S., and Paarsalu, M. E. (1980). Perception in sport: Basketball. *Journal of Sport Psychology*, **2**, 14–21.

Beal, A. L. (1985). The skill of recognizing musical structures. *Memory and Cognition*, **13**, 405–412.

Berliner, H. (1978). A chronology of computer chess and its literature. *Artificial Intelligence*, **10**, 201–214.

Binet, A. (1894). *Psychologie des Grands Calculateurs et Joueurs d'Echecs*. Paris: Hachette.

Burns, B. D. (2004). The effects of speed on skilled chess performance. *Psychological Science,* **15,** 442–447.

Calderwood, R., Klein, G. A., and Crandall, B.W. (1988). Time pressure, skill, and move quality in chess. *American Journal of Psychology,* **101,** 481–493.

Chabris, C.F., and Hearst, E. S. (2003). Visualization, pattern recognition, and forward search: Effects of playing speed and sight of the position on grandmaster chess errors. *Cognitive Science,* **27,** 637–648.

Charness, N. (1979). Components of skill in bridge. *Canadian Journal of Psychology,* **33,** 1–16.

Charness, N. (1981). Search in chess: Age and skill differences. *Journal of Experimental Psychology: Human Perception and Performance,* **7,** 467–476.

Charness, N. (1992). The impact of chess research on cognitive science. *Psychological Research,* **54,** 4–9.

Charness, N., Reingold, E. M., Pomplun, M., and Stampe, D. M. (2001). The perceptual aspect of skilled performance in chess: Evidence from eye movements. *Memory and Cognition,* **29,** 1146–1152.

Chase, W. G., and Simon, H. A. (1973a). Perception in chess. *Cognitive Psychology,* **4,** 55–81.

Chase, W. G., and Simon, H. A. (1973b). The mind's eye in chess. In: W. G. Chase (ed.) *Visual information processing*. New York: Academic Press, pp. 215–281.

Chi, M. T. H. (1978). Knowledge structures and memory development. In: R. S. Siegler (ed.) *Children's thinking: What develops?* Hillsdale, NJ: Erlbaum, pp. 73–96.

Church, R. M., and Church, K. W. (1983). Plans, goals, and search strategies for the selection of a move in chess. In: P. W. Frey (ed.) *Chess skill in man and machine* (2nd edn). New York: Springer-Verlag, pp. 131–156.

Cleveland, A. A. (1907). The psychology of chess and of learning to play it. *American Journal of Psychology,* **18,** 269–308.

de Groot, A. D. (1946). *Het denken van den schaker*. Amsterdam: Noord Hollandsche.

de Groot, A. D. (1965). *Thought and choice in chess*. The Hague: Mouton.

de Groot, A. D., and Gobet, F. (1996). *Perception and memory in chess*. Assen (The Netherlands): Van Gorcum.

Djakow, I. N., Petrowski, N. W., and Rudik, P. A. (1927). *Psychologie des Schachspiels*. Berlin: de Gruyter.

Egan, D. E., and Schwartz, B. J. (1979). Chunking in recall of symbolic drawings. *Memory and Cognition,* **7,** 149–158.

Ellis, S. H. (1973). Structure and experience in the matching and reproduction of chess patterns. Unpublished doctoral dissertation, Carnegie-Mellon University. Diss. Abstr. 73–26, 954.

Elo, A. E. (1965). Age changes in master chess performances. *Journal of Gerontology,* **20,** 289–299.

Elo, A. E. (1986). *The rating of chessplayers, past and present,* (2nd edn). New York: Arco chess.

Ericsson, K. A., and Charness, N. (1994). Expert performance: Its structure and acquisition. *American Psychologist,* **49,** 725–747.

Ericsson, K. A., and Simon, H. A. (1993). *Protocol analysis: Verbal reports as data (Revised Edition)*. Cambridge, MA: MIT Press.

Ericsson, K. A., and Smith, J. (1991). Prospects and limits of the empirical study of expertise: An introduction. In: K. A. Ericsson and J. Smith (ed.), *Towards a general theory of expertise: Prospects and limits.* Cambridge: Cambridge University Press, pp. 1–38.

Ericsson, K. A., Krampe, R. Th., and Tesch-Römer, C. (1993). The role of deliberate practice in the acquisition of expert performance. *Psychological Review,* **100,** 363–406.

Gobet, F. (1998a). Chess players' thinking revisited. *Swiss Journal of Psychology,* **57,** 18–32.

Gobet, F. (1998b). Expert memory: a comparison of four theories, *Cognition,* **66,** 115–152.

Gobet, F., and Charness, N. (in press). Expertise in chess. In: K. A. Ericsson, N. Charness, P. Feltovich, and R. Hoffman (ed.) *Handbook of expertise and expert performance.* New York: Cambridge University Press.

Gobet, F., and Simon, H. A. (1996a). Recall of rapidly presented random chess positions is a function of skill. *Psychonomic Bulletin and Review,* **3,** 159–163.

Gobet, F., and Simon, H. A. (1996b). Templates in chess memory: A mechanism for recalling several boards. *Cognitive Psychology,* **31,** 1–40.

Gobet, F., and Simon, H. A. (1996c). The roles of recognition processes and look-ahead search in time-constrained expert problem solving: Evidence from grandmaster level chess. *Psychological Science,* **7,** 52–55.

Gobet, F., and Simon, H. A. (1998). Expert chess memory: Revisiting the chunking hypothesis. *Memory,* **6,** 225–255.

Gobet, F., and Simon, H. A. (2000). Five seconds or sixty? Presentation time in expert memory. *Cognitive Science,* **24,** 651–682.

Gobet, F., de Voogt, A., and Retschnitzki, J. (2004). *Moves in mind: The psychology of board games.* New York: Psychology Press.

Holding, D. H. (1985). *The psychology of chess skill.* Hillsdale, NJ: Erlbaum.

Holding, D. H., and Reynolds, R. I. (1982). Recall or evaluation of chess positions as determinants of chess skill. *Memory and Cognition,* **10,** 237–242.

Jacobs, A. M. (1986). Eye movement control in visual search: How direct is visual span control? *Perception and Psychophysics,* **39,** 47–58.

Jacoby, L. L. (1991). A process dissociation framework: Separating automatic from intentional uses of memory. *Journal of Memory and Language,* **30,** 513–541.

Jacoby, L. L., Ste-Marie, D., and Toth, J. T. (1993). Redefining automaticity: Unconscious influences, awareness and control. In: A. D. Baddeley and L. Weiskrantz (ed.), *Attention, selection, awareness and control. A tribute to Donald Broadbent.* Oxford: Oxford University Press, pp. 261–282.

Jongman, R. W. (1968). *Het oog van de meester* (The eye of the master). Assen (The Netherlands): Van Gorcum.

MacLeod, C. M. (1992). The Stroop task: The 'gold standard' of attentional measures. *Journal of Experimental Psychology: General,* **121,** 12–14.

McClelland, J. L. (1979). On the time relations of mental processes: A framework for analyzing processes in cascade. *Psychological Review,* **86,** 287–330.

McConkie, G. W., and Rayner, K. (1975). The span of the effective stimulus during a fixation in reading. *Perception and Psychophysics,* **17,** 578–586.

Milojkovic, J. D. (1982). Chess imagery in novice and master. *Journal of Mental Imagery,* **6,** 125–144.

Newell, A., and Simon, H. A. (1972). *Human problem solving.* Englewood Cliffs, N. J.: Prentice Hall.

Nodine, C. F., Carmody, D. P., and Kundel, H. L. (1978). Searching for Nina. In: J. W. Sanders, D. F. Fisher, and R. A. Monty (ed.), *Eye movements and the higher psychological functions.* Hillsdale, NJ: Erlbaum, pp. 241–258.

Rayner, K. (1998). Eye movements in reading and information processing: 20 years of research. *Psychological Bulletin,* **124,** 372–422.

Reingold, E. M. (1995). Facilitation and interference in indirect/implicit memory tests and in the process dissociation paradigm: The letter insertion and the letter deletion tasks. *Consciousness and Cognition,* **4,** 459–482.

Reingold, E. M., and Jolicoeur, P. (1993). Perceptual versus postperceptual mediation of visual context effects: Evidence from the letter-superiority effect. *Perception and Psychophysics,* **53,** 166–178.

Reingold, E. M., and Toth, J. P. (1996). Process dissociations versus task dissociations: A controversy in progress. In: G. Underwood (ed.), *Implicit cognition.* Oxford: Oxford University Press, pp. 159–202.

Reingold, E. M., Charness, N., Pomplun, M., and Stampe, D. M. (2001a). Visual span in expert chess players: Evidence from eye movements. *Psychological Science,* **12,** 48–55.

Reingold, E. M., Charness, N., Schultetus, R. S., and Stampe, D. M. (2001b). Perceptual automaticity in expert chess players: Parallel encoding of chess relations. *Psychonomic Bulletin and Review,* **8,** 504–510.

Rensink, R. A., O'Regan, J. K., and Clark, J. J. (1997). To see or not to see: The need for attention to perceive changes in scenes. *Psychological Science,* **8,** 368–373.

Reynolds, R. I. (1982). Search heuristics of chess players of different calibers. *American Journal of Psychology,* **95,** 383–392.

Saariluoma, P. (1984). Coding problem spaces in chess. *Commentationes Scientiarum Socialium,* **23.** Turku: Societas Scientiarum Fennica (Finnish Society of Sciences and Letters). Available from Exchange Center for Scientific Literature. Rauhankatu 15, SF-00170 Helsinki, Finland.

Saariluoma, P. (1985). Chess players' intake of task-relevant cues. *Memory and Cognition,* **13,** 385–391.

Saariluoma, P. (1990). Apperception and restructuring in chess players' problem solving. In: K. J. Gilhooly, M. T. G. Keane, R. H. Logie, and G. Erdos (ed.), *Lines of Thought: Reflections on the Psychology of Thinking.* Wiley: London, pp. 41–57.

Saariluoma, P. (1994). Location coding in chess. *Quarterly Journal of Experimental Psychology,* **47A,** 607–630.

Shen, J., and Reingold, E. M. (2001). Visual search asymmetry: The influence of stimulus familiarity and low-level features. *Perception and Psychophysics.* **63,** 464–475.

Simon, H. A., and Barenfeld, M. (1969). Information-processing analysis of perceptual processes in problem solving. *Psychological Review,* **76,** 473–483.

Simon, H. A., and Chase, W. G. (1973). Skill in chess. *American Scientist,* **61**(4), 394–403.

Simon, H. A., and Gilmartin, K. (1973). A simulation of memory for chess positions. *Cognitive Psychology,* **5,** 29–46.

Simons, D. J., and Levin, D. T. (1997). Change blindness. *Trends in Cognitive Sciences,* **1,** 261–267.

Stroop, J. R. (1935). Studies of interference in serial verbal reactions. *Journal of Experimental Psychology,* **18,** 643–661.

Tikhomirov, O. K., and Poznyanskaya, E. (1966). An investigation of visual search as a means of analyzing heuristics. *Soviet Psychology,* **5,** 2–15.

Toth, J. P., Reingold, E. M., and Jacoby, L. L. (1994). Toward a redefinition of implicit memory: Process dissociations following elaborative processing and self-generation. *Journal of Experimental Psychology: Learning, Memory, and Cognition,* **20,** 290–303.

Treisman, A., and Gelade, G. (1980). A feature integration theory of attention. *Cognitive Psychology,* **12,** 97–136.

Winikoff, A. W. (1967). Eye movements as an aid to protocol analysis of problem solving behavior. Unpublished doctoral dissertation. Carnegie-Mellon University, Pittsburgh, PA.

Wolfe, J. M. (1998). Visual search. In: H. Pashler (ed.) *Attention.* Hove: Psychology Press/Erlbaum, pp. 13–73.

Yarbus, A. L. (1967). *Eye movements and vision.* New York: Plenum Press.

15

Tracking the eyes to obtain insight into insight problem solving

Günther Knoblich, Michael Öllinger and Michael J. Spivey

Abstract

This chapter addresses the use of the eye-movement methodology in research on insight problem solving. First, we provide a short review of classical research and some definitions for insight. Then, two current theories of insight problem solving are introduced, the representational change theory and the dynamic constraint theory. In the following part of the chapter, we discuss the added value of eye-movement measures and describe recent empirical studies in which eye movements were recorded to investigate the cognitive processes underlying insight. The results show that the use of eye movements has had important implications for theorizing. Using eye-movement recordings it was demonstrated that (1) problem representations are sometimes biased towards certain elements; (2) insights are often preceded by impasses; and (3) effective solution hints to difficult insight problems can be derived from successful problem solvers' scanning paths. In the last part of the section, we discuss future research avenues, especially the possibility that eye movements themselves can, in a bottom-up manner, kick-start cognitive processes that lead to insight.

Tracking the eyes to obtain insight into insight problem solving

Insight in problem solving is a puzzling phenomenon almost everybody is familiar with. One can spend hours and days thinking hard without making any progress in solving a problem that looked quite easy at the outset. After all systematic attempts to solve the problem have failed, a sudden idea brings the solution. Often, such ideas occur completely unexpectedly and only after one reached the impression that a solution is not possible at all.

The Gestalt psychologists initiated the systematic investigation of insight phenomena (Köhler 1921). In their view, insight follows a sudden restructuring that radically changes the relationships between the elements of a problem situation (Wertheimer 1925, 1945, 1959). The Gestalt psychologists thought of restructuring as analogous to the sudden transitions that occur in the perception of ambiguous figures like the Necker cube. This can be well illustrated by the geometrical insight problem depicted in Fig. 15.1, Panel A (Wertheimer 1925).

The task is to calculate the sum of the areas of the square and the overlaid parallelogram. Only the lengths of the sides a, and b are given. Although it is easy to find the area of the square, by squaring the length of the side a, no further progress can be made, as long as the two areas are represented as a square and a parallelogram. According to Wertheimer, the problem can only be solved, when a radical restructuring occurs. In particular, the elements in the problem situation need to be regrouped so that they are perceived as two right-angled triangles with equal areas (Fig. 15.1, Panel B). After this restructuring the two triangles can be aligned and the solution is obvious (in Fig. 15.1, Panel C): The sum of the areas can be calculated simply by multiplication of the lengths of the sides of the rectangle a, and b.

Another famous problem that has been used in many studies of insight problem solving (Kershaw and Ohlsson 2004; MacGregor *et al.* 2001; Scheerer 1963; Weisberg and Alba 1981) is the nine-dot problem displayed in the left panel of Fig. 15.2.

The task is to connect the nine dots with four straight lines without lifting the pen. The right panel in Fig. 15.2 shows the solution. The classical explanation for the high difficulty of this problem is that problem solvers do not initially consider moves that go beyond the virtual square formed by the dots (Ohlsson 1992; Scheerer 1963). Accordingly, the insight needed for the solution is to realize that the lines can be extended to non-dotted locations outside the virtual square (in the meantime a

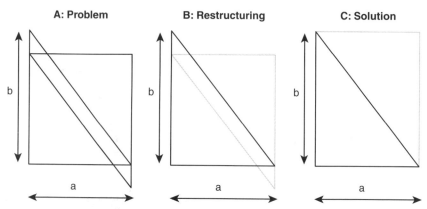

Figure 15.1 Werhteimer's (1925) square and parallelogram problem: how can the sum of the areas of the square and the parallelogram be determined from the lengths of the sides *a* and *b*? Panel A shows the problem, Panel B shows the necessary perceptual restructuring, and Panel C shows the solution.

A: Problem   **B: Solution**

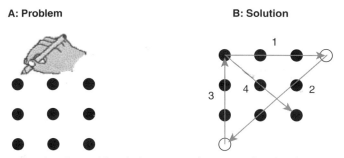

Figure 15.2 The nine-dot problem (Scheerer 1963): connect the nine dots with four straight lines without lifting the pen. Panel B shows the solution.

number of additional sources of difficulty in this problem have been identified, see Kershaw and Ohlsson 2004).

Recently, there has been a renewed interest in phenomena of insight, and cognitive psychologists have made significant progress in explaining sudden ideas in problem solving. The aim of this chapter is to provide an overview of current research on insight problem solving with a special emphasis on studies that have used eye movements as a dependent variable. We start with definitions of insight and a short treatment of two current theories of insight. Then, we discuss what eye tracking measures can capture in addition to what is captured by measures traditionally used in research on insight problem solving, as well as the limitations of this methodology. Next, we describe the results of three recent empirical studies that have used eye movements to test assumptions about the cognitive processes underlying insight. The results of one study (Grant and Spivey 2003) suggest that eye movements might actually be one causal factor in triggering cognitive insights. Finally, we discuss further research avenues and speculate about some future developments that might arise from a more extensive use of the eye-movement methodology in research on insight problem solving.

Definitions of insight

Providing a clear definition of insight has proven quite difficult. During the 1980s there was a heated debate among researchers over whether the term 'insight' would provide a useful concept in problem solving research at all (e.g. Dominowski and Dallob 1995, Metcalfe and Wiebe 1987; Weisberg and Alba 1981). At present, different definitions of insight focus more or less on three different dimensions: a *phenomenal* dimension, a *task* dimension, or a *process* dimension.

Phenomenally, insight can be characterized as the sudden, unexpected, and surprising appearance of a solution idea in the problem solver's consciousness. Most often, an 'Aha!' experience and positive emotions (Gick and Lockhart 1995) accompany the appearance of such an idea. The suddenness and ease of the solution is in stark contrast to the systematic, stepwise, and effortful progress made while solving conventional problems. Wegner (2002) has recently pointed out another important phenomenal quality of insight, namely its involuntariness:

> The happiest inconsistency between intention and action occurs when a great idea pops into mind. The 'action' in this case is the occurrence of the idea, and our tendency to say 'Eureka!' or 'Aha!' is our usual acknowledgement that this particular insight was not something we were planning in advance. Although most of us are quite willing to take credit for our good ideas, it is still true that we do not experience them as voluntary. (pp. 81–82)

Wegner's description nicely captures what could be called the paradox of insight (Ohlsson 1992): while conscious and voluntary effort does not lead to any progress, an involuntary and unexpected idea leads to the solution of the problem.

Insight has also been characterized on a task dimension. Weisberg (1995) has proposed a taxonomy for determining whether a problem requires insight. Other authors have used different criteria to distinguish between insight problems and non-insight problems (e.g. Chronicle *et al.* 2004; Davidson 1995, 2003; Metcalfe and Wiebe 1987; Schooler *et al.* 1993). However, it has proven difficult to come up with general and objective criteria for this distinction. The criteria often refer, in one way or another, to the phenomenal experience of the problem solver. In this case, the definition of insight and the definition of insight problem become circular: insight problems are problems that require insight, and insight phenomena occur when insight problems are solved (Dominowski and Dallob 1995). The most useful criterion seems to consist in the ratio of the problem difficulty and the number of problem solving moves that can be applied to a problem (the size of the problem space). If a problem is very difficult, although only a small number of moves can be applied to it, it is likely to be an insight problem. The rationale for this criterion is that the number of possible moves is assumed to be the main source of problem difficulty for conventional problems.

Recently, the definition of insight has been coupled to cognitive models of insight problem solving. These models postulate that the solution of insight problems requires different cognitive processes than the solution of conventional problems. Thus, insight is characterized on a process dimension. Two different approaches have been taken in developing cognitive models of insight. The core assumption of the representational change theory (Knoblich *et al.* 1999; Ohlsson 1992) is that unconscious processes altering the representation of a problem trigger insight by making additional problem solving moves available. In contrast, the dynamic constraint theory assumes that insight occurs when problem solvers abandon the use of misleading heuristics (MacGregor *et al.* 2001). However, as Jones (2003) demonstrated, these two theories are not mutually exclusive and most likely deal with different aspects of insight problem solving. In the next section, we describe both theories in more detail.

Current theories of insight

The representational change theory

The representational change theory (RCT) of insight (Kershaw and Ohlsson 2004; Knoblich *et al.* 1999, 2001, Ohlsson 1984; 1992, compare also Kaplan and Simon 1990)

starts with the observation that solutions to insight problems often exhibit a characteristic temporal pattern: problem solvers initially try approaches to the problem
suggested by their past experience with similar problems. When success does not
follow, they enter an impasse, a state of mind that is accompanied by a subjective feeling
of not knowing what to do next. While problem solvers are stuck in impasses, they
either persevere with solution approaches they tried earlier, or they do not show any
open problem solving behavior at all. However, continued attention to the problem
sometimes leads to the appearance of a new idea in consciousness. If the insight
turns out to be unhelpful, the impasse continues. However, sometimes the new
idea points the way to a solution. In this case, attainment of the goal is likely to be
purposeful and swift.

According to Ohlsson (1992), this impasse-insight sequence (cf. Wallas 1926) poses
two challenges for cognitive theories of insight problem solving. First, it needs to
be explained why solvers get stuck on problems for which they have the necessary
knowledge. Most insight problems have only a small problem space, the solution can
be achieved in a single step or in a couple of steps, and special knowledge is not
required. Thus, according to standard accounts of problem solving (Newell 1990;
Newell and Simon 1972), their difficulty should be very low. Nevertheless, the
impasses produced by such problems can last for hours. Second, it needs to be
explained how impasses are resolved. If certain factors prevent persons from applying
their knowledge to a problem, why is the impasse not permanent? Which cognitive
mechanisms allow one to break out of impasses?

The RCT addresses both challenges. According to this theory, insight problems are
problems that have a high likelihood of being inadequately represented during the
initial encoding of the problem. In particular, it is assumed that while encoding a new
problem prior knowledge with the solution of similar problems is automatically
retrieved. The initially activated knowledge elements bias the problem representation
and implicitly define a space of possible problem states. This problem space is only
a subset of the complete problem space and thus, may not include the solution,
especially if the solution of the current problem requires a different solution than
other superficially similar problems the solver has previously encountered. If the
initial problem representation does not include the solution, the problem solver
encounters an impasse.

The main assumption of the RCT is that impasses can only be resolved by changing
the representation of the problem. A change of the problem representation will alter
or extend the problem space by activating dormant knowledge elements. In some
cases, the change will activate knowledge elements that are essential for the solution.
The appearance of such unheeded elements in working memory can suddenly open
up a short and simple solution path. In this case, the problem solver will have the
experience of a sudden and unexpected thought that leads to the solution (the AHA
experience).

Proponents of the RCT have also specified cognitive processes that can change the
problem representation, including re-encoding, chunk decomposition, and constraint
relaxation. Re-encoding (Ohlsson 1992) is necessary, when the elements of a problem
situation are interpreted in a way that prevents the solution. Wertheimer's geometrical

problem depicted in Fig. 15.1 is a good example. As long as the problem elements are grouped to form a square and a parallelogram, no solution is possible, and the problem solver will encounter an impasse. During the impasse unconscious perceptual processes can lead to a different perceptual interpretation of the problem situation, e.g. the elements are grouped to form two right-angled triangles. This perceptual re-interpretation opens up a simple and short solution path to calculate the sum of the areas.

A second process of representational change is chunk decomposition (Knoblich *et al.* 1999). This type of change becomes necessary when the initial encoding of the problem elements results in meaningful semantic units that are inadequate to solve the problem. Consider the matchstick arithmetic problem in Fig. 15.3a. The task is to move one stick to transform the incorrect arithmetic expression into a correct arithmetic expression containing only numerals and the arithmetic operators *plus*, *minus*, and *equal* (sticks cannot be removed). The symbol X (10) is a tight chunk, because removing a stick from the X results in a slanted stick that has no meaning within the context of the task. In contrast, the symbol X and I together form the loose chunk XI. This chunk is loose because each of its elements is meaningful by itself. According to the RCT, the necessity to decompose tight chunks is another reason why problem solvers encounter impasses. In the example, the impasse can be resolved when the binding between the two sticks forming the X becomes weaker so that the chunk can be decomposed into its component features. It is assumed that chunk decomposition is triggered by unconscious processes that occur as a response to persistent failure to make any progress during an impasse. As soon as the tight chunk X is decomposed into its components, it is easy to see that the solution to the example is $VI = III + III$ (shift one of the sticks horizontally to align the lower ends of the two sticks forming the X).

A third process of representational change is constraint relaxation (Knoblich *et al.* 1999; Ohlsson 1992). In contrast to re-encoding and chunk decomposition, constraint relaxation does not affect the representation of the problem situation, but the representation of the *goal* of problem solving. Such a change becomes necessary when the goal representation formed during the initial encoding of a problem is overly narrow. The RCT assumes that the initial representation of the goal is also biased by prior knowledge with similar problems. Consider the matchstick problem in Fig. 15.3a. The task is again to move one stick to obtain a correct arithmetic statement. According to the RCT, this problem will activate one's prior knowledge about arithmetic statements, including the unnecessary constraints that only values can be manipulated and that an equation contains exactly one equal sign. Such unwarranted

A: Chunk decomposition   **B: Constraint relaxation**

Figure 15.3 Two problems form the matchstick arithmetic domain. The task is to move one stick resulting in a correct arithmetic expression. The stick cannot be removed.

constraints can also prevent the solution of a problem and lead the problem solver into impasses. To overcome the impasse in the example, one needs to relax these constraints. As soon as one realizes that sticks that form the arithmetic operators can also be moved and that an arithmetic expression can contain two equal signs, it is easy to find the solution $III = III = III$ (rotate the vertical stick that is part of the plus operator). Like re-encoding and chunk decomposition, constraint relaxation is assumed to be an unconscious process that occurs as a response to persistent failure during impasses.

In short, the RCT assumes that problem solvers encounter impasses, because their initial problem representation is biased and does not contain a solution to the problem. The resolution of impasses occurs due to unconscious processes changing the problem representation, such as re-encoding, chunk decomposition, and constraint relaxation.

The dynamic constraint theory

Like the RCT, the dynamic constraint theory (DCT) of insight (Chronicle *et al.* 2004; MacGregor *et al.* 2001; Ormerod *et al.* 2002) is an extension of Newell and Simon's (1972) problem space theory to cover insight phenomena in problem solving. The main assumption of this theory is that some problems trick the problem solver into using inadequate heuristics. Heuristics are rules of thumb or content-independent strategies that allow one to make progress in a broad range of different problems. One example is the hill climbing heuristic, where the problem solvers select the move that generates a problem state that is most similar to the goal. For example, in the nine-dot problem displayed in Fig. 15.2, problems solvers may always try to connect a maximum number of dots with each line. However, sometimes such a hill-climbing heuristic may not yield progress, for instance, if one needs to select moves generating states that are less similar to the goal than the current state. According to the DCT, problem solvers will encounter an impasse when they use a heuristic that is inadequate. Insight occurs when problem solvers find the appropriate heuristic for solving the problem. Thus, whereas the RCT links insight to a change in the *representation* of a problem, the DCT links insight to a change in the *strategy applied* to a problem.

Thus, the first step in obtaining insight is to notice that the use of the currently used heuristic will fail to produce a solution to the problem. The earlier the failure is noticed, the earlier the problem solver will consider alternative moves. But how does the problem solver notice that a heuristic fails? MacGregor and colleagues (2001) assume that problem solvers also use a progress-monitoring criterion, in addition to maximization heuristics, like hill climbing. The progress-monitoring criterion is applied to each currently available move and determines whether the resulting state is close enough to the currently active goal state. For example, in the nine-dot problem, problem solvers can use the ratio of the remaining number of dots and the number of lines still available. If none of the currently available moves fulfil the progress-monitoring criterion, the problem solver will start to look for alternative possibilities by relaxing constraints in the problem representation to extend the space of possibilities. Then, new sub-goals can be formed and these sub-goals will make new operators available, guide the further search for a solution, and narrow the problem space again.

A second important factor in the DCT is the problem solvers' mental look-ahead, that is, their ability to mentally simulate potential sequences of moves. It has been demonstrated that roughly one-third of problem solvers are able to plan only one move ahead, roughly one-third are able to plan two moves ahead, and roughly one-third are able to plan three moves ahead (Jones 2003; MacGregor *et al.* 2001). The mental look-ahead will affect how fast a problem solver will detect that the currently used heuristic will yield no progress. In general, the further she or he can plan ahead, the earlier she or he will notice that the heuristic fails and try to extend the space of possibilities.

Empirical support for the DCT has been obtained for variants of the nine-dot problem (MacGregor *et al.* 2001) and a number of coin problems (Chronicle *et al.* 2004; Ormerod *et al.* 2002). The DCT and the RCT are not mutually exclusive, although some alternative predictions can be derived (Jones 2003). Rather, they focus on different potential sources of difficulty in insight problems. Before we turn to a description of studies that have used eye movements to test theories of insight, we will shortly discuss the methodological and theoretical advantages of measuring eye movements compared with other measures used in research on insight.

The added value of eye-movement data

In the past, researchers have typically used simple performance measures to investigate their assumptions about the processes underlying insight in problem solving, such as the time to solution and the probability of finding a solution within a given time interval. However, these measures provide only relatively crude information about the underlying cognitive processes. The only information one gathers about a cognitive activity that extends over minutes, or even hours, is whether it finally was successful. This is not to say that the analysis of performance measures together with a careful task analysis (e.g. Knoblich *et al.* 1999), the construction of different task alternatives (MacGregor et. al. 2001), or the use of different hints (Kershaw and Ohlsson 2004; Ormerod *et al.* 2002) cannot be successfully applied to test theories of insight problem solving. However, the link between theoretical constructs and the observed measures is relatively indirect and auxiliary assumptions often have to be made to establish such a link.

We are not the first to notice these shortcomings, and to propose using more informative measures with a higher temporal resolution. Metcalfe and colleagues (Metcalfe 1986a, 1986b; Metcalfe and Wiebe 1987) asked problem solvers to continuously provide meta-cognitive judgments while they worked on insight and non-insight problems. Solvers provided 'feeling-of-warmth' ratings 4–6 times per second to indicate how close to the solution they felt. The results showed that these ratings accurately reflected the progress in non-insight problems, but not in insight problems. Although these results were very influential, the use of meta-cognitive judgments is limited. 'Feeling-of-warmth' ratings reflect only informational states that are consciously accessible to the problem solver. Also, they are highly disrupting and it has not been investigated to what extent they affect the problem solving process. In the worst case, collecting the judgments could alter the very processes they are thought to reflect.

Another data source that can provide continuous information about the ongoing problem solving process is the think-aloud protocol, where problem solvers concurrently verbalize their thoughts while solving a problem. Duncker (1945) was the first to extensively use such protocols in his famous 'studies on the tumor' problem. Later, the use of this method became very fashionable in problem solving research (Newell and Simon 1972). Following Duncker (1945), Ericsson and Simon (1993) provided a host of arguments to defend the claim that problem solving processes are not altered by concurrently thinking aloud. Nevertheless, the use of think-aloud protocols has proven problematic for insight problem solving research. First, the protocols contain only thoughts that can easily be verbalized and are therefore incomplete. (Duncker (1945) has already noted that 'a protocol is only reliable with regard to what it contains, but not for what it does not contain.') Second, Schooler *et al.* (1993) have demonstrated that concurrently thinking aloud largely reduces the probability of insight. This suggests that the think-aloud method alters the thinking process to be investigated when applied to problem solving, so that its use seems highly problematic.

Advantages of eye-movement data

Many of the disadvantages of these more conventional experimental measures are avoided when one uses eye-movement data as a measure of cognitive processing. As eye movements naturally occur 3–4 times per second, eye-tracking data provide a semi-continuous record of regions of the display that are briefly considered relevant for carrying out the experimental task. Crucially, this record provides data during the course of cognitive processing, not merely after processing is complete (as is often the case with more conventional measures). Moreover, eye movements exhibit a unique sensitivity to partially active representations which may not be detectable by most other experimental measures. Essentially, if one thinks in terms of thresholds for executing motor movement, eye movements have an exceptionally low threshold for being triggered, compared with other motor movements, as they are extremely fast, quickly corrected, and metabolically cheap. So, if the eyes fixate a region of a display that turns out to be irrelevant for the chosen action, a mere 300 ms have been wasted, and re-orienting the eyes to a more relevant location requires very little energy. Hence, briefly partially-active representations – that might never elicit reaching, speaking, or even internal monologue activity because they fade before reaching those thresholds – can nonetheless occasionally trigger an eye movement that betrays this otherwise-secret momentary consideration of that region of the visual display as being potentially relevant for interpretation and/or action.

Importantly, this sensitive semi-continuous measure of cognitive processing can also frequently be used in ways that do not interrupt task processing with requests for metacognitive reports or other overt responses that may alter what would otherwise be normal uninterrupted processing of the task. Thus, in addition to providing evidence for partially active representations throughout the course of an experimental trial, and not just after it, eye-tracking also allows for a certain degree of ecological validity in task performance, as the 'responses' it collects are ones that naturally happen anyway.

These 'responses' can be analyzed in a number of ways, most of which generally require the visual display to be segmented into different regions of theoretical interest – although fixation patterns on a blank screen can actually be informative under the right circumstances (Altmann and Kamide 2004; Spivey and Geng 2001). Importantly, without some form of linking hypothesis between fixations of certain regions and particular cognitive processes (e.g. Tanenhaus *et al.* 2000), the full, accumulated scanpath from any given trial will often be difficult to interpret (cf. Viviani 1990). With specific predictions for a preponderance of attention in certain areas under certain stimulus conditions, one can produce interpretable results from examining the mean durations of fixations in various display regions, or comparing the sum total of all fixation durations in different regions (total gaze duration). Total gaze duration can then be converted into percentage of total time spent fixating different display regions. There also are various types of time-series analyses of scanpaths that can test for particular eye-movement sequences. For example, Brandt and Stark (1997) used a method derived from ray-tracing (from computer graphics) to compare the similarity between a full scanpath during visual inspection and a full scanpath during visual imagery. In addition Richardson and Dale (2004) are exploring a categorical variant of recurrence quantification analysis (from dynamical systems theory) to test for coordination of fixation sequences between a speaker and a listener.

It should, of course, be acknowledged that visual attention is not always coincident with eye position. Ever since Posner *et al.* (1980) demonstrated that participants' covert visual attention can be effectively dissociated from the point of ocular fixation (when explicitly instructed to not move their eyes), the occasional cognitive psychologist has questioned whether eye movements are really indicative of cognitive processes at all. Of course, it would be a rather extreme claim to propose that movement of the eyes is purely random and not causally related to cognitive and neural processes. Even under the kinds of unpredictable visual search circumstances where variation in absolute eye position appears to exhibit noise consistent with a random walk process, saccade amplitudes exhibit long-range temporal correlations amidst the noise (Aks *et al.* 2002). In fact, a great deal of behavioral and neuroscience research has shown a very close coupling between movement of visual attention and movement of the eyes. Not only do the eyes generally follow where attention leads, with a typical latency of about 50 ms (see Henderson 1993, and Hoffman 1998, for reviews), but many of the same regions of frontal and parietal cortex that are involved in planning and executing eye movements are also implicated in covert visual attention (see Corbetta 1998, and Corbetta and Shulman 1999, for reviews).

Eye movements have a long history of being used as an unusually informative measure of perceptual-cognitive processing during a wide range of tasks (e.g. Buswell 1935; Delabarre, 1898; Dodge 1906; Totten 1935; Yarbus 1965; cf. Richardson and Spivey 2004a, 2004b, for a review). Within contemporary cognitive psychology, eye-tracking has produced important experimental findings in reading, visual search, and scene perception (cf. Rayner 1998, for an excellent review). Eye-movement methods have also been at the forefront of research in visual memory (e.g. Ballard *et al.* 1995; Richardson and Spivey 2000), change blindness (O'Regan *et al.* 2000), visual imagery (e.g. Brandt and Stark 1997; de'Sperati 2003; Laeng and Teodorescu 2002; Spivey and Geng 2001), spoken language processing (e.g. Griffin and Bock 2000; Tanenhaus *et al.* 1995), mechanical problem solving (Hegarty 1992; Hegarty and Just 1993; Rozenblit *et al.* 2001;

see also Hodgson *et al.* 2000), chess (chapter 14), driving (chapter 12), and video games (chapter 13). Quite recently, eye-movement measures have been applied to insight problem solving (Grant and Spivey 2003; Jones 2003; Knoblich, *et al.* 2001), where the advantages may be especially promising, as the intermediate stages of processing during the solving of insight problems have remained relatively opaque when examined by the more conventional measures.

What eye movements have revealed about insight: Three recent studies

Test of the predictions of the RCT

Knoblich *et al.* (2001) conducted an eye-movement study to test predictions derived from the RCT of insight problem solving. The participants attempted to solve matchstick arithmetic problems. In addition to problems that required chunk decomposition (Fig. 15.3a) and constraint relaxation (Fig. 15.3b), participants attempted to solve another problem that did not require a change in the problem representation, because the solution is consistent with the prior knowledge that values, but not operators, in an equation can be manipulated (value problem: $IV = III + III$ with the solution $VI = III + III$). All problems required moving exactly one stick to transform a false arithmetic expression into a true arithmetic expression. The participants watched a visual display of the problem while they attempted to solve it and their eye movements were recorded throughout the solution attempt.

Two dependent variables were derived, the mean fixation time and the proportion fixation time spent on each problem element (result, equal-sign, operand 1, plus-sign, operand 2). Before computing the proportion of fixation time spent on each problem element, a median split was used to categorize the fixations into short and long, the rational being that long fixations are more likely to reflect cognitive processing whereas short fixations are more likely to reflect lower-level processing. To trace the changes in eye movements over time, the problem solving process was divided into three intervals of equal duration for each problem solver and each task.

These data allowed Knoblich and colleagues (2001) to test three predictions of the RCT. The first prediction was that impasses should occur for problems that require a representational change. During an impasse, the problem solver does not know what to do next and should therefore tend to stare at the problem without testing particular solution ideas. Thus, the average duration of fixations should increase. The results showed that the mean fixation duration did not significantly increase across consecutive intervals in the value problem that required no representational change. However, mean fixation duration significantly increased across the consecutive intervals (roughly from 450 ms to 550 ms) in the problems that required a change in the problem representation (decomposition of tight chunks, see Fig. 15.3a, and relaxation of unnecessary constraints, see Fig. 15.3b). This result supported the assumption that problem solvers selectively encountered impasses when attempting to solve problems that required a representational change.

The second prediction was that insight problems are initially represented in a way that does not lead to the solution. For the matchstick arithmetic domain, it was assumed that the values should be represented as variables and the operators should be represented as constants. Such a bias in the problem representation should affect attention allocation to the different elements in the problem display. In particular, during the initial phase of problem solving, the larger proportion of the fixation time should be spent on the values rather than the operators in the expression. This should be true for all problems, regardless of whether a representational change is required. The results also supported this second prediction (see Fig. 15.4). During the initial phase of problem solving, problem solvers spent much more time looking at the values than at the operators in the equation. In fact, they spent only half of the 20 per cent fixation time on the operators that would be expected if attention were equally distributed across each of the five problem elements. This was only true for the long fixations assumed to reflect cognitive processing. The short fixations reflecting lower-level processing were almost equally distributed across the problem elements.

The third prediction was that in the course of problem solving, differences between successful and unsuccessful problem solvers would develop. Successful solvers of the constraint relaxation problem (see Fig. 15.3a) should show a smaller or even reversed bias towards overemphasizing the values when the constraint against altering the operators is relaxed. In contrast, unsuccessful problem solvers presumably never relax that constraint, so they should continue to spend more time on the values than

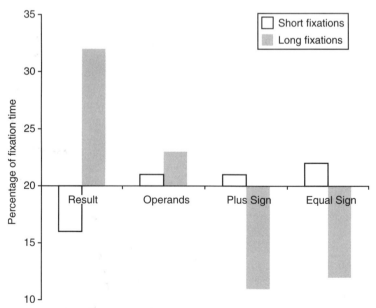

Figure 15.4 Attention allocation to different problem elements during the initial phase of solving matchstick arithmetic problems. The long fixations illustrate a strong bias towards attending the values in the equation.

on the operators. The results confirmed this prediction. Whereas the percentage of fixation time spent on each operator increased from 12 to 24 per cent in the successful problem solvers, from the first to the third interval, it did not change at all for the unsuccessful problem solvers. In the chunk decomposition problem (see Fig. 15.3b), the result should be the crucial element, because it contains the tight chunk X that needs to be decomposed in order to solve the problem. Successful problem solvers presumably decompose the tight chunk, and thus the percentage of fixation time spent on the result should largely increase. Unsuccessful problem solvers presumably fail because they never decompose this chunk. Accordingly, they should not show the same increase in fixation time on the results. Again, the results confirmed the predictions. Whereas the percentage of fixation time spent on the result increased from 36 to 67 per cent in the successful problem solvers, from the first to the third interval, it did not change at all for the unsuccessful problem solvers. Note that the decomposition required the problem solvers to almost completely focus their attention on the crucial chunk. Together, the results of this study provided support for several predictions of the RCT.

Testing predictions of the RCT and DCT by defining impasse

Jones (2003) recently conducted a further study in which he used eye movements to test the predictions of the RCT and the DCT in the car park game. The object of this game is to maneuver a taxi car out of a car park crowded with other cars blocking the exit route. Specifically, one needs to figure out how the cars blocking the exit route can be moved so that the taxi can leave the car park. In some problems, the taxi itself needs to be moved before an exit route has been created. Jones (2003) suggested that these problems require insight. Following the RCT, he expected problem solvers to impose the unwarranted constraint that the taxi can only be moved after an exit way has been created. Accordingly, he hypothesized that problem solvers should encounter impasses before relaxing this constraint.

In order to test this prediction, he asked 37 participants to try to solve a computerized version of the car park problem that required a taxi move. The participants watched the current state of the problem on a computer display and their eye movements were recorded in addition to the moves they carried out. From the eye movements it was determined whether problem solvers encountered impasses before they carried out the crucial taxi move. Jones (2003) used the following criterion for defining impasse:

> A participant has reached impasse for the current move if the fixation time for the move is greater than or equal to the mean fixation time for the participant plus or minus two standard deviations. Under this definition, impasse is sensitive to the individual differences in fixation time across participants.

The rationale behind this operationalization of impasse was the same as in the earlier described study (Knoblich *et al.* 2001): When problem solvers get stuck, cognitive processing comes temporarily to a halt. This, in turn, results in very long fixations, because information uptake from the problem display is reduced.

The results showed that all participants who successfully solved the problem (30) encountered one or more impasses before they moved the taxi for the first time.

In addition, the time spent fixating the problem before the taxi move was more than five times longer (> 12s) than the time spent fixating the problem before the three preceding and the three following moves (between 2–3 s). Thus, the prediction that solvers encounter impasses before carrying out the taxi move was confirmed.

In a further step, Jones (2003) tested the assumption of the DCT that problem solvers having a greater look-ahead value should be more successful in solving insight problems, because they should encounter impasses earlier than problem solvers with a smaller look-ahead value. This could be tested, because moving two of the cars blocking the exit way was trivial whereas moving the third was very difficult. Accordingly, Jones (2003) hypothesized that problem solvers who plan three moves ahead should encounter impasses even before they have moved the first car. In contrast, problem solvers who plan one or two moves ahead should encounter impasses only after they have moved the first car. In addition, problem solvers with a higher look-ahead value should be more successful. Both predictions were confirmed. Roughly one-third of the problem solvers showed their majority of impasses before they had moved the first car, implying a look-ahead value of three. These participants completed the problem significantly faster and needed significantly fewer moves to complete it.

Further (non-eye-movement) measures were collected to test opposing predictions of the RCT and DCT. The outcomes were more in favor of the RCT. However, because the independent predictions of both theories were confirmed, Jones (2003) suggested merging them. In particular, he suggested that the DCT assumption of individually differing look-ahead values should be added to the RCT to explain why impasses are not always encountered right before the insightful move needs to be carried out.

Eye movements as a trigger for problem restructuring

Under certain circumstances, however, eye movements may not merely be a convenient measure of cognitive processes for testing theoretical predictions, but in fact they may occasionally be a trigger for certain cognitive processes themselves. For example, Grant and Spivey (2003) suggested that fixation of certain regions of a diagram during problem solving may actually instigate insight. Grant and Spivey first recorded participants' eye movements while they attempted to solve a diagram-based version of Duncker's (1945) classic radiation problem. The highly schematic diagram was simply a solid oval, representing the tumor, with a circumscribing oval representing the skin. Participants were told 'Given a human being with an inoperable stomach tumor, and lasers which destroy organic tissue at sufficient intensity, how can one cure the person with these lasers and, at the same time, avoid harming the healthy tissue that surrounds the tumor?'.

As this problem is traditionally a very difficult insight problem, only 36 per cent of the 14 participants solved it without needing hints. Nine of the participants gave up or ran out of time, and were then given the hint that they could adjust the intensity of the laser; if this did not work, they were given the hint that they were allowed to use more than one laser. Although the eye-movement patterns were rather similar for successful (hint-free) solvers and unsuccessful (hint-needing) solvers, one difference stood out. Successful solvers tended to look at the skin portion of the diagram more than unsuccessful solvers. During the first 30 s of working on the problem, paticipants who eventually solved it without hints spent 16 per cent of their time fixating the skin, whereas participants who required hints spent 8 per cent of their time fixating the skin. This difference was only marginally significant ($p < 0.1$). However, a similar difference during the last 30 s immediately preceding discovery of the correct solution showed that successful solvers spent 20 per cent of their time fixating the skin, and participants who had just received hints were still spending only 9 per cent of their time fixating the skin ($p < 0.02$). Thus, when participants were linguistically instructed, via hints, to consider multiple weak incident rays, they produced the correct solution without increasing the time spent fixating the skin. However, if a participant happened to be fixating the skin more than usual to begin with, then she was likely to discover the solution on her own.

Grant and Spivey (2003) then examined the eye-movement patterns at a slightly finer grain, looking for a particular sequence of 2–3 fixations that crossed over the skin in either direction, possibly mimicking a 'perceptual simulation' (Barsalou 1999) of multiple incident rays converging on the tumor. Such skin-crossing fixation patterns were abundant among the successful solvers, happening 17 times, on average, per participant during the first 30 s, and 19 times during the last 30 s. In contrast, unsuccessful solvers exhibited an average of 6.4 skin-crossings during the first 30 s, and 14.4 skin-crossings during the last 30 s. Thus, it looked as though participants' eye-movement patterns were reflecting their development of the correct solution (a similar observation of sensorimotor information playing an important role in cognitive problem solving was reported by Glucksberg (1964), where participants who were soon to solve the candle-mounting problem tended to incidentally brush their hands and arms against the box significantly more frequently than participants who were soon to fail).

Of course, these kinds of results and observations constitute little more than a correlation between correct solutions and certain sensorimotor movement patterns. The direction of causality is unclear. Did the five successful participants in the radiation problem arrive at the correct solution via a purely abstract cognitive domain of processing, and did the emerging solution cause their attention and eye movements to then exhibit the observed pattern? Or did paying more attention to the skin, and even executing oculomotor patterns that might simulate multiple incident rays, perhaps help cause subjects to then see the correct solution?

One way to distinguish between these two alternatives would be to implement an attentional manipulation as the independent variable in a new experiment, and see if different attentional patterns affect the frequency of correct solutions. For example, if the tumor-and-skin diagram is presented in a way that biases attention toward the skin, will participants more readily discover the correct solution? Grant and Spivey's (2003) Experiment 2 tested exactly that, by inducing a kind of perceptual priming for the appropriate attentional profile (not unlike Gick and Holyoak's 1983, diagrammatic priming of the concept of 'convergence' for the same problem). In Grant and Spivey's second experiment, the schematic diagram was animated on a computer screen (with a single pixel increase in diameter pulsating at 3 Hz) to subtly increase the perceptual salience of either the skin or the tumor. A third, control, condition had no animation. In the control and pulsating-tumor conditions, one-third of the partic-ipants solved the problem without hints, as expected from Experiment 1. However, in the pulsating-skin condition, two-thirds of the participants solved the problem with-out hints. Based on these findings, Grant and Spivey (2003) suggested that the increased perceptual salience of the skin helped elicit patterns of eye movements and attention, which could trigger a representational change resulting in a perceptual simulation of multiple weak lasers from different locations converging on the tumor. Thus, it would seem that eye-movement patterns may not only pose as a useful window into the cognitive processes of insight during problem solving, but indeed may even assist in the very generation of it.

Future research avenues

Future work in this area will need to focus more on the underlying mechanisms that allow a problem solver to go from a state of not knowing the solution for an insight problem, and even reporting very low 'warmth' estimates, to quite suddenly being able to report and carry out the correct solution. This apparently fast and dramatic rearrangement of one's conceptualization of the problem space poses a challenge for many traditional, linear, additive kinds of theoretical frameworks for describing problem solving and even cognition in general. In contrast, a wide range of complex nonlinear dynamical systems in nature produce these types of abrupt qualitative changes in state on a regular basis (e.g. Bak 1996; Prigogine and Stengers 1984; Van Orden *et al.* 2003). What is noteworthy in all of these natural cases of sharp sigmoidal state-transitions over time, nonetheless, is that a small gradual change in some related parameter or substance always precedes the dramatic transition. That is, to state the obvious, the qualitative change in state does not come from nowhere. Subtle quantita-tive monotonic changes in state, sometimes quite gradual over time, do precede the sudden, nearly discrete shift. Identifying these subtle preconditions for a qualitative re-conceptualization of the problem space is the challenge that research on insight problem solving now faces.

An intriguing possibility for one of those preconditions, as suggested by Grant and Spivey (2003), is that certain patterns of eye movements, triggered by low-level sensory cues, may be able to 'jump-start' high-level cognitive strategies (see also Noton and Stark 1971), For example, future work in this area may benefit from perceptually inducing fixations of regions of a display that previously contained diagrams (cf. Richardson and Spivey 2000) that could provide analogical transfer or interference with a current insight problem.

As evident in some of our descriptions of eye-movement patterns during insight problem solving, implicit cognitive processes may be 'working on' the conceptual rearrangement necessary for solving the insight problem well before the participant suddenly has explicit knowledge of the correct solution. Eye movements may provide a particularly dramatic unveiling of the gradual accumulation of the correct solution to an insight problem, but they are not the only indicator. As a related example, Bowden and Jung-Beeman (1998) have used lexical decision times to show significant semantic priming effects for the undiscovered correct answers to compound remote associate problems, such as 'what one word makes a compound with the words *sense*, *courtesy*, and *place*?'

Moreover, 8 h of sleep can facilitate insight for an unsolved problem better than 8 h of wakefulness (Wagner *et al.* 2004; see also Mazzarello 2000). This is likely due to a process of consolidation and restructuring of representations of the stimuli and task that occurs during sleep (e.g. Maquet 2001; Wilson and McNaughton 1994; see also Hinton *et al.* 1995). Thus, during sleep or a similar 'mental incubation' period, it appears that something implicit is taking place that sets the stage for a representational change in the problem space when the task is faced once again after waking. It would be interesting to compare eye-movement scanpaths on the same insight problem diagram before and after an incubation period with those from two adjacent time blocks.

Ken Bowers and colleagues (Bowers *et al.* 1990, 1995) have argued that incremental implicit cognitive processes, possibly in the form of spreading activation, may continuously – rather than discontinuously – guide one toward correct solutions to insight problems. To test for evidence of partial activation of a solution, Bowers *et al.* (1990) presented participants with a pair of remote associate problem word triplets, a coherent one which has a solution and an incoherent one which does not (e.g. still/pages/music, and playing/credit/report). Participants were asked to find the solution to the coherent triplet, and barring that, at least select which word triplet has a solution. Even when participants could not find the solution to the coherent word triplet, they could reliably identify which triplet had a solution, with significantly above-chance performance.

Thus, despite the phenomenological 'Aha!' experience associated with discovering the solution to an insight problem, it does not appear to be the case that insight into solving a problem truly takes place in as instantaneous a fashion as typically reported. Implicit cognitive processes may be gradually preparing the problem solver for the required representational change long before the solution becomes apparent. In this chapter, we have described a number of experiments demonstrating that these implicit cognitive processes (which do not show up in 'warmth' ratings or verbal protocol) may be observed by recording participants eye movements during the problem solving process, along with other implicit measures which avoid the problems associated with meta-cognitive reports.

Conclusion

Only recently, researchers have started to record the eye movements of individuals who try to solve difficult insight problems. Nevertheless, the use of the eye-movement methodology has already had at least three important implications for theorizing in insight problem solving research. The first is the demonstration that the representation of a problem can be biased towards certain elements of the problem display. Here, the recording of eye movements enabled a diagnosis of whether the initial representation of a problem was biased and how attention allocation to different problem elements changed in the course of problem solving. Second, by analyzing fixation duration in different phases of the problem solving process, it was demonstrated that insights are often preceded by impasses, phases in the solution process in which problem solvers do not know what to do next. Third, a diagnosis of eye-movement patterns in successful problem solvers provided a way to derive effective attentional cues that boosted the solution rates for the tumor problem which had proven to be very resistant to explicit hints in prior research. This raises the most exciting possibility that eye movements themselves can, in a bottom-up manner, kick-start cognitive processes that lead to insight, an idea that so far has hardly been considered. We are very optimistic that the further use of eye movements in research on insight problem solving will enhance our understanding of the processes that provide us with sudden ideas for the solution of difficult problems.

Acknowledgements

We would like to thank Peter Chapman and Monica Castelhano for their helpful comments on an earlier version of this manuscript.

References

Aks, D. J., Zelinsky, G. J., and Sprott, J. C. (2002). Memory across eye-movements: 1/f dynamic in visual search. *Nonlinear Dynamics, Psychology, and Life Sciences,* **6,** 1–25.

Altmann, G. T. M., and Kamide, Y. (2004). Now you see it, now you don't: Mediating the mapping between language and the visual world. In: J. Henderson and F. Ferreira (ed.) *The interface of vision language and action.* New York: Psychology Press, pp. 347–386.

Bak, P. (1996). *How nature works.* New York, NY: Copernicus Books.

Ballard, D. H., Hayhoe, M. M., and Pelz, J. B. (1995). Memory representations in natural tasks. *Journal of Cognitive Neuroscience,* **7,** 66–80.

Barsalou, L. W. (1999). Perceptual symbol systems. *Behavioral and Brain Sciences,* **22,** 577–660.

Bowden, E. M., and Jung-Beeman, M. J. (1998). Getting the right idea: Semantic activation in the right hemisphere may help solve insight problems. *Psychological Science,* **6,** 435–440.

Bowers, K. S., Regehr, G., Balthazard, C., and Parker, K. (1990). Intuition in the context of discovery. *Cognitive Psychology,* **22,** 72–110.

Bowers, K. S., Farvolden, P., Mermigis, L. (1995). Intuitive antecedents of insight. In: S. Smith and T. Ward (ed.) *The creative cognition approach.* Cambridge, MA: MIT Press, pp. 27–51.

Brandt, S. A., and Stark, L. W. (1997). Spontaneous eye movements during visual imagery reflect the content of the visual scene. *Journal of Cognitive Neuroscience,* **9,** 27–38.

Buswell, G. T. (1935). How people look at pictures: a study of the psychology and perception in art. Chicago, IL: University of Chicago Press.

Chronicle, E. P., MacGregor, J. N., and Ormerod, T. C. (2004). What makes an insight problem? the roles of heuristics, goal conception, and solution recoding in knowledge-lean problems. *Journal of Experimental Psychology: Learning, Memory, and Cognition,* **30,** 14–27.

Corbetta, M. (1998). Frontoparietal cortical networks for directing attention and the eye to visual locations: Identical, independent, or overlapping neural systems? *Proceedings of the National Academy of Science, USA,* **95,** 831.

Corbetta, M., Shulman, G.L. (1999). Human cortical mechanisms of visual attention during orienting and search. In: G. Humphreys and J. Duncan, John (ed.) *Attention, space, and action: Studies in cognitive neuroscience.* London: Oxford University Press, pp. 183–198.

Davidson, J. E. (1995). The suddenness of insight. In: R. J. Sternberg, and J. E. Davidson (ed.) *The nature of insight.* Cambridge, MA: MIT Press, pp. 125–155.

Davidson, J. E. (2003). Insights about insightful problem solving. In: J. E. Davidson, and R. J. Sternberg (ed.) *The psychology of problem solving.* Cambridge: Cambridge University Press, pp. 149–175.

Delabarre, E. B. (1898). A method of recording eye-movements. *American Journal of Psychology,* **9,** 572–574.

De'Sperati, C. (2003). Precise oculomotor correlates of visuospatial mental rotation and circular motion imagery. *Journal of Cognitive Neuroscience,* **15,** 1244–1259.

Dodge, R. (1906). Recent studies in the correlation of eye movement and visual perception. *Psychological Bulletin,* **3,** 85–92.

Dominowski, R. L., and Dallob, P. (1995). Insight and problem solving. In: R. J. Sternberg, and J. E. Davidson (ed.) *The nature of insight.* Cambridge, MA: MIT Press, pp. 33–62.

Duncker, K. (1945). On problem-solving. *Psychological Monographs* **58**(5): ix, 113.

Ericsson, K. A., and Simon, H. A. (1993). *Protocol analysis: Verbal reports as data* (rev. edn.). Cambridge, MA: MIT Press.

Gick, M. L., and Holyoak, K. J. (1983). Schema induction and analogical transfer. *Cognitive Psychology,* **15,** 1–38.

Gick, M. L., and Lockhart, R. S. (1995). Cognitive and affective components of insight. In: R. J. Sternberg, and J. E. Davidson (ed.) *The nature of insight.* Cambridge, MA: MIT Press, pp. 197–228.

Glucksberg, S. (1964). Functional fixedness: Problem solution as a function of observing responses. *Psychonomic Science,* **1,** 117–118.

Grant, E., and Spivey, M. (2003). Eye movements and problem solving: Guiding attention guides thought. *Psychological Science,* **14,** 462–466.

Griffin, Z. M., and Bock, K. (2000). What the eyes say about speaking. *Psychological Science,* **11,** 274–279.

Hegarty, M. (1992). The mechanics of comprehension and comprehension of mechanics. In: K. Rayner (ed.) *Eye movements and visual cognition: Scene perception and reading.* New York: Springer-Verlag, pp. 428–443.

Hegarty, M., and Just, M. A. (1993). Constructing mental models of machines from text and diagrams. *Journal of Memory and Language,* **32,** 717–742.

Henderson, J. (1993). Visual attention and saccadic eye movements. In: G. d'Y dewalle, and J. Van Rensbergen (ed.) *Perception and cognition: Advances in eye movement research. Studies in visual information processing, Vol. 4.* Amsterdam: North-Holland/Elsevier, pp. 37–50.

Hinton, G. E., Dayan, P., Frey, B. J., and Neal, R. M. (1995). The wake-sleep algorithm for unsupervised neural networks. *Science,* **268,** 1158–1160.

Hodgson, T. L., Bajwa, A., Own, A. M., and Kennard, C. (2000). The strategic control of gaze direction in the Tower of London task. *Journal of Cognitive Neuroscience,* **12,** 894–907.

Hoffman, J. (1998). Visual attention and eye movements. In: H. Pashler (ed.) *Attention.* Hove: Psychology Press, pp. 119–153.

Jones, G. (2003). Testing two cognitive theories of insight. *Journal of Experimental Psychology: Learning, Memory, and Cognition,* **29,** 1017–1027.

Kaplan, C. A., and Simon, H. A. (1990). In search of insight. *Cognitive Psychology,* **22,** 374–419.

Kershaw, T. C., and Ohlsson, S. (2004). Multiple causes of difficulty in insight: The case of the nine-dot problem. *Journal of Experimental Psychology: Learning, Memory, and Cognition,* **30,** 3–13.

Knoblich, G., Ohlsson, S., Haider, H., and Rhenius, D. (1999). Constraint relaxation and chunk decomposition in insight problem solving. *Journal of Experimental Psychology: Learning, Memory and Cognition,* **25,** 1534–1555.

Knoblich, G., Ohlsson, S., and Raney, G. E. (2001). An eye movement study of insight problem solving. *Memory and Cognition,* **29,** 1000–1009.

Köhler, W. (1921). *Intelligenzprüfungen am Menschenaffen.* Berlin: Springer.

Laeng, B., and Teodorescu, D-S. (2002). Eye scanpaths during visual imagery re-enact those of the perception of the same visual scene. *Cognitive Science,* **26,** 207–231.

MacGregor, J. N., Ormerod, T. C., and Chronicle, E. P. (2001). Information processing and insight: A process model of performance on the nine-dot and related problems. *Journal of Experimental Psychology: Learning, Memory, and Cognition,* **27,** 176–201.

Maquet, P. (2001). The role of sleep in learning and memory. *Science,* **294,** 1048–1052.

Mazzarello, P. (2000). What dreams may come? *Nature,* **408,** 523.

Metcalfe, J. (1986a). Feeling of knowing in memory and problem solving. *Journal of Experimental Psychology: Learning, Memory, and Cognition,* **12,** 288–294.

Metcalfe, J. (1986b). Premonitions of insight predict impending error. *Journal of Experimental Psychology: Learning, Memory, and Cognition,* **12,** 623–634.

Metcalfe, J., and Wiebe, D. (1987). Intuition in insight and noninsight problem solving. *Memory and Cognition,* **15,** 238–246.

Newell, A. (1990). *Unified theories of cognition.* Cambridge, MA: Harvard University Press.

Newell, A., and Simon, H. A. (1972). *Human problem solving.* Englewood Cliffs, NJ: Prentice Hall.

Noton, D., and Stark, L. (1971). Eye movements and visual perception. *Scientific American,* **224,** 34–43.

Ohlsson, S. (1984). Restructuring revisited: I. Summary and critique of the Gestalt theory of problem solving. *Scandinavian Journal of Psychology,* **25,** 65–78.

Ohlsson, S. (1992). Information-processing explanations of insight and related phenomena. In: M. Keane and K. Gilhooly (ed.) *Advances in the psychology of thinking.* London: Harvester-Wheatsheaf, 1–44.

O'Regan, J. K., Deubel, H., Clark, J., and Rensink, R. A. (2000). Picture changes during blinks: looking without seeing and seeing without looking. *Visual Cognition,* **7,** 191–211.

Ormerod, T. C., MacGregor, J. N., and Chronicle, E. P. (2002). Dynamics and constraints in insight problem solving. *Journal of Experimental Psychology: Learning, Memory, and Cognition,* **28,** 791–799.

Posner, M. I., Snyder, C. R., and Davidson, B. J. (1980). Attention and the detection of signals. *Journal of Experimental Psychology,* **109,** 160–174.

Prigogine, I., and Stengers, I. (1984). *Order out of chaos.* Toronto: Bantam Books.

Rayner, K. (1998). Eye movements in reading and information processing: 20 years of research. *Psychological Bulletin,* **124,** 372–422.

Richardson, D. C., and Dale, R. (2004). Looking to understand: The coupling between speakers' and listeners' eye movements and its relationship to discourse comprehension. *Proceedings of the 26th Annual Meeting of the Cognitive Science Society.*

Richardson, D. C., and Spivey, M. (2000). Representation, space, and Hollywood squares: Looking at things that aren't there anymore. *Cognition*, **76**, 269–295

Richardson, D. C., and Spivey, M. (2004a). Eye tracking: Characteristics and methods. In: G. Wnek and G. Bowlin (ed.) *Encyclopedia of Biomaterials and Biomedical Engineering*. Marcel Dekker, Inc, pp. 568–572.

Richardson, D. C., and Spivey, M. (2004b). Eye Tracking: Research Areas and Applications. In: G. Wnek and G. Bowlin (ed.) *Encyclopedia of Biomaterials and Biomedical Engineering*. Marcel Dekker, Inc, pp. 573–582.

Rozenblit, L., Spivey, M., and Wojslawowicz, J. (2001). Mechanical reasoning about gear-and-belt systems: Do eye movements predict performance? In: M. Anderson and B. Meyer (ed.) *Diagrammatic representation and reasoning*. Berlin: Springer-Verlag, pp. 223–240.

Scheerer, M. (1963). Problem-solving. *Scientific American*, **208**, 118–128.

Schooler, J. W., Ohlsson, S., and Brooks, K. (1993). Thoughts beyond words: When language overshadows insight. *Journal of Experimental Psychology: General*, **122**, 166–183.

Spivey, M. J., and Geng, J. (2001). Oculomotor mechanisms activated by imagery and memory: Eye movements to absent objects. *Psychological Research*, **65**, 235–241.

Tanenhaus, M. K., Spivey Knowlton, M. J., Eberhard, K. M., and Sedivy, J. C. (1995). Integration of visual and linguistic information in spoken language comprehension. *Science*, **268**, 1632–1634.

Tanenhaus, M. K., Magnuson, J. S., Dahan, D., and Chambers, C. (2000). Eye movements and lexical access in spoken-language comprehension: Evaluating a linking hypothesis between fixations and linguistic processing. *Journal of Psycholinguistic Research*, **29**, 557–580.

Totten, E. (1935). Eye movement during visual imagery. *Comparative Psychology Monographs*.

Van Orden, G. C., Holden, J. G., and Turvey, M. T. (2003). Self organization of cognitive performance. *Journal of Experimental Psychology: General*, **132**, 331–350.

Viviani, P. (1990). Eye movements in visual search: cognitive, perceptual, and motor control aspects. In: E. Kowler (ed.) *Eye movements and their role in visual and cognitive processes*. Amsterdam: Elsevier, pp. 353–383.

Wagner, U., Gais, S., Haider, H., Verleger, R., and Born, J. (2004). Sleep inspires insight. *Nature*, **427**, 352–355.

Wallas, G. (1926). *The art of thought*. New York: Harcourt Brace Jovanovich.

Wegner, D. M. (2002). *The illusion of conscious will*. Cambridge, MA: MIT Press.

Weisberg, R. W. (1995). Prolegomena to theories of insight in problem solving: A taxonomy of problems. In: R. J. Sternberg, and J. E. Davidson (ed.) *The nature of insight*. Cambridge, MA: MIT Press, S. 157–196.

Weisberg, R. W., and Alba, J. W. (1981). An examination of the alleged role of 'fixation' in the solution of several 'insight' problems. *Journal of Experimental Psychology: General*, **110**, 169–192.

Wertheimer, M. (1925). *Drei Abhandlungen zur Gestalttheorie*. Erlangen: Philosophische Akademie.

Wertheimer, M. (1945, 1959). *Productive thinking*. New York, Harper.

Wilson, M. A., and McNaughton, B. L. (1994). Reactivation of hippocampal ensemble memories during sleep. *Science*, **265**, 676–679.

Yarbus, A. L. (1965). *Role of eye movements in the visual process*. Oxford: Nauka.

Author Index

Adams, M. J. 239
Ady, R. 286
Ahissar, M. 205
Aks, D. J. 364
Alba, J. 239, 304, 356, 357
Allard, F. 328
Altarriba, J. 63, 64, 141
Altmann, G. T. M. 364
Andrews, R. 215, 216, 222
Andrews, S. 85, 86
Andriessen, J. J. 4
Anes, M. D. 217, 222
Angelone, B. 253
Antes, J. R. 176, 191
Antoinetti, A. 307, 312
Arai K. 263

Baayen, R. H 86, 91, 100
Baccino, T. 41, 42
Bacon, W. F. 285, 293
Bahrick, H. P. 223, 224, 246
Bak, P. 370
Ball, K. K. 290
Ballard, D. H. 190, 314, 364
Balota, D. A. 3, 4, 56, 64, 138, 139, 141, 200
Bar, M. 176, 191, 200, 205, 206
Barenfeld, M. 330, 345
Barsalou, L. W. 369
Bayle, E. 2
Beal, A. L. 328
Beauvillain, C. 37, 138, 140, 148
Becker, W. 6, 7, 13, 148
Belky E. J. 261, 262, 274
Bennett, S. C. 143
Berliner, H. 325
Berntsen, D. 242
Berry, D. C. 304, 312
Bertera, J. H. 134, 135
Bertram, R. 82, 83, 84, 85, 86, 88, 90, 91, 92, 93, 95, 96, 98, 100, 115, 142
Bichot N. P. 272
Biederman, I. 168, 169, 170, 174, 175, 181, 184, 191, 192, 193, 218, 311
Binder, K. S. 138
Binello A. 261
Binet, A. 325
Blanchard, H. E. 63, 64, 68, 135, 136
Bock, K. 364
Boland, J. E. 108
Boucher, B. 223, 224, 246
Bouma, H. 2, 3, 55, 133

Bowden, E. M. 370
Bowers, K. S. 371
Boyce, S. J. 175, 176, 184, 191, 192, 198
Brackstone, M. 284
Brandt, S. A. 364
Bravo M. J. 267
Breitmeyer, B.G. 215
Brewer, W. F. 224, 239
Bridgeman, B. 215, 216
Broadbent, D. E. 304, 312
Brysbaert, M. 3, 58, 59, 61, 64, 65, 71, 140, 141
Burke, A. 242
Burnham, C. A. 304
Burns, B. D. 349
Buswell, G.T. 1, 2, 55, 310, 364

Calderwood, R. 349
Calvo, M. G. 64
Candel, I. 242
Carlson-Radvansky, L. A. 216, 218
Carpenter, P. A. 2, 3, 6, 8, 34, 41, 42, 57, 58, 106, 107, 132, 142, 150, 177, 178
Carpenter, R. H. S. 115, 119, 264
Carrasco M. 267
Carroll, J. B. 17, 306
Carroll, P. J. 164, 165, 167, 177, 184
Caspi A. 271
Castelhano, M. S. 224, 226, 227, 228
Cave K. R. 272
Cavegn, D. 194
Chabris, C. F. 349
Chaille, C. 306
Chance, J. E. 239
Chapman, P. 190, 240, 242, 244, 245, 289, 292, 298, 299, 314
Charness, N. 325, 327, 328, 329, 331, 344, 345, 346, 347
Chase, W. G. 177, 178, 325, 327, 328, 329, 330, 333, 338, 348
Chelazzi L. 261
Chen, H-C. 135
Chi, M. T. 305, 328
Chou I.-H. 263
Christianson, S. Å. 243
Christie, J. 199
Christie, J. M. 41, 42
Chronicle, E. P. 358, 361, 362
Chun, M. M. 251, 275, 276
Church, K. W. 348
Church, R. M. 348
Clark, H. H. 177, 178

Subject Index